EMILY TENNYSON:
THE POET'S WIFE

Ann Thwaite was born in London, but her parents came from New Zealand and she spent the war years there, returning to finish her education at Queen Elizabeth's, Barnet, and St Hilda's College, Oxford. She has lived in London, Tokyo, Benghazi and Nashville, Tennessee, and has lectured in many countries, but most of her life has been spent as a writer. She published many children's books before writing her first biography, *Waiting for the Party: The Life of Frances Hodgson Burnett* (1974, reissued by Faber in 1994). *Edmund Gosse: A Literary Landscape* won the Duff Cooper Prize for 1985 and *AA Milne: His Life* was the Whitbread Biography of the Year, 1990. She is a Fellow of the Royal Society of Literature. A Churchill Fellowship in 1993 allowed her to travel widely for the Tennyson research. She is married to the poet Anthony Thwaite. They have four daughters and live in a mill house in Norfolk.

Emily Tennyson:
The Poet's Wife

—

from

ANN THWAITE

Ann Thwaite
for
Catherine ~
with many thanks
and good memories.

ff

faber and faber

First published in Great Britain in 1996
by Faber and Faber Limited
3 Queen Square London WCIN 3AU
This paperback edition first published in 1997

Typeset by RefineCatch Limited, Bungay, Suffolk
Printed in England by Clays Ltd, St Ives plc

A CIP record for this book is
available from the British Library

ISBN 0-571-19059-6

2 4 6 8 10 9 7 5 3 1

This book is particularly for
five women
Gill Frayn, Sue Gates, Anne Harvey, Emily Thwaite, Hilary Tulloch
with different sorts of gratitude

Many who knew her thought it a pity that so substantive and rare a creature should have been absorbed into the life of another, and be only known in a certain circle as a wife and mother. But no one stated exactly what else that was in her power she ought rather to have done.

George Eliot, *Middlemarch*, 1871–2

Mrs Cameron . . . used to say to me, that, though unknown, 'she was as great as he was' . . . The poet himself was aware that these words were truly spoken . . . It was a wonderful life – an effaced life, like that of so many women . . . He could never have been what he was without her.

Benjamin Jowett to Hallam Tennyson, 1893

She was ready to sympathise with every form of emancipation; but for herself, her poet's life was her life, and his necessity was her great opportunity.

Annie Fields, *Authors and Friends*, 1897

She too was a poet in her life and fervent feeling, though she did not write it down.

Anne Thackeray Ritchie to Reginald Smith, 1899

'The Victorians,' Mrs Swithin mused. 'I don't believe . . . that there ever were such people. Only you and me and William dressed differently.'

Virginia Woolf, *Between the Acts*, 1941

Contents

━━

Illustrations

——

ILLUSTRATIONS AND FACSIMILES IN TEXT

ACKNOWLEDGEMENTS

Tennyson Research Centre, Lincoln, by permission of Lincolnshire
County Council (Plates 1, 6, 10, 13, 19–23, 26–29, 31, 33, and most
illustrations in the text); Beinecke Rare Book and Manuscript Library,
Yale University (Plate 2); National Portrait Gallery, London (Plates 7,
32); Conway Library, Courtauld Institute, London (Plate 9); Watts
Gallery Archives (Plate 11); Board of Trustees of the National
Museums and Galleries on Merseyside (Walker Art Gallery, Liverpool)
(Plate 17); Reading Museum Services (Plate 24); Department of Rare
Books and Special Collections, Library of Rochester University (illus-
tration on page 266).

Emily Tennyson's setting of Tennyson's early poem 'Break, break, break', one of about twenty of his poems his wife set to music.

Preface

———

> Emily jump? Emily jump? She has lain on her sofa for
> fifty years. She took to it on her honeymoon, and I
> should be surprised, nay I should be shocked, if she
> ever got up again.

These absurd words were put into Tennyson's mouth by Virginia Woolf
in *Freshwater*, the farce she wrote to entertain her friends. Woolf was
the great-niece of Julia Margaret Cameron, the photographer, who was
one of Emily Tennyson's closest friends. In extreme form, this is one
view of the poet's wife. In 1950 (a hundred years after their marriage),
Philip Larkin's verse expressed more accurately, as well as mockingly,
how much the poet depended on his wife:

> Mrs Alfred Tennyson
> Answered
>   begging letters
>   admiring letters
>   insulting letters
>   enquiring letters
>   business letters
>   and publishers' letters.
> She also
>   looked after his clothes
>   saw to his food and drink
>   entertained visitors
>   protected him from gossip and criticism
> And finally
>   (apart from running the household)
>   Brought up and educated the children.

While all this was going on
Mister Alfred Tennyson sat like a baby
Doing his poetic business.

I have always been interested in the lives of nineteenth-century women who managed, in spite of the restrictions they suffered, to live full and fulfilling lives. A few, such as Frances Hodgson Burnett (the subject of my first biography), were able to do so because they were themselves successful and famous. Many more could achieve fulfilment only through 'planting their own happiness in the happiness of another' (as Leibnitz put it in another language). Some feminists may dislike it when we 'structure our view of women through their relation to male achievers', but it is often both realistic and inevitable that we should do so, considering the history of so many women. If it is repellent – and amazing – to hear women a hundred years later still accepting (as one Tory MP's wife did on a recent television programme) that women live 'mainly through their husbands and children', historically they very often had little option. The last thing we should do is to undervalue and forget women who lived 'hidden lives'. I have used a quotation from *Middlemarch* as one of my epigraphs. 'The growing good of the world', George Eliot went on, 'is partly dependent on unhistoric acts.' It is worth celebrating those who 'rest in unvisited tombs'.

Emily Tennyson's grave in Freshwater churchyard on the Isle of Wight is not entirely unvisited. I once heard a local woman point it out to her grandchildren: 'She used to live at Farringford,' not mentioning Tennyson. But it is Tennyson, of course, who made it possible to write this book. It is usually impossible to retrieve the life of someone who is not famous and, even in Emily Tennyson's case, where so much material survives (see the Acknowledgments and Sources at the back of this book), it has been difficult not to be depressed by the evidence that few people imagined posterity could have any interest in *her*. Again and again, accounts of visits to Aldworth or Farringford contain pages about the poet and a single sentence (or nothing) about Emily Tennyson herself. Even those who valued her did not find it easy to write about a woman. When Frederick Locker (whose daughter married Lionel, Emily's younger son) was writing a piece for the *Memoir* of Tennyson, he ended: 'I am painfully conscious of its inadequacy. Lady Tennyson's name is not even mentioned, but there is little need. Is not there a Book where all noble actions are recorded?'

It is interesting Locker uses the word 'actions', for Emily herself lamented on one occasion: 'My want and my trial have been that I have been, as a woman, debarred from action.' Unfortunately, for those who would like to recruit her as an active feminist, twenty years later she said that she believed in those rebarbative words of St Paul in his first letter to the Corinthians that 'the head of the woman is the man'. She thought there should be 'no competition between the two, though we would have both developed to the utmost.' She considered that in 1896 – she was writing in the last year of her life – 'the order of the world' allowed women to possess a great deal of subtle power and influence. As the American Annie Fields put it, 'his necessity was her opportunity'. It was Tennyson himself who wrote of the total unity of a 'true marriage' – of the 'two celled heart', of the relationship there could be between woman and man, 'like perfect music unto noble words'. This was an image which became reality as Emily set many of her husband's poems to music over the years.

The biographer's job (like that of the historian) is to examine the evidence, to see the life as it was lived and not to twist the facts to fit a preconception. Biographers of Tennyson himself seem to have made little effort to understand his wife, important as she obviously is in his story (a contemporary even going so far as to say that it was 'to his wife's perpetual and brooding care and love of him . . . the world owes . . . many of his immortal poems'). She is often ignored, but sometimes betrayed. It was Harold Nicolson who saw her binding, 'with little worsted strands', 'what was most wild in him and most original'. There is no relationship between the real passionate Emily (who felt the prick of a thorn as if it were a dagger wound) and Nicolson's 'wistful lady' at the Farringford tea-table. Even Robert Bernard Martin, in his far more substantial and very useful biography *The Unquiet Heart*, describes the remarkable subject of this book as 'deeply conventional'. But how could anyone 'conventional' have so triumphantly survived marriage to Alfred Tennyson? Edward Lear once said that no one but Emily could have put up with him for more than a month.

Emily Tennyson's contemporaries could also criticize her. I challenge (as based on too little knowledge) Frederick Tennyson's accusation of her worldly ambition, Edward FitzGerald's suggestion that Tennyson would have been far better off with 'an old Housekeeper, like

Molière's' and Elizabeth Barrett Browning's idea that Emily was too much Tennyson's 'second self' and too indulgent for the good of his work.

Christopher Ricks told me he agrees with T.S. Eliot that 'people are only influenced in the direction in which they already want to go. AT's exacerbated sensitivity to criticism ante-dates the marriage, and so do all the things which might on their own have worked to curtail many aspects of his nature as man and poet (and allowed the development of other aspects).' It was also Ricks who encouraged me to allow Emily's sons to play such a major part in this biography. Too many biographers underestimate the importance of children. Ricks once said: 'Parents are formed by their children as well as children formed by their parents. In life, though not in Lives, children are formers . . .' Emily's relationship with her two sons was in many ways as important as her relationship with their father. This is the story of a family as well as of the life of one woman.

But Emily Tennyson's work was, above all, for Tennyson. A black lifeguard at an American hotel swimming pool (after my day in a university library), found Emily Tennyson's job, and my interest in her, totally understandable. 'Oh I see,' she said. 'She was the poet's manager.' Emily herself believed this was as important as any work could be. Idleness, in particular the idle lives of many Victorian women, distressed her. She agreed with Carlyle, who said. 'Blessed is he', or indeed *she*, 'who has found his work; let him ask no other blessing'. On her marriage, 'after so many years of trial', Emily thought herself blessed – and the anguish of her ill health was not just that it distressed Tennyson, but that it meant she was unable to work. Many have assumed that her work stopped in 1874, when she had some sort of breakdown, but it was only an interruption. Her work as the poet's wife, and as his widow, continued until shortly before her own death in 1896.

The wife of an American poet once wrote: 'Poets' wives, like coal miners' wives, or the wives of other men engaged in dangerous occupations, feel a certain solidarity.' I have certainly felt a deep sympathy for Emily Tennyson. But I should not say more here. In December 1885 Hallam Tennyson wrote to Edward Lear from Farringford: 'My mother thinks that the preface is a little too long and that if you wrote a short preface, people would read it. The public are wont to skip long prefaces.' As I have often done in the five years I have been working on this book, I recognize Emily Tennyson's good sense.

'Words in enigmas', Emily wrote in her journal in February 1867 – the most gnomic phrase she ever wrote. I end with two stanzas by a living poet which say something I want to say, better than I can say it:

What drops, and sticks, and stays
(These words that seem so frail)
Settles. It makes its stand.
Through brief and shifting days,
Fading, receding, pale,
It shows the living hand

That wrote them, transmits the voice
That spoke them. So we see
Years later what was said,
Written or spoken, choice
Not theirs to oversee,
Not theirs, who now are dead.

Beginning near the end

In the autumn of 1892 Alfred Tennyson lay dying at Aldworth, the house near Haslemere that he and his wife had planned together. Emily, in all the accounts, is a shadowy figure, led back and forth from the sickroom to her own nearby room by the devoted son, Hallam. She seems to be passive, to need protection from the nastier side of death. Her daughter-in-law, sensible, helpful Audrey, records nearly everything. But the vomiting and enemas will be left out of the son's account, the massive *Memoir* for which Audrey is keeping these notes, just as Emily herself had recorded over the years, at Tennyson's suggestion, the 'something-nothings' of the poet's life – and of her own life with which for forty-two years it had been so intricately entwined. In this deathbed diary, Emily Tennyson is not described. She is hardly there. All the attention is of course on the poet himself.

It was as she wished. Benjamin Jowett, the Master of Balliol, once said in exasperation that she had hardly enough 'self-love to keep herself alive'. But it was he who recorded the remark of their friend, the photographer Julia Margaret Cameron, that Emily Tennyson, though unknown, was undoubtedly 'as great as he was'.

'Should this remark of Mrs Cameron's ever fall into Lady Tennyson's hands,' Jowett wrote, 'she will only wonder that anyone should seriously have thought that her husband shared his greatness with her, yet one who knew them both intimately is conscious that the poet himself was aware that these words were truly spoken.' Jowett wrote of her preserving 'not only life, but almost youth, on her sofa'.

Many recorded that sofa. Thomas Hardy had spoken of Emily in 1880 rising from it, to welcome him as if from a coffin. Edmund Gosse described her seven years later as 'lying flat on her back', 'a quite angelic old martyr sort of lady'. These are misleading images; there was never anything martyred about Emily. Edward Lear's wonderful exaggeration must have alerted many over the years to the fact that Emily Tennyson deserves attention: 'I should think computing moderately that 15 angels, several hundreds of ordinary women, many philosophers, a heap of truly wise and kind mothers, 3 or 4 minor prophets, and a lot of doctors and school-mistresses, might all be boiled down, and yet their combined essence fall short of what Emily Tennyson really is.'

On 28 September Tennyson's 'sickness had gone on so long' – an aching throat and jaw and other things too – that it was decided to summon to Aldworth Sir Andrew Clark, the distinguished physician whom Tennyson had first met socially at the Gladstones'.

'He arrived in the evening with Lady Clark, and seemed quite annoyed at not finding him, as he considered, more ill,' Audrey wrote in her diary. It was Dr Dabbs, George Dabbs, arriving from the Isle of Wight, who realized how serious things were. At this stage the plan was to move Tennyson to Farringford, if he was fit to be moved. It was certainly in Emily's mind that that was where he should die, if the time had really come for him to die. Twenty years earlier, in Vienne, in the 'old damp church' of St Maurice and St Pierre, Emily had seen a sarcophagus with 'two places in it and two skulls side by side. No wonder I thought this is how I should like A. and myself to lie in our grave.' She had imagined them side by side in Freshwater churchyard, not far from Farringford, where the graves are in grass running down to the River Yar, a peaceful, unspoilt place even now. 'Two graves grass-green beside a gray church-tower.'

But Tennyson was too ill to be moved. Jowett wrote to Emily every day, reminding her one day to 'think over the blessings of the past' and rejoice in Alfred's 'simple and absolute love of you.' And saying the next:

I am grieved to hear that life is slowly passing away. No-one at this hour has a greater sorrow than yours – to lose the partner of your life who was also the most distinguished man of his age. And no-one has a greater consolation in the remembrance of the happy unclouded past, and in the unshaken faith that you are rendering him up to God.

It is better that you should survive him and not have been taken first. For he could not have borne to live without you and would not have known how to do so . . .

I bought the single-volume edition of the poems today and began to read them through again. Will you do the same, beginning with In Memoriam . . .?

It was what everyone seemed to think she should be doing. Over the years many grieving people had spoken and written to her about the comfort they found in *In Memoriam*, but she had said – and Tennyson had agreed – that true consolation, like true faith, comes from within and not from the thought of another's loss.

The real consolation now, as it had been so often in that by no means unclouded past, was to be found in the words of the prayer book and the Bible, which had become part of her very self. Over the days of Tennyson's dying, Emily sat for the most part alone, praying and reading. 'I went in to see my Mother in law,' Audrey wrote in her diary, 'and asked her if she would like me to sit in the room with her, but she said tho' grateful she would rather be alone.'

Emily's own book of prayers was a collection of loose pages enclosed in a black binding with ELEGIES in gold on the spine. It had originally held manuscript pages of *In Memoriam* and on the inside of the cover there still remained some lines in Tennyson's neat young hand:

> Thou seemest human & divine
> Thou madest man without, within:
> Yet who shall say thou madest sin.
> For who shall say 'it is not mine'

On 4 October Dr Dabbs told them 'there was no hope'. Emily believed that in fact that was just what there *was* – 'the sure and certain hope' of eternal life. Immortality had been Tennyson's great theme all his mortal life. 'The only tolerable view of this life is as the vestibule to a better.' He had once told William Allingham: 'Two things I have always been firmly convinced of, – God, – and that death will not end my existence.'

That same day, Audrey Tennyson wrote in her diary that her father-in-law kept 'talking about a journey'. 'When H. went in, he told him he must not take him on his journey today; he could not bear it.' There was no question now of travelling to Farringford and the journey he was to go on was not one which Hallam or Emily could take with him. 'If thou shouldst never see my face again, Pray for my soul . . . I am going a long way . . . where falls not hail, or rain, or any snow, nor ever wind blows loudly . . .'

3

There was a story of journeys Tennyson had often told. Carlyle had chided him for all that talk about immortality:

'Why should we expect a hereafter? Your traveller comes to an Inn and he takes his bed, it's only for one night, and another takes it after him' – To which Alfred answered, 'Your traveller comes to his Inn and lies down in his bed almost with the certainty that he will go on his journey rejoicing next morning.'

Without that almost certainty how can he fear the grave as little as his bed? The thing was, as young Arthur Hallam had put it to Alfred sixty years before, to look to a future life 'as calmly as to a future day'.

They tried to keep calm at Aldworth. The grandchildren, Hallam's children – Lionel who was nearly three and Aubrey who was eighteen months – had been sent off with their nurse to their uncle, Cecil Boyle, on 1 October. Lionel had been allowed to say goodbye to his grandfather. He understood he was very ill and that he would soon be going away too. Telegrams kept arriving – including one from the Queen. 'O, that Press will get hold of it now,' Tennyson said. The newspapers and periodicals were alert for the death of 'the greatest living' Englishman, as a *Times* leader had described him not long before, 'greater even than Gladstone'.

In Tennyson's earlier dangerous illness he had wanted Emily with him all the time, even when he was asleep. Now she accepted Hallam was in charge – or so it seems from Audrey's diary, though it is difficult to believe. Was Emily willingly being pushed to the edge of her own life? Perhaps it was that, as Tennyson's earthly end approached, Emily was trying to detach herself from the world, longing to go with him.

On the day when Dr Dabbs had given up hope, Emily wrote a list of her own small bequests and requests – to her grandsons, to their mother Eleanor, to her niece Agnes Weld. She asked her son to give something to her sister Anne ('Nanny') and to Horatio Tennyson's daughters, Cecy, Maud and Violet.

'God's Infinite blessing to thee and thine and love and gratitude beyond all words to thyself,' Emily wrote to Hallam. To her sister, Anne Weld, she wrote: 'I had been joyful in the hope of going with Him' – writing of Alfred, as she had often done before (and had been teased for it) as if he were Christ, at least as far as the capital letter went. Now she feared she was not dying, but she looked with hope to an eventual 'eternal reunion'.

Oct. 14th 1892

Aldworth,
Haslemere,
Surrey.

To our Lionel's dear boys wheel
you think best with my blessing

Please my Hallamee
give my little Heartsease
ring to Eleanor —
The Jessamine Brooch I
promised long ago to Agnes.

Harriette from mybeloved
to give any memorials
you like to my Nanny &
to Cissy Manel & Violet

God's Infinite blessing
to thee & Chevie and
love & gratitude beyond all words

Elizabeth

As he watched by the bedside, Hallam knew that Tennyson's death would not free him. It would not be his mother but the biography, the *Memoir*, the book he had to write, which would hold him in thrall (and often enthralled) for years to come.

Wednesday, 5 October, was Tennyson's last day alive. Audrey recorded her father-in-law asking for a Shakespeare and lying with his hand resting on the open page, discouraged by Hallam from trying to read. The lovely book had once belonged to his dearest brother Charles and carried the book-plate of their Turner great-grandfather. It was open at *Cymbeline*, the first Shakespeare play Emily had read, as a child of eight, and at a tender passage they had both loved:

> Hang there, like fruit, my soul
> Till the tree die.

Hallam would write to the Queen: 'This must have been in answer to a message from my mother.' (Had she felt excluded like Imogen – 'Why did you throw your wedded lady from you?') Tennyson was finding it hard to talk and when he did they could hardly understand what he was saying, 'owing greatly I think to his having no teeth in,' noted the unpoetic Audrey. 'My mother is crushed but brave and thankful that he does not suffer,' Hallam replied to the telegram from the Queen.

At ten past four in the afternoon Dr Dabbs gave Tennyson some drops of laudanum and they heard him say, after drinking it obediently, 'Very nasty' – again a small remark, but one that seems to hold within it all his feelings about the drug that was its main ingredient and the damage it had done to the life of his brother Charles. 'Take no opium,' Alfred had written to their Cambridge friend William Brookfield sixty years before. 'It were better that a millstone were hung about thy neck and that thou wert thrown into the Cam.'

At quarter past five 'Hallam fetched his mother in that he might recognise her,' Audrey recorded. Hallam wrote later: 'My father's last conscious effort was to call "Hallam" and whisper to his wife, "God bless you, my joy".' Audrey's diary does not record this. Perhaps she felt the words too private for her pen. Perhaps she did not hear them. We know a little more about them from a letter written by Tennyson's sister Matilda: 'Oh, Hallam, those words of Emmie's ring in my ears. "His last most tender words were said not sadly, but with an inexpressible gladness on his beautiful face."' Alfred's physical beauty had always been an intense pleasure to Emily. 'One of the finest looking men in the world,' Carlyle had called him long ago. Emily felt his splendour endured to the end.

So did all those gathered round the bed. Sir Andrew Clark would speak of 'a Rembrandt picture'. 'In all my experience I never witnessed anything more glorious.' Tennyson's hand was still lying quietly on his Shakespeare, not, in its 'last heat' picking 'at the deathmote on the sheet', as he had imagined in his misery after Arthur Hallam's death so long before.

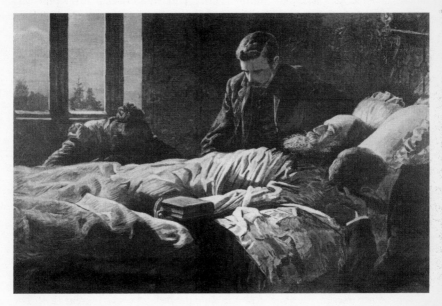

At half past five a harvest moon, a huge full moon, rose, illuminating the amazing 'Italian' view far across Sussex, beyond the cypresses, to a glimpse of the sea, not grey but silver on that October evening. At six 'the moon which had been straight in front of him suddenly lit up the whole of his face and bed, and he looked grand and peaceful.' Eight years earlier Tennyson had said he felt every day 'as though I stood at the gates of Death and the light of the morning is not always upon them.' He was writing to his brother Frederick at the time of his wife Maria's death. 'But you have a strong faith to light you through the dark hour.'

So, of course, had Emily and it did not fail her now, although she admitted she was not really ready – how could she ever be? – to let Alfred go. 'But no-one, I think, could look on his face when the grand eyelids veiled his eyes, without feeling that there were depths there not to be fathomed, that there was a communion in which no mortal could hold part . . .'

'It is seldom', one of the papers said, 'that so ideal a life has been crowned by so ideal a death.' Certainly it seems that the *death* was ideal, though perhaps not as ideal as Hallam wanted to suggest. Dr Dabbs' medical bulletin included a comparison with Tennyson's 'own "Passing of Arthur"' but the death certificate records that the poet was unconscious for fifteen hours before he died in the early hours of 6 October 1892. Hallam took his mother out of the room before the heart finally stopped beating 'for fear there should be anything to pain her'. Now Hallam was protecting her as she herself had so often protected Tennyson, over and over again down the years. But 'without pain, without a struggle, the greatest of England's poets passed away.' 'May my end be as calm as his,' Tennyson had written from his own father's deathbed. There had been three great men born in 1809: Darwin, Tennyson and Gladstone. Now only one was left.

Gladstone was one of the problems Emily had to face immediately. Was he or was he not to be asked to be a pallbearer at the funeral? Tennyson's relationship with Gladstone (and Emily's too, for she was much involved) was complex and at times very close. They had all – sixty years before – loved Arthur Hallam. On his deathbed – wandering a little in his mind – it was Gladstone Tennyson had imagined walking with him in the garden at Aldworth. Only the previous June Hallam had written a letter for him to *The Times:* 'I love Mr Gladstone but hate his present Irish policy.' Home Rule for Ireland was the great issue that divided them, and in the notes for the funeral in the Macmillan archives – it was the publishers who made all the arrangements – there are, among all the instructions about tickets and wreaths, the three words 'No Home Rulers'.

But the decision was made on 7 October that the Prime Minister must be invited. He made an excuse and did not accept, suggesting that he was 'at this moment' particularly burdened, that he had to work on a lecture to be delivered in Oxford twelve days later. There is a telegram from his daughter – whom Hallam Tennyson had once loved – saying simply, 'Heartbreaking but duty gives us no choice. Mary Drew.'

The pallbearers were altogether something of a problem. Thomas Woolner died himself between Tennyson's death and the funeral; George Watts was 'laid up' in bed. These were the two artists who did more than any others (and there *were* many others – photographers as well as painters and sculptors) to preserve Tennyson's likeness for future generations. Both have also given us images of Emily and both were friends. Of the twelve pallbearers who lined up on the day, only three are part of this story: Benjamin Jowett, the Duke of Argyll and the Marquis of Dufferin and Ava. There was not a poet among them.

The newspapers, among a number of other inaccuracies, described the widow as 'completely prostrated by grief' and attended by nurses. Certainly she had a fear of what she called a 'deadly faintness' and she had never contemplated attending the funeral herself. No-one expected her to do so. But she was in fact 'bearing up wonderfully', able to cope with all sorts of arrangements and letters as long as she was away from the crowds of sympathizers who flocked to Aldworth with their wreaths and offers of help. There was a notice and a basket on the gate in an attempt to discourage condoling neighbours and the general public from coming up to the house – but many people did.

Emily was living in Tennyson's study with one of Watts' portraits of Alfred for company. She had always loved solitude, her 'old friends, the empty room and the sofa in the corner' but she was of course glad of Hallam's company whenever he could be there. 'His study is my room. Hallamee's and mine. God bless him. He alone knows what our boy has been to us and is to me.' Graham Dakyns was making himself indispensable as he first had when he came thirty years before to Farringford as the boys' tutor. Even Audrey felt Dakyns was 'one of us'. Maud Tennyson, Alfred's niece, one of Horatio's daughters, was also making herself useful and so too were their friends May and Andrew Hichens. They all dealt with piles of letters; even one of the nurses, who had been kept on in case she was needed, was recruited. But Emily seems to have gone through everything first herself, picking out the ones she felt she should answer personally. She wrote vividly, for instance, to the Lushingtons at Park House about the last days, knowing that they would value something not in the newspapers. 'Excuse the paper,' she wrote to her sister, Anne Weld, 'I write on any I can find.' It was with a narrow black border, not the heavy band that was appropriate and which she had used to Anne three days earlier. It was in one of these letters that she asked her sister to address her as 'Emily,

Lady Tennyson. We both of us dislike the word dowager . . . A small matter but there seems to be in it – a feeling that one is still his wife as one feels that one is.' The word widow was as bad as dowager.

'Audrey has slaved in the most loving way for us,' Emily wrote more than once. It was the word 'slave' Tennyson himself had used to his son; but the 'us' was now Emily and Hallam. Audrey wrote to an American friend that her 'mother-in-law's health has never suffered in the least, which is such a mercy and has lessened Hallam's anxiety enormously.' Mary Brotherton, whom they had known for years on the Isle of Wight, suggested that Emily was indeed not only 'wonderfully strong and courageous in her sorrow' but was 'made of far sterner stuff than poor Hallam'. 'For all her bodily fragility,' she 'will not be beaten down while there is anything she can or should do.' Champagne was a help. 'I have had champagne for years, as you know,' she wrote to her sister. The prospect of the *Memoir* also 'buoyed her up', as Hallam said, writing to Frederick Locker as early as 17 October for a contribution, a chapter about his travels with Tennyson. Hallam himself was kept afloat by Audrey's selfless support, as well as his mother's resolution. There was also his joy in his sons. 'Hallam's little boys are great darlings,' his aunt Tilly wrote to a friend. 'It is a comfort that he is married else he would have felt his Father's loss still more than he does, poor thing!'

Dr Dabbs, worrying about what was in the papers, said that his own account in *The Times* had been checked – before publication – by Lady Tennyson as well as Hallam. It was not his fault that the *Pall Mall Gazette* made him say lots of things he hadn't actually said. Emily went through with Hallam all the arrangements for the funeral. Though it was Audrey who wrote out the lists of names and addresses for Macmillan, Emily made a great many suggestions. 'No Home Rulers' had been one of them. She also made sure a memo was sent to the India Office asking for the addresses of three 'Indian gentlemen' she wanted invited to the funeral.

The decision had now been made that Tennyson was to be buried in Westminster Abbey. There was really never much doubt that that was the place for the Poet Laureate, who had himself supported the petition for the burial in the Abbey of his friend Robert Browning just three years before. There was a space waiting beside him, an appropriate juxtaposition for the two poets who together would always mean Victorian poetry. Emily wrote to Sarianna, Browning's sister, in Venice: 'In one way you know more of our loss than any other can, and also of our consolation, in the feeling that the world is, by God's blessing, the better for him and your brother.'

Emily still thought of the quiet churchyard at Freshwater. Marian Bradley (her friend, the wife of the Dean of Westminster) saw the great sacrifice involved in 'giving him to a grave so far from you'. Emily had jotted down on an envelope the words to send to Westminster – the draft for a telegram presumably: 'If it is thought better, let him . . . rest in the churchyard of the dear place where His happiest days have been spent.' It was not just that she wanted her bones to lie one day beside his, but she must have remembered the letters he had written to her at the time of his mother's burial in Highgate Cemetery: 'We all of us hate the pompous funeral we have to join in, black plumes, black coaches and nonsense. We should like all to go in white and gold rather – but convention is against us,' and 'I could have wished for the country churchyard.'

'Decide as you think best,' Emily had told Dean Bradley and natur- ally the Dean had decided on the Abbey. He wired: 'Quite understand your feeling but share national wish present and future for burial Poets Corner.' It had been for eleven years his Abbey and Tennyson had been for thirty-five years his friend. They had walked hundreds of miles together over the years. They had been particularly close when Hallam had been at school with him at Marlborough.

Hardwick Rawnsley – the son of Emily's cousin, Kate – walking to Aldworth from Haslemere station, met a local roadworker, who had his own views on the subject: 'I suppose they be agoing to tek him away today and bury him in London – he'd a deal better bide with us . . . he was quite a home man, was Lord Tennyson.'

> Sunset and evening star
> And one clear call for me!
> And may there be no moaning of the bar
> When I put out to sea.

There was, Emily wrote, 'a glorious sunset' when Tennyson's body left Aldworth. Moonlight as he died, sunset as he left the house, and the brilliant stars for the long silent walk to the station. 'God moves in a mysterious way.' It was the eve of the day when 'our Lionel left his home for the last time' seven years before, Emily reminded her sister. (Her son Lionel was seldom far from her thoughts.) She had agreed to the Abbey for the Poet Laureate, but there would be no nonsense about black plumes and coaches, no 'doleful crape' round her cap.

The plain oak coffin was carried to Haslemere station in their own wagonette, made beautiful with ivy, stag moss, the bright leaves of the Virginia creeper and the scarlet Lobelia Cardinalis. The coffin was covered by the white pall brought from Keswick by the Rawnsleys – which must surely have been begun when Tennyson was so ill in 1889. Emily described it as 'woven by working men of the north' and embroidered not only with a stanza of 'Crossing the Bar' but also with wild roses 'forty-two in number' for 'the years of his Laureateship and his married life'. If it had not been for Kate Rawnsley, Emily had often thought, there might have been no married life.

The wagon was pulled by Robin Hood, one of the Tennyson horses, with William Knight, coachman and old friend, walking beside him. Behind them there was a cart, loaded with wreaths, wreaths of the roses Tennyson most loved, of laurel said to be from Virgil's tomb and of the Alexandrian laurel too, from their own garden. The cart was drawn by Dumps, the grandchildren's pony, and behind that on foot followed Hallam and Audrey, Maud Tennyson, the Rawnsleys, Graham Dakyns, Andrew Hichens, Annie Andrews the housekeeper, Herbert Godsell the butler, the two nurses and a crowd of other servants and schoolchildren and villagers.

And next day at Westminster (12 October 1892), for all the huge crowd – eleven thousand had asked for tickets and ten thousand had had to be refused – there was still a simplicity that made a man, recently returned from Renan's funeral in France, comment: 'These English hate a show. It's like a country funeral,' he said. 'No military band, no speech, no flags, no plumes.' It was as Emily wanted, although she was not there.

The music included Emily's own setting of 'The Silent Voices', arranged for four voices by Frederick Bridge, the Abbey organist. 'Though the harmonies were his, not a note of Lady Tennyson's own music was changed.' The anthem opened in the key of F minor 'with solemn chords from the organ' and ended with 'a jubilant transition in the key of F major, the music now almost triumphant.'

> Call me rather, silent voices,
> Forward to the starry track
> Glimmering up the heights beyond me
> On, and always on!

Emily chose for the final hymn Bishop Heber's joyful

> Holy Holy Holy Lord God Almighty . . .
> All Thy works shall praise Thy name in earth and sky and sea.

Tennyson had written, and the choir sang: 'May there be no sadness of farewell, when I embark.' And still the weather played its part. 'The sun, which was shining all the time and picking out rare points of beauty in its progress, filled Poets' Corner with a lively light while the coffin was lowered into the grave.' Dean Bradley, his old friend, could scarcely find voice to utter the closing words of the service.

In the midst of the great congregation in black there was the 'little white-frocked thing, seen first between dear Lionel's fine boys and then lost past me down the long choir,' as F.T. Palgrave, another old friend, described it. This was three-year-old Lionel, Hallam's son, now the heir to the title, hand in hand with his cousins Alfred and Charlie, his nurse behind him 'carrying his hat'. The one grandson who carried Emily's name, her son Lionel's third son, Michael Sellwood Tennyson, aged nearly nine, was not in the Abbey. His behaviour was always unreliable. They had said – before they realized how much there was to worry about – that he looked the most Tennysonian of all the grandsons. Nobody seemed to know quite what was wrong with Michael; Emily worried about him a great deal.

Michael's bright brother, Alfred, the eldest grandson, Browning's godson, celebrated by his grandfather as 'golden-haired Ally', had just started his first term as a scholar at Eton and hoped his new suit didn't make him look like 'a seedy waiter'. The middle brother, Charlie, then nearly twelve, 'an excellent little fellow', had recently won the first Classical Prize at Summerfield, three volumes of Virgil bound in white vellum. One day, as Sir Charles, he would do more than anyone else in his generation for his grandfather's reputation.

Their small cousin Lionel was at this stage a credit to the family. Told that his grandfather was in Heaven, the child had said complacently: 'I was very good to him. I always showed him all my toys.' Marian Bradley, the Dean's wife, reporting on the funeral to Emily, praised Hallam and then said, 'The child was wonderful throughout and bids fair to be another such.' Fortunately Emily never knew how wrong that prediction turned out to be. Fortunately, too, she knew very little about their nephew, the third Alfred Tennyson, Frederick's wastrel younger son – and heir – who redeemed his reputation briefly in the Abbey that day by being kind to dear Aunt Tilly, the only one of the poet's ten siblings who was there, whatever else the papers reported. Matilda Tennyson felt: 'It was a solemn awful heart-shaking day, but I would not have missed it for worlds . . . The universal homage paid to his goodness and greatness help to give one hope for England.' But for our hope of another life, Emily wrote, three days after the funeral, 'the void would be unendurable'.

The man was dead. The great poet survived. It is not necessary to be a Christian to realize that 'no man dies less than the great poet who dies when his work is done,' as Hall Caine put it. 'Thy life outlives the life of dust and breath.' At the beginning it was not only in his poems but in the newspapers and magazines. It would be difficult to exaggerate the amount of space they gave to Alfred Tennyson that October. They described in detail not only the deathbed and the funeral, but everything marginally connected with the great man. There are three fat family scrapbooks stuffed with cuttings.

There were photographs of places: the room in Somersby where Tennyson was born, the Sellwoods' house in Horncastle, 'Holywell Glen', The Brook, The Moated Grange (Emily must have heard Alfred's voice in her ears denying the identifications), lodgings in Louth and Cambridge, the dining hall at Trinity, and, over and over again, views of Aldworth and of Farringford. There were pictures of everyone: engravings after Watts' portraits of them all, the boys with their frilly collars, Emily herself in profile, the whole family photographed by Rejlander, the *Illustrated News* version of them all greeting Garibaldi, and of course every possible portrait of Tennyson himself.

There were dozens of artists' impressions of scenes from the previous few days – of the deathbed (with no sign of Emily), of the 'Last Journey over Blackdown', of the arrival of the coffin at Waterloo, of workmen excavating the floor of the Abbey, of wreaths in the Jerusalem Chamber (being set out on trestle tables as if at a charity bazaar), of the huge congregation at the funeral, women with handkerchiefs to their faces, men clutching top hats. And in *Punch* there was a cartoon of Tennyson standing up in a rowingboat, with a laurel wreath on his head, precariously 'crossing the Bar'. 'There was no particular Bar,' Emily wrote to her sister a few weeks later, rather impatiently, for it was something she had said many times before. 'It is curious how little credit people give to the Imagination of a Poet.'

The Times said the funeral, the 'solemn ceremony', formed 'the strongest possible testimony of the national belief that the late Lord Tennyson is distinctly and emphatically one of the Immortals.' But it was Franklin Lushington, whom Emily – and Edward Lear – both loved (brother-in-law of Tennyson's frail sister Cecilia), who wrote the words Emily most wanted to hear: 'I never was at any funeral ceremony which was so impressively filled with a strong note of hope "swallowing death up in victory", or so noble in every respect.'

There were dissenting voices, but Emily probably did not hear them. There was a suggestion that Tennyson's publishers, Macmillan, who had organized the occasion, were 'trying to make the thing a mass advertisement for their "shop".' Edmund Gosse lamented that it seemed to be chiefly a 'crowd of perfectly callous nonentities' celebrating the death of English poetry. 'Tennyson had grown to be by far the most mysterious, august and singular figure in English society. He represented poetry, and the world now expects its poets to be as picturesque, as aged, and as individual as he was, or else it will pay poetry no attention.' It was as if Gosse thought that Tennyson, by being so extraordinary, had made it impossible for everyone who followed after.

Thomas Hardy, who had lunch with Gosse after the funeral, thought the music 'sweet and impressive, but as a funeral the scene was less penetrating than a plain country interment would have been.' He told his wife there was 'some slight confusion in the arrangements. Many people who should have been in the procession were not.' (Emily had had to warn her niece, Agnes Weld, that 'only men can go in the procession', but that that would not stop her from being counted as a mourner.) Henry James found it difficult to define exactly what was wrong: 'It was a lovely day, the Abbey looked beautiful, everyone was there, but something – I don't know what – of real impressiveness – was wanting.' There were 'too many Masters of Balliol, too many Deans and Alfred Austins.'

Emily would have hated the slur on her devoted Benjamin Jowett, on faithful Dean Bradley – but Austin was another matter. He was certainly a nonentity – and it was he who, to general dismay, would eventually, in the year Emily died, succeed as Laureate, after Kipling had turned it down. Many favoured Swinburne who was, after all, 'no longer a Red Republican, nor a social rebel of any sort'. He had refused the invitation to the funeral, hating 'all crowds and all functions, but especially the funereal kind, beyond all decent expression.' But he did write 'a little word to Lady Tennyson' and later an elegy, which Emily thought a 'splendid tribute, so full of life'. They had had a soft spot for Swinburne ever since he first visited Farringford 'when little more than a boy', had listened to Tennyson read, but 'did not press upon me any verses of his own', as Alfred had written gratefully at the time.

Alfred Tennyson had hated letters of condolence – both writing them and the thought of receiving them. 'I myself have always felt that letters of condolence when the grief is yet raw and painful are like vain voices in the ears of the deaf, not heard or only half-heard. The heart knoweth its own bitterness.' When Jane Carlyle died in 1875, he had thought with horror of all the letters Carlyle had received. He told a story of an old aunt of his in Lincolnshire, who said when she lost her husband, 'I get so many letters I can't eat my dinner in peace.' He had said, 'When my wife dies, I want no letters.' But it was Emily who was left and she treasured them, particularly the ones that reminded her of days long ago. One read, 'I have him still before my eyes pushing your bath-chair up Freshwater Cliff and then it was first I fully realized how lovable he was.' Another, 'Kindness to the young is always indelible; and how could it be otherwise when it came from him . . . I remember one moonlit walk back to Alum Bay, when he was good enough to accompany me –' And from Anne Thackeray Ritchie: 'I can hear him still saying of you – she is almost too delicate and tender for this world.'

Emily presumably did not see the more disturbing letters, such as one from an undertaker in Ryde offering his services, suggesting in detail how the body could be preserved with damp salt, a method apparently approved by Herodotus. Graham Dakyns, helping out with the letters, scrawled 'No answer' across the top of that one, and kept it.

This letter, like many of the others, was actually addressed to Hallam, the new Lord Tennyson. Emily, far from being prostrate, was answering, or at least drafting answers, even to many of the letters written to her son. This is one of the most curious things, among many curious and confusing things, about the Tennyson archive. Emily had often written for Alfred over the years. Now she was writing for Hallam as well as for herself. There was a joint general statement, which was presumably sent to many of the sympathizers. The draft is very difficult to read but looks like this:

Hallam's contribution is conventional enough; Emily's continuation reaches strangely convoluted heights – or depths:

We would desire to thank each kind hand that closed a shutter or tolled a bell or weaved a wreath or wrote words of sympathy or by presence shewed it but this is impossible. We can but pray God bless all for the love and reverence shewn to the Memory of one who loved all who love. Your deeply grateful His wife and son Hallam.

That is what it seems to say. Another version of it adds 'yesterday' after 'expressed it by their presence'. So obviously this must have been written on 13 October, the day after the funeral. That scrap adds: 'We live with him in spirit. We desire always to live with Him and we believe in doing so we . . .' There she broke off. But she could cope. She who had been married to 'our greatest poet of intimate bereavement' was now herself bereaved but still full of energy. Years before Thomas

Woolner had spoken of her 'naturally energetic temperament'. James Spedding, one of Tennyson's Cambridge friends, had also recognized that energy – a mental and spiritual energy she had almost always had, even when quietly lying on her sofa. He wrote to her: 'Energetic people can of course never understand the case of the unenergetic.' With her energy went a passion she herself recognized could make life hard. She had once written to Hallam when he was still a schoolboy: 'I am so made that what to many is but the prick of a thorn is to me a dagger wound.' It was prayer that had made life possible.

The numerous surviving drafts of letters written after Tennyson's death are an extraordinary indication of Emily's determination to involve herself in everything. Aldworth, she told her sister, was full of people working away ('some sat upstairs ... some in the drawing room'), but there were still many letters, which 'Hallamee and I must write together'. The drafts show that these were not just letters to personal friends and the Royal Family (never of course chiding them for not appearing at the funeral), but to all sorts of organizations and, though this must have been later, to admirers all over the world. They were dashed off in Emily's own hand – and then were presumably copied, signed by Hallam and addressed and put into envelopes by their team of helpers around the house.

The recipients ranged from the Vestry of St Pancras and the Birmingham Book Club to a 'provident institution' and the Trustees of Shakespeare's Birthplace. Each one got an appropriate message. In some Emily writes as herself – presumably those were in reply to letters addressed directly to her. More often she writes as if in Hallam's voice: 'Let me say for my Mother and myself how very grateful we are for the expression of kind sympathy of the Council of the Royal Colonial Institute.' And in that letter she did not stop there but went on at length about Tennyson's desire, 'one of the deepest desires of his life', to help the realization of 'an Empire in the most intimate union . . . a leader to all that is good'; to which Hallam added the three words 'throughout the world'. One can imagine them, mother and son, poring over the letters together, writing the sort of letters Tennyson would never have written himself.

The Trustees of Shakespeare's Birthplace got the whole story of the volume of Shakespeare on the deathbed: 'We could not part from this volume but we buried another, with the passage marked, in the grave.' And Emily wrote to the Greenock Burns Club, again as if from Hallam:

'My mother bids me to convey to you her heartfelt thanks . . . Of his great admiration for Burns I need scarcely speak.'

There were a lot of crossings-out in these drafts, but the writing is bold and determined and, at almost eighty, it was only as difficult to read as it had always been. There was nothing new for Emily in this daily writing; she had done it throughout most of her life. She was a natural writer, if often rather a clumsy one. ('I have begun such a weak sentence, I found it irremediable,' she had once written to Thomas Woolner.) Her instinct – unlike Tennyson's – was always to keep closely in touch with those she loved, even when so many business letters had to be written. When the boys were at school and at Cambridge, they had to beg her to save her strength and not write to them so often. When she and Alfred were apart, they exchanged daily letters until Hallam took over Alfred's side of the exchange. And for nearly twenty-five years Emily had kept a regular journal, which would inform much of the narrative of the *Memoir*.

Nor had Emily's writing been confined to letters and diaries. Her record-keeping was formidable. She had written lists of everything possible – inventories of furniture and linen, catalogues of books. Even the surviving lists of wine and spirits in the cellars and side-boards at Farringford and Aldworth are in Emily's hand, not in that of the butler – and only once, when she was not well, in Hallam's. She had kept the family accounts. She had written 'subjects' which she hoped might inspire Alfred, though they seldom did. She had copied out for him thousands of lines of his poems. He had called it 'a weariness of the flesh writing out my own things.' To Emily it was often a weariness, particularly of the wrist – an early injury sometimes caused problems. But she wrote and wrote, for his sake. And very occasionally she worked at her own things, not only the musical settings of his songs but also her own hymns – Palgrave published two in his *Treasury of Sacred Song* in 1889. And she even wrote fiction, but this seems to have been a secret, not only unpublished but unmentioned.

Now ahead of her was the task of helping Hallam with the *Memoir*, a task which would both crown and record her life's work. Marian Bradley wrote: 'How thankful we are, dearest Emily, for you that you have your Hallam and I am sure you will find new life and comfort and hope in writing the Life.' Mrs Bradley saw that it should be Emily's life as much as his – Tennyson's life, their lives together, written by his wife and son. There were plenty of examples of widows writing their husband's lives, collecting their letters, with help from their friends and relations; but it does not seem that the question of whether Emily's name would appear with her son's on the title page was ever discussed. Hallam needed the credit, and Emily certainly wished him to have it. She had fretted for years that devotion to his parents had deprived him of his own career.

She had been sad that Alfred had never got round to writing a poem celebrating their son's devotion. Now, when a new edition of the poems was being discussed, she wrote to George Craik at Macmillan: 'I should like that "To Hallam Tennyson" should be added to "De Profundis" . . . Perhaps it is a foolish thought but I should wish our Hallam's name to appear among His poems, tho' of course his Father's entire trust in him is proved by his having left him Sole Literary Executor and by his having desired that if a Memoir of him had to be written Hallam should write it.'

Now perhaps the *Memoir* would not only celebrate appropriately the great poet, but at last provide a stepping stone for the son into a wider world, as the peerage he had inherited would also do.

'What I feel most strongly,' Marian Bradley added in her letter to Emily that October, 'is that I should like the world to realize what *you* have been to him and for him and in him from first to last. I could say so many things about it – but can't and mustn't, I suppose – so many little passing words of love and reverence for you, his sacred wife – I can recall.'

With their team of helpers, Emily and Hallam acknowledged the great piles of letters of sympathy, the hundreds of letters, extremely quickly. Ahead of them there were tens of thousands more, letters from the past – a lifetime's letters – which needed to be read and sorted in case they could add to the story of Tennyson's life. As early as 9 October, F.T. Palgrave had been asking if he should come to help with the *Memoir*. There was a feeling of urgency about it – so many people whose memories were needed were frail and aged, not least Emily herself. And Hallam had the original intention of publishing for Christmas the following year. Audrey and the children went off to stay with friends to be out of the way, and on Thursday, 20 October, exactly a fortnight after Tennyson's death, Emily and Hallam and the entire household left Aldworth and set off by special train for Farringford, their house on the Isle of Wight, the 'dear place' where the family had spent their happiest days.

The Duke of Argyll had worried about the return: 'I have been so sorry for you going back to Farringford. It must have been a sore trial. I think of it myself with tears. Going back to the year when we first saw you there with your two Boys . . .' He always remembered 'the lovely boys with their hair falling down to their shoulders' in the days before they went off to school. Going back to those years – the Argylls had first visited them in 1862 – was in fact just what Emily longed to do and if there were tears, and there must have been, no traces of them survive. Going back to Farringford had always been a joy. She had always preferred it to Aldworth. 'Farringford was pre-eminently home,' she wrote, 'the happiest days of our lives having been spent there before partings began.' 'This is the old beloved home to me, the dearest spot on earth.' Returning once from the Continent, she had written to Graham Dakyns: 'I felt lost in a perfect ecstacy on Sunday, the ecstacy of being at home and in such a beautiful home; for indeed much as you may be disposed to laugh at me, I have seen no place in our wanderings where I should so much like to live. The boys were *wild* with delight.' Even when the boys calmed down, growing older, Emily's feelings remained the same. It was the right place to begin work on the *Memoir*. 'Hallamee and I live in the past, those happy days of our journals and journal-letters – a past made wonderful by the glorious skies of October.' She was inspired – it was as if Tennyson's death had lifted her up rather than cast her down.

Mary Watts, the artist's wife, wrote to Emily in November in the effusive terms so many people used: 'May God comfort you who made his home an earthly heaven.' She and Watts had spent a fortnight with the Tennysons two years before, when Watts was working on the final portrait, the one in the dining hall at Trinity College, Cambridge. 'May the gratitude of millions of hearts help you through your days of desolation,' Mrs Watts added. But it was work, not gratitude, that helped Emily. She had entirely put off the idea of dying. There was a job ahead. 'I am thankful for what is left of me, for there is something I have to do, I think.' Her dearest friend, Edward Lear, had agreed exactly with her feelings about work, writing to her not long before his own death, from the Villa Tennyson, San Remo: 'The longer we are permitted to live, the more we ought to work.'

Letters were confirming Emily's belief, encouraged by Hallam, that she had survived Alfred for a purpose. 'Hallam is right in feeling that God in his infinite mercy has left you for a time that you may help him to fulfil all that your loved one wished,' wrote Emily Lushington, sister-in-law of Tennyson's sister Cecilia. Wife and son, the survivors, set to work immediately, with Jowett encouraging them to get on and catch all the old men before they were in their graves. Emily wrote to her sister: 'My Hallam tells me that I can be a help in the work to be done and nothing I can do is too much to be done either for the Father or the devoted son of our love . . . He and I feel that we live with Him still and that in this is our best hope of a fuller life in God.'

It was a dangerous mood to be in for the writing of a biography. Emily seems to be admitting that they were embarking on a process of deification, or at least of glorification, a deliberate campaign to protect Alfred from the image of the gossips, by stressing not only the greatness of his poetry but also the greatness of his character. 'Fain would we leave his memory embalmed in his own poems.' (The sentiment is less sententiously echoed in her version of the preface written to help Hallam: 'I feel strongly that no biographer could so truly give my Father as his own poems give him.') 'But people will not let us. They say things so dreadful that we must speak . . .' In this letter to Mary Watts she is not specific about the dreadful stories that were going about – or how she had heard them. Hallam referred to 'spiteful voices' too in a letter to the Lushingtons; Edmund said *he* had heard nothing but 'unmixt admiration and eulogy'. But it is clear there *were* other voices. A little later George Gissing would write of Tennyson to Edward Clodd: 'I have such admiration and love for his work, that I loathe to hear such things as are constantly being told. If he was *not* in essence a grand creature, well, it makes the world a little more inexplicable and unpleasant.' Emily must have been aware that people talked about Tennyson's coarseness, his taste for infantile obscenity, his drinking, his 'petting' of young women visitors. Edward Lear, years before (suggesting that no-one but Emily could have stayed married to him for more than a month), had confined his observations of the worst things to entries in his diary in Greek. Other visitors were less discreet. Even Jowett would confide from time to time in Florence Nightingale a view rather different from the one he would write for the *Memoir*.

In fact it seems Emily was not primarily worried by gossip about Alfred's behaviour. He had been the man he was and she had loved him as he was – not some imaginary ideal man, let alone a plaster saint, but his extraordinary reality. What did worry her was James Knowles's article in his *Nineteenth Century* only three months after Tennyson's death – not the irreverent reference in it to Tennyson using his bottle of port 'as a sort of counsellor' – but his diminution of Tennyson's faith to a quoted sentence: 'There's a something that watches over us; and our individuality endures: that's my faith and that's all my faith.' Nothing but God and immortality – Emily and Hallam must have heard Tennyson speak of these two pillars of his belief a hundred times, but in cold print it seemed a denial of Christianity. The Duke of Argyll urged Hallam 'to speak out plainly and specifically on what he knows to have been his Father's faith in Christ.' Emily's sister wrote to her of Knowles' 'treachery', which had Emily quoting Dante: 'Non ragionam di lor, ma guarda e passa'. This might have been just the tag 'let's not speak of *them*', but might have held the fact – for Emily knew Dante well – that Virgil was suggesting that that particular lot were neither for nor against God, but for themselves.

It was 'the melancholy, long, withdrawing roar' of the Sea of Faith that chilled her. She wanted to believe that Tennyson's poems were holding his readers in the love of God. She could not bear to face Alfred's doubts – what Lord Acton called 'his grave groping for religious certainty'. She knew the strength of Alfred's need to believe in a loving God. Not long before he died, he had been pondering the painful world and the problems of man's capacity to multiply ('the torrent of babies') and had then exclaimed, 'Yet God *is* love, transcendent, all-pervading. We do not get *this* faith from Nature or the world. If we look at Nature alone, full of perfection and imperfection, she tells us that God is disease, murder and rapine. We get this faith from ourselves, from what is highest within us, which recognizes that there is not one fruitless pang, just as there is not one lost good.'

> A warmth within the heart would melt
> The freezing reason's colder part,
> And like a man in wrath the heart
> Stood up and answer'd 'I have felt'.

This was the Tennyson Emily wanted the world to know. She had *felt* with him 'as a child that cries, But, crying, knows his father near.'

Tennyson had often said he hated biographies. William Allingham had recorded that direct assertion when he asked the poet in 1887 whether he had read the new life of Darwin. There had once been – and surely more than once – 'rollicking' talk after dinner about great men being treated 'like pigs to be ripped open for the public'. Tennyson had apparently 'thanked God Almighty with his whole heart and soul that he knew nothing, and that the world knew nothing, of Shakespeare but his writings; and that he thanked God Almighty that he knew nothing of Jane Austen, and that there were no letters preserved either of Shakespeare's or Jane Austen's, that they had not been ripped open like pigs.'

Their neighbour Julia Margaret Cameron had written this down one night, after dinner at Farringford – with her typical verve – in a letter to her great friend Henry Taylor, late in 1862. Tennyson had been appalled to see it, many years later, quoted in *The Times* from Taylor's autobiography. 'It is very possible that I went on in a rollicking way after dinner . . . I can quite fancy myself saying it,' he wrote to Taylor in protest. What was the world coming to that one should find long-ago dinner-table talk in the newspaper for all to read? 'I could never have imagined that such a man as yourself would have so far chimed in with the bad taste of the age.'

It is interesting to think that what would certainly have annoyed Tennyson most was the way 'dear old Julia Cameron' (as he called her) continued: 'Then he said that the post for two days had brought *him* no letters, and that he thought there was a sort of syncope in the world as to him and to his fame.' Tennyson had always had mixed feelings about fame, hating recognition in the street or on the downs, yet needing praise from the critics and in the post. He wanted both sorts of immortality; he needed constant reassurance that his work would endure, that people read him and loved what he was doing. Only a year after that protest at a sudden brief dearth of praise, he was saying: 'Modern fame is nothing. I'd rather have an acre of land. I shall go down, down! I'm up now. Action and reaction.' Emily had always had to cope with action and reaction, the see-saw of his moods.

Tennyson was quite right, of course: there would be a reaction to the extraordinary fame he had achieved in his lifetime, and Emily and Hallam saw the *Memoir* as a way to preserve for ever the admiration of his contemporaries as well as so much else. (Fortunately Henry Sidgwick would eventually encourage them to 'diminish the amount of laudation' and Hallam would ask him 'to eliminate any "praising" words of mine you may find'. 'From a *literary point of view* the book will gain.') As early as 1853 Henry Hallam, Arthur's father, had written of Tennyson, 'How his name is in the mouths of men; and how he seems to mark an epoch.' As the years passed, the public's interest in Tennyson had become quite ridiculous, as his brother-in-law Edmund Lushington had mused in 1879: 'What a strange thing fame is. This morning a neighbour tells me he has seen a Bible printed in Amsterdam in 1715 recommended by the bookseller on the grounds that the fly-leaf has "some of Tennyson's writing about his account with his washer-woman".' And Lady Dorothy Nevill had recalled visiting Lord John Russell when he had rented Aldworth one year: 'I especially remember someone pointing out a writing-table in the library with two enormous stains of ink splashed on each side of the blotting-book. "They are rather remarkable ink-stains" said my guide; "the Poet Laureate made one and the Prime Minister has made the other".'

There was bound to be a reaction against this sort of thing – but there could also be an extension. A public interested in his laundry bills and his ink blots could be fed with every sort of vulgar information. Hallam was certainly not prepared to accept the fact that sooner or later all would become known, though he must have realized what crowds of witnesses there were. It is easy for us to feel he should have known that his father's character and poetry were great enough to survive, not only any revelations that Hallam himself might make, but also the ghouls he imagined were waiting to devour the corpse.

Tennyson had been going on about the ghouls for years. 'When I am dead they will tear me to pieces, limb from limb,' he told one of the Rawnsleys, one of the little girls who had been Emily's bridesmaid nearly forty years before. Her brother Hardwick recorded Tennyson saying:

> In my youth the growls!
> In mine age the owls!
> After death the ghouls!

(One can hear how he pronounced them.) Hallam was determined to anticipate the ghouls. In January 1893 he wrote a stiff letter to Hard-wick himself:

My mother and I are taken aback by the news that you – who knew next to nothing of my Father – are going to write his Life . . . My mother and I are preparing the only authorized Life. Perhaps the 'news' is not true. My Father expressly desired that if any Memoir were written – it should be written (so as to preclude the necessity of any other Memoir) by those who knew him best – We alone have the documents on which an authentic Memoir can be founded.

The news was indeed true and Rawnsley had been busily writing round and gathering all sorts of memories for which future biographers would thank him. It was hard for a Rawnsley to be told that he knew 'next to nothing', when he had been brought up to understand just how much the Tennysons owed to the Rawnsleys. There was a note of desperation in Hallam's letter. When he read it through, he added, placatingly, 'You are a good fellow. I am sure you will not mind me telling you the truth.'

Hallam would tell James Knowles after Emily's death, when their own *Memoir* had *still* not appeared: 'You little know how much I have tried to carry out my Father's exact wishes. The work has been done with intensest anxiety on my part and with the intent to make it as exact and true as possible and pardon me if I say that I know better than anyone else what he wished me to do.' Emily had known, as well as Hallam did, that Tennyson had wanted the *Memoir*, if there really had to be one, to be 'final and full enough to preclude the chance of further and unauthentic biographies' – to keep out 'penny-a-liner lies' as Hallam said to Anne Thackeray Ritchie.

Despite Tennyson's mutterings and growlings about biographers, there had been talk for years of some sort of official family *Memoir*. Years before, it had been Tennyson who had first encouraged Emily to keep a record of their life. There exists a note in Emily's hand, written as if she were Hallam, of the journal 'which my Father had wished my Mother to keep,' to which in Hallam's hand is added 'for his private use'. She called these journals 'the authority for a good deal of the story of our lives'. Emily had always thought of 'our life', but Hallam, devoted son of his mother that he was, was yet enough of a man of his time to rewrite 'our' as 'his'. Hallam told Anne Thackeray Ritchie that 'they kept journals – in view of the "ghouls".'

For years Hallam himself had been keeping notes of Tennyson's talk, as well as more structured notes on the poems, these primarily for an eventual annotated edition. So many people kept notes of what Tennyson said – Audrey, Agnes Weld (Emily's niece), William Allingham, as well as dozens of more casual visitors – that it is a wonder that Tennyson was as unselfconscious as he was. Self-absorbed, yes; self-conscious, no. Over and over again people stressed his 'naturalness', how he always said exactly what he thought.

Why should we want to know that Dr Johnson stirred his lemonade with a dirty finger? Tennyson would ask, not accepting that it is these little infirmities that endear the great to us. 'What business has the public to want to know about Byron's wildnesses?' Tennyson won-dered. 'He has given them fine work, and they ought to be satisfied.' But Tennyson knew perfectly well that they would *not* be satisfied and that his own life would inevitably be written: 'The worth of a biography depends on whether it is done by one who wholly loves the man whose life he writes, yet loves him with a discriminating love.' There was definitely the suggestion that the biographer should not tell all, not even as much as he knows. They were at hand, those who wholly loved the man, to take on what Gladstone called 'doubtless an arduous task'. Where they went wrong was in deciding on the sort of biography that would best help to preserve and enhance Tennyson's reputation after his death. In that same passage Tennyson had suggested, 'If one knew all one would pardon all.' Emily had always not only accepted and pardoned but, in a curious way, particularly valued even Tennyson's most difficult behaviour. But she was nervous too of how strangers would interpret him. She shared Hallam's 'intensest anxiety', if only because he communicated it to her.

Long after Emily's death, at a time when Tennyson's reputation was in eclipse, Edmund Gosse ruminated on Lytton Strachey's *Eminent Victorians* and regretted the unnecessary transfiguration of Alfred Tennyson in the *Memoir*:

Thus the priesthood circled round their idol, waving their censers and shouting their hymns of praise, while their ample draperies effectively hid from the public eye the object which was really in the centre of their throng, namely, a gaunt, black, touzled man, rough in speech, brooding like an old gypsy over his inch of clay pipe stuffed with shag, and sucking in port wine with gusto –'so long as it is black and sweet and strong, I care not!' Their fault lay, not in their praise, which was much of it deserved, but in their deliberate attempt in the interests of what was Nice and Proper – gods of the Victorian Age – to conceal what any conventional person might think not quite becoming. There were to be no shadows in the picture, no stains or rugosities on the smooth bust of rosy wax.

Certainly Hallam Tennyson felt himself appointed to write that sort of Life, though he *said*, 'I only want the true and full picture to be given.' Gosse mocked the homage to the Nice and the Proper. Sir Alfred Lyall – and he was certainly not alone – praised Hallam for his portrait of a life 'free alike from adventures and eccentricities, tranquil, blame-less and nobly dignified.' Reading the *Memoir* now, in the light of subsequent revelations about the Tennyson family, we find it impossible to suppose that anyone (least of all his son Hallam) could have imagined Tennyson's life as tranquil and free from eccentricities. But the real Alfred Tennyson is undoubtedly there, in spite of the nervous cuts and alterations. The *Memoir* is full of rich material, and not nearly as bland as Gosse suggested. Anne Thackeray Ritchie would say how Tennyson could never be 'chipped to the smooth pattern of the times'. He was always 'a poet leading a poet's life'. There was no possibility, however the material was arranged, of Alfred Tennyson looking like an immaculate saint; there was every possibility of Emily, the poet's wife, looking like an angel.

Already, incredibly, on 14 October, just two days after the funeral, Arthur Waugh's respectable (if inevitably inadequate) biography was in print. Waugh remembered later the 'sense of shame' he had felt when he read in the papers Tennyson's deathbed words: 'Oh, that Press will have me now.' 'Sincerely loyal as my own tribute was to be, the sentiment of that time was so strong against an alien intrusion that I felt, for

...ofession.	Residence at the Time of Marriage.	Father's Name and Surname.	Rank or Profession of Father.
...ie	Shiplake	George Clayton Tennyson. Clerk	
	Shiplake	Henry Sellwood. Organ...	

...of *Shiplake*   in the County of *Oxford*

...Shiplake Church   by me,   D. Rawnsley, ...

...Cecilia Lushington
...Edmund Law Lushington
Catherine Anne Rawnsley   C.R.Weld
Henry Sellwood.

the moment, like some sort of skulking hybrid between Iachimo and Peeping Tom.' However, the book was already in proof. Waugh travelled to Edinburgh on the day Tennyson died, worked with the printers, and the book was in the hands of the reviewers before Hallam and Emily arrived in the Isle of Wight. There were three editions in quick succession, six altogether: 'Everyone was talking about Tennyson that autumn.' Less respectable books would undoubtedly follow.

Even Waugh's *Alfred Tennyson* must have given Emily some misgivings. She opened the book and saw a facsimile of that most intimate document, her own marriage certificate – scarred by the way that Drummond Rawnsley, who had married them, had started to write her name and then had had to scratch it out, because the man's name is supposed to come first. One can see quite clearly how Rawnsley had begun to write over Emily's name but decided it was too much of a mess, and began again on the line below. There were those long-ago signatures – and not only their own but those of her cousin Kate Rawnsley, her father Henry Sellwood, of the Lushingtons, and even that of C. R. Weld, her sister Anne's husband, whose eventual disgrace would wipe him entirely out of the *Memoir*, in spite of his long close involvement in Tennyson's affairs.

Emily's role in Waugh's book – in his version of Tennyson's life – was marginal, a scatter of tiny references. Even her own mother's death was related to Alfred ('When Tennyson was but seven years old.') This was to be Emily's fate in numerous biographies, most written by men, when it was not the worse one of a few paragraphs suggesting that she had tamed his wild spirit and flattered him too much for his own good.

In one of his first letters after the return to Farringford Hallam had written to his cousin's wife, Sophie Tennyson: 'I am going to write a short life of him.' No need to say to whom the 'him' referred. 'This is to prevent other irreverent hands doing it. Has Uncle Frederick any letters? . . . Ask Uncle Frederick for any reminiscences of Somersby or Florence.' This casual reference to Frederick (Tennyson's eldest brother) and Somersby suggests Hallam had little idea of what had gone on there in February 1829, how George Clayton Tennyson had threatened to stab his son Frederick 'in the jugular vein and in the heart'. (The phrase was their mother's, reporting to the grandfather in Tealby.) The reference to Florence was because Alfred and Emily had stayed with Frederick there in 1851. 'My mother's help as to early days will be invaluable,' Hallam wrote. But violence and separations and illegitimate sons were obviously not going to be part of the story.

Emily was extremely wary of causing the sort of anguish Robert Browning had felt when Aldis Wright had published his edition of Edward FitzGerald's letters in the last year of Browning's life – and had revealed with what cool callousness Fitz had thought of Elizabeth Barrett Browning's death. At the time Emily had tried to soothe Browning, but he, who had always loved her 'singularly', refused to be soothed even by her. Hallam Tennyson remembered too his own revulsion when reading a volume of Jane Carlyle's letters, which he felt had damaged both her and Carlyle himself. Hallam hated the idea of washing any sort of linen in public. There would be a lot of bonfires. There had been bonfires already – destroying some of those 'chips of the workshop', Tennyson's 'additions and subtractions' – and Hallam was determined to burn freely, thinking it was what his father had wanted him to do.

Thousands of letters to Tennyson went up in smoke, and many he had written as well. The saddest destruction was of most of the letters exchanged between Alfred and Emily in the years before their marriage. There are some remarkably intimate fragments surviving, which makes one wonder if the destruction was rather to wipe out references to family 'scandals' – to opium, to alcohol, to marital breakdown and the lunatic asylum. The most poignant passage in the first part of the *Memoir* comes, very little altered, from Emily herself, not from one of the brothers.

In 1869 she had written for her sons about Tennyson's father, whom she had hardly known: 'You know how owing to some caprice on the part of your great-grandfather your grandfather was disinherited and . . . put into the church for whose duties he felt no call. This preyed upon his nerves and his health and caused much sorrow in his house. Many a time has your Father gone out in the dusk and cast himself on a grave in the little churchyard near wishing to be beneath it.' Hallam's version is more dramatic. Of his grandfather he wrote: ' . . . the sense of his father's unkindness preyed upon his nerves and his health, and caused him at times to be terribly despondent. More than once Alfred, scared by his father's fits of despondency, went out through the black night, and threw himself on a grave in the churchyard, praying to be beneath the sod himself.'

Very often in the early part of the *Memoir* Hallam quotes Emily's words unchanged, without saying whose they are. Sometimes, after the marriage, he gives credit to her journals. Tennyson certainly had not realized how actively Emily would be involved. He had, indeed, hardly imagined that he would die first. In 1875, after she had collapsed apparently from overwork, he had written: 'It will be a long time before she recovers her old self, and be able to write letters for five hours a day, not that I shall ever let her do so again.' But now Tennyson was not there to stop her and Emily gladly worked for hours on end, day after day, preparing material for the book.

First there was the problem of finding all the old diaries. A letter to her sister contradicts the suggestion that their whole purpose had been towards a telling of the life. On 1 November, Emily wrote to Anne: 'You must forgive me if I do not write much. Almost all my strength I have to give to the *Memoir*. We have not yet found nearly all the journals, but they were not cared for as they ought to have been and would have been had a memoir been thought of in [the] old days.'

The idea was that she should reduce the journals to an epitome for Hallam to use when writing the *Memoir*. She was not concerned only with giving information; one can see her crossing out a repetition, improving a cadence, making things clearer, not to Hallam, but to other readers who would not have known the things Hallam knew. What the original journals were like – how much else they contained – we have no idea, for it seems that nearly every scrap was destroyed, just as so much else was destroyed. What is more extraordinary is how much remains. Apart from the journals and her early letters to Alfred, it would seem Hallam could not bear to destroy anything in his mother's hand – so that there are surviving not only all those lists and the scraps of poetry and fiction, but also such things as instructions to the servants and her address book.

What survives of her biographical writing is considerable. There are several different versions of the Narrative for her sons, originally dated 9 December 1869, which supplies a highly selective version of Tennyson's early life. When she wrote it first, the boys were adolescents, Hallam seventeen and Lionel two years younger. The sons already knew a good deal about their father's background. Emily throws in the words 'as you know' or 'you know how' every now and again, but there was certainly a limit to what she wanted them to know. To suggest – as some have done – that *she* did not know what she left out is absurd. Emily's life was far more involved with that of the Tennysons in these early years than the *Memoir* allows. Her understanding of what Tennyson had endured at Somersby strengthened her long relationship with him.

But there were good reasons why she avoided telling the whole true terrible story. The sensitive boys were not to be burdened yet with knowledge of the 'black blood' of the Tennysons, of the 'old calamity', of their grandfather's epilepsy and alcoholism, their various uncles' madness and instability, opium addiction and violence – or of the mental breakdown of their aunt, Emily's own sister Louisa. She did not want to go into the details of the distresses and despairs of what Arthur Waugh had called so inaccurately Tennyson's 'serene and unblemished life'. The original 'censorship' was not for the *Memoir*, but for the boys.

Part of one version of Emily's Narrative for her sons is now bound in the first of the two green volumes, which hold the epitome of the main journal. This covers the period up to 1874, before the breakdown in her health. There follows, also entirely in Emily's hand, but written as if she were Hallam, a sixty-page outline of the main events from 1874 up to the time of Tennyson's death, presumably taken from memoranda books or pocket diaries which have also been destroyed. The whole thing was a remarkable achievement for someone in poor health and over eighty by the time she completed her task. Much of the later material goes straight into the *Memoir* without any reference to 'my mother's journal', the phrase used with the quotations from the main journal between the marriage and 1874. But it was certainly written by Emily and not dictated by Hallam, who had quite enough to do encouraging all the other contributors and putting together the fragments of the jigsaw. 'It is very difficult to piece things neatly together,' as Emily wrote when they had only just started.

Emily made various attempts, when writing, to use the third person, obviously with the intention of making it easier for Hallam to transfer material straight into the *Memoir*. But she found it difficult to do so, and in her condensation of the main journal she gave it up after a while, turning her 'they' back into 'we', and 'their' into 'our'. In this rewritten journal Alfred is consistently A., but it was her idea that in the *Memoir* itself Hallam should call him, not A.T., as he had originally, but 'my father'. There is a manuscript page in Emily's hand, writing as if she were Hallam, which largely became pages 220 to 221 of the *Memoir*.

That Emily herself saw her contribution to the *Memoir* as central is shown in her version of the preface, where she writes for Hallam: 'I have therefore relied to a great extent on the simple facts of his daily life recorded in a journal not meant for publication.' And although Hallam writes his mother almost entirely out of the first part of the book – before the marriage in 1850 – he does say in *his* preface: 'The picture of his early days has been mainly sketched from what he and my mother have told me.'

The *Memoir* is essentially a scrapbook, a collection of relevant papers – mainly letters and diary entries and contributions from friends – linked together with some narrative. Emily wrote a title page at one point:

Memorials and Reminiscences

of

Alfred Lord Tennyson

edited by his son

Hallam Lord Tennyson

It is obviously Hallam who has crossed out the word 'edited', even though he admitted it was his father's wish that his hand should be as 'seldom seen as maybe' which 'accounts for the occasionally fragmentary nature of the work'.

A certain Dr Allen, the physician of an Asylum for curing diseases near Beech Hill, with whom this family became acquainted, had either conceived or adopted the idea of wood-carving by machinery. At all events he was possessed by it, and inspired my father with so great an enthusiasm for it that by degrees he persuaded my Father to give him not only all the money (for which I was careful I agent) he had put his little estate at Grasby, since I was born) but all else he had besides not merely this, but some and but for my Father's intervention apparently all the family belongings of such of the family as were at Beech Hill, so fascinating was the prospect of carved oak-panels for rooms & carved oak furniture to be done by machinery & made by its cheapness within reach of numbers, while adding to the wealth of the family.

The entire project collapsed My Father's worldly possessions were gone and part of those belonging to all at Beech Hill. The only tangible good which came of the trouble was that my father had the opportunity of seeing something of Dr Allen's patients which enabled him to write "the mad scene in Maud".

My uncle Edmund Lushington generously insured the life of Dr Allen by annual insurance for part of his debt to my Father. The letter which appeared afterwards in these volumes was written on occasion of the news of the Doctor's sudden death reaching my Father.

34

The surviving Materials – ten manuscript volumes – must have been based on some earlier compilation, for they contain hardly any original material but lots of copies (mostly in Audrey's hand, some in Emily's, with links in Hallam's hand), bits of paper pinned with now rusting dressmaker's pins on to the foolscap pages. Much of this material never reached the final *Memoir*. Hallam had always wanted it to be 'short', and Henry Sidgwick urged him not to make it longer than Trevelyan's *Macaulay*, which he thought the best biography written in his time – 'two moderate-sized volumes, of something under five hundred pages each'.

Emily copied some letters, but mostly she was working away 'in Ally's study' on the primary task of condensing her journals. A few pages of the new version have been cut, but Hallam appears to have believed it valuable to preserve his mother's record. Rather than chopping it up, he has copied it or had it copied yet again, with inevitable variants. Sometimes Emily cannot read her own long-ago handwriting. She had complained to her sister how small it was and how bad the winter daylight.

There are also surviving, together with her preface, a number of short essays in Emily's hand written as if by Hallam. There are, for instance, two on Tennyson's faith, one beginning 'that my Father studied the Bible, all who knew his poems know.' This seems to be a direct answer to James Knowles' essay, as Emily attempts to reconcile 'the teaching of Nature' with the God of Love, and ends up by resorting to the suggestion that Tennyson 'bowed before the mystery'. There is also one where she writes: 'I for one rejoice in the hints I have heard of National Insurance for old age pensions' and goes on about a hope to 'free Ireland for ever from the curse of double ownership'. None of these 'essays' is dated; all of them are very confusing biographically, for it is often difficult to be sure whose views they are, though they are all written in Emily's unmistakable hand.

As she was so involved and so many of her own words are used, both in direct quotation and in Hallam's version of her Narrative, the *Memoir* seems as much Emily Tennyson's book as his. Would it have been the same book if it had been hers alone? There is plenty of evidence that she would have been more obviously present. For all her self-abnegation, Emily saw herself, as indeed she was, at the heart of Tennyson's life. It was not that she wanted more credit for what she had done; she just wanted to be there at Alfred's side. But again and again where she had written 'We' or even, trying to help Hallam 'They', Hallam has changed it to 'He'.

Hallam, keeping his eye directly on his father, is inclined to eliminate other women too. For instance, in her journal Emily makes it clear that Alfred's sister, Mary Ker, travelled with them in August 1872. Mary was important to Tennyson, but her appearance in the *Memoir* is restricted to a mention of her marriage.

It is not necessary to examine in detail all the numerous instances in which Hallam has reduced Emily's presence in the narrative or overruled her version of what might appear. I will give just two examples. For his own reasons, Hallam decided to underestimate Emily's early friendship with the Tennysons, which will be explored, as far as is possible, in the next two chapters. He wants – and many subsequent writers have followed too closely in his footsteps – to suggest that Alfred's meeting with Emily in the 'Fairy Wood' in 1830 was a first meeting – an isolated chance encounter, not part of a family friendship. One of the results of this is that Emily Sellwood becomes an unnamed friend in the 1834 scene when Alfred's sister Emily makes her first appearance after the death of Arthur Hallam, to whom she had been betrothed.

In her first version of the Narrative for her sons Emily, the poet's wife, wrote: 'The next visit to Somersby I remember was after the fearful cloud from Vienna. It was the first night that Aunt Emily appeared among their friends after her unspeakable loss. She came slowly in, dressed in deep mourning, a skeleton of her former self, with one white rose in her raven black hair as Arthur Hallam liked to see it.' In the *Memoir* this becomes ' "We were waiting for her", *writes one of her friends*, "in the drawing room the first day since her loss that she had been able to meet anyone and she came at last, dressed in deep mourning, a shadow of her former self, but with one white rose in her black hair as her Arthur loved to see her." ' This not only wipes out Emily Sellwood's presence but increases the poignancy of the relationship between the betrothed pair – ('as *her* Arthur *loved* to see *her*'), an important consideration for Hallam's namesake, the son, who was always nervous of the interpretation that could be put on his father's passionate friendship with Arthur Hallam.

Emily is also left out of the *Memoir* at a point when it would be particularly reasonable for her to be there, the time of her own wedding. Hallam published Alfred's brief sweet thank-you note to Emily's cousin Kate Rawnsley, but leaves out Emily's half of the letter. He also adds a postscript about the Shiplake poem which does not belong to this letter at all. We will look more closely at these matters later.

Of course it was Tennyson's own early life that mattered – it was Tennyson's life that mattered – and his widow obligingly wrote and rewrote the story as it was going to be told: the official record. In 1869 she had written: 'I was thinking in bed last night of a time that must come and it struck me that when your Father and I are gone you will be glad to have some record of his early days and I resolved to leave you one.' But there was another story of those years and she could tell that separate story, unimportant as it might seem – her own brief outline of the long years before her marriage.

Now, after his father's death and near the end of her own life, at last Hallam asked her for her own story. She agreed to write her Recollections. She began:

You ask me to tell you something of my life before marriage. It would be hard indeed not to do anything you ask of me if within my power. To say the truth this particular thing you want is somewhat painful . . .

CHAPTER ONE

The girl at the Market Place window

All of Emily's earliest memories were painful. She was in a house, the house where she had been born, in the Market Place in Horncastle and she spent a lot of time looking out of the window. She remembered her mother 'passing the window in a crimson velvet pelisse' and then they were together in the house, and her mother was lying on a sofa, with a white shawl round her. Lying on sofas: it was something that women did.

This early memory of her mother lying on a sofa must have been of a time just after the birth of Louisa, the youngest sister, the third of the Sellwood girls, after Emily and Anne. Four months later, on the 30 September 1816, their mother was dead of typhus fever, aged twenty-eight. Emily was three years old.

The child's first memory of her father, Henry Sellwood, was of him looking at her 'with sad eyes' after her mother's death. He carried Emily in his arms to the funeral in the church across the lane, around the corner from the Market Place. She asked what they were doing 'and in all this had no idea of death', though she had been held up to see her mother in her coffin, 'crowned with roses' and beautiful. They were the last roses of summer. All through her life Emily would have a particular sympathy with the motherless, knowing what it meant.

Years later Bertrand Russell would say, not remembering his mother, that 'I have loved a ghost and in loving a ghost my inmost self has become spectral. I have therefore buried it deeper and deeper beneath layers of cheerfulness, affection and joy of life.' Emily had that obvious joy of life too, but Tennyson would sense that sadness at the heart of things, that overwhelming need for love the motherless must always feel. Her own mothering of her sons would be self-taught, instinctive and passionate.

Emily Sarah Sellwood was born on 9 July 1813 in the house in Horncastle, Lincolnshire where her father carried on his business as an attorney. She was baptized the same day, which may suggest the fragility which was to burden her all her life – an almost unbearable delicacy at times, but one which she bore with a Christian fortitude her father encouraged and a calmness that was never a simple passivity. The winter of 1813–14 was a hard one; indeed Emily's first January was said to have been the coldest month of the entire nineteenth century.

Henry Sellwood had been born in Berkshire on 10 November 1782. He had arrived in Lincolnshire, early in the new century, optimistic, eager, energetic, determined to make his way in the world. There is a Bible surviving, a present from Henry's mother, with the inscription: *Henry Sellwood, Horncastle, May 1808*. He joined the legal practice of Robert and Richard Clitherow in 1809, eventually setting up on his own in the Market Place. Seven miles away at Somersby, just at this time, George and Eliza Tennyson were moving into the newly refurbished Rectory.

Emily would say that her father, knowing he needed to earn his own living (the dramatic phrase was that the family were 'on the road to ruin'), had wanted to be a soldier, but his mother had got it into her head that he 'would be slain if he went to the wars'; she persuaded him to take up the law instead. The Sellwoods had owned a considerable amount of land in Berkshire, but the inheritor of the family estates, Colonel Sellwood of Brightwalton, Commander of 'the Berkshire Militia at the period of the American War of Independence', had been merely a cousin of Emily's grandfather, Henry Sellwood. This grandfather had acquired Pibworth (a house still standing) on his marriage to a Rowland, together with over six hundred acres of woods and farmland near the village of Aldworth in Berkshire. Why they were on 'the road to ruin' is not at all clear.

In her Recollections, Emily recalled childhood visits to her Sellwood grandparents:

I remember that in Berkshire we often used to wander up to a tower among our woods, where a gaunt old lady lived called Black Jane, who told our fortunes. We had our private theatricals too, like other children. Our dramatic performances were frequent and our plays inexhaustible for we drew on Miss Edgeworth's tales. I was always fond of music and used to sing duets with my soldier-cousin Richard Sellwood.

The duets – like Black Jane – were undoubtedly in Berkshire for that was where Richard Sellwood lived when he was not serving King and Country. But the theatricals presumably took place in Horncastle as well.

Printing Emily's recollections in his 1911 volume *Tennyson and his Friends*, Hallam added an extract from a letter Emily wrote in 1873 to Marian Bradley, who had just been to St Mary's, Aldworth and seen the extraordinary Crusader effigies which still inhabit the place:

To think of your having been among our Aldworth giants . . . Pibworth belonged to my grandmother, a Rowland from Wales. I am glad you did not go there, for all the grand pine grove, which backed it, was cut down as soon as it was bought, some years ago, by some London man and I hear it has sunk into a mere commonplace house. The little estate, in which were the ruins of Beche Castle, was ours. The tombs are those of the 'de la Beches'. Their pedigree was said to have been taken down to show to Queen Elizabeth . . . and never to have been replaced, so that no more is known of the giants than that they were 'de la Beches'. Neither do we know if they were really our ancestors, as they were reported to be, or whether the report came from our having owned the remains of the castle.

Naturally Emily would have liked the idea of having these huge five-hundred-year-old knights as ancestors, even if they survive with some mutilation, but there is no evidence of any connection. Her father was inclined to trace his family's origins to Somerset, where Hallam claims an Abbot, John de Selwode, as 'of the same name and race as my mother' and appropriately buried beside the reputed tomb of King Arthur at Glastonbury.

If Emily thought the birthplace of her father – a substantial country house – had become commonplace and unimpressive, what would she have thought of her mother's birthplace in Spilsby, Lincolnshire, which now carries the sign TREV'S FRANKLIN HOUSE BAKERY?

Emily was often in Spilsby, not far from Horncastle, before her marriage and must have had pointed out to her the humble shop on the main street which had belonged to her grandfather. There, it seems, all the Franklin children were born, though by the time Henry Sellwood arrived in Lincolnshire, looking for a bride, they had moved to a country house a few miles from Spilsby at Mavis Enderby. It was in the church at Mavis Enderby that Henry Sellwood and Sarah Franklin were married on 15 September 1812, less than ten months before Emily was born.

Henry Sellwood had certainly not married for money, but his new wife did bring a network of Lincolnshire connections extremely useful to a rising young lawyer. Sarah was the fifth daughter and tenth child of Willingham Franklin, and we know that around this same time her brother John, later to be as famous as any man in England, had to live entirely on his naval pay and at least once had sent £5 home from his midshipman's pittance to help his parents in Lincolnshire. (Their mother died just two years before Sarah's marriage.) John would become one of Henry's 'dearest friends'. 'My father was much beloved by his wife's family,' Emily said.

There is little evidence of what sort of person Sarah was. One of the surviving books with her name, a French course 'à l'usage des enfants', dated 1796, when she was eight, suggests that her education was not neglected. Like her brothers, she was apparently intelligent and religious. There is a copy of Vicesimus Knox's *Considerations on the Nature and Efficacy of the Lord's Supper* inscribed 'Sarah Sellwood with Diana's affectionate love'. She may never have read it, but it is unlikely that Diana, whoever she was, would have given it to Sarah unless she knew that it was a subject likely to interest her. Not long before her marriage she acquired ('Sarah Franklin. March 30.1812') Lucy Aikin's *Epistles on Women*, exemplifying their character and conditioning in various ages and nations, with miscellaneous poems. Emily as a girl must have pored over these books of her mother's, as we can, trying to imagine the lost, unknown woman who had owned them.

The Franklins had also apparently come down in the world – a natural claim for people whose situation is not exactly what they would wish it to be. Emily's Franklin great-grandmother – a widow 'of masculine capacity and great resolution' – had apprenticed her eldest son Willingham to a grocer and draper in Lincoln, and when he was out of his indentures the family moved to Spilsby and opened a shop, which flourished on their hard work. They added to it a banking business – it was a time of great expansion in small rural banks – and Willingham enhanced his good fortune by marrying Hannah Weekes, the daughter of a substantial farmer.

There were twelve children born over or behind the Spilsby shop. The eldest, Thomas, apparently got involved with a dishonest partner, the Spilsby bank failed and the Franklins were again in financial difficulties. He and another of the brothers and two of the girls died before Emily was born, and her mother, as we have seen, died when she was only three. Of the ones who remained, all of them were important to the Sellwoods in one way or another.

Most important was the brother closest in age to Sarah: John, the fifth and youngest son, born in 1786, two years before his sister. As a boy he went to the grammar school at Louth, a generation before Tennyson's own brief and unhappy time there. At fifteen he went to sea. By the time Henry Sellwood arrived in Lincolnshire, Franklin had already been engaged in two of the greatest naval battles in British history: Copenhagen and Trafalgar. Emily was throughout her life constantly

43

described as the niece of Sir John Franklin; his statue dominates Spilsby today: DISCOVERER OF THE NORTH-WEST PASSAGE. There is still a high school carrying his name in Yellowknife, North West Territories. Tennyson would write the epitaph for his memorial in Westminster Abbey. 'My husband talks of the heroic Franklin blood,' Emily wrote in 1871. It was always a connection which made her proud. A second Franklin uncle was also knighted: Sir Willingham Franklin, ONE OF THE JUDGES OF THE SUPREME COURT OF JUDICATURE AT MADRAS it says on the memorial in Spilsby church.

Of the Franklin aunts, we shall hear more later. Only one was un-married: Elizabeth, or Betsy, as she was often known. It was she who came to the rescue of her brother-in-law, Henry Sellwood, after his wife's death and agreed to move to Horncastle and help to bring up the three small motherless girls, Emily, Anne and Louisa. Sadly she had, as Emily said, 'no instinctive love of children', and had long been used to a quiet life. She was eleven years older than Sarah and nearly forty when her sister died. She was set in her ways and did not like them disturbed. If the little girls were too merry and noisy in the mornings, they were summoned by their aunt, all three of them, into her room, where they had to hold out their 'small hands for stripes from a certain little riding-whip'. If, later in the day, their needlework was not well done, the horrid aunt would prick their fingers with their own needles as a pun-ishment. (Emily never enjoyed sewing.) In the days before they went to school, Aunt Betsy taught the sisters herself and if she did not approve of their work, they had fool's caps put on their heads and were ban-ished to a corner of the room. Emily excuses her aunt, saying her nature 'was by no means cruel' – it was simply the way she believed children should be brought up.

Their father had very different ideas. 'No-one could have had a better father,' Emily said, more than once. 'He was my idol.' She saw him as 'kindly, cultivated, unaffected and above all a good friend'. But he was busy, and presumably too grateful for his sister-in-law's help to interfere very often with her methods.

The position of an attorney in a nineteenth-century market town was a little ambiguous. He was not necessarily a gentleman, which was presumably the reason Henry Sellwood was so often described as gentlemanly. Sellwood was always tall (six foot two or three) and thin and always gentlemanly: 'the model of an English gentleman'. It may be remembered that Tennyson's grandfather was also an attorney in a

Lincolnshire market town. Years later a visitor to Tennyson's uncle at the grandiose folly Bayons Manor would comment: 'Whoever would think for all the pomp and circumstance and pretended ancestry of Bayons Manor that its owner was the son of my grandfather's attorney at Market Rasen?'

In the Horncastle Directory the clergy were listed with the gentry but the attorneys were not. They were listed with the auctioneers, bakers, bankers and basketmakers, and only at the head of the list for alphabetical reasons. Henry Sellwood became a sort of banker as well. He was one of three local directors of the Lincoln and Lindsey Bank in the Cornmarket in Horncastle, of which he was a shareholder – at the same time as 'John Fytche, Esq.', Tennyson's mother's brother, was a local director of the Louth branch of the same bank. It was a period when a trusted attorney in a country town could easily make a fortune. His dealings went far beyond writing wills and conveyancing, and included many activities that would today be handled by a building society or a land agent. Sellwood had a finger in every pie in Horncastle, and contacts all over the neighbourhood.

At a public meeting on 12 October 1813, Henry Sellwood was one of the 'gentlemen' elected to a committee with the intention of establishing the first National School in the town. It was a time when 'the education of the poor was beginning to excite so much attention in all parts of the kingdom'. The meeting was chaired by the Vicar, the Reverend Clement Madeley, who had baptized Emily just three months before. Sellwood's interest in education may have been stimulated by the birth of his first child – but it was not, of course, a school the child could ever go to, established as it was for the education of the poor. The following year the National School was built on land given by Sir Joseph Banks, the botanist who had travelled round the world with Captain Cook. It was just round the corner from the Market Place, next to the church and opposite the Manor House, just a minute's walk from the Sellwoods' front door. Sir Joseph headed the list of benefactors to the new school with a handsome thirty pounds, matched by the Vicar. In comparison, Henry Sellwood's three guineas was modest, but it stands out among the mass of single guineas in the subscription list.

Henry Sellwood kept his connection with the school throughout his time in Horncastle, as a member of the governing committee. He also became a governor of Horncastle Grammar School and was for many years solicitor to that school. A later report on the National School spoke of the 'absolute necessity' of such institutions. 'In a Christian point of view they are imperatively called for as matter of *duty*.' The writer urged his readers to 'Train up a child in the way he should go' and to make sure children's minds were 'early imbued with the principles and doctrine of the Gospel of Christ'.

The Sellwood children in the house on the Market Place were certainly being trained in the way that they were intended to go as devoted servants of Christ until their lives' end; but there was plenty of contact with the world. Horncastle life teemed outside their windows. Everyone came into town and many people knocked on the Sellwoods' door, looking for advice of one sort or another. There was a great deal of work for an efficient lawyer. Everyone admired his integrity, as Alfred Tennyson himself would do. Sellwood prospered, gradually buying 'real estate at Horncastle, Coningsby and Ingoldmells in the county of Lincoln' – and becoming able to afford to keep a phaeton and horses, and to build stables to house them.

Horncastle was not only a market town, a centre for agricultural produce and the sale of animals. It had its own breweries and tanneries and candlemakers. Its resident population of three thousand multiplied when the fairs were on. There were twenty-one public houses or inns in Horncastle, four of them in the Market Place itself: the Black Horse, the Lord Nelson, the Punch House and the Queen's Head – and many more were only a minute away in Bridge Street, the High Street and the Bull Ring.

The town was famous for its fairs – indeed the Directory once declared that the one held each August had 'long been celebrated as the largest fair for horses in the kingdom, perhaps it may be said in the world.' It would go on for ten days, much of it outside the Sellwoods' windows, with the inns all round them doing a roaring trade. It was hardly a sheltered life.

The Market Place in those days was not as large an open space as it is now. The Sellwoods' house faced on to some ancient shops. Though much of the town had been redeveloped in the eighteenth century and contained some handsome buildings (including the Sellwoods' own house, with its nine sash windows and three dormers), there was still an almost medieval jumble of narrow lanes, through which, when the fairs were on, people and animals jostled. Henry Sellwood took a great interest in the horses. He had been a daring rider in his youth. On one visit to Berkshire the children's grandmother told them of a time 'when

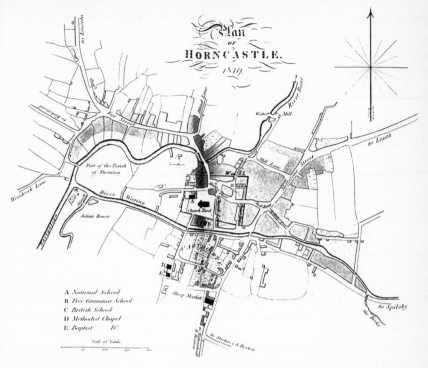

all the gentlemen of the county were volunteers' and 'he could ride horses which no-one else could ride,' adding proudly, 'your father and his brother (both six foot three) were the handsomest men among them all.' At that time, apparently, during the Napoleonic wars, 'he kept guard with his fellow-volunteers over the French prisoners' and would say they were 'always singing their patriotic songs'. Both riding and singing were part of Emily's childhood. Much as her father wished it, she said, she never became a good horsewoman. 'I well recall my dislike of riding when my pony was fastened to an iron stake, which I had to go round and round' – presumably on a long rein.

When her uncle, Captain Franklin, visited he told his nieces not only of his own adventures in the great sea fights, but also of Cromwell's battles in the area. 'Horncastle and its vicinity were fields of much contest in the days of Cromwell. One of his hardest fought battles took place between Bolingbroke and . . . Winceby, but as no political results followed from it, the details . . . have been omitted in the page of

47

History' – but relics of this period were still often found. Emily began a lifelong interest in history. Horncastle was a Roman town – traces of the Roman wall remained a hundred yards or so from the Sellwoods' house and 'urns, coins, fibulae and other Roman vestiges' were found from time to time. Emily learnt Latin with her father enthusiastically. She was also learning French. Later there would be German and Italian. She discovered very early the delights of Shakespeare; we know she read *Cymbeline* when she was only eight.

But music began to be – and would remain – at the centre of her life. Piles of sheet music survive from these early days, including *The Scholars' Daily Practice* and *Preparatory Exercises for the Pianoforte*, calculated to form the hand and give a correct idea of fingering. Practising her scales regularly, she was soon able to play the songs her mother left behind, 'songs from Walter Scott's poems: The Song of Fitz Eustace, A Tale of Flodden Field, The Last Words of Marmion', and much else besides. There was a lot of singing round the piano. Later she would learn the harmonium and play trios with her sisters. Her teacher may well have been the same Miss Tonge who taught the Tennyson girls. Emily was a diligent pupil. All her life she would see 'Idleness as the Root of all Evil'; there was a worrying picture with this caption in the front of a book on the Sellwood children's shelves called *Education at Home*.

Emily would always remember an early visit to Harrington Hall – though it was a house that seems to have meant more to Alfred Tennyson than it ever did to her. There was a family connection at this point – before Rosa Baring lived there – for the house belonged to Robert and Augusta Cracroft and Robert was a first cousin of Emily's uncle Thomas, the husband of her mother's sister Isabella. Towards the end of her life Emily thanked her sister Anne for sending a picture of the house, and wrote:

Do you remember our being there when we were tinies and that the tapestry half frightened us. I remember too my great admiration of Arabella Cracroft and her great dog. She was a lovely creature.

Arabella, twelve years older than Emily, was Robert's younger sister. It may have been another visit to Harrington – or perhaps the same one – to which Emily refers in an earlier letter to Anne. (Her references to the past in letters, though frequent, are always tantalizingly brief – often in response to remarks in her sisters' letters.) 'Oh yes,' she wrote in 1889, 'I well remember how we quivered in the drive tho' we did not dare to show it, our dear Father caring so much that we should be brave.'

Henry Sellwood, excellent father of daughters, always encouraged them to live up to his expectations of them; they certainly grew up confident of their brains and of their talents. The sisters were used to speaking up and being listened to – in a way that might not have been so if Henry Sellwood had had a wife and sons. If Aunt Betsy believed in keeping children subdued, Emily's father had a different attitude. Theodore Watts-Dunton would one day say that Emily Tennyson seemed to him 'destined from birth to hold a high place as a conversationalist, brilliant and stimulating.'

If there were some advantages in not having brothers, there is no doubt that to Victorian girls the sister/brother relationship was particularly important. Girls without brothers were deprived of a natural continuous relationship with the opposite sex, what one feminist has called 'the rough and tumble sexuality of the nursery'. The brothers of their schoolfriends would become important, not only because of the dangerous chance of finding husbands among them, but also for the welcome possibility of getting to know boys and young men as friends.

Some time in the autumn of 1822 Emily, aged nine, was looking out of the window. There was always so much to see. One day there was a carriage drawn up at the door and in it was a boy of 'about thirteen' waiting for his father, who was talking to Henry Sellwood. The boy was Alfred Tennyson. She remembered him clearly. The house had no front garden, just an area and railings, so he was very close to her, she said. He was pale in those days but with 'the same very refined features' – features 'full of strength and spirituality and tenderness' – a remarkable boy. This is the most tantalizing of all Emily's passing references to the past. She tells us so little of what we want to know. The reason in this case is that she was writing only about his appearance. Alexander Macmillan, the publisher, had asked for her opinion of a crayon sketch purporting to be Alfred when he was twenty-two or three, which Macmillan wanted to use in a new edition of Palgrave's *Golden Treasury*. Everyone thought the drawing was of Tennyson, but Emily wrote decisively: 'I think of it now as I did at first – that whether meant for him or not, it is certainly not he.' *She* knew what he looked like, had known ever since she was a child when she first saw him from the window of the house in the Market Place in Horncastle.

We know nothing else about this encounter – whether the boy in the carriage noticed the girl at the window, whether Emily asked her father who the boy was. Whether indeed she knew already that the Reverend George Clayton Tennyson was seeing her father on business. We wonder what that business was. A bright child of nine, an eldest child with a lonely talkative father, may pick up a lot about what is going on in the neighbourhood. Emily may well have looked with particular interest at this boy, knowing that he came from that crowded un-conventional Rectory at Somersby, one of the seven brothers and four sisters. If she knew nothing of drunken rages, Emily could certainly have heard of the tame owl and of the monkey 'whose prime luxury was to singe the hair of his back at a candle', and of the tender-hearted boys who were notorious for springing the gamekeepers' traps and so addicted to reading that the carrier and carters in the lanes had to beware of running them down.

Frederick, the eldest Tennyson brother, was now at Eton, but Charles and Alfred had been brought home from their chilling experience of the Grammar School at Louth to the sporadic but brilliant and demanding teaching of their father. The Rectory teemed with children. Mary, Emilia (but usually confusingly known as Emily too) and Edward were just a little older than Emily Sellwood. Arthur had been born in 1814, the same year as Emily's sister Anne, then there were Septimus (the seventh son, the first-born having died in infancy) and Matilda (who was Louisa Sellwood's age), and after that Cecilia, who was five, and Horatio the baby of the family, three years old in the September of 1822. Cecilia gives a picture in the *Memoir* of the boy Alfred at around this time, 'in the winter evenings by the firelight', taking her, his small sister, 'on his knee, with Arthur and Matilda leaning against him on either side, the baby Horatio between his legs' and fascinating 'this group of young hero worshippers' with legends of knights and heroes, dragons and demons and witches.

It is a charming picture and was certainly a cherished memory. But we now know much more than Emily and her son Hallam wanted us to know of what was going on at Somersby. Alfred must have been glad to sit quietly on his own waiting for his father. His need to escape from the reality of life at Somersby from boyhood 'frequently' took the form of 'a kind of waking trance', which he described years later. 'This has often come upon me through repeating my own name to myself silently, till all at once as it were out of the intensity of the conscious-ness of individuality the individuality itself seemed to dissolve and fade away into boundless being . . .' It is tempting to think of the boy sitting in the carriage repeating his own name to himself – 'Alfred Tennyson, Alfred Tennyson' – while the girl at the Market Place window watched so intently that every feature of his face was engraved in her memory for the rest of her life.

And in the office the two fathers talked to each other – both tall, impressive men, but deeply different: Henry Sellwood, attorney-at-law, so energetic, spry, sane, sanguine and abstemious; the Reverend George Clayton Tennyson, so indolent, bitter, despondent and hard drinking, who had energy only for his quarrels with his father, his wife, his eldest son. They were quarrels well known in the county. In a letter in August 1820 Alfred's father had specifically accused his own father of humili-ating him in public, 'holding me up to utter derision', greeting him in front of visitors with the words, '*Now you great awkward booby are you here?*'

We do not know what business the Reverend George Tennyson had with Henry Sellwood on that day in 1822 or how well the two men knew each other. Sellwood had undoubtedly heard Tennyson preach, if only when he gave the special sermon on 24 October 1817 for the Horncastle Dispensary Meeting, with which Sellwood was deeply in-volved. Whether he was acting generally as Tennyson's lawyer at this point we do not know. Later his involvement in the Tennysons' affairs was considerable.

This was a bad year, 1822, for Tennyson's father. He was in a con-stant state of anxiety and fret, pain and anger. It was Emily who was responsible for establishing so firmly in the *Memoir* the idea that George Clayton Tennyson had been 'disinherited' by his father. (Was it a word Tennyson himself ever used?) It was a convenient explanation for the dramatic contrast in lifestyle between the two brothers, George and Charles, and for George's anguish. There is no question that Charles, the younger, was his father's favoured son. He was a public man. Henry Sellwood knew of him as Member of Parliament for Grimsby, a force in the county, with a house in London and a rich wife. But old George, Alfred's grandfather ('the old brute', as Arthur Hallam would call him) was endlessly generous to the Somersby family, even if he did anger his elder son by keeping him in the dark about the child-ren's 'future prospects'. It was always known that they did have 'future prospects' and that the eldest son himself would at least inherit the family property if not anything that old George had acquired in his lifetime. He was certainly not cut off without a shilling, as the phrase 'disinherited' conventionally suggests. Alfred's father's difficulties were always as much of his own making as of the grandfather's, but compounded by epilepsy and the fear of epilepsy. It is difficult to distinguish cause from effect. In 1822 ill health was the public explanation of his problems – of the missed services, the unpaid bills, the bizarre treatment of troublesome servants and sons.

That spring George Tennyson had written to his mother from Cheltenham where he and his wife had both gone in search of healing, leaving the small children in the care of the servants and their burdened older brothers. The physician, he said, 'gives me great hopes that the waters will re-establish my health and says that a schirrus has not as yet formed upon my liver, but that he could not have answered for the consequences if I had not immediately come here.' But that November – presumably after the visit to Henry Sellwood – Alfred's father was back in Cheltenham, accompanied this time by his son Charles, aged fourteen (he was only thirteen months older than Alfred), whose asthma had also been causing concern. Everyone was worried about George, not least his brother Charles, with whom most of the time he maintained a good relationship, in spite of his jealousy over their relative stations in life.

Their mother wrote to Charles the following January: 'We will, if we can, get him freed from the noise of his children.' Charles's wife said: 'So many boys to teach is really too much and with his weak nerves and delicate health I fear it will upset him.' George himself said that teaching the boys gave him some purpose in life. 'Phoenix like, I trust . . . they will spring from my ashes in consequence of the exertions I have bestowed upon them,' he wrote to his brother. But increasingly the exertion was too much for him. He confessed he had become overwhelmed by his low spirits 'and a crippling inertia'. He would sometimes sleep until three in the afternoon and drank more and more as if alcohol could solve his problems. 'I never set myself about anything that I can possibly avoid,' he admitted.

In her Narrative for her sons, Emily, who hardly knew him, reflected on his undoubted intellect and the energy he had once showed in teaching 'himself Hebrew and Syriac and so far perfected himself in Greek that he taught Uncle Charlie and your Father all they ever learnt of this and of all other things that they did not learn of themselves (unless it be dancing) until they went to Trinity.'

The dancing days and Cambridge are still far off. In 1823 we have a chance to get some idea of Emily's Lincolnshire relations through the surviving letters of Eleanor Porden and John Franklin, who were married that August, having been secretly engaged when Emily's uncle left for his first Arctic expedition in 1819. Eleanor, another brotherless daughter, seems to have had considerable influence on Henry Sellwood, who became her brother-in-law, and this network of Franklin relations and connections was immensely important to his prosperity as a lawyer; there is evidence that he acted for nearly all of them at one time or another.

Eleanor Porden was a remarkable woman, a Londoner who had always taken a keen interest in the scientific discoveries of the day since as a girl of nine she had, with her father's encouragement, attended lectures at the Royal Society. It seems no coincidence that that spring, when he visited Horncastle, John Franklin had given his small nieces the Reverend Jeremiah Joyce's *Dialogues in chemistry intended for the instruction and entertainment of young people* – a fourth edition had come out the year before. Both volumes carry on the fly-leaf: 'To Emily, Anne and Louisa Sellwood with their Uncle John Franklin's affectionate regard. May 14. 1823.'

Two days later John Franklin wrote to Eleanor Porden, his betrothed:

You are mistaken, my dear friend in supposing the members of my family are ignorant of Miss Porden's existence, they have known of you for some time from your literary productions, and have been made acquainted within these few days of our intimacy.

Eleanor Porden had published an erudite poem 'The Veils', written when she was only sixteen, which had earned her 'the honour of having her work crowned by the Institute of France', not long before Waterloo. When she sent John Franklin her huge poem on Richard Coeur de Lion – published in two volumes – she told him: 'I have learned from experience that it is sometimes inconvenient to be acquainted with an Author, and I have also been taught not to feel affronted if my friends should be the last to read any work of mine.' It was tactful of John Franklin (and lucky for him if it were true) to tell her that his family knew her work.

She intended to continue her literary career after their marriage. When he had said he hated the idea of 'seeing the name of anyone connected with himself in print', she had said that out of loyalty to her father, who had so encouraged her and had died two years before, she would choose her art rather than marriage. She was wary of accepting Franklin, fearing the 'narrow, provincial society' he came from, his puritanical religion, his enormous love of Lincolnshire, his hordes of relations. What she did not fear was his dangerous profession; she would scold two of his sisters, Emily's aunts Betsy and Isabella, for *their* fears.

In 1823 John Franklin told Eleanor Porden about his 'very much attached family':

I should certainly ask you to find room in your heart for each of my relations or at least to keep a corner vacant for them, and I should trust after you are known to them they would for their own sakes be cheerfully admitted to fill up the space. That you may know how large a portion to keep unoccupied I will give you some account of them. My Father as I have already told you is very old, supporting the infirmities of blindness and deafness with a truly Christian calmness and resignation. His family now consists of seven persons. My two brothers who are in India, and four daughters. My eldest sister is unmarried, having been for the greater part of her life an invalid, and she is now only in a state of convalescence, after a severe illness. She will, I hope, be quite restored to health by the time *we* can visit Lincolnshire, and I am sure no person will more gladly and cheerfully welcome you as my wife.

My other sisters are married and have each some charming little girls and boys who are playfellows and who will be delighted to receive a new aunt into their society. Of the occupations which my brothers-in-law follow, Mr. Booth and Mr. Cracroft each farms a large portion of land. Mr. Wright is a Clergyman. I have also two other brothers-in-law but my sisters are dead, the one Mr. Sellwood is a solicitor and lives near here, the other lives in London. The former has three daughters, and the other three sons.

This is the state of my family. You will find them all mild and amiable and I am sure affectionate.

Emily was, of course, one of the three daughters of the solicitor, and Aunt Betsy, of the little riding-whip and the needle-pricks, was the invalid unmarried sister. The other unnamed sisters were Hannah Booth, ten years older than Emily's mother, Sarah, and her two younger sisters, Isabella Cracroft and Henrietta Wright.

Franklin mentioned that he had 'to make some arrangements' about getting the invalid sister Betsy to London. Her problem was 'shortness of breath', continual coughing, the fear of consumption.

I am extremely desirous she should have the benefit of better medical advice than can be procured here and I also hope change of air may be of service. One of my nieces requires some medical advice likewise. Neither of them can at present bear the fatigue of travelling up in a chaise but I think they might be got by water conveyance to Hull, and from thence in the steam vessel to London.

This was it seems Emily's first visit to London. The niece who required the medical advice was undoubtedly her. Were there already fears that *her* lungs were weak? Or was this advice in connection with the damaged wrist, from which she would suffer from time to time for the rest of her life? Emily's health would always cause concern, more often to other people than to herself. The letter suggests how remote this part of Lincolnshire felt from London, though some people, including Tennyson's uncle Charles, travelled regularly back and forth. The Horncastle Navigation Canal had been opened twenty years earlier; the railway would not reach Horncastle until after the Sellwoods had left.

Captain Franklin was back in Lincolnshire in July for a family reunion to welcome his brother James back from India. 'We mustered very strongly at my sister's today and only wanted your society to complete a happy family circle,' John wrote to Eleanor, who was busy with preparations for their wedding on 6 August. Emily was now ten and the interest in India she showed all her life may date from the traveller's tales of her uncle James, and from stories about her uncle Willingham's family in Madras.

When the newly married pair visited Lincolnshire in September, for a prolonged visit to the family, we get a picture of Emily's grandfather and assorted other relations from Eleanor's first letter to her sister from the Cracrofts' house at Keal, near Bolingbroke – not far from Spilsby.

I have passed my time very pleasantly since I left London and on the whole find cause to be very well pleased with those I am brought amongst. Old Mr. Franklin is as you know totally blind and nearly deaf. His faculties also, particularly his memory, are much impaired by age, but his eyes are clear and bright, and there is no indication of his infirmities in his appearance. When he gets reminded of the early pranks of his sons or anything that has passed more than twenty years ago, his speech flows on in an easy and cheerful strain of anecdote; and his spirits seem to be uniformly good. My elder brother-in-law, the most worshipful judge Sir Willingham, is indeed a constant theme and source of merriment with every one in this part of the world, for he appears to have been the veriest little pickle that ever lived, and as hard to catch or confine as Wayland Smith's dwarf assistant in Kenilworth.

Henry Sellwood was closely in touch with his brother-in-law Willingham Franklin. 'Tell me all about my own affairs as well as those of your family,' Sir Willingham had written to him in November 1822, soon after he had arrived in India. 'I hope to be able to send home some money which you will apply to the purposes specified.' Sir Willingham, his wife and three of his children would all be dead in Madras before another year was out, leaving Emily's cousin Kate a surviving orphan of not yet six years old. She would become immensely important to Emily, but they would not meet for another dozen years.

Emily's Franklin grandfather died, perhaps fortunately, in April 1824, before his son's family was almost wiped out. His blindness, Eleanor had been told, was attributed to 'incessant reading'. His son the sailor was also a reader, reporting from his ship on Shakespeare, Junius, Pope, *Roderick Random* and *Peregrine Pickle*. Eleanor continued her 1823 report on the Franklin family:

As to Brothers and Sisters Booth, Cracroft, and Wright, and brother Sellwood, and all the descendants and relatives of all these, it is in vain for me to attempt an enumeration of them. Mrs Booth I have yet seen but once, but the Captain's two younger married sisters are both very pretty and very pleasant women, particularly I think Mrs. Cracroft with whom we now are. The four children she has are very pretty, well taught, intelligent animals, the second girl is so like my husband as to be generally called Johnny. Mr. Cracroft I thought vulgar at first from his shooting dress and Lincolnshire dialect, but I have since corrected my opinion and find him intelligent and well informed. He is a farmer on a large scale, and a great sportsman . . .

Thomas Cracroft's slightly ambiguous position on the social scale is nicely indicated by the clergyman's annotation of his rank or profession in the Parish Register of his children's baptisms. He is variously described: Farmer, Gent., Farmer, Gent., Gent. He was, in fact, very well connected and could most accurately be described as a gentleman farmer. In Lincolnshire accent was no indication of class. Eleanor went on:

I am making great progress in my knowledge of cattle and sheep about which he has taken particular pains, and I believe has been of great service to the whole country; and those are not unwilling to profit by his result who had neither spirit nor intelligence to make his experiments. The house here is something between a farm house and a gentleman's residence, situated on a hill side and covered with roses in full blossom above the bedroom windows. My worst complaint is that one cannot stir without going up or down hill, not perhaps a general grievance in Lincolnshire; however we have a fine prospect over the low lands to Boston Church, whose tower sticks up like a great tree on the horizon.

We are to be a family party of 14 though neither the Booths nor Wrights are included. Of Cracrofts and Brackenburys there seems to be quite a clan, and the children have such a lot of Aunts and Uncles that if they are not by nature good arithmeticians they will be sadly puzzled among them. This house is always full of company, and it is only a morning of continual rain which gives me leisure for this long letter.

Captain Franklin and his bride visited each of the families in turn. On 9 October 1823 they arrived in Horncastle to stay with the Sellwoods. They were there for the annual Horncastle Dispensary Ball and the description is worth including, for though Emily, at ten, was too young to go in 1823, in the years to come she and the Tennysons would go to many others of which we have no descriptions.

Eleanor Franklin wrote to her sister on 20 October:

I would not dine out, reserving myself for the Ball on Thursday, and the Ball cured me. At half past twelve was a sermon for the benefit of the dispensary, attended by all the grandees for twenty miles around. Then at 3 o'clock the gentlemen dined at the Inn. The Captain had his health drunk, and made a speech. The prosperity of the town of Horncastle was also given, but no-one returned thanks! The toast was addressed to Mr. Sellwood, and he not perceiving it, spoke not, and of course no-one else did, but we have had a fine laugh against him for it. The ladies used formerly to dine with the gentlemen, till Mrs. Dymoke changed the arrangements because it was a bustle for those three or four miles off to drive home and get dressed and back by 8. However it is to be resumed next year, as it is found that those who come from a greater distance, and are at the Inn, are in danger of starving, while their spouses are stuffing. After dinner, business was discussed. Now you must know that the physician of this place died last week, since when the whole neighbourhood has been as much distracted between two rival candidates as if the contention were for a seat in Parliament. A ci-devant apothecary, recently dubbed physician, had canvassed and secured the Champion and the gentry five months ago; while the town have espoused the cause of Dr. Bousfield, a clever man at Spilsby, who held back out of delicacy to the dying man. To save ill blood, *both* were proposed for the post (which is honour and not profit) and so I suppose both will settle here to try their rival skill.

At eight o'clock came the ball, and a very good one it was. Mrs. Dymoke, Patroness. She had promised better music than usual, and sent 100 miles for a harp, but no harp was to be had, no, nor even a flageolet, and as she disdained a drum we were forced to be contented with the scraping of some half score of boys who were almost lost behind their fiddles. All else however was well. The Horncastle Ball is only reckoned second to the Stuff Ball at Lincoln and this was an unusually good meeting. Every one seemed to enjoy it, and so did I, but I almost knocked myself up with a Country Dance. Quadrilles however prevailed. The supper is a picnic, furnished by the neighbouring gentry, and their cooks display all the mysteries of their craft on the important occasion. Lord Yarborough's death kept the whole of that family away, and I understand that Sir Joseph Banks is much missed on the occasion, but nevertheless all was very gay and very pleasant.

There are a number of interesting things about this letter, not least the fact that it was Henry Sellwood who was expected to respond to the toast to the prosperity of Horncastle. It was only about fifteen years since he had arrived in Horncastle from Berkshire and here he was, not only one of its leading citizens, but brother-in-law of the distinguished sailor Captain John Franklin, survivor of Copenhagen and Trafalgar, wounded and decorated in the 1814 attack on New Orleans and an Arctic explorer who had charted thousands of miles and imposed Lincolnshire names along the northern coastline of Canada.

Henry Sellwood's house near the church, on the corner of the Market Place, was one of the most prominent houses in the town, its rate assessment one of the highest. Mrs Dymoke, patroness of the Ball, was the wife of the hereditary Champion of England. The Dymokes had been defenders of the sovereign's title (if any should deny it) since the days of Richard II. Mrs Dymoke apparently did not know that she might have found a harp at Somersby just a few miles away. Emily would one day tell her sons: 'Your Aunt Mary played on the harp as her father used to do.'

Dr William Bousfield, named by Eleanor as the town's choice as official physician to the Horncastle Dispensary, was already the Tennysons' family doctor, riding regularly from Spilsby to Somersby to attend his difficult patient. As early as 1816 Mary Tennyson, Alfred's grandmother, mentioned Dr Bousfield of Spilsby in a letter to Charles about his brother's alarming symptoms – which they still hoped might be 'catalepsy rather than epilepsy', but which in any case were aggravated by alcohol. Dr Bousfield prescribed some pills which might have helped if George Tennyson had remembered to take them, but after a fit 'he knows not how he has been affected – or that anything has been the matter.'

Late in 1823 Dr Bousfield's sisters advertised in the *Stamford Mercury*, the paper that was circulated all over Lincolnshire:

HORNCASTLE SCHOOL

The Misses Sophia and Mary Bousfield respectfully announce to their friends, that they have taken the house at Horncastle lately in the tenure of Miss Falls, which they intend opening, after the Christmas vacation, for the reception of young Ladies. The terms of the School may be known by applying to Miss S. Bousfield, Boston.

Boston, November 3rd. 1823.

The next Horncastle Directory shows the Bousfield sisters teaching in Far Street, not only Sophia and Mary, but also, in another house, their older sister Frances. Their brother William was practising from an address in the same street. That Dr Bousfield in 1824 also became the Sellwoods' family doctor seems certain. When he eventually died in 1836 both Henry Sellwood and Charles Tennyson Turner were among those who contributed to a fund for the bereaved family.

Emily says in her Recollections that 'at eight years old I was sent to some ladies for daily lessons.' The most likely ladies in 1821, the year Emily was eight, were the Misses Falls of Far Street, whose school was taken over by Dr Bousfield's sisters at the beginning of 1824. Emily was an excellent scholar, who had already learnt a great deal at home. On 22 December 1824 'the 1st Prize for Application' was awarded to 'Miss Sellwood'. It was a really solid book for an eleven-year-old: *Les Protégés du Dix-Huitième Siècle: Histoire Religieuse et Morale* by an anonymous Madame D., printed in London in 1820 'pour l'amusement des jeunes demoiselles, mais aussi pour les perfectioner dans cette langue presqu'universelle'.

We know there is a link between Emily Sellwood and the Miss Bousfields, not only that they lived a few minutes' walk apart. A miniature, surviving at Yale among a miscellaneous collection of Tennyson material, is in a wrapper marked 'Miss Sellwood – Horncastle' – and tucked in between the ivory of the miniature and its backing is an invitation to a New Year's Eve party from a Mrs Fawsett to Miss and Miss Sophia Bousfield. It is dated 29 December 1835. Miss Bousfield was Frances, born in 1787, and Sophia was two years younger. The portrait is certainly not of either of these middle-aged women. Almost certainly it is a portrait of Emily, aged twenty-two, by one of the Miss Bousfields. Amateur and ill drawn as it is, it seems to give a convincing picture of the young Emily, whose appearance is otherwise entirely unknown. Mrs Fawsett, presumably Charlotte Fawsett of Bridge Street, was a close friend of the Sellwoods. John Franklin enquires after her family in one of his letters.

In the *Memoir* the second letter of Alfred's that Hallam Tennyson publishes is an extraordinary effusion sent, with some of his own poems, to 'My dear Dulcinea', signed 'Yours ever, Don Quixote'. Hallam identifies this as 'a piece of nonsense with which he favours his sisters' governess'. This letter also is at Yale where one can see it is addressed to 'Miss Bousfield – Horncastle'. The paper is watermarked 1824, the year the Bousfields opened their school in Far Street. The letter could well have been written the following year, the year of Alfred Tennyson's sixteenth birthday. As we saw, the family had been saying of the father, 'we will if we can get him freed from the noise of his children'. Everyone was urging George Tennyson 'to put out my children to school' and he was refusing, or at least refusing to allow his sister, to pay the fees.

By March 1825 Dr Bousfield was saying, 'so long as he will continue to teach his children, so long he will be disordered.' His fits were increasing in number and severity; the children must have heard him calling out, 'I am dying'. In May one of the grandfather's friends reported, 'Dr Tennyson had given up the Education of some of his children, which would be a great relief to him in his weak state.' To get the girls out of the house each day must have seemed an excellent idea. How likely it seems that Dr Bousfield finally persuaded George Tennyson to let the Tennyson girls, Mary, Emilia, Matilda and even six-year-old Cecilia join Emily, Anne, and Louisa Sellwood at his sisters' school in Far Street, Horncastle. Dr Bousfield, looking at the Tennyson family, wrote of 'a most promising and highly gifted set of children', not of *boys*. And Aunt Russell had offered to pay the school fees for the *children*, not the boys.

In the Census the word used to describe each of the Misses Bousfield is 'governess', the term Hallam also uses in the *Memoir*. There is no evidence at all that Miss Bousfield of Horncastle taught the girls in the Rectory at Somersby, though they were later certainly to have a governess at home, the notorious Miss Watson, who purchased things on credit in one shop and sold them 'for ready money' in another. She was so lively and amusing that the family worried that young Charles had fallen in love with her. It was while she was there in 1827 that the Reverend William Chaplin wrote of George's worrying behaviour: 'He will not allow them to go to school and he will not clothe them.'

The Sellwood girls certainly established at some point a close friendship with the Tennyson girls and it seems likely that it dated from a time before the Sellwoods went off to boarding schools in Brighton and London. Emily says specifically that her father 'disliked having a governess in the house', and surely George Tennyson must have felt the same, as his weak state and deplorable habits – indulging 'too much in malt liquor' – affected the entire household. When the cook burned herself to death, he was certainly blamed for that. Indeed the girls may well have gone to school in Horncastle in 1825 because the Tennysons could not persuade a governess to stay in the Rectory.

It is likely that by now the Sellwood girls had a fair idea of what was going on at Somersby. Mary Anne Fytche, Mrs Tennyson's sister, had railed at George for his treatment of her sister, subjecting her 'to the caprice of so dreadful a temper as yours for twenty-two years'. He was accused of having encouraged the servants to insult her and he had apparently refused her any money 'in such language as I should be ashamed to transcribe'. She wrote from her home in Louth, where Tennyson's young brothers were now at the grammar school in spite of what Alfred had gone through there. Their aunt said, 'These circumstances are so public that your poor children here are told of them everyday by their schoolfellows . . .' If rumours had reached Louth, which was so many miles further away, how much more gossip must there have been in Horncastle.

Late in 1823, just as the Misses Bousfields' advertisement was appearing in the newspaper, there was a great deal of space devoted to a matter that also affected the Sellwood household. There was an election pending in the county. On 2 December John Franklin, always interested in Lincolnshire affairs, wrote to his sister Betsy in Horncastle:

I am glad Mr Sellwood has received the appointment of agency to Sir Wm. Ingilby, he I hope will derive benefit from the contest, whoever may win the Election – there seems however little reason to fear Sir William being unsuccessful as he started with a great preponderance of interest and so much in advance of his competitor . . .

Eleanor joins me in the most affectionate love to my Father, yourself, Mr Sellwood – and the little girls.

It seems very likely that the eldest little girl, Emily, at ten, took a keen interest in this election, watching from the window all the increased comings and goings. She was always interested in politics and may well have begged in vain to go with her father to Lincoln for the hustings.

Sir William Ingilby (whose sister Augusta was married to Robert Cracroft of Harrington Hall) had a passionate belief in radical reform. He was also a close friend of the Tennysons' uncle Charles and had been at school with him at Westminster. Ingilby was a lively fellow, well known for his outrageous clothes and particularly for a curious green hat. The by-election had occurred because the sitting member, the Hon. Charles Pelham, had been elevated to the peerage on the death in September of his father, Lord Yarborough. 'To fill this high situation, one of the most extraordinary and protracted contests that was ever witnessed took place.' Ingilby had the support of the new Lord Yarborough, but certain elements in the county were worried that 'a great Whig lord is resolved to force an unknown stranger upon us . . .' Ingilby was reviled as 'the Yorkshire baronet'. That his election agent, Henry Sellwood, was also an incomer might not have helped. Samuel Wells, attorney, agent for the rival candidate, the Tory Sir John Thorold, was described as 'the unfeed, unbought, legal adviser for the cause'. Sellwood's role was the same. The candidates' seconders are interesting. Sir William Ingilby's was, unsurprisingly, Robert Cracroft of Harrington Hall. Sir John Thorold's nomination was seconded by John Bourne of Dalby, Alfred Tennyson's uncle – married to his father's sister Mary.

It was a rough election with no insults spared and a lot of noise. There were mock funeral processions, muffled drums, flags galore and a lot of hissing and cheering. Thorold's agent's abuse was imaginative; Sellwood's is not recorded. His candidate, Ingilby, stood as 'a true and honourable Whig and a real friend to constitutional reform', but he was also denounced as an 'amphibious politician who has the ability to make every Tory believe him to be a Whig – and every Whig a Tory'. There was an outcry when it was suggested that the new Lord Yarborough had spoken up for him (cheers and cries of 'That is against the law'). Peers must not 'interfere in the election of members of the House of Commons. (Applause.)'

Polling went on for ten days with mounting tension. Ingilby was overwhelmingly elected (3,024 votes to 1,074) after fighting 'fairly and manfully (cheers)'. Ingilby declared himself 'an enemy to rotten boroughs and the dictation of an individual'. He was 'a friend to free and open elections and thought there ought to be a more equal representation of the people (cheers).' There was no secret ballot yet, so we know that among the votes cast for Sir William Ingilby were not only of course those of Henry Sellwood and Robert Cracroft, but also those of George Clayton Tennyson DD of Somersby and Thomas Hardwick Rawnsley of Spilsby.

The following year, 1824, was full of deaths. The deaths of her uncle and aunt and her little cousins in Madras were at least far off, and perhaps dulled for Emily by the fact that she had not seen the family since they had left England in 1822. Her Franklin grandfather's death in April was not unexpected; he had been born as long ago as 1739, but she would miss his stories of her mother as a child.

The death she remembered all her life ('among my early tragedies') had a particular power to remind her of the fact that 'in the midst of life we are in death'. The children were so totally unprepared for it. Five of them – the three Sellwood girls and their closest cousins the two eldest Cracroft girls – were in a tent at a sheepshearing, 'the great rustic festival of that day'. These cousins were two of the 'intelligent animals' who had delighted their new aunt Eleanor the year before: Sophie and Isabella, aged nine and eight years old. It was Isabella, called after her mother, who was so like her uncle John she was 'generally called Johnny'.

A 'village boy' had come into the tent where the sheep were being shorn, swarmed up the pole in the middle and shouted out to the bewildered children: 'I know something; your father is dead.' For a moment, Emily must have thought that it was *her* father, Henry Sellwood, the boy was talking about. Thomas Cracroft had been on his way home from Lincoln, had called in, feeling ill, at the house in the Market Place where his children were visiting. He had died of 'Asiatic cholera, a solitary case of it'. Describing that alarming day – 11 July 1824 – seventy-two years later, Emily Tennyson focused, as she had as a child, not on the terrible death of her uncle Thomas Cracroft, the one with the

Lincolnshire dialect and the vulgar shooting dress, but on what happened after they heard the news.

'We hurried home', Emily remembered, all those years later, 'and we three sisters were put by my aunt (to keep us quiet) to the hitherto unwonted task of stoning raisins. This made me so indignant that I threw my raisins over the edge of the bowl – and forthwith, my aunt caught me up, and, so rough was the treatment of children then, banged my head against the door of our old wainscoted rooms, until I called out for my father, crying aloud "Murder", when he rushed in and saved me.' It seemed typical of poor Aunt Betsy to have so misjudged the children's feelings and to have set them to such a trivial and inappropriate task in that house of death. It was significant too that it was Henry Sellwood who was her saviour.

Thomas Cracroft had been not just the father of Emily's favourite cousins, but a kind and interested uncle. There survives just one book he gave her: the Reverend Isaac Taylor's *Scenes in America*, 'for the amusement and instruction of little tarry-at-home travellers', inscribed: 'Emily Sellwood's. The gift of her Uncle Cracroft. 1823'. One immediate result of his death was that Henry Sellwood took over the business of the Harrington estate. Robert Cracroft appointed his dead cousin's brother-in-law in his place, and, soon after Thomas Cracroft's death, Robert and Augusta decided to live at Hackthorn, the Cracroft family home, which had been available since Cracroft's father's death in 1821. It was Sellwood's job to find new tenants for Harrington. The first tenant was a Colonel Thoroton, but when he left in 1830 an advertisement appeared in the *Stamford Mercury*:

To be let

A handsome FAMILY RESIDENCE, completely Furnished, called Harrington Hall, 8 miles from Horncastle, and 6 from Spilsby. The shooting is excellent, extending over from 3000 to 4000 acres of land.
For particulars enquire of H. Sellwood, Esq. Horncastle.

It was not until 17 May 1831 that the lease was signed by Arthur Eden of Wimbledon and witnessed by T.H. Rawnsley, Tennyson's father's close friend. Eden was to bring with him to Harrington, his wife, widow of William Baring MP, a member of the banking family, and her three daughters, Fanny, Georgiana and Rosa. Rosa was almost exactly the same age as the agent's daughter, Emily.

Eleanor Franklin, the lively writer the Sellwood girls had got to know so well when she and their Uncle John stayed at the time of the Horncastle Ball, produced a daughter in London on 3 June 1824. Even so, John Franklin rushed up to Lincolnshire again (he had been there not long before for his father's funeral) as soon as he heard of his brother-in-law's death. His sister Isabella was inevitably in a sad state. They all seem to have been at Harrington Hall. Betsy had also rushed to her sister's side from Horncastle – leaving the Sellwood girls, one suspects, rejoicing at her absence. Eleanor wrote to John from London on 20 July: 'I am not surprised that Betsy is so well, nothing is of more use to a nervous invalid than to feel that others are dependent on them for support. It is not only the pleasure of paying off part of a debt of kindness, but that most delightful feeling of being useful once more.'

It was just as well Eleanor realized the delights of being useful. She was being extremely useful herself in her husband's absence, but her own health was giving great cause for concern. All through the year her cough was troublesome; she never recovered her strength after her child's birth. Her sister and the rest of her family grumbled that the Franklins in Lincolnshire 'fell back upon John for everything, quite regardless of his wife's claims'. While John was supporting Isabella Cracroft at Harrington, Eleanor was coping in London, not only with their new baby, with her vaccination, with plans for her christening (as another Eleanor), but also with arrangements for her husband's new Arctic expedition. 'The boats are building at Woolwich.'

'Eleanor', John had written proudly the year before to Betsy, 'is as warm in the cause of Arctic Discoveries', as he could possibly wish. She had herself said to Betsy: 'If evil should come, it will come soon enough. We have no occasion to cloud the present hour by anticipating it.' Even so, she could not help grumbling as her own health deteriorated and John Franklin lingered in Lincolnshire on family business. 'It seems that none of your family can do anything without you, and your self-love is flattered by it, you vain animal! How will they get on when you have taken wing? I wish you would come home and do your own business for I feel it very ridiculous to have all these gentlemen coming to me to try the effect of petticoat influence.' John was back again in Lincolnshire staying with the Sellwoods in December, but he did get home to London to spend Christmas with his wife and little daughter. Eleanor realized how much he minded missing the large family party in Lincolnshire. Should she send them oysters for Christmas Day? she asked.

The baby had hardly time enough to enjoy riding on her Papa's shoulders ('I'm not sure whether horse or rider is best pleased', Eleanor wrote) before it was time for him to leave England. Eleanor was extremely ill as the date for the departure of the Expedition approached. As his wife lay dying, John Franklin wrote to his brother-in-law, Henry Sellwood, whose wife had also died young, as 'My dearest friend'. He spoke of 'the awful trial I have got to witness'. He did not have to witness the very end for Eleanor would not let him change his plans. On 16 February 1825 the ships left Liverpool. On 22 February, Eleanor Franklin died aged twenty-eight, just the age her sister-in-law, Emily's mother, had been when she died nine years earlier.

Emily was thirteen when, in the April of 1827, Jackson's, the booksellers at Louth, published anonymously *Poems by Two Brothers* – half of them by seventeen-year-old Alfred Tennyson and most of the rest by his brother Charles, with three or four (in spite of the title) by the oldest brother, Frederick. The authorship seems to have been known; like so much else about the Tennysons, it was talked about. It is just possible that the bookish prosperous attorney in Horncastle bought a copy of the poems; there is no evidence of this. Tennyson called them 'early work', but everyone began to think of the boys as poets – even their grandfather. 'It is very extraordinary', he wrote to his daughter, Mrs Russell, the following New Year's Day, 'that Alfred never wrote to you, but indeed nothing is extraordinary the poets do.'

Emily, Anne and Louisa Sellwood were at boarding school by this time – and indeed they did not return to Horncastle in the Christmas holidays. There seems to be little more to be discovered than Emily herself recalled, though the choice of Brighton must surely have been, not just for the sea air, but because their widowed aunt, Isabella Cracroft, was living there at this period, and presumably their cousins attended the same school. A surviving sketchbook with one specific date – Stratford, Essex, 1827 – merely adds to our knowledge that Emily admired picturesque buildings. She sat down and sketched competently, not only in Stratford, but in Charing, Kent, Banstead, Surrey and Pulborough, Sussex. She was certainly studying Italian. A new edition of an Italian Grammar has the inscription 'Miss Sellwood August 1827', when she was just fourteen.

In her Recollections she says that after years with the Horncastle ladies the sisters went 'to schools in Brighton and London' because of that dislike her father had, with no wife, of having a governess in the house.

So, much as he objected to young girls being sent from home, school in our case seemed the lesser evil. My sisters liked school; to me it was dreadful. As soon as I reached the Brighton seminary, I remember that for weeks I appeared to be in a horrible dream, and the voices of the mistresses and the girls around me seemed to me all thin, like voices from the grave. I could not be happy away from my father, who was my idol. The result was that I became ill. After a while I grew better, and more accustomed to the strange life. My father would never let us go the long, cold journey at Christmas-time to Horncastle, but came up to Town for the vacation; and took us for treats to the National Gallery, and other places of our interest. Great was the joy, when the summer-holidays arrived, and after travelling by coach through the day and night, we three sisters saw Whittlesea-mere [near Peterborough] gleaming under the sun-rise. It seemed as if we were within sight of home.

Eleanor Franklin had been strongly against boarding schools, and had suggested that 'a schoolgirl may always be known all her life from one educated at home, by the commonplace ideas and the habits of petty deception and chicanery, which they always get more or less.' The Sellwood girls entirely escaped this infection, which Eleanor seemed to think so inevitable. The two schools would seem to have been rather good ones but not one word about them occurs in any of Emily's letters, even when her own sons are at school. It was as if, like Alfred, who refused after he had left even to walk down the street in Louth where his school was, she could not bear to think about her schooldays until, right at the end of her life, her son Hallam asked her to recall her childhood and that school life so long unmentioned.

On their return from school in the summer of 1828 the girls must have read with avidity John Franklin's *Narrative of a Second Expedition to the shores of the Polar Sea*. A surviving copy is inscribed to Aunt Betsy at Horncastle: 'Miss Franklin with her Brother's love. John Franklin, 6th June 1828.' He was knighted on his return from this expedition and married again in November, 1828. Jane Griffin became his second re-markable wife, 'an indomitable woman and cleverer than her husband', according to her husband's niece Kate at the end of Lady Franklin's life. In 1828 she had just returned from Russia and had already travelled throughout – and made notes on – every European country. In the early 1830s she would accompany her husband – in command of his frigate

Rainbow – to the Mediterranean and then in 1836 go with him to the other side of the world when he was appointed Governor of Van Die-men's Land. They took with them two of Emily's cousins, Sir John's own motherless Eleanor and the fatherless Sophie Cracroft. Lady Franklin in her widowhood would become 'a great favourite' with Tennyson and Emily's closest aunt – though often far away, as she journeyed not only in search of her lost explorer but to Calcutta, Abys-sinia, California, Hawaii, Japan, Alaska, and all around South Ameri-ca. She was an enthusiast for female education and corresponded with Elizabeth Fry about the welfare of female convicts.

These two wives of Sir John Franklin must have had a considerable influence on their niece's idea of what women could be and do.

In the Narrative Emily wrote for her sons in 1869 there is nothing at all about her own childhood, but she is there herself right from the beginning of the story she is telling of Tennyson's life. 'You have seen a sketch of the house in which he was born', she began, 'and if you had known it as I knew it you would have a loving recollection of the sweet woodbine that peeped into the bay window of the nursery, of the vault-ed dining room with the stained glass in its arched windows and the beautiful stone chimney-piece carved by your Grandfather, of the pleasant drawing room furnished with book-shelves and yellow cur-tains and furniture, which looked out on the beautiful lawn over-shadowed on one side by a Which [*sic*] Elm walk and on the other by a fine Larch tree and a Sycamore.' It was not an elegant description but it was of a house and garden Emily knew well for, I think, a dozen years. Everything was sweet and beautiful and pleasant to look at (and beauti-ful again) and every description of the house and garden is lyrical.

Thirty-six years after the family left Somersby Tennyson received a letter from America, from the son of a local bricklayer who had emi-grated. He recalled 'the apple-trees that bore such fine yellow apples running up from the stables to the house, the broad lawn . . ., the Sibe-rian crab tree down the garden, the old Scotch firs at the house end where the rooks used to build . . . Many a speckled trout and silver eel have I caught in the brook running through the meadow below.' And Alfred wrote back, delighted to hear 'a voice so far away calling to me, "over a vast" as Shakespeare says, and speaking of the old things': the brook, the golden apples, the Scotch fir with the rooks. Alfred remem-bered too 'the coachman who always seemed to me half-mad, though I fancy he was generally half-drunk'. This was Horlins who, memorably, when blamed for not keeping the harness clean, was said to have rushed into the drawing room, flung all the tackle on the floor and roared out: 'Clean it yourself then.' Hallam told that story in the *Memoir*, but left out any comment on Horlins's drinking habits. Alfred does not mention his father when writing to the bricklayer's son – but the master and the servant seem to have been drinking together. In letters written at the time it is the Rector, not the coachman, who is generally half-drunk, and often entirely so. Alfred told his grandfather he could see that 'most diseases' that flesh is heir to were exacerbated in one who 'inundates his stomach with half a cellar'. It is a vivid image. Tennyson himself was suffering from 'a determination of blood to the Head' and from the 'motes in the eye' which were to bother him all his life.

In the autumn of 1827 the Reverend William Chaplin of Thorpe Hall, Louth, described a state of affairs at Somersby which was giving everyone who knew the family, including, surely, Henry Sellwood, great cause for concern. Chaplin suggested to Charles Tennyson, the uncle, that his brother should be certified as insane and confined. Not only was his conduct singular, but he was now 'dangerously disposed to his wife and children . . . His excessive habit of drinking brings on such repeated fits, that he is as deranged as madness can be described . . . The children are alarmed at him and the wife is . . . in daily danger of her life . . . as long as he is under the uncontrolled power of liquors.' Chaplin was sure Dr Bousfield would be ready to certify the Reverend George Clayton Tennyson insane, a resolution that would be a great relief, not only to his family but to the whole parish. 'Everyone is afraid of him . . . The only person having influence with him is a faithful servant, a coachman – he can stop some violent paroxysms but that cannot last long . . . Mrs Tennyson cannot get the children away, and will not leave them – she has spent a most dreadful life for some years. George's violence is well known in all the adjoining villages and his horrid language is heard wherever he goes.'

Dr Bousfield, at Charles Tennyson's request, took a fresh look at his patient and could not see that he was really any worse than he had been for many years, but he also managed to talk to Mrs Tennyson alone and saw that her 'placid disposition' was indeed 'greatly unhinged'; she was alarmed at what might happen to her children. Dr Bousfield advised travel rather than confinement. Elizabeth Russell, George's sister, had always believed in the efficacy of 'locomotion' 'for spirits like ours when depressed'; and her nephew Alfred, now at Cambridge (and wishing for 'a fairy carpet to transport' him away from the monotonous revelry of the place) agreed that the 'constant variation of scene and ideas should operate as an infallible restorative'. He would maintain a belief in that family solution for the rest of his life, with Emily's encouragement.

In the years that the girls were away at school it seems likely that Henry Sellwood in his letters made reference from time to time to the Tennysons' problems. Emily in her Recollections writes that: 'Among our neighbours', in Lincolnshire, 'we had as friends the Tennysons, the Rawnsleys, the Bellinghams and the Massingberds.' This is not the place to re-examine the much examined vicissitudes, the accusations flying back and forth, the comings and goings of letters and persons between Somersby, Tealby, Louth and Cambridge. Emily Sellwood probably knew only as much as I have told, perhaps less. There was gossip certainly – from servants and neighbours; there was also a great deal of tactful reticence. We can guess that even at this stage Henry Sellwood may have been worried. Was this friendship with the Tennyson family a suitable one for his beloved daughters? Rumours of Frederick's behaviour, added to the knowledge he already had of the father's excesses ('known for many years, by many witnesses'), must surely have disturbed Sellwood.

Frederick, Alfred's eldest brother, was not the first-born. There was an absent George, who died when a few weeks old. When dealing with turbulent Frederick, must not his father have dreamt of how different the lost George might have been, having himself such strong feelings about primogeniture, boiling with anger at the way the Old Man of the Wolds (as the grandfather was known at Somersby) had favoured his younger brother Charles?

Sellwood must have heard both sides of the story. As Emily said, the Rawnsleys were also friends (they would later be connected by marriage), and Thomas Hardwick Rawnsley, Rector of Halton Holgate, remained loyal to his friend Dr Tennyson, seeing much fault on Frederick's side – at least on the occasion, which must have been the talk of the county, when it was said that father and son had threatened to kill each other, that Frederick had been turned out of the Rectory and taken into the care of the local Constable and that the whole family had eventually walked out, leaving the Rector, as Thomas Rawnsley put it, 'under the most deplorable state of mental depression and wretchedness'.

Their grandfather thought Frederick's brothers Charles and Alfred were just as much of a problem. 'Those three boys so far from having improved in manner or manners are worse since they went to Cambridge.' 'They are so untoward and disorderly and so unlike other people I don't know what will become of them, or what can be done with, or about them.' They were all poets; Alfred had already told his younger brother – if we are to believe him – 'Well, Arthur, I mean to be famous.'

At Cambridge all three tall brothers made friends they would know all their lives. Edward FitzGerald would say of the Tennysons: 'I see so many little natures about that I must draw to the large, even if their faults be on the same scale as their virtues.' In 1829 Alfred's marvellous new friend at Trinity, Arthur Hallam, was already writing to his old schoolfriend William Gladstone, 'I consider Tennyson as promising fair to be the greatest poet of our generation, perhaps of our century.' It was an extraordinary prediction about an extraordinary young man.

In Lincolnshire Dr Bousfield, looking at the whole family, had seen that 'highly gifted set of children', and presumably Henry Sellwood was inclined to agree that there was much to compensate for the deficiencies of their parents. It seems he did nothing to discourage Emily's friendship with the Tennyson girls after she was allowed to return to Horncastle. She was back permanently at sixteen to continue her education with her father. She played the piano and read a great deal – in Italian, French and German as well as English – while he was busy about his business, and she talked with him in the evenings about what she had read.

The Tennysons, as she said, were still neighbours and family friends, whatever terrible things had been going on while she was away at school. Everything was now quiet, or as quiet as a house full of young people and children could ever be said to be. There was a curate taking services at Somersby and the Rector was far away, safely distant across the Channel, but feeling such a void in his heart, as he wrote to his friend Thomas Rawnsley, that one can only feel sorry for him.

From time to time Emily Sellwood (presumably with Aunt Betsy) would pay a morning call at Somersby and the older Tennyson girls – Mary and Emily – would also pay calls in the Market Place when they were in Horncastle to exchange their books at the Literary Society, to which they all belonged, or to post letters.

The Tennysons also came to Horncastle for music lessons – Alfred, for a time, as well as his sisters. And there was always shopping. The Market Place alone contained not just market stalls on market days, but a variety of useful shops – not only a butcher, a baker and a chandler, but also a bootmaker, druggists, glass, china and earthenware dealers, a milliner as well as two straw hat makers, a toy seller, a confectioner, a fruiterer, a watch and clockmaker, a glover and breeches maker and, most important of all, several sellers of music, books and stationery.

The Tennyson girls – like Emily herself – were great readers. They were described by someone in the village as almost as clever and 'high-larnt' as their brothers – 'but nothing with their hands – you know – nivver could sampler, nor knit, nor sew, nor nowt.' They all read poetry, of course (not least their brothers') and they wrote it as well. It was even said that one of Mary's poems had crept in to *Poems by Two Brothers*. At some stage they established what Alfred and Emily's grandson Charles Tennyson would describe as 'a romantic circle of friends and correspondents, known as the Husks, the main function of which was the writing and study of poetry'. The circle included Mary Massingberd – also mentioned in the Sellwood list of family friends. It surely included the Sellwood girls too, though Alfred's sister Emily's friendships were 'not very lasting' and it is difficult to follow the course of the relationship between the two 'Emmies'. At a later stage it was a younger sister, Cecilia, who seemed closest to Emily Sellwood, but in 1830 she was only twelve: four years make a lot of difference when you are nearly seventeen.

We know at any rate that the Tennysons used the Market Place bookshops – indeed it would be odd if they had not. Long before this the Rector had grumbled about their prices. 'All country booksellers are rascals. Babbingon of Horncastle has charged me always one fourth more, sometimes half more' than the price of the book when ordered from a London dealer. (In the same letter he called Jackson, the bookseller in Louth, 'an infernal rogue' – but that didn't stop his sons publishing their first book with the firm fifteen years later.) Country booksellers might be rascals and rogues, but Market Place, Horncastle, was conveniently close. There was always the chance that the girl at the window might see the Tennysons crossing the square.

It was in April 1830 that Emily Sellwood received her first invitation to stay overnight at Somersby. Possibly Anne and Louisa went too – they would have been on holiday from school – but that seems a rather large addition to an already overcrowded house. 'How they could have all got in, I do not know', as Emily's and Alfred's son would say over sixty years later. Alfred and Charles were on vacation from Cambridge and had brought home with them their dazzling friend Arthur Hallam, who was very much Charles's friend as well as Alfred's. Little has been made of the love between Charles Tennyson and Arthur Hallam, over-shadowed as it has been by Alfred's. But they wrote sonnets for each other; one of Arthur's ends:

> Then trust me, Charles, nor let it cause thee smart
> That seldom in my songs thy name is seen –
> When most I loved, I most have silent been.

Alfred's new book *Poems, Chiefly Lyrical* would be out in two months. Arthur Hallam's father had dissuaded him from sharing Alfred's volume and encouraged him merely to print, not to publish, a small selection of his own. Hallam loved Charles but he saw that 'though he burns and shines', he 'is a lesser light than Alfred'. Charles had himself just published a much-praised book of poems – a volume called *Sonnets and Fugitive Pieces*, dedicated to his sister Mary, 'in sign of my deep love'. Arthur Hallam was quite convinced of Alfred's genius, even though he knew 'friendship can play sad pranks with one's judgement in these matters.' He told Alfred's mother he feared the new book (*Poems, Chiefly Lyrical*) would be 'far too good to be popular', but knew that it would 'throw out sparks that would kindle somewhere and will vivify young, generous hearts, in the days that are coming, to a clearer perception of what is beautiful and good.'

It was not only Alfred's poetry, avidly as she read it, that would kindle a spark in one young and generous heart in that spring of 1830. 'Poems are good things but flesh and blood is better,' Arthur Hallam wrote to Tennyson two years later, and Emily's description of Alfred Tennyson at this time shows how much she agreed with this. The ethereal Emily Sellwood was intensely aware of the flesh and blood Alfred Tennyson. Emily described Alfred as he looked at the time when she began to love him: 'When I think what he was between twenty and thirty in face and form I can scarcely imagine anything more glorious in human form.' He had 'a graceful carriage of the head'; he was broad-chested with a 'tapering waist'. 'His face was long of the Elizabethan type, his forehead ample, his eyes long and dark, having a liquid light and very deep eyelids, which veiled them when thoughtful. His nose aquiline, his hands the admiration of sculptors, long fingered with broad tips.' Artists would say that 'the union of strength and delicacy and the continual change of expression made it difficult to take his portrait.' He was 'kingly', with 'masses of fine wavy hair, very dark, with a pervading shade of gold, and long as it was then worn'. 'His smile most beautiful.' 'His manner was kind, simple and dignified, with plenty of sportiveness flashing out from time to time.'

'He was about six feet and strong in proportion,' could 'put a stone' against any of the strongest men in the village and 'hurl a crow-bar further than the stalwart blacksmith.' But 'he always seemed to me a mysterious being lifted high above other mortals.' Charles, his brother, captured some of that mystery:

> Thought travels past thee with intenser glow,
> And nobler visions burn upon thine eye
> Than other souls e'er knew of, or can know:
> Massing delicious thought and fancies high
> From hour to hour, thy spirit teems with joy
> Not seldom with unrest.

Only the previous year, on a rare visit to London, Alfred had had one of those appalling visions that would stop him in his tracks from time to time:

I used to feel moods of misery unutterable. I remember once in London the realization coming over me of the whole of its inhabitants lying horizontal a hundred years hence. The smallness and emptiness of life sometimes overwhelmed me. I used to experience sensations of a state almost impossible to describe in words; it was not exactly a trance but the world seemed dead and myself only alive.

They were all intensely alive that spring at Somersby among 'the leafiness and luxury of all the happy banks and lanes', but there was a presentiment that it could not last. 'I cannot be happy without forecasting unhappiness,' Arthur Hallam said. 'There is a cold speck on the heart, even when it glows with enjoyment.' Glow with enjoyment they did, these brilliant young men, the clever, hero-worshipping girls and the undisciplined children, so 'strangely brought up' – as their grandfather said. (Horatio was still only ten this spring, and Cecilia and Matilda not much more.) There was a feeling of licence, a special sense of relief and gratitude in the father's absence, remembering the perils of the year before. Hallam wrote from Somersby to his friend Joseph Blakesley: 'My life here has been one of so much excitement and enjoyment . . . If I die I hope to be buried here: for never in my life, I think, have I loved a place more . . . I have floated along in a delicious dream of music and poetry and riding and dancing and greenwood-dinners and ladies' conversation till I have been simply exhaled into Paradise.'

Alfred's sister Emily, to whom Arthur Hallam eventually became engaged, would wonder afterwards why it was not Mary, the oldest sister (nineteen and a half that spring), who won his heart. Arthur certainly admired Mary's looks, as all their friends did. When she went to London with Alfred, Blakesley (who would one day be the Dean of Lincoln) wrote of her 'noble countenance and magnificent eyes'. It was also Blakesley who said, 'She is really a very fine looking person, although of a wild sort of countenance, something like what Alfred would be if he were a woman, and washed.'

Arthur Hallam seems to have loved them all: Alfred and Charles and their sisters, their mother Eliza, complaisant and pious, and their friend Emily Sellwood. Even the two awkward indolent adolescents Edward and Arthur could not spoil things. Edward was sixteen, the same age as Emily Sellwood; he was 'chippy and unmanageable' and already on the verge of the breakdown that would confine him shamefully to a York asylum for the rest of his life. Arthur was a year younger, 'as idle as a foal', irritating his grandfather with his 'gestures and his twitchings' and an inability to master the multiplication tables 'or indeed anything useful.'

The four youngest ones – Septimus, Matilda, Cecilia and Horatio – were all considered too old now to be packed off to bed. So it was a large party on that April evening in 1830 enjoying the dancing, the fortune telling, the composing of verses and the other games. Emily Sellwood remembered particularly playing 'The Emperor of Morocco'. It was one of those games where everyone in the room tries to make the chosen player laugh. She was proud that, when it was her turn, Arthur Hallam was pleased with her because she went through the whole thing 'with so much gravity', carrying her two big candles, one in each hand.

'The Emperor of Morocco is dead,' she was told.

'How did he die?' she asked.

'Shaking one hand, just like I', came the answer. And everyone in the room gave some ridiculous reason for his death, trying to make her laugh – until the whole room was full of people shaking hands or heads, winking eyes, twisting their mouths, and waving their feet around. And it seemed a triumph not to laugh, among all the giggling children, the teasing Tennysons.

'Next morning some of us went to Holywell,' Emily Sellwood wrote, a whole crowd of them, wandering in the wood, like the lovers in *A Midsummer Night's Dream*, though it was spring and not summer. Emily found herself not with Alfred but with Arthur Hallam. 'His manner was very kind and chivalrous and I was not afraid of him,' the shy girl remembered, 'as I thought I would be.' And then, suddenly, there was Alfred making his appearance from behind a tree, wrapped in his cloak and laughing at Emily: 'Are you a Dryad or a Naiad or what are you?' There was something about the wood and the girls that made the young men think of nymphs.

The other Emily was there too, of course, Alfred's sister. Two years later Arthur Hallam would write to her, his 'dearest Nem' after he had sent her a copy of de la Motte Fouqué's *Undine* – together with some gold earrings – for her twenty-first birthday. 'Your hearty welcome of poor Undinchen is very gratifying to me. Cannot you indeed find any one like her in the world? So I thought for a good many years; but one fine spring I came to a wooded glen among wolds, where I saw a being more like Undine than I had ever thought to see.' This comparison with Undine emphasizes just how deeply unconventional Arthur thought Alfred's sister was.

Love – and the love of love – was in the air. But if Tennyson's use of tree nymph and water nymph had been casual, Arthur Hallam's use of the comparison was much more specific. How deeply disturbing Undine's behaviour is. The strange thing about the Undine story is that Undine herself disappeared on 'the journey to Vienna' and it is Huldbrand, with whom Hallam had identified himself, who swoons in anguish.

Arthur Hallam's encounter at Somersby with Emily, the sister of his dear friends, led to their engagement. Emily Sellwood's meeting with Alfred Tennyson in the wood that day was not so significant to Alfred as it was to Emily herself. She remembered his words and the way he had looked at her and, from that day on, her devotion to him was deep and entire. But more than twenty years would pass, with a great deal of anguish, before they were finally united in marriage.

CHAPTER TWO

'The sharp desire of knowledge'

Years later Emily Sellwood, when she was the poet's wife, twice described the 'meeting' in the wood in different versions of the Narrative for her sons. Hallam Tennyson, using his mother's description in his *Memoir*, changed 'Naiad' to 'Oread' (rather inappropriately, for there are no mountains in Lincolnshire) and diminished Arthur Hallam's role in the story. And it was the namesake son who made the suggestion, so often repeated since, that it was his parents' *first* meeting, rather than that it was, as Emily herself made clear, simply her first overnight stay at Somersby. It was also Hallam Tennyson who said they met in the 'Fairy Wood'. Emily and Alfred always thought of it as Holywell, an appropriate place for such a significant exchange. (Surely it was the way he looked at her, the way he looked, rather than the words he used, which made it seem in hindsight to Emily no less than an epiphany.)

Describing Somersby in 1846, Tennyson wrote:

My native village is secluded in a pretty pastoral district of softly sloping hills and large ash trees. There is a little glen in it called by the old monkish name of Holywell ... and within a stream of clear water gushes out of a sandrock and over it stands an old school house almost lost among the trees and used in my time as a woodhouse, its former distinction only signified by a scripture text 'Remember thy Creator in the days of thy youth.'

Emily never forgot her Creator, but the days of her youth were long past when she wrote down what had happened – so little had actually happened – in Holywell. It was important for Emily, thinking about this time nearly forty years later, to include Arthur Hallam in her relationship with Alfred. She knew that he had been the most important

Arthur Henry Hallam

person in Tennyson's life, not only at that point, but for long afterwards, an importance increased rather than diminished by his early death, so short a time after those happy games and woodland wanderings at Somersby in the spring of 1830.

We can see Arthur Hallam as he was then in a drawing by Emily's sister Anne, probably made on that same visit. The contrast between the two young poets was vivid. Arthur certainly thought of himself as a poet too, but not with Alfred's genius or with his inclination for poetical behaviour. Whereas Alfred liked to surprise his family by arriving without warning, 'My maxims of conduct are extremely different,'

Arthur Hallam wrote to Charles. 'I confess to an avaricious appetite for the sight of sympathies excited, necks stretched out, and butlers looking round the corner, not to mention a well-aired bed, and a providently augmented dinner.' At Somersby Hallam could write: 'I do feel rather mad at times here,' but he was usually full of common sense and good advice. And if at times he shared Alfred's morbidity, his nature was basically 'sanguine and hopeful' and 'not framed for despondency'. The physical contrast was striking too. Alfred was tall, dark and strong; Arthur was slight and fair, 'a very delicate, interesting-looking young man', as he was described that summer by one of their fellow passengers on the boat that brought the two friends back from their rash adventure (their 'wild bustling time' as Arthur called it) in the Pyrenees, when they had carried mysterious dispatches and money to the Spanish revolutionaries.

Arthur's sister Ellen wrote of Arthur's possessing an eye and voice that revealed 'the angelic spirit within – the deep feeling impassioned soul'. Alfred said of his friend that he was 'as near perfection as a mortal man can be'. Similar praise would come to Emily herself in time, but Alfred did not yet realize he had met 'the noblest woman of them all', with 'one of the sweetest and justest natures in the world'. She was, after all, just seventeen in that summer of 1830, a young girl, pale, shy and quiet beside the brilliant beloved Arthur Hallam, 'teeming with talent', the centre of attention.

> O bliss, when all in circle drawn
> About him, heart and ear were fed
> To hear him, as he lay and read
> The Tuscan poets on the lawn.

It was Emily Sellwood, when she was years later Alfred Tennyson's wife, who wrote of Arthur Hallam that they were 'all in love with him from the first'.

Far more is known of the progress of Arthur's love for his friend's sister, Emily, than of what was going on in the heart of Emily Sellwood in these years. If she was keeping a diary, it no longer exists, and the earliest surviving letter in her hand dates from the summer of 1839. This letter was to 'Dearest dear Emmie' and her mocking reference to herself as 'thy old torment t'other Emmie' emphasizes how well she knew the Tennyson sisters in the days before they left Somersby. Nearly all Arthur Hallam's letters to *his* beloved Emily, Alfred's sister, survive and so a great deal is known of that inefficiently forbidden relationship – with the young people not able to marry, foreshadowing the situation in which Emily Sellwood and Alfred would find themselves many years later.

In Horncastle the Sellwoods must certainly have known of Dr Tennyson's return from abroad and been relieved that the family was apparently sufficiently restored to normality to attend the annual Horncastle Dispensary Ball in September 1830, in the same series as the one the Franklins had attended with Henry Sellwood in 1823. Emily's father was still deeply involved, and this may well have been his daughters' first Ball. Certainly Mary, Emily and Charles Tennyson were there with their parents.

Despite this brief appearance of normality, the gossip continued. In February 1831 Eliza Massingberd (and the Massingberds were on that short list of the Sellwoods' friends in the neighbourhood) was considering a move and wrote to her son Frank – who would eventually marry Rosa Baring's sister – that she balked at the idea of living at Bag Enderby, the neighbouring parish to Somersby, and also in the charge of George Clayton Tennyson, 'for I should not like to spend my latter days in a place where the Clergeman is so strange a man as Dr Tennison, and having his strange family our readiest neighbours would be a great objection.'

Dr Tennyson was certainly strange, but Mrs Massingberd's anxieties on that score were unnecessary, for within five weeks he was dead. Dr Bousfield tactfully gave the cause of death as typhus fever, the same disease from which Emily Sellwood's mother had died, but he knew, as everyone knew, of other causes, other shames – alcoholism, epilepsy, laudanum – which were not mentioned, but could never be forgotten. The body was apparently removed from the house before the funeral, but Alfred's claim, rather surprisingly noted in the *Memoir*, that he had slept in his father's bed within a week of his death, 'earnestly desiring to see his ghost', suggests not only some identification with Hamlet but no fear of an infectious disease.

Dr Tennyson was dead. His eldest surviving son Frederick, with whom he had most often clashed, wrote that he was: 'All his life a man of sorrow and acquainted with grief'; his brother said that George had had 'a thousand kind and good qualities'; Arthur Hallam remembered 'that heart so tender-feeble, yet so wild', and even Mrs Massingberd, though she had been reluctant to be his neighbour, felt much compassion for 'poor Dr Tennison' and the fact that he had been forced to take orders without a true vocation. 'His father has indeed much to answer for.' Everyone was asking, 'What is to become of his unfortunate family?' The question was asked in the most exact sense, for there was a real possibility that they might have to leave Somersby immediately. This worry was soon resolved, fortunately, as the incoming clergyman was single and had no need of such a large rectory – small as it had seemed for a household that at one stage numbered twenty-three. If the Tennysons had left the area at this point, it is unlikely that Emily Sellwood would ever have become the poet's wife, for all her continually developing friendships with the poet's sisters. The Tennysons were to be at Somersby for another six years.

The Reverend Thomas Rawnsley, their father's old friend, who had taken his funeral service, had been named as guardian of the minors in the family (along with their mother and their uncle Charles). Now he urged the older boys to 'put their great Talents into exercise, and to exert them for their own maintenance and Respectability'.

'Poor Alfred has written to me a very melancholy letter,' Arthur Hallam wrote to the eldest brother Frederick in July 1831, 'What can be done for him? Do you think he is really very ill *in body*? His mind certainly is in a distressing state.' Soon after Dr Tennyson's death, Arthur had urged on Alfred the 'consolation and hope' of 'religious feelings. Struggle as we may Christianity draws us all within its magic circle at last.' It was the struggle that would, among so many other things, keep Alfred and Emily apart year after year and draw them into its magic circle at last.

But at this time the consolation and hope of Christianity, and even Arthur Hallam's abiding concern and friendship, seemed to have little effect on Alfred's mood. In January 1832 Arthur wrote in their separation to Alfred's sister – who was also having religious doubts – to assure her that 'all our unhappiness comes from want of trust and reliance on the insatiable love of God' and to suggest 'I do not think women ought to trouble themselves much with theology', a view that would have irritated Emily Sellwood, reading William Paley in Horncastle. In the same letter Arthur was, as usual, worrying about Alfred: 'I am very, very much grieved at the account, given by Fred, of Alfred's condition of mind and body. What can be done?' It was a question he and many others, including Emily Sellwood, would ask again and again.

I do not suppose he has any real ailment beyond that of extreme nervous irritation; but there is none more productive of incessant misery, & unfortunately none which leaves the sufferer so helpless. I trust my coming will be beneficial to him: but meantime nothing should be left undone that may wean him from over-anxious thought. It is most melancholy that he should have so completely cut himself off from those light mental pleasures, which may seem insignificant in themselves, but in their general operation serve to make a man less unhappy, by making him more sociable, and more disposed therefore to receive satisfaction from the numberless springs of enjoyment which the mechanism of society affords. Unfortunately the more morbidly intense our inward contemplation of ourselves is, the more hollow & delusive we consider any temporary & apparently irrelevant diversion: yet, in fact, such may often be the only means of habituating the mind to a more healthy, that is, a clearer & truer view of its own condition.

It has been said that Emily Sellwood was the only person capable of replacing Arthur Hallam in Alfred's heart and this analysis of how Arthur himself saw Alfred's needs reveals how closely, through a lifetime, Emily, as the poet's wife, followed Arthur's own suggestions.

Arthur now showed himself immensely energetic in another area where Emily would also excel. He became Alfred's agent and business adviser, just as she would later be. Hallam, as an unrelated poet and critic, was in some ways in a stronger position than Emily would ever be. She could hardly, for instance, propose to Edward Moxon, as Hallam did in 1831, that he should publish 'an article of mine on Tennyson's Poetry'. Nor would she be as rash as Hallam was in sending off sonnets without Tennyson's permission. ('I confess this is a breach of trust . . .') But Hallam's activity on his friend's behalf about what to publish, what to include, and how to title his books foreshadows years of similar involvement from Emily. He would urge Alfred to publish, just as she would, because he was never easy 'about your MSS until I see them fairly out of your control.'

Arthur Hallam returned to Somersby a year after Dr Tennyson's death, when he was at last twenty-one and his father's ban on his seeing Alfred's sister, Emily, was lifted. In March 1832 Arthur, though joyful in loving and being loved (and pleased with the new curtains in the dining room), found Somersby not quite the Paradise he had remembered. There had been a feeling of marvellous freedom when George Tennyson was away on the Continent; now he was dead, the atmosphere was different, even though the anxiety over leaving the Rectory had at least temporarily been lifted. The girls' music had deteriorated. ('They sung six times as well two years ago'.) There were no rideable horses, Mary's considerable beauty had diminished and though Charles was sleeping 'much less than he did', Arthur was inclined to believe not only that his beloved Emily herself lacked enough perseverance to tackle German, but that her brothers were 'lazy loons' with very little to do. There was an air of listlessness and lassitude that had often been remarked at Somersby, not least by the grandfather.

Unlike some of the Tennysons' friends, Arthur Hallam was never 'too magnificent for a little Parsonage in a remote corner of Lincolnshire'. Even so, he wrote lightly to William Brookfield, 'I must try to reform things.' He was thinking of the music – and indeed perhaps that they needed Emily Sellwood – but his words had wider implications. He was nervous generally about things at Somersby in 1832, and even more anxious about Alfred himself. It is important to remember that Tennyson's huge gloom and despondency were not caused by Arthur Hallam's death, nor indeed by clashes with his father and grandfather, though his acute sensibility and inherent despair were naturally exacerbated by outward circumstance. In the summer of 1832, when the two young men were held together in quarantine in Rotterdam, instead of enjoying the chance to talk for hours on end with Arthur, Alfred typically (Arthur reported) 'howls and growls sans intermission'. He 'complains constantly and eloquently of total decay' though 'his genius grows brighter and more vigorous every day'.

For all the howling and growling, Alfred was immensely popular among their Cambridge friends, who were already being accused of 'spoiling the young man with [their] absurd flatteries' and tolerance, and encouraging the poet's self-absorption, just as Emily herself would come to be accused as an over-indulgent wife. The young men worshipped and bowed down, addressing him constantly, and not entirely as a joke, as 'O Alfred', 'O King' and 'Alfred the Great'. There *was* something kingly about him; Emily Sellwood had used the very word.

In between Dr Tennyson's death and his own, Arthur Hallam's view of the Somersby Tennysons is a sad one. (Emily Sellwood's view must surely have been similar.) For all the fascination the family held for him, for all his acceptance of their idea that it was 'the only desirable place on earth', there was every reason for anxiety. He saw his beloved, the other Emily, nursing 'a cruel melancholy'. She suffered from all sorts of physical maladies, but more worrying was her 'overwrought sensibility'. Arthur Hallam had given her some excellent advice for that Tennysonian self-absorption, advice not suitable for poets. 'Think more on subjects unconnected with yourself.' That was certainly not advice the poet's wife would ever give him.

Arthur used the word 'melancholy' again when writing of Septimus Tennyson, 'who was going the way of us all, poor fellow', writing sonnets, but also following his siblings in less desirable paths. 'Sep. is at an age,' Arthur Hallam wrote – Septimus was then seventeen – 'when feeling hearts are touched with melancholy ... The tendencies of indulged sensibility are best counteracted, as they would have been prevented, by early contact with the world and a course of laborious exertion in some definite pursuit.' Septimus would make some attempt to train to be a doctor – apprenticed to a practice in Louth – but would end up, like most of his brothers, without a profession and famously self-characterized, as 'the most morbid of the Tennysons'.

Then there was Frederick, the eldest, whose behaviour, even after his father's death, continued to be outrageous. Henry Sellwood (and his daughters) must certainly have heard of Frederick's quarrel with his grandfather in July 1832 at Bayons Manor, for it was witnessed by Sir William Ingilby and Colonel Cracroft, both friends of Henry Sellwood. The grandfather reported on Frederick to his son Charles in London: 'He is a savage. Sir William and Cracroft observed his conduct ... On his leaving me I said he would kill me by his conduct. His answer was, you will live *long enough*. I have been at Rasen today and given instructions for an alteration in my will. He governs the whole Somersby family and said when you were there you acted so improperly *he* would take care you should not be admitted again. It is high time that house should be shut up.' Then he went on to say that he was only allowing his grandson Charles to have one bedroom in Grove House in Tealby, where he was living as a curate, 'so that he cannot entertain this brute'.

While the grandfather was calling his grandson Frederick a brute, Arthur Hallam was using the same word of the grandfather. The old brute was 'bruter than ever' – for it was his opposition (what the young Tennysons and Arthur saw as his meanness) that was blocking the marriage of his grand-daughter. The only good thing about him, Arthur said, 'is his relationship to the person I love best in the world,' and of course he meant Alfred's sister, not Alfred.

The situation of Charles would be of more concern to the Sellwoods than that of Frederick, Septimus or Arthur Hallam and his betrothed.

Everyone loved Charles, just as they all loved Arthur. William Brookfield said, 'I love the wretch.' Julia Cameron would say, 'Really who could help it?' After Charles's death, Alfred told Gladstone, 'He was almost the most lovable human being I have ever met' – Arthur Hallam and the poet's wife obviously accounting for the 'almost'. Charles was the brother between Frederick and Alfred – the three of them were born within two years and three months. When they were young, Charles and Alfred were as close in every way as brothers can be. 'All my griefs were shared with thee, As all my hopes were thine,' Alfred wrote.

William Allingham described Charles as 'like Alfred, though of shorter stature', plumper too, with a 'manner peculiar to the family, at once dignified, odd, very easy and natural.' His way of talking was 'odd but distinct, and the phraseology always original . . .' He was a good poet too. Coleridge had thought Charles's 1830 sonnets showed even more promise than Alfred's *Poems, Chiefly Lyrical*. Frederick said of Charles: 'He always was a good kind creature – liker my dear mother than any of us.' Like his mother, like all her children, he was self-indulgent. At Cambridge he had a taste for 'books with indecent titles and indecent pictures', a taste he put aside, growing resolutely 'pure and good' after his decision to take orders.

But what he could not finally put aside was an attraction to laudanum. It was just at this time that his friends were first commenting on his use of laudanum. His great-nephew, another Charles, long after would suggest that a doctor had prescribed the drug for some complaint which caused 'a good deal of severe neuralgic pain', but there is no surviving evidence for this. Alfred, in a letter from which the relevant sentence was almost entirely obliterated, told James Spedding that, 'I believe his spirits are pretty good, tho' he sometimes takes some drops of laudanum by way of stimulus.' Spedding told another friend the following month that Charles 'denies laudanum, except in asthmatical intervals.' So it may have been asthma – the illness that had taken him to Cheltenham as a boy with his father – that started him on the dangerous slope. Neither Alfred nor Spedding seems particularly worried at this point, though we know from Alfred's letter to William Brookfield his own fear of the drug. He told his friend that if he did not leave it off, he foresaw nothing for Brookfield 'but stupefaction, aneurism, confusion, horror and death.' Arthur Hallam also equated the drug with dissipation rather than medication. 'I trust you are not seeking relief in dissipation,' he wrote to Brookfield. 'Remember you promised me to take no more opium.' Opium or laudanum (of which opium was the main ingredient) was readily available in Cambridge market at this time – and often home-produced in Lincolnshire, from white poppies grown in cottage gardens, as a general medicine and tonic.

On taking orders, Charles had become the curate at Tealby, under the thumb of his grandfather. Arthur Hallam commented that he 'appears worn with the duties of his new state'. He was the only one of the Tennyson sons to go into the Church, though it was proposed – as a slightly desperate solution and in spite of the example of their father – for many of the seven brothers, including Alfred. Their elders were anxious to see them in respectable independence. Charles's real independence, and his escape from Tealby, would come later.

The worst situation of all was that of Edward, the brother closest in age to Emily Sellwood. He had been described by his father – in 1829, when he was sixteen – as 'unmanageable', 'a very awkward . . . fellow who fancies himself to be a superior Genius'. Nearly four years later, after his father's death, his mother wrote of poor Edward's mind as 'so unnotched he is scarcely able to endure his existence'. Dr Bousfield called in a colleague, who considered Edward's state would terminate in hopeless insanity and wanted him removed to the asylum at Lincoln. Lincoln seemed a little too near to his uncle Charles, who considered also that the boy's treatment should be disguised in some way, that he should suppose 'he goes . . . as a Pupil for the purpose of initiating him in the medical profession.' How soon Edward realized the deception is not recorded. 'A small and comfortable lunatic asylum' called Acomb House in York was chosen and in York he stayed for the rest of his life. In the public record he survives in a sonnet Alfred encouraged his young brother to send to the *Yorkshire Literary Annual* in 1831, the year before he was committed. In the *Memoir* he appears only in the family tree.

'Despondency and madness' – it was Arthur Hallam who quoted Wordsworth and urged Alfred not to accept them as the necessary end for 'we poets' who in our youth begin in gladness. But it is no wonder that Alfred feared his inheritance, his own future and that of the next generation. Any comment Arthur Hallam or Alfred himself may have made on Edward's committal has been destroyed, but it is certain that Alfred's brother passed his idle days in exactly the unstructured way Hallam, the concerned friend, thought most inappropriate for the mental health of the Tennysons. An 1837 report on the asylum says that 'male patients amuse themselves with walking, reading and the pianoforte occasionally'; clearly, there was a great deal of time for introspection. In the 1841 census Edward Tennyson was described as a 'Gentleman', by 1851 as an 'insane patient', in 1871 he is a 'Lunatic' and in 1881 an 'Imbecile'.

Arthur Hallam felt strongly 'the importance of regular occupation, the danger of indulging desultory and moody trains of feeling, which always arise in the absence of such occupation'. Seven miles away from all that self-indulgent behaviour at Somersby, in the house in the Market Place in Horncastle, the Sellwood girls were well aware of the importance of routine and regular occupation. Emily, the eldest, had become eighteen in the year of Dr Tennyson's death, and had taken over the management of the household from Aunt Betsy, the reluctant and often ailing housekeeper, who took herself off initially to Lincoln.

Emily Sellwood's days were busy and well regulated. But it is tempting to imagine her at night – longing for love, lying in bed in her shadowy room in Horncastle and reading by candlelight or moonlight words that had not long before been written by Alfred Tennyson seven miles away in Somersby:

> And ever when the moon was low,
>   And the shrill winds were up and away,
> In the white curtain, to and fro,
>   She saw the gusty shadow sway.
> But when the moon was very low,
>   And wild winds bound within their cell,
>   The shadow of the poplar fell
> Upon her bed, across her brow.
>   She only said, 'The night is dreary,
>   He cometh not,' she said;
>   She said, 'I am aweary, aweary,
>   I would that I were dead!'

When she was nineteen, she could have read:

> And sometimes through the mirror blue
> The knights come riding two by two:
> She hath no loyal knight and true,
>   The Lady of Shalott.

But in her web she still delights
To weave the mirror's magic sights,
For often through the silent nights
A funeral, with plumes and lights
   And music, came from Camelot:
Or when the moon was overhead,
Came two young lovers lately wed;
'I am half sick of shadows,' said
   The Lady of Shalott.

Alfred Tennyson was only twenty-two when – in the disturbing year of his father's death – he wrote the first version of the poem by which he is still best known over one hundred and fifty years later. Is it any wonder that the girls of Lincolnshire – those few who knew what he was writing – were fascinated by him, this poet 'dowered with the hate of hate, the scorn of scorn, the love of love'. Who is not at nineteen, twenty, twenty-two 'dowered with the love of love'? They were all engaged in tentative approaches and retreats towards engagement.

The Tennysons' uncle John Bourne observed that their grandfather would take no interest at all in the goings-on: 'He seems to care nothing about the persons whom either the boys or girls choose to marry – Miss Bellingham, Kitty Burton or Kitty the cookmaid are equally the same to him.' Frederick, having been thrown over by the frail and faithless Charlotte Bellingham ('that vixen' Hallam called her), would also be refused by his cousin Julia, soon go off to Corfu and later settle in Italy. Charlie, not really having been in love with the governess, seems to have behaved so badly towards Catherine Burton (daughter of the owner of the Rectory at Somersby), that Arthur Hallam thought him 'decidedly to blame'. The Tennyson girls were much sought after by their brothers' Cambridge friends. Robert Tennant found the whole family 'enchanting' and was sad when Cecilia (who would later marry another of the group, Edmund Lushington) was not at sixteen attracted to him. Tennant continued his Tennysonian connection mainly by tutoring Horatio, the youngest boy, 'a good lad', though not much given to study. Mary would actually engage herself to John Heath, whose inconstancy would make them all sorry when he became tutor at Cambridge eventually to Arthur Hallam's young brother Henry.

There is only one outsider's view of the Sellwood family at this period – the exact date is impossible to guess, but the use of the word 'girls' and the suggestion that they were rather small may indicate that it was before they were all fully grown. Emily at any rate was tall as an adult. These memories, written down soon after Emily's death, are those of someone called Robert Roberts, who lived in Horncastle. They may be trivial but they are at least the result of 'personal observation'.

I well remember 'Lawyer' Selwood, the father of the late Lady Tennyson. He was a tall, thin, gentlemanly man, with a pleasant expression and quiet manners, always dressed in a black frock coat. Almost every day, about three o'clock, it was his custom to take a country walk past our house, which was in the outskirts of Horncastle, and he always had a daughter on each arm. The daughters were rather small, shy, sensitive-looking girls: and as their father was tall, and walked with a long springy step, or, as our townspeople said, 'with a loup', they had great difficulty in keeping up with him. His devotion to his motherless girls and their affection for him were subjects of general remark.

With customary exaggeration a recent writer says that Mr. Selwood's house is 'one of the best in Horncastle, and easily recognisable as the residence of the principal inhabitant.' This is all stuff, and of a piece with Lord Houghton's description of the father of Keats as a member of the 'upper middle class', when he was in reality a livery stable keeper, or something of the kind. It is a fairly good house, but there are many better in the town, and Mr Selwood, though always recognised as a gentleman, and respected by every one, could not correctly be described as the 'principal' inhabitant.

An old lady of more than eighty years of age, the wife of a respectable tradesman, and who had been parlour-maid in the family many years, remembers the Miss Selwoods as very kind and gentle. 'One of them made me this,' said she, pointing to a little card-board figure standing on her chimney-piece, representing an old woman seated darning a stocking. She is wearing a blue gown, checked apron and mob cap. By pulling a string the arm can be made to move. It is fixed in a broad piece of wood painted black, to enable it to stand up securely. On the back is written, 'A. Selwood.' I was so much amused with it that the old lady (to whom I had been a friend) begged my acceptance of it; and when I expressed reluctance to deprive her of it, she pressed it upon me, saying, as she was an old woman some one would soon be getting it, and I might as well have it as any one else. I have it now, and esteem it an interesting relic.

Roberts is anxious to counteract any suggestion of Henry Sellwood's importance in Horncastle, writing nearly fifty years after Emily and her father left the town, but, as we have seen, he was, if not the principal inhabitant, at least a prominent one – and his house on the Market Place, if not the best in Horncastle, certainly a highly rated one, as the rate books of the period confirm. If Henry Sellwood had 'a daughter on each arm', it is of course possible that the observer is remembering him walking with just Anne and Louisa, his younger daughters, and that Emily was already deprived of these brisk daily walks by her ill health. There are a number of references to the problems she had with illness after the time when she went with Aunt Betsy, as a girl of ten, to consult a London doctor. But Emily does mention 'long country walks' in her Narrative, and in her Recollections, her late summary of her life, walking is listed among the other occupations that made up her daily round.

There is no doubt that, from an early stage, the three Sellwood girls were deeply attracted to the unconventional way of life at Somersby and not only to the young people themselves. But in the quiet house in Horncastle, letter writing, reading, studying modern languages, painting, needlework, music making and entertaining formed part of a regular unsurprising pattern, with little room for what Arthur Hallam called 'violent whims' ('Tennysonian whims').

We spent rather recluse lives, but we were perfectly happy, my father reading to us every evening from about half-past eight to ten, the hour at which we had family prayers. Most delightful were the readings; for instance, all of Gibbon that could be read to us, Macaulay's *Essays*, Sir Walter Scott's novels. For my private reading he gave me Dante, Ariosto, and Tasso, Molière, Racine, Corneille. Later I read Schiller, Goethe, Jean Paul Richter; and for English – Pearson, Paley's *Translation of the Early Fathers*, Coleridge's works, Wordsworth, and of course Milton and Shakespeare. We had walks and drives and music and needlework. Now and again we dined in the neighbourhood, and some of the neighbours dined with us; and once a year my father asked all the legal luminaries of Horncastle to dinner with him.

In the 1830s there was one main topic of conversation at the Sellwood dinner table. 'Here the people are all radicals,' Mrs Massingberd wrote to her son, and they certainly were in the Sellwoods' house. The burning question was the likelihood of the passing of the Reform Bill. Emily's father had been closely involved from before the 1823 election when he had worked as Sir William Ingilby's agent. Now he was Chairman of the Horncastle Reform Committee. In 1831 Sir William's great friend, Alfred's uncle Charles, had missed his brother's funeral because of a crucial vote in the House of Commons. Lord Grey had been returned the previous November and in March the Bill passed its second reading by just one vote – three hundred and two for the Government and three hundred and one against. 'If I had not gone,' Charles wrote to Alfred's grandfather, who had also not attended the funeral, 'the Speaker's casting vote would have thrown out the Bill.' It was not yet a time for rejoicing in Lincolnshire or anywhere else. Indeed the following June Alfred's uncle Charles (not yet d'Eyncourt) found himself involved in a duel at Wormwood Scrubs, with Sir William Ingilby as his second, as a result of insulting remarks he had made about the Cecils and the Marquis of Exeter, who had evicted tenants who did not give them their votes. There was widespread unrest. Henry Sellwood chaired a large public meeting at the Bull Hotel in Horncastle. In June 1832 the Bill was finally law and power passed at last to at least some of the people. One in five adult males had the vote – twice as many as before. In Somersby, the story goes, Tennyson and his brothers rang the church bells.

When Ingilby stood again in 1835 John Franklin would write to his sister Betsy, 'I dare say our good brother Booth will make all the interest he can muster against Sir William Ingilby and I fancy Mr Sellwood will not be as zealous on his behalf this time as the last. Conservatism prevails very strongly in Essex.' Ingilby lost his seat in 1835, but Henry Sellwood still voted for him and apparently remained a devoted Whig for the rest of his life.

In 1833 Emily acquired a copy of Alfred Tennyson's new book of poems, the volume that includes 'The Lady of Shalott'. It would seem likely that she had also read the earlier books, the shared volume with his brothers and *Poems, Chiefly Lyrical* in 1830. But this is the first of Tennyson's books to survive with her ownership signature: 'Sellwood' in Emily's hand. That summer Arthur Hallam's lengthy, discerning praise of Tennyson in the *Englishman's Magazine* may well have reached Horncastle. Henry Sellwood was certainly aware of his daughters' interest in the brothers of their friends at Somersby, and interested himself. Hallam had welcomed

a poet in the truest and highest sense . . . He has yet written little, and published less . . . There is a strange earnestness in his worship of beauty, which throws a charm over his impassioned song, more easily felt than described, and not to be escaped by those who have once felt it . . . The features of original genius are clearly and strongly marked . . .

Hallam ended by commending the book to readers with 'feeling hearts and imaginative tempers'. Perhaps too the Sellwoods read

'Christopher North' in *Blackwood's Edinburgh Magazine* in May 1832 or J.W. Croker's unsigned article in the *Quarterly Review* in April 1833. In the latter Tennyson himself could not recognize 'one spark of genius or a single touch of true humour or good feeling.' It was this review, with its stricture on his first Arthurian poem ('it hardly avails to enchant us'), that Tennyson blamed for disheartening him so much that it delayed *The Idylls of the King* for years. It may well have been as early as this that Emily began to understand the complex, agonizing relationship between the poet and his critics.

Forty years after this time, Emily said to her son Hallam, 'I am so glad I did read a great deal when I was young. I bless my Father for this, as well as for so many other good things.' Her reading list shows not only a love of poetry, but also that her languages were excellent. Her copy of Schiller's *Werke* was published in Stuttgart in 1834 and given to her by Emily Tennyson. She would read all her life French, German and Italian. Her copy of Tasso's *La Gerusalemme* was inscribed 'Emily Sarah Sellwood from her Father. 9th July 1834'. That was her twenty-first birthday. Italian was always to be her favourite language. It was something she shared with the other Emily, Alfred's sister, who had been learning Italian from her fiancé. Arthur Hallam had spent some time in Italy between Eton and Cambridge. He had quoted Tasso to her early in 1833.

In that same letter Arthur Hallam had begged his Emily, as he had so often, to take care of her most precious health: she was often worrying him by her evident frailty, 'not coming down to breakfast and not going into dinner.' 'Do not give way to an idle nervousness,' he wrote rather sternly to her in February 1833. 'Sii pietosa del mio male, se nol sei del tuo proprio.' 'Have pity on my unhappiness if not on your own.'

Two months later it was Arthur himself who was seriously ill, after a visit from Alfred and Mary in London. His 'influenza fever turned into an ague' and he was longing for Somersby and 'the cool shades of Holywell' in the tedious unbearable nights. He was longing for his 'only beloved' – for his Emily, of course, not Alfred – 'with a sad and feverish eagerness hardly supportable.' He was there at Somersby in July – for the first time without Alfred – and by the autumn he was well enough to travel with his father to Vienna.

Before Emily Sellwood was twenty-one, before he and his own Emily were twenty-three, Arthur Hallam was dead. 'His Spirit departed without Pain,' Arthur's uncle wrote to Alfred, hoping to ease *his* pain. John

Kemble, another of the Cambridge friends, wrote to his sister Fanny that though Arthur's death 'was always feared by us as likely to occur, the shock has been a bitter one to bear. Never was a more powerful intellect joined to a purer and holier heart.' Arthur had 'the most sparkling yet the kindest wit.' All their friends were 'mourning for him as if he had been our brother.' Frederick anticipated Alfred by thinking of Arthur as 'he who was more than Brother to us.' 'More than my brothers are to me,' Alfred Tennyson would write, asking his closest brother, Charles, to forgive him, for 'thou and I are one in kind' whereas Arthur 'supplied my want the more

As his unlikeness fitted mine.'

Frederick, wrote of 'the affliction into which our family, especially Emily, has been plunged. We all looked forward to his society and support through life in sorrow and in joy, with the fondest hopes, for never was there a human being better calculated to sympathize with and make allowance for those peculiarities of temperament and those failings to which we are liable.' There *was* one other – though Frederick would never properly appreciate her – who would through life understand and make allowance for those same peculiarities of temperament, those same failings.

We know that Emily Sellwood was at Somersby on the evening that Emily Tennyson, with one white rose in her black hair, saw her friends again for the first time after Arthur's death, that 'unspeakable loss'. 'There could not but be a reverent hush in the room and all rose, all the gentlemen at all events.' Who was there on that evening in 1834? We know nothing else about it. If Alfred was there, it seems certain he had no time for Emily Sellwood. 'Give as little way to grief as you may,' Henry Hallam, Arthur's father, wrote, fearing 'the solitary life you both lead in the country' – the bereaved friend and the 'widowed' fiancée. '"Vienna, September 1833" were words printed in fire on the poet's memory.' At the time, he recollected later, 'I suffered what seemed to me to shatter all my life so that I desired to die rather than to live.' He would find his way through that black despair as his poetry would help many others to do – but towards Arthur Hallam himself Alfred's feelings would never alter. He said in his latest years to his friend Mary Brotherton, 'I feel just the same.'

It was Francis Garden, another of the Cambridge friends, who would write from Italy, seeming to know already that Alfred would turn his grief into great poetry. 'They that sow in tears shall reap in joy.' He suggested that the poet, by exploring the principles of doubt, 'which I have heard you apply to Christianity', might discover that God's unseen love is as sure as the reality of a friend's affection. 'There is hardly any misfortune that cannot be borne by a heart that looks to God as the doer of all.' Grief would turn into poetry and not only into *In Memoriam*. 'Ulysses', Alfred said, 'was more written with the feeling of his loss upon me than many poems in *In Memoriam*'.

> Some work of noble note, may yet be done . . .
> Though much is taken, much abides; and though
> We are not now that strength which in old days
> Moved earth and heaven; that which we are, we are;
> One equal temper of heroic hearts,
> Made weak by time and fate, but strong in will
> To strive, to seek, to find, and not to yield.

In her Narrative for her sons, Emily goes on to write, after her description of the sad evening at Somersby, of her friendship with the two younger sisters, then sixteen and seventeen: 'Dear Aunt Cecilia and Aunt Tilly often came to my Father's house and the brothers also came sometimes.' The brothers certainly included Charles, not yet at Caistor. After more than one doomed relationship with girls, he was becoming very interested in Louisa Sellwood, Emily's younger sister. She was eighteen that May, and looks delightfully, unconventionally attractive in a painting by her sister Anne.

As 'the fearful cloud from Vienna lifted', they returned to the sort of evenings they had enjoyed before, 'evenings of music and singing' at Somersby, with Mary, the eldest sister, playing the harp. We know that the Sellwood girls were at Somersby for instance on 18 June 1834 when the Heath brothers were visiting and Charles and Alfred were 'very witty'. There were dances again at the Rectory, at Halton (the Rawnsleys' home) and in Horncastle. Emily recalled, with an irritating lack of detail: 'We had several dances at our home. Two fancy dress dances I well remember.' Emily loved dancing. Thirty years later she would say how much sympathy she felt with 'all young things that love it' and would admit that even at Farringford 'many a time I have danced in a room alone for the pure pleasure of it,' an image of physical joy not usually associated with her.

'Society' itself was another matter. Emily wrote of this time: 'Louy and I disliked visiting in London and in country houses so we always refused, and sent Anne in our stead. My first ball I thought an opening of the great portals of the world and I looked forward to it almost with awe. It is rather curious that at one of my very few balls Mr Musters (Jack Musters his intimates called him), who married Byron's Mary Chaworth, should have asked for and obtained an introduction to me.'

That Emily should have mentioned Jack Musters in her brief Recollections (only two foolscap pages) of the first thirty-seven years of her life – from her birth to her marriage – seems highly significant. Jack Musters' interest in her – his noticing her and wanting to be introduced to her – was obviously important to her at a time when Alfred Tennyson, since that exchange of glances in Holywell, seems to have been taking no particular notice of her at all. Emily must certainly have read, as everyone read, Thomas Moore's *Life of Byron* – the biography of Byron, epitome of the romantic poet, whose death Tennyson himself at the age of fourteen had famously mourned by carving his name in sandstone. Moore's *Life* – published in 1830 – may well have been one of the books that had passed between the Rectory at Somersby and the house in the Market Place at Horncastle (Emily Sellwood tells us that they used to lend each other books). Alfred's sister Emily was filled with envy when Ellen Hallam, who became her friend after her brother Arthur's death, wrote of meeting Byron's daughter Ada in London. ('They say she cannot bear poetry, is this true?' Emily Tennyson asked Ellen.) Emily Sellwood needed at this point to be assured of her own beauty, her desirableness – and here was Jack Musters, who later married Mary Chaworth, whom Byron loved, asking for an introduction to her. Emily does not say anything about the encounter. What mattered was that he had singled her out.

Whether Alfred Tennyson was there on that occasion, we do not know; but Emily tells us that he too was 'fond of dancing and especially of waltzing and he waltzed well and was a very coveted partner.' Sophy Rawnsley, daughter of the Rector of Halton Holgate, agreed with her friend Emily Sellwood that he was 'a splendid dancer', but added that they preferred to talk. 'He always had something worth saying and said it so quaintly. Most girls were frightened of him. I was never afraid of the man, but of his mind.' Did she mean his intellectual powers or his despondency, his moods?

Tennyson himself would remember that 'sometimes in the midst of the dance a great and sudden sadness would come over me, and I would leave the dance and wander away beneath the stars or sit on gloomily and abstractedly below stairs. I used to wonder then, what strange demon it was that drove me forth and took all the pleasure from my blood.' Later, unromantically, he would name a physical demon: gout. At the time, his behaviour (like so much else) would be attributed to the black blood of the Tennysons, to the unstable, despondent mind.

William Allingham would record, years later, Tennyson being 'amusing in his vehement denunciation of the old Tory aristocracy of his boyhood', of the 'county families' who were not really aristocratic at all: their pride, prejudice, narrowness and bitter partisanship. At a public ball 'the Whig families would sit by themselves on one side of the room, Tory on the other, noticing each other as little as possible. But the youth of each sometimes danced together in the middle.' This must refer to many balls. At the annual Ball in support of the Horncastle Dispensary at the Bull Inn on 4 October 1832 – 'one of the largest and most brilliant assemblies of rank and fashion ever known' – the *Stamford Mercury* lists most of the characters in our story of this period: the Massingberds, the Reverend Thomas Rawnsley, the Cracrofts and, most importantly, not only 'Mr and two Misses Sellwood', 'Mr and two Misses Tennyson' but also 'Mr Eden and three Misses Baring'.

The 'Mr Tennyson' should properly be the eldest son Frederick but local newspapers are often to be forgiven similar errors and Alfred was certainly at Somersby in October 1832, working on his new book of poems. The Misses Tennyson were undoubtedly Mary and Emily; the Misses Sellwood Emily and Anne. There is evidence that it was on this occasion that Emily Tennyson, Alfred's sister, made friends with the Baring girls. Mary was 'astonished' to find her sister so rapidly taking to these new friends from 'their great house at Harrington'. Their stepfather, Arthur Eden, had rented the house, as we saw earlier, from the Cracrofts in May the previous year, but they had apparently not had the chance to get to know the Tennysons until now. Emily Sellwood had probably met them already; her father was, after all, agent for the estate they rented. Did Emily Sellwood introduce them and then look on, in concealed distress, as Alfred danced with the beautiful Rosa Baring? Was it because of Alfred's evident interest in the other girl that Emily needed – and always remembered – the admiration of Jack Musters?

We have independent evidence of Rosa's striking appeal from the diary of John Rashdall, a Cambridge friend of the Tennysons, who came to be curate at Orby, beyond Spilsby, in 1833. In November 1834 he wrote of Rosa, not knowing of any interest Tennyson had in her, as 'the prettiest and most elegant girl I ever was intimate with.' How intimate Alfred Tennyson was with her has aroused endless speculation. Rosa Baring was the grand-daughter of Sir Francis Baring, chairman of the East India Company and founder of Baring's Bank. At his death in 1810, not long before Rosa's birth, he left a fortune of more than two million pounds, an even vaster sum, of course, than it sounds. Rosa was part of a glittering, extremely rich family.

It was in September 1834 that Alfred Tennyson wrote in Rosa Baring's album these commonplace lines:

> Thy rosy lips are soft and sweet,
> Thy fairy form is so complete,
> Thy motions are so airy free,
> Love lays his arrows at thy feet
> And yields his bow to thee;
> Take any dart from out his quiver
> And pierce what heart thou wilt for ever.

They are conventional lines for a girl's autograph album and far less poignant than an equally pretty verse Tennyson wrote for Sophy Rawnsley probably at the same time, a year after Arthur Hallam's death:

> Sweet, ask me not why I am sad,
> But, when sad thoughts arise,
> Look on me, make my spirit glad
> To gaze upon thine eyes.
> For how can sorrow dwell in mine
> If they might always gaze on thine?

Sophy was only sixteen in 1834, the youngest child of the Reverend Thomas Rawnsley, the old friend with whom the Reverend George Clayton Tennyson had sought refuge when his 'whole family quitted' in 1829. Rawnsley had become deeply involved in Tennyson family affairs – particularly in the negotiations towards Emily's marriage with Arthur Hallam, so tragically ended by Arthur's death. Rawnsley was one of the guardians of the younger Tennyson children. Contact between the two families was intimate and frequent.

We have Alfred's sister Emily's authority for the fact that Alfred was fascinated by Sophy –'the lightest and most indefatigable dancer I ever saw', 'a very nice amiable girl, and so cheerful and happy that it brings sunshine into one's heart, though it were gloomy before, to look at her.

Alfred is delighted with her. I sometimes fancy she is the prototype of his "Airy Fairy Lilian".'

'All the Rawnsleys are dear to me,' Alfred would write years later – and at this time, just after Arthur's death, refusing an invitation to visit, he said that their house was the place he visited 'with greater pleasure than at any other in the country, if indeed I may be said to visit any other.' Alfred even went so far as to say Mrs Rawnsley 'was always like a mother to me', and she would treat him like a son, on one occasion urging him, however much he felt at home, not to put his feet up on the sofa. The Rawnsley relationship, enriched undoubtedly by his particular feelings for Sophy, would ultimately prove more important to him than his attraction to Rosa Baring.

Any evidence that Rosa was his first real love – his only real love apart from Emily Sellwood – comes from the poems. That Tennyson was always so anxious to distance himself from the biographical interpretation of his poetry is perhaps negative evidence that he had deeply personal feelings he wished to hide. Certainly he said to Laura Gurney, Julia Cameron's great-niece, when he was an old man, that 'he had never kissed a woman, in love, except his wife.' There is no reason to disbelieve him, but unrequited passion, particularly unrequited first love, can be as disturbing, as over-powering – indeed more significant – than many encounters that end in kisses.

There are endless unimportant poems at this period addressed to young women – under a series of mainly fictional names. Edward Fitz-Gerald called them 'that stupid Gallery of Beauties': Marian, Lisette, Margaret, 'My Rosalind, my Rosalind' – dreams of fair women. The poem for 'Kate' was an exception. Arthur Hallam had hoped she would be 'sufficiently distinct from Rosalind' and she was indeed, with her angry air and unbridled tongue:

> None are bold enough for Kate,
> She cannot find a fitting mate.

If she suggests the heroine of 'The Princess', she suggests even more Shakespeare's Shrew. Finding a fitting mate was on all their minds, and for Tennyson the quest was fraught with his own particular problems and dangers.

It may well be true that without Rosa Baring Tennyson could not have written 'The Gardener's Daughter', 'Edwin Morris', 'Locksley Hall' or 'Maud', the poem to which he was most deeply attached, reading it over and over again throughout his life. The identification of the garden at Harrington Hall with 'Come into the garden, Maud' is widely accepted. But the idea that (until the late poem 'Roses on the Terrace') Tennyson thought of Rosa Baring every time he wrote of roses is not convincing on the evidence we have. Negative evidence for Tennyson's love for Rosa comes from the fact that there is no mention of her at all in the *Memoir*. It was their grandson Charles who decided that 'there is little doubt that Tennyson was in the early 1830s seriously in love with Rosa Baring.' In fact there must be some doubt, for there is no evidence outside the poems.

Indeed one piece of evidence from a poem seems to suggest just the opposite. If he had really loved Rosa, he would have been unlikely to recite to Francis Palgrave in 1854, in the year of his son Lionel's birth, of his deepest devotion to his wife, 'Early Verses of Compliment to Miss Rose Baring'. They are more conventional 'album' verses, trivial and sweet.

> Rose of roses, bliss of blisses
> What care I for others' kisses?. . .
> Rose of roses, bliss of blisses,
> Were not thine the kiss of kisses?
> Ah! For such a kiss is that!
> Ah! For such a rose as this is!

Alfred Tennyson was working on 'Maud' at the time, embedding the admired lyric 'Oh! that twere possible' in the complex new poem. He was, it seems, transforming the passions and distresses of twenty years before. But if there had really been long embraces, kisses 'sweeter than anything on earth', if Rosa had really been the love of his young life, would he have quoted these long-ago verses to Palgrave, whom he must have known would eagerly write them down? If there had been anything serious to remember, anything that might have pained Emily, his beloved wife, he would not have mentioned Rosa, 'shamed' perhaps, like the hero of 'Locksley Hall', 'through all my nature to have loved so slight a thing.'

Tennyson pulled out the old unimportant verses for Palgrave because Rosa Baring, now Shafto, was on the Isle of Wight in 1854. Tennyson mentions her to Sophy Elmhirst, who had been Sophy Rawnsley, in a letter mainly about the new Tennyson baby. 'I did not know that Rosa was at Ryde. I hope that you will be coming to see her and if so that you will come on here.' Sophy was their friend and they wanted to see her. Rosa was someone he and Sophy had both known long ago, who meant little to him now.

Looking at all the Rosa poems, all the poems full of roses in the 1830s, it is easy to believe that Tennyson was fascinated by Rosa Baring and deeply attracted to her, but it seems most likely that the relationship went no further than she herself says it did. In *her* memories, she and Sophy Rawnsley – who was Rosa's bridesmaid when she married Robert Shafto on 25 October 1835 – are the inseparable ones. Rosa Shafto's memories in her old age were recorded by Hardwick Rawnsley, Sophy's nephew, son of Emily's cousin Kate.

Rosa Baring, I only knew as a sweet old lady . . . Often would she speak of the way in which she and her companions round Somersby, who were not too frightened of him, hung upon the words of the quaint, shy, long-haired young man, who had in his boyhood's day made an impression of being more learned and more thoughtful than was common, and seemed wise beyond his years. She would tell of how she and one of her girl friends, in admiration of the young poet, would ride over to Somersby, just to have the pleasure of pleasing him or teasing him as the case might be. From time to time he would write a verse or two for one or other of the girls who had been with him at a picnic in the woods, or send some little birthday poem of congratulation or some verse of reconciliation after a tiff at a dance; and although she confessed that all poetry in those days seemed to her mere 'jangledom', yet it was always delightful to her to believe, that the 'rose of the rosebud garden of girls', had reference to her. Alfred, as we all called him, was so quaint and so chivalrous, such a real knight among men, at least I always fancied so; and though we joked one another about his quaint, taciturn ways, which were mingled strangely with boisterous fits of fun, we were proud as peacocks to have been worthy of notice by him, and treasured any message he might send or any word of admiration he let fall.

The public nature of the poems with their declarations of love ('my whole heart is vassal at thy feet' and so on) is confirmed by the fact that the poems Rawnsley quotes 'were given to my mother by Rosa Baring.' She must have been flattered to have inspired his poems. When he became famous, she may well have treasured an admiration she scorned a little at the time. Even if Tennyson's feelings were indeed deeper than these poems suggest, if they did, as some think, have their true expression in 'Maud', they surely never brought him to the point of declaring them and asking for that unattainable hand in marriage. He knew he was not in a position to marry a Baring. Even after his grand-father's death in 1835 he was left with only a small estate in Grasby, valued at about three thousand pounds, which brought him an income not quite adequate for his own needs. 'An advantageous settlement in marriage is the universal prize, for which parents of all classes enter their daughters upon the lists,' as a writer of the period declared. Un-equal means could be as much of a problem as insufficient.

Love, if not marriage, was in the air. It was safer for Alfred Tennyson, who could see a multitude of reasons why he could not marry, to in-dulge his sensuous imagination over Rosa Baring rather than over Emily Sellwood. It would be his feelings about Emily that would soon cause the real sorrows, the days of loneliness and affliction. Let a few lines from 'Tithonus', which may have nothing to do with either of them (though probably dating from 1833), indicate the passion of Tennyson's imagination. (Rose-buds do not open in April – but an earlier reading of line four has 'And after many summers dies the rose'.)

> The woods decay, the woods decay and fall,
> The vapours weep their burthen to the ground,
> Man comes and tills the field and lies beneath,
> And after many a summer dies the swan . . .
>
> Ay me! Ay me! with what another heart
> In days far-off, and with what other eyes
> I used to watch – if I be he that watched –
> The lucid outline forming round thee; saw
> The dim curls kindle into sunny rings;
> Changed with thy mystic change, and felt my blood
> Glow with the glow that slowly crimsoned all
> Thy presence and thy portals, while I lay,
> Mouth, forehead, eyelids, growing dewy-warm
> With kisses balmier than half-opening buds
> Of April, and could hear the lips that kissed
> Whispering I knew not what of wild and sweet,
> Like that strange song I heard Apollo sing,
> While Ilion like a mist rose into towers.

The view of Alfred Tennyson as cold-blooded, low-pressured, even asexual (because of his apparent chastity for many years), seems to be totally denied by the poems themselves. All the major poems of this period are sensuous and so indeed are some of the fragments, which were not published until after his death. Did Emily read this at the time and recognize what lay behind it, its note of unsatisfied yearning for sexual experience?

> Why suffers human life so soon eclipse?
> For I could burst into a psalm of praise,
> Seeing the heart so wondrous in her ways,
> E'en scorn looks beautiful on human lips!
> Would I could pile fresh life on life, and dull
> The sharp desire of knowledge still with knowing!

CHAPTER THREE

'Learning to love and weep'

At the end of 1834 there was another of the annual balls at Horncastle in aid of the Public Dispensary. Charles Tennyson and his young brother Septimus, now aged nineteen, were there and so was Henry Sellwood with Emily, Anne and Louisa, now aged twenty-one, nineteen and eighteen. Charles had come over from his lonely curate's lodging in Grove House at Tealby, desperate for some diversion. Earlier that year, in April, his cousin Clara had written to her brother George with a show of sympathy: 'I pity poor Charles who is almost killing himself with laudanum and suffering so much from lowness of spirits.' What state he was in on the 18th December we do not know, but we can imagine him as, years later, he described himself, standing in the balcony of the Horncastle ballroom looking down on the long lines of the dancers in Sir Roger de Coverley – among them Louisa Sellwood, Emily's sister:

> He has not woo'd, but he has lost his heart.
> That country dance is a sore test for him;
> He thinks her cold; his hopes are faint and dim;
> But though with seeming mirth she takes her part
> In all the dances and the laughter there,
> And though to many a youth, on brief demand,
> She gives a kind assent and courteous hand,
> She loves but him, for him is all her care.

Charles was Louisa's first love, though she was not his. She must have known about the laudanum. She thought she could help him ('for him was all her care'), as many loving girls have thought about one bad habit or another – but there were years of anguish ahead. The problems would always be more hers than his, as we shall see. In 1834 she was, her sister says, 'the loveliest girl'. 'She had a delicate aquiline nose, dark brown hair and dark eyes with a beautiful complexion and a pretty shy manner.'

In March 1835 the way was opened for Charles's marriage, with what his sister Emily called 'the sudden dissolution' of their great-uncle Samuel Turner, whose heir he had always been known to be. Turner, the Tennysons' grandmother's brother, was a childless, card-playing, heavy-drinking parson, who had acquired a great many benefices and a great deal of land. He was a local worthy, president of this and vice-president of that. He was the founder of the Caistor Society of Industry, to promote 'industry, economy and morality amongst the labouring poor', and had built and sustained the local poorhouse. He had married Barbara Haddelsey, the landlady of the George Inn, Caistor, and acquired a stepson also called Charles. Charles Haddelsey, a lawyer (who had been left nothing but his house by his rich stepfather), would become much involved in the Tennysons' business affairs. His daughter Susan, born in 1822, became a close friend of both Charles Tennyson Turner and his sister Cecilia.

He was Charles Tennyson *Turner*, because – in order to inherit some fine property, together with all sorts of complications and obligations – he had to take his great-uncle's name. He inherited the best house on the market square in Caistor, in the north of the county, and – when the Vicar of Grasby died that May – the welcome chance to leave his curacy at Tealby and take over a benefice which was in his own gift. All might have been well if he had not also inherited a habit of self-indulgence.

Our knowledge of what was happening in 1835 and 1836 owes a great deal to a series of surviving letters from Alfred and Charles's sister Emily to her new friend Ellen Hallam, sister of the dead, lamented Arthur. Emily had spent the winter of 1834–5 with the Hallam family, who treated her with 'truly parental kindness' as the daughter-in-law she had so nearly become. Indeed Henry Hallam had settled three hundred pounds a year on her. At the time of Arthur's death he had written to Alfred: 'All that remains to me now is to cherish his memory, and to love those whom he loved.' Ellen became Emily's closest friend – evidently replacing as first in her affections both the Baring girls and the Sellwoods. 'I am a different being since I have known thee, all my friends say the same thing.' Emily's feelings for Ellen were sensual as well as emotional. She wrote: 'Oh! Darling that thou art! How I love to see thy handwriting – how I long when thy letters are put into my hand, to have thee near me to fumble unmercifully.' Though the dictionary does not give this meaning, she means apparently to caress and to hug. It is even clearer when, in another letter, she writes: 'Alas! For me, there are no very patient subjects for fumbling here. Mary is not always disposed to have her ringlets disordered and Bill, the monkey, might answer my caresses by a bite.'

Emily Tennyson tells Ellen Hallam she has started singing again, having gone one day to the piano 'in a listless way' and found herself able to play pieces which, six months earlier, before her strengthening visit to the Hallams, she had been quite unable to face. She thanks Ellen for giving her the name of the author of *The Book of Taste* and says she will 'endeavour to get it from the Horncastle Book Club.' This library was kept at the Dispensary, contained a thousand volumes and was opened to members two days a week. It was obviously a place where the two Emilys must have met from time to time.

The Reverend T.H. Rawnsley wrote to the Tennysons' uncle Charles the following month: 'They are all well at Somersby, but I wish they were earnest more either of fame or profit, but then they are leading a *harmless* and *quiet* life, & this is what the Antient Poets and Philosophers say is after all the happiest state of permanent enjoyment.' Sadly, Alfred Tennyson, harmless and quiet though his life might seem, was not finding it conducive to much enjoyment. His sister told Ellen, when she read out Ellen's account of pouring tea for Wordsworth, that he growled as 'Tennysons are apt to do sometimes, and said he was cut out of all society worth living for – he finished by venting his spleen upon harmless, stout fox-hunting Lincolnshire squires . . . Remember such lions as Wordsworth and Coleridge etc are never seen in our part of the world – scarcely ever anything comes over our bleak wolds, but bleak winds, upon bleak-feeling people; sometimes indeed a determined hunter is seen swiftly crossing the field at the bottom of the garden, but these eager life-taking beings you must own are even worse than nothing.' And this was the girl who had thought Somersby the dearest place on earth.

Alfred also grumbled about Lincolnshire in occasional letters to his friends – 'this land of sheep and squires', with a 'dearth at once of books and men'. Charlie, he told William Brookfield in May, had inherited a house in a 'wretched market town' at the 'limit of the civilized world'. 'The country about him is dreadful – barren rolling chalk-wolds without a tree.' Alfred had been to see the Caistor house and admired only 'a watercloset with a recumbent Venus in it'. It was a house of some significance. Their grandmother had lived there as a girl and had told her grandson Alfred how once she had been sitting, 'courting', on the steps of the house in the market square, with his grandfather Tennyson, when a piece of stone parapet had crashed to the ground, narrowly missing being the cause of their destruction. With the difference of a few feet, none of the family would have existed.

Alfred was staying with James Spedding in the Lake District when he wrote the letter to Brookfield. Edward FitzGerald was there too; it was the beginning of an important friendship. 'The sooner I see thee again the better,' Alfred wrote. There is a minor mystery about whether Tennyson actually saw Wordsworth when he was in the Lake District, though his name is certainly in the Rydal Mount Visitors' Book for May 1835. Wordsworth was one of the 'lions' Alfred's sister Emily longed to see, but Alfred himself was already becoming something of a lion. Indeed one of the Spedding family called him 'James's great Lion of a friend, Mr A. Tennyson' and people were already beginning to value and collect his letters, which may well have had something to do with his increasing reluctance to write any. Lady Mary Vivian wanted to buy a note Alfred had written to one of his friends, but thought it 'worth more than a pound', which was all she could afford to spend on it – and was much gratified to accept it 'upon a long loan' instead.

In June 1835 the Franklins, Sir John and his second wife, paid a visit to Lincolnshire, laden with 'poor relics' of their travels in the Middle East. 'Even the Damascus Mishmish was highly valued,' Jane Franklin wrote in her diary, sharing her souvenirs among Booths and Wrights and Sellwoods. She wrote a great deal about Emily Sellwood's relations, her husband's sisters and their husbands, Emily's aunts and uncles and the country cousins, whom Jane Franklin, sophisticated survivor of a hundred exotic journeys, observes with cool precision as Henry Sellwood kindly drives her and her husband around in his phaeton to visit them. Most vivid of all the descriptions is Jane Franklin's picture of Mary Booth, married to Emily's cousin Tom, the Vicar of Friskney. She is 'a pleasing and rather pretty-looking person' until she opens her mouth. 'Her face is rather long and elegantly shaped, but is spoilt by a set of large discoloured teeth, some of which are black and rotten and the others have a blue livid hue of strange effect – yet it never occurred to me that they were false teeth which appears to be the case. She has lost her own some years' – she was only about thirty – 'owing it is supposed to having taken acid medicines. Her manners are timid and gentle and wholly unpretending, and her most objectionable peculiarity is her mode of speaking which is exceedingly rustic and mean-sounding; some words are minced and others drawled and the effect of the whole is something quite low-bred and provincial.' Fortunately, to make up for all this, poor Mary Booth has a 'little fat baby Thomas, lying in a corner of the Dining room in his rose-coloured basket-cradle' – which is more than Lady Franklin ever had, and even she does not bring herself to suggest in her diary he should rather be confined to a distant nursery.

If only Jane Franklin had had the chance to describe Emily Sellwood in such detail on that visit in 1835. It is the very year of the miniature which seems to be of her and a description might confirm the identification. The Franklins stayed at Horncastle with their brother-in-law, Henry Sellwood, and the diary records that Aunt Betsy has returned after four years in Lincoln. Her brother John had encouraged her to do so. She had been ill again and he thought it was a good idea for her to be nearer her relations and under the eye of her 'excellent friend and brother' in-law. But she was obviously not getting on any better with her nieces. She did not return to the house in the Market Place, but took lodgings, 'two small and respectable rooms in the house of the people who make boas out of goose and other feathers and of whom my white-goose-feather boa was bought,' Jane Franklin records. Were two small rooms, however respectable, in the house of a feather-boa maker in East Street really suitable for the sister-in-law of one of Horncastle's leading citizens? There must surely have been gossip. Tennyson would say: 'There is nothing to equal the smallness of a small town.'

Lady Franklin records that at this point in June 1835 all Henry Sellwood's 'daughters are still absent from home. Ann remains in Guernsey for several months longer, and Emily and Louisa are in Berkshire, preparing to return home.' It was in this year that all three girls visited Guernsey. John Franklin was rather hurt that his nieces had passed through London without spending more than a few days and had not got in touch with him. 'I should certainly have called to see them if I had been informed of their intention,' he wrote to their Aunt Betsy on the 26 March. 'I shall be glad to hear of their safe arrival at Guernsey. I think they will enjoy themselves there very much. Bell continues to write very favourably of the Island and of the society.' The girls stayed with 'Bell', their widowed aunt Isabella Cracroft, whose husband had died in their house in Horncastle ten years before. She had tried Brighton for a while but had then removed to the Channel Islands with her family. Many years later, when another girl set off on a similar journey, Emily would remember 'our voyage – when we three young creatures crossed together to Guernsey.'

As for Berkshire, their Sellwood grandparents were both dead by now; Emily and Louisa probably stayed with their cousin Richard Sellwood, whom Emily would see as a family hero all her life, as 'noble' and fine a character as the much-adored Henry Sellwood himself. He was the 'soldier-cousin' with whom she remembered singing duets. When he left the army there was a disastrous attempt at farming in Australia, after which he returned to Berkshire and lived at Southern Hill, Reading for the rest of his life. He never married and Emily writes of him as the last of the Sellwoods.

The Sellwood girls returned to Horncastle to news of the death of the Tennysons' grandfather on 4 July, his grandson Charles's twenty-seventh birthday. The *Stamford Mercury* reported the funeral, saying that 'a vast multitude (estimated at two thousand)' assembled in the grounds of Bayons Manor and followed the body across the valley to the parish church at Tealby. No-one from Somersby was there. If the general idea in the county was that the older brother's branch had been entirely passed over for that of the younger, this was not in fact true. The grandfather had 'done what he always said he would do.' He had bequeathed to the Somersby family the whole of his inherited wealth, so enabling them all to live independent lives without having to earn their own livings. Only Charles and Alfred would add to their inherited wealth; the others lived, some of them sometimes a little precariously, for the rest of their lives on the bequests of the old man who was said to have disinherited them. They had hoped for more and had been disappointed, but, as Emily would put it to her sons, Alfred had 'the manor of Grasby' and an estate there, Frederick considerable property at Grimsby, 'your grandmother her jointure and each one of her younger children his or her portion'.

On the last day of the month, July 1835, a Royal Licence was issued to change the name of the Bayons family to Tennyson d'Eyncourt, even though the grandfather's first reaction to this had been unequivocal: 'It would hurt my feelings to lay aside the name of Tennyson for this Frenshyfied name & should not we be laught at and held in derision for so doing?' There would be laughter and derision for their uncle Charles, though he had managed to give the impression that the change of name was a condition of the inheritance and more his father's idea than his own. Their cousin Edwin wrote: 'I am very glad we have changed our name, as it gives us a good position ... Besides which it will keep us in a great measure clear of the Somersby family who really are quite hogs.' This hardly fits in with the bland words Emily Sellwood wrote on the subject years later as the poet's wife; when saying that the Somersby Tennysons thought it better to leave the county, she added, 'though the children of the two families were then and always have been on the most friendly terms.' This was certainly not always so; she could not have guessed we would read not only porcine insults, but also such letters as cousin Clara's, who must have been very relieved when young Charles took himself off to Caistor, for she had hated having 'a tribe of Somersby people' coming and going and had been relieved that Charles's lodgings in Tealby had not allowed his siblings to stay, 'as of course Mary would expect to go everywhere we did.' Clara's dislike of being seen in Mary's company may well have had something to do with Mary's beauty.

Charles was particularly devoted to Mary, the eldest of the four sisters, two years younger than he was, just a year younger than Alfred. He had dedicated his first book to her and a copy of Thomson's *The Seasons* (the poem that influenced young Alfred's first verses) is inscribed in Charles's hand: 'Charles Tennyson and Mary. The gift of my mother.' A copy of Cowper's poems at Lincoln contains the inscription: 'Mary and Charles Tennyson. Somersby.' A considerable number of Mary's own poems survive. One of the joys of the move to Caistor, on his great-uncle's death, was the chance the spacious house gave Charles to invite his family to stay with him. At the time of his grandfather's funeral, he was ill apparently, and his mother had come over from Somersby to look after him.

Alfred said that Charles was talking 'of travelling for three years', an odd suggestion when he had just taken on a new parish, and of 'afterwards taking a wife'. We do not know if Alfred suspected already that that wife would be Emily Sellwood's sister, Louisa; the talk of three years' travel may indicate that Charles himself had not yet finally decided. In 1835 he inscribed his name in a copy of Sir John Carr's account of a tour along the Rhine, a book he had bought at Jackson's of Louth. The Rhine journey would be his honeymoon.

By the end of September Charles Turner (as he must now be called) was indeed engaged to marry Louisa Sellwood, the youngest of the three sisters. On the Sunday before Christmas Charles seems to have been rehearsing the future by writing in a book he was presumably giving Louisa for Christmas, a volume of Buffon's *Natural History*: 'Louisa Turner. Caistor. 1835, Dec. 20th.' It was six months before they were married. That this is not a slip for 1836, when Louisa Sellwood really was Turner, we can be sure, for on the same day Charles wrote his own name in a volume of John Amory's *Life of John Buncle*: 'The Rev. Charles Turner, Caistor, Lincolnshire, 1835, December 20th Sunday.'

Ten days later Charles's sister Emily wrote one of her long letters to her friend Ellen Hallam. She had just returned to Somersby from staying with her in Molesey, having spent Christmas Day in Cambridge on the way. Alfred had travelled with her from London, but had a rather miserable Christmas with a cold in his head while his sister relished the glorious music – Trinity Chapel in the morning and King's College in the afternoon. Alfred was always getting colds – at one point he writes of his thirtieth. They returned to Somersby to find Frederick back from Corfu, and a new piano he had bought since his return. There was a lot of music making going on at Somersby – one of Emily Sellwood's Booth cousins looked 'more frenzied than ever behind his violin cello' and was heard exclaiming to himself, 'Oh Music!'

Emily Tennyson's next surviving letter to Ellen shows how short a time her good spirits survived the return to Somersby. Dr Bousfield has been; she is suffering from headaches and the same 'old pain in my side', which had troubled her long before Arthur Hallam's death, when Alfred took her to Cheltenham in 1831. Five years later Dr Bousfield's verdict is that 'these grievances were brought on by agitation and distress of mind.' It was certainly already 'well established that the connexion between the mind and the body is of so close and reciprocal a nature, that the health of the one materially depends upon the vigorous condition of the other.'

The poor girl was so 'steeped in misery' that it was no wonder that she felt ill and that when she played the piano 'the airs do not sound near so nice as they did at Molesey.' Mrs Tennyson has also been ill. Even so, in this house of sickness, Alfred's sister announces suddenly towards the end of the letter, without any more detail:

Emily Sellwood has been staying a fortnight with us – I have not been able to enjoy much of her society – she is a very delightful person – Thou wouldst love her if thou wert acquainted with her.

Alfred's sister had not been able to enjoy much of Emily Sellwood's society, confined to her room as she was by her headaches and the pain in her side. But Alfred was there. It was probably on this visit that the two of them really got to know each other. Emily would always remember Alfred reading to her Thomas Campbell's poems, as they sat comfortably 'on the little yellow sofa at Somersby.' Their relationship was obviously rather different now that his brother was engaged to her sister.

Three years later, in one of the few scraps of their early correspondence that survives, Alfred remembered another occasion when they sat together:

I saw from the high road through Hagworthingham the tops of the elms on the lawn at Somersby, beginning to kindle into green. I remember you sitting with me there on the iron garden chair one day when I had first come from London (and when Miss Bourn of Alford called). It was earlier in the year than now. The morning three years back seems fresh and pleasant; and you were in a silk pelisse, and I think I read some book with you.

James Spedding would say of Alfred that he was 'a man always discontented with the Present until it has become the Past, and then he yearns towards it and not only worships it, but is discontented because it is past.' It is easy to believe that that unexpectedly warm early spring morning meant more to Emily at the time than it did to Alfred, fresh and pleasant as it was in retrospect. Emily must have been well aware, staying in the house for a whole fortnight, of the plans for leaving Somersby, plans that must have chilled her heart as much as the iron garden chair chilled her body through her silk pelisse.

The other Emily wrote to Ellen Hallam later in March of the possibility of them all going to live abroad. Ellen herself suggested Pau, on the edge of the Pyrenees, and the Rawnsleys recommended Lausanne. Mrs Tennyson apparently was 'not a person who likes much heat and in all our manoeuvrings she is the prime object to be considered.' Now Emily, who a few months earlier had longed to be in Molesey again and had grumbled with Alfred over the years about their rural remoteness, was lamenting the possible departure. 'What pain it will be to leave Somersby, to know that we leave it for ever, this peaceful spot – where every lane and every tree teems with our earliest recollections – but this event must take place, therefore the sooner the better.' But it would still be another fifteen months before they would finally leave. And in the meantime there was music ('music mad' their sister called Frederick and Mary), and excursions to Mablethorpe: Alfred had 'immense satisfaction in seeing a rough sea' and was even prepared to go with Cecilia in the open pony chaise – 'wretched work' in his sister Emily's opinion.

It was a fine spring and Somersby was particularly beautiful – Emily Tennyson wrote to Ellen of 'most glorious humming days', explaining that 'humming' 'signifies with us the most perfect weather that can be conceived.' Two and a half years after Arthur Hallam's death Emily wrote to his sister of how much she relied on her letters. 'When sorrows come thick and my mind gradually darkens thy calm mild eyes come before me and gloomier thoughts depart.' The glorious weather and her brother Charles's happiness seemed to remind her of what she had lost. Charlie was over from Caistor. She said she never remembered to have seen him in better spirits. 'Yesterday', 23 March, 'he went to Horncastle and brought Emily and Louisa Sellwood back with him – their society is always a great pleasure to us. Louisa is looking very pale and thin, but she says she is quite well. Emily played several beautiful waltzes to us in the evening.' Alfred was certainly there too; he and Cecilia had returned from Mablethorpe two days before.

It would seem Emily and Louisa Sellwood stayed only the one evening on this occasion for the next day Emily Tennyson suggests the house is empty and she takes a solitary walk. 'Not having been to Holywell for a long time, I bent my steps in that direction, and visited that part of it which I had not seen since the time dear Arthur was my companion. It seemed strange to me – the dark firs were looking exactly the same, and the cascade was still dashing and sparkling.' Did Emily Sellwood and Alfred Tennyson ever walk again in Holywell? It seems likely.

Emily Tennyson was still not at all well when she wrote to Ellen again on 14 April. Less than six weeks before his wedding, Charles was finding his loneliness in the large house at Caistor unbearable. He had begged his sister Emily to join him, but she had not felt up to leaving the comfort of her own bedroom, and Matilda, the youngest sister, and their mother had gone instead. In this April letter Eliza Tennyson, the mother, becomes a more central and less ineffectual figure than she is often imagined to have been – and the interdependence of the family is seen even more clearly than usual. Charles dilated so much on his extreme loneliness when away from all of us that Mamma's maternal feelings could endure it no long[er], and she therefore yielded to his entreaties to go and stay a month with him. Yesterday, a woeful day! for those who remained behind; Mamma set off with Matilda. Thou must know that we are all sad melancholy birds when her consoling voice is not heard, nor her cheerful smiling face seen about the house.

On another occasion she had told Ellen how much she delighted in her mother's 'elasticity of mind', and commented, 'Oh! If God had not blessed her with this cheerful, hopeful spirit, she would never have borne up under the trials which she has had.' The gloom and despondency which were undoubtedly the Tennysonian inheritance were fortunately mixed in both Alfred and Charles with a good helping of their mother's humour and cheerfulness.

Emily Tennyson continued her letter to Ellen Hallam by recalling another Sellwood visit a little earlier in the month.

Emily and Louisa Sellwood have again been here, both of them nicer in every way than ever – I was not sufficiently well when they were with us to go down to breakfast, so Emily, kind thing, came and sat with me in my room, as thou wert wont to do. A few days ago Matilda and Cecilia called on them soon after they had left us – they found poor Emily very pale and languid, and suffering pain in her side and chest. Though so afflicted, she remembered my love for flowers, and sent by Matilda a most brilliant and fragrant nosegay.

It is the first clear picture of Emily Sellwood's ill health, which in one form or another would plague her for the rest of her life. It is curious that it matches so almost exactly Emily Tennyson's own symptoms – the 'debility' (that is the word Alfred's sister uses of her own demon) and the pain in the side. It is also significant that Emily Sellwood's condition does not prevent her kind act. Even in her illness, she thinks of others, not herself – sending brilliant flowers from her town garden to Alfred's sister in the country.

Emily Tennyson, herself, is acutely aware of her own self-obsession. In this same letter after praising Emily Sellwood, she continues by observing the 'happiness' of the rooks in the elms, and 'other people's' joy in the spring, 'while I feel inexpressible yearnings for something beyond all this, beautiful though it may be.' Next day she looks back on what she has written and regrets it. 'Don't think me decidedly crazy. It was wrong of me to talk to thee in this maudlin manner – to cloud thy dear mind by such morbid feelings, and cause thee to sigh over the ill-regulated mind of a Tennyson.'

Meanwhile at Caistor another ill-regulated Tennysonian mind was writing to his beloved 'Looloo', telling her how he had complicated the lives of his fellow citizens by his jokiness.

As soon as we descended, I introduce Tilly to my housekeeper, as Mrs Turner in joke. Well, some bystander of the commonalty took up the word, heard I suppose with some distinctness in the stillness of Evening and very soon after the church bells began to chime very nuptial-wise . . . No application followed for ale or pence as, I believe, they were undeceived and ashamed of their prematureness. Caistor, as I have told you, I think, is a small and, as Miss Bousfield will tell you, a very primitive place. Therefore the mob, in their feudal respect for me, as occupier of the house of a long sojourner amongst them, metamorphosed my sister into my bride and made an entry into the church to ring her in and a false entry into their cajoled craniums. Matilda is also fully convinct that she over heard a peasant woman pronounce her to be *Miss Sellwood*.

Charles, oddly, does not seem to blame himself for setting the false rumour of Matilda's identity in motion. He, if any of them, should surely have been 'ashamed' of the 'prematureness'. This glimpse of Caistor seems worth recording for the suggestion it gives of how much gossip there would be about the Turners over the years, both here in Caistor, and in Grasby and Horncastle – where of course it would have affected Louisa's sisters.

At Horncastle, the month before the wedding, Anne was working on a portrait of Louisa. 'Dearest, how does thy miniature proceed?' Charles asked his fiancée. 'Be sure to let the paintress have the full advantage of every sweet light and shade of thy countenance, so that I may in absence look on some memorializer (tho' that is not com-plimentary, you said) of thy mysteriously-shaped head and thy kind affectionate features.' He was of course not to know how much absence and separation there would be.

It is clear that Emily Sellwood spent much more time at Somersby before the marriage of Louisa and Charles than the *Memoir* suggests. ('They had rarely been in each other's company since their first meeting in 1830.') When her sister married his brother, Emily and Alfred already knew each other very well. Even so, it may well be that it was on the wedding day itself, 24 May 1836, that Tennyson first felt strongly drawn to Emily. *He* dated her devotion from 1836, writing in 1850 that he had married a woman who had loved him 'for fourteen years without variableness or any shadow of turning.' We can imagine, from her description of Alfred in Holywell, in that already distant spring, that *her* love for him had begun as early as 1830.

If we are to use poems as biographical evidence – always a dangerous thing to do – we should read now the sonnet of this same period which some assume sprang from Tennyson's disillusionment with Rosa Baring. It is quite possible that this contempt for outward show and frivolous chatter, for conventional beauty, skin-deep and cold, may have nothing to do with Rosa at all, but with a general revulsion from the ill-read, glossy, rich-husband-seeking young women who could be found at any of the country balls and dinner parties.

> How thought you that this thing could captivate?
>   What are those graces that could make her dear,
>   Who is not worth the notice of a sneer
> To rouse the vapid devil of her hate?
> A speech conventional, so void of weight
>   That after it has buzzed about one's ear,
>   'Twere rich refreshment for a week to hear
> The dentist babble or the barber prate;
> A hand displayed with many a little art;
>   An eye that glances on her neighbour's dress;
>   A foot too often shown for my regard;
> An angel's form – a waiting-woman's heart;
>   A perfect-featured face, expressionless,
>   Insipid, as the Queen upon a card.

'True feeling is all that is really valuable on the windy side of the grave,' Alfred Tennyson had written to his aunt Elizabeth Russell, and it was Emily Sellwood's display of feeling as her sister married his dear, unreliable brother, that plucked at Tennyson's heart on that May Tuesday in Horncastle.

> O Bridesmaid, ere the happy knot was tied,
> Thine eyes so wept that they could hardly see;
> Thy sister smiled and said, 'No tears for me!
> A happy bridesmaid makes a happy bride.'
> And then, the couple standing side by side,
> Love lighted down between them full of glee,
> And over his left shoulder laughed at thee,

'O happy bridesmaid, make a happy bride.'
And all at once a pleasant truth I learned,
For while the tender service made thee weep,
I loved thee for the tear thou couldst not hide,
And prest thy hand, and knew the press returned,
And thought, 'My life is sick of single sleep:
O happy bridesmaid, make a happy bride!'

Emily's Narrative confirms that the tears were not only in Alfred's poetic imagination. Both sisters and their father Henry Sellwood must have felt deeply uneasy at the marriage. Louisa was so young; she was just twenty. Charles, ten years older, though warm and funny and financially secure, was so obviously a Tennyson, indolent, careless, self-indulgent (even self-deluding), given to fits of gloom and despondency – and with a well-known disastrous habit, his fondness for opium, which he could never quite give up. A letter twenty-three years later gives us an indication of Louisa's attitude to opium. Emily wrote to Alfred: 'Poor Charles. Perhaps we shall be able to do something towards convincing Louy, but I fear not because she is fully aware of what has been so often said by others that abstinence is easier than moderation.' These sentences, which somehow escaped the flames of their son Hallam's censorship, can, of course, be read in different ways. They could mean that Louisa was throughout their married life to be indulgent of Charles's habit, counselling only moderation. They could mean that Emily and Alfred believed Charles should be allowed to indulge occasionally in opium, but that Louisa constantly nagged him about total abstinence. Or, and other evidence suggests that this could well be true, they can suggest that Louisa came to share Charles's addiction, even if only by moderate indulgence.

Certainly Louisa Sellwood, motherless daughter of a fond father, was temperamentally entirely unsuited to what lay ahead. No wonder Emily wept. If Louisa was seen by the Somersby Tennysons as an answer to their worries about Charles's loneliness and dejection, the Sellwoods must certainly have realized how emotional, self-critical and perfectionist Louisa was and how unlikely it was that the marriage would work. She showed over the years an extreme form of self-deprecation and introversion that was also characteristic of her older sister. She became as deeply neurotic as any Tennyson. The first Sellwood–Tennyson marriage would prove disastrous and naturally affect the chances of happiness for their sister and brother.

The wedding itself went off smoothly enough on 24 May. Many of Emily's friends and relations were there in Horncastle to see the marriage of the youngest sister to the Reverend Charles Turner, who everyone knew to be, in spite of his name, one of that strange family of Tennysons at Somersby and related to an equally curious crowd at Tealby. Charles's uncle, now MP for Lambeth, was at that time busy with the creation of the extraordinary castle Bayons Manor – complete with moat and drawbridge – and had now adopted the supposedly glorious name of d'Eyncourt. Both Tennysons and d'Eyncourts were the subject of much gossip. Louisa may well have been grateful for Sam Turner's will and the less distinctive name. But it seems that her sister Emily never quite accepted it. Many years later, when Louisa had been 'Turner' for over thirty-five years and Alfred had made the name of Tennyson glorious, Emily found herself writing a letter inviting a friend to meet 'Charles and Louisa Tennyson' – and having to cross it out and substitute that prosaic 'Turner'.

Emily remembered that their 'dear old Vicar', Dr Clement Madeley, who had buried their mother and watched the Sellwood girls grow up, pronounced Louisa 'the loveliest bride he had ever married'. The bridesmaids were Mary Tennyson and Emily and Anne Sellwood. Frederick, not Alfred, was best man, though the tradition was certainly that it was Alfred who took Emily into the church.

Writing about it years later, Emily thought Mrs Tennyson, the mother ('who went out nowhere'), was not present, but in fact she signed the register. 'Aunt Louy's loss to me was dreadful,' Emily told her sons in 1869, saying nothing of the worries about the marriage itself. 'I got a bad chill arranging flowers' in the cold church 'and was very ill afterwards' – but she obviously did not collapse immediately as Arthur, one of the younger brothers, remembered Emily reading Milton's 'Comus' to him. At the wedding reception? Surely not. Arthur wrote this in his memories for the *Memoir*, at his nephew Hallam's request, and he may well have been confusing two occasions. But it is a significant memory all the same. Emily Sellwood introduced 'Comus' to Arthur, aged twenty-two (less than a year younger than she was herself), a poem he had not known before 'and which I have loved ever since'. We know Alfred himself was devoted to Milton – he called 'Lycidas' 'a test of any reader's poetic instinct'.

'The bride and bridegroom went off in the family coach with four horses and white favours, after the manner of those days, for the

Rhine,' Emily recorded. The 'peace and glee' which Charles rejoiced in (Alfred had used the word 'glee' too) was to be short lived:

> Farewell! It is my parting hour:
>   Thy sister wends her way with me,
> To spend far off, by land and sea,
>   Those first fair moons of peace and glee
> That shine upon the orange flow'r.

The orange blossom had hardly faded and the honeymoon was still in progress when the two families – the Tennysons and the Sellwoods – came together again in Horncastle. Sir John and Lady Franklin were in Lincolnshire for a final visit before Emily's uncle took up his appointment, on the other side of the world, as Governor of Van Diemen's Land, now Tasmania. They brought with them another niece, Emily's cousin Kate, the surviving daughter of the family of Willingham Franklin who had died in Madras in 1824. She was now seventeen and had been staying with the John Franklins in London for three months. Since her return to England as an orphaned child she had lived with her mother's brother's family, the Burnsides, in Nottinghamshire. Now Sir John brought her to Lincolnshire to meet her father's family. There were her aunts Hannah Booth, Henrietta Wright and Betsy Franklin and her Sellwood cousins. Kate was to meet most of them for the first time, though she said Anne Sellwood was 'well known to her' from her visits to the Burnsides (Emily and Louisa had always preferred to refuse such country house invitations), and she had seen her uncle Sellwood when she was still a child. Sir John was to be godfather at a Booth baby's christening and to be the guest of honour at a Horncastle dinner organized by his brother-in-law, Henry Sellwood.

It seems they did not arrive in time for the wedding of Louisa and Charles. Many years later, and not long before her death, Kate – by then a Rawnsley – answered what she called an examination paper for her son Hardwick, who was gathering material for his book *Memories of the Tennysons*. From our point of view, the long letter is a little disappointing. She does not describe Emily Sellwood. Hardwick Rawnsley was not really interested in Emily – his mother's cousin – and his mother dutifully directed her answers to his exact questions. What were the *Tennysons* like in their early days? She herself had never met their father, but of course she had heard talk and tells her son 'the less said of him the better'. Skeletons in family cupboards were best left there – a feeling she shared, of course, with her cousin Emily's son, Hallam, who was working on *his* book, the *Memoir*, at the same time. Kate, in the privacy of this letter to her son, says something which seems to contradict the general impression Emily herself tried hard to give in her Narrative, echoed of course by her son in the *Memoir*. Kate says quite bluntly of George Clayton Tennyson, 'I never heard his son Alfred speak pleasurably of him, indeed much the reverse.' This also contradicts the idea that his grandson Hallam had not heard much of Tennyson's feelings about his father. If Kate Rawnsley had heard Tennyson speak bitterly of his father, might not others close to him also have done so?

Kate found Frederick's 'fairness' – his lighter colouring – something of a relief in contrast to his swarthy siblings, but she thought all of them good-looking, except poor Matilda, the youngest sister who was not there that evening. She was said to have suffered from a collision with a coal scuttle, or the after effects of measles, or both. Mary, Kate described as 'singularly beautiful', indeed, she thought her 'the hand-somest woman I ever saw' – though she was not long afterwards mauled by a family mastiff and was never quite the same. Kate found them all, the brothers and sisters, disconcertingly unconventional. The girls were 'untidy and forlorn in dress and in their ways . . . The men almost, if not quite, rude at times, but there was a charm in their thorough ability and in their power of language – to those able to appreciate it. To such as could not they were too peculiar to be agreeable.'

Alfred's behaviour at the Sellwoods' that evening in June 1836 was certainly not agreeable to young Kate and can hardly have been so to her cousin Emily either. Kate reported Alfred sat opposite her and stared at her 'to find out what manner of girl I might be.' She actually heard him ask his neighbour in a sepulchral undertone, ' "Is she a Hindoo?" ' Was it that he had heard talk of her childhood in Madras? Whatever it was, Kate 'felt very much out of it all the dinner and was thankful when we went to the drawing room – where, after a time, we were joined by the gentlemen, Uncle F. rather indignant at Alfred's cool proceeding of stretching himself across 3 chairs to smoke as soon as we left the dining room. The stringent etiquette of those days could not brook such an offence against good manners and respect for elders and betters.'

Kate, not Emily, was the one who was asked to play the piano. Indeed Emily must have pressed her young cousin to play, having heard she was 'a fair performer'. Alfred drew his chair close to the girl 'to see, as he said, the sparkling ornaments' she was wearing. Perhaps he realized she had overheard the remark about the Hindu, and wanted to soften it by calling her 'Zobeide' and saying her garnets were fit for an Eastern princess. 'I was I believe considered to be somewhat Eastern-looking as a girl,' Kate commented mildly. From Kate's description, Alfred appears to have taken no notice of Emily, his hostess, whatsoever. Can that really have been so? Emily had certainly not seen the 'bridesmaid' poem, if indeed the lines of it were yet already in Tennyson's head. There was another short poem, closely related to this evening, which began 'Woman of noble form and noble mind!' and continued in praise of 'as pure a heart as e'er beat time to Nature'. But the heart and mind were not Emily's, nor even Kate's, but those of Mary Neville, another guest on this occasion. She had come apparently with the Tennysons, and Kate described her vividly as 'a very remarkable looking Mrs Neville, sister to the present and former Mr Massingberd of Gunby, tall as a Giraffe, graceful and with a beautifully shaped head and delicate features – a pleasant and clever woman but born to trouble as the sparks fly upwards.'

Since the Massingberds were close friends of the Sellwoods, Emily would certainly have heard stories of Mary Neville's trouble. Emily, Alfred's sister, had told Ellen Hallam at the end of 1835 that Mary, who had grown up in Germany at the court of the Grand Duchess of Baden, had just returned from America. Apparently she had been abandoned there by her husband, William Hastings Neville, who had fled the country, leaving a great many debts. Somehow she had managed to get back to England with three small children, 'one quite an infant', and had arrived at her father's door almost dying from 'fatigue and distress of mind'.

So there were four rather remarkable women guests in the Sellwoods' house that night: Lady Franklin, forthright, sophisticated, much travelled; Mary Neville, 'full six feet high', romantic survivor of a disastrous relationship; Mary Tennyson, whom nobody could see come into a room 'without being struck by her beauty,'; and the shy, dark Kate Franklin, at this point a stranger to Lincolnshire and to Emily Sellwood – someone to whom Emily would become extremely close, so that for the rest of her life she would think of her as a 'sister-cousin'.

It cannot indeed have been an easy evening for the young hostess. It was then a month before Emily's twenty-third birthday. She must have noticed her famous uncle's disapproval of Alfred Tennyson's casual habits. There must have been a great deal to hinder her from enjoying the company of the young poet she so much admired. Kate commented that the evening broke up without a great deal of chance to talk, as the visitors who were not staying in the house 'had some miles to drive home to Somersby.' Perhaps Emily Sellwood breathed a sigh of relief as the two 'remarkable-looking' Marys and the two 'disconcertingly un-conventional' Tennyson brothers got into their carriage and drove away. But her deepest feeling must surely have been of anxiety over the family's impending move from Lincolnshire.

There was a great deal of talk about it and at last, in June 1837, it happened – what Emily Sellwood called 'the dreadful departure from Somersby', after an auction and all sorts of 'huddle and confusion'. It was the very month that Victoria, the new young queen, came to the throne, an appropriate time for a new beginning. But it was a hard time for Alfred. It was now, Emily said (in her Narrative for her sons) that, with Frederick abroad and Charles involved with his parish, 'on your Father devolved the cares of the family, an anxious task where all have nerves shattered in childhood and none of the sons any work in life', except of course Charles. 'People are apt to glance at Poets as unpractical; all I can say is that your Father furnished the house at Beech Hill throughout, not forgetting the kitchen, and very pretty and inexpensive all I saw of the furniture was except, I think, one bed with drab curtains.' Was that the bed she slept in herself? She did stay at Beech Hill, on more than one occasion, and remembered once staying up after Alfred had gone to bed and watching 'a magnificent Aurora. It was like rose-coloured lightning, making everything in my room bright,' even perhaps the drab curtains.

Beech Hill, this house the Tennysons finally decided on, was at High Beech in Essex. Emily's description of Beech Hill, with its inexpensive fittings and furnishings, gives a rather false impression. In fact, the house they were renting was a splendid one, on a hill, with a view of Waltham Abbey, and a pretty verandah hung with creepers. It was far more spacious than the Rectory they had left at Somersby. There was a greenhouse with grapes and a walled garden. There is even the sugges-tion that what Tennyson would call a 'muddy pond' was actually an ornamental lake. High Beech was a village between Chingford and Waltham, on the edge of Epping Forest. Its chief advantage for Alfred was its proximity to London. 'One gets up to London oftener,' as he said, but he found the society in Essex 'artificial, frozen, cold and life-less'. The sad disadvantage of Beech Hill for Emily Sellwood was its huge distance from Horncastle.

For the last year Emily and Alfred 'had naturally met more fre-quently and on more intimate terms' since the marriage, as Emily her-self said. Charles and Alfred were as close as Emily and Louisa. Charles was, Emily said, 'the brother who from childhood had been his chief friend among his brothers and so remained to the end.' When the Tenny-sons moved to Essex 'between Alfred and Emily a correspondence had been allowed.' Emily Sellwood was by now, in the summer of the move to Beech Hill, twenty-four. Even so, with 'the stringent etiquette of those days' young women did not write to young men without their father's permission. Henry Sellwood, in the happy immediate after-math of the marriage between Louisa and Charles, must have agreed, perhaps with some misgivings. Emily had never, it seems, been inter-ested in anyone else since that day seven years before in Holywell. Did it matter to Henry Sellwood that Tennyson's manners had shocked Sir John? Alfred Tennyson was, after all, a fine poet and Henry Sellwood had a great respect for poetry. He must have been more disturbed by other things. Living in a gossiping community, Sellwood had certainly known of the Rector's epilepsy and alcoholism, of Edward's confine-ment in the York asylum, of the indolence and self-indulgence and constant ill health of so many members of the family. Most of all, he had become aware of Charles's opium habit and of Alfred's own 'ner-vousness', which must have given him, as Emily's father, cause for con-cern. How could it be otherwise when 'he smokes the strongest and most stinking tobacco out of a small blackened clay pipe on an average nine hours every day', as a friend observed.

Emily must surely have pleaded very eloquently to be allowed that correspondence. *She* saw the joy of Alfred's company – his wit, his warmth, his marvellous talk, his poems – 'the magic music' between the growling and the foul smoking. Emily Sellwood loved him. He was indeed the most glorious human form she could possibly imagine and he possessed 'a well of love whose depths were not often revealed, but when revealed, dwarfing other love, not easily dwarfed.' So Emily said rather awkwardly. Jane Carlyle paid her own tribute to Alfred's attrac-tions. She was sure anyone would fall 'in love with him on the spot, unless she be made absolutely of ice.'

It is very difficult to determine how the relationship between Emily and Alfred progressed. No letters from Emily to Alfred survive from this period. From Alfred's letters to Emily we have only a few tantalizing scraps, largely undated, which somehow escaped their son's bonfire. Hallam Tennyson wrote in the *Memoir*, referring to this time, 1838 to 1840, 'I have not felt able to include the many passages which would show the intensity of feeling expressed in these letters, but have burnt the correspondence according to my father's directions.' We do not know what Emily herself felt about the burning; but some moving and passionate words of Alfred's did escape the flames – words, one can imagine, that Emily had kept in her heart all her life – for instance, 'Trust in me always and trust me always thine.'

One fragment, which seems to date from the end of 1837, suggests there was as yet no sort of commitment. It reads as if Emily had already been to Beech Hill – perhaps ostensibly to visit Alfred's sisters – and had seen the unimpressive pond and heard the noisy little dogs. It seems likely that Emily was there in the autumn of 1837, for that is the date of the inscription in the copy of Schiller, 'ES from ET. October 1837'. Could Emily have been there to help distract Alfred's sister at a time of further appalling loss? For it was in 1837 that her closest friend, Ellen Hallam, died suddenly aged twenty-one, of complications from measles. It was just four years after her brother's death.

Alfred had published the month before the lyric 'Oh! that 'twere possible'. One can imagine the girls – the two Emilys, Cecilia, Mary – reading it together, perhaps even listening to Alfred reading it. He was already a compulsive reader of his own poems. It appeared in *The Tribute*, a miscellany for which Richard Monckton Milnes had badgered his friend for a contribution. Perhaps Alfred did not read it aloud; he was not entirely satisfied with it. Years later it would become the heart of 'Maud'. Tennyson had written it as early as 1833 or 1834, soon after Hallam's death, but Emily Sellwood no doubt hoped in 1837 that it had at least something to do with her, that reading it he might think of her.

> Half the night I waste in sighs,
>   In a wakeful doze I sorrow
> For the hand, the lips, the eyes,
>   For the meeting of the morrow
>   The delight of happy laughter
> The delight of low replies.

The words that Tennyson actually addressed to her, the words that survive, are very different. Indeed this first censored scrap suggests he had not written before.

I have been at this place . . . all the year, with nothing but that muddy pond in prospect, and those two little sharp-barking dogs. Perhaps I am coming to the Lincolnshire coast, but I scarcely know. The journey is so expensive and I am so poor.

It was not an encouraging letter for Emily to receive, whatever else was in it. 'I am so poor,' he said. Yet he did nothing to change the situation; not long afterwards he would turn down £60 Edward Moxon had offered for a preface to a life of Beaumont and Fletcher. To say he had been 'all the year' at Beech Hill was a typically Tennysonian exaggeration, whenever it was written, for Alfred – restless as he always was – spent a good deal of time away from Essex in all three of the Beech Hill years: 1837, 1838 and 1839. He used rooms the family rented at 12 Mornington Crescent in Camden Town, he visited Cambridge and Devon in 1838, and in 1839 he was not only in London, but spent a large part of the summer in Wales. 'My mother is afraid if I go to town even for a night,' he wrote to Emily at one point. 'How could they get on without me for months?' They had to manage as best they could – but how, indeed, could they get on if he ever married? And how could *he* get on, if he had to settle down and live in one place?

'Perhaps I am coming to the Lincolnshire coast,' he wrote and to Lincolnshire he certainly did go from time to time. Emily would write to Alfred in April 1857: 'These days are always in a manner more sacred to thee than any others because two or three years thou didst spend them with me at Horncastle. The statute folk did them honour, fiddling and dancing then, and now the dove coos in our own elm-tree.' The annual 'statute' fairs were for the hiring of servants and farm workers. Imagine a scene such as that in Thomas Hardy's *Far from the Madding Crowd*, when Gabriel Oak tries to find work, and think of Alfred Tennyson and Emily Sellwood walking the crowded streets of Horncastle, or watching the dancing from the window in the house in the Market Place.

The spring was always also Alfred's favourite time for Mablethorpe and April 1838 may be the date of the one glimpse we have of the four of them together: Charles, Louisa, Alfred and Emily. It was in her

Narrative for her sons, years later, that Emily wrote: 'Once we see the four together in the old vicarage at Grasby with its surging floors.' In November 1837 Charles and Louisa had moved out of the fine stone house on the market square at Caistor and into the cramped old vicarage in his parish three miles away at Grasby. Cecilia Tennyson wrote to her friend Susan Haddelsey in Caistor: 'so Charles and Louisa are at Grasby. I am sorry on *thy* account but I am glad for one thing, Louisa will not have that long walk to take on Sunday which I think did her serious harm so weak as she is.'

The most vivid picture of life at Beech Hill, and a certain amount of information about what was going on in Lincolnshire, comes from these long letters from Cecilia Tennyson to Susan Haddelsey in Caistor. Susan was the daughter of Charles Haddelsey, Charles Tennyson Turner's attorney, who also dealt with Alfred's Grasby rents. If Cecilia (or indeed Emily Tennyson) was also writing to Emily Sellwood, as seems likely, the letters have not survived. The reason Emily in her Narrative recorded only the 'surging floors' (their creaks, their unevenness?) was perhaps that there was much talk in 1838 of the inadequacy of the vicarage and of building a new one. The year before, Charles had written to young Susan Haddelsey, at school in the Pas de Calais – a rather flirtatious letter from 'a respectable married man' – 'If I build at Grasby, I shall soon want you in England with architectural specimens from St Omer . . .' Charles Tennyson Turner would build a new vicarage at Grasby, but not for another dozen years. It would be finished soon after the marriage of Alfred and Emily in 1850. The cause of the delay is so closely related to the cause of the delay in that marriage that we must now look in as much detail as we can at Charles and Louisa's own relationship.

In February 1837, just before the family's move from Somersby, there is a happy glimpse of the two of them (in Charles's letter to Susan Haddelsey) enjoying the social life of Caistor. It is nine months after their wedding and they are giving a dinner party for some of their neighbours, including Susan's parents. They are also learning Italian together – there are joint Italian exercises surviving in an exercise book. There were problems in the parish. Most of the inhabitants were 'rough and illiterate almost to brutality', his namesake great-nephew would say, but he loved them and 'his sensibilities always remained open to the pathos and humour of their lives.' Many of them still believed in witchcraft and there was a great deal of riotous behaviour; even so,

Charles thought it unlikely he could find a living that would suit him better than Grasby, whatever Alfred thought of its bleak situation.

But Louisa, his wife, does not seem to have been able to assuage Charles's loneliness for long. There were always Tennysons coming and going, his loving sisters but also the difficult, lazy younger brothers, Arthur, Septimus, Horatio. Most of the Tennysons, most of the time (perhaps as a result of that crowded rectory in which they had been brought up) seemed to need great crowds around them. ('I feel quite melancholy,' Cecilia wrote to her friend Susan from Beech Hill at one point, 'having only so small a party about me.') If the young men had been just coming and going, it might have been all right, but they often stayed for weeks, even months on end, lounging about the place, writing poetry, especially Septimus, smoking and drinking too much, especially Arthur. Arthur even managed to catch smallpox ('but not severely') and needed nursing. Louisa, unused to idle young men about the house, must have found it all extremely difficult. She must have also found it difficult as the months and years went by and there was no sign of a child. Charles, we know from his sonnets, was extremely fond of children. He wrote of them, of children he knew, with an aching tenderness, of 'little Sophy by the seaside'; of the boy employed to scare the rooks away, of three-year-old Letty patting the globe of the world:

> And, while she hid all England with a kiss,
> Bright over Europe fell her golden hair.

Reading one sonnet, about the mother of a child who died in infancy ('She could not dream her little child would die'), one cannot help wondering whether a miscarriage or a child born dead or at least a resented childlessness, was perhaps at the centre of their own unhappiness, the canker at the heart of the marriage. Could Charles's history of taking opium have caused infertility or even impotence? It is possible.

In the *Memoir*, Hallam Tennyson, as one would expect, says very little about the marriage of Charles and Louisa. There is nothing from the wedding in 1836 until Alfred stays with them in 1852 and finds them both 'very well, only Charles rather low as it seems to me.' He was often very low. It was his great-nephew, Sir Charles Tennyson, more than a century later who gave what has become the accepted version of what went wrong in the late 1830s. 'Within three years of their wedding Charles and Louisa's marriage had been tragically wrecked ... The excitement of his engagement and marriage proved too much for him, and he began almost immediately to give way once more to the dreaded opium habit. Louisa struggled bravely and devotedly to free him, but the effort was too great. She succeeded, but at the cost of her own health. This completely broke down and, soon after the family moved from Somersby, she had to leave home and her husband with, as it seemed, little chance of returning to him.'

There is a late letter from Emily to Louisa (written in the year of her grandson Charles's birth, which was also the year of Charles and Louisa's deaths) which tries to calm Louisa's terrible guilts, her feelings of total unworthiness, when her husband had died miles away from her and she herself had been confined to an asylum. Emily's letter would seem to be the source of her grandson's analysis of the sad situation so long before he was born. 'Through thy help he came out of a state, brought on chiefly by illness, from which scarcely any other human being has been known to be freed . . .'

This was certainly how Emily wanted to see what had happened all those years before. But, looking at the evidence at the time and of Louisa's character throughout their married life, there is no doubt that the faults were as much on her side as his – indeed, that far from it being the 'excitement' of his marriage that made Charles return to the solace of opium, it was the difficulties of their relationship that made him turn to the drug again. 'Try to forgive C.', Louisa used to write in her diary, but she also needed Charles's forgiveness over and over again. 'My darling,' he wrote to her towards the end of their lives, 'Try to think always that our sins are blotted out.' He thought of her sins as well as his own. 'Deary Louie,' Emily wrote, 'God bless you. Look to Christ alone not to your sins.'

That was impossible for Louisa. Her diaries, which are not really diaries at all but confessions, reveal how obsessed she was with her own faults and failings and how the sins of the flesh dominated her life. Perhaps the lack of a child was the result of a revulsion from Charles's flesh; perhaps she was revolted by what he wanted her to do, unprepared as she had been for marriage, with no mother from her smallest infancy, a spinster aunt, unmarried older sisters. Certainly she came to consider the taking of food and drink (except the minimum to maintain life) was a weakness, if not a sin. 'I despise my natural instincts,' she once wrote, chillingly. We know all this from a series of memoranda books and a number of loose undated pages from later in their lives, which were not destroyed, I think, only because they were never read. They are very difficult to read, and confusing. Louisa uses a sort of shorthand or code, so that even when one can read what is written the sense is often elusive. But the same words crop up over and over again: confess, sin, judgement, forgive, fear, temptation, disturb, vex, pain, distress, grief, unbelief. And occasionally a clear sentence stands out: 'I was angry and angry at being angry.' Louisa was often angry and distressed and disturbed, complaining and impatient, and impatient with herself for being impatient. At one point she writes of 'C's want of love' and once there are the stark words 'Feel no-one cares for me.' She is 'very, very desolate'; she cares 'so much for love, praise'.

There are eighteen little diaries, crammed full of Louisa's inmost thoughts – but mostly illegible, as she intended them to be, even with a magnifying glass and endless patience. She keeps her secrets all these years afterwards. What was it that made it impossible for Charles, whom everyone described as the most delightful of men (of 'unfailing sweetness'), to soothe his wife's troubled soul? His sister Emily actually called him a saint. Was it because he had put up so cheerfully with so much? Certainly Louisa's constant self-recrimination, her moral anguish, must have driven him distracted. There seems to be just one critical phrase in his own diaries:

> Louisa's lachrymosity me miserrimo atq. irato

That was written in 1866, nearly thirty years later. 'No tears for me,' Louisa had said on her wedding day, or so Tennyson recorded in his sonnet. There must have been many tears in later years.

On 11 April 1838 Cecilia Tennyson wrote happily enough to Susan Haddelsey in Lincolnshire of a pleasant visit from Anne Sellwood. She had stayed at Beech Hill on her way to Guernsey, where she and Mary Tennyson were to spend some months. Anne – frail like all the Sellwood sisters – was going for her health. 'She was advised to bathe to strengthen her spine.' On the Sunday night before the girls left, Cecilia said they had some 'wild fun'. 'We sat up till one o'clock, Alfred amusing us all the time by taking different characters. He made us laugh so much you should have heard him – would have amused you so.' She went on: 'Has Charles been in any of his ridiculous moods lately? Tell me Susan when you write, and let it be soon, how Louisa is. I fear from what I have heard that she has not been at all well.' Anne must have told

Cecilia that there was some cause for worry; one wonders what effect Charles's 'ridiculous moods' were having on Louisa.

At Beech Hill Alfred was certainly in a more buoyant mood. He was still working on the poems that would eventually make up *In Memoriam*.

> Yet less of sorrow lives in me
>> For days of happy commune dead
>> Less yearning for the friendship fled
> Than some strong bond which is to be.

'The current of his mind no longer ran constantly in the channel of mournful memories and melancholy forebodings,' but he had not published anything substantial for years and his friends were becoming impatient. George Venables wrote: 'Do not continue to be so careless of fame and of influence. You have abundant materials ready for a new publication, and you start as a well-known man with the certainty that you can not be overlooked, and that by many you will be appreciated. If you do not publish now when will you publish?' There is no trace of a letter in reply to Venables's question. To Emily he would say, 'My friends have long ceased to write, knowing me to be so irregular a correspondent.' It was a theme that would run throughout his life.

Irregular his letters may have been, even to Emily, but the few that survive and the scraps of others, are eloquent not only of their own deepest feelings, but of the forces driving them apart. 'In letters,' Alfred wrote, 'words too often prove a bar of hindrance, instead of a bond of union.'

Her words, her love, only seemed to convince him that he was not worthy of her. He actually says to her at one point: 'How hast thou come to me. Thou didst make thyself wings of love and of faith and hast flown over the interval betwixt thee and me and settled in my bosom. But how thou should'st have found thyself there, without those wings, I know not.' *He* could not have bridged the distance between them. He knew she hated to hear him run himself down 'so that I will not speak of what I deeply feel thy superiority in all that is good and yet, see, I have spoken it but thou wilt forgive me by this written kiss, for alas I can but write it.' They were nearly always apart.

One scrap contains only the words: 'A good woman is a wondrous creature, cleaving to the right and the good in all change; lovely in her youthful comeliness, lovely all her life long in comeliness of heart.' Was

Tennyson worried that Emily Sellwood was *too* good for him, that her standards, her attitude, her perfect faith, not only in God but in him, would be too much to live up to, to live *with*, all their lives long, for one with his worrying inheritance, his fear of madness and of epilepsy? 'There is heredity; it counts for so much,' he said many years later. It always counted; he was always aware of it. That the Sellwood inheritance was also worrying became increasingly apparent in 1838 and 1839 as Emily's own health deteriorated and Charles and Louisa's marriage reached breaking point.

Certainly what he saw in Grasby must have reminded Alfred alarmingly of the only other marriage he had known so well. There were stormy quarrels – at Grasby about religion. We know they *were* stormy; years later Emily would say with relief that 'the theological discussions are not stormy now.' It was impossible to imagine quarrelling with Emily – however much Charles and Louisa stormed – but it is not only quarrels that cause noise. As a boy Alfred could never remember a time when his mother was not pregnant – year after year a baby had replaced the earlier baby, often before it was even walking. Mary and Emily followed his own birth so rapidly that his earliest memories were of five children in the house at Somersby – noisy and jostling for attention – and then six more by the time he was ten. Was he appalled by his own parents' fecundity, by the long line of children born to suffer their father's wayward ways?

'The thought of annual infants would drive me wild,' their friend Edward Lear, the twentieth of twenty-one children, would say. 'In my case I should paint less and less well . . . And alas! And seriously – when I look around my acquaintance – and few men have more, or know more intimately, do I see a majority of happy pairs? No, I don't.' Alfred might not have put it quite like that – though Lear loved children as much as he did – but he seems certainly to have feared that if he married he would write 'less and less well'. In 1850 Tennyson would write to the young poet Coventry Patmore, after his second child, with astonishing frankness even for him: 'Come as soon after the birth as you can. I wish you had been content with one.' Annual infants were hardly compatible with Tennyson's deepest needs – least of all infants with such dreadful heredity.

'I require quiet, and myself to myself, more than any man when I write,' he wrote to Emily. It is the writer's constant cry. Emily might have said that she could give him quiet and other things he needed as well, but he would have found it hard to believe her, however much he needed and said he needed 'the glory of being loved', and craved her 'assurances to make up the deficiencies in my own strength.' Elizabeth Barrett (not yet Browning) had heard gossip, she told her friend Miss Mitford soon after this, that Alfred Tennyson, the handsome, mysterious poet, was 'separating from his family because they distracted him.' She had obviously heard nothing of any 'engagement'. There was really never a formal engagement – with a ring, public announcements and a date for a wedding. There was simply an understanding, that permitted correspondence. Emily thought herself engaged.

Emily Sellwood stayed at Beech Hill again in November 1838, returning to Lincolnshire in early December. Alfred could particularly enjoy being with Emily in the company of his sisters. They were all more relaxed. Jane Carlyle would observe in him a not unusual ambivalence. 'Alfred is dreadfully embarrassed with women alone – for he entertains at one and the same moment a feeling of almost adoration for them and an ineffable contempt! adoration I suppose for what they *might be* – contempt for what they are!' Emily Sellwood, clever, well-read, sympathetic, quick, was already so much what she might be. Though she might sometimes have aroused his impatience (if not contempt) with the limitations of her experience, and her modest assessment of her own worth, she was accustomed to talking with her father about the very things that interested Alfred most. Men in general might adapt 'their conversation to what they *take to be* a woman's taste' but Henry Sellwood had never done so. And we know – from one of the scraps of paper that escaped the flames that burnt so much we would like to know – that Tennyson 'honoured Sellwood's integrity and cultivated his confidence'.

It was probably on this visit that Emily and Alfred first discussed *The Princess*. It is a poem full of humour and strong women, and surely owes a good deal to the 'Husks', the group of young poetry-reading women attracted to his sisters: Mary Neville and the Sellwood girls among them. *The Princess* was not published until 1847, by which time Mary Neville (six foot high like Lilia) was dead. It was Lilia who spoke up for the women beaten down by convention, by men:

> O I wish
> That I were some great princess, I would build
> Far off from men a college like a man's

> And I would teach them all that men are taught;
> We are twice as quick!

Julia Hallam had now replaced her dead brother and sister as Alfred's sister Emily's chief correspondent and confidante. On 12 December Emily wrote to Julia of the horrors of Beech Hill in winter. Trudging daily along the damp walks in the garden with Cecilia and Aunt Mary Anne Fytche (her mother's sister who was often with them), she thought longingly of London and 'streets full of warm smoke'.

Our home circle is now much reduced, Emily Sellwood, Mary and Matilda having gone into Lincolnshire, and Alfred having taken up his lodgings in town – Don't you agree with me in thinking that of all seasons in the year, this is the least suitable to the separating of dear friends? – dear friends however should never separate.

In the same letter she records that Louisa has had 'two very narrow escapes from destruction lately – in the first instance she was tossed by a savage beast'; in the second she and Charles, returning from Hull in a small boat, were run down by 'a Scotch coal vessel'. 'The mast was shivered all to pieces' and Louisa 'nearly lost all consciousness'.

Emily Sellwood's own physical health was such that it seems to have become a sort of bench mark with the Tennysons, against which all other invalids might be measured. When Mary Neville, their tall friend, is staying with them at Beech Hill, having come over from Guernsey to see a Dr Curie in London, Cecilia tells Susan Haddelsey that poor Mary is 'in a very very weak state of health, indeed almost nay I think quite as weak as Emily Sellwood.'

'Dear friends should never separate,' Emily Tennyson had written in December 1838. But the only surviving letter of Emily Sellwood's from this period was written to Emily Tennyson only about seven months later, and its tone suggests that there had been some problem between them which was part of a larger problem between the Tennysons and the Sellwoods. It seems significant that in her Narrative, all those years later, Emily would single out Cecilia (now twenty-one) for her love and understanding at this period. She wrote that Cecilia was 'very dear to me and most faithful thro' all to us'. Then she crossed out 'most' and added 'as was Aunt Tilly' – with no mention of Emily or Mary.

Emily Sellwood, longing for news of Alfred, who was presumably showing his usual disinclination for letter writing, seems to have written importunately – perhaps more than once – to his sister Emily and she had replied impatiently. There seems too to be an apology for having teased her about what was going on in her heart. Alfred's sister had already met Richard Jesse, a young sailor, at the Hallams' dinner table it seems, but it would be several years until their marriage. It was a delicate subject, for she was receiving a considerable annual allowance from Arthur Hallam's father and was regarded – certainly by some – as permanently betrothed to the dead son. Was it at this point that she was trying to brace herself to tell the Hallams and her own family that she was *not* going to spend the rest of her life in mourning for Arthur? And had she shown some natural inclination to take her brother Charles's part and criticize Louisa? Did Louisa really love Charles, one Emily had asked the other? Or had their marriage been a great mistake? I give the letter in full, as it is the very first of Emily Sellwood's letters to survive.

Dearest dear Emmie,

I fear I have been very selfish. I have pressed thee too much to write. I have not enough remembered that One alone can measure the capabilities of any living creature and Wo Wo to the man who dares pronounce his fellow can do this or that if he would. Forgive me, dearest Emmie, it has been selfishness all – a selfish fear lest thy love for me had departed; a selfish desire to have those anxieties relieved which sprang from my interest in another. And yet strange that it should have been thus! I so often thought of thee much as thou really wert. Oh well do I feel from this, and numberless things, that there are thoughts opposed to the ruined nature of man which he may constantly entertain in his mind and still they will have no effect because He the Life Giver is not invoked to give them a quickening power.

Dearest Emmie, I know that to none canst thou describe those things which are now passing within thee. I hope I shall not teaze thee again. Only promise me that if any day thou shouldst feel it would be a comfort to open thy heart to me thou wilt speak; indeed, indeed I shall not be wearied or at least I would fain flatter myself I shall not be such a wretch.

Wilt thou not go with Alfred into Wales? Thou knowest I am very jealous that he is thine brother and thou mayst go. And would he not cheer thee and would not mountains and free air cheer you both. And what shouldst say Nemmy to meet thy old torment t'other Emmie in a Welsh vale? We have speculated on a tour in North Wales. Somewhat wildly, it may be though, but perhaps the autumn may tell one.

And wilt thou say whether it bores thee to read my scrawls. Tell truly whether I shall write – ay or no. I will do either and ask no reply. For fear however the no's should have it, I had better not prolong this. Indeed I began it on this small sheet thinking thou art probably rather I should say possibly on thy way to Paris – for I do not much expect it is so – yet it may be.

One question nevertheless I will answer. I do think 'she loves him'. Not that I would depend on myself in this matter. I might so easily believe what I wish – but I never hear anyone mention her without noticing the change for the better in her health and spirits and Anne, who has been some days with them when together, feels certain her affections are there where they ought to be. Yet do not think she ceases to be really interested in you. You would not if you could hear her speak of you. And now dearest Emmie – Fare thee well. From my heart I thank thee for having made that painful effort to write to me. I hope I shall not drive thee to it again. Only love me still and believe me.

Thy very affectionate
Emily S. Sellwood

It is a relief to discover that Alfred did write to Emily Sellwood from Wales – though what survives is only a fragment from Aberystwyth, full of jokes about Welshwomen's hats and leeks, lobsters and provincial pianos. At this point Louisa was still in Grasby with Charles, who was, according to Cecilia, 'enjoying himself on the sofa – with his books – listening to sweet airs and songs' and putting aside all gloomy thoughts. 'I doubt there will be a Revolution in England soon – but I hate boding ill and had rather not be ominous,' he wrote to Beech Hill at the end of May. Did it drive Louisa mad seeing him sitting around on his sofa, given up to what Frederick had called the 'tyranny of dreams'?

Emily Sellwood's letter to Emily Tennyson was written from Horncastle. It was not very long afterwards that she set off on a tour, not to North Wales, but to Berkshire, Devon and London, that would keep her away from Lincolnshire for most of the rest of the year. The evidence is sketchy but it seems that, not long after Emily wrote that Louisa loved Charles, Louisa left Charles (still loving him but finding it impossible to live with him) and travelled west with Emily and their father. There is an inscription in a book to suggest they were staying with Richard Sellwood at Hermitage in Berkshire that summer. Then there is the address on a letter from Alfred written on 24 October 1839. It is to Miss Sellwood, Mrs Branchs, Linton, Linmouth, Devonshire. There is no greeting and it would seem one page has been destroyed, but there is an odd reference to 'Daddy's sojourn with thee'. (In later years Tennyson always called Henry Sellwood 'Daddy'; it is interesting that he does so as early as this.) Emily has been 'tongue tied' about it, as if perhaps she has been supposed to be broaching some awkward financial discussion. The bulk of what survives is another sort of discussion, responding obviously to something Emily has been saying, about God's reasons for sin and suffering, about free will – and how the happiness resulting from choosing good over evil must far exceed 'the mere physical happiness of breathing, eating, and sleeping like an ox'. 'Can we say that God prefers higher happiness in some to a lower happiness in all?. . .' 'What reasonable creature, if he could have been askt beforehand would not have said "Give me the metaphysical power, let me be the lord of my decisions: leave physical quietude and dull pleasure to lesser lives –" to animals.' Tennyson would conclude, as he often did in such discussions: 'We know nothing of these things and we trust there is one who knows all.'

Emily must have told Alfred, in the letter he was answering, of a visit to Glenthorne House, just four or five miles from Linton where she was staying. The Sellwoods had presumably had a letter of introduction to the Hallidays at Glenthorne from their mutual friends the Rawnsleys. Had she heard something from her host about Alfred which made her worried? Alfred's response must have been exactly what she longed for:

I have written but a stale sort of letter, let thy love cover its defects. Knowest thou that I am pleased with thee for feeling movements of jealousy about Glenthorne. I can't very well say why I am pleased. I suppose because it is a proof of love, dearest: yet I have proof enough, it may be

> That truth can never be confirmed enough
> Tho doubt should ever sleep,

but certain it is that I am gratified by thy jealousy. I hope to have a nice summery letter from thee enclosing full forgiveness for all my bantering and grumbling. Farewell – dearest – dearest – trust in me always and trust me always thine AT

There is one tiny scrap of evidence of Emily's state of mind in that autumn of 1839 when Henry Sellwood had returned to his work in Horncastle and Emily was in charge of her troubled sister Louisa. Late in life Emily wrote to her sister Anne with her remedy for sleeplessness. 'Take a cup of arrowroot and brandy the last thing at night. It has done Ally good. I could not sleep without it. You know how to make it. A great Exeter chemist taught me. In those days I took it made with milk.'

Picture them, the two young women, thinking of those Tennyson brothers, stirring the milk into their arrowroot and longing for sleep.

Louisa was also apparently longing to return to Charles. Henry Sellwood wrote to his brother-in-law John Booth on 4 November, ten days after Alfred's letter.

I heard a few days ago from Emily who considers Louisa quite right in her mind but it seems she is very anxious to rejoin her husband either at Grasby or to travel abroad. The latter I should think much preferable but I have written to say that she ought not by any means to go without a female companion. It seems she would like to spend this [time] in Italy.

Emily might consider Louisa 'quite right in her mind'. Charles obviously did not, though he seems to have wavered over whether separation was the answer. He described Louisa's condition a little later as of a kind 'which, from its mild tho' unchangeable character of monomania, offers but little hope of amelioration.' From those later diaries we have some idea of what was going on in her mind. Her father naturally enough was inclined to put all the blame on Charles.

Emily and Louisa, Charles and Alfred were all in London in November 1839. On the 29 November, Henry Sellwood wrote to John Booth:

I have now got Emily and Louisa home again but I was obliged to go to London and fetch them on account of the extraordinary conduct of Mr Turner. He is in fact quite demented by his opium and yet poor Louisa insists upon rejoining him unless he were absolutely to say that he would not take her in. Except this I consider her mind quite restored. Emily's health is rather worse than better and she had when in London a sharp attack of illness but I do not understand the nature of it.

It was not something a modest young women could discuss with her father, apparently, and the nature of her illness is confirmed by a chance reference in a letter from Robert Cracroft, writing from Harrington Hall two days earlier to his agent Henry Sellwood. Cracroft had happened to run into the Vicar, Clement Madeley, and said to Sellwood: 'I was sorry to hear that you had been in London on account of the health of your eldest daughter and I hope you are satisfied with the opinion of Dr Sir Charles Clarke and that his opinion has been favourable.' Clarke was a leading gynaecologist, who had published *Observations on those Diseases of Females which are attended by Discharges*; it had gone into a third edition in 1831. Poor Emily was presumably experiencing menstrual problems which cannot have been helped by the worries over Louisa.

A week later, back in Horncastle, Sellwood told John Booth that Emily was a great deal better and that Louisa also was 'in tolerable health and very good spirits'. Her father it seemed had been working on her to accept that she was better off without Charles. 'I have applied to Haddelsey (Mr Turner's friend and attorney) to try to arrange a separation from which (I fancy) Louisa is by no means averse. But nothing is settled as yet.'

Nothing would be settled for some time. There must have been considerable gossip in Horncastle. Charles and Louisa's wedding had, after all, taken place in the parish church, Dr Madeley's church, only three and a half years before, and everyone in Horncastle had known the Sellwood girls all their lives. Aunt Betsy, who was at this point, 'tolerably well', was undoubtedly in favour of the separation and of having nothing more to do with that 'extraordinary brood' to whom her nieces seemed so foolishly attracted. It also seems likely that (as well as Tunbridge Wells – where they were about to move) it was Horncastle that was in Tennyson's mind when he vowed never to live in a small country town. 'God made the country; man made the city and the Devil made the little country town.' He wrote to Emily once: 'Of all horrors a little country town seems to me to be the greatest, and I can never be thankful enough to Providence that I was not born in one . . .'

Nothing was settled. Louisa went back to Charles on New Year's Day 1840. Her father wrote to John Booth on 2 January:

Poor Louy. She went back to her husband yesterday and she has been in most excellent spirits ever since her return was determined on. Mr Turner would never say that he would consent to a separation and in fact I think he feels his utter inability to take care of himself. I really think he has no evil dispositions except his great vice which nullifies most of his inherent good qualities.

She has not raised her expectation of domestic Comfort very high and has promised if she should find matters worse than she expects [she will] return to us again or to go and visit with the Cotterills at Brigg. Mr Cotterill has the school there . . .

P.S. It is fully understood that Louisa is not to reside permanently at Grasby.

The following week Emily received a New Year letter from Alfred which must have chilled her heart. What had happened in London in November?

I send thee all the sweetest and tenderest wishes for thy happiness here and hereafter, and if my wishes could make thee happy thou shouldst leap all day long like a lamb new to the field and the world; but though my wishes have little power on thy constant wellbeing yet let me wish thee a happy new year from January to December: may thy sisters and thy Father and thy Father which is in Heaven love thee more and more until thou rest satisfied in their love. I am sometimes killed with sadness when I think of thee, but I always hope that thou keepest within thee a clear faith in good things, which shall come to thee in time or out of time – it makes little difference, so that the result be good. Bless thee therefore as thou wilt be blessed. I bless thee [who] am not worthy to bless thee, for I know thy worth.

There is another fragment, equally sad, which seems to date from the same time:

I murmured (like a hen in the sunshine) lines and half lines of some poem to thee, I know not what: but I could not think of thee, thou white dove, brooding in thy lonely chamber without movements of the truest affection toward thee and an admiration of thee which no years can render less. God bless thee, sweetest, and God will bless thee for thou seemest to me such as pure eyes delight to dwell on.

Was Emily really now to rest satisfied only in the love of her sisters, her father and her Father in Heaven?

Louisa's return to Grasby does not seem to have helped either Charles or herself. Later the same month, January 1840, there is a letter from her doctor, R.H. Paterson of Brigg, to the Bishop supporting Charles's application for 'non-residence at Grasby', because of 'the peculiar state of health (mental) of Mrs Turner . . . I deem change of abode, imperative, as an essential step towards her recovery.' The Bishop was 'considerate of his case' but it was not until 1843 that Charles finally got permission to put his parish in the hands of a curate and join, not Louisa, but his mother and sisters, in order to superintend their affairs 'as most of my brothers are not in a situation to do this.' He gave no list of the reasons for his brothers' inability to help; it would have made sorry reading.

As late as August 1840 there is a reference to the situation in Lady Franklin's diary, written in Van Diemen's Land, which suggests Louisa must have remained at Grasby after Charles's first application. Lady Franklin is commenting on a newly arrived letter from Emily Sellwood to her cousin Sophie Cracroft, which, even allowing for the slowness of mail between England and the Antipodes, surely cannot have been written earlier than March or April: 'Louisa Turner and her husband are living together again at Grasby,' Lady Franklin wrote. 'She is better in mind and health, and they are living more comfortably.' It was not to last.

Writing to the Bishop three years later, Charles reminded him he had been living as 'a widower virtually, – as it is not thought safe for my wife and myself to live together.' 'It was not thought *safe*' – it was the very word his mother had used of his father in 1829: 'I do not feel it safe to remain any longer in the house with him.' The pattern was repeating itself, with some variation. Louisa, after the separation, was spending most of her time with her family in Horncastle, with occasional visits elsewhere, for instance to the Cotterills at Brigg. It was the Reverend Charles Cotterill, headmaster of the Grammar School, who would later take responsibility for Grasby and allow the unhappy vicar to leave Lincolnshire. Charles Turner wrote to the Bishop:

I cannot but say that distressful circumstances have made Grasby a lonely place for me and as my wife resides with her father and at times, being on a visit in the neighbourhood (for it is deemed right and serviceable for her not to continue too long a period together even in her father's house), comes even nearer to me – viz. within a very few miles – this sad proximity I should much rejoice to dispense with by a change of residence. Even if, eventually, (a case perhaps not at all probable) she could return to me, the loneliness and wants of neighbourhood of Grasby would throw it quite out of the line of a medical adviser's suggestions . . . Her religious views, with which I could not concur or sympathize, seem to keep her heart at a distance from me and therefore of course no motion is made or is likely to be made on the part of her friends to reunite us.

Louisa seemed to believe in some dire sort of Calvinism, and to see both herself and Charles predestined for damnation.

Emily Sellwood's letter to Sophie Cracroft on the other side of the world also gave rise to this comment in Lady Franklin's diary entry for 20 August 1840: 'It appears she is farther off than ever from giving up her engagement with Alfred Tennyson.' By now then, in the spring of 1840 when Emily was writing, her family, and certainly Emily herself, saw the two of them as pledged to marriage. Emily would *never* give up her devotion to Alfred Tennyson. Her aunt's comment suggests that her family wanted her to do so. Emily felt herself permanently 'bound by the golden cord of her first love'. But any idea of real deep happiness she would have to abandon for ten more years. To go on loving when all hope was gone, that was her triumph.

I had, as I suppose most young creatures have, a thorough belief in happiness and a real longing for its topmost heights in this world. Yet I never dreamt of pursuing it for myself, though, strange contradiction, it seemed then and it seems still, lawful to seek to give it to others, if it be but of the right kind.

This was Emily's central statement of how she would live her life – not seeking happiness for herself, echoing Alfred (in his October 1839 letter about free will) in believing that happiness only comes from doing what is right. However Alfred saw his own 'onward progress', Emily knew that any happiness for her with him was now not to be counted on. It was not possible for her to abandon Louisa; it was not possible for her to oppose her father when he said he wished the correspondence between Alfred Tennyson and his daughter to come to an end. Above all, she had to accept what Alfred was saying more and more clearly throughout 1840. He felt that the road he had to travel was not one he could ask Emily to travel with him. He felt 'mists of weakness, or sin or despondency' swirling around him and, pulsing through his veins, the black blood he shared with Frederick, Charles and Edward, Arthur and Septimus – with Cecilia too, though that was not yet obvious. Even Horatio, about to try his luck at farming in Tasmania, also displayed, according to FitzGerald, to 'an extreme degree, the other worldliness of the Tennysons'.

Arthur was drinking too much and in debt (in Horncastle, of all places, as well as Caistor); by the end of 1842 he would be drying out in Crichton Institution, an asylum primarily for the insane, in Dumfries. In 1840 itself Alfred would be visiting Septimus in Dr Matthew Allen's madhouse in High Beech. (It would give him material for 'Maud'.) In June 1840 the first child of the new generation was born: Frederick's son Giulio. He was the fruit of an Italian union and illegitimate – and not only as far as English law was concerned. Problems were beginning already for the next generation. The Sellwoods probably knew nothing about this. Alfred may have known a good deal.

Dr Matthew Allen, the owner of the asylum at High Beech, became a major character in Alfred Tennyson's story. Soon Alfred would foolishly sell the Grasby estate he had inherited in order to raise money to invest in Allen's woodcarving scheme – an optimistic plan to produce by machinery elaborately carved screens and choir stalls, lecterns and chairs, fit to ornament the cathedrals and bishop's palaces of England. 'Never was any thing more promising,' Dr Allen wrote to Tennyson. 'All things are a lie and all things are false if this fails.' Alfred was so impressed he at first encouraged all his gullible family to speculate, with the promise of easy money. Tennyson himself lent Allen 'all I had in the world', seeing it as a way to escape his 'honourable poverty'. He thought Allen the goose that laid the golden eggs, but he was another sort of goose altogether. 'I have not been laying awake this three months to leave a screw loose. If you think I have, call me a Goose.' Alfred would have reason to call him worse things than that.

Tennyson's attempt to make himself financially sound, which would eventually result in 'an entire loss of property', became the official reason for the break with Emily Sellwood. In her Narrative she writes of the Allen disaster *before* she says her father thought it best the correspondence should cease. In 1869 she certainly wanted to give her sons the impression financial problems had something to do with the long-delayed marriage. She did not wish them to know the story of the early years of the marriage of their aunt and uncle. Nor did she want the world to know it in the 1890s after Tennyson's death. Money troubles were an acceptable reason for the long separation.

'Men of genius have never anything to keep wives upon,' as Jane Carlyle put it, and Hallam Tennyson quotes this in the *Memoir*. 'They were not able to marry owing to want of funds.' Emily's mention of Tennyson's mother's offer to enable them to marry, by giving up some portion of her own income, follows immediately after an account of one of Emily's visits to Beech Hill, as if the offer had been made while she was staying with them, perhaps in November 1838. The offer was turned down as unfair to the rest of the large family and indeed Eliza Tennyson, whose 'portion' came mainly from Frederick, could ill have afforded to help them.

Money *was* a factor. Alfred had always complained of a lack of money. In 1835 he had had to sell his Cambridge poetry medal to be able to join FitzGerald at Mirehouse, James Spedding's home in the Lake District. FitzGerald would come to his rescue over the years. But the end of the correspondence between Emily and Alfred came before the worst financial problems – subsequent on the failure of Tennyson's investment. The separation of Louisa and Charles was a more important element in Emily's and Alfred's own separation. 'Circumstance arose for which neither of them was responsible, which made her father desire that the correspondence should cease. She never doubted his love ... It was done for good motives but caused many miseries,' Emily wrote, and on another day, a slight variation: 'Great family sorrows made my father deem it advisable that the correspondence which he had allowed between us should cease. In ourselves there was no change.' Here are two surviving fragments of some riddling letters Alfred wrote before the ban, suggesting surely that, although he still loves her, he would make a hopeless husband – self-absorbed, helpless, financially and emotionally insecure, devoted above all to his art – unhealthy in mind, body and inheritance:

If I have written aught of this from vanity may thy love leave me when I want it most. I scarce expect thee to agree with me in many things I have said – believe only that all is kindness to thee, to her, to Anne, to thy father and that I have but one wish with respect to them all, that they may be blest by the Father of all and that they may see the truth, (not as I see it, if not the truth) but the truth. Thine, dear,

(till the age of ages commonly translated ever and ever)   A

I need thy assurances to make up the deficiencies in my own strength: thence most likely comes my preaching. If thy love for me is a strengthening influence to thyself, so shall mine for thee be to myself – if thy love makes thee dis-comforted I pine in discomfort and if thou diest oh wherefore should I live? how should this dependence on thy state coexist with my flying from thee? ask not, believe that it does. Tis true, I fly thee for my good, perhaps for thine, at any rate for thine if mine is thine. If thou knewest why I fly thee there is nothing thou wouldst more wish for than that I should fly thee. Sayest thou 'are we to meet no more?' I answer I know not the word nor will know it. I neither know it nor believe it. The immortality of man disdains and rejects it – the immortal-ity of man to which the cycles and the eons are as hours and as days. Thinkest thou not I hope some day to return to thee, as one that has wandered comes home with pleasure. Would to Heaven thou could'st be comfortable, that I might know thou wert in a restful state, not bowed beneath the burthen of the days. Ah that is a painful thing not to find sympathy by our own fireside, but if it cannot be, if God has varied his creature man in a million ways, what help but in ourselves? We must bear or we must die. It is easier, perhaps, to die but infinitely less noble so do thou, who art the noblest, live. Be thou bold, thro' the God thou trustest, to endure whatever may chance. I will use another argu-ment, ungracious as coming from me, but not the least with thee – lest thy sorrow leach on to me and draw me down. Fine is it, that I should preach to thee, so much stronger and holier than I am. Thou knowest it is my vice of old, however much the 'Physician heal thyself' may apply to me.

Perhaps Henry Sellwood heard his eldest daughter, as she read these pages, weeping over Alfred Tennyson in her room, brooding in her 'lonely chamber', as Alfred had imagined her. Sellwood had so often that year comforted his youngest daughter, in despair over herself and Charles. Perhaps he now saw Emily's 'streaming eyes'. It is easy to sympathize with the father's resolve to put an end to the arrival of such letters, though it seemed the letters were themselves putting an end to a good deal, including the thought of a shared fireside. Years later Emily would wonder whether she had done the right thing in deciding to accept the situation. 'I cannot tell.' In writing for her sons she wanted to reassure them about her father's role. 'My Father's love I never doubted and he had an affectionate appreciation of your Father.' Though Tennyson had written those words that had escaped burning, 'I fly thee for my good, perhaps for thine . . .', she insisted it was she who had come to a decision.

She wrote: 'Days of affliction were at hand.' 'Both might have been spared much suffering.' 'Years of great misery were consequent on my decision.'

'Living so long unmarried . . .'

Whether it was Emily's decision or Alfred's lack of decision, whether it was money or heredity and family circumstance or primarily none of these, there were now many years ahead of separation and pain. 'The far future has been my world always,' Tennyson wrote, and in the far future they would see each other again and experience a union strengthened by the separation.

Not long after they parted, it seems Tennyson wrote 'Love and Duty', which appeared in the two-volume *Poems* in 1842, his first publication for ten years. He would say he hated the book, but he hated even more to hear it abused – and abused his friends for persuading him to publish. Tennyson always said 'he forgot praise and remembered all censure.' But now there was more praise than blame and he was widely accepted as 'by far the most eminent of the young poets'. Granville Bradley said that when he went back to Oxford in October 1842 Tennyson's 'name was on everyone's lips, his poems discussed, criticised, interpreted; portions of them repeatedly set for translation into Latin or Greek verse . . . read and re-read so habitually that there were many of us who could repeat page after page from memory.'

Tennyson's grandson Charles would say that the poem 'Love and Duty', 'to a degree unusual in the poems of his maturity, has the ring of bitter personal experience.' James Spedding, reading it when it first appeared, commented, 'I was surprised with the power and beauty of it . . . The imagining of such situations for the mere purpose of entering into the feelings which belong to them has something unwholesome in it, to my fancy; but the situation being given (whether in fact or fiction) there is no harm in turning it into poetry.' 'Whether in fact or fiction' – there is no evidence that Tennyson ever discussed his relationship with Emily with any of his friends, except the Lushingtons, of whom more later. The only mentions of Emily Sellwood in letters surviving from before 1850 are in his sisters' letters. It seems, in his daily life, almost as if she had never been. But in his heart? And what of hers?

> Of love that never found his earthly close,
> What sequel? Streaming eyes and breaking hearts?
> Or all the same as if he had not been?. . .
>   For how hard it seemed to me,
> When eyes, love-languid through half tears would dwell
> One earnest, earnest moment upon mine,
> Then not to dare to see! when thy low voice,
> Faltering, would break its syllables, to keep
> My own full-tuned, – hold passion in a leash,
> And not leap forth and fall about thy neck,
> And on thy bosom (deep desired relief!)
> Rain out the heavy mist of tears, that weighed
> Upon my brain, my senses and my soul!
>
> For Love himself took part against himself
> To warn us off, and Duty loved of Love –
> O this world's curse, – beloved but hated – came
> Like Death betwixt thy dear embrace and mine,
> And crying, 'Who is this? behold thy bride,'
> She pushed me from thee.
>   If the sense is hard
> To alien ears, I did not speak to these –
> No, not to thee, but to thyself in me:
> Hard is my doom and thine: thou knowest it all.
>
> Could Love part thus? was it not well to speak,
> To have spoken once? It could not but be well.
> The slow sweet hours that bring us all things good,
> The slow sad hours that bring us all things ill,
> And all good things from evil, brought the night
> In which we sat together and alone,
> And to the want, that hollowed all the heart,
> Gave utterance by the yearning of an eye,
> That burned upon its object through such tears
> As flow but once a life.

The trance gave way
To those caresses, when a hundred times
In that last kiss, which never was the last,
Farewell, like endless welcome, lived and died.
Then followed counsel, comfort, and the words
That make a man feel strong in speaking truth;
Till now the dark was worn, and overhead
The lights of sunset and of sunrise mixed
In that brief night; the summer night, that paused
Among her stars to hear us; stars that hung
Love-charmed to listen: all the wheels of Time
Spun round in station, but the end had come.

O then like those, who clench their nerves to rush
Upon their dissolution, we two rose,
There – closing like an individual life –
In one blind cry of passion and of pain,
Like bitter accusation even to death,
Caught up the whole of love and uttered it,
And bade adieu for ever.
                    Live – yet live –
Shall sharpest pathos blight us, knowing all
Life needs for life is possible to will –
Live happy; tend thy flowers; be tended by
My blessing! Should my Shadow cross thy thoughts
Too sadly for their peace, remand it thou
For calmer hours to Memory's darkest hold,
If not to be forgotten – not at once –
Not all forgotten. Should it cross thy dreams,
O might it come like one that looks content,
With quiet eyes unfaithful to the truth,
And point thee forward to a distant light . . .

They would hardly see each other – Emily and Alfred – in the long decade ahead, years of increasing fame, health cures and restless wandering for Tennyson, his soul 'revolving in itself, in idleness and tobacco smoke', as FitzGerald said, 'thin and ill and no wonder', 'ruining himself by mismanagement and neglect of all kinds'. He would alternate between shutting himself away from the world in hydropathic establishments, 'cursed watering places' (where he 'rusted in ignorance of all things') and periods in London, where he had a dozen different addresses in fewer years, drank and smoked too much and either dined out every night for months, 'talking like an angel', or refused to dine at all, once, in a fever, eating nothing but eighteen lemons for three days – enough to make anyone 'miserably imbecile about the knees'.

Tennyson's behaviour was often imbecile or at least foolish, but nearly always lovable. He had many devoted old friends and made more friends all the time. Most of them pondered on how they could save him from himself and wondered at the 'heart so large and full of love' in someone so totally ill-organized. Charles Dickens, meeting him in Switzerland (offering Tennyson Liebfraumilch and unsweet hard biscuits), would see his carelessness, his unsuitability to be in charge of himself. He watched Tennyson pull from his pocket a five-pound note 'which he had worn down, by carrying about, to some two-thirds of its original size, and which was so ragged that, when he took it out, bits of it flew about the table.' Tennyson was travelling with his publisher, Edward Moxon, on that occasion. Dickens thought Moxon, in his 'limp and melancholy straw hat', an 'odd companion for a man of genius'. There would be others, even odder, over the years, but the travelling was better and the arriving more certain than when two geniuses travelled together.

William Brookfield, rather doubtfully encouraging Ralph Waldo Emerson to take Tennyson to France, said he needed someone to tell him what to do. 'That is the way we do with him. We tell him he must go, and he goes. But you will find him heavy to carry.' Robert Browning praised Moxon's care of Tennyson: 'He seems to need it all – being in truth a long, hazy kind of a man, at least just after dinner . . .' In theory, Tennyson wanted companions; he wanted to travel. He was always on the verge of going to Italy. He said he longed to go to Italy – or Switzerland, or Cornwall or somewhere. But when, at long last, he told FitzGerald he really was setting off with his brother Frederick for Florence, two days later he was back in Fitz's rooms. He was in a hopeless state, this 'really great man', thinking far more about his bowels and his nerves than about 'the Laureate wreath he was born to inherit'.

Tennyson *was* writing, from time to time. He was forever adding to and tinkering with *The Princess* and with the elegies that would one day become *In Memoriam*. But often the same idleness that stopped him writing letters – so that his friends grumbled about his elusiveness – prevented him even putting his poems on paper. He admitted he had lost any number of poems simply by not writing them down. One of the notebooks containing some of the elegies became 'foul with the rust, dust and mildew of innumerable moons', and was left behind, mislaid, on more than one occasion.

Tennyson considered his ill health was his inheritance. He would often refuse to connect it with his smoking and drinking, though he said he knew that 'wise men say that our happiness lies in our own hands.' He knew that 'health of mind is so involved with health of body' and took his water cures for months on end (a misery of cold baths and wet sheets) to try to achieve a quiet mind as much as a fit body. In the months taking cures at Prestbury and Umberslade, he was often forbidden 'the excitement of composition'. He was always worrying about his eyes. His doctor, he said, 'forbids me to read, even to think.' 'They tell me not to read, not to think: but they might as well tell me not to live.' All the same, he never seems to have come near suicide.

In the early poem 'The Two Voices', written not long after Arthur Hallam's death, Tennyson seems to see the human spirit, tempted to suicide, 'restored to courage' by the sight of a man and his wife and child walking to church:

> These three made unity so sweet
> My frozen heart began to beat
> Remembering its ancient heat . . .

He had told Emily: 'We must bear or we must die. It is easier, perhaps, to die but infinitely less noble.'

And what of Emily? He had told her, when they parted, 'to endure whatever may chance'. Was he still sometimes 'killed with sadness' when he thought of her? She was indeed 'so much stronger and holier' than he was. Did she cherish 'the hope that conquers all things'? We know very little. There is no mention of Tennyson in the few letters of hers that survive from the 1840s. 'Live happy', he had said in the poem 'Love and Duty'. 'Tend thy flowers.' In the Narrative, years later, Emily would say that she and her father were as happy as a father and daughter could be together. But there were tensions, unadmitted at the time, between Henry Sellwood and Louisa. She was often with them, though nearly all traces of her movements in these years have been destroyed. In her Narrative Emily gives the false impression that she lived alone with her father for the eight years between her sister Anne's marriage in 1842 and her own.

In this time, Alfred's shadow must indeed have frequently crossed Emily's thoughts, not least when she read his poems ('"I am half sick of shadows," said the Lady of Shalott.'). But both brothers, Alfred and Charles, remained in 'Memory's darkest hold', as she and Louisa talked together, over the years, of their lost loves. Tennyson had written to Emily that 'all life is a school, a preparation, a purpose: nor can we pass current in a higher college, if we do not undergo the tedium of educa-tion in this one.' Emily certainly saw her quiet life as a time of self-education and preparation – for life eternal if not first, as it actually turned out to be, for life with Tennyson. She had considerable persever-ance and self-discipline – in marked contrast to Alfred's sister Emily, who had once declared herself, aged twenty-three, too old 'to begin an entirely new language'. Emily Sellwood read a great deal both by her-self and with her father. Her friend Marian Bradley would consider Emily's well-stocked mind, her ability to talk on equal terms with men, a fine reward for marrying late.

Emily would say that in whatever ways she would make Tennyson a suitable wife, she owed it to Henry Sellwood, 'who so lovingly trained me by reading to me the best of historians and poets and encouraging me to read them myself, and books of science and theology and all that could help life besides.' Dante remained a consolation – and always associated with Tennyson, with whom she had first read him. Goethe would become equally important. She spent many hours at the piano, not only playing but beginning to compose. She continued to manage the Sellwood household, as she had done since she was eighteen. At the time of the 1841 census there were four servants, three young women and a young man who looked after the phaeton, the horses and did all the heavy work in house and garden. Emily kept the household accounts, tended her flowers and made her father's life as comfortable as possible.

Although Emily and Alfred did not see each other, there remained many links between their lives, the most important Emily's continued contact with Tennyson's sisters and their mutual friendship with the Rawnsleys. Late in 1840 Kate Franklin, Emily's orphaned cousin (the one with the dark complexion and the garnets who would record that 1836 dinner party) came to live with the Sellwoods in Horncastle. She 'lived by her own choice in my father's house, the refuge of all his wife's family who wanted one,' as Emily wrote, thinking also of Aunt Betsy. Kate became so close that Emily in the future would often sign off her letters to her as if they were indeed sisters. There were now four young women in the house on the Market Place: Emily, Anne, Louisa and Kate.

In 1842 two of them, Anne Sellwood and Kate Franklin, would marry and so too would two of Alfred's sisters, the two closest to Emily Sellwood: Emily and Cecilia Tennyson. Alfred was a witness to the beginning of the relationship between Emily Sellwood's cousin Kate and his own close friend Drummond Rawnsley, son of the man who had stood by his father through all the family troubles and who, as the guardian of those who were still under age at their father's death ten years before, had been deeply involved in the Tennysons' family affairs.

Kate tells the story of meeting Alfred Tennyson at Halton Holgate in Lincolnshire, the Rawnsley family home, in the same long letter for her son in which she remembered the dinner party five years earlier. It was February 1841; she was now twenty-two and had just recently come from Nottinghamshire to live with the Sellwoods. She was on her way to stay with the Booth family at Friskney – with the cousin whose wife's discoloured teeth had so amazed Lady Franklin. 'Tennyson had then been at Mablethorpe some weeks, revising and adding to his Poems with a view to bringing out an edition in two volumes.' At Halton Holgate Kate Franklin commented on Alfred's appearance, as so many people did, favourably, or unfavourably – according to the light and to his mood. He could appear to be 'one of the finest looking men in the world'. Kate saw him looking

very much like the old man of the sea as if seaweed might cling to him, unkempt and unbrushed, altogether forlorn as to the outer man. When told he had seen me before, he looked hard at me and said 'Now who are you and what are you? Where do you come from?' to which my reply was 'Catherine Anne Franklin, spinster – Nottingham –' the curtness of the answer appeared to amuse him – he had I suppose thought to bully me, as I was young-looking, but I was too old for that and, seeing his engagement with Emily Sellwood was then in abeyance, I cared nothing about him personally, though delighting in his poetry.

Next morning Alfred, Drummond and Kate walked together in the Halton garden, among the first yellow crocuses of spring. (Tennyson called them 'torches of flame' and Kate thought his line in 'Œnone' might have been suggested by that garden.) Kate called that walk 'the most eventful one of my life – and Alfred Tennyson with his short but keen sight was the first to perceive what was to come of it.' Eighteen months later, on 15 September 1842, Kate married Drummond Rawnsley from the Sellwoods' house in Horncastle. Tennyson confirmed Kate's observation, telling Drummond's father in a letter not long afterwards that he had accused Drummond of loving Kate 'in your little study and the sort of denial he made was as good as a confession.' There is a sighting of Drummond and Kate in Florence in February 1843 in a letter from Frederick Tennyson also to Drummond's father. 'I think his wife is a lively and agreeable person,' Frederick said, apparently forgetting he had met her in Horncastle. Emily had said how 'wealthy' Kate was and it seems they spent a long time abroad immediately after their marriage, before Drummond settled into the life of a country clergyman, like his father and his older brother Edward. Kate said Tennyson had 'no truer or more devoted friend' than Drummond Rawnsley and he and Kate herself were to play a crucial role in finally bringing Alfred and Emily together again.

Emily's sister Anne and Alfred's sister Emily married on successive days in January 1842. Both Kate and Drummond, not yet married, signed the register for Anne in Horncastle, and so did 'Louisa Turner'. Unsurprisingly there were no Tennysons present. It was not only Louisa's name, of course, that divided her from the family into which she had married. Charles – her separated husband – was at his sister's wedding. In spite of her ignominious status, Louisa apparently attended her sister with Emily. In 1879, not long before Louisa's death, Emily wrote to her of that snowy day in 1842. 'Dost thou remember thy pink silk and mine (not our favourite colour) with our swansdown and how nice she looked, poor child, in her white one!' The 'poor child' was Emily's retrospective feeling; at the time everything seemed set fair.

Charles Weld, Anne Sellwood's husband, was born in Windsor in 1813, the same year as Emily, and had respectable connections in both Dorset and Dublin. He was brought up mainly in France, had studied at both Trinity College, Dublin and the Middle Temple, but was not called to the Bar until 1844. He never practised as a barrister and, at the time of the marriage, was secretary to the Statistical Society in London. For many years he would be Assistant Secretary and Librarian of the Royal Society, a job that came with free apartments in the centre of London (where Tennyson would often stay), coals and candles. His time there ended in scandal, as we shall see, but his history of the Royal Society, with some illustrations by his wife, would win him his space in the Dictionary of National Biography. Emily was immensely fond of this second brother-in-law called Charles. She would indeed love them both, Charles Turner and Charles Weld, and forgive them much.

One letter from Louisa to her sister Anne, written apparently just after Anne's marriage, has escaped destruction. She shows how, like Emily, she was immensely attracted to 'Mr Weld' when she first saw him.

I do not think I ever told you, a little thing, which shewed, either the bond of sisterly sympathy, or the sympathy produced by a love 'stronger than the love of woman'. The day Mr Weld arrived here, I remember remarking the colour coming into my face just about the time, I rather guess, you were similarly affected. Mr White was beginning his sermon – the colouring and a sort of feeling of Mr Weld's arrival were irresistible.

Louisa goes on to domestic matters. She is obviously writing from Horncastle and passes on a message from Emily asking for instructions about a 'puce dress' Anne is to have made and 'a little light cloak and a long white cape' she has left behind. Louisa is glad to think of them established as 'the upholders of a household'. 'Already I am delighted you like servant house bedroom bed presents. I suppose Charles has begun his labours and you yours.' She slightly misquotes Keble's morning hymn to encourage Anne in her housework, but does not seem fanatically religious, as her husband had suggested to his Bishop that she was.

> The trivial round, the daily task,
> Would furnish all we ought to ask;
> Room to deny ourselves; a road
> To bring us daily nearer God.

On 24 January 1842, the day before Anne Sellwood's marriage to Charles Weld, Alfred's sister Emily married Richard Jesse, a Lieutenant in the Royal Navy. They had apparently first met at the Hallams' dinner table late in 1834, more than a year after Arthur Hallam's death. Even so, when the engagement was announced in October 1841, there was a storm of gossip and indignation. Elizabeth Barrett thought that Emily had shown herself far too prosaic for the sister of a great poet – 'What a disgrace to womanhood!' she exclaimed, rather unfairly, really knowing very little about the case of the 'lubberly lieutenant'. Emily Tennyson herself, years before, but after Arthur Hallam's death, had written to his sister, pleading forgiveness for the character Philip van Artevelde, in Henry Taylor's verse play, for his 'second attachment', on the grounds that his spirits are still entirely bound up in his first love and he sees 'in Eleanor, who is almost her prototype, but a second Adrianna'. Now it was this that worried poor Emily Tennyson's critics. There could be no second Arthur Hallam and to contemplate Richard Jesse – 'a boy in the Navy' – as a substitute, seemed unbelievable to Arthur's cousin Jane Elton, who would marry Tennyson's friend William Brookfield just the month after she wrote to him: 'Is it not extraordinary – painful – unbelievable, this intended marriage?' She remembered Arthur's sister Julia saying Emily 'would never *dream* of marrying – that she was a kind of Nun now, and that nothing was more impossible than her marrying . . . and can you conceive anyone whom he had loved, putting up with another?'

There was a good deal of putting up to be done over the years. Some say Richard Jesse was a brave and handsome man, but Jane Brookfield, a prejudiced witness, thought he had only 'a pale good-humoured face' to recommend him. He had a large mouth, which talked a great deal, and weak eyes behind spectacles. It was the talk that was the main problem. George Venables, one of Tennyson's Cambridge friends, found him 'a great bore' and Tennyson did too. In spite of writing about his sister's 'perpetual maidenhood', he apparently accepted the marriage sufficiently to give her away, but he 'clearly disliked' Jesse, calling him 'that cackling fellow'. In years far ahead his wife would need to keep the two of them apart.

A surviving letter from Emily Jesse to a friend gives an idea of how Tennyson's sister was herself feeling at this time: 'When girls marry how utterly ignorant they are of the almost awful responsibilities which will be theirs – 'tis all mercifully arranged by our Heavenly Father – if they knew beforehand what they were going to undertake, the conscientious and sensitive (those who are really worthy and capable of taking upon themselves the cares of a household and the holiness of matrimony) would not easily change their free girlhood for chains.' Horatio, writing his mother an unsatisfactory cadging letter from Australia, said he had heard of his sister's marriage. 'Thou sayest they are happy. God keep them so now and ever; kiss her for me.' Many thought it 'an unnecessary match' but Emily Jesse herself made the best of things and produced two sons.

'Poor Emily!' the next Emily Tennyson would say of her sister-in-law more than once. It was not a good marriage; it cannot have helped that she called their first son Arthur Henry Hallam Jesse, undoubtedly to please Henry Hallam, who generously continued the allowance he had given to her on Arthur's death and who agreed to be the boy's god-father, as nine years later he would be Hallam Tennyson's. That Emily may have married to get away from the Hallams and Tennysons, to have a life of her own, as her grand-daughter suggested, is not very convincing, when one knows that the Jesses, who always had finan-cial troubles, spent a great deal of their lives sharing houses with Tennysons, at one stage with Emily's mother, Aunt Mary Anne and Matilda, at another with Mary. Indeed Emily continued to live with her own family immediately after her marriage while Richard Jesse went off to Caen for three months to learn French, 'which seems a funny plan' as Jane Brookfield commented. And when they went on holiday to Scarborough that summer, not long after his return, her sister Mary went too. But it is true that on her grave in Margate cemetery (and perhaps by her wish) there is no mention of the Tennyson connection. It is also odd that her son told his daughter that he never remembered being caressed by his mother – and this was the same woman who, as a girl, had longed for tender 'fumbling'. Had Richard Jesse destroyed her sensual nature? 'I know what it is to feel like a stoän,' she would tell Blanche Warre-Cornish in her strong Lincolnshire accent.

The fourth wedding that year was on 14 October 1842, when Cecilia Tennyson married Edmund Lushington. 'It will be good for all parties,' Mary Tennyson wrote optimistically to Matthew Allen's wife. It is the best documented of the four, though it was not until 1845 that Tennyson said to his friend, 'I have brought in your marriage at the end.' He was talking of his sequence of elegies, that loose collection of poems which would become *In Memoriam*. The Tennysons had left Beech Hill in February 1840 for somewhere that was supposed to be both cheaper and healthier, but it was 'a mere mouse-trap' of a house in Tunbridge Wells and by November 1841 they had moved again. This time it was into a house called Boxley Hall, less than two miles by footpath from Park House, near Maidstone in Kent, just one and a half hours by express from London. Park House was the home of the Lush-ington family, already close to Tennyson and to become much closer.

Visiting Boxley Hall in 1866, Emily makes a tantalizing reference. 'I have been there before but not to A's room. A delightful room looking upon the bright garden with its fir trees and its crystal stream.' Is she talking about a visit in 1842 or 1843, before the Tennysons' further move to Cheltenham? In the epitome of her journal, her son Hallam (we assume) has actually cut out a short passage at this point, as if there is something he does not want us to know. Certainly he gives the impression, and Emily's Narrative supports it, that there was no meeting or correspondence between Alfred and Emily at this period.

But in December 1842, Alfred's sister, Emily Jesse, sent on to Emily Sellwood a copy of a splendid letter of praise from Thomas Carlyle to Alfred Tennyson – apparently at Alfred's request, though his sister does not actually say so. To the other Emmie, Emily Jesse said 'I should like to look in on you. With my kind remembrance to Mr Sellwood. All send love. Thy very affectionate Emily.' Whatever it was in 1839 that estranged the two Emilys, that made Emily Sellwood so nervous about writing to her, apparently no longer kept them cool in 1842. And yet it was not only geographical distance that made it difficult for them to 'look in' on each other.

There was a good deal of 'looking in' going on between Boxley Hall and Park House, just two miles away. Tennyson had been at Cambridge at the same time as the brothers Edmund and Henry Lushington. They were fellow members of Trinity and fellow Apostles, sharing many friends including Richard Monckton Milnes, Francis Garden and Robert Monteith, James Spedding, George Stovin Venables and, of course, Arthur Hallam. Edmund was not particularly close to Hallam (who had written to his sister: 'He drank my wine and I drank his. I am not likely, I think, to know him more intimately'). But the link was there and the two brothers together were in some sense a replacement for the dead friend, as Emily herself would eventually prove able to be. The much younger brother, Franklin Lushington (born in 1823), would become a particular friend of Emily. It was through the Lushingtons that Emily would meet Edward Lear, who loved both her and Frank Lushington, and also Granville Bradley, who had been at Rugby with Frank.

Edmund had inherited Park House in March 1839 on the death of his father. He was twenty-nine and had recently been appointed to the Chair of Greek at the University of Glasgow, a position he would hold with great devotion and distinction for thirty-seven years. His mother had died in 1841, but he had four sisters all unmarried – Maria, yet another Emily, Ellen and Louisa – who continued to live in the house they had grown up in. Even if Cecilia Tennyson had been stronger and more resilient, and had detested Glasgow less, she would have found herself married into a difficult situation. George Venables was not at all sure whether to be glad about the marriage. He worried about 'the losers', among whom he thought that he, as well as Edmund's sisters, might be numbered.

Edmund would speak kindly of Cecilia's 'highly strung nature'; others with justification would be less kind. She became extremely neurotic, a lifelong invalid, without the courage and spirit to make such a role tolerable. The Lushingtons' biographer would call the marriage 'generally sad'. At times it would be much worse than that. The girl who had once felt 'quite melancholy' at having so small a party about her at Beech Hill would now find the large household at Park House difficult to cope with. The difficulties would increase rather than diminish.

Emily Sellwood and Cecilia Lushington remained good friends. Emily described Cecilia as 'true and trustful and loving through all' the problems of these years. Emily must have realized the problems and tensions in this other marriage of close concern to her. Her suggestion in her Narrative that Cecilia 'reigned as a Queen to whom all did homage' was far from the truth. She was never really mistress of a house that hardly seemed hers; indeed she was rarely there.

In spite of her friendship with Cecilia, it was obviously impossible for Emily Sellwood to be present at her wedding. There is no surviving letter of description of it to the Sellwoods, but Emily Jesse, Alfred's sister, wrote to Julia Hallam a letter full of the sort of details she thought everyone would want to know: it was one, she said, of 'numerous notes similar to this'. She described the bride's dress ('a very light new fashioned sort of spotted net over a rich white satin slip'), her jewellery ('chased silver'), her seven bridesmaids, the Lushington sisters in blue and the Tennysons in pink. 'My brother Charles married them' and 'twenty-six with the bride and bridegroom sat down to breakfast.' In the evening, long after the bride and groom had gone, 'a large party sat down to dinner,' followed by music and dancing. 'Nobody left till near midnight.' Alfred, who had given away another sister, stayed on at Park House. Next day he wrote to Edward Moxon, his publisher (asking him to send no more reviews), with his 'head yet vertiginous with the champagne I drank yesterday at my sister's wedding.'

Park House at this point seemed to symbolize all sorts of hope for the future. Tennyson used the wedding poem, his epithalamium, to suggest that a time had come at last, nine years after Arthur Hallam's death, when he could feel happiness again.

> Nor have I felt so much of bliss
>> Since first he told me that he loved
>> A daughter of our house; nor proved
> Since that dark day a day like this.

Such lines would make difficult reading for Emily Sellwood, who had shared dark days with him and thought she had also shared some moments of bliss. Now Cecilia, his sister, was the rose, whom Arthur Hallam had seen as a young girl in bud.

> O when her life was yet in bud
> He too foretold the perfect rose.

'The white-favoured horses wait' and take another bridal pair off on their own, just as they had taken away Charles and Louisa six years before. And now it was Charles who read the solemn words: 'First it was ordained for the procreation of children', and asked Edmund Lushington: 'Wilt thou love her, comfort her, honour and keep her in sickness and in health . . . so long as ye both shall live?' He must have thought of his estranged wife, Louisa, far away in Lincolnshire.

Alfred Tennyson would say, late in life, 'I rather avoid weddings as a rule. They are somewhat flexible affairs – tears and smiles – April weather.' But in this case the tears came only afterwards, when things did not turn out as they had hoped. The mingled blood ('Thy blood, my friend, and partly mine') brought much grief and pain, but at the time Alfred felt a moment of 'colossal calm', of hope and happiness and of respite from the worry over his financial affairs.

The calm did not last long. Even as the shadow of Arthur's death at last began to lift (the grief in some sense assuaged by the experience of writing about it), Tennyson was oppressed not only by his loss of Emily (a self-inflicted wound though it may have been) but also by his mounting worry over the woodcarving scheme. He already realized how rash he had been to have allowed Matthew Allen – who had become a friend – to beguile him and his family into investing so much money in the speculation.

In February 1844 Alfred Tennyson wrote to Edward FitzGerald: 'It is very kind of you to think of such a poor forlorn body as myself. The perpetual panic and horror of the last two years had steeped my nerves in poison: now I am left a beggar.' He said he had been through Hell. Two years took him well back before the Park House wedding and indeed in July 1842 his sister Mary was telling Matthew Allen's wife that Alfred 'fidgets himself to death' and that they were all in a state of uncertainty and suspense. In September 1842, the month before Cecilia's wedding, Alfred had written to Edmund telling him that Moxon said his new books had made a 'sensation' – even if they had sold only five hundred copies – and how much he wished the success of the woodworks would be equally sensational. 'What with ruin in the distance and hypochondriacs in the foreground,' he felt 'very crazy'. He had got himself into an awful mess.

Emily Sellwood knew exactly what was going on, for the Tennyson girls had asked for her father's support the previous year in trying to get their trustees to release some security so they could invest in the scheme and increase their thin fortunes. Henry Sellwood may well have had his doubts but he was prepared to act for them. He specifically said to Charles Tennyson d'Eyncourt, one of the trustees, 'Altho' I am not entirely ignorant of the purpose for which the money is wanted yet I ought to state that I have not been consulted on the subject but have merely been applied to within a few weeks for the Loan' of £1,900. He was able to find one of his own clients prepared to put up the money with the security of some property – but the unnamed speculator was 'resident in another county and he would not be satisfied without the deeds being lodged either in his own hands or in mine, nor indeed could I ask him to consent to any other arrangement. The money I understand is for the use of the four Miss Tennysons and there can be no doubt therefore that they would wish the deeds to be handed over to me and I apprehend that their two brothers who are in England would readily consent to it.' This referred to Arthur and Septimus and it suggests how much the whole family knew and trusted Henry Sellwood. Their uncle Charles was rightly – as it turned out – suspicious of the whole business. He had been reluctant himself to raise the £1,900 the girls wanted even after their brother Charles added his tribute to Matthew Allen's new woodcarving scheme and the safety of the investment. ('There can be but little, if any doubt, of the prudence of the speculation.') The four Tennyson sisters, 'your distressed nieces', all signed a letter to their uncle abusing him for 'withholding from us what is our own' and asking him what difference it made to him where the deeds were placed, 'so long as the person is trustworthy. The latter qualification no-one denies to Mr Sellwood.'

Their uncle agreed. Mr Sellwood was not the problem. 'I have not objected to the Deeds being given up to Mr Selwood,' he said, but he could not 'permit anyone to write offensive letters to me.' He washed his hands of the affair, and sent his own solicitor Thomas Rhodes to Horncastle to deliver the documents to Henry Sellwood. This was in November 1841.

Matthew Allen himself wrote to Tennyson that month in a state of high excitement. 'Orders are flowing in from all the great ones – Never was any thing more promising. All things are a lie and all things are false if this fails . . . My friend Clissold has just ordered a screen. The Bishop of London's brother two more chairs, and the Bishop of Chester has sent for two choir-stalls etc two screens – finials etc etc . . . In fact it is and will be the great rage of the Town soon. The Kingdom talks of it.'

The Sellwoods themselves must have been tempted by the invest-ment. There is an unclear passage in a letter – undated but water-marked 1843 – from Emily to her sister Anne which suggests it was Anne's husband, Charles Weld, who warned the sisters to steer clear of putting any of their own money into the scheme. (Or had he merely foiled a dishonest servant?) The passage suggests other things too and seems worth giving in full – so rare are letters of this period – even though we do not really know what Emily is talking about. 'Nanny' was her pet name for her sister. Weld had certainly known all about the woodcarving scheme for he was by now working at the Royal Society. Mrs Tennyson's sister, Mary Anne Fytche, wrote excitedly to Susan Haddelsey: 'There is going to be a Lecture at the Royal Society on this beautiful discovery.' Emily wrote to Anne:

I give my little Nanny so much credit for curiosity that she has no need to be told her Charlie's 'few lines' were very full of kindness and interest and she knows well they have not come to ungrateful hands. If she thinks, as well she may, I cannot thank as I ought for them I will depute her to thank for me and I dare say the wild puss will instantly seize a certain friend of mine by the coat sleeve and make the strokes of that small hand of hers resound as loudly as may be. This is her notion of gratitude and its expression.

Oh Charlie we will let the onyx pin and the pencil case and the bracelet and all things go whither they list. Shall we grudge those hands something which have given us so much? Enduring possessions of the mind, we will philosophic-ally hold, are cheaply purchased by fleeting perishable material ones. I at least who, thanks to thee, have lost nothing not even a manteau bleu, will boldly preach this, receive it who may.

All the Tennysons lost a great deal in the collapse of the venture. Dr Allen had boasted to Frederick Tennyson late in 1841: 'In twelve months your share would be worth Ten Thousand Pounds and that in five years it ought to give you that yearly.' By March 1843 Allen admitted he was 'utterly ruined'. Emily Sellwood learned from the failure of the woodcarving scheme, as they all did. Years later she would write to Anne and Charles Weld's daughter: 'Do not hunt after high investments. It is so easy to lose all one has in these and have nothing left for oneself or anyone.'

In this case, Tennyson's own small fortune was almost entirely restored to him only a few years later. It has often been said that Edmund Lushington took out an insurance on Allen's life. In fact, the insurance policy already existed. It had been given to Tennyson (dated 23 November 1840) by Allen as security. When Allen was ruined, he naturally could not keep up the premiums as he had promised. It was then that Lushington stepped in and went on paying the necessary £80 a year (a considerable sum) until Allen's opportune early death. He was, as Emily said, 'that most loving and generous of brothers-in-law.' When Allen 'dropt down dead' Emily saw it as 'a tragic end, is it not, to speculation?'

Henry Sellwood maintained a business relationship with his son-in-law Charles Turner at this period too, in spite of his separation from Louisa. Charles Haddelsey, stepson of Samuel Turner (Charles's great-uncle and benefactor), had turned out to be a rogue. It was extremely embarrassing, to say the least, for the Haddelseys had become close friends of Charles Turner and indeed all the Tennysons, after the move to Caistor and Grasby. Both Charles and Cecilia were particularly fond of his daughter Susan.

We have seen that Charles Tennyson, as he was then, inherited a great deal on the death of Samuel Turner, whereas Charles Haddelsey, whose mother had been married to him, and who knew him a great deal better than the great-nephew did, inherited only the house he lived in. As the lawyer in charge of the estate, Haddelsey was in an excellent position to compensate himself for what he felt he deserved and had been denied. He was deeply involved in the Tennysons' financial affairs. There is a sentence in a letter from Matthew Allen to

Frederick oddly echoing Charles Tennyson d'Eyncourt's objections to the way his nieces wrote to him: 'Mr Sellwood writes to me just in the same style as Mr Haddelsey and I neither can, nor will bear it' – which seems to suggest at this point that both Haddelsey and Sellwood were trying to stop the Tennysons' foolish investment. But at the same time Haddelsey was apparently fraudulently appropriating a good deal of money. He had disposed of £2,000 worth of shares for his own use, writing of 'a claim for services to the late Mr Turner'. In September 1843 Charles Turner appointed a new agent, Joseph Burkinshaw, in his absence from Grasby. But the attorney who handled the legal work involved in the recovery of the embezzled money was his father-in-law, Henry Sellwood. The proceedings lasted through the whole of the 1840s. The case was finally settled out of court in 1850. The restoration of Grasby Church was carried out with the money retrieved from Haddelsey. No wonder that when Henry Sellwood eventually died one bell in the new church was dedicated to his memory.

Alfred Tennyson's friends and admirers, known and unknown to him, were well aware of his financial problems, problems that would be partially alleviated by the sales of his 1842 poems and by Matthew Allen's death in 1845, but never solved. Tennyson had got into the habit of worrying about money; he would find it hard to give up worrying, even·in more prosperous times. In May 1843 he described himself, a little conventionally, as 'poorer than a church mouse'.

There was some attempt to obtain for him the Laureateship when it became vacant in 1843 on the death of Robert Southey. There survives in the Peel papers an eloquent plea from Francis Egerton dated 27 March, asking Sir Robert to consider the name of Alfred Tennyson. 'I am privately informed that the salary would save him from *absolute starvation*. I never saw him, nor does he know that I am aware of his wishes or his difficulties.' The following week, on the 3 April, the Laureateship was offered to William Wordsworth. Tennyson's time would come.

In the meantime, influential friends – Henry Hallam, Arthur's father, and the rising politician William Gladstone, Arthur's schoolfriend – were pressing Peel to grant Tennyson a pension, a reward for literary distinction and achievement. At first a single payment of £200 was offered and declined, with Hallam suggesting to Peel that what the young poet needed was a small regular addition to his annual income. 'He is not destitute of means,' he admitted, but he had far less 'than his position in society requires.' Certainly he needed more if he were again to consider marriage as all his friends hoped.

When the Civil List pension was finally granted in September 1845, Henry Hallam calmed Tennyson's reluctance:

Your scruples about the pension need not molest you much. Peel, as I told him, will be applauded on all sides for such a distribution of patronage. It is not the habit of anyone to find fault with the disposal of public money in reward of literary merit . . . however like Orpheus you may be in other respects, you will never be torn to pieces with sharp female claws.

Tennyson had sent Arthur's father some of his elegies but understandably Hallam found it difficult to read them. It was *his* dark house, in the long unlovely street, where Alfred Tennyson had stood and heard in his heart those most simple and moving of all the lines in that long sequence. It was *his* son who was no longer here.

> He is not here; but far away
>   The noise of life begins again,
>   And ghastly through the drizzling rain
> On the bald street breaks the blank day.

Henry Hallam paid to Alfred Tennyson the most vivid tribute anyone could pay: 'Of the Poems I do not yet speak as another would, to praise and admire – few of them indeed I have as yet been capable of reading, the grief they express is too much akin to that they revive. It is better than any Monument which could be erected to the memory of any beloved Son. It is a more lively and enduring testimony to his great Virtues and Talents that the world should know the friendship that subsisted between you, and that Posterity should associate his name with that of Alfred Tennyson.'

When Thomas Carlyle heard the news of the pension, he wrote: 'Poor Alfred – may it do him good; – "a Wife to keep him unaisy" will be attainable now, if his thoughts tend that way.' Jane Carlyle, herself a mild cigarette smoker and married to a smoker, said she thought Tennyson was 'unlikely to marry, as no-one could live in the atmosphere of tobacco-smoke, which he makes about him from morn to night.' Tennyson's thoughts were of Horncastle when he wrote to Thomas Rawnsley in October 1845:

I am glad to hear of your quadrilling at Horncastle. . . I should like to have been amongst you as in old times but

> The days are awa' that we hae seen

and I begin to feel an old man myself. I have gone through a deal of suffering since I saw you last, and would not have it over again for quadruple the pension Peel has given me.

He went on to say how the news would undoubtedly disgust a number of people, including 'certain crones in or about Horncastle . . . causelessly bitter against me and mine as they have always been.' There seems no doubt that these crones were Emily's Aunt Betsy Franklin and her friends, who must have lamented loudly at the involvement of the dear Sellwood girls with those disreputable Tennysons and would now lament the government's recognition of his poetry. Alfred was forgiving, wishing them no worse punishment than that they should read 'the very flattering letter Peel wrote me.'

Tennyson's 'I begin to feel an old man myself', in this letter, is sadly matched by some lines in a letter Emily Sellwood wrote to her sister Anne, returned from travel on the Continent, at about the same time.

Right glad I am to hear you speak so ecstatically of mountain glories. They were the dreams of my childhood and youth but I suppose I have grown somewhat prematurely old – for I am no longer beckoned by snowcapt giants, summoned by them in tones irresistible; such is only the fate of the young in years, of the young in heart though aged in days. How we long for the good gossip you talk of! Daddy the other day spoke much of his desire for it.

Gossiping, not mountain viewing, was now the appropriate pleasure.

Travelling with his publisher Moxon at this period, Tennyson was also 'disappointed' with mountains. Elizabeth Barrett once commented sadly: 'Is it a good or bad sign when people are disappointed with the miracles of nature? I am accustomed to think it a bad sign . . . A man sees with his mind, and mind is at fault when he does not see greatly, I think.' Apart, it seemed that both Alfred's and Emily's minds were 'at fault'. It would be different when they were together.

Emily seemed to be settling into an accepted bookish spinsterhood as she wrote her name on the 24 March 1845 in each of three bound volumes of *The Friend*, a new edition of Samuel Taylor Coleridge's periodical, packed with essays 'to aid in the formation of fixed principles in politics, morals and religion.' Emily was certainly keeping herself 'unspotted from the world' and 'visiting the fatherless and widows in their affliction.' She was also studying the New Testament, as she did all her life, and cultivating the grace which enables us to bear tribulation 'with constancy and calmness of mind, and a ready submission to the will of God.' She knew that 'tribulation worketh patience; And patience experience; and experience, hope.'

Did hope remain? Certainly Alfred Tennyson was seldom far from her thoughts. Three months later, on 15 June 1845, George Venables ran into her in Park House, as he records in his diary, perhaps without any idea who this 'Miss Sellwood' was or the part she had played already in his friend's life. Old Mrs Tennyson and Franklin Lushington were at Park House too that June, with Cecilia and the resident Lushington sisters. Tennyson was in Eastbourne, but he had been at Park House not long before. There must have been much talk about the long poem he was working on, which was still going under the title 'The University of Women'.

It would become *The Princess* and would contain some of Tennyson's most memorable lyrics: 'Tears, idle tears', written at Tintern Abbey long before and 'Blow, bugle, blow' with its 'wild echoes flying', its echoing answers dying, which dates from his visit to Killarney the following year. It would become particularly important to Emily, including as it does some of Tennyson's most resonant statements about women and marriage. It was now already nearly seven years since they had first talked about the poem at Beech Hill.

There is just one indication that there were others who sought Emily's hand in marriage in her early years. It is in a letter to her son Hallam when he is coping at Cambridge with his first unrequited love. 'Hadst thou been five years older,' his mother writes and goes on to admit her own very limited experience of affairs of the heart. She writes a little awkwardly and obscurely:

I suppose it very much depends on character whether love begets love. The love which sought to make me all its own, from those who in mind and character did not suit me, was repellent to me, but I believe it is far from being always so and I quite think that if the person be to be respected and admired, heart and mind, though not naturally the very person most attractive to one, it is quite possible to be won entirely by love for that person.

As the years passed and she remained totally devoted to Tennyson,

Emily's situation in the 1840s seems to be summed up in the words of
Christina Rossetti:

> I love you and you know it – this at least,
> This comfort is mine own in all my pain:
> You know it, and can never doubt again,
> And love's mere self is a continual feast:
> Nor oath of mine nor blessing-word of priest
> Could make my love more certain or more plain.

As for Tennyson himself, many seem to find it impossible to believe
that he remained chaste during these years when we see him only
through a cloud of his own tobacco smoke, appearing and disappearing, of no fixed abode, finding his family at times intolerable, dossing
down in friends' lodgings, drinking too much, worrying about money
and his health. But we have his own word 'that he had never kissed a
woman, in love, except his wife' and if that suggests there might have
been kissing without love, there is his strong statement recorded by
James Mangles in his diary, as he thought of his youth. He was showing
Mangles 'his' chambers in Mitre Court Buildings at the time – the
rooms shared by Henry Lushington and George Venables, where he
had so often smoked and spent the night in the 1840s. Mangles says
Tennyson 'discoursed for some time on the panacea for the world's ills
– viz. Chastity. Why should not young men be chaste? Doctors said
"No" – he did not believe them.' He knew the power – he would say so
in *Guinevere* – of the passion for one woman 'to keep down the base in
man.' There is also his odd statement, again recorded by Mangles, that
'scratching beats fornication all to pieces'.

However much Tennyson believed in the possibility of chastity, there
is plenty of evidence that marriage, the need for marriage, was in his
mind. Aubrey de Vere, the Irish poet whom Tennyson had met in Mitre
Court Buildings, usefully kept a diary at this time. On 16 July 1845,
just a month after Venables had seen Emily at Park House, de Vere
wrote

On my way in, paid a visit to Tennyson, who seemed much out of spirits, and
said he could not longer bear to be knocked about the world, and that he must
marry and find love and peace or die. He was very angry about a very favourable review of him. Said that he could not stand the chattering and conceit of
clever men, or the worry of society, or the meanness of tuft-hunters, or the
trouble of poverty, or the labour of a place, or the preying of the heart on itself

... He complained much about growing old, and said he cared nothing for fame, and that his life was all thrown away for want of a competence and retirement. Said that no-one had been so much harassed by anxiety and trouble as himself. I told him he wanted occupation, a wife, and orthodox principles, which he took well.

The following October Jane Welsh Carlyle wrote to her husband from Chelsea, reporting that her friend Lady Harriet Baring, some kin of Rosa's, had told her that Alfred Tennyson wanted to marry, 'must have a woman to live beside; would *prefer a lady*, but cannot afford one; and so must marry a maid servant'. That this gossip was light-hearted enough, that they did not really think Alfred's situation was distressing, is shown by Mrs Carlyle's also passing on Mrs Henry Taylor's offer of her rather superior housemaid. The gossip was in any case out of date because Alfred's financial situation had just improved dramatically as Mrs Carlyle knew.

Emily Sellwood in Horncastle in 1845 had had other things on her mind as well as Alfred Tennyson. Her uncle, Sir John Franklin, had returned in 1843 after seven years as Governor of Van Diemen's Land. His achievements there had been considerable, as far as the develop-ment of education and science in the young colony was concerned, and he had been personally popular, but he did not enjoy administration and was glad to return to the Navy when the Admiralty – urged by the Geographical Society – proposed a new expedition to try to discover an Arctic waterway between the Atlantic and the Pacific, in other words to determine that there was a North West Passage. Franklin himself was quite convinced that there was. Indeed Emily always said that the last words he ever spoke to her were: 'If I am lost, remember, Emily, my firm belief that there is open sea at the North Pole.' He was in Lincoln-shire in March and attended the christening of his godson Willingham (named for the grandfather, John Franklin's brother), the child of Kate and Drummond Rawnsley, at Little Hadham, Hertfordshire on 23 March 1845.

Sophie Cracroft, another of the cousins, who had gone to Van Die-men's Land with the Franklins, had been delighted with Charles Weld, Anne's new husband, on her return. She found Anne 'just the same as ever and affectionate to the last degree.' She made them laugh a lot. Charles's appearance 'I like extremely.' Charles Weld had been appointed to the Royal Society late in 1843, not long after Sir John's return and it seems likely that Franklin had something to do with the appointment.

On 26 May 1845 Sir John Franklin sailed from Sheerness in command of two ships, the *Erebus* and the *Terror*. There were one hundred and thirty-eight officers and men on board, with enough provisions for three years. The ships were last sighted, moored to an iceberg at the entrance to Lancaster Sound, beyond Baffin Bay on their way west; not one of the men was seen alive again, and the mystery of what happened has fascinated people ever since. Charles Weld would become deeply involved in helping Lady Franklin, who would not for many years admit herself a widow, to raise funds and plan search after search. It was eventually discovered that Rear Admiral Sir John Franklin had died on 11 June 1847. His memorial in Westminster Abbey carries these lines by his niece's husband, who had offended him by putting his feet up on the chairs at that Horncastle dinner party long before:

> Not here! The white North has thy bones; and thou
> Heroic sailor-soul
> Art passing on thine happier voyage now
> Toward no earthly pole.

Franklin had made an indelible impression on Emily. His visits to Horncastle before his appointment in the Antipodes had been his nieces' earliest contacts with a more exciting world than the 'narrow provincial society' they had grown up in. He remained Emily's hero ('simple, noble, devout') and she loved the fact that Alfred Tennyson would talk of the 'heroic Franklin blood'. Their little boys would one day thrill to the tales of his adventures.

Emily Sellwood's life even at this period was not entirely restricted to Horncastle. In her journal of later years she refers briefly to a visit she and her father, possibly Louisa too, made with the Welds to France, to Tours. And she reveals when in St Lawrence on the Isle of Wight in 1857 for Horatio's wedding that she and her father had been there twelve years earlier. There were seaside holidays – in August 1844 at Trusthorpe, just south of Alfred's favourite Mablethorpe. And there were those visits to Cecilia at Park House in Kent.

But for the most part Emily was at Horncastle. Among the handful of letters surviving from before Emily's marriage, there is one that gives a strong impression of how devoted Emily was to her father and how central was the part the family played in the life of Horncastle. The letter can be dated precisely from the date of the funeral it describes. Emily was writing to her sister, Anne Weld, on 28 March 1845 from the house in the Market Place across from the Parish Church. Louisa Dymoke had died aged thirteen. She was the grand-daughter of Clement Madeley, Emily's 'dear old Vicar', who had baptized the three Sellwood girls and married two of them. Madeley had died himself that Good Friday, four days after his grand-daughter, a few days before her funeral. His daughter, Mary Ann, had married John Dymoke, Rector of Scrivelsby, younger brother of Sir Henry Dymoke, Champion of England, whose mother had presided over the Horncastle Ball Lady Franklin had described twenty-two years before.

Emily's father, as the Dymokes' agent, lawyer and friend, had made all the funeral arrangements. 'Now I will begin after my last,' Emily's letter starts. After answering Anne that their 'Daddy dearest did not take cold at the little girl's funeral' she plunges straight into a description of the coffin: 'pale blue or french grey cloth with a white plate – very pretty'. Obviously Emily wrote to her sister regularly every few days, as indeed she would all her life, and at this time she expected Anne's husband – 'Charlie boy' – to read the letters. This one survives, among hundreds of early ones that have not – perhaps for its compliments to Henry Sellwood.

I think I said our Daddy and Sir Henry were the only people who followed with Mr Dymoke, who feels his child's loss exceedingly. The Archdeacon read the service . . . excuse me if I have told this before (some of it) –Yesterday at the Dymokes' request our Daddy went to call on them, he sat talking a long time – found Mrs Dymoke in a much better state. Today she spoke as if she had liked her talk very much. She said 'What a noble mind! It is one I bow down to.' Charlie boy must not laugh at Daddy's daughter for repeating this to another daughter. This morning she came before eleven, staid till just one before one – she told Daddy she was comforted. I do not know how she expressed it exactly. I drew up a very little the blind and we peeped under. Previously she had for some time paced up and down the room, but after the first she had talked to me. When she had watched the pall into the porch – we could see no more – she took up a prayer book and I read, rather whispered, part of the funeral service. She said if my Father can see me now he will be pleased I am with you. By degrees she talked more and at last she certainly seemed better.

When the carriage was announced, we went down and found Mr Dymoke and our Daddy in the drawing-room. So the first meeting is over with him too. I do think our Daddy has been a great comfort to them. You will be pleased to hear both Sir Henry and Mr Dymoke commended the arrangements. I am thankful our Daddy's fatigues and anxieties on this score are at an end. The organ played, the church was hung with black, the vicar's pew in addition to the normal hangings. All the chief householders in the town followed of their own accord. After the funeral, this afternoon, bread was given to a great many – two hundred or more poor families.

Emily went on to write of the dear child, who had spent some time with her while staying at her grandfather's Vicarage – but had been at school in Switzerland and had spent very little of her life in Lincolnshire. Emily remembered above all her 'over sensitivity', 'her horror at the thought of anything displeasing to God.' Their total faith in eternal life is expressed in Emily's comment:

Dr Madeley seemed to have gained a grand-daughter, not lost. He felt himself belonging to another world when the news came and was so completely dead to all the affections of this he smiled at it and said 'So my little Louisa is gone to her rest before me.'

There would be a great deal of regret in Horncastle in September 1846 when Henry Sellwood announced his retirement. Robert Cracroft called it 'the worst piece of news' Sellwood could give him, that he was retiring from a 'Profession of which you have so long been an honor to.' 'I fear you will leave the county,' he added. Sellwood had his sixty-fourth birthday that November and had practised as a lawyer in the town for thirty-eight years. In December a four-year partnership with J.W. Conington was dissolved. Sellwood had done well out of all his hard work and owned considerable property in the county. He could look forward to a comfortable retirement, but it seems likely that his decision to retire was at least partly due to Emily's health. She had never been strong and now, she wrote years later, 'The doctors believed I was going into a consumption.' That old debility, the pain, the ache in the side, that the other Emily had described in 1836 was always feared as a sign of 'a consumption' (tuberculosis) – but in Emily Sellwood's case it seems the fear was never justified. A move south was suggested: 'The Lincolnshire climate was pronounced too cold for me.'

On 30 December 1846 Emily was in Hertfordshire as godmother at the baptism of her 'sister-cousin' Kate's third child, named Emily

Margaret. There must have been some talk on that occasion of forth-coming moves. The child's father, Tennyson's good friend Drummond Rawnsley, gave his farewell sermon at Little Hadham, Hertfordshire on 13 June 1847, and moved to take over the living at Hartley Wespall in Hampshire, just a few miles from Charles Kingsley's parish at Eversley. For the next couple of years Emily would see a good deal of her small god-daughter and the rest of the Rawnsleys. There is a copy of Drummond's sermons with the inscription: 'Emily Sellwood with D. Rawnsley's fond love. March 1848'. She would also hear a good deal about Charles Kingsley.

In 1847 the Sellwoods were in London, probably staying with the Welds, and looking for a suitable house in the south of England. 'We found one at last at Hale, near Farnham,' less than twelve miles from the Rawnsleys. Tennyson would call it Emily's 'Paradise'. Emily loved Hale House. In years to come she would remember birds (a blackbird, a nightingale) that sang there with sweet, sad notes as they sang, she said, nowhere else, and peaches and flowers that flourished there, as they flourished nowhere else. She felt at home in that part of England: the Hale house would play a major part in the decision to build, years later, near Haslemere.

Alfred Tennyson was also thinking about namesake godchildren. He wrote to Charlotte Burton at Somersby Rectory in July 1847: 'I shall be very happy to be godfather to your little one . . . Call your child Alfred if you will – he was born in the same house, perhaps the same chamber as myself and I trust he is destined to a far happier life than mine has been – poor little fellow.' Dickens had called his fourth son Alfred D'Orsay Tennyson Dickens, not long before that meeting with Tenny-son in Lausanne. Soon Coventry Patmore would be naming his second son Tennyson Patmore. It was not Alfred's fame but his charm that made them do it. Groaning, growling, indolent, careless, pleading both poverty and depression, Alfred remained above all lovable. There are countless witnesses to that and the few voices that seem to speak against him turn out to have little substance.

Take for instance the allegation that his constant visits to Park House became unwelcome. This comes from a letter from Arthur Hallam's younger brother Harry to his cousin Jane Brookfield, the one who had been so appalled at Emily Tennyson's decision to marry Richard Jesse. Harry told Jane that he had drawn from Franklin Lushington 'the grand fact that the Tennyson habit of coming unwashed and staying unbidden was, is and will be the great burthen and calamity of the Lushington existence, socially considered.' Further references to 'M.' (who could be Mary or Matilda) in the next sentence and to 'E.' and 'Mr J.', Emily and Richard Jesse, indicate that it was probably not Alfred himself whom anyone was objecting to. Cecilia Lushington did have rather unfortunate siblings, socially considered. But she herself could be as impossible as any of them. There survives a moving letter from her younger brother Arthur to her husband Edmund years later, when Cecilia had evicted him for smoking inside Park House.

Arthur said how often he had wanted 'to say furiously honest passionate things to Cissy on your account', but had always checked himself, 'fearing it would do more harm than good.' He observed 'the sorrowful state of things between you and Cissy', but knowing how drink could make him, himself, 'capable of all hideousness', he felt he was hardly the best person to protest at his sister's behaviour, much as it saddened him.

Edmund Lushington seems to have been wonderfully long-suffering. Certainly he always welcomed Alfred to Park House, though his smoking may well have caused some tensions with Cecilia. In September 1847 Alfred Tennyson arrived unexpectedly, as he so often did. Arthur Hallam had noticed this 'poetic' penchant for unannounced arrivals as long ago as 1830. On this occasion, Tennyson found to his surprise (when he arrived 'before breakfast') that Emily Sellwood was visiting his sister. It seems to have been the first time they had met for seven years. Recording this meeting, years later, Emily said that they met unexpectedly at Park House at a time when everyone thought Alfred was in Italy – and that finding him there 'she soon returned to her Father at Hale House, near Farnham'. Fortunately we know a little more as George Venables turned up and recorded the meeting in his diary. In fact, although she says 'I returned to Hale, as soon after as I could', they spent the weekend together in the house and must have had plenty of chance to talk things over. They were both there when Venables arrived on Friday, 17 September. On Monday, 20 September, after a midday dinner, it was Tennyson who left, surprising Venables by doing so – as if the relationship between Emily and Alfred over the weekend had not seemed to him an awkward one. Emily stayed at Park House all the week, and 'returned home', Venables said, on Saturday, the twenty-fifth. Alfred turned up again that evening, perhaps expecting to find Emily still there. Both he and Venables left after a further week, on 4 October. When Venables returned to Park House on 10 October, a Sunday, he found Emily Sellwood there again. On the twelfth 'Miss Sellwood went'. That is all we know from Venables, but it must certainly have been the beginning of the renewed contact between Emily Sellwood and Alfred Tennyson.

That Emily made considerably more of an impression on Tennyson's friends than the brief diary entries reveal is suggested by two books. One is a copy of Johann Fichte's *Die Bestimmung des Menschen*, which carries on the first flyleaf the inscription 'F. Lushington March 1847' and then in Emily's own hand, on the back of the endpaper, 'Emily Sellwood, Sept. 1847'. The blank pages carry some verses in Frank Lushington's hand, apparently his own translation from the German, including

> Work, and watch, and love, and trust,
> Carve the cradle, weave the pall:
> Earth to earth, and dust to dust
> Life to God, and God in all.

It is easy to imagine Emily and Frank translating the German together, sighing over it. He was already becoming one of her closest friends. When she died, he would say they had known and loved each other for nearly fifty years.

George Venables, too, must have found Emily an interesting companion. The following March he published some privately printed poems that he and Henry Lushington had produced together over the years, dedicated to the four Lushington sisters. The book was printed solely 'for the amusement of some of those who may be acquainted with either or both of the writers.' He sent off copies to a number of friends; one was Emily Sellwood.

In the absence of any other evidence of how Tennyson himself was feeling about Emily in 1847, we must consider a letter he had written from Park House that spring to his father's old friend Thomas Rawnsley, Drummond's father. Alfred was regretting his inability to accept an invitation to Lincolnshire to see the 'old familiar faces'. He wrote: 'Well, I can't help it – I love my old friends as much as ever – recent friendships may be broken thro' but old ones early-made are a part of one's blood and bones.' It seems likely, seeing Emily Sellwood that September, he felt a shock of recognition that she was indeed still part of his blood and bones, inextricably his.

Emily herself does not tell us explicitly that Tennyson proposed again and she refused him. She does say that they met again at Park House and that Edmund Lushington (devoted to them as he was, and a generous man) 'offered to give up his carriage horses that he might help them. But this, of course, could not be allowed.' There remains the suggestion (which Emily was always keen to promote as thoroughly respectable) that money was the main problem, but there were others, variations on the ones that had kept them apart in 1840. Emily realized that her life as the wife of Alfred Tennyson would be far more demanding, far more difficult (whatever the compensations) than her life as the daughter of Henry Sellwood – difficult as that must have been at times with the still unresolved problem of Louisa and her marriage that was not a marriage.

Tennyson was in every sense a challenge. Would he ever really want to settle down? And what about his religious attitudes? He never seemed to go to church. Was he perhaps tempted to abandon Christianity altogether, like so many of his friends, disturbed by the new book *Vestiges of Creation*? This book by Robert Chambers, fifteen years before Darwin published *On the Origin of Species*, dealt, as Tennyson told Moxon, with 'many speculations with which I have been familiar for years'. Did Emily have the strength to take Tennyson on, much as she longed to do so? Could she cope with the religious doubt, the smoking, the drinking, the black moods, the responsibility of looking after a genius?

It was Willingham Rawnsley who recorded the fact that Emily said 'in a letter to my mother', her cousin Kate, 'that she had even definitely refused him.' This is confirmed by his younger brother, Hardwick – who, as Canon Rawnsley, would become famous as one of the founders of the National Trust. He had seen the same letter and said that for seven years after 1840 'the lovers ate out their hearts of love in secret'. 'Then Tennyson again came forward, and this time was refused on the highest and noblest principles of self-abnegation by the woman who loved him. Emily Sellwood had grown to feel that they two moved in worlds of religious thought so different that the two would not "make one music" as they moved . . . She was happy in having as confidante a cousin whom she could trust, and in whom her lover, the poet, also confided.'

I had hoped to find that 'letter to my mother' Rawnsley paraphrases, but it seems to have disappeared, like so much else. 'Make one music' is

a quotation from the first part of *In Memoriam*, not yet published in
1847. That there were religious differences cannot be doubted and
reminds one sadly of the overt cause of the separation between Charles
and Louisa. That there *were* relevant letters is also certain, for an existing letter from Willingham to Hardwick refers to them. It is undated but
was written by one brother to the other when they were working together
on *Memories of the Tennysons* from which the quotation above is taken.
In a postscript, Willingham Rawnsley scrawls across the top: 'I have
letters from Emily to the mother' (their mother Kate obviously), 'before
the marriage, which are too private to be exhibited . . . but I should like to
show them to you.' If only he could have showed them to us.

A short time later – it was published in December 1847 – Tennyson
gave Emily his new book *The Princess*, inscribed simply in his own
hand 'Emily Sellwood from A. Tennyson'. It was just three months
since they had spent that weekend together at Park House.

They had first talked about the poem as early as 1838, at the time of
their most intimate relationship. Now, with the long poem in print,
Emily read words that must have stirred her profoundly:

> Let . . . this proud watchword rest
> Of equal; seeing either sex alone
> Is half itself, and in true marriage lies
> Nor equal, nor unequal: each fulfils
> Defect in each, and always thought in thought,
> Purpose in purpose, will in will, they grow
> The single pure and perfect animal,
> The two-celled heart beating, with one full stroke,
> Life.

Emily in later years would quote that image of the 'two-celled heart'
when writing to a young couple about to be married. The poem em-
bodied the ideal of unity in marriage, of the two making one whole, and
would have a great deal to do with Emily's final acceptance of Alfred:

> Not like to like, but like in difference,
> Yet in the long years liker must they grow;
> The man be more of woman, she of man;
> He gain in sweetness and in moral height,
> Nor lose the wrestling thews that throw the world;
> She mental breadth, nor fail in childward care,

> Nor lose the childlike in the larger mind;
> Till at the last she set herself to man
> Like perfect music unto noble words.

Whose mind was actually 'childlike' and whose 'the larger mind' was open to discussion. 'He is as simple as a child': Aubrey de Vere would not be the only one to suggest that that was true of the man, great as he was. But it was no chance that after writing about *The Princess* in the *Memoir*, their son would add this central statement of his father's attitude to women: 'He would say "I would pluck my hand from a man if he were my greatest hero, or dearest friend, if he wronged a woman or told her a lie".'

There were also in *The Princess*, most stirring of all, many lines of a sensuous romanticism that would always appeal to Emily:

> Now sleeps the crimson petal, now the white;
> Nor waves the cypress in the palace walk;
> Nor winks the gold fin in the porphyry font:
> The fire-fly wakens: waken thou with me.

CHAPTER FIVE

'Round my true heart
thine arms entwine'

In November 1847 Tennyson had undergone another 'water cure', as if he were determined to make himself fit for marriage. He was cheered that Dr Gully seemed to dismiss his fears of epilepsy. Gully told him briskly that his health problems would be largely solved if he stopped smoking; yet he could not stop. The following month he said to Edward FitzGerald, 'My Book is out and I hate it and so no doubt will you.' He was right. FitzGerald, loving him, despaired – not only of what he was writing but of the man himself. He commented that nothing less than 'the invasion of England' would rouse Tennyson 'from his inglorious pipe, petty digestive solicitudes, and make him burst the whole network of selfishness twined about him by so many years of self-indulgence and laziness.' One should remember this sort of premarital remark of Fitz-Gerald's when later he regrets Emily's handling of the poet.

Tennyson's mother wrote from Cheltenham to Frederick in Italy on 7 December 1847: 'Alfred has been spending a short time with us. He has been in the water cure at Malvern with Dr Gully, who is a very clever man. He talks of going to Rome after Christmas so that ye will see each other ere long.' Mrs Tennyson had presumably not yet heard of the turmoil in Rome, where the Pope had fled from the Vatican after the assassination of Count Rossi, and a republic had been proclaimed. Alfred was always planning that Italian journey. It would take Emily to get him there.

Eliza Tennyson's letter was accompanied by some lines from Aunt Mary Anne Fytche, her sister, whom Arthur Hallam had called 'the life of the family', years ago in Somersby. Now she reported on a visit to Malvern with Aunt Russell, who had also 'made a trial of the water cure'. But 'as soon as it was known in the Hotel we were politely told by the Master of the Hotel we must move off as they never took in Water Patients! We were at a loss to account for this Hydrophobia till we heard he was a Wine Merchant.'

After *his* cure, in the early spring of 1848, Tennyson was in Ireland staying at Curragh Chase in County Limerick with Aubrey de Vere for no particular reason. At least it was a safer destination than Paris where his sister Emily Jesse apparently narrowly escaped death from 'a Revolutionist's bullet' and wrote a hair-raising letter home about the ruffianly drunken mob chanting the 'Marseillaise' under her window.

Tennyson in Ireland made a powerful – and not unusual – impression on his host:

Alfred Tennyson is very little restive, and I hope I shall make this visit pleasant to him. I wonder why he came, and whether he is fond of me. I fear not much so. Yesterday when I looked up at dinner, and saw him sitting between my sister-in-law and her sister, in this remote land, strange to him, I felt all at once such an affection for him as made his noble face look very dim and misty. He has, indeed, a most noble countenance – so full of power, passion, and intellect – so strong, dark and impressive. I find I am growing very much attached to him. He is as simple as a child, and not less interesting for his infirmities. He is all in favour of marriage, and indeed will not be right till he has some one to love him exclusively.

It would seem he had not given up all hope of Emily Sellwood, even if she had refused him the year before.

As a guest, as a friend, Alfred Tennyson would need some tactful handling, as he would as a husband. The secret was often not to be cowed by his words, but to speak out boldly as he himself would do. De Vere gives a good example at Curragh Chase in 1848.

Another night there was a dance which he denounced as a stupid thing, while a brilliant and amusing person, Lady G., who was accustomed to speak her mind to all alike, scolded him sharply. 'How would the world get on if others went about it growling at its amusements in a voice as deep as a lion's? I request that you will go upstairs, put on an evening coat, and ask my daughter Sophia to dance.' He did so, and was the gayest of the gay for several hours, turning out moreover to be an excellent dancer.

There were also charades at Curragh Chase. One night Tennyson turned his own poem 'The Day Dream' into a sort of play, taking himself the part of the Prince. Did he remember the acting games at

Somersby and think of Emily Sellwood who was still alive, while Arthur Hallam was not?

Another night a young lady sitting next to him at dinner spoke of a certain marriage, which had just been announced, as a very *penniless* one. 'He rummaged in his pocket, extracted a penny, and slapped it down loudly close to her plate, saying, "There, I give you that, for that is the God you worship".' The relationship between marriage and money was a sensitive subject for Tennyson, though he must have known that it had nothing to do with Emily's failure to renew their engagement, if indeed she had really been given the chance. His own feelings about marriage continued to be ambivalent. Two years later, writing to Aubrey de Vere, he would comment on the recent wedding of Caroline Standish – de Vere's sister-in-law's sister, who had been one of the house-party at Curragh Chase: 'I don't know but I feel quite sorry that Caroline Standish is married. She did so well unmarried and looked so pure and maidenly that I feel it quite a pity that she should have changed her state.' Had he consoled himself with that thought if Emily Sellwood did indeed turn him down at Park House in 1847? Long after he would return to this theme, praising 'the spinster's sweet-arts'.

At some point, probably in the summer of 1849, it would seem that Alfred Tennyson came to visit Emily Sellwood at Hale House. Their grandson once stated, with such exactness that it is difficult to disbelieve him, that Tennyson had stayed 'at an old inn at Farnham, now 21 West Street, and walked daily across the Market-Place and past the castle to visit her.' This makes the house opposite the church at Hale sound much closer to the centre of Farnham than it really is – though Tennyson was always a good walker. The appeal of Hale House for Emily was above all that it was *not* in a market town, but in what she called 'this wild region', with its 'heather-scented air'.

At Lincoln there survive a number of unfinished stories in Emily's own unmistakable hand, undated, unrecognized. Rather than drawing conclusions from them, always a risky thing to do with fiction, I simply quote from two of them here, for readers to draw their own parallels, such as there may be. The stories are written on blue-grey paper, sewn with pink wool into neat little booklets. It is impossible to be sure when they were written. They have no titles. I identify them from the names of their heroines; the second story is written in a man's voice.

From the Madeline story:

For many a day, yes, many and many a month had she schooled her sadness and gone cheerfully about her daily tasks, making these as many and engrossing as could be, so that her father scarcely noticed anything weighed on her spirits or, if the thought crossed him, he would put it by, saying to himself, years make her graver and when the painful certainty that her tall graceful form was growing too slender and her cheek too pale would force itself upon him, as it had done of late, he attributed it to overwork in the school and parish . . . He thought a little rest will soon restore her bloom and now Madeline addressed herself with characteristic energy to placing geraniums, verbenas, nemophila, to best advantage . . . Then she took her book and went to one of the bowers of roses made in her own rose-hedge, the admiration of the neighbourhood . . .

She regretted the happy days that had been . . . but she rose suddenly and said this must not be. God has ordered it thus. All is certainly well, though I see it not and what right have I to feel so lonely and desolate with such a father? Her own movement had prevented her from hearing footsteps on the grass . . . In a moment she was clasped in his arms. 'Madeline, dearest. You are not married then? I may yet, oh say I may, hope to call thee mine. Forgive me what I have done, agitating you thus,' he said, frightened by the dead pallor which came over her face. He bore her back to the seat and put her gently down. He spoke soothing words, and encouraged by the sight of a Dante in his hand, in a little while she regained her self-possession to listen to his explanation . . . 'How often I cursed my folly that not having spoken to you before I left England, thinking surely she would have had some pity on her early friend had she known all . . . How absurd did my notions of fortune necessary for a married man seem . . .'

From the Agnes story:

All I know is that suddenly your letters ceased. That you had forgotten me I would not believe . . . I, poor groveller, was falling ever lower and lower, sinking deeper and deeper in utter selfishness. I lived all I could of my life among the talking-machines of London and joined in their hollow brilliant clatter until it seemed to me I had talked away my soul when I awoke as I did, you will believe, sometimes to a sense of things as they were and had a glimpse of how they should be. Well, I went on nevertheless in much the same course until I first met Agnes. I will not attempt to describe the wild rush of passion that shook my whole being . . . You know how of old you would chide me for talking of Christianity as the religion of the people . . . You know at the worst of times there must always have been a little grain of honesty in me. This forbad me from disguising in any way my thoughts from Agnes on what I soon found was to her the supreme theme, the living life-giving cup of her existence. I knew she loved me, though all my wild prayers and most passionate entreaties could not prevail upon her to say she would be mine in the present state of my mind.

Think not she assumed anything to herself so doing. No, none could be sweeter and meeker than she. She would ascribe all sorts of nobleness and goodness to me, say she knew well how much better I was than she, but that there could be no real highest union between us if I denied the master she most desired to serve, if, in fact, we were not one in Christ. I saw her sentence was irrevocable unless I changed, but whether it was pride or obstinacy or what it was I cannot say. I only hardened myself more and more in my own conceits and with frenzied impetuosity I rushed into all sorts of unnameable evils. I drank. I betted. I gambled, but I will not fill up the loathly list of my doings. Soon I found myself in the Fleet . . . Left to myself my wild feelings for her drove me almost to madness . . . And so days went on, I, raging within myself, until at length suddenly a voice seemed to say, more inwardly still: 'I will arise and go to my Father . . .' I told her of the voice. I entreated her to help me obey its call. She took up the Bible which had of late been my constant companion. A light dawned on me from the words she read and from that moment I felt she was mine . . .

We were married as privately as possible . . . When I asked her how she could marry one so soiled, she said: 'God loves the soul made new by repentance. Why would not I?'

In 1849 there were a number of important developments in the two already linked families. On 8 February Anne Weld gave birth at Somerset House, in the Assistant Secretary's apartments of the Royal Society, to her only child, a daughter, Agnes Grace. Emily Sellwood undoubtedly spent some time with her new niece and her sister, though London – never a healthy place – was threatened by a cholera epidemic. A letter in *The Times* that summer would describe the city as 'a gigantic sickhouse'.

Tennyson, after yet another water cure the previous November, had reverted to his old ways, according to FitzGerald, and was back on a bottle of port a day and the constant pipe smoking Dr Gully had so deplored. In his London chambers, he was himself deploring the bachelor life: 'The room smokes like the vestibule of ovens, the laundress is a Roman Catholic and has gone to her chapel . . . The lock of the door is spoilt, so that I cannot fasten it up when I go out, and I couldn't leave open chambers in London.' There he was hungry, 'alone, the rain falls, the bells are tolling.' He was in a mood to talk over his problems with his brother Charles.

In the month Agnes was born to Anne, Charles had asked his Bishop for an extension of his non-residence licence on account of the continued ill health of his own wife, Louisa. But things were changing. They were in contact again that spring. It is even possible to imagine all four of them, the sisters Emily and Louisa and the brothers Alfred and Charles, meeting by chance or design at Somerset House. Tennyson already knew Charles Weld. Everyone was worried about Alfred and realizing how much he needed a wife. He knew it most of all himself. If Emily did not see him in London, she must have heard some painful talk about him.

Tennyson's new friend Francis Palgrave (who would become devoted to both Alfred and Emily) described Tennyson in March as 'bearing the look of one who had suffered greatly'. He was actually going down with what he himself called 'a six-weeks-long influenza'. But he was also going through a recurrent recital of the pros and cons of publishing his elegies, the poems in memory of Arthur Hallam on which he had been working ever since Arthur's death fifteen years before. As long ago as January 1845 FitzGerald had said that that 'A.T. has near a volume of poems – elegiac – in memory of Arthur Hallam.' He himself believed 'Lycidas is the utmost length an elegiac should reach. But Spedding praises: and I suppose the elegiacs will see daylight – public daylight – one day.'

Was the time at last approaching? Tennyson had wanted to read them aloud in February, when he was staying on the Isle of Wight with his friend Edmund Peel, and had not been able to put his hand on the text. There were a number of manuscripts and Tennyson was careless with them. The one he was looking for was in a long butcher-ledger-like book. He wrote to Coventry Patmore about it: 'I have some obscure remembrance of having lent it to you.' 'If not,' he continued, 'will you go to my old chambers and institute a vigorous enquiry?' Patmore made a drama out of a crisis and told William Allingham in August a heightened version of his brilliant retrieval of the lost poems. If he had not rescued the book, he suggested, Tennyson's elegies might have been lost for ever and used for butter papers. 'It is the best thing he has ever done,' Patmore said. By now – August – Emily Patmore had 'copied it out for the press'.

Patmore's delight in his own marriage must have had an effect on Tennyson at this time. Emily Patmore would become celebrated as 'the Angel in the House'. Already her husband was writing in a letter: 'Is not the highest unwedded love shallow and trifling compared with the deep and always deepening devotion of marriage?' Patmore would suggest that within the bonds of marriage there were delights and discoveries more rewarding than the adventures of Don Juan. The two Emilys, who would both be commemorated in medallions by the new young sculptor Thomas Woolner, would become good friends.

There is no record of exactly when Emily Patmore did her copying, but in March 1849, through the intervention of Kate Rawnsley, Tennyson lent Emily Sellwood a manuscript of his elegies, which may well have had a great deal to do with her final decision later that year to marry him. Many of the elegies were already familiar to her. In the 1830s, at the time of her closest relationship with Tennyson, Emily had copied out seventeen sections of the poem, twelve of which do not appear in any other earlier manuscript. Her fair copy, surviving at Harvard, is on paper watermarked 1833. Those pages may well have been among the pile of manuscript she was given to read in that spring of 1849. Her letter to her cousin Kate Rawnsley survives only in Kate's sons' *Memories of the Tennysons*, where it is dated simply April 1st. It was a Sunday and she had promised to keep the elegies only until Saturday. Emily's feelings were still in a state of turmoil. She had by no means made up her mind to marry Tennyson when she wrote this letter. Dating it in 1850, as has been generally accepted, does not fit in with the rest of the evidence. It was in the course of 1849 that Emily, with the encouragement of the Rawnsleys, of Charles Kingsley and of her own family, came to accept what she herself called 'the great responsibility'. The 1 April letter, returning the manuscript of the elegies to her cousin, appears in the Rawnsleys' *Memories* like this:

April 1st.

My dearest Katie,— . . . . . Do you really think I should write a line with the Elegies, that is in a separate note, to say I have returned them? I am almost afraid, but since you say I am to do so I will, only I cannot say what I feel. . . . You and Drummond are among the best and kindest friends I have in the world, and let me not be ungrateful, I have some very good and very kind. The longer I live the more I feel how blessed I am in this way. Now I must say good bye.—Thy loving sister, EMILY.

I thought I would write my note before the others came. Here it is, no beginning nor end, not a note at all, a sort of label only. "Katie told me the poems might be kept until

Saturday. I hope I shall not have occasioned any incon-
venience by keeping them to the limit of time ; and if I
have I must be forgiven, for I cannot willingly part from
what is so precious. The thanks I would say for them and
for the faith in me which has trusted them to me must be
thought for me, I cannot write them. I have read the poems
through and through and through and to me they were and
they are ever more and more a spirit monument grand and
beautiful, in whose presence I feel admiration and delight, not
unmixed with awe. The happiest possible end to this labour
of love! But think not its fruits shall so soon perish, for
they are life in life, and they shall live, and as years go on be
only the more fully known and loved and reverenced for what
they are.
So says a true seer. Can anyone guess the name of this
seer? After such big words shall I put anything about my
own little I?—that I am the happier for having seen these
poems and that I hope I shall be the better too."
I cannot enter into things more particularly with him. I
only hope he will not be vexed by this apology for a note.

Charles Kingsley has been identified as 'the true seer'. Kingsley
would tell the publisher of *Fraser's* when he was asked to review the
poem the following year: 'I had rather not; for though everyone knows
that the latter is Tennyson's, I do not like breaking the incog, especially
as *he* told me, and told me, too, private histories connected with the
book, so that I should be hampered . . . with the fear of . . . a breach of
confidence.' Kingsley *did* review the book and his words of praise justify the assumption that Emily was quoting him in her letter. Emily had
talked over the poem with him and, though much of it must have been
painful reading for her, Kingsley's view of it must have reinforced the
Rawnsleys' urging and her own increasing recognition that she should
marry. Kingsley in his review would call Tennyson 'the willing and
deliberate champion of vital Christianity and of an orthodoxy the
more sincere because it has worked upward through the abyss of
doubt.' Emily felt 'the happier for having seen these poems.' Perhaps it
was indeed possible to believe that she and Alfred could be 'one in
Christ'.

The reconciliation of Charles and Louisa this spring was also an
important factor. On 21 May 1849 Charles's curate, James Douglas,
wrote to the Bishop from Grasby Vicarage: 'The principal cause of
Mr Turner's non-residence having been happily removed he intends

to reassume the management of the parish himself and dispense with my services. I therefore beg to inform your Lordship that I shall probably leave in the course of two months for an incumbency in Scotland.'

Forty-five years later, writing to Hallam Tennyson, a friend of Charles Turner (A.J. Symington) said he could hear Charles's own words clearly in his mind. Tennyson's feelings were now, after Emily's reaction to the elegies, that there really was a chance for him.

Alfred went to Charles – explained the situation – thought the engagement might now be renewed, and asked Charles to arrange a meeting for that purpose.

Charles told me that he took a firm stand – spoke earnestly and almost sternly – that though Alfred was his dear brother he had also to consider his sister-in-law – that he could easily bring about a meeting but would not move an inch in the matter till he was satisfied that Alfred had firmly made up his mind to go through with it, and that there were to be no more morbid doubts, conscientious changes, shilly-shallying and such like nonsense.

Alfred assured him that all in the past that had laid him open to such mis-interpretations had been done solely in the interests of his sister-in-law ['If thou knewest why I fly thee there is nothing thou wouldst more wish for than that I should fly thee'] – was on his part a sacrifice of self-renunciation and that he could not live without her – so, *now*, that a way was opened up, all would come right again.

Charles was satisfied; and he added to me that *all along* he believed that they were mutually made for each other. A meeting was arranged, with satisfactory results to all concerned.

Charles, talking years later to his friend Symington, seems to have taken a little more credit for the reunion than was really his due. It was always the Rawnsleys Emily felt were most responsible for bringing them together again and it was at their vicarage at Shiplake that Emily and Alfred met more than once that summer. There is also the sugges-tion – both from their grandson and from Emily's own story – that Alfred visited Emily at Hale, before the move to Eastbourne in the autumn of 1849.

There was as well, inevitably, the money factor. At some point in 1849 Tennyson's publisher, Edward Moxon, also saw copies of the elegies and promised Tennyson not only a lump sum but also a yearly income, which made it seem that at last a way really was 'opened up'. Money had always to him been part of the problem, however much he despised the worship of Mammon. In one copy of the proof of the printed Materials for the *Memoir* at Lincoln there are the words 'a yearly income' added in Emily's own hand in the margin, to the sentence about a lump sum. Any self-employed writer knows the importance of some regular income, however small. Correcting these proofs was one of the last things Emily did before her death; her mind was as sharp as ever and all her corrections and alterations are pertinent. In the *Memoir* this passage becomes: 'Moxon had promised a small yearly royalty on this and on the other poems, and so my father had decided he could now honourably offer my mother a home.' Not that he actually had a *home* to offer.

Tennyson was in Cheltenham with his mother in October 1849, but he never stayed long. As Matilda put it: 'We never keep him long; he does not like the place, it makes him shy meeting so many people, he says.' It was with strangers and acquaintances he would feel most lonely. The family, to whom he was drawn by both love and duty, were no substitute for a family of his own. 'I am off again in a day or two into Lincolnshire,' he told Patmore on 2 October.

In Lincolnshire Tennyson must have seen Charles and Louisa back in the old vicarage at Grasby and building a new one. There was little sign at this point that Louisa's mind was still disturbed. She seemed able to confine to her diaries evidence of what would become again a seething misery, while giving a superficial appearance of calm and competence. As for Charles, he had said to William Brookfield, with whom he had shared the opium habit at Cambridge long before, 'We used to be wits, now we're going off, I think, nothing but languid commonplaces.' There had always been something languid about Charles but he would never be 'commonplace', though it seems that now, like his brother, he was preparing to settle down.

In Lincolnshire Alfred was seeing a great many people, but old friends, with whom he was not shy. 'I have a love for old Lincolnshire faces and things which will stick by me as long as I live.' There must have been talk of Emily Sellwood as he stayed overnight and dined with Rawnsleys and Cracrofts and Booths. They were all connected with her in one way or another. Weston Cracroft wrote in his diary: 'I was amused when the Poet put his feet up on the sofa and Mrs Rawnsley, careful soul, whom I had observed to grow fidgety, all of a sudden quietly warned him off.' This Mrs Rawnsley – Sofia – was the mother-in-law of Emily's cousin Kate, and the wife of Tennyson's father's old friend. Tennyson long ago had said he visited her house with greater pleasure than at any other in the country, and that 'she was always like a mother to me,' though he still had one of his own. Mrs Rawnsley could certainly ask him to remove his feet from her sofa; somehow the incident shows how little he had changed, how little he had grown up, since he left Lincolnshire a dozen years before.

In November 1849, returned from Lincolnshire, Alfred sent Emily two different versions of the lullaby 'Sweet and Low' for her to choose which should be published. It suggests to me that they had already seen a good deal of each other, had talked over *The Princess* (which Alfred had given her himself when it was published and to which he was now adding) and that, as he always would do, he valued her literary judgment, the greatest tribute any poet can pay. It seems an extremely intimate gesture, sending for an opinion this song:

> Sweet and low, sweet and low,
>   Wind of the western sea,
> Low, low, breathe and blow,
>   Wind of the western sea!
> Over the rolling waters go,
> Come from the dying moon, and blow,
>   Blow him again to me;
> While my little one, while my pretty one, sleeps.
>
> Sleep and rest, sleep and rest,
>   Father will come to thee soon;
> Rest, rest, on mother's breast;
>   Father will come to thee soon;
> Father will come to his babe in the nest,
> Silver sails all out of the west
>   Under the silver moon:
> Sleep, my little one, sleep, my pretty one, sleep.

This was the version Emily Sellwood chose and which appeared in the third edition of *The Princess* in 1850. When she received the lullabys, Emily sat down at the piano and set the words to music, as she would often do in the future. She would always try to make 'perfect music unto noble words'. In her surviving manuscript book of her own music, Emily wrote by 'Sweet and Low' : 'Music written before publication of the words.'

Emily's delight in the elegies, the union of words and music, the reunion of Charles and Louisa, Alfred's views on marriage – and babies – in *The Princess*, above all their discovery that their feelings for each other had not changed – everything was combining towards one end. 'Let them be married soon,' Emily would write to Julia Margaret Cameron in 1858, when her daughter became engaged. 'I may be pardoned for a horror of long engagements.'

'Are you well? Are you happy?' the Lancashire handloom weaver Samuel Bamford asked Tennyson in December 1849, thanking him for a signed copy of his poems. Tennyson had sent it after Mrs Gaskell had told him that the old man had been learning the poems by heart in other people's houses (as many as twelve were in his head), because he could not afford to buy them. Tennyson reckoned Bamford's 'admiration as the highest honour I have yet received'. It was just the sort of thing to appeal to Emily, but would she have the power to keep the poet well and happy?

Emily Sellwood was now thirty-six; Alfred Tennyson was forty. Emphasis has always been given to Alfred's indecision, but there may well have been 'the wild prayers and passionate entreaties' Emily wrote about in one of her stories. He had after all told Charles that he could not live without her and he would, not long after the marriage, tell Alfred Gatty, in an intimate late-night talk, that he 'would have broken stones on the road to have had her as his wife'. It was Emily who remained longer uncertain about taking this momentous step, after all the years of separation, after the years of devoted care of her father. She had never stopped loving Alfred; there was no doubt about that. But could she leave her father? There is just one hint that he encouraged her to do so.

Henry Sellwood was not well in 1849 and a painful decision was made, I think, just at the time Louisa returned to Charles and the large house at Hale seemed much too big for them. They had at one time intended to stay there permanently, Emily, Louisa and Henry Sellwood. He had planted a St George peach tree for Emily, as she would recall in a letter to him from Italy two years later. You do not plant a peach tree if you intend to stay somewhere for only a couple of years. They had settled down at Hale when Tennyson appeared on the scene again – and Louisa returned to Lincolnshire.

Neither Emily nor her father was well and it was decided they would rent a house in Eastbourne for the sea air. Emily's friend, Alfred's sister

Cecilia Lushington was there with some of the others from Park House. It seemed the natural place to go. In 1892 Emily would write to her sister Anne. Her niece, Agnes, was by then over forty, but there had been an offer of marriage. Emily was anxious to know whether Agnes would accept – after the long years as her mother's companion:

The longer one lives, the more one feels how serious, nay how momentous an affair it is. Well do I remember my father's sad eyes when, being ill himself, he thought of me left alone in the world. It is of course different with Agnes. She is strong and has a better fortune and so more means of doing good in the world. Still for most people I think it is best to be married.

Was that really how, looking back, Emily saw herself in 1849, lacking in the strength and fortune to do any good in the world unless she married? Did she see marriage to Alfred – whom she had always loved – as a means of doing good in the world, of saving him from himself, of restoring him to health and happiness and giving him the sort of peace he needed to write? It was indeed 'a great responsibility'. In all those years, she admitted, she had 'lost courage', but her friends and her family encouraged her.

Charles Kingsley's counsel had been a source of particular strength to Emily. He was a great believer in marriage and a powerful advocate. She wrote: 'Kingsley not merely encouraged but urged me. Thank God.' Just before Christmas Kingsley and Tennyson met at the home of Drummond and Kate Rawnsley, the vicarage at Shiplake, and talked a great deal together. Charles Kegan Paul, who would years later become the Tennyson boys' first headmaster and, later still, one of Tennyson's publishers, gives a vivid impression of Kingsley at this time, which makes it easy to see how much he and Tennyson had in common.

We went into the study afterwards while Kingsley smoked his pipe, and the evening is one of those that stand out in my memory with peculiar vividness. I had never then, I have seldom since, heard a man talk so well.

Kingsley's conversational powers were very remarkable. In the first place he had, as may be easily understood by the readers of his books, a rare command of racy and correct English, while he was so many sided that he could take keen interest in almost any subject which attracted those about him. He had read, and read much, not only in matters which every one ought to know, but had gone deeply into many out-of-the-way and unexpected studies. Old medicine, magic, the occult properties of plants, folk-lore, mesmerism, nooks and bye-ways of history, old legends; on all these he was at home . . . The stammer, which in those days was so much more marked than in later years, and which was a serious discomfort to himself, was no drawback to the charm of his conversation. Rather the hesitation before some brilliant flash of words served to lend point to and intensify what he was saying . . .

It must not be supposed that he ever monopolised the talk. He had a courteous deference for the opinions of the most insignificant person in the circle, and was even too tolerant of a bore.

Kingsley naturally had an even more courteous deference for Tennyson's opinions. There is no record of their discussion, but a few days later – it seems on Christmas Day itself –Tennyson wrote to Emily's 'kind and clever' cousin, Kate Rawnsley, at Shiplake: 'I have made up my mind to marry in about a month. I have much to do and settle in the mean time. Pray keep this thing secret. I do not mean even my own family to know.' Of course Emily knew of the decision. It was hardly one that could be made unilaterally. She was certainly keeping her side of the secret and so was Kate. Though Charles Weld was at Shiplake on 29 December, there is no reference to Tennyson or their marriage plans in a letter Emily wrote to her sister Anne in London from Eastbourne on 11 January 1850 to tell her that Aunt Betsy was dead.

This was the aunt, Elizabeth Franklin, who, years before, had banged the child Emily's head against the door in angry punishment. Emily had long since forgiven her. If Aunt Betsy was, as seems probable, one of the 'Horncastle crones' who had been so 'causelessly bitter' against the Tennysons, her death would be yet another factor in making Emily feel easier about this marriage.

Elizabeth Franklin, who had lived for years in Horncastle, was to be buried with many of the rest of her family in Spilsby. Emily herself was apparently not well enough to make the winter visit for the funeral; her father would break his journey in London on the way. Emily wrote to Anne:

One cannot mourn that poor Auntie is after her long sufferings at last at peace, though very often we shall miss her warm hearty sympathy with us all. I am sorry Louie did not see her, very sorry. Will you be so kind, Nanny, as to have a comfortable bedroom secured for Daddy in an hotel near you. He means to go up by the twelve o'clock train tomorrow and spend Sunday with you. I am sure you will take care he has a good fire in his bedroom and that this should be as warm and quiet as may be. I would he were better able to bear the fatigue of his journey and I wish I were coming to see you too.

I must avail myself of your kind offer to shop for me. I suppose a black corded silk handkerchief would be right for Daddy's neck. Is cloth or crape proper for his hat? Four sufficiently good cambric handkerchiefs he would require, never yet having had those replaced he lost in his Horncastle journey.

For myself I imagine a Saxony cloth dress perfectly plain will be correct and I thought a gray tweed or an Irish duffle cloak would do for me. I thought of having it made like two large capes, the biggest quite covering my petticoats. I do not know the width but if it be that of mousseline de laine I suppose six or seven yards would do. Neither do I know the width of Saxony cloth but you know I require rather a long length for my dresses. Kate was so good as to give me a pair of black gloves too large for her . . . so I think I shall not need anything else unless it be some white crape or thin muslin flowers for inside my bonnet.

Now that we know that Emily Sellwood was in mourning for her aunt – the one who had brought her up – in the early part of 1850, it becomes clear that the further delays in fixing a date for the wedding after Tennyson's firm announcement in his Christmas Day letter to Kate, may have had nothing to do with any last-minute hesitations on his part. The 'shilly-shallying' Charles spoke of was all ten years earlier. There *would* be a wedding, when it was possible to have one without offending everyone even more than they intended to do anyway by making it as small, quiet and secret as possible. Tennyson had a great fear of it getting into the papers. Indeed he told Edmund Lushington he would gladly give '7/6 out of his limited income . . . to every penny-a-liner who will keep it *out of the papers*'.

The fact that Emily was in mourning meant the marriage could not take place until the summer. The Victorians took mourning very seriously indeed. As Elizabeth Franklin had brought Emily up, the period of mourning should really have been close to that for a mother. When one of Tennyson's cousins died in Italy in 1872, Emily told her son Hallam she would have to wear mourning 'and use a black seal', even though she barely knew the dead woman.

It was not the postponement that made Kate Rawnsley anxious, but rather a worry as to whether Emily was doing the right thing. Writing to Kate long afterwards, Emily said, 'I can never forget how much yourself and Drummond and Kingsley (then only as far as I was concerned as your friend) had to do with our life and with what anxiety to yourself.' Kate was anxious whether the union they were all encouraging really would prove a blessing to Emily. There was the problem of marrying someone whose 'formative influences had also been deformative'. There was the problem of habit. Alfred expressed it: 'My only fear is that I have lived so long unmarried that I may have crystallised into bachelorhood beyond redemption.' He hoped he still had some 'plasticity' left. He had. Kate Rawnsley would be able to say, just before her death, 'I have never regretted or in fact done otherwise than rejoice in the part I took in helping to smooth away difficulties . . .'

There is little trace of what Emily was doing in the early months of 1850. Did Tennyson go to see her in Eastbourne? Surely he did, but there is no evidence of the fact. The date 'March 1850' is in a copy of Goethe's *Faust* given to Emily Sellwood by Ellen Lushington. Both Emily and Alfred may well have been at Park House that month. 'Goethe thought it a sign of weakness to lose faith in immortality,' Tennyson would say. 'I hope that I shall never be so weak-minded as to let my belief in a future life be torn from me.' The elegies were now constantly in his mind. He had at last – perhaps partly as a result of the combined reaction of Emily and Kingsley – decided to have them printed. Trial copies were produced. On the 21 March Patmore said he had one of the half-dozen copies Tennyson had asked Moxon to print. Emily claimed some influence on the final title. Perhaps she had said clearly one day, 'Why not make the dedication the title?' The working title had been *Elegies*; *Fragments of an Elegy* and *The Way of a Soul* had also been considered. The dedication was 'In Memoriam A.H.H.' Years later, in June 1864, when they were considering titles for some of the Idylls, Emily said to Tennyson: '*In Memoriam* has proved a good title so perhaps I may be right in this too.'

Tennyson took out the marriage licence in Oxford on 15 May and it must have been around that time, 'a month before the wedding', that there was a meeting at Shiplake to discuss the arrangements for the day. The idea that Tennyson gave Kate trouble by his inability to 'make up his mind' comes solely from Willingham Rawnsley, who was far too young at the time (he was five that March) to have any clear idea what was really going on. Writing many years later, he did not realize the Sellwoods were in mourning and suggests that Tennyson's indecision was about the marriage itself, rather than about the problems of fixing an exact date and keeping the whole thing as quiet as possible.

The licence allowed the marriage to be at any time within three months. Mary had been grumbling about her brother's keeping 'silence about his engagement, which I think is not fair towards his family, especially as the Rawnsleys know it.' She was still unmarried herself and determined to take a gloomy view of the step he was about to take: 'Poor thing, I dare say he is miserable enough at times, thinking of what he is about to do.' There is no other suggestion that Tennyson was anything but happy that at last he was to be married, but he was enormously busy with last-minute negotiations over the elegies.

His friends who had been sent the trial copies were still making suggestions for alterations, or trying to. Aubrey de Vere was too late with his. His letter on 21 June (exclaiming 'Married!! is it possible?') suggests the final rush to publication.

You stole a march on me – publishing before I was aware and not letting me know where you were, or how I was to send you such suggestions as occurred to me. I have marked many passages . . .

Tennyson had decided to press for a five thousand printing at his own risk and could hardly bear to leave Moxon's side until the first copies were in the shops at the end of May. *In Memoriam* was published anonymously but it was probably Moxon himself who made sure, in the *Publishers' Circular* of 1 June, that Tennyson was named as the author. Tennyson was not at all well – which may have been another reason for the late decision on the exact date. It might have been only a heavy cold, but he feared it was his old enemy hay fever. 'I shall get quite afraid of the summer if I am always to be treated in this fashion.' Being Tennyson, he even feared it might be 'something worse'.

A summer wedding had been decided on back in the winter, at the time of Aunt Betsy Franklin's death. It was probably only when *In Memoriam* was safely published that Alfred wrote to Kate: 'It is settled for the 13th, so the shirts may be gone on with.' This is the one sentence that survives from what was certainly a longer letter. Tennyson's shirts were always rather a problem, keeping him in clean ones, but there were other things to be thought about. Emily's family were of course doing most of the thinking and arranging. It was only 'by dint of very great exertions' that everything was ready in time.

The place had seemed a natural choice, a lucky chance, as Tennyson would say. *That* had been decided much earlier. They wished to be married in the country, Emily said. She and her father had been living in Eastbourne, the Welds were in London and the Turners' new vicarage in Grasby was remote and hardly yet habitable. (Louisa would buy carpets and a tea-set in Brigg that very month. They had moved in only in May.)

Shiplake on the Thames, near Henley, where Drummond Rawnsley was the Vicar, was an appropriate place for the wedding. Drummond and Kate had been so deeply involved in bringing Emily and Alfred together again. The surroundings of the old Vicarage have not changed much to this day. There is still the triple-terraced garden above the chalk quarry and the wide splendid view of the Thames valley with the shining river flowing through the water meadows. In June 1850 Emily said, wild 'snowflakes' grew – a large summer version of the snowdrop. In the garden now, high above the river, there are huge cedars, just as there were a hundred and fifty years ago. The church across the lane from the Rawnsleys' Vicarage was then covered in ivy and famous for its medieval stained glass, brought from a ruined French abbey and installed just twenty years earlier, 'long before such adornments were fashionable,' Miss Mitford said.

'The thing is to come off on the 13th, Daddy says,' Charles wrote. He could not get away from Grasby but he and Louisa wrote warm letters to be given to Alfred and Emily on their wedding day. Alfred arrived at Shiplake on the 12th and Emily now moved into Holmwood, a short distance away at Binfield Heath, for her last night of single solitude. It was a house that would become famous later on for another connection. Swinburne's parents would move there in 1865 and the young poet would spend a great deal of time there.

Emily would speak of Kate 'crowning' her on this wedding day. She was thinking of those lines in *In Memoriam*, of the

> maiden in the day
> When first she wears her orange-flower!
> When crowned with blessing she doth rise
>   To take her latest leave of home,
>   And hopes and light regrets that come
> Make April of her tender eyes . . .

Willingham Rawnsley remembered himself, aged five, walking across the lane to the church with a sprig of syringa in his button-hole. Emily remembered the syringa too, the mock orange blossom; she said the smell and sight of the flowers was almost the only thing that made it look like a wedding party. The Rawnsleys' nurse, Rebecca Self, had helped her to dress. Hardwick Rawnsley said the servant always 'spoke of the beautiful eyes and hair and the sky-blue dress and she always ended by saying "Ah how she loved him and how proud he seemed of her".' The servant may have said such things but what she *wrote*, in a surviving letter to Rawnsley at the time he was working on his *Memories,* is quite different. 'She wear a silver grey silk dress and something whit on her shoulders and a white nice straw bonnitt and white ribbon and viel. She told the wedding had been put of for ten years . . . she went away in a dark dress Mr Tennyson he looked very noble and was well dress. he went in to the gargen and got her sum flowers and give to her when I had dress her . . . She was so place and look so happy. It was your mother's doing that they was made happy.' Whatever the colour of the dress, the last statement has the ring of truth and fits in with things as we know them to have been. Emily would say over and over again throughout her life how much she owed her happiness to her cousin Kate.

Emily Sellwood and Alfred Tennyson stood before the altar, and 'were made one forever'. Their lives would now run together until and beyond that day when Tennyson would write:

> She with all the charm of woman, she with all the breadth of man
> Strong in will and rich in wisdom . . .
> Very woman of very woman, nurse of ailing body and mind,
> She that linked again the broken chain that bound me to my kind.

'You must be so full of strange thoughts and feelings,' Louisa wrote to Emily in her letter to be read that day. She was an expert in such things. Charles hoped that all would be well for 'a brace of amiable and remarkable people', his 'double sister and long-single brother'. As that brother at last took his vows he said, 'The peace of God came into my life before the altar when I wedded her.'

Years before he had written:

> Look through mine eyes with thine. True wife,
> Round my true heart thine arms entwine
> My other dearer life in life,
> Look through my very soul with thine!

It was as if he had come at last to the place where he had always wanted to be; he had always imagined what a good marriage was and could be.

They were both happy to have a quiet wedding. Tennyson said, to the amusement of those around, that it was 'the nicest wedding he had ever been at'. There would have been even fewer around if he had had his way. Emily told Louisa and Charles:

It was very pleasant to have Cissy and her husband there. They were good to me more than I can say. They offered to come to Shiplake, K[ate] and D[rummond] having said it was not their fault they were not asked. Then I begged for CW, who was very anxious to be there and the only one who could come . . . I bought a seal ring brooch, *the* veil and nearly a shawl with your five pounds.

Anne Weld presumably could not leave sixteen-month-old Agnes, but Charles Weld was certainly there, signing the register along with the Lushingtons, the Rawnsleys and Emily's father, Henry Sellwood. Emily added the tedious curate, Greville Philimore, to her list of those present, though he did not sign the register. She remembered the two little Rawnsley girls, Mary, who was six, and Emily Margaret, her god-daughter, as her bridesmaids. But Margaret was only three and was too small; she was just carried into the church in her nurse's arms so she could see what was going on. The second bridesmaid was Jenny Elmhirst, the Rawnsley children's cousin, Sophy's daughter, who was staying in the house.

We know of other presents besides the £5 from the Turners – Tennyson's mother gave them a 'tall crimson glass vase' – perhaps other things as well. Kate gave Emily a leather-bound Bible with brass edges and clasp. Henry Sellwood would give them some furniture, including a huge dresser from Horncastle, which now belongs to their great-grandson Hallam. Mrs Burton of Somersby commissioned a bread-board from T.W. Wallis of Louth, carved out of a section of a sycamore tree from the lawn of the Rectory, near which they had read Dante together on an iron garden seat fourteen years before. Best of all, rich Aunt Russell gave them 'a present of £50', a much appreciated bounty.

Reports of the wedding are rather confused. Mary Tennyson, who was not present, would write to Mrs Burton: 'Well it is all over. Alfred was married to Emily last Friday. Friday and raining . . .' Willingham Rawnsley, quoting her letter, said that later she found it had been a Wednesday and said, 'I hope they will be happy but it is very doubtful.' Yet even she reported 'Emily looked bright, they say.' It was a word often used of her. ('Bright with something of an angel light.') In fact, 13

June 1850 was a Thursday and not raining, which is typical of the whole confusion surrounding this happy day. Tennyson would celebrate 'this sunny spot'.

Four days later Emily told Charles and Louisa she was 'baby enough to be sorry I did not wear my white dress. Ally would have liked it but I took him literally about travelling dress.' Nearly twenty years later she would give a version of why she had not worn her white dress, which would be repeated over and over again. She wrote in her Narrative for her sons: 'The cake did not arrive in time nor the dress and the white gloves disappeared in the depths of a carpet bag.' But apparently at the time she had actually made a decision (the wrong decision she felt) to be married in the same dress – sky blue, grey or dark – she went away in. Many years later she would mention her *two* wedding dresses in a letter to her son Hallam at school. She had been doing a great clear-out and discovered: 'My poor wedding dresses are both spotted with the damp – so now if only luck comes when the wedding dress is worn out [she had first written 'dresses are' and then thought that this bit of folk-lore must relate to the more normal situation of having only one] mine must come now – but what better can I have than I have had with my Husband and my boys.'

Moreover, not only was it Emily's decision not to wear the white dress, but there definitely *was* a cake, and gloves too, at some point anyway. Mary says: 'We received this morning a beautiful piece of bride cake,' and Emily says to Louisa and Charles, 'I hope you have got cake, gloves, favour ...' 'We went after breakfast to Pangbourne,' Emily said. The well-known lines Tennyson wrote for Drummond were partly written 'more than half a year' later but seem appropriate at this point, as they leave Shiplake to start their married life.

> Vicar of that pleasant spot,
>   Where it was my chance to marry,
> Happy, happy be your lot
>   In the Vicarage by the quarry:
> You were he that knit the knot.
>
> Sweetly, smoothly flow your life.
>   Never parish feud perplex you,
> Tithe unpaid, or party strife.
>   All things please you, nothing vex you;
> You have given me such a wife.

Have I seen in one so near
    Aught but sweetness aye prevailing?
Or, thro' more than half a year,
    Half the fraction of a failing?
Therefore bless you, Drummond dear.

Good she is, and pure and just.
    Being conquer'd by her sweetness
I shall come thro' her, I trust,
    Into fuller-orb'd completeness;
Tho' but made of erring dust.

You, meanwhile, shall day by day
    Watch your standard roses blowing,
And your three young things at play,
    And your triple terrace growing
Green and greener every May.

Smoothly flow your life with Kate's,
    Glancing off from all things evil,
Smooth as Thames below your gates,
    Thames along the silent level
Streaming thro' his osier'd aits.

We naturally know nothing of the intimate sexual relationship of Alfred and Emily, this newly married pair, and speculation seems even more inappropriate than it usually is. They were both totally inexperienced, but things appear to have gone well. Tennyson was certainly used to women. He had lived at very close quarters with four sisters for years and undoubtedly was well acquainted with the problems of menstruation. His sister Mary's loving remarks seem relevant at this point: 'What creatures men are!' Alfred she saw as an 'exception to this general rule' and 'one of the noblest of his kind. You know my opinion of men in general . . . they are not like us, they are naturally *more* selfish and not so affectionate,' but Alfred was different –'universally beloved by all his friends, and was long so before he came to any fame.' He was, it was often said, both 'natural' and kind. He was not easily embarrassed. 'It is clothes', Tennyson would say, 'that make the immodesty, not the want of them. There is nothing immodest in your natural skin.'

Emily's use of the word 'comfortable' the day after the wedding, writing to her dear sister-cousin Kate, is reassuring to us as well as to her. 'I know you and Drummond will rejoice to hear I am as happy and comfortable as even you could wish me. I owe you a great deal.' They wrote a joint thank-you letter, though their son Hallam would put only Alfred's bit in the *Memoir*, telling Kate she had managed it all very well and admitting he knew he still owed money – for those shirts she had organized apart from everything else. The envelope contains an almost illegible little note, a postscript in both their hands which seems to read: 'No.1. Married life. So save please.' It was indeed saved.

Emily wrote to Charles and Louisa thanking them for writing for the wedding day. 'Yours is the only note I have yet seen with my new name. I cannot tell you how good Alfred is to me. Poor thing! he has got such a bad cold; he will take all the care of me and none of himself.' It was, in fact, his hay fever and it would haunt the first part of his honeymoon. Louisa said the happy strain of Emily's note 'did only answer my expectations. I thought Alfred would pet and nurse and take care of his wife. I hope his cold is better.' Alfred wrote briefly and frivolously to Sophy Elmhirst, Drummond's sister: 'We seem to get on very well together. I have not beaten her yet.'

'Did you feel *very* nervous?' Louisa asked Emily. However nervous Emily had felt on her wedding day, it seems certain that she never for one moment regretted the step she had taken and that their physical union – at least when they were both well – was as happy as she could have wished. Even so, it was perhaps a little difficult for Emily to start her married life at the very moment when the literary world's attention was focused on Tennyson's friendship with Arthur Hallam.

'What passions our friendships were,' William Thackeray would write, looking back to their Cambridge days, and of no friendship could this be said more truly than that of Alfred Tennyson and Arthur Hallam. In the elegies Hallam figures as not only friend, but lover, husband (or indeed wife) and God. Tennyson found in him all the things he longed to find in a friend. That sex was neither sought nor found is quite clear. Tennyson was surely unconscious of what is now seen as the sexual imagery of the poem and of what some future readers might make of his words. Tennyson would say that of course he had never called Hallam 'dearest' in real life. He would come to regret the tone of 'amatory tenderness' *The Times* commented on the following year. James Mangles would report Tennyson in 1870 saying 'they have called it weak, cowardly, effeminate and I know not what. It is true I should not write so now.' But when Mangles said, 'Nevertheless, I hope you stick to it,' it was Emily who said, 'Yes, I say, let them rave.'

Emily certainly saw in *In Memoriam* nothing to rouse her jealousy. She was, it seems, never jealous of Arthur Hallam. She saw herself, I am sure, not as a rival of the dead beloved, but as a successor, who could benefit from that marvellous well of tenderness and love Alfred had shown himself capable of feeling, and in ways that had not been open to those long-ago friends. When Alfred gave her her own copy of *In Memoriam* that month he wrote in it the simple words

AT to his best loved.

Emily had no doubt that she was just that, his best loved. The elegies had suggested the possibility that the highest form of love, such as Tennyson's love for Arthur Hallam, means the repression of physical sexuality. But there is, despite claims to the contrary, little evidence that for Tennyson the marriage of true minds was what mattered above all. Certainly Tennyson was nervous of a great brood of children, but there is nothing to suggest that the long delay in their marriage had dulled the passion of its consummation. One can imagine Tennyson's contemptuous snort at a critic who quotes from 'Happy' (a late poem) the line 'This wall of solid flesh that comes between your soul and mine' to suggest that Tennyson saw 'marriage as more a spiritual than a physical communion'. For 'Happy' is a dramatic monologue and the speaker is a *leper*'s bride. The relevant quotation from that poem might rather be, if quotation there must be: 'I loved you first when young and fair, but now I love you most.' A biographer's suggestion that Tennyson had *chosen* an 'invalid wife approaching middle age' is odd; Tennyson had first chosen Emily in 1836, when she was indeed 'young and fair'. Even now she looked younger than her years. (Patmore would guess 'about thirty-two'.) 'She has loved me and prayed for my earthly and spiritual welfare for fourteen years,' Alfred wrote to one friend, and to another, 'I . . . am married to a lady only four years younger than myself, one who has loved me for fourteen years without variableness or any shadow of turning. She has the most beautiful nature I have met with among women.'

Certainly Emily's health was indifferent, but so was Tennyson's own. They would cosset each other over the years ahead. Her ill health never ruled out passion. She was, in fact, a passionate person, often using the word of herself in one way or another. She felt strongly about all sorts of things and most of all about Tennyson. In 1871, when she was nearly fifty-eight, she would say that love seems to grow even stronger as we grow older. 'A. never seemed to me so beautiful and touching,' she wrote in her journal.

Marian Bradley, Emily's close friend, would record in her diary her own secret dread of pregnancy, of the thought of another child, of the fear of death in childbirth, as she waited for the arrival of her sixth child, conceived because of 'the temptations of strength and health' on a happy summer holiday in Switzerland. She would envy Emily's late marriage for other reasons than that it had made her so well read. It was to Mrs Bradley that Alfred Tennyson confided in 1869: 'There are moments when the flesh is nothing to me, when I feel and know the flesh to be the vision, God and the spiritual only the real and true.' But in 1850 it had surely not been so. The flesh was important. In spite of the hay fever (or 'something worse') the first child must have been conceived very soon after the wedding. In November Alfred would write to Thomas Rawnsley that he and Emily expected 'an heir to nothing about next March or April'.

Alfred had a great many letters to write to his friends, having told so few of them before he married what was going on – but from now on he would leave as much letter writing as he possibly could to his wife. 'I hope,' Louisa wrote to Emily, 'I hope, Emmy dear, you will not follow your good man's example about letter writing.' She would not, luckily for her story. But before she had really taken over, Tennyson, in that same November letter to Thomas Rawnsley, would show just how much she was needed:

You do ill to seem as though you blamed me for neglect and forgetfulness of you and yours: you know it is not so and can never be so, but I confess that in the matter of letter writing I am in arrear to everybody: I have dozens of letters to write this afternoon and I cannot help wishing I could hire the Electric Telegraph once a month and so work off my scores with the wires at whatever expense. This old world pen-and-ink operation is behind the age.

They travelled extensively that summer, though they had assured Louisa and Charles they would settle down and take a house. 'It sounds more cozy', Louisa wrote, 'than roaming about – more as if you expected to find that in one another which would take away the necessity for running about for amusements.' They would eventually settle down and always find a great deal in each other. But it was difficult to know where to settle. 'Probably near Town,' Emily said. Before settling, there was much that they wanted to see together that summer. They went first to Clevedon, to 'the obscure and solitary church' above the Bristol Channel, 'where repose the mortal remains' of Arthur Hallam, 'snatched away by sudden death' in the twenty-third year of his age, more than sixteen years earlier. Someone at Thackeray's dinner table reported seeing them 'walking on the terrace at Clevedon Court' – the home of Arthur's grandfather. 'It was my wish', Emily told Charles and Louisa, 'to see Clevedon and AHH's tomb.'

Tennyson himself wrote calmly from Weston-super-Mare to John Forster in London, 'I have just been to see AHH's tomb. The tablet is not (as I supposed) in the chancel but in a transept.' He would alter the word 'chancel' to 'dark church' (echoing that 'dark street') in future editions of *In Memoriam*. The tablet spoke of 'the brightness of his genius, the depth of his understanding, the nobleness of his disposition, the fervour of his piety and the purity of his life.' Alfred realized he had just another such beside him: bright, understanding, noble, pious and pure. It was Emily, knowing how significant the visit was for her own relationship with Alfred, who wrote: 'It seemed a kind of consecration to go there.'

CHAPTER SIX

'Happiness after so many years of trial'

━━━

Alfred and Emily spent the best part of a week alone together in lodgings at Weston-super-Mare. They stayed on there because they both needed a rest, not because it was beautiful. They failed to go and see the Elmhirsts, who were on holiday in Devonshire. Tennyson gave one of those elaborate excuses which would make Sophy feel that she meant less to him than she wished she did, even though she was a Rawnsley and 'all the Rawnsleys' were dear to him, as he always said. It was only at the last minute that the Tennysons agreed to go west to Linton. In Bristol on 22 June they had almost decided to make for Tintern Abbey instead. Both places had connections with their separate pasts. Alfred had written to Emily at Linton in 1839; at Tintern he had written 'Tears, Idle Tears'.

At Linton the weather was atrocious; Alfred talked of 'the weeping Devonshire climate'. But they had one fine day when they hired a horse and a donkey and set off for the Valley of the Rocks. When the donkey Emily was riding 'proved rather an unmanageable beast', Alfred had no hesitation in swapping mounts, however ridiculous the sight of the large man on the small donkey. 'To my delight', Emily wrote in her journal, 'when we met country people they evidently quite understood the state of things and bowed to him most respectfully.' She would always care more than he did about what other people thought, but not about what they thought of *her*.

Charles Kingsley gives a picture of the idle holidaymaker of this period. 'A great deal of dressing, a lounge in the club-room, a stare out of the window with the telescope, an attempt to take a bad sketch, a walk up one parade and down another, interminable reading of the silliest novels, over which you fall asleep on a bench in the sun.' Kings-

ley was advocating a study of the wonders of the shore to fill the holiday hours: 'stranger than ever opium-eater dreamed'. 'Happy truly is
the naturalist . . . everywhere he sees significances, harmonies, laws,
chains of cause and effect.' Emily and Alfred shared not only the pleasures of the most serious literature, an interest in history, theology,
metaphysics, but also an intense interest in the natural world. Kingsley
writes of the delight of finding 'the solemn spot where the stag's horn
clubmoss ceases to straggle across the turf' and there, in Emily's journal, is the stag's horn moss itself, together with the grass of Parnassus.
In Tennyson's poetry there is not only grass but oat-grass and sword-
grass; there are not just flowers but sunflowers, hollyhocks and the tiger
lily.

Over and over again people comment on Tennyson's habit of saying
whatever came into his mind, whoever was present, whatever it was.
'He was almost like a child in saying everything that passed through his
head.' 'Only in an entirely noble nature can this power of giving utter-
ance to the feeling of the moment . . . increase its lovableness. With him
it was an irresistible characteristic.' It was never, at least at this stage, a
monologue. He would flash round with a sudden question; he would
draw Emily in. Imagine them riding side by side in Devon and, a little
later, crossing Coniston Water in a rowing boat with this marvellous
talk in her ears. 'Tennyson is the most delightful man in the world to
converse with,' William Allingham would say. Emily would jot down
in her journal: 'Conversation never commonplace where he is.' Jane
Carlyle had said with surprise that Tennyson talked to her 'like an angel
– only exactly as if he were talking with a clever *man*.' Emily was used
to equal talk with her father and there is evidence that she was not just
an excellent listener, an admiring audience. Anne Thackeray Ritchie
would have 'a special memory of once dining with the Tennysons in the
company of George Eliot and Lord Acton, but it was Mrs Tennyson's
gentle voice which seemed to take the lead.' Emily's confidence and
power would increase over the years, but even in this summer of their
marriage she could speak up boldly, as we shall see.

They travelled slowly to the Lake District from Devonshire. They
crossed Exmoor and had lunch in Glastonbury because of its possible
connections with Emily's family. There was that fifteenth-century
abbot John de Selwode. 'In after years,' Emily wrote, making the epitome of her journals, 'it seemed a very pleasant coincidence that he, the
last Abbot but one, should have been the only Abbot buried in the

chancel near the real or reputed grave of King Arthur.' Alfred had first written about King Arthur soon after Arthur Hallam's death. The lines of 'Morte d'Arthur' must have been in their heads at Glastonbury:

> The old order changeth, yielding place to new,
> And God fulfils himself in many ways . . .
> Pray for my soul. More things are wrought by prayer
> Than this world dreams of.

'Long they stood', surely, at Glastonbury as at Clevedon, 'revolving many memories'.

In Clifton there were more prosaic pains. Alfred was having problems with a toenail and 'a painful little operation' was necessary. Great was Emily's horror when 'the doctors gave him chloroform, then a new thing'. She was turned out of the room and through the wall 'heard him shout as if hallooing the hounds. The chloroform was not of the best and had blistered his poor chin.' Alfred was in rather a bad way with the hay fever and the blistered chin when they reached Cheltenham to visit his family and to try to make up for having not invited them to the wedding. His sister Mary seems to have been the most upset about that – but perhaps all his siblings were and only the evidence is lacking. It may well have been the first time Emily had seen Tennyson's mother since the Beech Hill days, over ten years earlier. Certainly Tennyson had kept her in the dark about his plans. That placid 'female fortitude' Tennyson had celebrated in his poem 'Isabel' stood her in good stead, as it always had done. 'She was not angry,' Tennyson told Forster, writing from Cheltenham that week. It was from Cheltenham too that Tennyson asked Edward Moxon to send an unbound copy of *In Memoriam* to Henry Sellwood – who had been at the wedding and was now living in Grasby with Louisa and Charles. It sounds as if he had already had a copy of the first edition but now planned to have one specially bound in Caistor or Brigg. Writing to Moxon, Tennyson sent his wife's regards and said she 'hopes to make your acquaintance'. It was an indication of how much Tennyson expected to involve Emily in his professional affairs.

Moxon responded by sending Mrs Tennyson a personal copy ('with the publisher's regards') of William Wordsworth's *Prelude*, posthumously published that month. Wordsworth had died on Shakespeare's birthday, just seven weeks before the wedding. Now with the immediate success of *In Memoriam* there seemed no doubt that Tenny-

son would be approached to succeed him as Poet Laureate. The first
edition of the elegies had sold out immediately. By the time they
reached the Lakes, Moxon was preparing a third edition. The reviews,
by friends and strangers alike, were excellent. Charles Kingsley called
Tennyson without any hesitation 'our only living great poet'. G.H.
Lewes called him the 'greatest living poet'.

Everyone was writing and talking about the poem. There were few
dissenting voices – some in letters unread by Alfred. FitzGerald told
Frederick he found it 'monotonous' and with 'that air of being evolved
by a Poetical Machine of the highest order'. Charlotte Brontë also used
the word 'monotonous' and was 'sceptical of a grief that could command such a flow of words' – which seems to show an odd lack of
understanding from a fellow writer. Elizabeth Barrett Browning defended Tennyson in one of her letters to Miss Mitford: 'The monotony
is a part of the position – the sea is monotonous and so is lasting grief
. . . He appeals heart to heart, directly from his own to the universal
heart and we all feel him nearer to us.' Emily had felt just that, reading
the extraordinary poem in its entirety the year before. Now every day
she came nearer and nearer to him.

In the public estimation *In Memoriam* was standing comparison
with Milton's *Lycidas* and Shakespeare's sonnets. Everyone was buying
it. There had been nothing like it since Byron's popular success. It was
twenty-six years since the boy Alfred Tennyson had carved 'Byron is
dead' on the soft sandstone near Somersby. Emily, who had first loved a
penniless young poet from a nearby village, found herself married to a
man almost universally recognized as a fit successor to William
Wordsworth.

On one of their drives they passed Rydal Mount 'but did not go in'.
Wordsworth was dead. They saw Fox Howe too, where Matthew
Arnold had grown up. They were 'rambling about the Lakes', 'flitting
from place to place'. Tennyson wrote to Sophy Elmhirst on 21 July
from a hotel near Patterdale, overlooking Ullswater, saying they would
soon be going to Tent Lodge, a 'pretty little villa' on Coniston Water.
But first they took lodgings at Keswick. Emily wrote years later in her
summary of this time: 'James Spedding discovered that we were at an
hotel in Keswick, called on us and pressed us to go to Myer House, my
first acquaintance with this good and wise and delightful friend.' 'All
that is best in Heart and Head', FitzGerald said of Spedding. 'A man
that would be incredible had one not known him.'

Isabel Spedding, James's niece, remembered what had happened in 1850 rather differently. She said the Tennysons had taken lodgings with the Miss Robsons, three sisters who kept 'a milliner's shop below the Queen's Head Inn . . .' Tennyson approached the Speddings' carriage one day, when it had halted outside the milliner's, and asked about Mirehouse. The result was the same, they were pressed to go and stay there. What is interesting is Isabel Spedding's comment that it was 'rather to Miss Robson's relief, who thought the poet rather a formidable person for her little lodgings, but was charmed with Mrs Tennyson; she was so sweet and gentle.' Both Isabel and her sister, aged eleven or twelve, were much excited 'as it was a very rare event for perfect strangers to come and stay at Mirehouse' – the long low house below Skiddaw on Bassenthwaite Lake. Tennyson was not a stranger to Mirehouse; he had stayed there with FitzGerald in 1835 – but that had been before Isabel and Mary were born. James Spedding was indeed 'much pleased' with Emily, as he told FitzGerald in Suffolk and FitzGerald told Frederick in Italy. There is a story told in the Spedding family that James laid out on their bed all the unmended socks Tennyson had discarded over the years while staying with him in Lincoln's Inn Fields 'to emphasize his friend's change in fortune'.

The Robsons' lodgings in Keswick must have been the 'rough accommodations' Tennyson mentioned in his letter to Coventry Patmore, urging him to visit the Lakes while they were there. By the time Patmore arrived in August, too soon after the birth of his second son, Tennyson Patmore, Emily and Alfred (the child's godparents) were well settled in Tent Lodge. Tent Lodge was a pleasant square house, marvellously situated high above Coniston Water on the Marshalls' estate, with a castellated boathouse on the shore. Mary and James Marshall themselves lived at Monk Coniston, a neo-Gothic house, also high above the lake and a hilly ten-minute walk from Tent Lodge. There was much going back and forth between the two houses and a great deal of entertaining. Mary Marshall – to whom Emily would be particularly devoted, though they spent most of their lives many miles apart – was a sister of Stephen Spring-Rice, who had been at Cambridge with Tennyson. James was a benevolent landowner and industrialist, MP for Leeds. Both were deeply concerned with social reform and were admirers of F.D. Maurice, the Christian Socialist.

Coventry Patmore had been an admirer and disciple of Tennyson's since he first read the 1842 poems when he was nineteen. His own first volume had been published by Moxon when he was only twenty-one; Ruskin said his poems were a little too like Tennyson 'to attract attention as they should'. Like Edmund Gosse, who would one day write his biography, he worked as a cataloguer in the British Museum. Already in 1850 he was showing signs of what Gosse called 'that lofty, moral arrogance' and slashing stringent tongue, so at odds with the sensitive tenderness of such poems as 'The Toys'. He reveals his arrogance in writing about Tennyson to his wife from the Lake District in 1850:

I cannot enough value my advantage in seeing so much of Tennyson. It is a great good to me to find that I have my superior, which I have never found in the company of anyone else . . . In Tennyson I perceive a nature higher and wider than my own.

This valuation of Tennyson makes particularly impressive Patmore's judgment that Emily 'seems to be in all respects worthy of her husband'.

Coventry Patmore wrote constantly to his wife, another Emily, the angel confined to her house in North London. Patmore was considered an expert on women. Like Charles Kingsley, he was always celebrating 'the never failing freshness and mystery of marriage'. Gosse once cut him down to size, calling him 'this laureate of the tea-table'. When Tennyson read 'The Angel in the House' he would say, 'I admire it exceedingly and trust it will do our age good, and not ours only. The women ought to subscribe for a statue to you.' (Virginia Woolf, in another age, would write of the need for women writers to 'kill the Angel in the House'.)

It seems worth quoting, at this stage when all Tennyson's friends were peering curiously at the poet's new wife, everything that Patmore has to say about Emily Tennyson, however much his attitude and assumptions can be questioned. What did he mean by saying Emily was 'not literary at all'? She was certainly, as he admits, 'familiar with the best modern books', and many older ones as well, and she was used to talking about them as well as reading them. His own dear wife Emily was certainly not literary; she published one book: *The Servants' Behaviour Book*. To Patmore, a 'literary lady' was perhaps one who presumed to publish novels or poems.

Mrs Tennyson seems to be a very charming person, and I have already seen enough of her to feel that any description of her from a short acquaintance is sure to be unjust. Her manners are perfectly simple and lady-like, and she has that high cultivation which is only found among the upper classes in the country, and there very seldom. She has instruction and intellect enough to make the stock-in-trade of half-a-dozen literary ladies; but she is neither brilliant nor literary at all. Tennyson has made no hasty or ill-judged choice. She seems to understand him thoroughly, and, without the least ostentation or officiousness of affection, waits upon and attends to him as she ought to do.

She is of very pleasing appearance, and looks about 32. Tent Lodge is the prettiest place in the world. A moderate sized house, built and furnished in quiet taste, standing on the foot of a hill that shelves to Coniston Lake, along which a small park, which belongs to the house, extends. There is a boat belonging to the house, and last night Tennyson rowed me half way down the Lake.

Two days later Patmore wrote again to his wife:

After dinner, we go out (mind I generalize from two days' experience) again till dark, and after tea Tennyson reads aloud, or we talk till half-past ten or eleven . . . I have just had a long talk with Mrs Tennyson. She seems to be in all respects worthy of her husband. She is a thorough lady – according to my standard. She is highly cultivated, but her mind seems always deeper than her cultivation, and her heart always deeper than her mind, – or rather constituting the main element of her mind. She is familiar with the best modern books, Ruskin, Maurice, Hare, etc. Her religion is at once deep and wide; so that upon this and most subjects I feel that I am most fortunate in having many opportunities forthcoming of talking with her.

Four days later Patmore was still enthusiastic about her:

I like Mrs Tennyson more and more every day. She seems to like me, as she talks more freely than a woman of such character would without a considerable faith in her hearers.

Patmore was delighted to tell his wife that the Tennysons were 'thinking of taking a house near London. They have asked me to look for one for them about Mill Hill or Barnet' – then, of course, country villages. They had been kindly pressed by the Marshalls to take Tent Lodge permanently, but much as they loved rowing on the lake and driving among the mountains, 'the damp climate did not suit either of us very well'. Patmore told his wife that Tennyson 'seems to have talked so much to his wife about you that she already knows you and counts on you for a friend . . .'

Once, when the two poets were out walking and had been talking for hours about other things, Tennyson suddenly turned to Patmore and said,

'What do you think of her?'

'Who?' Patmore asked, rather stupidly.

'Her, my wife,' Tennyson said. 'She is a perfect woman.' Then he added kindly, 'She is a good deal like your wife.'

It was true that these two poets' wives had a good deal in common; they would become friends over the next few years. Emily Patmore was even more remarkably selfless than Emily Tennyson. When she died, Patmore would read in her will, 'I leave my wedding ring to your second wife with my love and blessing.'

That neither Emily was priggish about drink is suggested from Patmore's description of the climb he and Tennyson made up Coniston Old Man – 2,700 feet, the ascent five hours' hard walking; Tennyson was feeling fit at last and free from his hay fever in the Lake air. Patmore tells his wife, 'Being obliged to take a great deal of spirits to keep up our strength, we both became rather glorious, and descended the mountain "charioted by Bacchus and his pards", at any rate six times faster than we had ascended.' Since his marriage, Tennyson had been trying (as he had so often before) to cut down on his drinking, but without much evident success. In a letter to someone he had met on one of his water cures, he wrote: 'I had hoped great things from your leaving off wine ... you know I always intend to, but whether I shall do so, know not and what I ought to do, being the son of a man who had his bottle of port daily, I know not.' There was heredity again. 'It counts for so much', as he said. Tennyson was to follow his father's example, as far as the port was concerned, throughout his long life. In most other ways, fortunately for Emily, he was very different from his father. Whether that reflected in part the difference between Emily and her mother-in-law, it is difficult to say, but there *was* a great difference, however often it has been suggested that Tennyson chose a wife as admirable and sweet-natured as his mother.

Admirable and sweet-natured she certainly was, but as well there was a glittering edge to her, an outspokenness and a keen confident intelligence that appealed greatly to Alfred's friends. There is a good example of how much she was herself, however eminent the company, at Monk Coniston that summer. Alfred was listening as his new wife talked at her first meeting with the great Thomas Carlyle. Emily herself put it like this for her sons:

Your father made me rather nervous, I dare say, listening to what I said to him at dinner, and no doubt was rather nervous himself when he heard me say, 'Mr Carlyle, you know that is not sane.' Next day, I think, he came to call and hearing me cough and seeing a window open behind me he quietly shut it. He was ever invariably most kind to me.

Long before, Carlyle had 'seemed to take a fancy' to Tennyson, admiring 'the pulse of a real man's heart' in the 1842 poems. Now Emily's response to one of his wilder grumbles seems to have pleased Carlyle too, and she agreed entirely with the view that 'virtue and beauty and faith are as real as vice and ugliness and unfaith, nay, perhaps more real.'

Carlyle wrote to Jane:

Alfred looks really improved, I should say: cheerful in what he talks, and looking forward to a future less 'detached' than the past has been. Poor fellow, a *good* soul, find him where or how situated you may! Mrs T also pleased me; the first glance of her is the least favourable. A freckly round-faced woman, rather tallish and without shape, a slight lisp too: something very *Kleinstädtisch* and unpromising at the first glance; but she lights up bright glittering blue eyes when you speak to her; has wit, has sense, and, were it not that she seems to be very delicate in health, 'sick *without* a disorder,' I should augur really well of Tennyson's adventure.

To FitzGerald, Carlyle wrote: 'Mrs Alfred is a very nice creature, cheerful, good-mannered, intelligent, sincere-looking.' To FitzGerald, Carlyle did not mention Emily's health. She *was* provincial (*Kleinstädtisch*), certainly, but the shapelessness Carlyle noticed was more to do with the unfashionable, comfortable clothes she favoured, than to any defect of her body in its 'natural skin'. And her mysterious delicacy at this point was perhaps nothing more than the early stages of pregnancy, perfectly described by the phrase 'sick without a disorder', though Carlyle would certainly not have known that she was already with child. The phrase has often been quoted out of context to suggest that Emily's health problems were largely psychosomatic.

The company was excellent at Coniston that summer and Emily would spend time with three of the men who would become particularly important to her: Thomas Woolner – who was trying to finish a medallion of Tennyson – Edward Lear and Franklin Lushington. Emily already knew Frank, Edmund's younger brother, from her visits to Park

House. (When she died, he would say she had been 'one of the stars of my life for more than fifty years'.) Lear would regret Frank's profession, that he was involved 'in this accursed *Law*!' He would regret many things through a lifetime's friendship, in which Emily's sympathy (for them both) would become deeply involved. Lear had returned the previous year to England, after travelling around the Mediterranean. He had decided at the age of thirty-seven to take a place in the Royal Academy Schools – a dramatic decision for one who had published three books about his travels and a celebrated *Book of Nonsense* and had indeed been briefly drawing-master to the Queen.

It was through Woolner and Lear that the Tennysons would become closely aware of Millais, Holman Hunt and Rossetti, all of whom would later illustrate Tennyson poems, though not on as extensive a scale as Lear himself. The summer of 1850 was the very time when the meaning of the letters PRB became known and the Pre-Raphaelite Brotherhood first made an impression on the world. Lear himself was never a member of the Brotherhood, but had much sympathy with them. And it was Patmore who would persuade Ruskin the following year to take up their cause in *The Times*. There is no record of what Lear and Emily thought of each other on this first meeting, but it was the beginning of a friendship that they would both value for the next thirty-seven years until Lear's death far away in the Villa Tennyson, San Remo, on the Italian Riviera.

If neither Woolner nor Lear recorded their early impressions of Emily, others beside Coventry Patmore did. Aubrey de Vere, who was staying with the Marshalls at Monk Coniston, wrote to a friend:

You will be glad to hear that the Poet's wife is a very interesting woman – kindly, affectionate . . . and, above all, deeply and simply religious. Her great and constant desire is to make her husband more religious or at least to conduce, as far as she may to his growth in the spiritual life. In this she will doubtless succeed, for piety like hers is infectious, especially where there is an atmosphere of affection to serve as a conducting medium. Indeed I already observe a great improvement in Alfred . . . She thinks always of what is *good for him* . . .

One night at Tent Lodge – it was about ten o'clock and Emily had already gone upstairs – Alfred said to de Vere: 'I have known many women who were excellent, one in one way, another in another way, but this woman is the noblest woman I have ever known.' It was a quiet and solemn statement – 'not apparently to me,' de Vere noticed. When he knew Emily better, a few years later, de Vere would use the same word Alfred had used, 'noble' – one of the words on Arthur Hallam's memorial. In 1854 he wrote: 'Certainly A Tennyson has been very greatly blessed in his marriage; and he deserved it; for he seems to have been guided by the highest motives, and to have followed the true wisdom of the heart in his choice. He is much happier and proportionately less morbid than he used to be; and in all respects improved.' De Vere suggested that even his most admiring friends, 'much as they like him, they like his wife not less. I can hardly say how deeply interesting she is to me. She is a woman full of soul as well as mind, and in all her affections, it seems to me that it is in the soul, and for the soul, that she loves those dear to her. She would, I have no doubt, make any imaginable sacrifice of her happiness to promote the real and interior good of her husband, and not of her happiness only, but of his also . . . I regard her as one of the 'few noble' whom it has been my lot to meet in life; and with a nature so generous, and so religious a use of the high qualities God has given her, I cannot but hope that the happiness accorded to her after so many years of trial, may be more and more blessed to her as the days go by. She is a person to whom you will be greatly drawn whenever you are near her . . .'

Aubrey de Vere remembered a very different Alfred staying with him at Curragh Chase in 1848 and visiting him in London more recently – groaning and growling in the way he had, smoking and drinking too much. Alfred had 'always been, to an extraordinary degree, human' and strongly sympathetic to his friends. De Vere decided that at the root of Tennyson's problems, of his hesitant faith, were those young men who believed 'no more in Christianity than in the feudal system', and filled his mind with attractive contradictions. T.S. Eliot memorably suggested that *In Memoriam* is 'not religious because of the quality of its faith, but because of the quality of its doubt'. But if it is his doubt that speaks most strongly to the twentieth century, it was certainly his faith that appealed to Emily and to most of his readers.

'I hate unfaith,' Tennyson would say. 'I cannot endure that we should sacrifice everything at the cold altar of what they choose to call truth.'

> We have but faith: we cannot know;
>   For knowledge is of things we see;
>   And yet we trust it comes from thee,
> A beam in darkness: let it grow.

As Aubrey de Vere saw, Emily could help Tennyson's faith to grow – but it would *not* be by any crude attempt 'to make her husband more religious'. Emily, of course, trusted in God, who works in mysterious ways. 'It is He that hath made us and not we ourselves.' She had also come to trust Alfred. 'I cannot understand: I love' he had written in *In Memoriam*, and she seemed to know exactly what he meant.

Coventry Patmore recorded on 19 August: 'Yesterday it was too wet to go to church, and Tennyson read prayers, lessons and a sermon by Maurice' – F.D. Maurice, the Christian Socialist, Kingsley's hero, who meant so much to Emily. If Maurice or Kingsley had been regularly in pulpits close at hand, Tennyson's churchgoing habits over the years would probably have been very different. He would one day tell James Mangles, his neighbour at Aldworth, that he had been driven out of the Church by 'a narrow-minded parson'. In later years there seems to be no record of Tennyson actually taking a service as he did that day at Coniston; Emily regularly led family prayers. But some surviving pages in their grandson Charles's young hand, headed 'Grandpapa's Prayers', suggest that Tennyson did on occasion take her role.

Tennyson would always need both solitude and more physically energetic company than Emily's – companions to climb mountains and walk long walks over downs and moors. He would also always need the stimulus of other talk than Emily's. Emily knew this and accepted it. But what she herself always loved most was what she called the 'double solitude', with which she was now so often blessed – time alone with Alfred.

One day, she recorded in her journal, they crossed Coniston Water, he rowing, she steering among the water lilies and past a clump of firs where the herons were watching them until they came to the further shore where they found 'a scrap of paper left by some picnic party'. Names caught their eyes. The newspaper, it turned out, contained, by an odd chance, the names 'of his uncle and one of mine'. How strange this linking of the two families on one scrap of faded newspaper. There was still a hope, the newspaper suggested, that Sir John Franklin was alive. A reward had been offered. And in the House of Commons the Rt. Hon. Charles Tennyson d'Eyncourt voted 'Aye' in a division 'that leave be sought to bring in a bill to protect the Parliamentary electors of Great Britain and Ireland from undue influence by the use of the ballot.'

One day there was a rainbow strangely reflected in the flat surface of the lake. One night – when Edmund Lushington was staying – there was a wild storm and the window of the room where Emily and Alfred were sleeping was broken, letting in the wind and the rain. Rather than wake the servants, they moved themselves into another room – but Alfred seems to have been so hopeless at bedmaking that they ended up with a 'sort of apple-pie creation' and a lot of suppressed laughter.

The mountains were 'a continual source of delight', as mountains had not seemed they ever would be again. But the climate really did not suit them. It was time to move south. On 13 October Mary Marshall inscribed for Emily a copy of Henry Taylor's *Notes from Life in six essays* and the following day they travelled, by chance perhaps, with Matthew Arnold as far as Cheltenham. Arnold was then, Emily said, 'in the heyday of youth'. He was twenty-eight. The year before he had published his first book, *The Strayed Reveller*. At Shiplake, reading aloud 'The Forsaken Merman' from that book, Tennyson had said 'he always felt that *he* ought to have written it'. On the same occasion Tennyson had spoken of young Arthur Clough's poems with much admiration. Arnold and Clough had been close friends at Oxford. It was Clough who would become closer to the Tennysons. Patmore had written to his wife from the Lakes: 'Do you not think yourself happy at having got among the poets?' – an odd question for poor Emily Patmore, at this point stuck in an August London with her new baby and a two-year-old. But Emily Tennyson had certainly 'got among the poets' and would remain so for over forty years.

In Cheltenham there would be some house hunting. Alfred had rashly written, his sister Mary said, 'to say that he should like to live by his Mother or in the same house with us, if we could get one large enough and he would share the rent, which would be a great deal better. He wishes us to take a house in the neighbourhood of London, . . . or to take a small house for him and Emily on the outskirts of Cheltenham till we can move; so what will be done I know not.'

Alfred did not seem to have a very clear idea of what he wanted. But Emily knew the Tennyson family well enough to have a clear idea that it would be foolish to share a house with them. They did look at an old house at Dowdeswell, with a beautiful view, but by 21 October they were staying with the Welds, Emily's sister Anne and her husband, in their Royal Society apartment at Somerset House in central London.

From there they visited Henry Taylor and his wife at Leyden House in Mortlake on the Thames and Emily met for the first time the Taylors' friend Julia Margaret Cameron, plain faced but striking in dark green silk – with whom they would later be, as Emily said, 'so intimate'. At this stage she lived near by in East Sheen – at Percy Lodge in Christchurch Road. Immediately south London seemed a more attractive place to settle than the villages just to the north of London that they had suggested to the Patmores. They looked at several 'likely houses', but nothing suited. They were not at all sure they wanted even 'to be so near London as Croydon' – where Lord Ashburton had offered them a house he had not yet bought. London is 'rather a horror to me', Alfred said to Emily, remembering days he had put behind him.

Tennyson told Walter White, his brother-in-law's assistant at the Royal Society, that he needed all the upper part of a house to himself 'for a study and smoking room, etc., and to avoid noise above his head and indoor privacy, as he is accustomed while composing to walk up and down his room loudly reciting the flowing thoughts.' A garden seemed important too for a poet's house. He had said at Shiplake that a poet ought not to have 'any other intellectual employment' – but that 'poetry ought to go hand in hand with digging.' Emily insisted on 'good airy rooms, particularly good bedrooms'. She apparently had had from her father some rather large four-poster beds.

There were all sorts of connections among these new people Emily was meeting. Henry Taylor had been a senior colleague of James Spedding at the Colonial Office, and indeed had secured Spedding's appointment. Taylor's wife and Mary Marshall, who had just given Emily one of Taylor's books, were both sisters of Stephen Spring-Rice, who, like Spedding, had been at Cambridge with Tennyson. Spring-Rice was a particularly close friend of Edward FitzGerald. Julia Cameron, not yet a photographer, was a devoted admirer of Henry Taylor's poetry; she put him in the same class as Tennyson. FitzGerald, more realistically, lumped him in with Richard Monckton Milnes and Aubrey de Vere, who could be consumed 'like stubble' by a breath of genuine poetic fire. Julia Cameron's older sister, Maria Jackson, was one of Coventry Patmore's closest friends – and long afterwards the grandmother of the girl who became Virginia Woolf.

People kept offering them hospitality while they were looking for a place to live. Nothing seemed quite right. They took refuge at Park House, the Lushingtons' place near Maidstone, a house very familiar to both of them. It was just over three years since that accidental yet momentous weekend reunion in September 1847. Their stay at Park

House this winter was sadly overshadowed by the extraordinary tragic news that Harry Hallam, Arthur's young brother, had died on a continental journey with his father just as Arthur had died seventeen years earlier. Harry had been a close friend at Cambridge of Frank Lushington. His father had seen, to his joyful amazement, how like the younger brother was to the older; now he too was dead. Of all his children only Julia was left. Years later, when Julia stayed with the Tennysons, Emily would write: 'For ourselves it is of course something apart from all other feelings to have Arthur Hallam's sister as our guest.' Harry died while everyone was still talking about *In Memoriam*.

They heard the news at Park House just a few days before a letter arrived on 9 November 1850 from the Queen's equerry offering Tennyson the Laureateship. The night before, he had had 'a dream that the Queen and the Prince had called on him at his Mother's and been very gracious, the Prince kissing him, which made him think "very kind but very German".' He had just been telling Emily about it when the letter was brought, offering the position 'as a mark of Her Majesty's appreciation of your literary distinction.' It took Tennyson four days to make up his mind about it, as both Emily and George Venables wrote in their diaries. (Venables was staying at Park House, as he so often did.)

Tennyson wrote two letters, one accepting and one rejecting, and finally sent off the acceptance, he said, because Venables told him at dinner that if he were Poet Laureate, 'I should always when I dined be offered the liver-wing of a fowl.' Emily recorded that he had been assured that 'no birthday ode would be required'. Emily did not yet realize that she would herself suffer from the fact that everyone in England who wrote poetry would send it to Tennyson, 'sucking at [his] time and leisure' and hers too, until he would in 1858 call it 'the eighth year of my persecution'.

The laurel wreath would become a crown of thorns. There were many times when Alfred wished he had sent the other envelope; 'his dread of levées and court balls and increased publicity' had almost made him refuse in the first place. I think Emily herself never did wish that he had, even when it was she who had to cope with acknowledging what Alfred called the 'shoals of trash', the 'wretched little books' that arrived by every post. Of course Emily felt that it was right that Alfred was Poet Laureate. The Queen and everyone else could accept that Tennyson was the foremost poet in the land. Sales of *In Memoriam* were already more than double the sales of Wordsworth's *Prelude* by the end of the year.

Edmund Lushington was away in Glasgow that November as he always was during term time; Alfred was often out looking at possible houses. At Park House the old friends and new sisters-in-law, Emily and Cecilia, talked by the fire. After the Shiplake wedding, Edmund and Cecilia had visited Lincolnshire; it had been Edmund's first sight of Somersby. But there 'the week's excitement and exertion' had 'brought on a very early miscarriage'. Hearing about Cecilia's loss, Emily must have felt particularly conscious of the vulnerability of the new life within her as she played with the small Lushingtons. Edmund arrived back on Christmas Day itself. It was little Eddy's seventh birthday on New Year's Eve, celebrated with a 'children's tea'. There would not be many more birthdays to celebrate. The image of the boy that survives is of a marble head by Thomas Woolner. Cecilia and Edmund Lushington, like Henry Hallam, would outlive all but one of their children.

On 20 January, seven months after their marriage and after nearly three months at Park House, Emily and Alfred moved into their first home. It was the Hall at Warninglid, on the road between Horsham and Cuckfield, north of Brighton – and a long way from London, both north and south. It was a disastrous choice. As Emily put it in her journal: 'The first result of our house-hunting was not flattering to us.' She uses the plural, not wanting to blame Alfred entirely; but she may not have made the fifty-mile journey from Park House herself until Tennyson had already signed the lease. They knew almost immediately that it was a mistake. If only they had been more experienced, Emily said, they might have realized the disadvantages (as well as the pleasures) of the remote rural situation – seven miles from the doctor at Horsham, with no mail delivered, 'not even a carrier'. They stayed at two nearby hotels, one in Cuckfield and one in Horsham, while they supervised the unpacking, and the Lincolnshire servants got things into some sort of order.

Emily says that she had the good fortune to bring with her from her father's house 'an excellent Cook and Housemaid', Martha Milnes and her sister Matilda. They were with them when the Census was taken later that year, so we know they were from Long Bennington and that they were then twenty-seven and twenty-one years old. Presumably they had moved from Horncastle with the Sellwoods and had been with them in Hale and Eastbourne. (Had they travelled too to Tent Lodge? It

is probable. Emily's servants would always be important to her, however shadowy they are now.) It is likely that Martha and Matilda were
younger sisters of 'poor Milnes', the servant who wept and wailed
when the Tennysons left Beech Hill in 1840.

All their servants' best efforts could not make the house at Warninglid the home they had been longing for. The birds sang; there were
good walks. But that was all there was to be said for the place. On the
second night – 'Alas! a storm came and made a great hole in the wall of
our bedroom.' The storm was so loud that they could not sleep and
Tennyson got up 'and read some of the books we had unpacked the
evening before.' Soon they would be packing them up again. Rain
poured in. Rooms were full of smoke from defective chimneys. As if
that was not bad enough, 'the bell which we had been told was an
alarm bell was in fact the bell of a Roman Catholic chapel, of which our
dining room was one part and the bedroom over another and that there
was a baby buried in the garden. We thought it all rather uncanny.' 'It
was even worse than we knew, for we afterwards learnt that one of the
famous or rather infamous Cuckfield gang, as it was called, lived in our
lodge. This perhaps saved our plate and maybe our lives, but at the time
it seemed gloomy enough.'

We may tend to think of 1851, the year of the Great Exhibition, as
the heyday of Victorian confidence and prosperity. In fact, Emily's
remark about the danger to their lives was not idle. Fanny Kingsley
would write of this winter: 'The state of the country was ominous. In
[Kingsley's] own parish there was still low fever and a general depression prevailed. Work was slack, and . . . gangs of house breakers and
men who preferred begging and robbery to the workhouse, wandered
about Hampshire, Surrey and Sussex. No house was secure. Mr Holl-
est, the clergyman of Frimley, was murdered in his own garden while
pursuing the thieves . . . The future of England looked dark.' Kingsley
himself, sick at heart, slept with loaded pistols by his bed and 'had to
send a charge of slugs, not deadly though unpleasantly straight' after an
intruder 'the other night'. He returned ten per cent of his tithes because
of the agricultural distress in his parish. He believed the Christian
organization of labour might have prevented all the unrest: 'Increased
police is a mere ruinous driving inward of the disease.'

In *Alton Locke*, which Emily and Alfred would read together the
very month they left Warninglid, Kingsley had shown the progress of a
working man from revolutionary Chartism to his own restrained

Christian socialism. The novel burned with his idealism and his concern for the souls of ordinary men and women. Carlyle had helped him to get the book published by Chapman and Hall. The Tennysons' grandson Charles would one day suggest that the social denunciations in 'Maud' sprang from Tennyson's 'long talks with Charles Kingsley and F.D. Maurice about the terrible conditions in the rapidly growing industrial cities.' Maurice, who had 'one of the most daring minds of the century', was Kingsley's dearest mentor. He had called his eldest son after him. Tennyson had always admired him too, and it was Maurice who had stimulated Emily's abiding interest in comparative religion, her wide tolerance of others' faiths. Maurice's view that the Church must address the social needs of man, as well as the spiritual, may seem obvious. (Did they not sing every Sunday that God had 'put down the mighty from their seats and exalted them of last degree'; had He not 'filled the hungry with good things' and sent the rich empty away?) But to many in the Church, Maurice and Kingsley were dangerous radicals. Their refusal to believe in a literal hell, where souls were damned for eternity, caused consternation.

All the clergymen who became the Tennysons' closest friends – Kingsley, Maurice, Benjamin Jowett, Arthur Hugh Clough, Arthur Stanley and Granville Bradley – started out as opposed to the establishment in one way or another. That they would end up as Professor of Moral Philosophy at Cambridge, Master of Balliol, Deans of Westminster, says more about the changing Church in the nineteenth century and their own remarkable talents, than any resemblance to the Vicar of Bray. F.D. Maurice would soon be dismissed from King's College, London for his unorthodox views; Jowett would have years in some sort of Oxford wilderness. Emily Tennyson is often depicted as a conventionally pious woman, but there was nothing conventional about her choice of friends or her religious views in the context of her time.

The Tennysons decided to abandon the Hall at Warninglid almost as soon as they got there. It was really an impossible place to live. How could they be comfortable seven miles from a doctor when their child was expected in just over two months' time? The day after they moved in Tennyson wrote to John Forster: 'I am going today in two hours perhaps to Twickenham to look for a house. I am in such a peck of troubles that you might get figs from thistles as soon as sense from me.' Emily packed his bag for him to go house hunting once more, while Alfred wrote out the 'Sorcerer-Cataleptic alterations in *The Princess*' –

for the fourth edition of the poem. His own 'waking dreams' and 'weird seizures' were in his mind as he awaited the birth of his first child – however much Dr Gully had calmed his fears of inherited epilepsy. How could he work at such at time?

While Tennyson was away, Emily had workmen hammering away to try and make the place more weatherproof and habitable. But on his return more noisy, stormy nights, 'in which we could not sleep', determined them to leave on 2 February, less than two weeks after they moved in. It was a drastic and expensive decision. They would end up paying the landlord who had deceived them a year and a half's rent – £85 – and they had not yet another house to go to. Tennyson had seen one he loved and wrote to Emily from the Castle Hotel in Twickenham in anguish that it seemed already taken: 'O dear how grieved am I that I did not look at Chapel House when I was here before. The most lovely house with a beautiful view in every room at top and all over the rooms are so high that you may put up your beds. A large staircase with great statues and carved and all rooms splendidly papered . . . and all in for 50 guineas.' It was the same rent Henry Sellwood had paid for their 'Hale paradise': 'I hope thou hast had a good night . . . O dear how I groan over Chapel House – *every* room bright and light and lofty and gay . . . Is it not enough to make one rage? Is the little mouth pretty quiet?' He was thinking of their unborn child, kicking and keeping Emily awake even when the storms did not rattle the windows. The owner of the Twickenham house had really wished them to have it, recognizing the name and telling Tennyson he had had a rage for poetry in his youth 'but married a poetical wife and they neutralized each other.' 'O dear! O dear! O dear! can't be helped . . .' Tennyson even toyed with gazumping. 'I was wicked enough to want him (as he said the agreement was not settled) to let me have the house but he said sharply My word's my bond!' Then Tennyson revealed they were still in with a chance – their rival's doctor 'wanted to keep her near *him*'.

While Tennyson described himself as 'half crazed' at missing, as he thought, the chance of renting Chapel House, Emily remained remarkably calm. Indeed, as he admitted she saved him from going entirely mad. 'If she were not one of the sweetest and *justest* natures in the world I should be almost at my wits' end (as the saying is) but she bears with me and with her troubles and mine.' By the time Tennyson wrote this to Sophy Elmhirst (Sophy Rawnsley, Drummond's sister) things were a great deal worse.

Sophy must have shown that she felt herself unfavourably compared with Emily as Alfred chided her for not being able to understand their inability to accept an invitation to Shawell, but he calmed her down in a later letter. 'You have known me from your cradle', 'You *know* me incapable of saying unkind things,' he said, sending Emily's love. Sophy had invited them for New Year and Alfred and Emily had written a letter together. Alfred wrote: 'It is very kind of you to remember us but Emily does not think she will be able to travel: and as for myself I think that . . .' at which point Emily took up the pen and wrote: 'I have too much to do, I am told to say,' and some more including, 'Take this not unkindly therefore.' Sophy *had* taken it unkindly – and there would be others in the future, thinking themselves Alfred's particular friends, who would resent Emily taking over the correspondence, and the way the two of them would seem to be so totally in each other's pockets, acting together, united against the outside world, as lovers often seem to be.

They consulted a doctor at Horsham who decided it was safe for Emily to leave Warninglid, heavily pregnant as she was. Tennyson apparently thought it better to draw her in a garden chair over the rough local road, rather than entrust her to a carriage. Emily remembered that 'with his accustomed tenderness' he guarded her from every jolt.

Sophy had felt particularly hurt when she heard the Tennysons had arrived at her brother's house at Shiplake. If Emily could travel from Park House to Warninglid and from Warninglid to Shiplake, why not to Shawell? That Emily had been right to fear travel would soon become clear.

The Tennysons reached Shiplake Vicarage on 3 February 1851. It was their first visit since the wedding. There was a cheering house party – a reunion of Franklin cousins as well as Rawnsleys, as Kate and Emily were joined by lively young Alice Wright, from Wrangle; Drummond's father was there too and Charles Kingsley came over from Eversley to see them. Although it was so early in the year 'the birds sang delightfully and the buds of the lime trees were crimson in the sunlight.' It was even possible for Emily to walk on the terrace. She read a good deal on the sofa. Drummond gave her a copy of his sermons, which had just been published, inscribing the book for her on 4 February. She ordered 'by the Henley carrier' Ruskin's *Stones of Venice*, Leigh Hunt's *Autobiography* and Howitt's *Year Book*. 'Mrs Tennyson particularly wishes for Ruskin.' She longed to go to Italy.

Meanwhile, she enjoyed at Shiplake the 'three young things' Tennyson celebrated in his poem for Drummond: Mary, Willingham and her god-daughter, Emily Margaret. She must have thought a great deal of their own child within her. Tennyson listened solemnly while seven-year-old Mary stood before him 'in a white pinafore with her fair little face and golden crown of plaits and her dark blue eyes fixed upon his face while she repeated some Latin ode to him' at her father's request. She was just the age he had been himself when he had repeated Horace to *his* father before going off to school at Louth. Willingham had his sixth birthday while they were there and Alfred and Drummond returned from Reading laughing over some rhymes. Tennyson said to the little boy:

> And oh, far worse than all beside,
> He whipped his Mary till she cried.

The child did not know what he was talking about until the next day he received *The English Struwel-Peter* as a birthday present. Emily, who very much disapproved of whipping, may have disapproved of Tennyson's choice, but she could hardly complain as she was in no state to go shopping herself – or indeed house hunting.

Tennyson was still looking at houses and getting extremely tired of it, but constantly thankful for Emily's equanimity and good humour. It was presumably on one of these occasions with Kate in the carriage, between Shiplake and Reading, that Tennyson added the stanzas to the wedding poem in the previous chapter. More than one person remembered Kate saying the poem had been written on a return visit, 'more than half a year' after the marriage, and in the carriage to Reading. (That convenient rhyme is not in the poem.) One of Kate's friends declared ('I remember it all *so distinctly*') that Kate had told her the coachman brought the lines back to Shiplake, saying, 'Mr Tennyson said I was to give you this paper and you was not to show it to anyone,' which fits in with the surviving letter to Drummond: '*Keep it to yourself*, as I should have kept it to *my*self if Kate had not asked for it . . .'

Hardwick Rawnsley published the story of his mother, driving to Reading with Tennyson, noticing the poet was very silent. 'As he left the carriage, he put a bit of MS, into her hands with the words "Give that to Dubbie"' – Drummond's pet name. But what about the letter? Did Tennyson press that into Kate's hands too? It sounds a little unlikely. In an unpublished letter, Willingham tells Hardwick he could hear their mother's voice telling him that she had challenged Tennyson:

'Now I know what you have been doing you must give me a copy of that.' This suggests something much more convincing – that Tennyson was silently composing the stanzas in his head – and wrote the poem out later and sent it with the letter to Drummond, when he next had a spare moment. Whenever it was written, it is the poem that matters. It certainly mattered to Tennyson. He worked on it, over several years, writing a number of different versions, some with all six stanzas, some with four and one with only three.

Coventry Patmore had written to Emily that their 'serious inconveniences' at Warninglid would have been worth it from his point of view if it meant they would now be living nearer London. The Twickenham house was still a possibility but nothing was certain. After a fortnight at Shiplake, Tennyson thought it was sensible for Emily to return to Park House until everything was sorted out and he had made a dutiful appearance as Poet Laureate at a court 'levée' which was to be on 6 March. For some reason, they decided not to go to Kent via London, where a night at Somerset House with the Welds would have been easily arranged, but via Reigate in Surrey, halfway to Maidstone from Shiplake, by a rural route. Emily's journal records that they 'slept at the Clarendon'. The journal, which seems such direct and concrete evidence, reminds us now of its fallibility. Perhaps in the original diary Emily made no mention of the name of the hotel. When she was copying out the epitome in 1893 she may have added the name of the hotel she thought they stayed at. At any rate in an 1847 Bible surviving at Lincoln there is the clear inscription: *Emily Tennyson, White Hart, Reigate, Feb 19/51*. More significant is what happened in the hotel.

There was a tiny two inch step leading out of one of our rooms. He said to me take care you do not fall down. I naughty creature forgot and did fall and had such a bad sprain that I could not get up and had to go to bed and for a time was very ill indeed.

He doctored the sprained foot water-cure fashion with loving care.

'Water-cure fashion' presumably meant wrapping it in cloths soaked in cold water; Dr Gully, who had treated Tennyson, believed in the healing power of cold compresses, regularly changed. So there was Alfred lovingly changing the cloths round Emily's ankle, sitting by her bedside – and having to go out to the local bookseller for a Bible when they found they had let all their books go on to Park House with their main luggage.

The unborn child was still kicking vigorously; there was no cause for alarm. On 20 February they arrived back at the Lushingtons' house, just a month after they had left with such high hopes of their own home at Warninglid. Fortunately, Alfred's pessimism and anguish over Chapel House, Twickenham had not been justified. By the end of February he had agreed terms with the owner. On 6 March he signed the lease. That was the very day that, as Poet Laureate, wearing trousers borrowed from Samuel Rogers (which were 'not hopelessly tight'), Tennyson kissed the Queen's hand for the first time. 'Joyful news for us both,' Emily wrote in her journal about Chapel House, but she was feeling nervous. Tennyson was so thrilled with Chapel House after the miseries of Warninglid that he had rashly taken a lease for five years – which would also prove to be a mistake.

Emily was at Park House and had still not seen their new home, when Alfred wrote to their landlord. After asking for the name of a good coal merchant in Twickenham or Richmond, he said:

My wife begs that I will petition of you to send her some little plan of the disposition of the rooms at C.H. for I myself (who have what the Phrenologists call a deficient locality) could not tell her very distinctly about this. Any little scratch upon paper would serve the purpose. She only wants to know where her servants are to put up her beds. She is a little afraid too that you may not be stringent enough with the tenants of the cottage about keeping their drains and sewers in order. If they should take a fancy to keep a dung heap by their door they might annoy one.

Emily might be the one who was fussing and making what she herself felt was a 'troublesome request' for the plan of the house, but they would both be annoyed if things were not ideal. Was Tennyson really going to be able to live in such a situation? Emily had been used to it in Horncastle, living close to other people. Tennyson had had all sorts of cramped urban lodgings over the years – but for both of them their ideal house was somewhere more like Hale House, Park House, the Shiplake Vicarage. Could they settle down in the last house in a terrace – by the Chapel – in Montpelier Row, Twickenham, however fine the eighteenth-century houses, however green and open the views from the top floor? From Tennyson's study there they would see across the grounds of Marble Hill (General Peel's Park) in one direction and those of Orleans House – the Duc d'Aumales's place – in the other. The river was not far away – but neither were a great many other people.

They spent the night of 10 March at Rochester according to Emily's journal, which seems an odd thing to do as it is so close to Park House. But two initials beside the date in Emily's tiny Pocket Almanack for 1851 suggest a possible reason. 'F.D.', she notes. Was F.D. Maurice lecturing in Rochester that evening? It seems likely. He was on a lecture tour at the time 'to gather and spread information in relation to working men's co-operative societies'. It was well worth making a special effort to hear him, though it hardly seems likely that Emily herself went. Kingsley had spoken of his reducing Chartists to tears: 'The man was inspired – gigantic.' Emily was certainly throughout her life inspired by Maurice's ideals – the brotherhood of Man and the fatherhood of God inextricably linked.

Next day the Park House coachman arrived in Rochester to escort them and help with their luggage. They took the train to London Bridge station where the Marshalls' 'delightfully luxurious carriage' met them and took them the rest of the way to their new home, Chapel House, where the servants had already settled in with the furniture from Warninglid. Tennyson had always had devoted friends and now everyone seemed delighted that he and Emily were settling within easy reach. 'About ten miles from London,' Tennyson said. There were regular omnibuses and trains too. Alfred copied out the times ('Omnibus hourly from the Bank' and so on) and sent them to potential visitors. Emily's journal from now on is studded with the names of visitors, many of whom have already appeared in these pages and many others who do not need to be recorded.

When the Census was taken on 31 March, there was one important visitor staying in the house: Emily's father, Henry Sellwood. The only servant apart from the Milnes sisters (who had come from her father's household) was an eleven-year-old errand and odd-job boy, Thomas Metcalfe. Sellwood no longer needed servants of his own for he would, though not like King Lear, spend the rest of his life living with daughters. Emily, though the eldest, was undoubtedly his Cordelia, but she would see much less of him than the others. Henry Sellwood's first visit to the Tennysons' home was marred by an unfortunate accident. Stepping back to admire a mitred Bishop, halfway up the stairs – one of the 'great statues' Tennyson had mentioned in his first letter about the house – Sellwood fell downstairs 'and bruised his eye and his legs'.

The house was quiet as both father and daughter rested, with wild March outside, the 'throstle' calling, the sunlight occasionally on the almond blossom. At the top of the house, Tennyson wrestled with his first poem for the Queen and hoped his children's children would have reason to be grateful to her. Henry Sellwood left on 12 April. Emily valued too much her 'double solitude' with Alfred, for which she had waited so long, to welcome even her beloved father as a regular member of the household. She knew too how much real solitude poets need. She regretted that almost immediately Tennyson found that the walks – so important a part of his creative life – around Twickenham were drearily suburban and uninspiring – 'dirty walks', Emily called them.

The child, the 'heir to nothing' Tennyson had joked about, started making his way into the world early on Easter Sunday, 20 April. The whole night before he was born he was vigorously alive but Emily's labour was long and difficult. Alfred asked the bellringers to stop the bells in the chapel next door but 'the organ rolled – the psalm sounded – and the wail of a woman in her travail – of a true and tender nature suffering, as it seemed, intolerable wrong, rose ever and anon.' The terrible time lasted nearly the whole of that Easter Sunday and 'all the turmoil' was in vain. 'My poor boy died in being born'; he was strangled by his own cord. Tennyson wrote in one letter: 'Had he lived the doctor said he would have been lusty and healthy; but somehow he got strangled.' They all blamed the fall Emily had had at Reigate two months before 'which shook him out of his place,' but, in fact, it could not have had anything to do with it.

Emily 'has borne all with the utmost fortitude'. As Alfred said, 'There is hardly any misfortune that cannot be borne by a heart that looks to God as the doer of all.' Emily's own health of course worried Alfred. He reassured Emily's sister Anne that the doctor said she was 'going on as well as can be'; more than twenty-four hours after the birth he had 'only seen Emily for a moment' – that was the way it was. He was extremely anxious. The following day he told John Forster: 'My wife is safe as yet'; he was dreading a relapse.

Mary Marshall had been with Emily. She thought, Alfred said, that 'the poor little fellow was nobly made and she having had a family of her own ought to know; but that perhaps made it all the sadder.' Alfred thought: 'Perhaps if he had been a sickly 7-months spindling, I should have minded it less – but I don't know: and they tell me that if he had not been so large a child he would have had a chance for his life.' Alfred grieved for the 'nine-months neighbour of my dear one's heart', more than ever he would have believed possible for a child stillborn.

At first he 'refused to see the little body, fearing to find some pallid abortion which would have haunted me all my life – but he looked (if it be not absurd to call a newborn baby so) even majestic in his mysterious silence.' 'I nearly broke my heart with going to look at him. He lay like a little warrior, having fought the fight, and failed, with his hands clenched, and a frown on his brow.' His father kissed the poor, pale hands and came away. 'I wept like a child for the child that was dead before he was born.' The memory *would* haunt him all his life, bringing tears to his eyes forty years later. Emily never saw the dead child. 'Well for her,' Tennyson said.

In one of her fictions, not yet quoted, Emily wrote: 'We lost our first-born – a sore blow to us both, as you may imagine. We grew but the more closely together for it. We felt, as it were, lifted up somewhat higher above the earth by our trust in the Father who chastened us.' 'Shadow and shine is life ... flower and thorn.' She could try to feel 'happy in the thought that it has (if there be truth in revelation) gone to God.'

Alfred could not bear to put a notice in *The Times* and wrote sixty letters instead. Only a few survive – to John Forster, Robert Monteith, Anne Weld, Emily Patmore. Each one is entirely different, detailed and heart-breaking. 'Dead as he was I felt proud of him ... dear little nameless one.' Tennyson hated gossip. ('Gossip is my total abhorrence. I wish it were some living crawling thing that I might tread it out for ever.') There would be gossip; it could not be avoided by keeping their misfortune out of the papers. Lucie Duff-Gordon wrote a little crudely to one of her friends: 'Tennyson is married to a woman who is so ill that she cannot walk, and he wheels her about. She has had a dead child, and he is very unhappy at it, I hear.' Coventry Patmore told William Allingham: 'Mrs Tennyson has had a son born dead; I am very sorry for this, as I think that the sooner Tennyson has a few children about him the better it will be for his mental health and comfort.'

There were two significant visits in that summer of 1851, before they went abroad. Francis Palgrave, who had first – as a passionate admirer – met Tennyson at the Brookfields two years before, was now Vice-Principal of Kneller Hall, not far from Chapel House, at that time a 'training college for schoolmasters'. Just five years earlier, Palgrave had taken a year out of his Oxford degree course to act as an assistant private secretary to Gladstone. He and Tennyson had many friends in common – and above all there was in his favour his tremendous enthusiasm for Tennyson's own poetry. He would become equally enthusiastic about Emily. Yet it had to be admitted that Francis Palgrave was a bore. Edward Lear would confide to his diary that he found him 'literal-minded to the point of fatuity', 'of all men the most frightfully antipatico to me, his voice and gross vanity'.

Was it any wonder that Tennyson greeted this unannounced arrival on the doorstep of Chapel House, with the 'somewhat gruff-sounding' words: 'So you have found me out.' Palgrave looked guilty. Emily ('his bride, long sought and lately won', as Palgrave called her) immediately retrieved the awkward moment, as she would often do in the future: 'You need not take Ally literally,' she said from her sofa. 'He is glad to see you: but we came here to escape from the too frequent interruptions of London.' So Palgrave wrote, not realizing they had actually escaped the draughty, smoky isolation at Warninglid. But it was true they had imagined Twickenham would exclude the threat of too many uninvited guests. Palgrave made himself extremely agreeable and enlisted Emily as an ally. She became after that first meeting 'a friend no less loved and honoured'. Palgrave is most remembered now as an anthologist, for his *Golden Treasury*. One day he would dedicate to Emily his selection of Tennyson's *Lyrical Poems* and pay tribute to her as 'the Wife whose perfect love has blessed him'. One day he would include in his *Treasury of Sacred Song* two short hymns written by Emily herself. Tennyson said to Emily in 1853: 'I think he improves as one knows him better.'

But that was all in the future. Another visitor would play an equally important part in their lives – and in our knowledge of those lives. On Coniston Water the year before Alfred had read from the first book of young William Allingham – poems such as 'Evening' and 'The Pilot's Daughter' 'aloud among the water-lilies of the Lake'. Coventry Patmore had been 'quite jealous of Tennyson's admiration of them'. But now that Allingham was in London, Patmore kindly arranged an introduction for him. The appointed day was 28 June. Allingham walked in the warm afternoon 'from Twickenham Railway Station to Montpelier Row', to the row of houses 'that seemed dropped by accident among quiet fields and large trees.' As so often happens, the diarist describes Tennyson –The Great Man – in detail. Of Emily he says very little: 'Mrs

Tennyson came in, very sweet and courteous, with low soft voice, and by and by when I rose to take leave she said, "Won't you stay to dinner?" which I was too happy to do.'

After dinner the Patmores were announced – and there is a glimpse of Emily in the garden 'with Mrs Patmore and her sister'. Allingham seems extremely relaxed in the great man's presence, laughing at his jokes and even turning into a joke Alfred's obsession with a ridiculous statement in *Critical Strictures on Great Authors*, which had just arrived in the post. 'What are you laughing at? You don't know what I'm saying.' 'O yes, I do,' says Allingham – a typically spirited response. On 1 July Allingham sent Emily a 'graceful little bracelet', presumably as a thank-you for her hospitality. The acknowledgment, for some reason, was written by Alfred; very soon Emily would be doing the same for him.

Emily's little Pocket Almanack records the cost of a good deal of local travel that May and June of 1851: 'Fly to Hampton Court 4s 6d; 'Fly to church'; 'To Kneller Hall'; 'Fly to Mortlake and East Sheen – three hours.' That would have been a visit to Mrs Henry Taylor and Mrs Cameron. There were several visits to Mortlake, and a visit to the Exhibition; one fly was for taking Drummond Rawnsley to the station. Twickenham station was a little too far for anyone with luggage. Some of these vehicles may have been only for Alfred. It seems unlikely that Emily would have felt up to visiting 'the great Glass House' in Hyde Park – but perhaps she did.

Certainly by July she felt ready for the visit to Italy she had often longed for – and which Alfred, so many times in the 1840s, had failed to make. Before their departure they tried in vain to let the house for the months they would be away, making inventories and leaving everything in order. Apart from the financial considerations (that £85 for Warninglid rankled), it seemed a good idea to have someone in the house to take care of it and to give the servants something to do – Emily's love of that 'double solitude' seems to have stopped her travelling with a maid, as so many women did. They packed a good many books: some novels, but mainly the classics – Virgil, Horace, Theocritus. They took 'a little Shakespeare and a little Homer', Dante and Goethe too.

On 8 July they went to Park House, expecting to travel with Cecilia and Edmund to Paris, but the Lushingtons were apparently not ready to leave and the Tennysons waited for them for several days at

Sandgate. Emily was strong enough to walk 'up the hill of the camp' with Alfred. When the Lushingtons arrived on Tuesday the 15th, the Channel was 'stormy or at least rough' and they did not cross until the following day, 'nor was it smooth then,' Emily wrote to her father, 'but the illness of none of the party amounted to sickness, however nearly it approached in one case at least that I can answer for. Alfred was heroically well, as well as yourself even Daddy.' Just before they left England they had heard of the marriage of Alfred's sister Mary to a barrister who apparently had not had a brief for years.

'Ally likes Alan Ker much as you know, but he cannot but feel the step he and Mary have taken is bold almost to madness. We have written to them,' Emily told her father. It was Mary who had been so doubtful about Alfred's marriage the previous summer. Ker's prospects might not have been marvellous, but Mary was now nearly forty-one and must have realized it was her last chance to have a family. Their son Walter would be at Cambridge one day with his Tennyson cousins. (Her confidence in Ker seems to have been justified. They went to the West Indies and two years later he was acting Attorney-General of Antigua.)

This visit to Paris with Emily and Alfred was Cecilia's 'first abroad-ing', Emily said. 'She enjoys it tolerably I think.' Cecilia was not a great one for enjoyment; she would return to Park House 'much tired', and does not seem to have gone abroad again. As for the Tennysons, the joy of the Paris visit was not the sightseeing but an unexpected meeting with Elizabeth and Robert Browning, on their way back to England from Italy. The two poets, Alfred and Robert, whose names would always be linked as the greatest of their time, had first met ten years before – but they hardly knew each other. Elizabeth Barrett Browning, whose reputation as a poet was then much greater than her husband's, had never met the Tennysons, though she had followed the career of the 'true and divine poet' with intense interest for many years – from long before her marriage in 1846.

Browning was very little read in the 1850s. Aubrey de Vere told Allingham that the publisher of his poems said that 'in 15 years he had hardly sold 15 copies of them'. If that was an exaggeration, even so it was no wonder that his wife smiled wryly when Tennyson said he would be glad to be unnoticed in Italy. 'There was not zeal enough for literature among the English of Florence to persecute anybody by over worship.' They all got on extremely well, in spite of this difference in their reputations. Emily looked curiously at Elizabeth, whose name had 'gone the round of the English newspapers' with Alfred's the summer before, after Wordsworth's death, in all the gossip about who was to be the new Poet Laureate. Mrs Browning was tiny and thin, 'so thin that when she welcomed you she gave you something like the foot of a young bird,' and her curls were like 'the pendant ears of a water-spaniel'. Emily always remembered her 'wonderful spirit eyes' – though they never met again. As with Emily Patmore, Emily Tennyson had a strong sense of how much they had in common. An invalid, marrying late, Elizabeth Browning had herself lost a number of potential children before finally producing her healthy son, two years before. Now, 'deeply imbedded in a reclining chair', her form was so small that it amounted almost to nothing. Everyone noticed the great eyes and that thin hand held up to her cheek. Emily said that Elizabeth met her more as a sister than as a stranger – that 'in a few short hours' she 'could plant herself in the heart for life'. 'Whether she thinks being a poet's wife entitles me to rank with poetesses I know not,' Emily wrote to her father, 'but she has been extremely kind and even kissed me on parting.' 'They are just come from Florence where they have been living four or five years. We have got valuable hints and promises of assistance from them.'

The Brownings had spent the summer of 1849 at Bagni di Lucca in the valley of the Lima. Having expected it to be 'a sort of wasp's nest of scandal and gaming', they had become totally 'charmed by the exquis-ite beauty of the scenery, by the coolness of the climate and the absence of our countrymen.' Bagni, they told the Tennysons, lies 'at the head of a hundred mountains . . . The sound of the river and of the cicada is all the noise' they would hear. 'Mountain air without its keenness, sheathed in Italian sunshine, think what *that* must be! And the beauty and the solitude . . .' It sounded perfect and the Tennysons decided immediately to spend some time there before facing what they expected to be the heat of Florence – and the complications of staying there with Alfred's brother Frederick and his Italian wife.

In return for this helpful advice, the Tennysons offered the Brown-ings their empty house in Twickenham, giving them a note for the servants and encouraging them to stay there as long as they liked. As it turned out, the Brownings did not use Chapel House, but they were 'pleased and touched to the heart'. Elizabeth Barrett Browning said that they 'accepted the note in which he gave us the right of possession for the sake of the generous autograph, though we never intended in our own minds to act out the proposition.' Thirty-four years later, coming across the letter when sorting out some papers for destruction, Browning called it 'the kindest in the world' and said: 'Life is well worth living were it only for one such experience and all that it implies.' On their fifth and final day in Paris, the Tennysons found the Brownings had left twin nosegays for them at their hotel, as a farewell – not perhaps the most appropriate presents for travellers, but touching.

The Tennysons travelled slowly to Italy, sightseeing on the way. The route was Châlons-sur-Marne, Dijon, Lyon, Valence, Avignon, Aix, Fréjus, Nice, Monaco, Menton, Cogoleto, Genoa. It was now August. Emily jotted down all these names in her Pocket Almanack, without comment. On their return she would write to Emily Patmore, 'We went by the Rhone and the Riviera, taking the usual road, except that we did not go as far as Marseilles, but crossed from Aix to Frejus, and a pleasant drive it was a great part of the way. I looked for the first time on the stone pines and smelt their delicious odour, and we gathered our first wild myrtle ... The olives were more beautiful than I expected: they, with their soft gray and with their violet shades, had an inexpressible charm, growing down close into the blue sea.' There were palm trees 'against the sky on a projecting rock', high above the lemon trees. It was all unfamiliar – and yet familiar too, from years of reading. Nice, she would tell Edward Lear, she took a dislike to, 'in spite of the beauty of its situation'. It was something to do with Emily's dislike of society and fashion. Nice was the epitome of a fashionable resort.

In the Gulf of Spezia they spent some time on the blue sea itself and Emily was delighted to find her previously unspoken Italian (studied long ago as a girl in Horncastle and kept up mainly by reading Dante) was entirely adequate.

I am afraid our countrymen cannot be generally great proficients in Italian since mine draws forth compliments. However I commonly understand something of what is said to me and contrive to make answers that seem to be intelligible, whether I do or not. One very amusing conversation I had with the boatman who rowed us for three hours on the Gulf of Spezia. His father had been boatman to Lord Byron and on the strength of this and of the common freedom of England and Piedmont he seemed to embrace all English people most cordially in his affection ... But against the Austrians his good-natured wrath poured itself forth in torrents of words and he was specially eloquent on the subject of the stripes Austria knows how to give, 'if people sing they are beaten, if they speak they are beaten, if they look they are beaten, if they eat they are beaten' and so he went on with a long string.

A few days later on 12 August they arrived in Bagni di Lucca. They had known Alfred's old Cambridge friend Francis Garden would be there with his consumptive wife, Virginia. Garden had taken a chaplain's job in Italy – for the sake of his wife's health. Alfred happily called on Garden as soon as they arrived – but it must have been rather a shock when, on their very first evening, just as they finished tea, Richard Jesse walked in. Emily was charitable, writing to her mother-in-law in Cheltenham, 'He is very kind in helping us'. But the 'cackling fellow' was not Alfred's favourite brother-in-law. Fortunately the Jesses were often up in the hills. They were keen walkers and liked best to be 'out of doors roaming when and where we like independent of time and humanity', Richard armed with a dagger and a stout stick, in case of dangerous encounters.

The Tennysons were not as enchanted by the valley as the Brownings had been, nor were they as energetic as the Jesses. Emily told Eliza Tennyson that, although Ally described Italy with the words ' "flies, fleas, filth, flame" ' – 'and "fraud" perhaps he might say,' – 'You must not think there has not been much to delight us.' It was only the beggars she herself found 'particularly distressing'. 'One wonders how there should be so many for the people seem very industrious and, as most of the work appears to be done out of doors one has continually the cheering prospect of busy knots of people at the house doors. The women seem particularly active – some making lace, some knitting, some preparing flax etc. Many times we have seen the priest sitting with one of these groups or standing and listening with an air of interest to some poor man who has detained him in the streets.' The priests were making a particular effort to identify with the people, whatever was going on in Rome. She was also touched when on two occasions, 'the priests bowed as they passed us, a sort of acknowledgment of universal brotherhood.' But she added, 'Do not think from this I am likely to turn Romanist.' The Roman Catholic church was in fact in a state of disarray – standing as it did against national unity. Austrian power was already beginning to crumble in the north of Italy – but it would not be until 1858 that the Pope would lose his temporal power. Carlyle had seen a lot of Mazzini during his exile in London and Tennyson must certainly have at least heard talk of him, but it would be Garibaldi they would eventually welcome to their home.

Emily said that in Bagni di Lucca 'the rage against Austria is much more sullen' than that of the fiery fellow who had claimed to have been Byron's boatman. Emily Jesse had been at 'the ball of the Grand Duchess' the night before the Tennysons arrived, but Emily said the 'Tuscans will not come here until the Grand Duke is gone and those who happen to be here will not go to his balls or even bow when he passes. The other day an Italian told Mr Garden they had meant to have done something this year, but now it was to be next and something in earnest. The police they say will go first and then the priests. One cannot however expect much from plots so talkative.'

Meanwhile the travellers enjoyed quiet days reading and writing in their little brick-floored rooms with reed blinds to keep out the blazing sun. 'This is far better than being in a hotel. The old man and his pretty modest-looking daughter wait upon us, the wife cooks and does our washing for us.' Their house, Casa Gregorio Barsantini, was in the Villa, described in Murray's *Handbook to North Italy* as 'a long street of about twenty lodging houses'. 'The Trattoria Gregorio Barsantini sends out dinners to families, the most economical mode of living here.' Signora Barsantini specialized in 'English dinners' which apparently meant 'little bits of rather tough meat plainly roasted.' 'We get on very well for we can always make up with peaches,' Emily wrote to her father, reminding him of the fine St George peach he had planted for her at Hale. Their 'three rooms, living and lights' cost nearly nine shillings a day in English money. Emily did not think it cheap. 'Here we sit then, often both of us in veils (don't laugh) you would not laugh if the flies plagued you as they do us.' There were no mosquitoes apparently but the flies were a real nuisance. The Brownings had not mentioned flies. 'All day we looked out on a high hill clothed from top to bottom with chestnuts: every side we looked, if we stretched our heads out of the windows, there were similar green hills all clothed with chestnuts, so that I fear my husband's time was rather lost here.' Obviously Emily felt the poet needed scenic stimulus rather than the double solitude at this stage. 'The views from the heights are certainly delightful,' but then the heat forbade these being climbed except in the evenings.

They dined in the afternoon and then at about five the Gardens called in their carriage to take them for a drive. One day poor frail Virginia Garden did not join them for they were going up to Lugliano, a village on top of one of the higher hills. 'Mr Garden was humbly content with a donkey, Ally had a pony and I was enthroned in an arm-chair with a foot-board and two long poles and borne by two portantini.' Murray's *Handbook* suggests it was the normal way for 'ladies' to reach these high villages. 'There are many interesting points, accessible only by ponies, donkeys and portantini. One favourite spot is the village of Lugliano.' It defines the portantini as 'a species of palanquin' rather than as the 'poor men', who sweated as they carried Emily up to the village high above. 'I felt very much ashamed of making them so hot for me. However one of them', obviously delighted to find an English visitor speaking Italian, 'told me it was good to be made hot and both were very cheerful.' In Lugliano they saw the people at Vespers, for it was the feast of the Assumption, and then the beginning of a procession with white robes and crosses. 'We admired the sunset on the mountains far and near and then came down again with regret to the valley.'

They had had some good talk with Francis Garden in the evenings; sometimes his wife was there as well, but then, Emily admitted, 'we did not get into any conversation we much cared for or at least I did not.' They returned calls in the conventional way of avoiding involvement – merely dropping a card in acknowledgment. So they did not meet the local English residents, nor Mrs Trollope who was visiting from Florence. Emily confessed she found her books 'unreadable'. To avoid repeating everything, she asked her father and her sisters to send her letters on, first to the Lushingtons who would send to Kate and then Kate could send them on to Cheltenham. 'It is not that I think them worth anything. On the contrary, I fear they are stupid, but it is only to let those nearest us know about us.' Emily was always conscious of her own literary shortcomings, but if Alfred would not write, she had to do the best she could.

By the time they left Bagni di Lucca on 5 September the green hills felt more than ever 'like prison walls', shutting out the outside world. Emily Jesse travelled with them (somehow they avoided Richard's company). They visited Lucca to dine and see the Duomo, an extraordinary sight with every pillar 'cased as it is in crimson seamed with gold'. Emily was amused by the old sexton, who considered not only that his cathedral was the finest in the world, but that every picture in it was 'the finest specimen of each master's art'. Very fine they were, she agreed. They reached Pisa late the same night and saw the Campo

Santo for the first time by moonlight. 'Magic the effect was.' But next day, inside the Duomo, Emily's protestant soul was saddened by the 'great Juggernaut figure of our Saviour done in giant size in mosaic inside the dome just over the high altar,' and by 'the priests, some in scarlet, some in black and white, some in green and gold, bobbing about' among the candles.

They reached Florence on 8 September and Emily was dazzled and delighted by everything in Dante's city. Rumour had exaggerated the grandeur of the Villa Torrigiani, which Frederick Tennyson was renting. It was a splendid house but 'not one of the gloomy palaces of the middle ages, nor is it full of great marble halls as I expected, but there are several fine rooms in it and we – Ally and I that is, and Emily Jesse who came with us from the Baths – have a pretty little suite of four rooms looking into the flower garden.' Frederick would sublet it three years later, finding it 'larger than we require and inconveniently expensive'. In the meantime, Emily and Alfred were happily impressed. Emily was particularly delighted with the extent of the grounds, close up to the city wall, and the 'beautiful tower on a mound' from which you could see, in one direction, in the far distance, the mountains and, in the other, the turrets and domes of the great churches and palaces of the city. 'One seems to have gone into another age of the world while looking at them,' Emily said.

In Emily's letters there is no mention of Arthur, Alfred's younger brother, though he was thought to be in Florence at this time. Just over three years later an acquaintance wrote to Elizabeth Barrett Browning that Arthur was complaining of being 'chilled and stunted through the whole nature of him by the frosty atmosphere and Tenarian gloom of his elder brother.' Presumably it was Arthur's excessive drinking, not cured by his year in the Dumfries asylum, that caused the frosty atmosphere. Emily reported Frederick and Maria 'most hospitable', though she felt a little uneasy with Maria. Emily never says a bad word about her (it was very rare for her to say a bad word about anybody) – unless to say that Maria 'really behaves like a lady' suggests Emily was conscious she was not one. There seems to be no evidence that she was actually 'the daughter of the chief magistrate of Siena', as her great-nephew Charles Tennyson recorded. Frederick's close friend Mary Brotherton would years later tell Emily's son Hallam (in a letter marked 'BURN THIS', which uncharacteristically he ignored): 'My dear husband knew a good deal of [Frederick's] "life in Italy" in much

1 Henry Sellwood by his daughter Anne.

2 Emily *c.* 1835, watercolour on ivory.

3 Anne.

4 Louisa by Anne.

5 The Sellwoods' house in the Market Place, Horncastle (no longer standing). Emily lived there from her birth in 1813 until she left Horncastle in 1847.

6 The Rectory at Somersby about seven miles away; Tennyson lived there from his birth in 1809 until the family left in 1837.

Tennyson painted by Samuel Laurence *c.*1840. FitzGerald wrote to Emily in 1871: 'Very imperfect as it is, is nevertheless the *best* painted Portrait I have seen; and certainly the *only* one of old Days. "Blubber-lipt," I remember Alfred once called it.'

8 Max Beerbohm's own caption for his cartoon of Thomas Woolner working on his 1857 bust of Tennyson
Mrs Tennyson: 'You know, Mr Woolner, I'm one of the most un-meddlesome of women; but – when (I'm
only asking), *when* do you begin modelling his halo?'

9 Medallion of Emily Tennyson by Woolner, finished January 1859. In 1855 Emily had worried about him wasting time on 'my lean face'.

10 Alfred Tennyson, a photograph by James Mudd, 1857.

11 Emily Tennyson, a charcoal drawing by G. F. Watts, possibly 1858, printed from a glass plate made 1895. This is not the 'lean face' of Emily's comment to Woolner, but fits in with Carlyle's description of her in 1850 as 'a freckly *round*-faced woman'.

13 Emily by G. F. Watts, the most frequently reproduced image. The finished picture arrived at Farringford in June 1863. Tennyson's brother-in-law, Edmund Lushington, thought it a poor likeness, but it was much admired. 'All say it is a Gainsborough,' Emily wrote.

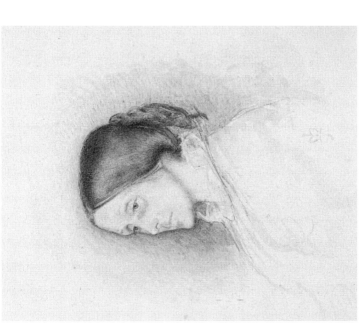

12 Emily by John Millais, perhaps November 1854, when she records him sketching her at Farringford. Millais gave this portrait to Lionel in 1879 and it is now in the home of his grandson, James Tennyson.

earlier days when [they] were living together unmarried ... and my husband thoroughly disliked and distrusted Maria and thought it a pity F.T. married her.'

Things were not entirely comfortable at the Villa Torrigiani in 1851. Emily Jesse would write after the visit: 'I am very sorry there ever should be misunderstandings – at any rate we always mean well.' And Emily Tennyson would write to her father: 'It makes me feel very nervous to know that while we are chattering in English, Maria sits at the head of the table not understanding anything that is going on.' Maria was extremely pregnant – her fourth child was born only a few days after the Tennysons left Florence. That may have made Emily a little nervous too, remembering her own recent labour.

They were hoping for another child. They had talked originally of spending the entire winter in Italy. They would return earlier because 'You see we fancied at the time that there was a probability of another little one and I did not wish her to be confined in Italy,' Tennyson wrote to Aubrey de Vere. In fact, Hallam, their second son, was not conceived until they had returned to England – but the 'probability' was presumably one of the reasons why they did not accept Frederick's invitation to stay longer. Emily said Alfred was talking of going north 'before the passes close. I rather fought against this, feeling he will regret not having seen Rome and Naples while in Italy, for I do not fancy we shall come back very soon, if ever.'

They stayed just over a fortnight in Florence, enjoying some intensive sightseeing, such as would have amazed the gossipers in England, thinking Alfred saddled with an invalid wife. 'Marriage is often a restorer,' Edmund Peel, Alfred's friend on the Isle of Wight, had said, 'at least has proved so in Miss Barrett's case, and may be expected to be no less so in this.' And so it certainly was for years.

'We have seen so many wonderfully beautiful things,' Emily said after their first day. 'We have been for hours' in what she called the Royal Gallery – the Uffizi – 'staying nearly all the while' she said, 'in the room where the Venus is' – as if there were only one Venus. She seems to speak, not of Botticelli's Venus, in her shell, but of the Venus de Medici – the one from Hadrian's Villa. Murray's *Handbook* describes the naked figure charmingly: 'She is evidently solicitous to discover whether she is observed. Yet the look does not indicate the timid modesty of a young girl, but the dignified anxiety of a noble married lady in such circumstances ... It is impossible to conceive more feminine purity than the statue displays.' 'My brain is quite overpowered,' Emily wrote to her father.

There followed the Pitti, the Boboli Gardens – very close to Frederick's villa – the convent and church of San Miniato al Monte, the Cascine – 'the Hyde Park of Florence' with equestrians and flower sellers – and, of course, the Duomo. The day they went to Fiesole they saw the Villa Goudi, with its cypresses, where Frederick had lived earlier. 'It seemed rather like a dream,' Emily wrote, 'to stand on that Fiesole hill and look over the rich plain and the towers and domes of Florence . . . which I had so often years ago pictured to my mind,' in those distant days when she had learnt Italian and read Dante and Milton as a girl in Horncastle. The autumnal leaves would soon be strewing the brooks in Vallombrosa.

Frederick was gloomy about the future of Italy and about the chestnut harvest. The wind was bitter; they had to have a fire one evening. Emily and Alfred left Florence on 24 September. Franklin Lushington's comments on their movements amusingly suggest the sort of whims and impatience Tennyson's friends thought Emily had to put up with: 'It was very stupid of him not to stay the winter in Italy while he was about it. The chief motive of his return appears to have been the want of English tobacco, but the immediate cause of his starting northwards from Florence was his having made up his mind to go southward to Rome or Naples on a particular day and packed his trunks accordingly. When the day came it happened to blow too hard for them to go by the Leghorn steamer southward, so instead of waiting with Christian patience till the weather was better, they immediately started northwards.' Emily's remark that she 'rather fought against' leaving Italy without seeing Rome and Naples, suggests that it was *her* idea to take the Leghorn steamer south, an idea quickly overturned by Tennyson himself when the wind blew hard and he thought of the effect of a sea journey on that possible new life.

The journey back to England took more than a month. They had wanted to see Venice, but were deterred by rumours of fever there. Emily would never see Venice, nor Rome, nor Naples. Florence would remain in her mind the 'enchanting city'. On the way back they admired Parma and Piacenza, in spite of continual rain. 'Poor things! How unfortunate . . . they have been with the weather,' Emily Jesse wrote to Frederick. They spent a great deal of time *inside* churches and galleries. Emily began to feel 'no church inside perfect without a dome'.

She thought, however much Ruskin might disagree, that Milan Cathedral 'is the most glorious of all temples inside'. From Milan they went beside the swollen lakes to Chiavenna, and stayed there in 'a suite of rooms'. (Their son would take the same rooms twenty-two years later.) Then they made their way over the Splügen pass into Switzerland. From Zurich they went west and up the valley of the Rhine to Heidelberg, where they stayed before travelling back to England via Antwerp.

They were back in Twickenham on 29 October, to what seemed 'rather a melancholy house'. In one of the books they had had with them, Emily had pressed a daisy Alfred had picked for her high in the Alps. It seemed such a little English thing to find. Two years later in Edinburgh, opening the book she had lent him, Alfred came across the daisy, where she had tenderly laid it by, and wrote a long poem for Emily, remembering that summer of 1851. Here are some of his stanzas for her:

O love, what hours were thine and mine,
In lands of palm and southern pine;
    In lands of palm, of orange-blossom,
Of olive, aloe, and maize and vine!

What Roman strength Turbia showed
In ruin, by the mountain road;
    How like a gem, beneath, the city
Of little Monaco, basking, glowed.

How richly down the rocky dell
The torrent vineyard streaming fell
    To meet the sun and sunny waters,
That only heaved with a summer swell.

What slender campanili grew
By bays, the peacock's neck in hue;
    Where, here and there, on sandy beaches
A milky-belled amaryllis blew. . .

Nor knew we well what pleased us most,
Not the clipt palm of which they boast;
    But distant colour, happy hamlet,
A mouldered citadel on the coast,

Or tower, or high hill-convent, seen
A light amid its olives green;
    Or olive-hoary cape in ocean;
Or rosy blossom in hot ravine,

Where oleanders flushed the bed
Of silent torrents, gravel-spread;
   And, crossing, oft we saw the glisten
Of ice, far up on a mountain head.

We loved that hall, though white and cold,
Those nichèd shapes of noble mould,
   A princely people's awful princes,
The grave, severe Genovese of old.

At Florence too what golden hours,
In those long galleries, were ours;
   What drives about the fresh Cascinè,
Or walks in Boboli's ducal bowers.

In bright vignettes, and each complete,
Of tower or duomo, sunny-sweet,
   Or palace, how the city glittered,
Through cypress avenues, at our feet.

But when we crost the Lombard plain
Remember what a plague of rain;
   Of rain at Reggio, rain at Parma;
At Lodi, rain, Piacenza, rain.

And stern and sad (so rare the smiles
Of sunlight) looked the Lombard piles;
   Porch-pillars on the lion resting,
And sombre, old, colonnaded aisles.

O Milan, O the chanting quires,
The giant windows' blazoned fires,
   The height, the space, the gloom, the glory!
A mount of marble, a hundred spires!. . .

Remember how we came at last
To Como; shower and storm and blast
   Had blown the lake beyond his limit,
And all was flooded; and how we past

From Como, when the light was gray,
And in my head, for half the day,
   The rich Virgilian rustic measure
Of Lari Maxume, all the way,

Like ballad-burthen music, kept,
As on The Lariano crept
   To that fair port below the castle
Of Queen Theodolind, where we slept;

Or hardly slept, but watched awake
A cypress in the moonlight shake,
   The moonlight touching o'er a terrace
One tall Agavè above the lake.

What more? we took our last adieu,
And up the snowy Splugen drew,
   But ere we reached the highest summit
I plucked a daisy, I gave it you.

It told of England then to me,
And now it tells of Italy. . .

Emily would always speak of Italy with love. While admitting she did not know a great many countries, she would write: 'Italy is the land I love next to England.' But she was never to see it again.

CHAPTER SEVEN

The births of the boys

——

Emily Tennyson told Emily Patmore, soon after the return from Italy, that she thought Alfred looked thin and 'not, I fear, the better for his journey'. He tried to settle down, but Twickenham was not really where he wanted to be and for the next two years he would be involved – and sometimes involve Emily – in 'this wretched house hunting business'. He would be 'so engaged in flying about the country – now in Kent – now in Surrey – now in Gloucestershire – now in Yorkshire' that he could never be sure of his whereabouts a day beforehand.

Emily was thankful that they were mostly quietly at Chapel House in the last part of 1851, though if it hadn't been for her, Tennyson said, he might well have gone off to Madeira with the Brookfields, or even to Australia with Thomas Woolner. Edward FitzGerald would report Tennyson 'ill at ease with his place of abode, though, I believe, happily married.' FitzGerald, that devoted chronicler of Alfred's ups and downs in the 1840s, had almost given up on Alfred's poetry by now. His disappointment had nothing to do with Emily, as some commentators have suggested. He was disappointed in *The Princess*; he was disappointed in *In Memoriam*. 'Had I Alfred's voice I would not have mumbled for years over them,' he wrote to Frederick Tennyson, leaving Alfred out of the list of people he really cared about: Frederick, Spedding, Thackeray and 'only one or two more'. He told his friend Elizabeth Cowell early in December, 'somehow I have no curiosity to see him any more.' But his old affection must have revived. When visiting his brother across the river in Richmond, Fitz called in with James Spedding, and felt sufficiently welcome to write to Emily on Christmas Eve, inviting himself and the Cowells the following week. He felt sure, as indeed was the case, that Emily would get on well with Elizabeth Cowell.

Emily was at this point endearing herself further to Edward Lear. They had first met in the Lakes the year before. Now Lear, back in England, wrote a note to warn her of the arrival of 'two volumes' of his 'own drawings and letter press', his *Excursions in Italy*. He realized it was rather late to be called a 'wedding present' but he would be very gratified if they would give a place to his books on their drawing-room table. Lear told Emily the 'superabominable' fogs and cold of England had made him resort to 'a kind of hybernating tortoise-ship' but he hoped to call at Twickenham, with or without Frank Lushington, when the weather improved. The books were a small return for the pleasure Tennyson's poetry had given him over the last eight years. It was 'quite beyond reckoning'. Emily wrote back warmly to encourage him to come to Twickenham 'not for a call but for Saturday to Monday and we will try to get Frank Lushington to come too that you may have the more agreeable recollections of Twickenham and be tempted to come again and again.' Lear would come to them again and again over the years, wherever they were. Though it was Tennyson's poetry that had drawn him to them, it was Emily herself who would keep him coming.

This winter many people were deeply disturbed by what was happening across the Channel. In December 1851 Louis Napoleon's coup had been endorsed by a plebiscite. He had not yet declared himself Emperor, but there was some justification for a responsive wave of English patriotism. *The Times* reported on 9 January 1852 that the new president had ominously alluded to Waterloo. Writing to William Brookfield in Madeira, Frank Lushington called it a 'National panic'. 'We are all on the point of becoming riflemen to resist the invasion which the French are going to try on. Among the most enthusiastic national defenders are Alfred Tennyson and Mrs A.T. At least they have been induced by Coventry Patmore to subscribe five pounds a piece for the purchase of rifles.' Lushington thought the Laureate should restrict his activity to the 'howling of patriotic staves'. Howl, Alfred certainly did and Emily found herself closely involved in the publication of several of his most hectic and jingoistic verses. Sending 'Rifle Clubs!!!' to Coventry Patmore, Tennyson said he had written it in two minutes. 'Really I think on writing it out it's enough to make a war of itself. My wife thinks it too insulting to the F. and too inflaming to the English.' Emily's feeling prevailed and the verses were not published at the time. Others were. Elizabeth Barrett Browning felt that when years later

Alfred complained about a fort being built on his doorstep on the Isle of Wight, he was only getting what he deserved.

Alfred was in Cheltenham visiting his mother and saying goodbye to the Kers. Emily was now in the early stages of her second pregnancy and feeling ill; she had been advised not to travel. Alfred had said he would be back in Twickenham on Saturday, but had postponed his return. He wrote to her on Friday 23 January, obviously a little exasperated by her longing for him:

Canst thou not hold on till Monday evening without me? . . . I fear thou wilt be bothered by my not coming – particularly as thou callest thyself unwell. The Kers and Cissy are *not* coming back with me so do not plague thyself about them . . . I have been out every day dining nearly and I am going out again today so that my reason for stopping is partly that I may spend *one* day alone with my family. And on Sunday all trains are so slow that I should be hours on the road. So rest thee perturbed spirit till Monday afternoon and sleep sound upon the *certainty* that I shall come then . . . Now bear up! be jolly – for to think of thee sad spoils me here for enjoyment of most things . . . John Rashdall wants us to go and spend 3 weeks with him at Malvern, which I think will be nice when thou canst move.

While she could not move, there were things she could do for Alfred. The very day after his return, thanking the Rawnsleys in Lincolnshire for a present of 'fowl, sausages etc' – 'so much better than anything of the kind we have here,' Alfred had protested, as he protested throughout his life, 'always I have had a hatred of letter writing'. One can imagine Emily saying that that was one letter he really *had* to write, knowing how hurt the Rawnsleys would be if he did not write himself. But she could deal with the correspondence with John Forster over the patriotic poems Tennyson wanted to appear anonymously in the *Examiner*, which Forster edited. Charles Weld, her brother-in-law, had in fact tried to get one of the poems into *The Times*, without revealing its authorship, but they ignored it. Alfred was genuinely most interested, it seemed, in awakening people 'to their danger'. Forster asked for a pseudonym and Emily herself objected to Merlin: 'One thinks of him more as the prophet. Taliessin the king of bards he objects to, to begin with, on the grounds of his being so. Would Aneurin do?'

The sequence of three letters shows how closely Emily was already involving herself in Alfred's professional life. She uses 'we' unselfconsciously. 'May we beg if the accent in Poesio be on the i "wrong'd" may be erased. We have not heard the name spoken and of ourselves call it Poèsio (as you can see).' The letters are typical of many Emily would write over the years. She is writing to a friend (as she often would be) and she apologized for a small burn by saying 'Naughty Alfred has tobaccoed my note. Forgive it,' and the sequence ends with a jokey deception. Emily writes: 'You will laugh at the thin disguise of the note and changed signature', when Alfred finally submits for publication a letter under the name 'Taliessin', commenting on his own poems which appeared as by 'Merlin', together with some lines by 'Taliessin', which are 'certainly not so good'. The manuscript of the poem at Harvard is written partly in Emily's hand, partly in Alfred's, with alterations. As she said in her letter, she did not have time to 'copy all this'.

James Spedding told Emily on 4 February he too would let Patmore have £5 for rifles. 'I think I could hit a Frenchman at 100 yards, if he did not frighten me.' She had encouraged him to turn up at a meeting about forming a club of volunteers. Emily told Patmore that there was not much point in Alfred getting actively involved as they were hoping to move soon to the country, indeed had already heard of a house 'extremely likely to suit'. She begged Patmore never to speak of Tennyson as an 'agitator' 'for any cause whatsoever . . . The word has come to have so evil a meaning, a sort of hysterical lady meaning if nothing worse.' Emily was herself never a 'hysterical lady'. She ended by saying, as again she would so often say, 'I know you will be disappointed at not getting an answer from Alfred but I thought these hasty lines would be better than nothing.'

Spedding's letter on 4 February was in reply to an invitation from Emily to dinner on the 10th at half past five. (They chose this hour for dining, Emily would tell the Brownings, because of the 'quicker' train which brings people down for that hour.) She had asked Thackeray too for 10 February, and he wrote an extremely warm reply – 'though I've seen you but once I consider you a friend too.' He asked her if he might bring his daughters, Anne and Minny, then aged fourteen and eleven:

I wonder whether I might bring my two girls? If you have a party, that of course won't be right: but if only a friend or two – these young women might have their dinner at home, and would sit quietly upstairs while we had ours. You will please not be displeased at this proposal, will you? But I get so hampered with engagements in London that I see the children very little; and had arranged to spend part of that evening with them.

Emily was, of course, delighted for the children to come. She must have been distressed by the knowledge that they were growing up motherless; their mother not dead but mad. By an odd chance, they were already familiar with Chapel House for it had once been the home of their governess's parents. Anne remembered the 'carved oaken figure of a Bishop with benedictory hands' all her life, and 'the panelled rooms and the dark hall and the oak staircase'. Years later, after her father's death, she would become one of Emily's closest friends.

In March they went, as Tennyson had said they would, to stay with John Rashdall, Tennyson's friend from Cambridge days, now the Vicar of Malvern. Tennyson had stayed with him in the past when he took the water cure. Now Emily, pregnant as she was, was temporarily under the care of Dr Gully's partner, Dr Marsden. When the time came to pay his fee, he suggested to Tennyson that he might 'come and mesmerise a young lady who is very ill'.

Tennyson protested: 'I can't mesmerise. I never mesmerised anyone in my life.' But the doctor insisted he would be able to do it. The first time it took Tennyson nearly an hour to put the girl to sleep; after that, miraculously, Tennyson's slightest breath, however full of tobacco smoke, would send her off. Emily told the story in her journal. She would herself have reason to thank Dr Marsden for teaching Tennyson to mesmerise. It had always fascinated him. He had recommended Harriet Martineau on 'Mesmerism' in the *Athenaeum* to Aunt Russell in 1844 and indeed it seemed to have some relationship with the sort of 'waking trance' he had been able to put himself into as a boy. Elizabeth Barrett Browning was only one of many Victorians who were extremely excited by it; it was somehow allied to the 'more difficult and more discomposing subject of spiritualism', about which Emily had very deep reservations. Several of Tennyson's siblings – Frederick, Emily Jesse, Mary Ker – would become obsessed with spiritualism. Later this year Emily Tennyson would recommend to Frederick, 'a collection of letters on Mesmerism from Edinburgh', by a Dr Gregory.

The house hunting went on and on. Emily must have begun to wonder whether they would ever settle. Was Alfred really happier con-tinuing the pattern of his wandering life as a bachelor? Or was it that he had in his head some ideal place he could never find? In Malvern they were disappointed in one house they had very much wanted. To the ones that were available, there was always some objection. They en-joyed Malvern all the same and stayed, it seems, more like two months than the three weeks originally suggested, perhaps largely because of John Rashdall, 'a man so beloved' (Emily said) 'that he had emptied the dissenting chapels,' as Charlie was trying to do in Grasby.

Then they had two weeks in Cheltenham with Alfred's mother and took Matilda, his youngest sister, back to Twickenham with them on 16 June. The baby was due in two months, but still Alfred could not settle down – and they were expecting to hear about another possible house. Emily mentioned it in a letter to Mrs Cameron on 25 June after a happy outing together to Kew Gardens, not far away – but added 'I am not going to drag you house-hunting even on paper'. To James Spedding, her favourite 'infidel', Emily wrote: 'We have most moving tales to tell of bad houses, and bad titles but no hint of some perfect home. I am only afraid of our taking up in despair with an exceedingly imperfect one.' Jane Carlyle told Emily she hoped none of the Gloucestershire houses would be 'feasible – and that you have made peace with the one you are in.' Emily might well have been prepared to do so.

It seemed unlikely that Alfred could make peace with any settled human habitation. On 7 July he was off again. After a night in London with Spedding, he made for Yorkshire. His excuse could not be house hunting in the colder north. His hay fever, which had been bad before he left, was atrocious on the railway, but he could not complain as the one other traveller in his carriage was in an even worse state with gout. He wrote funny long letters every day to Emily. A brawl, a funeral, an election, fossil hunting – Alfred made everything entertaining. Emily was at this stage – just two years after their marriage – still consulting him about spending. She would soon take over the accounts completely. From Whitby he said, 'You can send a sovereign if you like to the sapper and miner, but I think it is very hard that I am obliged to subscribe to all the bad poets' – as if there weren't already enough trash in the world. He was sure 'old Wordey' had been 'far too canny to do so'.

'I have seen no houses here to be sold, but then I have not looked out for them,' he wrote; he was still 'killed with hay fever'. By 22 July he was staying at Grasby with Charles and most of Emily's family. Henry Sellwood – 'Daddy' – took him over to see the new dock at Grimsby, which would have an effect on Frederick's fortune. This statement, in Alfred's letter written at the time, about her father in Lincolnshire contradicts Emily's journal where she says 'my Father remains with me during A's absence'. The discrepancy reminds us yet again of the unreliability of the 'epitome' – the rewriting of the journal after Alfred's death, forty years later, where, in summarizing and abbreviating, Emily often relies on her unreliable memory.

'Pray take drives every day,' Tennyson wrote from Grasby. There was not a great deal else Emily could do as she waited for his return and for the arrival of the longed-for child. She did arrange for a silver cup for their godson, Tennyson Patmore, in time for his first birthday. ('It was her thought, not mine,' Tennyson admitted to the Patmores.) She had no wish to entertain people while Alfred was away. Thanking her for a letter welcoming them to England, Elizabeth Barrett Browning agreed: 'No, of course we would not go down to Twickenham and find you incomplete . . . without Mr Tennyson. There is plenty of time . . . heaps of summer days to choose out of . . .' In fact, there was less time than they thought; Mrs Browning never got to Twickenham.

Alfred returned to Chapel House early in August. There is a brief glimpse of a visit to the geologist Professor Richard Owen, who had just moved into Sheen Lodge in Richmond Park. The fifth part of his *History of British Fossil Reptiles* appeared that year. Mrs Owen noted in her diary on 6 August: 'Today we had a visit from Alfred Tennyson. His wife sat in the carriage, being in a delicate state of health' – a usual Victorian euphemism for an advanced state of pregnancy. Matilda was still with them, which may well have been a mixed blessing. 'Miss Tennyson came in with her brother, who struck me as being a care-marked, dark-eyed, rather bilious-looking young man, with spectacles; middle height and rather thin.' So much for the eye-witness description of the 'noble' forty-three-year-old poet, who was over six foot tall.

As a result of the tragedy in April the year before, the plan had been for the Tennysons to move into lodgings at 37 South Street, Grosvenor Square, on 15 August 1852, a few days before the new child was due. There the birth could be easily attended by a 'great London doctor'. Emily wrote to Elizabeth Barrett Browning on 9 August, inviting them to come to dinner on the 13th. 'My Doctor names the 15th as the latest day on which I may move to town.' But two days after she had written, in the early morning of 11 August Emily went into labour at Chapel House. Mrs Cameron, alerted perhaps by young Thomas Metcalfe, the Tennysons' errand boy, apparently rushed off for Dr Anderson, 'the great London accoucheur'. 'Never till the hour of my death', Tennyson said, would he forget her 'great kindness . . . in the hour of my trouble'. He found a moment to write to the Brownings, putting off the dinner party: 'My wife is at this moment in labour.' Two doctors arrived in plenty of time. Dr Anderson was sure there was still a long way to go, that 'it would not come off till the afternoon'. But immediately the midwife was left alone with Emily she went into the final stages of labour. At '9½ a.m.' she was delivered of 'a fine boy', after 'a very easy confinement'. Alfred saw her and their son immediately, and then started writing to tell everyone the joyful news.

Tennyson wrote first to Kate Rawnsley at Shiplake, whom Emily and Alfred would always see as so largely involved in their happiness. He dated his letter 'half past nine a.m.' on 11 August, the very hour at which he told Aunt Russell the boy had been born. 'She got on very well with a nurse,' he wrote to Kate, 'Both she and the child are at present likely to do well. She *does* look so pleased!' To Elizabeth Barrett Browning, Alfred wrote, 'I never saw any face so radiant.' To John Forster he wrote immediately too, remembering how hurt he had been at not being told beforehand of the marriage. Alfred wrote more letters at this time, Emily would tell James Spedding, 'than ever he wrote his whole life before'. He told Forster:

Now I will tell you of the birth of a little son this day. I have seen beautiful things in my life, but I never saw anything more beautiful than the mother's face as she lay by the young child an hour or two after, or heard anything sweeter than the little lamblike bleat of the young one. I had fancied that children after birth had been all shriek and roar; but he gave out a little note of satisfaction every now and then, as he lay by his mother, which was the most pathetic sound in its helplessness I ever listened to. You see I talk almost like a bachelor, yet unused to these things . . .

Alfred soon became very used to being a father, inevitably a rather unconventional one for the period. Robert Browning, that other poetic, unconventional father, wrote: 'How happy I am in your happiness and in the assurance that it is greater than even you can quite know yet.'

'From the first', Emily said, Alfred watched the baby with 'profound and loving interest'. When there were no guests, he would take the baby in his bassinet into the drawing room, so that they might all enjoy each other's company. 'Some of his acquaintances would have smiled to see him racing up and down stairs and dandling the baby in his arms.' Tennyson was totally involved with his son from the beginning. On one occasion Emily wrote to the Brookfields, home from Madeira and wanting to show off their own new baby: 'Alfred would have enjoyed that meeting with you, but he was so good as to stay home and help nurse *our* baby.'

That was written the following year and there would be, as Browning saw, more and more happiness for them all. But the euphoria, as so often happens, was a little muted in the difficult second week. Alfred reported to Aubrey de Vere that they had a really terrible night – with Alfred trying to soothe Emily while the baby wailed 'his hard fate – which was not yet so hard as his mother's who suffers from an almost total want of sleep.' The wretched child set up a roar 'if he cannot get the milk in a moment out of the breast' and a terrible lamentation when Emily tried to brush 'his little demi-bald sconce' 'with a brush that would not bruise a midge'. The nurse tried to reassure these first-time parents by insisting that he was 'a very quiet child as children go', but Martha Milnes, the cook, cannot have helped by suggesting he was not nearly as splendid a baby as his 'poor little silent elder brother'. 'She thinks he looks so much less like the son of a king.' To Richard Monckton Milnes Alfred wrote, 'I was rather wishing for a little girl . . . Well, we will take the goods the gods provide us and be grateful.'

And they were indeed grateful and amazed. Tennyson said he had thought that the old painters overdid the expression and dignity of their Infant Christs, but now he could see that they did not. On their child's third day, Tennyson had gone into the nursery to look at him as he was lying alone and 'while I was looking at him I saw him looking at me with such apparently earnest wide open eyes I felt as awestruck as if I had seen a spirit.' It may well have been at this moment that the words that would become part of the poem 'De Profundis' came into the poet's mind: 'Out of the deep, my child, out of the deep . . .' After the 'nine long months of ante-natal gloom,' had come to them,

> a babe in lineament and limb
> Perfect, and prophet of the perfect man;
> Whose face and form are hers and mine in one,
> Indissolubly married like our love; . . .
>
> Out of the deep, Spirit, out of the deep,
> With this ninth moon, that sends the hidden sun
> Down yon dark sea, thou comest, darling boy.

There was some disagreement about that darling boy's name. Emily wanted 'Alfred', in spite of Alfred's insistence that it would interfere with their son's 'sense of personal identity' and cause 'double trouble in signatures etc all his life'. 'I cannot resist my desire to add the name of my old friend Hallam,' Tennyson said. When it came to the point, he was simply Hallam. 'They will not let me call him Alfred,' Emily told James Spedding.

Henry Hallam, Arthur's father, was approached and asked if he would be one of the godfathers of little Hallam Tennyson. He was happy to accept. 'That the names of Hallam and Tennyson should be united in the person of this infant will be to me a gratifying reflection for the remainder of my days.' The sad old man (only one of his own eleven children still alive) could joke that they would not call him Alfred 'because they were afraid he might be a fool'. Emily recorded this in her journal, but in fact, of course, nothing was further from their thoughts. William Allingham, calling at Chapel House on the day the child was born, saw that there was every chance he would be a remarkable boy, 'for his father is Tennyson and his mother one of the most love-worthy women in the world.'

Hallam did not seem to realize how lucky he was and was still crying a great deal. Elizabeth Barrett Browning encouraged Emily not to worry, though she admitted that when her own son cried she was always near crying herself. 'Only the fact is these little creatures *will* make much ado about nothing and we are wrong in reading their ills too large through our imaginations.' 'Let me be (why not?)', she signed off, 'affectionately yours always.'

At the end of September Alfred was not at all serene. (Was he ever?) He was worried about 'the state of things at Cheltenham' ('Tennysons never could live together', one of their wives would say years later) and even more about 'Emily and the boy. The first does not seem to get well at all. Perhaps she will have to give up nursing, which will be a great grief to her, and the child from having been walked out (the 2nd time in his bit of a life) on a dampish coldish day, has had what seems to us (fearful ones) a very bad cold. Nose stopt up so that he could scarce suck and mightily indignant he was against the whole order of things in this unjust world.' Then there was an alarming rattling that could have been croup. Emily was tense, which was not surprising, and 'her state reacts on the child. Ah well, we shall get on somehow,' Tennyson said, writing wearily to his Aunt Russell.

Two days later Emily wrote rather a cheerful letter to James Spedding, while admitting the child 'has taken almost all my time and strength'. She asked him to forgive her for writing of 'nothing but babies' and promised: 'I really would not talk much about them if you would come.' She wanted him to come to the christening, but he refused – busy with builders at Mirehouse: 'You will not expect me to think that so much depends on it as many people believe. Whatever my own deficiencies, I please myself with thinking that *he* has already all the immortal longings in him which he has a right to from both parents.'

Emily had told Spedding that 'in order to protect' the small boy 'against all you naughty infidels, we have been constrained to get Maurice to be one of the sponsors.' F.D. Maurice told his friend Charles Kingsley: 'It was to please his wife he asked me.' In fact, in a letter to Kingsley the following year – at the time of Maurice's dismissal from his chair at King's College, London (for unorthodoxy – for Christian Socialism itself), Tennyson showed how much Maurice had been his choice too. 'I will only add that the veneration for Maurice, which induced me to pass by all my family claims and select him as Godfather to my child remains unabated. I may say increased.' Maurice said at the time he was embarrassed to admit how great was his delight in being asked – which had more to do with Tennyson's poetry than anything else. He asked Tennyson to express to Emily how very much he valued 'this proof of her confidence'.

The third godparent (for whom the ceremony was delayed until she had returned from abroad) was Mary Marshall, who had been so good to them at Coniston just after their marriage and indeed had spent time with Emily when she lost her first child. There was an interesting connection between two of the godparents. In June the previous year James Marshall, Mary's husband, had invited Kingsley and Maurice to dinner. 'It is strictly for socialist purposes,' Maurice had said. 'They had 2000 men in their employ and really want to talk with us about them.' The dinner was actually something of a fiasco. James Marshall was 'a very shy man and never dared enter on the subject.' 'Had Mrs Marshall been present, things would have no doubt turned out quite differently.' So there is a suggestion surely that Mary Marshall's friendship with Emily was based on their sympathy for the Christian Socialism so energetically and inspiringly preached by F.D. Maurice. In the *Memoir* forty years later Maurice's godson, Hallam Tennyson, would sadly betray his godfather by not once mentioning his Christian Socialism.

They had a splendid christening party on 5 October 1852, though there were a number of missing guests at what Frederick, eager for a report to Florence, called 'the Baptismal Breakfast of Philosophers and Poets'. Sadly, Elizabeth Barrett Browning, who had delayed returning abroad ('we would not miss the christening for the world'), was not well enough to attend, her cough exacerbated by 'too late lingering in this cold, bitter England'. Charles Dickens very much regretted his inability 'to welcome a young Tennyson'. He would be in Boulogne, working on *Bleak House*, but promised: 'I shall drink his health on the 5th.' The Carlyles' invitation had somehow 'got thrown aside in the hurry of moving'.

The service was in Twickenham Parish Church at half past one. At the solemn moment of dedicating the child to be 'Christ's soldier and servant until his life's end', Emily thought it 'very pretty' to see Hallam's cousin, her three-year-old niece, Agnes Weld, 'kneel down and fold her hands at the font.' At Chapel House they had opened the doors between the dining room and the back room and filled the place with plants. Their cook provided such an excellent spread that people thought it had come from Gunter's, 'and we were very proud'. There were beautiful peaches and 'the best champagne we could get'. Champagne was Emily's favourite drink for most of the rest of her life.

Matilda Tennyson was already staying with them. Charles and Louisa came from Grasby, the Welds from Somerset House and Edmund Lushington from Park House. Charles said: 'There were poets there as thick as blackberries and radiant visions of fair women.' Venables was there and the Brookfields, Francis Palgrave, Aubrey de Vere, Henry Taylor and the Camerons. Drummond Rawnsley came with a haunch of venison ('the best I had ever tasted,' Emily said) – but without Kate, because she had recently produced her sixth child and now with the twins Fanny and Hardwick, born only the previous autumn, had, astonishingly, what Emily called 'three all in arms together'.

Anne Thackeray always remembered her father riding off to the christening on his brown cob, but his name was somehow not on Emily's list – but then neither was Henry Sellwood's, and surely *he* was present. He was at this point living at Grasby. Robert Browning was certainly there. Years later his friend Alfred Domett would record in his diary that Browning had known Hallam Tennyson since he was an infant. 'He was tossing him in his arms on one occasion and Tennyson, who was looking on, remarked "Ah, that's as good as a glass of champagne to him!"' The association with champagne makes one think it might have been at the christening, but a baby of eight weeks old is a bit young for tossing. If he did try it, it might have given rise to a later remark of Alfred's. When Allingham called Browning a *vivid* man, apparently Tennyson responded, 'How he did flourish about when he was here!' Elizabeth Barrett Browning suggests a quite different sort of behaviour. 'I could not go; it was not possible. Robert went alone, therefore, and nursed the baby for ten or twelve minutes, to its obvious contentment, he flatters himself.' That is obviously what he told *her*. Of Tennyson she said, 'I do like men who are not ashamed to be happy beside a cradle.' She was delighted at the joy his letters showed.

As things turned out, the Tennysons could not relax quietly together when the party was over. 'Mr Tom Taylor came next day by mistake,' Emily said. A letter written the following month suggests what she sometimes had to put up with. 'Don't bother yourself', Alfred wrote to Tom Taylor, 'with what happened at Chapel House. Any man (as I told you at the time) might be overset with shag upon port who was not used to the mixture.' Alfred himself was used to it, of course. What actually happened, how much Emily was involved or what she felt, is not revealed.

Alfred had already slipped down to the Isle of Wight to visit his friends there in September – perhaps with the excuse of house hunting, but if so without result on this occasion. It may have been to work further on his poem 'Out of the deep, my child', without the disturbing noises of the child himself. The poem did not come easily; it was not published until the child was long grown up. It was the poem Emily wanted to bear Hallam's name in the edition published after Tennyson's death. With the Duke of Wellington's death in that September of 1852, the poet put aside the poem celebrating a birth and turned to one marking the funeral on 18 November. Emily recorded that she dreamt of the Duke visiting them. 'I feared the cold hand of death but it proved a warm living hand.'

By the time of the funeral, the Tennysons had fled the floods and mists of Twickenham and 'the choking smell of dying leaves' – for Seaford on the Sussex coast, just west of Beachy Head, between Newhaven and Eastbourne. Hallam's cold continued and Emily had caught one at the christening. Sea air and the possibility of sunshine seemed a good idea. 'Yet I have been so happy here I do not want to go,' Emily wrote to James Spedding just before they left Twickenham, even as she struggled with a pile of 'bills and such disagreeable things'.

In Seaford they took a comfortable house by the sea – 'far from

Skeggie bareness and desolation,' Emily said, as if she had never really appreciated the uningratiating Lincolnshire coast. The garden was delightful with ivy-covered arches, urns and vases and balustrades, and the weather so mild that the scarlet geraniums were not taken out of the ground until it was already December.

'Twickenham is still our home,' Emily said, as they had not yet found a permanent alternative. But Seaford gave them a taste for exactly the sort of place in which they would eventually settle. She told one friend: 'I could live very contentedly here all my life looking on the sea and the headland and the bit of down.' To Frederick in Florence she wrote that the house 'looks pleasantly on sea and down, which has been fortunate for us since I, at least, have scarcely left the garden, the weather has been so stormy. The sea therefore of course fine. Great white-headed waves leaping up every moment from behind the shingle bank.' Malvern and such places seemed very tame. From now on, they would hope for sea views, though Alfred, gazing across the Channel, would still worry about invasion.

'The Ode on the Death of the Duke of Wellington' had taken Tennyson himself up to town – one note to Emily was scribbled 'at Dick's Tavern by Temple Bar where I dine' – but she had plenty of company at Seaford. Matilda was still with them, and Charles and Louisa came 'for two or three weeks'. (Charles seems to have been able to leave his parish whenever he liked.) Edward Lear, who had received his christening invitation too late to join them, came flying over the downs from Brighton, carrying in his carpet bag what Emily rather mysteriously described as a 'Roman Catholic doll' for Hallam – simply because Alfred had said that up to then the baby had enjoyed only 'the pure Protestant worship of morning light on the bed-post'. And now here he was with his first doll – an idol. They moved Hallam around to give him a variety of things to look at, as parents do. 'What a life of wonder,' Alfred said. 'Every object new.'

Lear had wanted to talk to Emily 'as soon as I thought you could think of any matters beyond the baby.' He wanted to discuss a project he had had in mind for 'a long while past' – a huge and challenging plan to illustrate Tennyson's poems 'so far as the landscape therein set forth admits of,' he said rather awkwardly. He had written out a lot of important lines and thought there might be '124 subjects in 2 volumes' – that was without either *The Princess* or *In Memoriam*. He was writing from the farm near Hastings where he was working with Holman Hunt

and his long letter contained the postcript 'I am becoming a Pre-Raphaelite'. He could not help thinking 'No-one could illustrate Tennyson's landscape lines and feelings more aptly than I could do,' but then, characteristically, he wondered if his 'powers of execution' were really equal to the task – and there were paintings he had to finish first.

Alfred was himself at this point attempting to draw his son's wonderful 'leg and arm' on a letter to Frederick in Florence, mostly written by Emily – only to find that the place where he had drawn was meant for the address. 'What if your Italians take the delineations to be political? PS I have spoilt the leg and arm (as well as I could) with the direction. I wish you could hear him shout.' He was a remarkable child already of course 'with a beautiful face for a mere babe'. Presented with one of his historian godfather's books, 'he seems more inclined to put the contents into his mouth than into his head,' but that was only natural. He was already enjoying 'walks near the sea and to Alfriston' with his nursemaid, Eliza Jeffries.

That December of 1852 Emily's name seems to have got into the papers in connection with an American petition, which she had actually not signed. It is best to give the story in her own words.

I expressly stated I thought the petition might possibly exasperate [*sic*] the evils, rather than diminish them and I have not signed and will not sign it. They should not have taken such unfair advantage of my saying I felt much interested in the subject. They ought only to have put my name to some general expression of such interest. However, it is best to let such things pass quietly, for with my whole heart I hate the idea of women obtruding themselves into Public affairs, and I do not wish to call anyone's attention to the fact of my name appearing as if I had been meddling with them. The only women who have anything to do with them further than thinking and feeling about them at home are heiresses who represent families. These I think should, when they have large estates, be allowed to have proxies in the House of Lords if noble, and proxies for votes if Commoners, or the interests of many may suffer.

So this was how Emily felt about votes for women in 1852. There would come a time when she could feel the need for a rather more active role in public affairs than 'thinking and feeling about them'.

They spent Christmas at Seaford. Just afterwards Edward FitzGerald visited them. (He had spent Christmas with his mother close by in Brighton.) He admired the baby and said that 'Alfred nurses him with humour and majesty'. As for Emily, he told Elizabeth Cowell, who had got on so well with her at Twickenham: 'As heroines go, I dare say she'll do as well for you as many another.' He was not himself quite sure she was the right wife for Tennyson, though it was twenty years later that he decided: 'An old Housekeeper like Molière's would have been far better for him, I think,' feeling that Emily's uncritical adoration had damaged Tennyson's poetry. On another occasion he wrote that, as far as his poetry went, Alfred might have done better to have remained 'single in Lincolnshire or married a jolly woman who would have laughed and cried without any reason why.' It was an odd thing for Fitz to write – but then he often wrote odd things. As we saw, he did not think much of either *The Princess* or *In Memoriam*, both written before the marriage. Indeed in the same letter in which he thought how good for Tennyson an old Housekeeper would have been he admitted: 'I can care nothing for his Poems since his two volumes in 1842', though he would admire parts of *Maud*. In 1853 he wrote that he 'nurses his Child delightfully. But he will never write Poetry again, as I believe. I mean such Poetry as he was born to write.' FitzGerald was always influenced by his feeling that Tennyson 'never writes, nor indeed cares a halfpenny about one though he is very well satisfied to see one when one falls in his way.' When Emily wrote to him, Fitz would feel how much rather he'd have had a letter from Alfred, rather than feeling that if Emily had not written, he would not have had a letter at all. To the Tennysons, FitzGerald remained 'dear old Fitz', however little they saw of him.

Early in 1853 they took a house in Marine Parade, Brighton, mainly because the Marshalls were there. Samuel Rogers, the aged poet, was there too and they took Hallam to visit him (when he had calmed down from his vaccination). They wanted to be able to tell the boy that he had met the poet. It was 'an interesting link' between the generations and made Emily think of the time when as a girl she had danced with the man who had married Byron's first love. Rogers kissed Hallam and said to Emily 'in his courtly way': 'Mrs Tennyson I made one great mistake in my life. I never married.'

They were back in Twickenham in February, but not feeling at all settled, though they had managed to acquire an excellent nurse for Hallam, Frances Gandy, 'fully capable of undertaking the entire management of a child seven months old'. In fact she would hardly get the chance to have overall control with such involved parents close at hand. It did not help when Edmund wrote on 31 March from Park House: 'Have you devised any means of getting away from that abominable Twickenham? I am very anxious to hear that you have, the sooner the better.' He felt sure Tennyson could not work properly until they were settled somewhere permanently.

All their friends seemed to be looking for the perfect home for them, though Spedding said there was no-one 'who knows less about the qualities of a house than I do'. Edward FitzGerald was also keeping his eyes open, though he knew they were 'afraid' of the east coast. 'Are you any nearer *fixing*?' he would ask. In spite of its lack of sea views, they were still attracted to the Farnham area and spent a little time there in the spring. Alfred walked over to Hale and 'looked into the old premises', and Emily had a chance to meet for the first time Charles Kingsley's wife.

As so many people did, Fanny Kingsley took immediately to Emily and wrote the next day: 'Your face is continually before me and so is the thought of your child. I cannot believe that I saw you yesterday for the first time. It seemed so very natural to me to know and to love you.' There was talk of Hallam's worrying lack of interest in solids – Fanny recommended a special kind of biscuit, obtainable in St Martin's Lane, which might suit the 'precious Babe'.

There must also have been talk of Maurice's *Theological Essays*, which had just been published to an outcry. Kingsley himself remained intensely loyal: 'I was utterly astonished at finding in page after page things which I had thought and hardly dared to confess to myself, much less to preach.' Now, he said, he would speak 'more and more boldly'. The Tennysons too remained totally loyal to their son's godfather. He had asked them to accept the book 'as a present to one of your name, in whom you have given me a very sacred interest'. Back in the Lincoln-shire days, all the Tennysons had 'digested' the 'admirable ethics' of Maurice's novel *Eustace Conway*, which James Spedding had given to Charles. On the return of it to its rightful owner, Charles had inscribed the book saying that, deprived of it, his 'careless' siblings had left 'their clerical brother to the exploded morality of all other centuries and treatises'. Now, nearly twenty years later, Maurice was being labelled crudely as 'the clergyman who didn't believe in Hell'. He would say that he did believe in some sort of hell, but that it was in the hearts and minds of those who cut themselves off from God. He was a Christian Socialist, not primarily because of any political or economic theory, but because he knew the tailors and the shoemakers were, like himself, sons of God. The storm had been gathering long before the publication of his essays, but it was just about to break.

There would be talk of Maurice at Grasby too, where the Tennysons had been invited to spend part of the summer. They had also been invited to Scotland to stay with Robert Monteith. When that invitation came, Tennyson wrote to suggest the expedition would be too expen-sive 'for self, wife, child and nurse'. By the time they got as far as Yorkshire, there was another reason for not travelling further. Emily realized she was expecting another child. They had gone first to Whitby, but it was extremely cold, and they did not stay long. From Redcar, they went across to Richmond. Years later Emily remembered watching with Alfred from high in the town the black fingers of a hailstorm sweeping over the plain from York.

Nobody was inclined to mention it, but it seems likely that Alfred himself – and perhaps Emily too – visited poor, mad Edward Tennyson on this visit to York. They certainly went to a service in York Minster. When she was very old, Emily recalled Hallam 'trying the congregation by crying out "cock a doodle" to the golden eagle' (the lectern), 'and saying good morning to departing worshippers'. A remarkable child, indeed; he would have his first birthday in Grasby a fortnight later. Alfred and Emily said goodbye on York station, for it was decided that Alfred should go on alone, and Emily, Hallam and the nurse, Gandy, would stay with Louisa and Charles – and Emily's father – in Lincolnshire. Alfred told Emily in his first letter that 'one of the guards at York spoke to me commiserating you and your looks at parting.' Emily was not inclined to hide her feelings.

'I did not get further north than Richmond in Yorkshire, not having been well enough to go with Alfred into Scotland,' Emily wrote to Spedding. 'He, poor soul, had small enjoyment of his sojourn there as he was shut up for three weeks under a doctor in Edinburgh.' It was in Edinburgh this August that Alfred wrote his 'Daisy' poem for Emily, missing her, 'when ill and weary, alone and cold' in that 'gray metropolis'.

Before these three weeks stuck in Edinburgh – after chloroform and an operation on a painful toe, presumably similar to the one he had had on his honeymoon – Alfred had travelled with Francis Palgrave and sent quantities of sweet letters to Grasby. One day he left out 'dearest', 'not liking to write it with people looking over one's shoulder' in the crowded public room of a hotel, and meaning to add it afterwards. 'Perhaps it has hurt thee and if so I am vext at myself.' On his birthday he met a three-months-old baby by the Sound of Mull and remarked that, though he was a very pretty one, he was 'not however near so pretty as ours was at his age'.

Hallam celebrated his first birthday surrounded by relations – his mother, his grandfather, his double-aunt and double-uncle. It was Emily's first visit to Grasby since before her sister's separation from Tennyson's brother, the first visit since the new Vicarage was built, where Charles and Louisa would spend most of the rest of their lives, until the last terrible time. It is a pleasant house, looking more Georgian than Victorian. Alfred called it 'a nice little place'. It was 'built at the foot of a high chalk ridge or wold, that ran like a backbone across the wide valley over which it commanded a magnificent view', some say to Lincoln Cathedral, twenty-five miles away, on a really clear day. The house has its back to the lane from the church and faces south over lawns and meadows. Already in 1853 there were roses and honeysuckle and clematis beginning to climb up the soft brick walls.

Beyond the vicarage gardens, Grasby remained a primitive place.

Agnes Weld, the niece, would tell years later of villagers, who, thinking a Sunday School teacher was actually a witch, 'finally killed her by a course of petty persecutions'. She told of people who believed in every sort of superstition, procuring the jaw of a female hedgehog as a cure for rheumatism, stealing sheep and cutting them in half on a scarlet cloth, waving branches of the rowan tree and even, perhaps, believing that the Baptists left their 'nasty sins' in the pond, and poisoned the cows.

Agnes said that on her long annual visits to her Uncle Charles and Aunt Louisa, 'I saw how ungrudgingly the gifts that would have made them shine in the most intellectual society were turned to the service of the poor villagers among whom their lot was cast.' Agnes did not report and Emily never mentioned the stresses and tensions between Louisa and Charles. They presumably did not know of her confessions, of the awful catalogue of sins and failings that Louisa scribbled continually in her memorandum books and on loose undated pages. 'I have not shewn my charity to those who stand in need and grudged what I did.' 'I have been harsh and cruel.' 'I have profaned the holy feast of Sunday.' 'I have not laboured to subdue my body but have pampered it.' 'I have been desirous to seem better than I am.' At least once she wrote: 'I am guilty of secret murder. I have wished Ch. death.' And it was probably on this visit in August 1853 that Louisa wrote: 'Did not come up to pray before lunch for fear of keeping E. waiting. She kept me waiting a long time . . . Constant judging and despising E. Perpetual murmuring at cold and accusing E. . . .'

On the surface certainly everything seemed fine in that chilly Lincolnshire summer. Was sad Louisa jealous of Emily's joy in her baby? Everyone else was delighted with little Hallam Tennyson. One of the Turners' servants, Pleasance Parkinson, was extremely taken with Emily and Alfred (who had been there the year before and now re-joined his family after his visit to Scotland). When Pleasance married a pig dealer, not long after this visit, she called two of her children after them: Emily and Alfred.

Emily was devoted to her sister, whatever might be going on in Louisa's mind. She was constantly concerned for her; there is no doubt about that. All through Louisa's life, when they were apart, Emily wrote to her regularly, though few of the letters have survived. One summer, for instance, Edmund Lushington refers to the fact that, while Charlie and Louisa are at Sandgate, Louisa is 'writing and hearing from you almost daily'. Edmund found much 'to admire and love' in Louisa, he told one of his sisters.

Frederick Tennyson was over from Italy in that summer of 1853 to make arrangements for the publication of his *Days and Hours*. He too joined them all at Grasby. So the three poet brothers were together in Lincolnshire again. Frederick had left his thirteen-year-old son Giulio with his grandmother's household now at Sion Row in Twickenham. One of that young Italian Tennyson's letters home to Florence has survived. But what did he really make of them all, meeting them in Twickenham? We have a report from William Allingham that November. He met Frederick and Edward FitzGerald on the doorstep of Chapel House. Tennyson had warned Allingham that Emily was not very well (she was now five months pregnant) and he found her pale, but also sweet and kind and particularly amused by Fitz's 'droll stories'. Tennyson carried Hallam to meet the men and the child amused himself – and them – by repeatedly dropping his ball on the floor with exclamations of satisfaction and delight at making the adults fetch it for him.

There is also a vivid glimpse this year of Horatio, Alfred's youngest brother, back from Australia and living again with his mother and aunt and his sister Tilly (Septimus too, from time to time), although he was now in his thirties. He writes to his sister Emily Jesse in Margate, after she has told him that her new baby, Eustace, is very like him to look at. Horatio tells her he can't visit her because of a 'want of the "Ready"' and bitterly laments the ill fortune of little Eustace: 'Is it black and pronounced with a look as if it had swallowed a draught of aloes? . . . Poor little devil! Let's hope not, let's hope it has a good dash of the Jesse to qualify the heavy leaven of the Tennysons – a little of the sprightly blood of the former House to quicken the black and sullen circulation of the "House of Tennyson". . .'

Henry Hallam also wrote to Emily Jesse about the new baby. He told her he had seen Alfred Tennyson at dinner recently. He was 'talking of buying a house. I think he should rent one first – he is not quite sure of keeping his mind.' Hallam did not think Tennyson was going mad. He merely thought that, after the way he had changed his mind about Warninglid and Twickenham, it would be as well to rent first.

On another visit to his friends in Bonchurch on the Isle of Wight Tennyson had seen – on a miserable October day – a house called Farringford near Freshwater Bay. It looked rather 'wretched with wet leaves trampled into the lawns.' But he liked it so much that, on his return to Twickenham, Emily wrote with a low offer for the freehold. The owner, the Reverend George Seymour, rejected the offer in a letter to Emily on 29 October, which shows how nearly the whole thing fell through before she had even seen the house. He produced a beautifully simple calculation. The rent of the house and ten acres of ground, including the garden, was £80 a year; 'The Park-side lets for 70 pounds.' That was a total rent of a £150. For the purchase price he multiplied it by thirty years and came up with £4,500. He agreed the house was looking a little neglected and not improved by 'the extra-ordinary growth of all the trees round the house' since the Seymours had lived there three years before. Turning down their offer, he said he would therefore 'consider anything further regarding it as terminated.' He regretted Tennyson had had a wet 'journey here for nothing'.

Farringford now seemed more desirable than ever. The privacy the trees provided was one of its attractions. To be concealed and yet to be able to see downs and cliffs and the sea itself – where would they ever find another place like it? The draft of Emily's further letter on 31 October shows much crossing-out, many second thoughts. They would suggest renting Farringford 'for one two or three years with an option of purchasing'. They would ask that if they did decide to buy 'the rent should be included in the £4500'. 'With these views,' Emily wrote, 'is it worthwhile he should come again to look at Farringford?'

Seymour agreed they should look at it together. The 'wretched house-hunting business' was nearly over. Emily wrote in her journal:

The railway did not go further than Brockenhurst then and the steamer, when there was one from Lymington, felt itself in no way bound to wait for the omnibus which brought as many passengers as it could from the train. We crossed in an open rowing boat. It was a still November evening. One dark heron flew over the Solent backed by a daffodil sky.

Was that Emily's phrase, that 'daffodil sky'? Or did Alfred describe the sky like that as they crossed the water? Did Emily write it in her diary in 1853 or add it only later after Alfred had written the line in 'Maud' – 'Beginning to faint in the light that she loves On a bed of daffodil sky . . .' It is impossible to know.

They landed at the little port of Yarmouth in the north-west of the island and stayed at Plumbley's Hotel in Freshwater, three and a half miles from the port and not far from the house. Freshwater, in those days, was not much more than a few houses and two hotels at the Bay, and a few more houses round the church by the river, with scattered farms and cottages on the lanes between them. The following day they were shown round Farringford. Looking from the drawing-room window, Emily thought, 'I must have that view'. She said so to Alfred, when they were alone. Emily had not seen either the Warninglid or the Twickenham houses before the agreements were concluded. Both times that had been because she had been heavily pregnant. So she was in November 1853; the third child was due in March. But she braved the long journey and open boat to make sure that this time they got things right.

On 8 November they were close to 'concluding what seems a perilous bargain,' as Tennyson put it. Emily said, 'I think it is really settled we take Farringford for three years with the option of purchasing it . . . I say think because the owner seems of changeable mind. We have settled the matter as far as we are concerned.' The agreement with the Reverend George Seymour is in Emily's hand, with a few additions by Seymour's solicitor and Tennyson's signature at the end. The annual rent was fixed at £104 payable half-yearly, plus 'all rates and taxes'. It was more than twice what Tennyson had been paying for Chapel House. (His mother agreed to take over that lease.) Farringford was furnished too, which was not really what he wanted. But the great thing was the option, built into the agreement, of buying at the fixed sum of £4,350, at any point during the three years of the tenancy.

On 25 November 1853 ('a great day for us') they moved into Farringford, the house that would be home to Emily for the rest of her life; 'the dearest spot on earth', she called it. Not everyone was pleased with their choice. John Ruskin grumbled: 'I don't believe in chalk and sand – and you have nothing else in the Isle of Wight.' He suggested they should have built their house on a rock or at least acquired 'a *granite* habitation', and one considerably more accessible. Of course the fact that Farringford was 'far from the haunts of men' was one of its great attractions. Tennyson had told Milnes that what he wanted was 'utter solitude in some country house'. Part of him wanted that certainly. 'In this lovely place', he told Moxon, with mixed feelings, 'one has nothing to look at but sea and stars'. Emily knew how much he also needed people, distraction, stimulation.

What Emily hoped was that the barrier of the Solent would mean they could choose who came and who did not. ('Has he invaded the Island yet?' FitzGerald would ask, speaking of Palgrave.) Sadly some of the visitors they most wanted (Spedding, Venables, the Brownings, Gladstone, FitzGerald himself) came rarely, if at all, put off by the distance. 'We feel there is one friend at least,' Emily said gratefully to Thomas Woolner, 'who does not find the Solent a Lethe.' There would always be, year after year (and more and more as the years went on), self-invited guests – Emily sometimes felt she was running a private hotel. There would always be some who called without any warning at all, with letters of introduction, or without. 'I wish we could lend you some of our company,' Emily would write to Mrs Gatty in 1859, 'since you say you sometimes feel the want of a little more.' One of their problems would be that the Isle of Wight was becoming more and more popular as a holiday place, made fashionable by Queen Victoria's residence at Osborne. Alfred would still grumble sometimes about living in 'such an out of the way corner'. He would apologize for its dullness (especially 'for a London man with no fishing') while boasting that it was indeed 'the prettiest place I know on this southern coast and only has to be seen to be appreciated'.

The view Emily saw from the drawing-room window was of Afton Down and Freshwater Bay and the long southern coastline of the island with St Catherine's lighthouse in the far distance. Again and again, visitors mention that view – the capes and the sea framed in 'the dear dark arched bow window'. Equally remarkable were the walks and sights that lay close at hand. There was a door in the garden wall behind the house and, beyond it, crossing a lane that led to the nearby farm, a path over the field called Maiden's Croft. Beyond that was the High Down (now known as Tennyson's Down), with the chalk cliffs – five hundred feet in places, plunging sheer to the sea, far below the wheeling gulls.

The house itself was very pretty but unpretentious. It would turn out to be not quite big enough, not for house parties anyway. 'We are very badly off for bedrooms,' Emily once told Venables. Already in 1853 the walls were covered in ivy and magnolia. It seemed to be part of the landscape, 'half hid in the gleaming wood' – as the brick boxes, which would spring up in Freshwater over the years, could never be. The picture overleaf, with its long greenhouse, dates from before the Waterhouse extensions in 1871.

Farringford had been built around 1806 and an engraving soon after shows a small Georgian country house, on an unrecognizably bare hillside, but already with some castellation and the Gothic windows. In the year of Waterloo, an ilex had been planted 'on a grassy island outside the front door' and nearly forty years later, when the Tennysons came, it screened that side of the house. There were enormous elm trees too, and a great cedar – trees cherished by the Tennysons, however much light they shut out of their rooms.

The place was always beautiful, 'but perhaps it is most beautiful in the spring when the woods are full of anemones and primroses; narcissus grows wild in the lower fields; a lovely creamy stream of flowers flows along the lanes; and then with a later burst of glory, comes the gorse, lighting up the country round about and blazing round the Beacon Hill. From High Down . . . you come at last to the Needles, and may look down upon the ridge of rocks that rise crisp, sharp, shining, out of the blue wash of fierce delicious waters.' Emily said Alfred would be reading to her and then be 'drawn down to the bay by the loud voice of the sea'. She would enjoy what she could see with her own eyes 'and so many other things with *his*, when he comes back from his walk'.

Seeing Emily burgeoning in the early months of 1854, Alfred would write to Frank Lushington: 'I pray God it be not twins.' It seemed a possibility, thinking of Henry Hallam's grand-daughters and the little Rawnsley pair, Hardwick and Fanny, whom Tennyson had seen when he went to Shiplake before Christmas, to stand as godfather to their even smaller brother, Alfred. Tennyson was worrying about money, as he was so often to do. It is inevitable for the self-employed writer. However temporarily successful, he knows there is no guarantee that it will last. They wanted to be able to buy Farringford, but both book sales and the interest on their shares seemed likely to be affected by the threat of distant war.

They also had problems with the servants. The Milnes sisters obviously thought the Isle of Wight was far too far from Lincolnshire. 'One cannot live without bore and bother of all kinds, daily frettings,' Alfred wrote to his Aunt Russell. He complained about the servants, not only quarrelling among themselves but being inconsiderate to their mistress 'who wanted great kindness' in her condition. He also complained about all the letter writing he had to do. In March 1854 Emily was not in a fit state to protect Alfred from all this 'house bother' – but she intended to make it her life's mission, as the poet's wife, to do just that.

There is a glimpse of happiness that winter in Tennyson's poem for Hallam's godfather, F.D. Maurice, inviting him to visit Farringford in the spring. It is a poem of support for their embattled friend (challenged by 'foaming' churchmen), but also of delight in the garden, the down, the groves of pine, 'far from noise and smoke of town', scandal and war. The godson, himself, now eighteen months, had taken easily to the new life in the country. Emily kept all her life a snowdrop he picked for her on 23 February 1854. On the envelope, she wrote: 'He said Mama when he passed the flowers.'

That spring Emily was frustrated not to be able to walk on the down herself. 'A week or ten days before the birth A. procured a small carriage in the village in which I could lie down.' It would prove a source of pleasure for years to come. Emily would also sit out, even in early March, in a 'bower of rushes' Alfred had made for her in the sheltered kitchen garden, where she said 'it was always warm'. But there was an ominous noise from the fort on Golden Hill – 'the sound of cannon practising for the Crimea'.

The papers were full of martial alarms. When the new child was born on the evening of 16 March, around nine o'clock, Tennyson was observing the night sky. 'Mars was culminating in the Lion,' he wrote in one of the letters announcing the birth. Emily wrote in her diary: 'This afterwards determined us to give our baby the name of Lionel.' The child was 'a strong and stout young fellow', another 'fine lusty boy'.

Emily was delighted with this son. When, nearly forty years later, Hallam himself had a second son, she said that it was: 'A great blessing – for an only son is a perilous gift, both for his own sake and his parents.'

'Emily has had a good deal of pain but no more I believe than is very common on such occasions,' Alfred told Emily's sister Anne Weld. Two days later he told Mrs Cameron he thought she had suffered rather *more* than is common. She was finding it difficult to sleep but Tennyson had at last been able to 'set her right by mesmerising', using the techniques he had learnt in Malvern, and Emily thought it had 'done her a great deal of good'. 'As for the little fellow, he is as jolly as can be.'

Tennyson described Hallam's first encounters with his small brother. 'He kissed him very reverently, then began to bleat in imitation of his cries; and once looking at him he began to weep, Heaven knows why: children are such mysterious things. I don't think the younger one will turn out such a noble child as Hallam but who can tell.' Predictions are often self-fulfilling, and would be in this case.

The family was complete. The home was found – if not yet bought. It was over ten years since Tennyson, revising an old poem 'The Miller's Daughter', had written some lines which now at last in 1854 seemed to have reality for him:

> The kiss,
> The woven arms, seem but to be
> Weak symbols of the settled bliss,
> The comfort, I have found in thee:
> But that God bless thee, dear – who wrought
> Two spirits to one equal mind –
> With blessings beyond hope or thought,
> With blessings which no words can find.

CHAPTER EIGHT

'Equally mated'

'People say they are winning children,' Emily wrote to Julia Margaret Cameron, who was still living in London in the 1850s. 'What would I do if I had not a poet's heart to share my feelings for the children?' What indeed would she have done? But the joy was that Alfred was as totally devoted as she was. They were united in their wish that the boys should have as happy a childhood as was possible. Alfred had bad memories of 'the brutality of old country nurses', of the Louth school at seven, bullied and kicked, as well as of other less mentionable violence. Emily remembered herself, at times it seemed so long ago that it hardly was herself, smarting – good child though she was – from the pricks of Aunt Betsy's needle.

Emily worried, naturally, about her children's health, both physical and mental. When they were three and a half and just five, she wrote to Elizabeth Barrett Browning (mother also of a precious child):

Yes, I do hope to see your little boy very soon. Our boys are healthy and merry and quite simple children with small inclination for anything but play and I feel it should at present be indulged, that they may have what chance we can give them of gaining strength to bear the weight of over – very, I will not say over – sensitive nerves that may have descended to them and that many signs make me believe have descended, and I cannot wish it otherwise.

She could not wish it otherwise; they were their father's true sons. Writing about the Somersby young, years later in her Narrative, Emily would describe the 'shattered nerves' of those earlier Tennyson brothers – Hallam would change 'shattered' to 'sensitive' in publishing the phrase. Sensitivity can bring rewards as well as pain. But what of the 'black blood' coursing through those little veins?

The weight of their parents' concern never seemed to afflict the happy boys. Observer after observer comments not only on their beauty but on their high spirits and their joy in life. One of the Bradley daughters, Edith, would write: 'I have never known a happier boyhood than that of those boys. Quarrels and discontents found no place at Farringford . . . This is no late idealization; we children knew it at the time.' Aubrey de Vere, who had now become a Roman Catholic, stayed at Farringford for two weeks in the summer of 1854 and was struck by Hallam's eyes – 'the most beautiful and the most contemplative I had ever seen.' He decided that Hallam would grow up to be a Carthusian monk. 'Nothing of the sort,' Emily retorted, 'but a happy husband and a happy father in a happy home.'

De Vere saw Farringford indeed as entirely happy – but Alfred had written to Coventry Patmore just a month or two earlier: 'When you call me a happy man you lie. I have had vexations enough since I came here to break my back.' There would always be vexations, however much Emily, as she got stronger after Lionel's birth, would try to shield him from them.

Emily wisely kept vexations and fears away from the children. 'God wills us to be happy – I often think one is not told of joy as a Christian virtue, as one ought to be.' Rejoicing in the boys – but seeing them as vulnerable possessions – Emily once wrote to Thomas Woolner, the young sculptor she and Alfred were encouraging: 'It is a shame that one should allow the very richness of one's possessions to disturb one, very faithless, I know . . . There can be no pale face that one does not think death is at the door, scarcely a little childish fault that one does not conjure up something worse far, a base life . . .'

At times she was worried. But mostly – trusting God as she really did – she seems to have been extraordinarily relaxed and her sons thrived on the unconventional pattern of their lives and saw far, far more of their parents than was usual at this period. It was one of Emily's triumphs that the boys grew up, for all their parents' adoration and spoiling (in the usual use of that word), completely unspoilt.

They were not always easy to manage, of course. Emily admitted as much in letters to Alfred when he was away, as he quite often was. There is a vivid scene when Lionel is four and Hallam five and they have just heard that Franklin Lushington is coming to see them. 'They took to beating me and kissing me and pulling all my hair over my shoulders calling out, "I am so glad, I am so glad," in the most crazy fashion.' She begs Alfred to bring home a 'dissected map of Europe' – a jigsaw puzzle – something new to hold their attention and calm them down.

Emily once wrote down Tennyson's views on how to handle children. 'Give as few commands as possible and if a child be stubborn about anything, divert his attention and wean him round to an obedience without tearfulness. The open effort and struggle to break the self-will of a child and beat him in the conflict makes his self-will stronger.' Tennyson questioned Plato's saying that 'of all wild beasts boys were the most unmanageable'. Their boys were managed with kisses, with diversions and uninhibited devotion. Emily would say: 'I do not think that anyone who has not had children can quite realize how much more painful it is to inflict even the simplest punishment on a child than it can be for the child to bear it. But the more loving the Mother the less she dare let a child' be unreproved. Hallam only once remembered being punished – and then in the mildest way – for some small discourtesy to a servant.

Both parents believed in 'the divine nature of childhood' and had little time for notions of original sin. They cherished their children's capacity for wonder, their curiosity, their trust and optimism. Curious once about whether the clouds were slippery, small Hallam said thoughtfully, 'I ought to know,' sure that he had come trailing clouds of glory from heaven which is our home. His awareness, at five, of his parents' devotion and unity is well suggested by another story. Emily wrote in her journal: 'I was telling Hallam what twins meant, saying that they came into the world together, that he came alone, that Lionel did, that I did, upon which he indignantly replied, 'Not *you*, you came down from Heaven with Papa.'

It was undoubtedly very good for the boys that they were not the entire focus of Emily's life. She was, in a real sense, a working mother. She saw herself like that and the neighbours understood the situation: 'They know I have too much to do to pay visits often.' She also, as did her neighbours themselves, ran her household and that could often be a complicated business, with huge numbers of visitors coming and going, not only eating large meals, but very often staying in the house. Emily would comment that she and Alfred had scarcely had an evening alone together in six months, which was not at all the way she really wanted life to be.

Even when they were alone, the house hummed with servants. By the time of the 1861 Census, the Tennysons had seven servants living in the house, including the 'first rate gardener', Charles Heard, a fifteen-year-old 'page' or odd-job boy, the nurse and the cook (the Andrews sisters, Elisabeth and Joanna – known as Annie), and three maids. At one point Emily would say to Alfred, as if it were something on which they entirely agreed, that 'one servant less is many cares the less,' but she felt it a duty to employ as many people as they could afford, however much emotional energy was involved in keeping a large staff happy. Alfred was inclined to suspect them of 'lighting fires with my library', tidying away or even purloining his papers. Allingham famously quoted one servant who described Emily (as so many people did) as an angel, whereas Tennyson himself was merely a 'public writer'.

Emily and Edward Lear saw eye to eye on their treatment of servants, as on so much else. Emily never expressed her feelings about them quite so overtly as Lear, but her practice went along with his. Many of them became close friends and her letters to the boys in the years ahead are full of references to the other occupants of the house. Lear wrote: 'I scout the notion of treating domestics less kindly than horses or dogs' – a too common practice among the English upper classes. 'Even when they are ever so much at fault I think it wiser to try to keep them from total ruin, than be indifferent to their welfare. And if I am laughed at for these ideas and acts, – I don't care for that the 999th part of a spider's nose.' At the end of her life Emily would consider perhaps that her employment policy had made it slightly easier than it might have been to enter the kingdom of heaven. She was acutely aware of Christ's talk about the camel and the eye of the needle. She wrote to her niece, Agnes: 'When I consider the eleven men and all their families and the seven women in constant employ and three others in frequent and the ten farm servants or so and their families, I cannot but feel this is a wholesome way of spending money to give to many every comfort now and means of saving for a time when they cannot earn.'

Emily was certainly a benevolent employer – and sometimes, as Alfred saw, taken advantage of for 'treating a coarse nature *too* kindly'. She would ask Alfred to bring the servants books from London; she would develop a conservatory by the back door, so that they would have vines and roses and myrtles and not flagstones to look out on; she would organize treats and outings for them and ignore as many faults as she could. When she felt the children's nurse, Fanny Gandy, had to go, for persistently favouring Lionel – whom she had had from birth –

over Hallam, Emily found the decision extremely painful. 'Dreary days of discomfort and sadness from parting,' she wrote in her diary – and later relented so far as to allow Gandy to take over as holiday relief, missing the children as she did.

For many nineteenth-century women, running a household was their only commitment. For Emily, it was subsidiary. Her grandson, Charles, would describe her as Tennyson's 'secretary and business manager'. She would herself use the word secretary. Emily always valued 'work' above 'society', not just for herself, but for other women. (And for men too, of course, with the example of those idle Tennyson brothers often in her mind.) Emily told Margaret Gatty, a keen worker (her *Parables from Nature* would soon be in every nursery) that, when 'people are equally mated in any degree', society cannot really do much for them. 'A good field for work is in this case, it seems to me, the greatest boon in life.'

For the next twenty years Emily was often 'overwhelmed with business'. She paid the bills and subscriptions, kept the accounts, and dealt with the entire money side of the marriage most of the time. She found tenants for the various houses they came to own (letting even Farringford itself so they could afford 'the necessary change'); she organized and supervised builders during the extensive additions that would be made in the years to come. She became deeply involved with the Farringford farm when they took it over in 1861. Emily would often consult Alfred – about the rent they should ask for the chalkpit, for instance – but he would say: 'I must leave it in thy hands to manage.' They were very capable hands; Tennyson would one day tell James Mangles that his wife was 'so clever in many things – could do almost anything'. Tennyson knew how lucky he was, however little Lear thought he showed it.

At one point in 1856, when Tennyson was away, Emily reported herself 'binding manuscripts for A and weeding his potatoes'. Soon after she is 'busy planning a new dairy'. Another time he was away she put 'his books in the new shelves' and he was surprised to find them done on his return. There survive a number of catalogues, or library lists, in Emily's hand, different attempts over the years to keep track of where the books were.

When a sudden thaw once brought floods of water through the roof, Emily said to Hallam, 'I am glad Papa is not here to be vexed by it.' She was always protecting him from bother of one sort and another. 'Is it not fortunate,' she wrote in 1856 to Thomas Woolner, 'I have been able to burn some insulting lies apparently from a newspaper sent anonymously to Alfred, and so spare him the sight of them.' She would pounce on abusive letters, but some of them got through. Tennyson would groan through his beard to James Mangles about libellous letters, addressed ' "Miss Alfred, the Poet Laureatess" and worse things than that.' Emily herself had the sustaining belief that one must expect bother in this world, that it was good for her 'in some way or the other' – as an idle, self-indulgent life would not have been. Reading once about the painter, 'poor Turner', she reflected: 'How one wishes one might have done something to soothe his spirit and make his life happy.' That was what she sought to do for Tennyson.

Emily would scheme to spare Tennyson the sight of guests who might bore or annoy him – though very few did, provided he was allowed to read to them. 'I must try and stop his return,' she says at one point when the Jesses are visiting, knowing his brother-in-law's 'chatter would drive him wild'. She would largely take over the burden of his family, not allowing the visits of his strange siblings and their mates to alter his routines. Unmarried Matilda lived with them for years on end.

Emily checked the linen, dealt with beggars, tried, with little success, to keep Alfred clean and tidy. She ordered fish direct from Grimsby (having discovered the Isle of Wight fishmonger procured Grimsby fish via a London wholesaler), and Parian marble from Frank Lushington in Corfu for Woolner's bust of Tennyson, the chippings to be made into marbles for the boys. She kept the wine cellar stocked and checked it regularly. There are many lists in her hand surviving. They consumed a vast amount, though Henry James's later report that Tennyson 'got through a whole bottle of port at a sitting without incommodity' was not always true. In 1863 he would be advised to give it up and Emily had the job of exchanging a quantity for Amontillado, which can hardly have been what the doctor intended.

Emily even sometimes ordered Tennyson's tobacco, much as she encouraged him in his frequent attempts to give up smoking. 'We make a bonfire of leaves and burn the box with all the pipes in it, he having put the last bit of tobacco into his study fire,' Emily wrote on 12 December 1855. 'Cardboard resolves,' his brother Frederick called them.

'I am writing in the greatest hurry in the midst of a thousand things,' Emily told Edward Lear. 'My brain is nearly riven. Proof sheets all around me.' Correcting proofs was part of the real work, that 'greatest boon' she had spoken of to Margaret Gatty: talking over ideas for poems with Alfred, listening to the poems as they were written, discussing them with him (Which line did she prefer? This one or that?), giving the encouragement Tennyson always so badly needed, copying the poems out for the printer, checking the proofs with him. 'It is a labour of love, dearest, and my privilege,' she told him. She would even check over some foreign translations of Tennyson's poems. 'A rather hopeless task', however, she said of one French version of one of the Idylls.

Tennyson disliked writing out his poems. Some poems disappeared entirely because, formed as they were in his head, he never got round to writing them out. 'Many and many a line has gone away on the north wind.' Even more, Tennyson hated making further copies of his poems once he had written them down. Emily spent a great deal of time writing things out for him. On one occasion, she wrote just the first words of every line – as a precaution in case the master copy of 'Enoch Arden' went astray. Tennyson obviously knew his own poem well enough to reconstruct it if necessary from those single words.

Letter writing Emily saw also as a labour of love, something she could do for him. She was a natural writer, if not an elegant one, with her pen running on, just as if she were speaking. But she often found the answering of letters tedious and it was extremely time-consuming. 'Reading, I grieve to say, is nearly impossible. My time is so occupied by the letters that must be written today.' Reading, she told Woolner, 'is so much better for you.' Lear would chide her for spending so much time 'answering fooly people's persecuting pain-provoking pages', but she felt it her duty to try to make sure Tennyson escaped criticism. Emily Jesse once wrote a violent letter to her husband from Farringford about an accusation that Alfred had taken no notice of a poem sent to him by Swinburne (who was *not* just one of the 'twenty million poets of Young England' whose volumes arrived by every post). His sister said the story was a 'wicked fabrication' and added: 'O how vile is human nature.'

His wife herself got into trouble when she answered one letter without due care and attention. She must have blushed to remember it ever afterwards. She wrote to Thomas Woolner:

Pity me! Behold my poor little note meant to be so courteous returned to me by some clown or the other named King who had joined the 'W' and 'K' together Wk so that ... I took the name for 'Whing'. I hope I do not often make mistakes in my letters to these strangers, at all events I have never been accused of any before. I do plead guilty to having looked at no more than the end of the letter at the time of answering it.

She had made two other mistakes in the letter and it had been very foolish of her to rely on a signature and not take a look at the title page of the book J.W. King had sent, but Alfred was so disgusted by King's letter he would not let Emily apologize in his name – 'and of course I will not sanction the man's impertinence by addressing him in my own,' she told Woolner rather surprisingly.

Occasionally a letter written failed to get posted and turned up months later. Lionel, when not quite two, began flying a letter of his mother's as a kite one day when their uncle, Charles Weld, had made one for Hallam. Emily's efficiency improved when Edmund Lushington presented her with a desk – chosen by Frank – full of lettered pigeon-holes; it can now be seen in Lincoln. 'It is of the greatest use to me. Before the burthen of undone work was immeasurable, now it is measurable.' 'My work does not seem so hopeless now that my longing to have it arranged can satisfy itself.'

The work would become more difficult for her to fit in once she started teaching the boys. She taught them herself, with some help from Alfred, until Hallam was eight and Lionel nearly seven. When they were small, she would sometimes write with the children in the room and confess the fact in letters to their father, or to Edward Lear, Benjamin Jowett or Thomas Woolner, all of whom were as devoted to the boys as Emily could wish. 'Very darling chaps indeed,' Lear called them. 'I heard little feet pattering which caused this disconnected sentence,' she wrote to Alfred. Her sentences were quite often a little disconnected, but she got through a dozen letters in a day, sometimes more. She told Lear, 'You know I have generally a hundred letters to write in ten minutes.' Only occasionally did she falter in her task of placating her correspondents, who often felt cheated at being deprived of a letter from their favourite poet or even their dearest friend. Edward FitzGerald and many others had to accept it was either a case of hearing from Emily, or not hearing at all. Before Tennyson's marriage they had generally not heard at all.

Apologizing to J.M.F. Ludlow, a close friend of F.D. Maurice, for the fact that *she* was writing, not Alfred, she said, 'Nothing in the way of written thanks ever comes to anybody in any other way, except when the sun has shone six months together.' Alfred told John Forster, 'I love you all the same tho' I should not write for 100 years.' Many of their friends and relations settled for an occasional correspondence with Emily. Many of the friends, as a result, became as much her friends as his. Woolner would not want to hear from Tennyson himself, knowing that if he wrote he would indulge in such an amount of grumbling 'as would supply *The Times* with enough matter for 12 months of leading articles.'

Even Alfred's brother Frederick, who would later make the only really derogatory remarks about Emily that anyone ever made, was full of admiration for what Emily was taking on. He wrote to Mary Brother-ton, who had asked for an example of Alfred's writing for a devoted admirer: 'I have some difficulty in hunting up an autograph of Alfred's – as he never writes to anyone – making over the whole of his cor-respondence to his unfortunate wife, who really is the best creature in the world and submits without a murmur.' Alfred was not alone in hating to write letters, Frederick said: 'Our family, with the exception of myself, are so little addicted to correspondence that the gravest vicis-situdes, short of death itself, might occur without finding an historian.'

It was in the 1850s that Alfred made his much reported statement that 'I would any day as soon kill a pig as write a letter.' He *did*, of course, write letters and not only his regular bulletins to Emily when he was away. Walt Whitman said of one letter that it was 'better than a poem'. But he was constantly exasperated by the 'plague' of the penny post, by the avalanche, the small mountain of mail that arrived for him every day. 'I am buried most mornings under a monticule of letters; I and my wife do our best to get them answered. We do our best but cannot get through them all,' he wrote to someone who had com-plained of not having had an acknowledgment.

Frederick Tennyson's statement that Alfred left everything to his wife was inaccurate. Emily and Alfred often tackled the mountain together. Some of the letters were actually written together, with contributions from each of them. Others written by Alfred have brief additions from Emily, sometimes across the top or even on the envelope – a warmer word of welcome, a kinder word of criticism, a gentler refusal. Many of the letters are completely Emily's, though dealing with his affairs. Others are entirely in her hand, but signed by Alfred and perhaps dic-tated by him – though probably not. He could generally rely on her to say what he wanted said. There is even one of this sort to a close friend,

John Simeon. There also survive both drafts and copies of Alfred's letters in Emily's hand – including ones to the Queen and to Gladstone. This suggests that Emily was not just making a copy for their files, so that they knew what had been said, but that the letters themselves were often joint productions.

Then there are some third-person notes in Emily's hand: anthology permissions, refusals of invitations, 'Mr Alfred Tennyson begs to enclose an order for 5/9 . . .' In these cases, a recipient unfamiliar with Alfred's own handwriting might well suppose he had written the note himself. Indeed Martin Tupper once wrote: 'As Tennyson autographs – so-called – are usually in his wife's handwriting, this holograph is worth keeping.' George Routledge told an enquirer after an autograph that he had no specimen of Tennyson's writing: 'His correspondence with us is generally managed by his wife . . .'

The Victorian passion for autographs (it is not unusual for letters to survive with the signature clipped off) and for the buying and selling of autograph letters undoubtedly contributed to Tennyson's distaste for letter writing. Very early on he got nervous about his letters being collected. A brief 1850 letter to Moxon, his publisher, now in the Morgan Library in New York, was in an 1878 Sotheby's catalogue and resold in 1880 for twenty shillings, considerably more than one of his servants would earn in a week. Writing to Emily, Alfred would sometimes disguise his handwriting on the envelope to fool the Yarmouth Post Office (the first time he did it, she must have thought he'd had a stroke).

He was concerned someone was out to steal his letters. On holiday he would sometimes get his companion, Francis Palgrave, for instance, to address his letters for him. Emily was also conscious that her letters might be read – but really it did not bother her. She wrote to her sister, Anne Weld, on one occasion: 'Burn this' – then crossed it out and wrote: 'Why should I say so?'

Work of one sort or another dominated Emily's life in these years. 'Society' meant very little to her, save the society in their own home which could provide Alfred with the diversion and audience he always needed. Of a visit to a nearby country house she would write in her journal, looking back: 'All there very kind and pleasant, but we are bad guests, for however gladly we welcomed our friends at home, we felt that our work, and therefore our chief pleasure, was there and that there we must for the most part be.'

There at Farringford in these years Emily mostly was. She did not leave the Isle of Wight at all for the first eighteen months they were there, partly, she said, because it was too expensive 'to allow ourselves much change'. But even when their financial position improved, as it very soon did, she was still not keen to go away. 'I find it hard work to leave home even for a night.' She was always at Farringford apart from a regular long summer break (from which she was always happy to return), and an occasional night at Swainston. Swainston was the home

of Sir John Simeon whom Tennyson had first met in London a few years earlier, at a time when he had represented the Isle of Wight in Parliament. Now, having taken the Chiltern Hundreds when he became a Catholic, he had a good deal of time on his hands.

Simeon's first call at Farringford happened to be on 6 June 1854, the day of Lionel's christening, and he arrived just as they were all returning from church. 'This was my first introduction', Emily wrote, 'to a friend who was to be so much to us both as long as he lived.' On the surface he was a surprising friend – a Roman Catholic convert, a Master of Foxhounds – but from his youth he had been a passionate and intelligent admirer of Tennyson's poetry and this was enough, with his obvious tenderness, charm, humour and liberal politics, to endear him to Emily, as well as to Alfred himself. There would be a great deal of coming and going between the two houses in the years ahead.

Simeon's son Johnnie was just two years older than Hallam. Emily observed the children at an early meeting 'wild with delight, Hallam much the wildest'. The eldest daughter, Louisa, then already ten, became to Emily, as Louisa herself put it, almost 'a daughter of the house', the daughter Emily never had. One of the child's earliest memories was of her father saying 'Morte d'Arthur' to her as she lay in his arms, enchantment to an infant. She did not know then what it meant ('So flashed and fell the brand Excalibur') but it stayed in her mind all her life.

Close as Emily would be to her sister Anne's daughter, Agnes, who was five years old that year, it was always a difficult relationship. Of Louisa Simeon, Emily would write, 'No-one except my own sympathises with me as she does.' Louisa would record their talks 'in the fire light by the side of her sofa – talks so helpful, so tender, full of the wisdom of one who had learnt to look upon life and all it embraces from one standpoint only – and that the very highest.' Louisa (a 'fine high-natured girl', 'decidedly clever' as Marian Bradley called her) became 'passionately attached' to Emily, whose talk and support would become crucial at a time, after her mother's early death, when Louisa contemplated becoming a nun. 'This makes me very sad. I tell her that I cannot part from her thus . . .' For all her love of God, central and unwavering, Emily never undervalued the world or human love. It was as Christ said, 'If we love one another thou dwellest in us and thy love is perfected in us.'

To Edward Lear she wrote that she agreed with him entirely about the remedy for the world's ills: 'Love Love Love, human and divine.' Louisa Simeon grew up loved but 'distressingly plain', Marian Bradley would record, apart from her abundance of 'fine fuzzy pale gold' Pre-Raphaelite hair. Alfred was very fond of Louisa too, 'but her face afflicts him,' Mrs Bradley said. Emily seems to have been less concerned with outward appearance, at least beyond her own beautiful family. It was a great cause for joy when Louisa left her convent after a few months and eventually married Richard Ward, the son of one of their neighbours on the Island.

Edward FitzGerald, that lovable man, was at Farringford at the time of Lionel's christening. 'He was in the most delightful spirits and as amusing as a man could be,' Emily told his friend Elizabeth Cowell. He

amused himself as well as Emily by playing 'one glorious air after another' on her surprisingly inadequate piano. There is not much to be
made of the fact that he never visited them again. As he himself said, it
was 'almost the last Visit I paid anywhere'. 'Maud, Maud, Maud' – (the
'birds in the high Hall-garden' calling) would ring in his ears ever after
– as they would for so many listeners. Emily always remained fond of
FitzGerald (and totally unaware of his feeling that Tennyson might
have been better off with some quite different kind of wife) – until the
sharp shock as she read, in letters published after his death, his callous
remarks about Elizabeth Barrett Browning.

A few years before Lionel's christening, FitzGerald (against a lifetime's habit) had agreed to be godfather to one of Lionel's cousins,
Frederick's daughter Elise, born in Florence in 1850. Now he stood
proxy for Drummond Rawnsley, who had married the Tennysons
almost exactly five years before. Drummond had been unable to get
away, but he had accepted Emily's invitation happily enough, in spite
of what Emily called his 'strong suspicions of our want of orthodoxy'.
This phrase of Emily's is worth noting – but after all F.D. Maurice had
been her choice as Hallam's godfather. It has been customary to imagine Emily Tennyson as conventionally religious, attempting to make
Tennyson himself appear respectably Christian when in fact he was
not. But here, as she often did, Emily identifies herself entirely with
Tennyson's 'want of orthodoxy'. Lionel's godmother was Tennyson's
cousin Emma, in token perhaps of Aunt Russell's continued generosity.
The second godfather was Franklin Lushington, one of the Park House
siblings who would all mean so much to the Tennysons.

The following letter from Emily suggests just how important Frank
was, just how much they trusted and valued him.

We ask of you the greatest favour we can ask of any one, that you will undertake the guardianship of our children. We are sure you will do your utmost to
have them brought up as Christian gentlemen, to give them the best education
that can be given them in the highest sense of the words, and in your mind as in
ours this we know implies a full persuasion of the sacredness of labour. You
will see our children are brought up to work. We wish them to share equally in
all we leave and to be separated as little as possible at school or college, to be
brothers indeed all their lives. God bless you and them.

Franklin Lushington – classicist, lawyer, judge of the Supreme Court
in the Ionian Islands, later Chief Metropolitan Magistrate in London –

was at this time not yet married. He was, and would remain all his life, Edward Lear's closest friend, causing him both more happiness and more pain than anyone else he knew. It is in that role he is now remembered. Emily's deep love for Frank and her tender understanding of Lear's love for him was part of the underpinning of Emily's long relationship with Lear.

Lear wrote to Emily of Frank, 'Say or think what one will, he is the most perfect character I have ever known,' a suitable friend for the woman Lear considered compounded of angels, doctors, prophets and philosophers. Emily wrote to Lear: 'I think we must found a Franklin Lushington Brotherhood,' a sort of fan club, 'but we will be very stingy of our honours.' It is significant that Emily's suggestion of this Brotherhood follows immediately on a reference to Arthur Hallam. Jane Brookfield, Emily told Lear, 'received me more as a relative than a stranger, from feeling herself one of the Hallams.' (She was Arthur's first cousin.) 'She thinks of Alfred as a brother, she told me.' Emily went on to write of the Brotherhood without a pause. There was this strong link in her mind: Lear's love for Frank Lushington reminded her, all those years later, of Tennyson's love for Arthur Hallam. As she understood that and accepted it completely, so she understood and accepted Lear's feelings. Frank, meanwhile, seemed to be oblivious of his sainthood and would write provocatively: 'All you *good* people have such an immoral wish to be always doing work and sacrificing yourselves – I believe immoral laissez-allez philosophic individuals, who have no turn whatsoever for sacrificing ourselves and a very distinct turn for doing no work at all, are the wisest and least troublesome set of the two.' He was teasing on paper.

Present, he was often silent. Emily warned Lear, 'Sometimes when with Frank, I grow just as silent as he is, unless it happen that I am with him alone and then I can generally conquer the shyness which his silence brings.' With Lear himself, Emily always felt entirely comfortable. She *was* shy; she loved to be entirely alone, when Alfred and the boys were not far away. To Lear she could write, 'I dare say you will do instead of being alone. I shall be helped by your presence instead of my old friends, the empty room, or the sofa in the corner or the solitary drive. Is not this the queerest compliment ever paid by one mortal to another? and yet is it not a very real one and a great one for a shy person?'

One of the bonds that bound them together, Lear and Emily, was

Preparing for Publication.

Poems and Songs
by
Alfred Tennyson,
Set to Music, and inscribed to
Mrs Alfred Tennyson,
by
Edward Lear.

N.º 1. *Flow down, Cold Rivulet &c.*
2. *Edward Gray.*
3. *Tears, idle tears.*
4 *Wind of the Western Sea.*

Price, 8 Shillings the set, or 2/- separately.
Applications for Copies to be made to
Edward Lear, Esq.re
65, Oxford Terrace, Hyde Park,
London.

their love for Tennyson's poetry. Emily already knew of Lear's grand long-term illustration plan and admired the first example he sold – 'Morn broadened on the borders of the dark'. She said it haunted her and: 'Were I rich, not one of all the set should belong to anyone but myself.' In October 1853 Lear sent her the prospectus for his settings of four of Tennyson's songs, which he had dedicated to Emily.

'I can only talk,' Emily would say, 'when I may say just what I like.'

To Lear she could always say anything, both face to face and in her letters over thirty-six years. Because he was often far away and in need of her love, her letters to him ('poor little scraps' as they sometimes were) tell us far more about herself than most of her other letters do – until the years when she is writing regularly to the boys at school. Lear would write to Emily at great length, even once when they were going to see each other the following day: 'Good gracious! you will say – does this man know we are come for a visit to London and have 14310 shops, 9000 exhibitions and 5 billion morning calls to make and yet sends such a long letter?' It was a measure of his need to communicate with Emily, to let her know what was going on in his life, sad as it often was and as funny as he could make it. 'If one were but a chimney pot, or a pipkin or a mackerel or anything respectable and consistent there would be some comfort.' But really there was not.

Edward Lear's diary is a source of some of the most revealing, un-censored observation of the Tennysons' marriage, as Lear became in-creasingly worried by the thought of an angelic wife slaving away – as he saw it – for an unappreciative husband. There he was, the outsider, 'the spectator – all through my life – of what goes on amongst those I know – very little an actor.' At times he would envy the family life he observed; at times it would repel him. Lear had gone off to the Mediter-ranean late in 1853 without seeing the newly acquired Farringford. 'I wish I could see you,' he wrote to Emily. 'But I shall wait to see my friends with comfort in heaven – for in England there is none for me.' England would draw him back all the same, though Emily found it hard to persuade him it was the best place in the world to live, 'barring bronchitis'.

Sometimes as Emily coughed and Alfred groaned about his own ills, it seemed surprising that the Tennysons themselves did not join the Brownings in Tuscany. But these years when the boys were small were the healthiest years of Emily's life. As often happens, childbirth had cured the menstrual difficulties she had suffered as a virgin and other gynaecological problems had not yet developed. The girl who had been a yardstick for delicacy ('quite as weak as Emily Sellwood', Cecilia had said fifteen years earlier), the woman so often portrayed as if she had spent her entire lifetime in an invalid carriage or on a sofa was at this period enjoying all kinds of activity. She was walking on the downs, scrambling over rocks, climbing a ladder to inspect a granary, playing a little battledore and shuttlecock, even letting both small boys at one time ride on her back. In October 1855 she recorded that they were seeing a good deal of the Simeons. 'One day we had an exciting slide down to Alum Bay, the clay path wet from recent storms. We came up with our feet in eel baskets.' Anyone who knows Alum Bay, where many visitors nowadays make the journeys both up and down by chair-lift, will realize what an extraordinary statement that is. There was some sailing too:

We all went and found the sea so very rough as we neared the point that we did not round it . . . Old Moyle (the sailor) laughed saying that the gentlemen were more frightened than the ladies and then defended them by saying it was on account of the ladies they were afraid. [His] remarks amused us.

Emily's grandson, Charles Tennyson, suggests that Emily developed a 'spinal complaint' soon after Lionel's birth, but I can find no evidence of this. Mysterious ailments dominated the lives of countless nineteenth-century women and it is difficult to be sure – over a hundred years later – exactly what was wrong with Emily. Certainly over the years she was often in pain and sometimes unable to walk. For years she had had a 'delicate chest and throat'. One of the attractions of the Isle of Wight was that it was supposed to be a good climate for people with weak chests. Twice in earlier years she had been 'shut up seven months' on end over the winter, because of her chest. The 'pain' she often mentions may have been in her chest from coughing, or from writing her letters and her journal day after day for hours with a bad posture. She mentions headaches and face aches and there may have been some sort of repetitive strain injury, which exacerbated an old injury in her hand.

But what was it that made it so difficult for her to walk? It is possible that in the years after Lionel's birth, as her muscles and ligaments weakened with increasing age, she suffered from a progressive prolapse of the womb. The treatment, in those days before effective surgery for the condition, was simply to wear some sort of truss and to 'abstain from motion'. A popular medical textbook of the time has a chapter on 'the descending or falling of the womb'. 'To treat this complaint, a broad bandage should be worn over the lower part of the bowels and drawn moderately tight, a strengthening plaster applied to the back and Restorative Wine Bitters used.' One of the ingredients of the Bitters was 'whitewood bark'. Several times Emily refers to taking 'bark'. No doubt it was recommended for many conditions. Retrospective diagnosis is impossible, but it may well be that in addition to her weak chest and the 'pain in the brain', always made worse by too many visitors, she was unable to walk much because of an unmentionable prolapse, progressively debilitating but not life-threatening.

Tennyson's own health was very often as much of a problem as Emily's, though both of them lived such long lives. Emily on the whole accepted she was 'delicate' and planned her life accordingly, often opting out of excursions she could have made – but trying to hide how she was feeling from her visitors. She more than once encouraged her sister Anne to be equally stoical; Marian Bradley said of Emily in these years that she 'never gives way to weariness or illness'. Alfred railed and fumed and worried constantly about his eyes, his hay fever, his teeth, his palpitations (blaming his smoking but unable to give up permanently), his gout. He attributed most of his problems to gout. When once, with a bad leg, he was advised, as Emily was so often, to rest on a sofa, Emily commented, 'Most unwise, considering his nature.'

Dr Ker, his sister Mary's brother-in-law, spoke of Tennyson's 'nervousness' and how 'it embittered his existence'. 'His waking hours in the morning were very miserable ones and he used to ask himself – "How am I to get through the day?"' A comment of Emily's confirms that grim picture of what Tennyson was like in the early morning. On one occasion when Emily was taking the little boys to Grasby for a summer holiday, it was Thomas Woolner who saw them off at King's Cross – such an early start, Emily considered, would definitely have been too much for Alfred: 'I will not let A. go, knowing that it would knock him up.' Against the idea that Alfred could never enjoy early rising is Emily's description of getting up with him to have breakfast at half past six with Lear and Frank Lushington before they caught an early boat. 'When they were gone we counted seven capes all glorious in the golden morning mist. Then we went up to the Attic and looked through the telescope to try and watch their boat.'

Tennyson has to be called a hypochondriac, for he *was* overanxious and preoccupied with his own health, though sometimes with reason. He once admitted, rejecting the suggestion of grosser problems before his marriage, that his own 'infirmities' were only 'short sight and hypochondria'. Even so, he was an excellent nurse, tender and loving. On one occasion, when Emily had sprained her ankle, she recorded him binding a cold water bandage inside oil skin 'every day for three weeks'. In her journal, Emily constantly records Alfred's thoughtfulness, piling on her 'numberless cloaks and wrappers' on boats, pasting up a window to keep the draught out and even sometimes sending people home if she seemed tired. Her intention in the epitome of the journal is certainly to present Alfred as a devoted husband. While she undoubtedly left out evidence of occasions when she felt neglected (and surely sometimes she must have done), she was not short of examples of his kindness and consideration.

In the summer of 1854 the Tennysons had moments of wondering whether they had done the right thing in coming to Farringford. There were upsetting 'household troubles'. Emily worried about the difficulties of getting to her father if he were taken ill. They were still hoping to buy the house when they could raise the money, but was it a sensible thing to do? Alfred fussed and grumbled, feeling cut off, pining for mountains, or at least for somewhere other than where he was. 'Ally says our friends will soon have forgotten us quite.' In the spring – before a brief visit to London – he had told Coventry Patmore that they had 'hardly seen a human face since we came here, except the members of our household.' Every letter he wrote – and he did write some – ended with invitations to people to visit them and relieve his loneliness and sense of isolation. 'I shall delight in welcoming you under my roof.' 'I and my wife will always be glad to see you here.' 'You know you have half-promised to come and see us.' There would soon come the time when they were overwhelmed by visitors.

Emily encouraged Alfred to take off for the west country in August. He was worried at not hearing from her and a surviving letter shows that it missed him at Wells and was returned to Farringford. She had written:

Own dearest,
    I feel sick at heart thinking of thy disappointment when there was no letter yesterday and of all thy anxiety the livelong day afterwards. I can only hope thou hast returned to Wells and hast found the two letters which wilt set thy mind at ease. Since I must love thee better than myself I cannot help hoping thou hast gone into South Wales or wherever thy fancy leads thee.

Emily had an admirable ability not to make Tennyson feel guilty about his absences, dreary as she would find them. She saw it as a weakness that she preferred not to leave the children and 'go with him without them'. She often urged him to go off somewhere because she thought he needed a break or some stimulus or a visit to the dentist. Once she wrote to Mrs Cameron, 'I want him to go to London but I cannot get him off.' 'Men need change,' she would say. For her, she said, a new book was sufficient change, though she reluctantly accepted that a change of air was necessary from time to time.

When he was in Somerset in 1854, Emily told him she was 'gadding' about in the donkey-chaise, calling on neighbours at Afton with the nurse Gandy and the children. 'Even we could not but have been satisfied with all that was made of our tinies.' In the evenings, she played Mozart to herself and read Ruskin. She told Tennyson that she disagreed with Ruskin's definition of architecture; she was apparently unaware that Effie Gray had just received a decree of annulment of their marriage on the grounds of Ruskin's impotence. The talk of the town had not reached Farringford.

Often when Emily was alone she would compose, improvise, with one of Alfred's songs propped on the piano in front of her and, in her mind, his voice as he read them. Rarely did she think what she was doing was worth writing down, but by the end of her life she had nearly twenty songs in manuscript, and half a dozen in print, tidied up by professional musicians. Emily also set a number of poems by the Lushington brothers, which Cecilia, on a good day, would sing to a drawing room of guests. Alfred was very loyal about Emily's settings of his poems – and could never see why other people needed to use poems she had already set quite satisfactorily. No fewer than thirty different composers produced settings of "Sweet and low", for instance, in Tennyson's lifetime, and the tune now familiar to many people is not Emily's. 'My wife has long since set 'Sweet and low' and very prettily too,' Tennyson said in 1852, while not refusing a permission, knowing that it was good for a poet to have his songs 'in people's drawing rooms', as Alexander Macmillan put it to Emily. Macmillan was asking Emily's opinion of a setting of 'What does little Birdie say?' – 'remembering your feelings on the subject'. Emily's reply was that 'the song was in four time not in three, according to my notion' and that particular setting was never published.

Even on holiday, in the summer of 1854, Tennyson was worrying about money and his new responsibilities. Taking a fly from Glastonbury to Yeovil, he counted the cost for seventeen miles and reminded Emily that their sons would have to be educated. Would they ever be able to afford to buy Farringford? He needed a new book with excellent sales, but he could hardly bring himself to finish 'Maud', aware already, it seems, that he would be 'beaten black and blue by the penny-a-liners'. 'People bother him so,' Emily told John Forster, 'that he doubts whether he will publish at all now'.

There was one possibly remunerative project in hand, a lavish illustrated edition of already published poems, which Moxon had suggested as a way of raising the capital sum they needed: 'I could by this means, I am almost sure, within a very short time too, put into your pocket at least a couple of thousand pounds' – a really huge sum of money of course in those days. Both Emily and Alfred had mixed feelings about the edition from the beginning and, as it turned out, it was the extraordinary success of *Maud* that enabled Tennyson to buy Farringford. The illustrated edition did not appear until 1857, was said by Holman Hunt to have been the death of Moxon, and would cause problems in which Emily would find herself deeply involved, as we shall see.

In May 1854 John Everett Millais, already famous at twenty-five, agreed to travel down to the Isle of Wight 'to take little Hallam as an illustration of "Dora"' – that is as William's child. It is difficult to believe that Emily could have been other than pleased with the engraving that resulted from the visit he finally paid to Farringford in November. She recorded 'Mr Millais comes on the 22nd and is beguiled into sweeping up leaves and burning them in the intervals of making sketches of Hallam and myself.' Millais' bonfires are better known than his pictures of Hallam and Emily. It must have been on this visit that he made the preliminary drawings for the previously unpublished portrait of Emily that appears in this book. Millais must have been in a curious state in November 1854. He had just finished his portrait of Ruskin and had severed his relationship with him in the aftermath of the annulment of Ruskin's marriage to Effie Gray; the following year Millais would marry Effie himself. Everyone was talking about it, but there is no mention of the scandal in what survives of Emily's journal.

What does survive of that November 1854 visit is interesting all the same. Emily records that 'we have had talks as to the limits of realism in painting. A. hates overrealism.' It seems likely that Tennyson thought the Millais portrait of Emily 'over realistic'. She is not flattered. She looks pale and too thin and there are dark circles under her eyes. It makes an interesting contrast with the much reproduced Watts painting of a few years later – so much loved by Tennyson. In this reproduction of Millais' illustration to 'Dora', the child is certainly the two-year-old Hallam; it seems possible, comparing the face with the portrait, that Emily posed for the sketch of Mary, the woman on the left. Emily would be particularly critical of Millais' contributions to the Illustrated Edition ('"The Miller's Daughter" I positively loathe'), but she said nothing against this illustration.

Tennyson had been working on and off on 'Maud', his new long poem, all through 1854. Indeed, as early as the previous October, when they were still in Twickenham, Emily had asked her father, living with Charles and Louisa at Grasby where there was a copy of the 1837 gift book *The Tribute*, to send Tennyson's lines 'Oh! that 'twere possible' ('after long grief and pain'), which had never been reprinted. 'Not knowing anyone who would work cheaper than myself,' Henry Sellwood wrote to Emily on 12 October 1853, 'I have copied and now send you Alfred's poem from the Tribute. I must take the cost out in good things when I come to see you in your new house.' The origins of

'Maud' – of this use of the early poem as the 'germ' of the later – form one of the many small puzzles in the Tennyson story.

Tennyson is on record as saying that John Simeon had 'begged him to weave a story round this poem.' But Tennyson did not really get to know Simeon until after June 1854 (eight months after Emily had written to her father), by which time Tennyson was already deep in 'Maud'. Kate Rawnsley also claimed to have suggested that the poem was far too good not to be revived and enlarged.

The date of Tennyson's taking up of the early lyric – before Simeon could have found it, as his daughter suggested, in 'some papers' at Farringford – is confirmed by a letter from Cecilia, Tennyson's sister, to her husband Edmund Lushington, visiting the Tennysons on the Isle of Wight for the first time that spring. She was delighted 'Alfred is bringing that poem up again. "Oh that twere possible." I always loved it so much.'

Tennyson was never so happy as when he was working on a long poem – or a series of linked poems. Such is the power and complexity of 'Maud' – that 'strange, wild story' – that it seems quite likely that it was fermenting in his mind for years before it took its final form. Emily's first mention of it in her journal is of Alfred reading from it to John Simeon in September 1854. She does not say when she first heard any of it herself. In February 1855 she records Tennyson reading to her 'the beginning of Maud and the Mad Song, and one night all Maud'. There is a vivid later reference to the 'mad scene' (beginning 'Dead, long dead'). In 1871 Tennyson told James Mangles that it was written in twenty minutes. Mangles wrote in his diary: 'He called out to his wife, "Now I am going to begin the mad scene" and in twenty minutes it was done.'

It is the 'called out to his wife' that is as interesting as the speed. At this stage, Tennyson's study was in the attic, a 'windshaken' attic with a 'little fire'. Many visitors climbed up there to smoke with him after dinner. It was too far away for 'calling out'. The house was extremely cold in that winter of 1854-5. (Benjamin Jowett, an early visitor to Farringford, complained of it.) February was the worst month of all, with water freezing on the shore of Freshwater Bay. Emily described in her journal 'the snow folding in and out of the hedge like drapery'. Surely Alfred was calling out only from the other side of the fireplace in the drawing room. It suggests he could write with Emily in the same room, so quiet she could be, so sympathetic and so still. Just at this time she recorded: 'A robin in the house so tame that it let me take it in my hand and when A. was reading to me it sat near us by the fire.' 'It seems that I am happy,' Tennyson wrote in 'Maud':

> I have led her home, my love, my only friend
> There is none like her, none.

Emily does not say what she herself thought as she heard him reading from 'Maud' in early 1855. She must eventually have known it off by heart, as it became Tennyson's favourite party piece, his 'poor little Maud', his 'pet bantling' so often abused. 'It requires immense strength of lungs,' he used to say complacently, and would interrupt himself with expostulations against his critics: 'That is what was called namby-pamby!' Emily would sometimes slip out of the room before he began on it yet again, or at least before he got to 'the sad part'. Of course he could make anything sound wonderful. Emily was acutely aware of that. She always wanted to read the poems to herself to form a proper judgment. 'It is well to read things to oneself without the glamour of his reading which may beguile one,' she wrote in her journal.

One suggestion that Emily found 'Maud' a little hard to take is in a letter from Robert Monteith, one of Tennyson's Cambridge friends. This was after its publication in the summer of 1855 and its huge sales. Monteith reported that Edmund Lushington was 'not so pleased with Maud as the British public seems to be: and the same, he says, is the case with Alfred's wife and most of his friends.' In fact, as a letter to James Spedding makes clear, Emily admitted only that there were 'a few things that were not admirable in it.' Many years later, in a letter to their son Hallam at Cambridge, she is more specific: 'The only failing point I see in any of Papa's works is the violent scenes . . . To me they are always just a little false.' She instanced parts of 'Maud' and then added, 'He is made for passion and indignation, not rage, rage belonging to small natures. But perhaps my criticism is false and it is that I have never seen rage.' It is as clear a statement as one could have that Emily had never seen Alfred angry and that she was not disturbed by the violence in 'Maud' because she, unlike so many of the critics, did not for one moment confuse the narrator with Alfred himself. She had said this directly to Forster in the summer of 1855, after reading his review of Maud in the Examiner: 'It is peoples' own fault or misfortune if they do not understand what manner of man the hero is.'

It is extremely unlikely that Emily was disturbed by any hint of the ingenious post-Freudian comparison between the first lines and a menstruating woman – that 'surrealistic lunacy' with which the poem begins:

> I hate the dreadful hollow behind the little wood,
> Its lips in the field above are dabbled with blood-red heath,
> The red-ribbed ledges drip with a silent horror of blood
> And Echo there, whatever is asked her, answers Death.

The comparison would not have occurred to Emily, I am sure. But she can hardly not have been worried about what had been going on in Tennyson's mind, however much he distanced himself from the hero/narrator, as he always emphatically did, however much he protested that the poem had 'nothing of Lincolnshire' about it. She may well have been uneasy about what a critic has called the poem's 'deeply pessimistic view of marriage'. She was astute enough to realize that, whatever else Tennyson was doing, he was also burying 'the dead body of hate', and freeing himself from the 'dead weight' of the past that had oppressed him.

Emily must also have realized that in the last section – for all that it was words in 'the mouth of a madman' – Tennyson would lay himself open to the charge of glorifying war. George Eliot, in the *Westminster Review*, actually suggested Tennyson saw war as the 'unique social regenerator'. We know from Emily's letters to Lear how much she sympathized with his pacifism, though she too could get carried away from time to time, wishing 'death and destruction to the enemy'. Years later she wrote to her sister Louisa: 'I want Ally to write a poem giving his true feeling about war. People call him so war-like that they wonder he has not made one of his sons a soldier. They do not see that he can admire heroism, which bravely devotes itself for country, without loving war itself.' Like her grandmother before her, the last thing Emily wanted was for her sons to become soldiers.

But in February 1855 even Lionel, aged eleven months, 'delights in warlike songs', and Hallam, at two and a half, had caught so much of the general atmosphere that winter that all his games were Crimean. Emily told Lear how the boy took up his drum and marched off, as he told her, 'to battle'. At least it was not a gun, but 'he falls down and says "This is the way the Russians fall when they are killed." He loves to talk of the poor soldiers who have no butter and no toast.' Emily naturally preferred the sweet behaviour Hallam had shown when the chimney sweep had come the previous summer, 'weapons in hand', and the two of them, dark sweep and golden lad, had exchanged courteous bows, as the child blew kisses over and over again. (Emily had first suggested a kiss to stop him staring.)

The whole household was stirred by the allied victory at the battle of the Alma River in September 1854. A Victorian history book called it 'the first great battle since Waterloo', nearly forty years earlier. Now the British and the French were fighting together far off on the shores of the Black Sea. Tennyson, who had often worried about a French invasion at home, wrote one stanza of a song celebrating the union, and gave up.

> Frenchman, a hand in thine!
> Our flags have waved together!
> Let us drink to the health of thine and mine
> At the Battle of Alma river.

It was Emily who finished the song and set it to music, adding two awkward stanzas of her own. The song was published eventually in 1864, after Alfred himself got A.H. Novelli's opinion of Emily's music. 'He is reported to be a great judge – he played it and pronounced it to be vigorous – broad and – English – three great merits, he said.' Emily told Alfred: 'I do not feel the words are properly mine. Thine is the keynote and thine the model.' She added their linked initials 'Æ', which she would nearly always put at the top of her manuscript settings of Alfred's poems.

Emily's words show clearly how she felt about war, reading of the battle in *The Times*, of 'three thousand dead and dying on the field'.

> Our flags together furl'd.
> Henceforward no other strife –
> Than which of us most shall help the world,
> Which lead the noblest life.

Then pledge we our glorious dead,
Swear to be one for ever,
And God's best blessing on each dear head
That rests by the Alma river.

'Henceforward no other strife,' Emily wrote, but knew it could not be so. What France and England should have been doing, Emily considered, was not fighting the Russians and killing each other's young (glorious or not), but 'helping the world' through peaceful colonization, bringing the benefits of civilization and progress to under-developed countries.

'Only one's friends', Emily wrote to Julia Margaret Cameron in London that winter, 'can take one's thoughts off the war ... Now indeed riches do seem to have a charm they never had before. To think of being able to send out a ship-load of comforts.' It was a dark time. 'We are almost afraid to open the newspapers now.' There was a false rumour that Sebastopol had fallen. There were 'painful tidings' about her uncle's Arctic expedition. It was the first real news of the fate of the crews of the *Erebus* and the *Terror*, who had disappeared seven years earlier. Some Eskimos had shown a surveyor from the Hudson's Bay Company 'certain articles of silver bearing Franklin's crest'.

At least Emily was able to walk on the downs 'almost daily' that winter, helped by a camp-stool Aubrey de Vere had given her, which allowed her to sit down whenever she needed to. The view from the Beacon, with the white cliffs reflected in a calm sea, seemed to Emily 'tender and sad'. 'Perhaps the landscape seemed so sad because of the sorrowful news of the death of our neighbour Colonel Hood in the trenches.'

The deaths of two men you know mean more than the deaths of six or seven hundred strangers. But *The Times* leader on 13 November 1854 on the hideous massacre at Balaclava, and the report the following day, inspired what still remains, though they would not have wished it so, one of Tennyson's most famous poems: 'The Charge of the Light Brigade'. *The Times* had referred to 'some hideous blunder', but the words that stuck in Tennyson's head were 'someone had blundered'. W.F. Rawnsley pointed out that in Lincolnshire 'hundred' is pronounced 'hunderd', an exact rhyme for 'blundered'.

Emily was closely involved in the fortunes of this poem. It was she who copied it to send to John Forster at the *Examiner*. That manuscript, a subsequent one, and the related correspondence are all partly in Emily's hand. She wrote to Forster on 6 December, saying the poem had been written 'yesterday on a recollection of the first report of *The Times*, which gave the number as six hundred and seven. He prefers "six hundred", on account of the metre, but if you think it should be altered to seven hundred, which from later accounts seems to have been the number, he says you are to alter it.' The original version was finally decided on. Forster, substituting it at the last moment, told Alfred: 'I am particularly glad that Mrs Tennyson thinks with you, with all of us, the original version the best.'

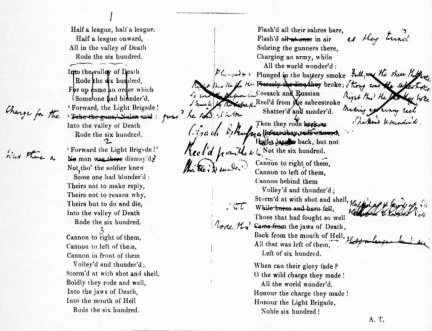

The regretted revised version somehow got into the collection with *Maud*, but it was 'the Newspaper version – or as near as may be' that was sent to the Crimea on thousands of printed slips. Tennyson drafted a letter addressed directly to the surviving 'Brave Soldiers!', which Emily discouraged him from sending. 'It would be pleasant to write to the soldiers only one is afraid it looks too regal to do so.' A proof, with a few lines in Emily's writing, reinstating some lines Alfred had crossed out, suggests not only the printers' problems, but the two of them talking over the poem together, as they talked over so many poems over the years.

CHAPTER NINE

Friends and relations

During the early part of 1855, when Tennyson was working on 'Maud', there had been, as there would always be, interruptions. Americans, Frederick Tuckerman and his brother, came, bearing a letter of introduction from a man who had been the Tennysons' vicar at Boxley, years before. It was a slender connection. But Tennyson was so delighted with their homage – in spite of an objection to the rhyming of 'blundered' and 'hundred' – that Frederick Tuckerman went away with the original manuscript of 'Locksley Hall'. Tennyson said he had never done 'such a thing in his life before', but he would do so again. Emily was never happy with Tennyson's generosity with his manuscripts. She saw them as part of the boys' inheritance. But she too liked the Tuckermans, spoke of 'the brotherhood of America and England' and would stay in touch with them for years.

Thomas Woolner was another visitor. He was working on a medallion of Alfred, which Emily thought 'very fine and strong, the best likeness that has been made'. Tennyson was still beardless in 1855; Woolner would preserve him like that, not only in the medallion, but in his 1857 bust. Tennyson's appearance would change dramatically by the time the bust was exhibited. In 1855 the sculptor told Emily: 'I never in my life enjoyed a fortnight more and shall always look back upon my visit as an isle of light in the general gloom of things.' Emily had taken to him when she had first met the short, impoverished, brilliantly talking, rather smug young man in Coniston in 1850. He must have had something in common with Alfred, for others found him too egotistic and outspoken and inclined to say, 'in the strongest words, what is uppermost in his mind.' Woolner was himself a poet, as well as a sculptor. Patmore said his poems were so good he was surprised they weren't much better.

Now Emily teased Woolner by saying, 'We cannot quarrel with you if you borrow a little sunshine from imagination to throw over your visit to Farringford, however puritanical we may be in our worship of truth.' Hallam was missing him, she said, and 'obliged now to make the best he can of his mother'. Woolner would make a medallion of Emily, too, though she had said she did not feel it right 'to let you waste your time on my lean face, which should have been drawn ten years ago, if at all.' When it was done, she joked that if he were going to make the fortune she would like him to make from copies, she would need to 'take to poisoning' to make herself famous. No-one would want to buy a medallion of the poet's wife.

That 1855 visit to Farringford established a lifelong family friendship. Woolner had made firm friends with the little boys, a sure way to Emily's heart. Emily would encourage Woolner to suggest subjects to Tennyson. 'I wish you would give Alfred something to do. He is pretty well but for want of this,' she would write a little later. She and Woolner exchanged regular letters; he appreciated her as much as Benjamin Jowett and Edward Lear did. Woolner wrote to Emily rather clumsily of one of her letters: 'Your last I keep always with me and read in choice moments; as one would look at a beautiful locket miniature, always in some strange way, hoping to get nearer the spirit of what the picture speaks of.' Emily would never miss an opportunity of trying to obtain commissions for Woolner.

The whole family left Farringford in the summer of 1855, the first time Emily had been away from the Isle of Wight since they had moved there late in 1853. She was with Tennyson in Oxford when he received an honorary doctorate in June. 'If I go I should like you to go likewise,' he had said. They both found it something of an ordeal. Emily wrote in her journal:

A. brings my breakfast to me in my room, both of us were terribly nervous . . . A. said that when he sat in the Balliol garden the shouts from the Theatre seemed to him like the shouts of the multitude in early Christian times when they cried 'Christians to the Lions'. In the Theatre these same shouts so overwhelmed me that I thought I must have left it, particularly those that followed A.'s name. However the great doors opened and he came in looking calm and dignified tho' pale. I grew calm too . . . I had first seen Oxford when six years old, posting into it when a summer's sunset gilded the domes and churches.

In London they had stayed with the Welds – Emily's sister Anne and her husband – in their apartments in the Royal Society in Somerset House. Tennyson always liked staying there; it was central and there was somewhere he could smoke. One day they 'took the children to Crystal Palace', though Lionel at fourteen months was a little young to appreciate it. They called on Lady Franklin too – Emily's aunt by marriage, who had now to be considered the explorer's widow. It was the first time Jane Franklin had seen Lionel, but she makes no comment in her diary. What she does reveal is how Henry Sellwood, who had been at Farringford in the winter, was helping her sort out a family feud: there were difficulties with her stepdaughter over the will Sir John had left behind. Sellwood had been Franklin's solicitor, as well as his brother-in-law and 'dearest friend'. The time had only recently come to prove his will, although it turned out he had died eight years before.

In 1855 Jane Franklin was still obsessed with finding out exactly what had happened to the 1845 expedition. There was no longer any hope that Franklin was alive, but she was determined to find out whether it had all been in vain and dispatched ship after ship, mostly at her own expense – even personally ordering the supplies (salt beef, dried apples, 'assorted soups', rum) – until McClintock's expedition in 1857 suggested Franklin had some claim to be as his Lincolnshire monument declares 'Discoverer of the North West Passage'. A picture of his birthplace – the little shop in Spilsby where her mother had also been born – would appear in the *Illustrated London News* and must have made Emily reflect on the difference between Sarah Franklin's childhood and that of her grandsons. Emily was immensely proud of the Franklin connection. Hallam and Lionel would grow up on tales of their great-uncle's adventures and his 'simple noble devout nature'. They never saw the shop, which still stands, with a plaque commemorating Sir John Franklin's birthplace.

From London in the summer of 1855 Emily took the little boys to grand Park House to meet their Lushington cousins for the first time. Cecilia and Edmund had three girls: Emily, Zilly (who was really also Cecilia) and Lucy – who was between the Tennyson boys in age. The only son, Eddy, was eleven and already seriously ill. 'Poor Eddy,' Emily wrote in her journal, 'Very patient and sweet. The devotion of his aunts very beautiful to see' – the lack of any relationship with his mother too painful to contemplate. There was one less aunt than there had been: the youngest one, Louisa Lushington, aged thirty, had died in France the previous summer. Alfred had then described Emily as 'writing and weeping at once'. She had written: 'There are few I love so well, scarcely any I admire so much,' remembering all her Park House visits in the years before her marriage, and the time they had spent together in Eastbourne.

Now, a few weeks after their Park House visit, the first of the four Lushington brothers, Henry, would also die in France, on the way home from Malta, where he had been Chief Secretary to the government. Emily wrote in her journal on 14 August 1855: 'His brother Franklin arrived too late to see him alive. A. reads Ecclesiastes to me, which he had once read to Henry Lushington. Also Solomon's Song.' Emily had not known Henry quite as well as she knew Frank and Edmund, but Alfred had been particularly close to him in the 1840s.

The Tennysons would go to Park House again, but from now on it would always seem 'unutterably sad'. The most crushing description of the survivors comes from Caroline Jebb, years later: 'The women are my portion in life and Mrs L. is too singular for anyone to enjoy her companionship. The Misses L., the single sisters, are muteness itself . . . They either knit or look at the carpet, but never talk.' That was how it would be and was beginning to be already with Cecilia depressive and fractious, Louisa dead and Eddy dying. In the summer just after Henry's death ('Courage, poor heart!' Tennyson had been writing when the news arrived), Emily wrote to Lear on 17 August encouraging him not to leave Park House.

Thank you for staying. You know I feel you ought. Frank will make it all easy for you and you will find you are a comfort and blessing to him and them . . . You must be good and not morbid and be with [Frank] as much as you can. I feel one (or at least I myself) often errs grievously through what in worldly parlance one calls shyness, what in higher and sterner language is want of faith in God and man and now you are giving me a good lesson which late events have made me more apt to learn. For how much is lost that can never be recovered now? My heart is stupid. I cannot write. Only I have a dim sad feeling we must help each other, those who at all understand each other and love each other . . . We shall look for you and Frank whatever you say to the contrary. Alfred and I are very grateful to you for all you have written to us of these sad times. Edmund's letter on Sunday was very touching. That from Mr Venables today terrible in its cold statue-like sadness. One knows all that is pressed down there. Forgive this note.

Exchanging letters frequently, Emily and Lear had become even closer. To him, she allowed herself to confide her loneliness at the end of August as Tennyson lost himself walking in the New Forest. She wrote to Lear:

I am sick at heart today not having heard from Ally though very likely I could not have heard and I had said so to myself beforehand telling myself it was then probably a two days' post; but then when the letter did not come it seemed as if it might surely only be a one day's post just to please me. What right have I to feel sad who have so unspeakably much to make me cheerful even when he is away; a love tried by all the changes and chances of a more than five years' marriage and tried only to prove its unimagined worth more and more. What of sorrow can this world hold which should not weigh light in the balance with this? But let me not talk of weighing and balancing, it is not good. I would rather feel that the God who has made me so rich in blessings will make me richer still. 'Open thy mouth wide and I will fill it.' None of the niggard measure of man this.

Dear Mr Lear, why do I say all this to you but from a feeling you are not to be always 'alone' and you must now sympathize prophetically with me.

When Tennyson's letter arrived, it was delightful and must have made Emily both smile and sigh as he told her of losing his umbrella *and* the tobacco case Simeon had given him ('so like the colour of last year's beech leaves that I did not see it . . .') *and* 'a lovely bit of forget-me-not' he had picked for her by the side of the river that runs from Winchester. It was a 'blotty' letter: 'Inn-ink, inn pens, haste, I writing obliquely, on sofa, recumbently, with half-palsied elbow.' He would come by the five o'clock boat from Lymington, 'Mind, meet me (if you can) Monday evening.' He was, 'Thine always, A.T.' 'It is a pity we are not rich enough to go about all together without scruple for he has not much pleasure in being long alone,' Emily wrote to Lear after Tennyson's return.

There seemed to be so many in need of comfort in the aftermath of Henry Lushington's death. Emily's letter to George Venables, his closest friend, gives a good idea why she was herself so much beloved. She thanks Venables 'for speaking out to me, if ever so little, of what is in your heart.' The 'cold statue' had at last allowed himself to confide in her, at least a little. And in return she told him what she felt he would want to hear. ('For my own part I can never hear too often what I love to hear.') Maria Lushington, Henry's sister, had written to Emily from Park House about how much Venables was missed. 'He helps everybody to bear the burthen which is so peculiarly heavy for himself.'

When he visited Farringford the following March, he talked to Emily alone for hours.

Edward Lear and Franklin Lushington did get to Farringford in the October after Henry's death. But first we must look at another developing lifelong friendship.

When George Granville Bradley was appointed Dean of Westminster in 1881, he would receive 'a vast pile of letters' of congratulation. Writing to Emily Tennyson, thanking her for hers, he said it was the only one he had opened. He told her how much their friendship meant to him. 'The Poems I should have known I dare say almost, not quite, as well as I do now . . . But the Poet is another thing, and not to have known you and the dear boys would have made life different.' The friendship had given him 'fresh life, fresh interest in every question that lies outside the petty round of things.' Bradley had been at school with Frank Lushington and had met Tennyson at Park House many years before. In 1855 on Tennyson's birthday, 6 August, the two families came into contact for the first time when the Bradleys were on holiday at Warren Farm, 'a short mile from the Needles and seven from the butcher's.' It was Edith Bradley's birthday too, celebrated with a picnic spread on a low hay-stack, where they had retreated from a flock of geese who were trying to get at the children. Edith was three, as Hallam would be a few days later. Edith was so beautiful a child 'a microscope could not discover a fault in her beauty. It rather alarms me at times,' her mother wrote in her diary. Emily felt rather the same way about Hallam – though some people found Lionel even more beautiful, as Edith herself would say when they were all a little older.

Marian Bradley, Granville's wife, was not yet twenty-four; Emily had just had her forty-second birthday. Marian had been engaged at fifteen, 'a poor little uneducated chit', and her dread was that her mind would become entirely cluttered with 'details of house-keeping' and with the demands of her ever-increasing brood of children. (There were eventually seven.) She worried that she would become 'Martha-like' and care less about 'books and intellectual things'. She envied Emily enormously for the well-stocked mind a late marriage had allowed her.

Even now, in these busy years, the Tennysons would still read Dante together, or Goethe perhaps, when it was a long time since they had read 'anything German'. When they had a quiet evening, Alfred would translate spontaneously the sixth book of the *Aeneid* or Homer's description of Hades, as Emily listened. Emily was aware of her little Latin and less Greek; Frank Lushington once lightly suggested she had complained of his 'supercilious habit of despising everybody who can't read the *Odyssey* in the original Greek.' She found Alfred's 'quite literal' rendering gave her 'as much as it is possible to have of the true spirit of the original' and was grateful. Sometimes perhaps she sewed, but she never says so. There is 'calico for Hallam's shirts' in her accounts, but a servant may have sewed them. Sometimes Emily took notes, the better to remember what she was hearing. There is a notebook of her own making – blue pages sewn together – full of her notes on Eckermann's conversations with Goethe. 'Error belongs to libraries, truth to the human mind,' Goethe said and Emily wrote it down. She and Tennyson also read together at this time Catullus, Molière, Chaucer, a life of Sydney Smith, Byron and, as always, Shakespeare. But sometimes, if Alfred's eyes were tired, they would play backgammon together.

Frank Lushington had written to Emily from Corfu to tell her she would 'find Mrs Bradley', though not actually 'extraordinarily superior' (not quite, was the implication, in Emily's class), 'very pleasant and conversible.' And so she certainly did. They would talk at great length over the years as the Bradleys, building a nearby holiday house in 1858, came regularly to Freshwater from Marlborough, where he was headmaster. The two women shared their fears of 'the dust of the world', of 'a sort of crust of conformity to the common dusty ideas of the world', where Mammon counted more than poetry. The children would play regularly together as they grew up, the Bradley girls, Edith and Daisy, the particular friends of Hallam and Lionel, sharing all the boys' games – the acting, the make-believe (often Arthurian), the hiding and seeking and running and climbing. Later there would be cricket and football and Arthur, the older brother, would consent to join them.

Marian Bradley naturally considered Emily Tennyson 'middle aged', but she found her 'charming, a beautiful combination of the intellectual and practical and earnest goodness, with a manner at once warm and gentle.' She described her 'soft white muslin dress, all folds sinking into each other, and no edges anywhere.' There was never anything hard or sharp or prickly about Emily. 'She is a first-rate wife to him, practical and devoted and fully able to sympathise with the Poet.'

Five years later, Marian Bradley wrote in her diary:

The more intimately I know her, the more I love and admire her, the more I incline to making her my ideal of all feminine loveliness of mind and manners, as well as of the highest standard of intellect and goodness. I think it most kind of her to admit me into the inner sanctuary of her thought and feelings as she does. It is a privilege I cannot sufficiently estimate and it does me a great deal of good.

One looks in Marian Bradley's unpublished, uncensored diary for any word of criticism of Emily, any sign of a clay toe – but there is none. Just once does Mrs Bradley regret Emily's situation, saying, without further explanation: 'It is a pity for such a lofty, lovely nature not to have room to blossom in.' Did she, as Lear certainly did, see Emily overshadowed and restricted by her life as the poet's wife? She never exactly says so, and it is she, Marian Bradley herself, who needs good done to her and contrasts herself with Emily. She sees herself as indolent, neglectful of the life of the spirit (a cause for great guilt in a clergyman's wife), as selfish, self-conscious, snobbish and harsh-judging. She had the self-doubting temperament of Emily's sister Louisa, and a strong sense of failure. She was always grateful for Emily's counsel and support. She is 'a sort of good angel to me'; 'my darling Emily T.' she calls her. In her turn, Marian Bradley would support Emily in 1867 at a time when she most needed her. 'No friends can be nearer to us,' Emily said of the Bradleys.

When Granville Bradley left his card at Farringford, with 'an appeal to the name of Franklin Lushington', in the summer of 1855, Tennyson invited him – the day before the two families met – to 'meet Lear, not the king but the artist'. It was a joke Tennyson would make many times. This was Lear's first brief visit to Farringford. Before he came again in October with Franklin Lushington, Emily wrote: 'I can scarcely think even yet that it is more than a dream that you and Frank are really coming . . . I trust the sadness of the past will but deepen the delight of our hours together.' They would all help each other, she suggested, as they mourned Henry Lushington, telling Lear, 'Between Ally and myself the sympathy is too intimate almost for us to help each other sometimes and we must rather be helped or hindered together.' It was a major statement of that unity and identification even small Hallam had noticed. And yet, over and over again, Emily shows herself strong enough to act independently and to help Alfred, not only with her devotion, but with a judicious mixture of solitude and stimulus, which was what he always needed.

Edward Lear would take to Corfu with him a chestnut Hallam had given him near the Beacon on the downs, and, turning it over in his pocket, would remember that visit in October 1855 as the best time he had passed 'for many a long day', with mushrooms and music, the lovely boys, and 'when they are gone, you, Alfred and Frank . . . talk-[ing] like Gods together, careless of mankind.' With Alfred and Lear there, and Frank eloquent, Emily obviously felt none of the shyness she said would sometimes overcome her. She would use any excuse to avoid a London party, but people would often comment on how good her talk was in her own home, until, at the end of her life, Theodore Watts-Dunton commemorated her as 'a conversationalist, brilliant and stimulating'.

Emily's sympathy for Lear's love for Frank Lushington was deep and must tell us something about her own love for Alfred:

One would be all and in that one cannot be, here is the loneliness. Is there a single soul on earth entirely exempt from this? The greater the heart with which one loves, the greater the heart one loves, the more does one long to bless with those infinite blessings which belong to God alone. I cannot tell if this must always be so, if it is not possible to attain to such a perfect oneness in and with God that one knows all the fulness of infinite and eternal blessing in ours and his and hers whom we love. I think it is possible to attain to this, I am sure it is the one thing worth striving for in life . . .

Emily's sympathy for Lear's yearning to be everything to Lushington did not stop her from teasing him about the effect his singing had on their young women guests at Farringford one evening. Emily had forgotten 'Friday and fish', in other words that Sir John Simeon was a Roman Catholic, which spoilt her dinner, 'theirs being spoilt' – but the evening had been redeemed by Lear's settings of Tennyson's songs. She wrote after the visit:

I am afraid you will not believe me when I tell you what a hero of romance you are at Afton. How Miss Cotton was found all pale after a sleepless night, how her companion came and poured into my ear a mighty river of thanks and praises and admiration of all sorts, even the very manner not forgotten. Why do I say 'even' when I think so much of manner myself?

Frank Lushington, writing from Corfu, would confirm Emily's ob-servation: 'I don't think I have seen anybody quite so wrapped up in his

singing as your friend Miss Cotton on that evening at Farringford.'
Emily has been accused of being ingenuous, of inappropriate match-
making, but she knew it was loving praise and admiration that Lear
needed. She was worrying about him and would go on doing so. His
response to Emily's words has been taken as some sort of coded message about his sexual preferences, but his bracketing of Lady Simeon
with Miss Cotton suggests much more that he was simply acknowledging to Emily the superficiality of his musical skills. (He had no musical
training and played by ear.)

Alack! for Miss Cotton! and Lady Simeon . . . and all admirers. But we all
know about a beautiful blue glass jar – which was only a white one after all,
only there was blue water inside it. But it's very kind of you to say what you do
for all that.

He would fantasize about marriage himself from time to time, particularly after Frank's marriage in 1862, but, after this visit to Farringford, he would think of a distant future living near the Tennysons in
his old age. He would imagine himself enjoying not only his friends, but
'Hallam and Lionel's children and Frank's grandchildren and so sliding
pleasantly out of life. Alfred by that time would have written endlessly
and there would be six or eight thick green volumes of poems. I –
possibly should be in the workhouse, but I know you would all come
and see me.' The thick green volumes of poems would be published, but
Lear would never see Hallam's or Lionel's children. He would end up in
the Villa Tennyson on the Italian Riviera, rather than in the workhouse,
but none of the family would ever go and see him.

Over the years he would regularly visit *them* and send presents to the
boys. At Christmas 1855 he gave them one of his nonsense alphabets, a
hand-drawn set of letters. Alfred took on himself the job of pasting the
paper pictures on canvas. Emily told Lear: 'The pasting and ironing
have been by no means so successful as they ought to have been, but
then I hope you will consider the remarkable fact of the Poet Laureate
being seen ironing by nearly the whole household as something of a
compensation. For what weighty lessons ought not housemaids and
cooks to learn therefrom. So that if the irons proved too cold and the
paste somewhat unmanageable I hope as a well-wisher to all housemaid and cooks, a man of universal humanity as I take you to be, will
not be too critical when you see the results. Hallam made no invidious
remarks, such as "Gandy or Eliza would have done this better" but

with rapturous delight pronounced all "bootful".' When Sotheby's auctioned these letters in 1980 (thirteen sheets in a folder, two letters on each) the catalogue described them as 'MOUNTED ON CANVAS. PROFESSIONALLY REMOVABLE.' No-one realized that it was Alfred Tennyson himself who had mounted them.

Emily would tell Lear stories about the boys and then stop, saying 'this is too Mama-ish'. There was a party on Christmas Eve and Alfred had broken up the quiet formal circle 'by insisting on our all joining in a game of Blindman's Buff,' Emily told Lear. 'I for my part thought it very good fun and I am only sorry Hallam was fast asleep and so did not come in for it.' She was rapidly getting to the point where she would say of the children, as she did on their Lake District holiday in 1857, that it was 'small pleasure to me to go anywhere without them'.

The Tennysons had their dinner at what we should think of as an extremely early hour – five or half past five. (In 1857 they changed to half past six.) Certainly the children were rarely in bed when their parents dined. Francis Palgrave would remember the boys racing 'round the table after dinner at Farringford for the raisins or walnuts which your father scattered.' And there was one dinner party, late in 1855, when the Simeons and some of the Camerons (visiting from London) were there. Emily wrote in her journal: 'The children were made to walk over the table, nothing loth. All very merry.' Not everyone approved of such merry behaviour, and one is reminded of the similar licence said to have been allowed to Wessex, Thomas Hardy's dog. When the Tennyson boys were a bit bigger, they dined with their parents when there were no guests. When there were guests, the boys would learn to wait at table, a pretty pair.

'We admire the place quite as much as we did at first and, if we were a little richer, we should not hesitate about buying it,' Emily wrote to Lear in April 1855. By the autumn of that year, they *were* a great deal richer, thanks to the huge sales of *Maud*. Emily had been prepared for the poem to be unpopular. She wrote to Edward Moxon, the publisher, in the month of publication, sending him the changes for the next printing of 'The Charge of the Light Brigade' and saying how pleased she was that the Brownings admired *Maud*. 'Mr Henry Taylor has also written very kindly about the poem, but I am prepared for a different tone of criticism from the many. It will take, I think, some time before they understand either the metres or the thoughts, but in the end I should not wonder at its being popular. So much for my prophecy!'

In fact, though most of the critics were harsh, *Maud* was immediately popular; eight thousand copies were sold in the first three months. Tennyson himself was always acutely sensitive to criticism. He told Charles Weld that October: 'I have generally (always when I published, I believe) had to run the gauntlet of much stupidity and some spite.' He said on another occasion, he could take 'the pen-punctures of those parasitic animalcules of the press' if only they would confine themselves to what he wrote and 'not glance spitefully and personally at myself.' It was easier, naturally, for Emily to take it all calmly though she identified so closely with Alfred that she could write, when terrible weather assailed them that same October that, 'The seven-inch hailstones' were nothing 'compared to those with which one is mercilessly pelted in the matter of *Maud*.' Emily was never herself attacked, of course, and she had tremendous confidence in her own judgment. She told Alfred: 'I do not as thou knowest very much care for what people say about thy things, being strong in the conceit of my own instinct . . .'

Elizabeth Barrett Browning once suggested that Tennyson was 'too much indulged. His wife is too much his second self; she does not criticize enough,' but Tennyson himself would say how much he depended on her judgment. 'I am proud of her intellect,' he wrote. She did not always get her own way. For instance, she was 'utterly against' Dr Mann's 'explanatory essay' *'Maud' Vindicated*, in which Alfred was deeply involved. Emily believed 'a thing should stand or fall of itself.'

However little she was affected by the criticisms, it was delightful, all the same, when people went into what she called 'high strikes' about Alfred's poetry. It was even more delightful when the books were bought in such numbers and Moxon paid over large sums of money. The Tennysons began negotiations in January 1856 to buy the freehold of Farringford. Emily seems never to have complained over the years of living with other people's furniture, but now she said how she longed for a settled home, 'our own things planted for life in their proper places'. They had left them behind when they moved from Chapel House as they had taken Farringford furnished. 'In spite of the difficulty of getting to and from we like it too well to wish to leave it.' The only thing against the Isle of Wight was the problem of getting quickly to her father if he were ill.

Buying the place was a long drawn-out process involving many visits and much correspondence with their solicitor, Charles Estcourt. (His 'horse hire' alone became a weighty item on the bill at 10/6 a time.) At

first he valued Farringford at below the asking price, which was eventually fixed at £6,750. Far higher than the figure mentioned in the 1853
agreement, it included much more land and a number of buildings
besides the house itself. Things did not proceed smoothly and there
were endless delays. Seymour, the seller, was discourteous; Estcourt, the
lawyer, was lazy – and they were obliged in the end to 'warehouse the
furniture from Twickenham'. Tennyson got so exasperated in March
(he was trying to work on 'my Merlin Idyll') that he thought they might
give up Farringford 'out of pure disgust' and a residual fear that the
cost of it would ruin him.

Contracts were not actually exchanged until 20 May, with a comple-
tion date as far distant as 23 November, but near the end of April Emily
wrote in her journal:

We have agreed to buy, so I suppose it is ours. Went to our withey bed, such
beautiful blue hyacinths, orchises, marsh marigolds and cowslips. Wild cherry
trees too with single white blossom. The park has for many days been rich with
cowslips and furze in flower. The elms are a golden wreath at the foot of the
down, we admired the mespilus in flower and the apple trees with their rosy
buds. He dug the bed ready for the rhododendrons. A thrush was singing
among the other birds, as he said 'mad with joy'. At sunset the burning splendour of Blackgang Chine, and St Catharine's, and the red bank of the primeval
river contrasted with the turkis-blue of the sea (that is our view from the
drawing-room) make altogether, a miracle of beauty. We are glad that Farringford is ours.

In fact, everything was not finally settled until 3 December. The
whole of 1856 had been dominated by the purchase. In January there
had been problems about where Tennyson's mother and his sister Tilly
were going to live, now that the lease of the Twickenham house had
come to an end. Emily wrote to Alfred, who was at Bonchurch with his
friend Dr Mann, working on 'Maud' Vindicated. The letter is worth
publishing as it rather surprisingly escaped Hallam's bonfires in the
1890s; most indications of family dissension were destroyed.

I fear Tilly has shown sad want of tact in what she has said to Mother. I said
what I did to Tilly when Mother had hurt me by speaking as if we were striving
with the Jesses to get her to live with us as matter of gain. Do not think
however I said anything in the very least unkind even then. It sounds harshly
put as Mother has put it but these were not my words.

I have written and said to her, 'It would be a source of unhappiness and reproach to me all the days of my life if I kept you out of our house when you wished to come and live with us. What I meant to express to Tilly was, that it rather hurt me you should have spoken as if you thought we wanted you to live with us as a matter of help in a money point of view when your comfort and happiness alone made us think of the plan. Dearest Mother and Tilly, I entreat you as far as I am concerned to do exactly what you like best.' Then I have added I was sure I spoke thy feelings too and I have said again that I had that perfect trust in herself and Tilly and that affection for them that I felt sure we should get on most lovingly together and that it would be a happiness to us to do anything we could to make them happy. I have said also that it was only the other day I had been speaking of writing to her and Tilly to ask whether they would like to come and live with us or in the house near if we bought this place.

I have told them as we should have to build and alter if they lived in the house with us I thought it best they should come first and try how they liked it, and I have added Mother must not think of that long journey to Twickenham for that I will look to the packing. Of course she is wholly unequal to it. I hope thou wilt approve of what I have done.

Alfred was totally supportive.

You have done quite right I think in respect to Mother. I believe I told her myself at Twickenham that I was afraid if she came to live with us the rest would flock there and that this was the sole objection to the plan of her living with us.

The flock included, as well as Tilly, Alfred's younger brothers Arthur, Septimus and Horatio, all as yet unmarried and coming and going mysteriously. Arthur was still mainly based (often to Frederick's despair) in Italy, but had spent six weeks with his mother at Twickenham in 1855 and was certainly still part of the flock. Emily was upset when she first saw their furniture after its service under the Tennysons at Chapel House, but begged Alfred to say nothing about it to his mother.

I pray thee say nothing of the bed and chairs and things that are spoilt by our brothers. She, poor dear, would live on bread and water to repair any loss. It is best she should not know of these . . . It makes me happier not to care about losses. I am grieved that in my first disappointment I grumbled. After all, did not Christ talk of moth and rust corrupting and the foolishness of valuing earthly treasures? 'Where your treasure is, there will your heart be also.'

'A bit of brass off and a handle off have been trifles indeed to us,' she said. Any idea of a Tennysonian invasion of the Isle of Wight was deflected in 1856; they stayed in London for the moment. Emily must have breathed a sigh of relief.

The nearby house she had mentioned – then known as the Red House – became their own home for the last half of May, as they had to move out of Farringford temporarily to allow the Seymours to sort out their furniture and effects for the sale. 'Pity us,' Emily said to Woolner. (There were some arguments about the fixtures. Were the iron railings included in the purchase or not?) The children were confused, not really understanding what was going on and the Seymours made things difficult by insisting the Tennysons left the servants behind at Farringford. Emily was coping with all sorts of problems. Unsurprisingly she told her sister Anne that she felt 'very much knocked up'. Edmund said he feared she was 'as usual' exerting herself too much. Woolner had sent some chest expanders. Emily's broke, but she told him 'Ally's big stretcher does quite well for me, holding it shorter than the handles.' She was trying to keep fit.

They were in chaos on 13 May, just about to move over to the Red House, when there was an unexpected visitor. Prince Albert, in Freshwater to inspect the new fort, had called in on his wife's Poet Laureate. The following week, by which time they had moved out, there were rumours of an even more illustrious visitor. Emily realized how ridiculous it was, the four of them (the boys in their best 'rose-coloured dresses') hanging around in the garden at Farringford for days on end, not liking to go into the house and disturb the preparations for the sale, waiting for a Queen who never turned up. Emily described the scene a number of times. To George Venables she said, 'I write to make you laugh.'

I would have answered your kind letter sooner and told you of the Prince's visit had we not been ordered to expect the Queen not by herself but only in this way. The Prince said to one of the gentlemen with him Farringford was a pretty place and he should certainly bring her to see it and there have been commands that the ports should be in readiness for her on Saturday, Tuesday and today so that, as we have since last Wednesday been in this red house, we have had to go to Farringford and spend hours in the garden waiting for her not liking to intrude into the house. Just now it rains so we have come away and I write to make you laugh at our want of etiquette and that I may do it I will begin at the beginning and tell you how every book was taken out of the room to be stowed away ready for the sale, how the chairs and tables were dancing, sofas and chairs stuffed with brown paper and all untidiness, the floor strewed with toys and cards and I know not what besides. Two loud rings at the bell. The house-maid with a face that terrified me coming close whispered in a mysterious voice 'His Royal Highness Prince Albert'. She begged me to go and speak with his gentleman. I came upon him near the stair-case. He said HRH being in the neighbourhood had asked was Mr Tennyson at home? 'Yes.' Could HRH speak with him! 'Of course.' I said 'I will go and fetch him, will the Prince (but some way I did not say the Prince) walk into the drawing-room', for it seemed to me more really civil to let him come in than wait at the door until Alfred came. I went upstairs and appeared no more but left Alfred to do the honours or receive the honour rather alone. The Prince shook hands and talked very kindly and pleasantly. He was looking out of the window when Alfred came in and there he remained for he never thought of asking him to sit down. He offered him wine. In going away one of his gentlemen brought him a large bunch of cowslips which he took into his own hands. Said they were finer than any others he had seen and that they made good tea. We have since heard that when he got on board he put them in water and said he meant to make tea of them for the Queen and himself. It is a pity that the expectation of seeing the Queen is so much spoilt by the uncomfortable state we are in. The Seymours still in the house, the entrance room nearly impassable from packages and the drawing-room stript of pictures and of some of its furniture. Alfred told the Prince there was to be a sale and apologized for the confusion but I suppose being a foreigner HRH did not well understand what was meant or he would not I should think have proposed to bring the Queen.

William Lambert, the landlord of Plumbley's Hotel, where they had stayed when they first came to Freshwater in 1853, bid for them at the sale on May 27 and 28. They bought some of the furniture, but not the pictures, and Emily was dismayed by the look of the main rooms, the faded patches where the Seymours' pictures had been. She told Thomas Woolner it looked ghastly but that Alfred liked the red wallpaper in the drawing room so much he refused to have it changed. 'Can you recommend him to any pawnbrokers for we must not look to finding our oil pictures in a more respectable quarter.' Fortunately Edmund Lushington let them have some of the Somersby paintings from Park House, ones that Cecilia had brought with her. Emily still dreamed of Holman Hunts and Edward Lears, which they had decided they could not afford.

Frank Lushington, sadly, had actually discouraged Emily from buying Lear watercolours at £12 each, reminding her that there was not only the purchase price of Farringford to be considered, 'but the whole house to patch up' and before long, he said, there would be

Hallam's school fees, 'a frightfully near prospect'. Hallam was now, in the summer of 1856, four years old and in fact did not go to school until he was nearly thirteen – but there would be tutors and a mass of other expenses. Emily was always determined not to 'overprize wealth', 'and it seems an overprizing to desire more than food and raiment and Farringford.' Neither she nor Frank, of course, realized at this point just how much *Maud* would earn by the end of 1856. Moxon had paid over only £445 in 1855, only a quarter of the previous year's royalties. In 1856 it was £2,058. 'We have so much,' Emily had said to Woolner that June. 'It is shameful to express even a half wish for more.'

In June 1856 Alfred and Emily were working hard together to get things straight when the Seymours' sale was over and they were able to move back into Farringford with their own things. Tennyson was magnificent, even though he was in the middle of 'Enid', as he called the Idyll 'Geraint and Enid' at this stage. 'Alfred has nobly stood out all the bustle of the removal, himself helping to unpack and to place the things,' Emily told Woolner. On the 4th, Emily herself helped Eliza, one of the maids, 'to make Hallam and Gandy's beds' – Gandy presumably being busy keeping an eye on the children, who were running about, delighted to be home again. 'May I stay?' Hallam asked. It was their 'home for life, I hope,' Emily said.

They left the children with Gandy and went back to dine for the last time at the Red House. Emily wrote in her journal (Merwood was their tenant farmer):

A beautiful evening. We stop at the barn and look at Merwood's bits of carpet, which he thought might do for us. I had sent to beg that he would not wait but there he sat in the barn his carpet spread out of doors. My A. gathered a rose and gave it to me as we walked through the kitchen garden. We went in at our back door. An evening to be remembered. A. gave me a welcome to our home which will be ever dear to memory. We had our tea in the drawing room. A. read me some of 'Enid'. It seemed as if we were the people of those old days. A stag's horn beetle (I think it was) came into the room with a harp like sound. We put it out and it sat on the window frame looking in at us and we admired its bright black eyes and its horns . . .

Writing to Edward Lear a year later Emily remembered the stag beetle, which came in and looked at them 'and played our welcome on its harp.'

There was an alarming time later that summer (before they knew what huge sums *Maud* would bring in) when it seemed that Oldings Bank had failed. On 2 July Alfred got back from London unexpectedly 'as I was getting into bed', told Emily the worrying news and showed 'noble disregard of it, much as the loss would affect our means.' 'I can never forget it,' she said years later. There is a nice glimpse of the two of them hanging up their 'Michael Angelo engravings' over some of the horrid patches on the red drawing-room walls the following day 'to divert themselves from dwelling on the possible loss.' The loss in the end amounted to £200, a large enough sum in those days, but 'we feared that it might have been much worse and we are glad and thankful.'

A day or two later, on Charles Turner's birthday (as Emily wrote in her journal), Alfred and Emily 'found the children playing in the chalk pit, as we went up the down, Gandy at her crochet work. Built a castle for them and shot it down, gave them wild roses and returned home with them.' The meadows and downs were full of flowers.

Five days later it was Emily's own birthday, but Alfred rarely re-membered. (He had no time for birthdays, particularly not his own.) Emily had delightful letters from her father and from her sister Louisa '– and from Alfred "Why did you not tell me?" –' which Emily con-sidered 'better than a hundred letters had he written them', rather an extraordinary remark even by the standards of one who lived at such a level of continued devotion, and acceptance of his curious ways. His birthday present the following year would be even more curious – the first lines he had written of 'Guinevere'. They might, as Emily felt with excitement, be 'the nucleus of a great poem', but they were hardly cheering words for a wife to receive from her husband. Arthur is part-ing from Guinevere, and says

> But hither shall I never come again,
> Never lie by thy side; see thee no more –
> Farewell!

Emily claimed to take the words in her stride, well schooled by Alfred to regard scarcely anything he wrote as in his own voice.

In August 1856 Edmund Lushington was at Eastbourne with his in-valids – his son, the patient Eddy, soon to die, and his querulous Cecilia – 'at times exceeding low'. He wrote to Emily, hoping the whole family would enjoy their two months in Wales – 'though why you should have abandoned English sea to find Welsh sea may puzzle the calculating brain.' He should not have been puzzled. They needed, of course, that panacea the 'change of air'. Alfred had been 'pining for mountains' for five years and the particular reason for Wales was that Alfred needed it for the Arthurian background of the Idylls. He had had the plan of an Arthurian epic over twenty years before when he had written 'Morte d'Arthur', not long after Arthur Hallam's death. That had been closely based on Malory and he always said its continuation had been killed by the *Quarterly* reviewer. It would eventually be incorporated in the *Idylls of the King* as 'The Passing of Arthur'.

Emily had been delighted that Alfred had decided to return to Arthurian themes. She realized some would say, 'Wherefore these idle tales of a day gone by?' But she was convinced they provided a worthy subject for Tennyson. 'By King Arthur', he said, 'I always meant the soul, and the Round Table the passions and capacities of a man.' Arthur's forgiveness of the adultery of Guinevere and Launcelot would move Alfred to tears when he read his own words. The stories surrounding Arthur might keep Tennyson going for years. He had written to the London Library some time before:

My wife has a great fancy for books about King Arthur, so oblige her as far as you can. She thinks I can write about the old king. I don't think books can help me to do it, nevertheless oblige her.

Alfred would say: 'I can always write when I see my subject, though sometimes I spend three quarters of a year without putting pen to paper' – walking, talking, smoking, feeling restless. Now he had his subject and was well into it. The books that could help him now, he felt, were the stories of the *Mabinogion* and the plan was to read them in the original Welsh, with the help of Charlotte Guest's recent translation. They also planned to study the *Book of Aneurin*.

It was hard work getting away from Farringford. Before they left there was the usual 'house bother' – a great well of water in the cellar and 'drains bad as they have never been before', their own responsibility now, not the Seymours'. Emily had to find time to solicit contributions for a fund-raising bazaar (the Turners sent things from Grasby) and to pack up a West Indian firefly and return it to Coventry Patmore. Alfred was persuaded to write the letter to go with that, worried as he was about the 'poor fellow' and whether 'he' would 'exhale before he gets back' to London. Hallam and Lionel enjoyed the firefly's 'side lights' anyway, without realizing how precarious his life was.

Emily spent a lot of time on 'an inventory of all the things in the house', for Alfred's plan was to let the house regularly for two or three months each summer, so they could afford to travel as a family. The lettings would always cause problems for Emily as Alfred refused to advertise, worried about getting the wrong sort of people who would open his drawers and steal his papers. In July 1856 it was a relief to leave the house, at least temporarily, in the safe hands of the Bradleys.

In years to come Emily would look back on the travelling summers of 1856 and 1857 as having undermined her health, precarious as it was, like that of the firefly. 'Both years,' she wrote to Elizabeth Barrett Browning, 'we had better have been in France or Italy.' They had bad weather in Wales – in the first fortnight at Llangollen only two fine days. 'The climate disagreed with me and spoilt my enjoyment very much,' Emily told Woolner. 'Still I am glad to have been there and glad to have seen even so little of the land of Arthur and Merlin and Taliessin.'

The children were 'wild with everything new', thriving on the journey but not so happy of course when it rained and they were confined to cramped lodgings and expected to play quietly, under Gandy's supervision, while their parents pored over their Welsh dictionary and a grammar, and even took lessons from a local schoolmaster in Dolgellau, setting 'boldly to work on *Aneurin*,' a Welsh bard who made one of the earliest mentions of King Arthur.

'Wales has been so crowded this year,' Emily told Edward Lear, 'we have been obliged to put up with poor accommodation. Ally's work has not proceeded in consequence.' But he had seen a great deal and shared some grand scenery with Emily. She liked Harlech 'best of all the places' she saw. At Barmouth she wrote in her diary: 'He said the drive here is beautiful when the tide is in and Cader Idris not veiled in clouds. I admired the place as much as he could wish me to do; I thought I never saw anything more beautiful in its way than the mountain bank with exquisite lights and shadows on crags and dark groves and fields. The sea and the sandhills radiant with sunlight. We had a delightful walk over the cliffs.'

Emily could walk over the cliffs but not climb Cader Idris. The day Tennyson went up, his return was much overdue. 'Pouring rain came on. We waited a long time for him. I heard the voice of the waters, streams and cataracts, and I never saw anything more awful than that great veil of rain drawn straight over Cader Idris, pale light at the lower edge. It looked as if death were behind it and made me shudder when I thought he was there. A message came from the guide that he had gone to Dolgelly.'

Another day Alfred took the little boys with him to the 'falls at Cynfael'. The guide, 'a widow woman', helped him carry them. The little boys were favourites wherever they went – Lionel in particular finding himself stroked or snatched up by completely strange women. One 'hugged and kissed him as if she were crazy'. He did not seem to mind.

In September Emily settled at Builth for two weeks with Gandy and the children while Tennyson went off to Caerleon. 'Our purse had grown so lean it seemed best for me to stay here with the bairns,' she told James Spedding. 'The little creatures are well and very good and pleasant,' she assured Alfred. 'Both are specially nice to me, so loving and gentle as if they felt I was alone', that they had to make up for Alfred's absence. But they were letting her get on with a history of Wales (*Hanes Cymru*) with her stumbling progress, following the *Aneurin* and the *Mabinogion*. She had always had a gift for languages, and liked to try the sound of Welsh on her tongue.

She told Edward Lear: 'You do not know how real the story of King Arthur looks, how awfully grand in Welsh, perhaps all the more because I spoke it out here all alone. There seemed to be a kind of communion with him as a real being. I think he must be a real being of some grand perfect kind. I am going to bring up the boys as Knights of the Round Table and initiated Hallam the other day. He was so interested at hearing about Caerleon and the round table, he said "Hush" to Lionel, "Let me hear." . . . Hallam described things in a strange picturesque way, he observes all things in nature minutely, but is not anxious to have much to do with books. I let him have his way at present.' He had just had his fourth birthday.

Not long after the Tennysons' return, the Patmores, who had 'improved' in Emily's opinion, visited Farringford for the first time. 'One knows they were always as good as could be *almost*, but they have gained in amenity of manner and he apparently in cheerfulness.' Emily set great store by cheerfulness. (Tennyson himself had an excellent habit of grumbling cheerfully – of making his gloomiest thoughts funny.) The Patmores were thoughtful guests, going for long walks in the morning so that Emily could get on with things that needed to be done. They further endeared themselves to Tennyson by offering to copy at the British Museum, where Patmore worked, a rare Welsh elegy on Geraint of Erbyn. Emily Tennyson seemed rather embarrassed about this. 'You both have a great deal to do of your own work,' she wrote after they had gone back to London.

Emily Patmore had decided the year before that Hallam Tennyson was 'without exception, the most splendid little fellow I ever saw. Exactly what King Arthur might have been at three years old.' The Patmores were connoisseurs of children, ending up with six of their own. Coventry had recently told the boy's godparents that five-year-old Tennyson Patmore stopped strangers with his beauty. But the younger poet may well have disapproved of the Tennysons' way of bringing up children. As we know from his poem 'The Toys', Coventry Patmore, though a devoted father, would in desperation resort to corporal punishment, which the Tennysons never did.

Emily Patmore's comment on Hallam comes just at a time when Emily Tennyson told Lear that 'almost everyone' 'admired Lionel most now, but we do not. He is very different from Hallam and we at least can well afford to admire both.' Emily was herself always extremely careful to be fair to both boys in every way, but other people seemed to find it difficult not to weigh up and analyse the comparative beauty of the brothers. The remarkable thing is their own lack of jealousy. Their devotion to each other lasted right through their lives. Before his second birthday Lionel had hated to see Hallam reproved – for being peevish – and showed his 'exceeding anxiety' that he should be good and that Emily should kiss him.

Emily's letters are full of stories about the boys, though she was well aware of the inherent dangers in telling such tales and spared many of her correspondents, as some readers may wish to be spared. Edward Lear was always interested; she knew that, but even to him she was cautious. In November 1856 she told him that, at two and a half, Lionel's heroes were Shakespeare and the Duke of Wellington. 'Indeed, both he and Hallam occasionally look grand and say "I am the Duke of Wellington". The other day Lionel went to Ally's room and seeing a medallion over the chimney piece he looked and said "Not Shakespeare". Is it not absurdly Mama-ish in me to repeat such things . . .?'

Emily was feeling particularly conscious – she was always conscious – of the preciousness and vulnerability of her sons in that dark November. The shadow of young Eddy Lushington's long dying had lain over their time in Wales. The boy, their only nephew, died on 20 October. He was twelve years old, 'a boy of great promise and Edmund's only son.' Edmund wrote: 'Oh my dear brother and sister may you be ever spared such a tearing away of life from life and love from love.' George Venables, who had mourned the child's uncle Henry so bitterly the year before, came to the funeral. 'It was certainly quite as well', Edmund wrote to Emily, 'that Cissy was altogether absent.' *In Memoriam*, he told her, seemed 'dearer than ever'.

Emily told Drummond Rawnsley two weeks later that she and Alfred had to hurry off to Park House. 'The entreaties are so urgent that we will go before Edmund leaves for Glasgow on the 20th,' returning to his work at the university, 'and poor Cissy is in so sadly depressed a state that refusal is out of the question, though we must leave our children behind.' It was, of course, a difficult visit. 'It is scarcely possible to express the sadness of the house,' Emily told Edward Lear. There was 'an almost hopeless sadness brooding over all things.' Cecilia would get worse and worse until a time when her husband said: 'Nothing can be made of her. She seems to want to go to Hampstead, then she fancies the sea might do her good, but more often she speaks as if she was sure nothing in the world could possibly do her good.' It sounds exactly like her brother Alfred in the 1840s, the gloom and indecisiveness from which Emily had rescued him. Nothing could save Cecilia now and Park House would never again be the haven it had been. Cecilia said to Edmund that she wished he had 'a good strong wife to take care of thee, to fondle and comfort thee. Well dost thou deserve it.' For all her lack of great physical strength, Emily was just such a wife to Alfred. Edmund would beg Emily to write to Cecilia to try 'to keep her up to' her promises to attempt to 'be as cheery and kindly as she can'. Emily did her best at Park House in November 1856 and Edmund was grateful. Their visit, he said, had been very precious and he hoped they were none the worse for it. At the risk of using 'a stale phrase', he could not resist comparing Emily to an angel.

'I always felt the ground hollow beneath me,' Emily would tell George Venables, after the death of yet another Lushington brother, Tom, whom they had seen with his children on that visit in 1856. 'And now this succession of open graves at Park House makes one live almost as much in expectation of death as of life. An awful world truly. I am not grown into a doleful heart for all I say. I think the boys find me not at all a bad playmate. I am only rather more nervous about illness than usual.'

It was a great joy to return from Park House to Farringford to a greeting from the healthy little boys, shouting 'I am very glad to see you!' as they ran and skipped, their eyes beaming, to welcome their parents home.

Two of the Idylls could have been ready for publication in June 1857, but Tennyson decided to withhold them – after some complex reactions from their friends – until he had enough for a bigger book. He asked that all the trial copies Emily had sent out should be destroyed, but apparently allowed Palgrave to retain one. Emily had some correspondence with James Spedding about 'Merlin'. Spedding had told Tennyson himself: 'I am still of the opinion that Merlin would not have been talked over by that kind of woman.' Spedding thought the effect of the poem was 'injured by the predominance of harlotry', and said to Emily: 'You agree with me I know about Merlin and Nimuë.' Emily was not at all sure she did agree, though she felt her own experience was too limited for her to have much confidence in her own opinion. Emily wrote to Spedding:

'Merlin' seems to me an awful tragedy. Do you not think that the higher and more imaginative the man, the more likely he is to fall, the lower he is likely to fall if he once yield ever so little to a base and evil influence? You think this, perhaps but think also that in the case of Merlin, Nimuë does not look, even at the beginning, enough the angel of light to have attracted him but it seems to me devotion, or an appearance of it, has more power over men than over women in itself. To a woman it is repulsive if she have no sympathy with him who pays it, but I do not think it is so with men. Only I have looked at the world through such a very little chink all my life that I feel I have small right to give any opinion at all on the subject. And yet I felt it so kind in you to say what you thought, I am in a way constrained to say what I think, however foolish my thoughts may be.

She told George Venables: 'I am quite sure that they are poems of a grand moral feeling. Others can judge better than I whether the manner of putting them is what the age will not bear.'

Emily could certainly 'bear' the poems herself. She was delighted that Robert Browning's reaction was 'so encouraging', but 'then the worst of it is', she told his wife, 'a grain of dispraise from almost anyone outweighs even your praise and people come and say these old stories will not do and he so far believes them that he stops work for months, perhaps for years, and life is so short.'

Emily was pleased anyway that James Spedding was *not* 'determined to write a book proving the poet's home is a nest of demons or he could not have written this' – which recalls the folly of the anonymous critic of *Maud* who declared that 'If an author pipe of adultery, fornication, murder and suicide set him down as the practiser of these crimes.' (To which Tennyson had responded: 'Adulterer I may be, fornicator I may be, murderer I may be, suicide I am not yet.' It was a remark his son would one day censor, just in case anyone took it the wrong way.)

Emily was very unhappy about the illustrations for the new Moxon edition, which had been in preparation since 1854. Her reactions were rather less explosive than Frederick's ('How vilely the Artists have treated my brother'), but she wrote to Thomas Woolner that she could not help fearing the illustrated book would be 'a failure, for even in those things that are fine in themselves, there is for the most part some departure from the story.'

For instance, in 'The Lord of Burleigh', what has the Lady to do when she is in a cottage surrounded by peasants instead of at Burleigh with her own weeping Lord by her side. Her face is beautiful and the group altogether good, it seems to me – if it had the remotest connection with the poem. 'The Miller's Daughter' I positively loathe. 'Locksley Hall' I like not. Hunt's things I delight in. What a pity he has put Oriana in an Eastern dress when she is an English woman ... You will think I am in a scolding mood, but is it not a pity that these artists should not have paid a little more attention to the letter of the poems?

Frank Lushington, writing to Emily from Corfu before seeing the book, said that he did not expect the illustrations to be worth looking at 'but one hopes at any rate that people enough will be foolish enough to buy the book to put a considerable sum into Alfred's pocket towards the improving of Farringford.' Moxon himself had been 'foolish enough' to put £2,000 into Alfred's pocket in advance of sales. Emily assured Woolner that when she spoke of the book being a failure, it 'was not exactly meant in a money point of view.' Described so often as an angel herself, Emily was now objecting to the hair of Rossetti's angel for 'The Palace of Art' being so 'coarse and rough'. She could also have objected that he appeared to be taking a great bite out of the forehead of poor St Cecilia, rather than simply looking at her. John Ruskin, while agreeing that the pictures were not really illustrations of the poems, thought there was much to be said for 'making people think and puzzle a little', but described Tennyson himself, predictably, as in a much worse state than Emily about the book, shaking like the 'jarred string of a harp', as he complained about it. There were more important reasons for complaint after Edward Moxon's death in June 1858.

For Moxon, the Illustrated Edition did turn out to be a failure from 'a money point of view'. He had been ridiculously optimistic and had printed 10,000 copies – far too many. The price was much too high for a large sale – he had been hoping to recover not only Tennyson's advance, but all the expense involved in the illustrations – payment both to the original artists and to the engravers. On Moxon's death, 7,790 copies remained unsold.

William Moxon, his brother, looked at the figures and decided that Tennyson owed 'the estate of the late Mr Moxon' the amazing sum of £8,886 8s 4d, a great deal more than the freehold of Farringford had cost. Charles Weld, the brother-in-law to whom they turned for legal advice, told Emily that William Moxon said the money was owed because the whole financial disaster was Tennyson's fault, that 'the Edition in question was published at Alfred's desire.' Moxon 'held him morally and legally responsible to stand by the venture.'

Weld asked Emily to try and find something that proved the edition had been Moxon's own idea. He did not think it would be a good idea for Alfred to come up to town 'for he would only worry himself and do no good.' Unused to dealing with women in such matters, he at first thought it would be unwise for Emily to 'interfere' or 'dabble' or take things upon herself. 'Forster and I think that in future you had far better *not* write . . . but allow *us* or your solicitor to act.'

Emily typically was not offended by this letter and was grateful to John Forster and Charles Weld, but she knew she was herself accountable: 'I will of course copy anything, answer anything, do anything I can . . . I will even come up to Burlington House alone if it would be desirable to question me personally.' She had a hard time looking for the relevant papers. 'My brain aches with vexation and much writing on the subject,' she told Woolner on 28 October. A few days later, she told Weld: 'Until eleven last night and again this morning, we were employed hunting up every letter that had been written by the Moxons and all the available accounts.' Her filing system was not as efficient as it should have been. 'I don't know how many times – 3 or 4 times – I looked in the drawer where the accounts were and did not see them before just now.' 'We have never been very careful of these things not foreseeing events and trusting to the fact that last year's settlement precludes all previous claims.' They did not live in a world of 'unearned advances' or 'returns' from the bookshops.

Emily sent John Forster a statement in her own hand of 'facts respecting the Illustrated Edition'. 'They must be taken as *mine* in which he, as far as he remembers, concurs.' She found no letters to prove the edition had been Moxon's own idea, but she simply stated that was so, and that Alfred had accepted £2,000 in lieu of a much larger sum he might have expected. He was 'heartily sorry if the speculation had proved a failure.' Emily herself told Weld that she understood William Moxon's position; she begged her brother-in-law not to be 'much annoyed by what he says. He is, I suspect, so angry that his brother has made a bad speculation that he does not know what he says. I am only sorry you should suffer from his wrath, as Ally's representative.'

Weld and Forster had in the end agreed that Emily's presence in London might help. Weld wrote: 'Should you decide on coming he will meet you here at breakfast on Saturday morning.' But Tennyson would not hear of Emily going; it was now November and the east wind was bitter. He insisted on going himself, knowing, however deeply Emily was involved, 'no agreement could be made without him.'

Matters were finally resolved, 'thanks to Charles Weld's energetic kindness,' which Emily would always remember. The exact terms of the settlement are not clear, but the Illustrated Edition was sold on to Routledge, just in time for it to be marketed as a guinea gift book for Christmas 1858. And Tennyson continued to be published by Moxon and Co., now managed by Bradbury and Evans, who had always printed Moxon's books. There would be more problems over the Idylls ('fresh troubles having arisen and old ones revived'). 'I wish you could persuade Tennyson to go to another publisher,' Woolner said to Emily, seeing it as 'some abstract amiability which keeps him to this ghost of Moxon's firm.'

One of the saddest things from Emily's point of view was that her plan for a penny edition of some of the most popular poems had been abandoned. Charles Weld had agreed with her that there should be 'a popular selection at 1d', so cheap that everyone could afford it. She imagined the edition prefaced by these words: 'A selection made at the request of some of the people and dedicated to the people by A.T.' Tennyson himself had sent Moxon 'a workman's letter' and suggested a *May Queen* at threepence or sixpence. In 1864 Emily would still be advocating a cheap edition. Eventually in 1865 *A Selection from the Works of Alfred Tennyson* did appear in Moxon's Miniature Poets series, dedicated to 'the Working Men of England'. There were eight parts and each part cost sixpence, not a penny. Sixpence was a considerable sum at a time when, for instance, the Tennysons' parlourmaid earned just £3 a quarter – only ten sixpences a week.

In 1857 Tennyson had gone up to London on 27 April for his dentist, the London Library and business in connection with the trial edition of *Enid and Nimuë*, which he was trying out on his friends. Emily ordered a carriage to take them all comfortably to the boat but when it arrived it was only a two-seater. Emily said: 'I fear there is no room for you, my children.' Poor Hallam's eyes filled with tears so they each took a child on their knees. There was excitement when they arrived at the dock for the ferry was just pulling out and Tennyson had to leap into one of the rowing boats and get the oarsman to follow so that he could shout at the ferry. 'It stops and he gets on board', as Emily and the children watched, waving. 'I did not see you waving the handkerchief for I am short-sighted,' his papa wrote to Hallam not long after. This was his next letter:

Dear Hallam

When you get this you must turn to Lionel and give him a nice little kiss and you must give another kiss to dear Mama.

This letter comes from

PAPA

At the bottom of this page, Alfred put five crosses and the one word 'Thine', which was obviously for Emily. The boys were becoming more and more intensely devoted to their father. Hallam evidently thought the kisses on the paper had some sort of magic power to 'bring Papa back in this drawing room.' Once when Alfred was about to depart, Hallam whispered over and over again, loud enough for him to hear, 'Why does he go?' 'Why does he go?', putting into words his mother's apparently well-suppressed feelings.

In Tennyson's absence, Emily recorded in her journal:

I look after calves, poultry and vine, plant roses and clematis and woodbine near his chair in the corner of the kitchen garden (I call it his but he put it there for me) and one rose tree near our arbour, tie up lettuces for him, put pine branches in the hedge near where it is thin and sow mignonette, get lilies of the valley for his room, write many letters and read a little.

Tennyson was in pain from another wretched in-growing toenail. ('Do not let anyone play tricks with that toe,' Emily said, dreading chloroform again.) There were also the tedious visits to the dentist; even so he was diligent in finding a new nurse for the boys, in trying to acquire more pictures for the faded patches on the walls at Farringford, and in commenting on Emily's choice of wallpapers for the Red House near by. They had rented it and were trying to get it in order for Tennyson's mother's household. In April Alfred and Emily had attended Horatio's wedding on the Island. He married Charlotte Elwes in the little church at St Lawrence on 16 April. Charlie, as Emily called her, came from the next village in Lincolnshire to 'my father and the Turners', and Louisa knew her well and liked her. She was a great deal younger than Horatio, the youngest of the Tennyson brothers, who was now already thirty-seven.

After the wedding breakfast Emily said: 'We all danced under the Verandah, A. and I arm in arm.' That night, Emily wrote: 'I sit near A at dinner to my delight.' One of the other guests observed the Tennysons:

I think I could be fond of him: all his friends are. One sees that he is simple and warm-hearted, and unspoilt by the world . . . Mrs Tennyson was there and charms me more than he does. She is tall, and slight, and simple, and sensible, with something of a thoughtful melancholy about her which interests one much; not that it is anything approaching unhappiness, and he seems quite devoted to her.

Emily's slightly preoccupied melancholy air may merely have meant she was missing the children and wishing they had been invited to the wedding too. 'Two days and nights from the children promise me small pleasure,' she had told Woolner before setting out. She was also not feeling at all well and would write to Venables in June, in confidence, that she might need to go to London to see a doctor. But she did not go. Perhaps it was simply that, as she told Lear that year, she was 'worn out in body and mind'. By June the house was full of people, the drains were causing problems again and the servants feeling 'rebellious'. The Tennyson family was at Farringford in quantity.

As it turned out, old Mrs Tennyson and Tilly for some reason did not get to Horatio's wedding and they never settled at the Red House. They seemed quite happy at this point to do without a great deal of Alfred's company. (In Wales, the year before, Emily had said to Alfred, 'It seems

to me such a pity that Mother and Tilly should not come to visit us when they are so near.') But they were at Farringford in June 1857, together with Charles and Louisa, Edmund and Cecilia, Horatio and his new wife. Tilly wrote to her cousin Lewis Fytche of being supported down the slippery slope at Alum Bay by 'Rashy and Edmund. I was afraid of rolling into the sea,' she said. She told him she and her mother were to share a house in Belgravia with Horatio and Charlotte. Emily told Edward Lear that if Farringford were still full of Tennysons, there would be a bed for him in the 'Red house just outside the gate'. Lear arrived on 4 July and it was probably on this occasion that he drew Hallam.

Edward Lear's singing was as usual a great success, and not only with

Miss Cotton. 'Lionel throws himself on my knee,' Emily recorded, 'and seems quite overpowered by music.' When everyone eventually departed, Emily wrote on 9 July: 'The first evening we have been alone for two months or more.' 'You know what it is to get into a crazy state from overwork,' she had told Woolner, even before the assorted Tennysons had arrived. 'I quite agree with what you say about big parties.'

Eliza Tennyson enjoyed her grandsons, aged just three and nearly five at this stage. She would see them again from time to time, mostly on brief visits when the family was in London. Her relationship with them is celebrated in her only surviving verse, written on paper watermarked 1859.

> My dear little Grandsons I love you both well,
> O, how much I love you mere words cannot tell.
> I wish I was nearer to see your dear faces
> Which bloom like the Rose when you quicken your paces.
> And are fann'd by the breeze that bends the tall trees
> As you gallop along or sit down at your ease.
> Now Papa's and Mamma's kind hearts it rejoices
> When they see your glad looks and hear your sweet voices.
> And now my dear boys I must bid you adieu.
> I hope soon you'll see me and I shall see you.

'A blessed solace to him'

<hr>

'We both sigh for the warm south,' Emily told Edward Lear in June 1857, 'but the Marshalls have been so kind as to give a yearly tenant notice for us' at Tent Lodge; that was the house on Coniston Water where they had stayed when they were on their honeymoon seven years before. They could not very well refuse. They would stay in Britain again this year and would be away from Farringford from July till early November. Three and a half months was a long time to be away from home and Emily was up till one or two in the morning the day they left.

They had a couple of nights in London. Emily saw her sister Anne. Indeed, Tennyson stayed with the Welds at Burlington House – where the Royal Society was now based – while Emily and the boys were at Draper's Hotel, presumably because there was not room for all of them in the apartment. On 17 July, after a brief call on Lady Franklin, Emily went to Little Holland House for the first time. FitzGerald, on Tennyson's earlier visit to London that year, had commented on the fact that the poet was 'staying at a great house in Kensington with which I won't meddle.' Little Holland House was not at all the sort of place that this suggests. Emily called it the Enchanted Palace and the boys loved swinging and climbing trees in the garden. It was a delightfully relaxed sort of paradise in Melbury Road – *rus in urbe* – the home of Thoby Prinsep and his wife, Sarah, who was one of Julia Cameron's sisters. It was also the home at this period of G.F. Watts, who would have so large a part to play in creating the images of the Tennysons handed down to posterity.

On this visit in 1857 they had hardly time to do more than admire the house and gardens, but they would all come to know the Prinseps very well and to spend a lot of time sitting quietly for Watts, and pondering, not just on his skill and his increasing fame, but on his temper (like summer lightning), his odd diet, his migraines and melancholia and, eventually his extraordinary marriage to Ellen Terry: the bride not yet seventeen, Watts more than twice her age. On a visit to Little Holland House on 28 July the following year, Watts sketched Emily for the first time. He drew her at least twice before the familiar 1862–3 painting, which has been so often reproduced (see Plates 11 and 13).

From London the Tennysons went into Lincolnshire and spent nearly two weeks at Grasby. Emily's expurgated journal naturally tells us nothing of any strains there may have been with Louisa. Louisa's own diary continues to show an extremely disturbed mind, her 'want of faith in Christ, Godhead and the Holy Ghost', her anger, her aggression towards both her husband and her father. The year before there is the brief unexplained entry: 'Very angry that Pa came home,' but Henry Sellwood was still living with them in the summer of 1857 and Emily records an interesting time with some exploration of the family past – visits to the Turner house at Caistor and to Bayons Manor. They all ('Lou, my father, A. and I') received communion from Charles – and the same afternoon Emily took the boys to evensong. 'Both very good but Hallam asks whether the man will soon let him out.' The following week, now recognizing the clergyman, he asked 'if Uncle Charley will leave his nightgown in church'. After some further attempts at church-going in the Lake District (when Hallam repeatedly asked 'What does that mean?' during the sermon, and, when hushed, could scarcely be restrained from dancing) Emily decided the children could make do with family prayers for the moment.

Edward Lear wrote sadly about visiting old friends – beautiful places, fine weather 'and people very happy and rich. Nevertheless I had rather be a cauliflower.' How could Emily reply to such a letter? She told him of the school feast at Grasby, of buying plumcakes and toys in Caistor for the village children. Emily had enjoyed the children's 'great fancy in their dances to the Hurdy-gurdy of a wandering min-strel' and their singing on the vicarage lawn. Tennyson had left Grasby on 27 July but, together with Woolner and two of their servants, he joined Emily and the children at Manchester station on the 31st. Emily's physical strength at this period – when less than two months before she had been thinking of consulting a London doctor – is sug-gested by the fact that she travelled across England from Lincolnshire to Manchester in the morning, spent the afternoon with her family at the Great Exhibition, looking at pictures, and then changed and went out in the evening to hear Charles Dickens read *A Christmas Carol* at the Free Trade Hall. Next morning, after breakfast with Woolner, they spent a few more hours at the Exhibition. Emily found a portrait of Alexander Pope showed a face 'so bitter' it 'almost makes me weep'. Tennyson told someone that Emily 'would willingly have spent a week there.' In the brief time they had, 'It was almost a mockery to try to look at anything,' Emily told Lear. 'We did however try to see Holman Hunt's picture and yours amongst other things. Your time of recognition will come some day I feel sure.'

Among the other things they saw was Woolner's recent bust of Tennyson. The now bearded Tennyson looked at the beardless bust. Emily much regretted the change, though beards were 'gradually appearing up and down the world'. Carlyle had grown one at much the same time. Emily had told Spedding, soon after Tennyson grew his the previous summer: 'Pray do not defend the beard; it will surely fall.' To Woolner she had said in March: 'I wish the public could compel Alfred by act of Parliament to cut off his beard!' When Lear had sent a cross from Mount Athos that June, he had told her he sent it as the bearded monks reminded him of Alfred's new appearance. Emily said she would tell Ally and that 'rather than be like the lazy monks, maybe he will cut it off.' Twelve years later, Julia Margaret Cameron's portrait of the bearded Tennyson was said by him, himself, to be remarkably like a 'Dirty Monk'. He never cut off his beard and, looking at the splendid photo James Mudd took of him that summer, one can see why. It seems apparent that Tennyson did not care what Emily felt about the beard.

Nathaniel Hawthorne and his wife, spotting him at the Exhibition, were impressed. Tennyson looked 'very handsome and careless looking, with a wide-awake hat, a black beard, round shoulders and slouching gait; most romantic, poetic and interesting . . .' 'I liked him well and rejoiced more in him than in all the other wonders of the Exhibition.' Hawthorne's one derogatory remark was that Tennyson's shirt (the only white thing about him) 'might have been clean the day before'. Hawthorne's comments were published in Tennyson's lifetime. 'I asked my wife if she could have let me wear a dirty shirt at the Exhibition and she said "No, certainly not".' Hawthorne was then American consul at Liverpool and already well known as a novelist, but he and his wife did not introduce themselves; they simply observed enthusiastically. Sophia Hawthorne wrote to her sister:

I wanted you to know how happy and loving they all seemed together. As Tennyson is in very ill health, very shy and moody, I had sometimes thought his wife might look worn and sad. I was delighted, therefore, to see her serene and sweet face. I cannot say, however, that there was no solicitude in it, but it was a solicitude entirely penetrated with satisfied tenderness.

The Hawthornes' own marriage had seemed a model, 'a vindication of true love and married happiness'. People would wonder, as they wondered about Tennyson, how Hawthorne could have 'such a taste for the morbid anatomy of the human heart, and such knowledge of it too.' Now it seems Sophia was not 'the angel of the house' it appeared – 'her pose of submission repressing overt rage'. Their marriage was to founder the year after this near encounter with the Tennysons.

There is a longer description of Emily and of the whole family in an earlier letter from Sophia Hawthorne to her sister. She noticed Emily's 'slightly peasant air' – the 'Kleinstädtisch', provincial look Carlyle had also commented on – which contrasted, she thought, with Tennyson's own aristocratic looks. 'I do not know whether she be born a lady or not,' the American observer wrote; Tennyson she knew was 'of gentle blood'. One wonders what the two Lincolnshire attorneys, Emily's father, Henry Sellwood, and Alfred's grandfather, George Tennyson, would have made of the distinction she drew between them.

Mrs Tennyson had a sweet face, and the very sweetest smile I ever saw; and when she spoke to her husband or listened to him, her face showered a tender, happy rain of light ... The children were very pretty and picturesque, and Tennyson seemed to love them immensely. He devoted himself to them and was absorbed in their interest ... Allingham, another English poet, told Mr Hawthorne that his wife was an admirable one for him, wise, tender, and of perfect temper, and she looks all this; and there is a kind of adoration in her expression when she addresses him. If he is moody and ill, I am sure she must be a blessed solace to him.

Sophia Hawthorne unashamedly followed the Tennysons round the Exhibition – perhaps other people were doing the same. She thought one of the servants was perhaps their 'eldest daughter' – a nice un-solicited comment on how they treated their employees. Tennyson had a horror of being recognized and must have winced when the boys, seeing James Mudd's portrait of Tennyson on display in the Photography Section, shouted 'That is Papa!'

When Lionel lingered with the servants, who were buying a catalogue, bold Sophia Hawthorne seized the 'youngest darling' with the golden hair, and kissed him to her 'heart's content'. Lionel had become used to this sort of treatment in Wales the year before and 'he smiled and seemed well pleased. And I was well pleased to have had in my arms Tennyson's child.'

Another admirer of the Tennyson children met them that summer. Charles Lutwidge Dodgson, not yet famous as Lewis Carroll, came to Coniston in September. The Tennysons had been at Tent Lodge for nearly two months by then and should have felt relaxed and refreshed, but there had been all sorts of strains and stresses. It had poured with rain on Hallam's birthday and the Marshalls gave him whips and a gun as well as the more welcome *Poems for Little Children*. (Emily actually crossed out 'whips and a gun' and substituted 'gifts' in her revised journal.) Then there had been an embarrassing incident when Alfred had grumbled about the house being 'too much shut up with trees' and the Marshalls, who had sent a woodman to improve the situation, found he had cut down a magnificent beech by mistake – instead of the small one they had meant. Another day, out riding (unusual for him) Tennyson lost his watch, an old favourite. Emily and the children and everyone else spent hours looking for it in vain.

To William Allingham, Emily wrote: 'I am stupid as weariness and aches can make me.' Edward Lear she congratulated on selling his great picture of Corfu, for £525, although, he said, it melted away in paying debts. 'One is so glad one can scarcely help crying for joy . . . Did I not say your day was coming?' But they were all ill, she told him, and had talked of returning only a week after they had arrived, if it had not been for fear of hurting 'those dear kind Marshalls'. Lionel was particularly unwell and both boys wept if their parents went off without them.

Things improved with some delightful expeditions and some extremely happy days. On one of them they returned to the little island where they had picnicked seven years before. The journal tells of drives and boating expeditions, of admiring Lingmoor 'couching magnificently like a lion at the foot of Langdale Pikes', as Alfred's arm supported Emily in the carriage. But it seemed, she told Lear, that 'We had scarcely a day alone for six months.' They were across at Monk Coniston, the Marshalls' own house, a great deal of the time and there were lots of visitors at both houses. Venables and Frank Lushington were among them, but not Edward Lear whom Emily most wanted to see. She always preferred her own house and wished she could take it with her 'like a snail, to moor alongside of that of a friend.'

Charles Dodgson had taken some photographs of the Tennyson's niece, eight-year-old Agnes Weld, that summer in Yorkshire. Anne sent them to her brother-in-law and Tennyson admired them. There is one of Agnes dressed up as Little Red Riding Hood, with her basket of goodies for her grandmother. It is technically excellent, the light catching the ivy leaves on the wall behind her, and every detail of the child herself. It was much admired when Dodgson exhibited it in London the following year. In the other photograph, where Agnes is wearing her best dress, she looks an unhappy child. She would become an unhappy woman. In a later photograph taken by Dodgson in 1862, Agnes shows a strong resemblance to her aunt Louisa, another unhappy woman, whose influence on her would be as strong as the resemblance. In that photo, the girl's fingers are pinching uneasily the stuff of her pelisse and she shows no interest in the pigeon on the table; perhaps it is dead.

Dodgson called at Tent Lodge on 18 September. It is not in the least surprising that Emily welcomed him. The children had not yet been well photographed. It would be years before their friend Mrs Cameron came to possess a camera. Dodgson wrote in his diary:

Only Mrs Tennyson was at home, and I sent in my card, adding (underneath the name) in pencil 'artist of "Agnes Grace" and "Little Red Riding Hood".' On the strength of this introduction I was most kindly received and spent nearly an hour there. I saw also the two children, Hallam and Lionel, five and three years old, the most beautiful boys of their age I ever saw. I got leave to take portraits of them . . . Both the children proposed coming with me when I left – how far seemed immaterial to them.

The Pied Piper's magic was already at work, as it was on the Liddell children – whom he already knew – and would be on so many other children over the years.

The Tennysons were spending their last few days in the Lake District at Monk Coniston, and it was there the photographs were taken over several days. Dodgson photographed everyone, including Emily herself. There were failures (the silver nitrate bath the wrong strength) and there were successes. In December Dodgson would record in his diary a letter from Emily 'begging me to destroy her picture', which presumably he did. She seems to have heard of Dodgson's habit of selling his photographs, not only to his friends, but also through Rymans, the stationers; she asked him to keep only three of Tennyson. The portrait of Hallam and Lionel wrapped together in a chair is extremely natural. The sitters apparently needed to be completely still only for forty-five seconds, but even that is a long time for small children. Dodgson was particularly interested in grouping and there was a dark but beautiful shot of Hallam on Alfred's knee, with James and Mary Marshall and their eleven-year-old daughter, Julia. Emily was presumably keeping the wriggling Lionel somewhere just out of view. In 1890 Dodgson would write to a friend: 'Any details of your visit to Tennyson and of his present self and his wife, would deeply interest me. I used to know him with considerable intimacy. She (then *Mrs* Tennyson) was *quite* delightful; and Lionel was, I think, the loveliest child, boy or girl, I ever saw.' For such a connoisseur of small girls as Lewis Carroll – as we tend now to think of him – that was a remarkable statement.

'We always are and are not going to Scotland next week,' Emily wrote, 'which we shall do remains to be seen. We have been very poorly almost all the while here and I rather dread moving further north.' They had been invited to visit the Duke and Duchess of Argyll at Inverary Castle, an invitation difficult to refuse. The Argylls were devoted admirers of Tennyson's poetry and Tennyson would regularly call at Argyll Lodge in London and read his latest poems. 'It takes superhuman strength of character not to love a duchess,' and Tennyson never resisted the appeal of the Argylls, though he always maintained he behaved exactly the same to everyone, painter, plasterer or peer. Emily seems to have thought it appropriate for the Poet Laureate to consort with Dukes from time to time. She encouraged him to call on them in London and was gratified that they were 'very kind'. But her sympathy always responded more eagerly to those who really needed her: Tennyson, of course, and others afflicted by what Lear called 'the Morbids' – including Lear himself, with his 'background of near destitution', Marian Bradley, so often reluctantly pregnant and so self-doubting, and plain young Louisa Simeon, the potential nun.

There was an embarrassing muddle when they did eventually get to Inverary – the only time Emily visited Scotland. A letter had gone astray; they arrived to find the Duke of Argyll at Balmoral, the Duchess with her mother, the Duchess of Sutherland, at Dunrobin. Emily felt extremely awkward and wished herself at home. 'I am homesick,' she wrote in her journal on 5 October – but presumably Farringford was let until November, for it was another month before she got there, after a few days at Carstairs with Robert Monteith, a look at the Marshalls' mills in Leeds, a week at Park House, and a visit to the Camerons in Putney – where they saw and went to see a great crowd of other people: the Carlyles (the Tennysons had been reading both *Frederick the Great* and *The French Revolution* that year), the Patmores, Woolner, William Rossetti, Holman Hunt – and dear Edward Lear.

'I cannot tell you how glad I was to get home,' Emily wrote to Lear, knowing he would understand. 'The boys went about patting their toys, and saying "My dear old Farringford, my own dear horse, my own dear cart."'

This would be the pattern for the next few years. The Tennysons would spend the summers away from home, with Farringford let, when they could find suitable tenants, at seven guineas a week. (This would often cause problems; Emily would write of being 'deluded by hopes of letting the house.') *Where* they would go was unpredictable up to the last moment. Emily never dissuaded Tennyson from going anywhere, but he would tend to use her as an excuse when he failed to go somewhere he did not really want to go anyway – to Australia (with Woolner), to Madeira (with the Brookfields) and to America, over and over again.

In unsatisfactory lodgings in north London, in July 1858, Emily wrote to Edward Lear: 'I have been trying to get Alfred to Corfu while you and Frank are still there, but I shall not manage it. Indeed today he proposed that we should take a house really on the Heath and send for servants and roam no further. Nevertheless he may find himself within the Arctic Circle, who knows?' Tennyson got to Norway that summer, to Portugal the following year (when Emily hoped he might join Lear in Rome), to Cornwall and the Scilly Isles in 1860, while Emily settled for London and family visits to Grasby and Park House. In London the Zoo was a constant attraction for the boys; one lion was 'so kind' as to make more of a roar for Lionel than Emily had ever heard before.

The boys were not yet ready, Emily felt, for long journeys abroad and she was not at all inclined to leave them, though sometimes she thought longingly of 'some near place on the continent', where they might be more sure of sunshine. At Park House the boys, playing cricket with their Lushington girl cousins, must have painfully reminded the family of the dead Eddy, who had once also been 'a little fellow with splendid long curls'. John Simeon regretted Emily going to Grasby 'for I don't think it ever agrees with you'. Measles in the village ruled out Grasby in that summer of 1859, but Park House hardly agreed with her either – Venables found the state of the Lushington sisters and their sister-in-law, Cecilia, 'most pitiable'. Frank would despair of them: 'They all seem to want good of some kind or other doing to them.' It was a house of invalids, heavy with depression, and Emily herself seems to have had some sort of collapse while she was there.

The doctor had forbidden her to write, she told Thomas Woolner, 'which indeed part of the time was needless as I could not write.' By September she was much better, and she wrote to Margaret Gatty: 'I get very crazy when I write. There is no saying what I might say if you trusted me long with a pen.' Margaret Gatty had become one of Emily's most regular correspondents. She had thrust herself unashamedly on their acquaintance the year before. Her husband, Alfred Gatty, would tell Hardwick Rawnsley how it happened. His wife, he said,

was a deep admirer of T's poetry and taught me to become so. She was staying in Hampshire, with a dear old friend, and resolved, to the horror of her hostess, to cross the Solent and invade the Poet's home. She reached Yarmouth, and was about to land when the skipper said "Here comes Mr Tennyson" and, sure enough, he appeared in cloak and wideawake (quite a Velasquez . . .) when she introduced herself, told him her errand and went back with him in the boat . . . He bade her come back in a week's time and stay with them and she did so. I may say she was worthy of this honour . . .

Her *Parables from Nature* had begun appearing in 1855 and Tennyson himself had not only written to assure her that his boys would read them as soon as they were old enough, but had told someone he admired one of the parables, 'The Unknown Land', 'as much as anything he had ever read.' There was no need for her friend's horror, and Emily said: 'We would by no means have so pleasant an acquaintance begin and end in this one visit.' It did not. Mrs Gatty showered the family with presents – not only books – and exchanged letters and occasional visits for years to come. She remained primarily an admirer of Tennyson and the large surviving number of letters from Emily to her does not reflect an intimate friendship of the sort Emily enjoyed with Edward Lear, though her letters were always frank and informal.

Emily ended one brief but perfectly sane letter to Margaret Gatty: 'Your poor mad woman.' It would be foolish to make too much of this.

No-one else ever called Emily Tennyson stupid, mad or crazy – but she would occasionally use the words of herself. She would say she was stupid or crazy with overwork. In 1859 she had had an unusually hectic time at Farringford even by her standards – and to take her holiday among the stresses and strains of Park House was obviously ill advised. There would come a time, not far off, when she would not even *write* to them, knowing that whatever she said would hurt or offend someone.

The Tennysons would be away in the summers ostensibly for a change and a rest. For the other nine or ten months of the year, Emily was almost always entirely at Farringford. There was the demanding work for Alfred, and not only the letter writing. She took a close interest in everything – making sure, for instance, that he held on to the copyright of 'The Grandmother', when he sold the poem to a magazine. She once said to Margaret Gatty: 'Perhaps you know I always disliked his sending poems to Magazines. He sent the first while away from home all unknown to me.' Whatever sums the magazines offered (and they would be huge), Emily always felt it best to keep the poems to increase readers' eagerness for his next book.

There were all sorts of purely routine tasks. That summer it would be Emily who packed up copies of the *Idylls* to send to their friends. G.F. Watts, thanking her, noticed 'the direction in your hand-writing'. She went on keeping the accounts, running the household, entertaining endless visitors. Then there were the seasonal tasks outside, with which she helped when she could, and the many hours spent teaching the boys. In addition, in 1859, Emily had embarked on some major improvements to the house.

Charles Weld, Emily's brother-in-law, had suggested making more of the attics, putting in 'oriel windows' and vaulting the ceilings. Emily told Margaret Gatty they were 'making Bay-windows in three of the attics and raising two at least of the ceilings.' The builders were also to put up a 'platform Ally has devised at the top of the house to look at once on the two seas' – and to observe the sky at night. Emily was also making changes on the ground floor, with a door into the greenhouse. The new door was an idea Emily had when Alfred was in London. 'I am very venturesome,' she wrote in her journal. She had said to Woolner not long before, when asked for a unilateral decision: 'I am not supposed to have a will of my own' – but of course she had. It was a relief when she could write after Alfred's return: 'He likes all that is done.' He usually did, and was glad enough, whatever society might say about women's wills, to leave all sorts of decisions to her. She would consult him regularly about most things ('I should not think of settling any-thing about Mathilde without thee' – Mathilde was a young German woman who helped teach the boys for a short time that year). But she also felt it 'not fair to trouble thee with plans while thou art away.' There were always so many plans.

The children were taking up more energy as Emily herself taught them regularly, and went on playing with them and reading to them whenever she had time. 'Hallam gets on but very little with writing and can only read easy stories,' she told Thomas Woolner in February 1858. When he was six, later that year, she was still guiding his hand, forming the letters herself. Woolner, receiving a letter from him, foolishly thought it Hallam's own writing and praised his progress, so that Emily had to explain. Hallam had apparently dictated: 'I read a little bit better now and Papa knew all his Latin grammar at seven and he went to school.' Hallam was certainly not following in his father's footsteps and Emily may have worried about her methods. 'Mamma means to teach me Latin when I am seven,' Hallam – still in Emily's hand – told his father once when he was away. 'Because I have not learnt French yet.' 'Every evening,' Emily wrote in her journal, 'the boys and I act fairy tales and nursery stories, being Mother Hubbard or her dog or the Frog Prince or the Bird and Mouse, or even Sausage as may be.'

An account of a bird's funeral suggests how much the middle-aged parents were at the beck and call of the little boys:

The boys find a little robin dead but still warm and Lionel kisses it over and over and makes me kiss it, and Hallam and A. make a grave for it in Hallam's garden between the Alexandrian laurel and the Russian violets and Lionel puts it in. They have made me carry it part of the way. A. tells them to say 'God bless you' to it and we put some of the feathers which have fallen off into Lionel's garden.

Emily was often not at all well – weak, coughing, unable to walk far. One day, Tennyson had taken over the boys to give their mother a little peace and quiet. They were blowing bubbles in the nursery, but Tennyson found the bubbles so beautiful, and the boys' joy in them so huge, that he longed to share the pleasure of it all with Emily. He went down to her with the bubbles and the boys; they were 'wild with delight'.

Emily's outings were now more frequently in the little carriage rather than on foot. The boys would help Alfred to pull Emily up on the downs – hard going uphill, but a wonderful race home again. They had learnt from Alfred's tenderness and would ply her with cushions and love and Lionel's special remedy when she coughed – gentle pats on the back. She was still walking, if not very far. There is a telling story from John Tyndall, the physicist, whom they first met in 1858 when he was staying on the Island. Tyndall described ascending a mountain pass with Tennyson's words in his head: 'O well for him whose will is strong!' Tyndall went on:

But wishing to be true to the science of the subject, I added that we must fall back in the long run on muscular force. This was a lowering of motive power from the moral to the physical; and, deeming probably that I had laid too much stress on the material side of the question, Mrs Tennyson turned towards me with that ethereal expression which Watts has seized so faithfully in his splendid portrait, and remarked quietly 'You can at all events walk till you die.' Taken in conjunction with her obviously frail physique, I thought the remark an impressive example of spiritual force and resolution.

It certainly suggests that Emily knew the importance of making an effort, of the power of the mind, of the need to keep going. The evidence is that she always tried not to give in – until a time, still far off, when the doctors' advice was to lie extremely still.

An entry in her journal has suggested to some that Emily's physical problems were largely a means of trying to keep Alfred at home, of holding his attention. On 8 April 1859 she wrote 'rather a wild night and day of pain, but it is almost worthwhile to have the pain to be so tenderly nursed as I am by A.' The pain may have been real enough, all the same, and there is a good deal of evidence to suggest that it was. Her power over Alfred came not from her submission to ill health but from her rising above it, and continuing to enjoy life, most of the time. He must have known how much she missed him when he was away. Sometimes he said he had to stay in London 'though unwillingly and longing for home', for one reason or another – the dentist or 'poor Watts' in the middle of a portrait. Emily's letters to Alfred are full of this sort of thing: 'I trust Saturday will indeed bring thee back, but do not come if there is anything for which thou wouldst wish to stay.' What *he* wished was what mattered to her, and she could enjoy what he enjoyed. When he went to the *Messiah* at the Crystal Palace, she wrote, 'Is it not a grand thing for me that one of the wishes of my life has been fulfilled for thee instead of me or me in thee rather' – 'the *Messiah* to my mind always the crown of things in music.' She liked to think they were one; his wishes her wishes, his enjoyment hers.

Emily longed for enjoyment for him, anything that might please and divert him. She must have constantly feared the possible consequences of his unhappiness. He had recently told Alfred Gatty in a late-night confessional session, which surprised Gatty who hardly knew him: 'I live under a constant sense of some super-impending calamity.' Gatty interpreted this as 'the Poet's heritage of woe', that black blood that would always flow through his veins whatever Emily did. Tennyson was even now groaning that his father had 'left him ninety pounds a year' and that because of the cruel delay in his marriage, his long separation from the woman for whom he said 'he would have broken stones in the road' to have had earlier as his wife, 'he should be old and incapable when his boys wanted his guidance.'

Emily's journal gives the background to the account in Edward Lear's diary of his visit to Farringford in June 1859. She had had 'six or seven weeks of rather sharp illness' that spring, something sounding like bronchitis. She told Lear in May she thought England the best place in the world to live 'barring bronchitis'; she was trying to persuade him and Frank to buy a place on the Isle of Wight, pushing aside the thought that Lear had told her that the two friends were 'best when not with each other . . . He has become 70 . . . I have stuck at 20.' (Lear was actually eleven years older than Frank.) 'If only Frank could be married . . .' Lear wrote. He would be, but not until January 1862.

In the early summer of 1859 there were builders in the house, working on the alterations to the attics and taking a long time about it. ('We are sadly troubled by workmen promising every day and never performing.') There were bees in the roof of the stable, and 'strong fears' that the new nurse for the boys would not do. (They still needed someone to keep an eye on them when their parents were busy.) That May Emily and Alfred were preoccupied with proofs. They were correcting the pages of the *Idylls of the King* together every day in the summer-house Alfred had built on Maiden's Croft, trying to get them finished before Lear's arrival.

Emily told Woolner that the proofs were really bothering Alfred and that she had so many other things to attend to she had not been able to help as much as she wished, 'in this work unfit for poets'. Woolner replied robustly that while the poet is 'down here upon the earth he must do something earthly', but Emily was not convinced he should be spending his time on proofs. If he had to do something earthly, she would rather, with his eyesight, that he mowed or sowed.

Was it any wonder that Lear found Emily 'pale and worn'? She would surely have denied his description of her as 'sad'. Alfred had taken her up to the attics to admire the view from a new window 'before the sash is put in'. The view from the window was 'enchanting'; it was 'a kind of drunkenness of delight,' she wrote extravagantly. They had also climbed out on to the new platform 'in its unfinished state' to admire those two sea views: the Solent in one direction, the Channel in the other. Two days after his arrival, Lear wrote in his diary, that there was 'a kind of sensitive excitement here always, which is not good for such an ass as I am.'

Lear was sorry he had shown his disapproval of the little boys joining the adults at dinner ('I think it a bad habit for children to come in then and feed'); he regretted distressing five-year-old Lionel's sensitive nature. Emily enjoyed Lear's singing. Lear himself, 'owing to the bad piano', found it a misery, though he did everything possible to amuse the guests 'for E.T.'. He loved the downs and found 'the two darling boys and their mother are as perfect a lot as can be.' Indeed Emily is 'certainly one of the uttermostly perfect women I have yet seen', 'assuredly a complete angel and no mistake'. Day after day, Lear repeats his praise – but Tennyson is 'so odd' and Emily seems ill and weary: 'Please God, if I live, one or two years more,' she said to him at one point – the sort of thing she said to no-one else. And he responded in his diary: 'What labour for him and how little he seems to regard it!'

When he left, Lionel, aged five, said, 'How I like him' and Emily wrote in her journal: 'One echoes the words in one's heart.' But it had obviously not been a comfortable visit for Edward Lear, however Emily felt about it. No visit ever was. Before Farringford he had visited another family at Lewes and had written in Greek in his diary: 'Certainly I should not go among them much more, these families that see nothing but themselves, as is natural.' Emily Tennyson at least saw Edward Lear himself and loved him and tried to cheer him. When he left he wrote that altogether the feeling of regret 'when I leave Farringford makes me sure I like it better than any other place I know.' It was painful that always for him, as he told Emily, 'such rare flashes of light make the path darker after they are over.'

There were American visitors the following month, more easily impressed by Alfred Tennyson than Edward Lear was, and strangely rejoicing in the Needles as equalled in beauty only by Niagara. Tennyson was now being published in America by Ticknor and Fields of Boston and it was James T. Fields and his wife Annie who visited Farringford in July 1859, with a letter of introduction from Longfellow. There was some confusion over their arrival – they arrived several days later than expected. There has also been some confusion about this friendship in general, for there were *other* American Fields. John W. Field and his wife Eliza of Philadelphia actually became closer to the Tennyson family over the years.

Annie Fields' description of this 1859 visit begins badly, for she guesses that the boys were 'of eight and ten years of age perhaps', when, in fact, they were five and not quite seven, a very different matter. This would suggest her memory was extremely poor, but most of the account is based closely on the diary she kept at the time, which presumably gives a reasonably accurate report from a romantic pen. Some of it is worth quoting:

Their house is very large, rambling and irregular, full of comfort, beauty, quiet peace I should say because Mrs Tennyson is a holy woman and diffuses her atmosphere throughout . . . There are hilly downs stretching far far away to the shining sea itself . . . The rose and ivy peep in at every window . . . The extremest simplicity [and] elegance are here combined in conversation, in manners and the minutest household arrangement. Indeed there is a rare union of negligence and care, which could not I fear be seen in the New World, implying intelligence and a certain refinement in the very servants themselves. We came to the house punctually at 5 as Mr Tennyson had said that was the dinner hour. Finding no-one in the drawing room however we looked about at all the pictures etc for a time. Presently Mrs Tennyson came in in her garden hat, received us most kindly with a gentle smile but few words . . . [in a] low faint voice and looking at me with weary eyes. She is slight and frail, but intellectually and morally strong and with a direct personal influence about her such as Shakespeare has in some ways contrived to express most remarkably in his female delineations. Her step is long in walking, full of native dignity yet perfect simplicity, while you feel her sincerity in every movement and expression. She reminded me of Millais's pictures, perhaps because the colors she wears are subdued and her postures striking and graceful . . . She wore white fastened with soft blue ribbon and a cashmere mantle because the evening was chill . . .

343

Annie Fields probably did not know that Millais had painted Emily. She certainly did not know that Edward FitzGerald would also agree with that Shakespearean comparison, but thinking Emily more 'of the Imogen sort', 'far more agreeable to me than the sharp-witted Beatrices, Rosalinds etc', quick-witted as she undoubtedly was. Annie Fields went on:

Just after the soup we heard tiny feet in the passage and two little boys with golden hair and dove-colored frocks and large white ruffles danced into the room. They ran quickly and without a word to kiss each one and then each put a chair by their mother's side. By and by they made fairy-like pages of themselves, serving their mother and father to the delight of both.

One can imagine Edward Lear's curling lip which had made Lionel cry.

Mrs Tennyson in her floating dress with her sweet boys upon each hand seemed more like a creation of some new Raphael than a living woman serving in this world . . . I fell asleep remembering the sister-kiss of Emily Tennyson.

Annie Fields reports a vivid moment when there were guests the following evening and Tennyson, as usual, insisted on slipping off with the men to smoke after dinner. He got his way 'in spite of Mrs Tennyson's imploring voice that he should omit it for once.' There was a 'sad English sunset' that night and Tennyson said, 'Do you see that cloud? . . . That was a dark black streak when I called you, the light only touched it on one edge, now it is perforated with light, as all dark things will be one day.'

Emily had obviously failed to tell the Fields what time she read household prayers and she had finished by the time they came down before nine o'clock next morning. 'Tennyson looked in with his hat on as if disturbed to find us there so early. After we had finished he came and took his breakfast' – Emily and the boys had already eaten – 'as if he did not wish to speak a word.' Annie Fields 'sat reading diligently in a corner. Soon he turned and said "Got something you like to read?" An answer in the affirmative satisfied him and he read The Times and took his breakfast in silence.'

Later that day the Fields left, Annie still feeling the poet's 'parting kiss on her cheek'. They went on their way, rejoicing in 'the privilege of having dwelt beneath a roof sheltering Wisdom and Holiness, the rarest and divinest attainments man can reach'. In a letter to her sister, Annie

Fields tells much the same story and describes Emily as her ideal woman, 'like what I believe Florence Nightingale to be', 'ready to sympathize with every form of emancipation' and having, though no longer young, 'the beauty of that eternal youth which never fades,' 'throwing into bolder relief the brown swarthy figure of our Alfred,' whom she saw as a combination of Milton and Shakespeare, and absolutely justified in avoiding conversation at breakfast.

It was around this time, when Benjamin Jowett was staying at Farringford, that the boys were tossed in his 'shawl'. 'They will long remember their tossing in the blanket,' Emily wrote, and they did, Hallam commemorating the occasion in the *Memoir* nearly forty years later. Emily was worried that Jowett, unused to children, would find the boys' 'affection' oppressive, but he loved it. He wrote them admonitory letters ('NEVER FEAR. NEVER CRY.' 'AVOID SWAGGERING.'), taught them how to make a Stonehenge with their bricks ('I have to make Druids for them,' Emily wrote) and said to their father that though Goethe says that if you are fond of children one child is as good as another, 'I have not seen any yet who have supplanted them in my affections.'

There was something nicely astringent about Jowett's affection. Hallam reported at six and a half that Mr Jowett had paid them each a penny to stop singing 'Ye Mariners of England' and 'Of Nelson and the North'. He took Hallam's penny away when the boy started up again, 'and he said it was not fair, so Boston' (the boys' nurse) 'is going to give me a farthing,' Hallam told Thomas Woolner, a little illogically.

The Reverend Benjamin Jowett was always the most welcome of visitors, though, like Frank Lushington, he was notoriously a silent man. His biographer wrote of his 'frightening taciturnity'. Jowett's father complained that on a five-day visit 'everything he has said might have been said perhaps in five minutes.' He found his own family completely unsympathetic and adopted the Tennysons as an alternative. Early in the friendship he had written: 'I often lament that I am so miserably shy with those whom I most desire to know.'

When Jowett did speak, he spoke in 'a peculiar, gentle soft voice' which went to Emily's heart. She wrote to Edward Lear: 'Tell Frank I think he would like Mr Jowett very much ... All the great questions which move the world appear to have an interest for him.' He had long ago discarded the notebook of 'jests' he had collected as a young man, hoping to lighten his conversation. He depended on others to draw him out. His intense admiration for Emily (it was he who recorded Mrs Cameron's remark that she was as 'great' as Tennyson was) may have been partly because she was so adept at making him talk. She first warmed to him – as she so often did with people – because of his admiration for Tennyson's poetry. ('I do not know of any verse out of Shakespeare in which the ecstasy of love soars to such a height,' he wrote of 'Maud'.)

Emily also appreciated Jowett's fight with the establishment, the lack of orthodoxy which kept him, for so much of his life, out of favour at Oxford, where he was accused of instilling doubt in his pupils' minds, especially through his stress on the metaphoric rather than the literal truth of the Bible. He once said to Margot Asquith, 'My dear child, you must believe in God in spite of what the clergy tell you.' He sympathized with Emily who remained faithful in spite of what the Reverend John Isaacson was telling her, Sunday after Sunday, in Freshwater Church. (Tennyson himself, of course, tried to protect *his* faith by not going.) Jowett would worry about his own 'self-indulgent life', especially when writing to his good friend Florence Nightingale. He found nothing self-indulgent about Emily who shared his concern for the 'awful contrast between the social lessons which the Gospel teaches and the social lessons which the world teaches.' It was Jowett who recorded Emily's love for 'the poor' – her love, not just her concern – regretting that some of her proposals for reform of the system were 'more than Political Economy can truly allow'. It was the male voice of reason squashing her idealistic ideas as impractical, much as he sympathized with her in theory.

There was another even more unconventional friend becoming increasingly important at this time. Julia Margaret Cameron, who had often come from London to stay at Farringford, had been particularly dear to the Tennysons, with her 'wild-beaming benevolence', ever since she had gone for the doctor at the time of Hallam's unexpectedly early arrival in Twickenham. Now, more than seven years later, she had come to live near by. Late in 1859 Emily was supervising the laying out of the garden of the two adjoining houses the Camerons had bought, just outside the Tennysons' boundaries, and named 'Dimbola' after their estate in Ceylon.

It is hard to better Anne Thackeray Ritchie's description of Mrs

Cameron. It is, as she says, 'very difficult to describe' someone so much larger than life, who roused such contradictory emotions.

She played the game of life with such vivid courage and disregard for ordinary rules; she entered into other people's interests with such warm hearted sympathy and determined devotion that, though her subjects may have occasionally rebelled, they generally ended by gratefully succumbing to her rule, laughing and protesting all the time.

She had 'a power of loving', her hero Henry Taylor considered, 'which I have never seen exceeded, and an equal determination to be beloved.' 'She thinks it a great honour to be done by her,' William Allingham would say, resignedly. 'Dark, short, sharp-eyed' and flamboyantly clothed, Julia Cameron was still not yet a photographer in 1860, but there were other reasons to protest. Emily would certainly object as she landed them with extraordinary presents: two legs of Welsh mutton, a violet poncho for Henry Sellwood when he visited, rolls of wallpaper ('of a vivid blue neither she nor we like'). 'We say that it is against our rule to receive gifts from her, dear generous creature that she is, but she persists.'

'What a dreadful friend Mrs Cameron must be,' Julia Wedgwood wrote to Robert Browning. He said: 'You exaggerate the horrors of Mrs Cameron.' 'In this dull world', as Jowett said, her faults were excusable. Edward Lear would ask Emily, 'Does Mrs Cameron rave?' William Allingham records her impulsiveness, her shrieking and gushing, seldom waiting for a reply. She was as different from Emily as a woman could be, but they appreciated each other, in spite of Julia Cameron's conviction that Henry Taylor was a poet as good as Tennyson – though it was Tennyson who had drawn her to Freshwater.

Emily loved her bright clothes, the sort of clothes she would never dream of wearing herself. 'Mrs Cameron comes across the Park,' she wrote in July 1862, 'looking gorgeous in her violet dress and red cloak, walking over the newly mown grass. Pleasant to hear the men cheering.' *Were* they cheering kindly – or mocking her? One wonders.

When Tennyson was away, the two women spent a good deal of time together. 'When your Father is with her,' she would tell Hallam, 'I do not often go up. They are so complete in their lives I always feel as if the presence of a third took something from and added nothing thereto, but when she is alone I go.' 'I should have been dreary,' Emily wrote in her journal during one of Alfred's winter absences, 'as I have to write all day and cannot see to read by candlelight, had not dear Mrs Cameron come to me night by night for an hour.'

Charles Cameron had gone off to his tea estates in Ceylon at the time when his wife moved to the Isle of Wight with the younger children. Charlie and Henry Cameron would become close friends of the Tennyson boys – a friendship Emily alternately encouraged and worried about. She welcomed 'playfellows for our boys', but Henry could be careless, letting the pet squirrel escape from its cage when he was cleaning it and then killing it with a stick when he tried to get it down from a tree. It 'makes us all sad,' Emily wrote. 'It had such pretty ways. We were all fond of it.' 'How dear it will be', Julia had exclaimed 'for our children to grow and live happy together playing mad pranks along the healthy lea.' 'I cannot trust their prudence,' Emily said regretfully, cautioning Lionel and Hallam. She found the Bradley girls, Edith and Daisy, better friends for the boys at this stage, though Lionel would remain close to Henry Cameron all his life. It was the Bradley children who played 'The Emperor of Morocco' at Farringford one evening – that same game Emily herself and Arthur Hallam had played with the Tennysons at Somersby thirty years earlier. 'A. generally succeeds' in making the children laugh, but Emily, joining in, managed to keep a straight face as the candles burned, just as she had all those years before.

Emily never knew what Julia Cameron herself would get up to next. There was the famous occasion – it was 18 June 1860 – when Emily, resting before dinner, heard a trampling on the drive: 'I think it is Americans coming as seven did the other day to ask for admittance, but find that it is Mrs Cameron's grand piano, which she has most kindly sent for Mr Lear,' realizing the inadequacy of the Tennysons' own instrument. Far from being offended, Emily rejoiced in the expressions of surprise on the guests' faces as they arrived for the evening's pleasure. 'Mr Lear sings a long time,' she added with satisfaction in her journal.

Lear was glad enough of the grand piano, but he hated the fact that the arrival of 'Mrs C. and her train' meant 'an odious incense palaver and fuss succeeded the quiet home moments.' His taste, like Emily's, was for talking intimately with one or two, not a noisy party. Their letters suggest that they enjoyed gossip as well as confession. That year one of Lear's best stories for Emily was of Archbishop Benson falling asleep with a full cup of tea in his hand while Lear was singing and tipping the entire contents into his lap – 'into the apron of the sleeping

Primate – like a lake embosomed in black rocks. Fellow guests held the four cornered garment till succour arrived – and we all laughed and rejoiced.'

Perhaps it is better now, Lear reflected in his diary, 'never to feel happy and quiet: so one gradually cares less about life. "We come no more to the golden shore where we danced in days of old".' Lear had found Tennyson querulous on the downs. He did not like to hear his repetitious, bawdy talk that night, after Emily had gone to bed; he made a vow (which he would break) that he would not visit Farringford again.

In Emily's journal, rewritten over thirty years later, it would seem the shore was still golden, but there is a constant sense of paradise lost, of the 'old ways' that were vanishing even as she enjoyed them. We know from her letters that she was aware of Alfred's restlessness and depression when he was not actually working on a poem, and she was trying hard to alleviate them. He needed to be working. Idleness, she suggested to Thomas Woolner, 'saps the very roots of life'. She would continue to try to find subjects for Alfred and encouraged their friends to suggest ideas, but she knew it rarely worked. Woolner, who claimed the slightly doubtful credit of suggesting the stories of both 'Enoch Arden' and 'Aylmer's Field', said to Emily: 'Poets are birds that will fly their own flight'. She knew it well.

When Millais wrote asking Tennyson to write some verses to go with thirty pictures by a new young artist, Emily replied: 'I am sorry to have to answer the thing is impossible. Poems do not *come* to him so, and if they did not come, you are, I flatter myself, too much his friend to wish them there or anywhere.' Millais was not convinced and muttered 'I should have thought it easy to write a few lines to each picture as I should find it easy enough to illustrate anything.' When committees asked the Laureate for odes, Emily would say, 'They do not understand that it is not easy to write "about 30 lines" on a given subject.'

Julia Margaret Cameron wrote to her husband in Ceylon with some acute observations just at this time, when she had first moved to the Island herself:

The trees too are luxuriant here – far more flourishing than they usually are by the sea – and Alfred Tennyson's wood may satisfy any forester. His place is in perfect beauty, but it does not satisfy him. His prairies are really enamelled with the purple orchis and golden cowslip . . .

He *sees* the beauty but he *feels* it not. His spirits are low, and his countenance serious and solemn. Every trifle of life disturbs him. The buildings *getting* up are a night mare to him, the work-men *not* getting on are a day vexation to him. His furniture has not come. The sculptures for his hall have miscarried or been delayed. The tradesmen cheat him. The visitors look at him. Tourists seek him. Americans visit him. Ladies pester and pursue him. Enthusiasts dun him for a bit of stone off his gate. These things make life a burden, and his great soul suffers from these insect stings.

What *is* the cure? I believe there is no cure. I believe it is a matter of temperament – of blood and bile . . .

He told us the other day not to pick the wild hyacinths out of his forest. We might at most have robbed him of six – Dear Mrs Tennyson *heard* and the next day sent us six dozen of the same and I am sure he would have been the first to repent.

The 'palaver and fuss' Lear disliked were part of an act. Mrs Cameron was actually very unhappy at this time when her husband was in Ceylon: 'I assume vivacity of manner for my own sake as well as for others,' she said, hoping to make time pass 'till I hear again'.

A year or two later, Lear would encourage Emily to buy Mrs Cameron's piano, should she leave the Island as seemed likely. 'It is really an awful shame that the P. Laureat hath only an ancient polykettlejarring instrument in his house. Neither is it moral, for it sets a bad example to others and flouts the musicle deities.' ('You know my exaggerated mode of writing and talking,' he once wrote to Emily.)

In the first months of the new decade Emily and the boys were ill. They were all coughing and the Newport doctor at first diagnosed whooping cough. Emily had had it before. It was finally decided that she was allergic to the new wallpaper, which on analysis was found to contain 'a great quantity of arsenic'. The paper was immediately 'stript off the walls' and gradually all the patients recovered, probably simply with the passing of time. On 16 April 1860 Alfred brought Emily down into the drawing room and then Hallam joined them and finally Lionel. 'So here we all are once more, thank God. How beautiful everything looks. There is enchantment about all.'

Looking back at the end of her life, Emily would see these early years at Farringford, when the boys were small (and the family circle had not yet admitted a series of tutors) as the happiest period of her life, a time full of beauty and enchantment. Tennyson's fame was at its height with the publication of the *Idylls of the King*. Its reception was a relief after all Tennyson's delays and hesitations about publishing, though he said perversely that it pained him 'to hear the Idylls praised, because he thinks how unlike they are to what he intended.' The sales excelled even *Maud*, with 20,000 copies sold in the first months, and there was a much more respectful reception from the critics.

This was delightful, of course, and exactly what Emily thought Tennyson deserved. But it would be the small things Emily remembered, looking back. 'Some pictures one longs to recall, one scarcely knows why.' One morning she had seen the boys in their blouses on the landing, walking hand in hand, playing at taking a morning walk. She had been at the bottom of the flight of stairs and they had suddenly realized she was there and had left their game and rushed into her arms.

There was another stranger, equally vivid memory. Emily had been alone late at night in her bedroom while Alfred was in London. In bed in the dark she had heard a small sound as of someone trying to cut the glass of the window. She had thought to herself that it was the 'villainous centre-bits' grinding 'on the wakeful ear in the hush of the moonless night' – Alfred's words in 'Maud' came to her mind. She got up to listen and felt more certain than ever that there was a 'distinct grinding of glass'. She wondered whether to ring the bell to alarm the thieves, knowing it would not wake the maids. No, she decided, she would light a candle and hope it would deter the intruders. 'I held it', she wrote to Alfred, 'and grew bolder and went to the window myself and saw a snail grinding the glass with its shell.' She stood there in the candlelight, smiling, and enjoying the snail's noise, which now sounded like a strange sort of music.

Emily also remembered playing merry old dance tunes for the children's dancing, 'Lionel almost flying as usual', and both parents reading to the boys, with an arm round each of them: *Reynard the Fox*, parts of *A Midsummer Night's Dream*. She remembered Alfred bringing her when she was ill a 'large root of primroses' he had dug up and planted for her in the very same terracotta pot which had, before her marriage, injured her arm – so now the 'happy primrose memory' replaced 'the unhappy accident one'. There were pictures in her mind of Holman Hunt having tea in the hayfield with the boys, of F.D. Maurice losing his hat and carrying his godson on his shoulders, of John Simeon helping her to rig a boat for the boys, of Hallam decorating the hall like a bowerbird with scraps of paper and material on his aunt Anne's wet birthday, of Hallam in the woods shouting to Lionel, 'Here's a crowfoot!', of both boys 'very happy getting jogged together' on their father's knees, and of them chasing each other and trying to gather all the daisies on the lawn. She remembered them listening to her playing Welsh airs on the piano and singing 'Too Late' to them, their faces wonderfully awed and sad. She remembered Alfred's huge snowlady one winter crowned with his own black hat; Alfred showing her the sea dragons he had painted on the windows of the summerhouse in Maiden's Croft; Alfred rolling the grass by moonlight, going out with her to see the first snowdrops of the year and later the banks brilliant with primroses and celandine; Alfred reading to her, talking with her, on those quiet evenings – at times so rare – when they were alone together.

'If it were not faithless,' Emily wrote in her journal, 'I should be afraid of so much happiness as I have.'

CHAPTER ELEVEN

'Before partings began'

'The boys are rosy and merry and hard to be tamed down to lessons. When people are here, very docile comparatively. When they are not!' Emily left it to Lear's imagination. To Thomas Woolner she said, 'All the company we have makes lessons hard work.' It was often difficult for their mother to calm their 'wild spirits and get a hearing for lessons', though she said she was not very 'exacting'. It made teaching simpler that Lionel insisted upon learning 'everything that Hallam learns'. Emily would try to fit in some of her letter writing when she had set the boys a task. Writing to Lear once, she had to break off: 'Hallam is shovelling cinders and I don't know what mischief he will be tempted to next if I do not attend to his lessons, so farewell.'

Teaching was hard work. When Hallam was seven and a half, in January 1860, Emily had told Lear: 'Hallam has only had two Latin lessons. I have nearly made him understand some French and English verbs, so I hope the Latin will not be so difficult.' He was now an avid reader, which was a relief, starting his History of Rome at the beginning again as soon as he had finished it, and taking his turn sometimes at reading aloud in the evenings. Their father was worried about their progress all the same; perhaps Emily really had too much else to do. His reasoning in a letter to Hallam does not sound calculated to appeal to a boy: 'Learn your lessons regularly: for gentlemen and ladies will not take you for a gentleman when you grow up if you are ignorant . . . I shall be glad to find you know more and more every day.' A little later, Edward Lear gave other reasons for asking 'Do they get on? Do they begin Greek?' Greek, he said, 'is the foundation of all knowledge and happiness and good in this world – far beyond cleanliness or Godliness.'

Reluctantly, Emily decided in January 1861 to look for a tutor for the boys. Both Jowett and Bradley were at Farringford this month and they were both consulted. On the 23rd, Bradley wrote to Graham Dakyns, aged nearly twenty-three:

Are you now bond or free?

Tennyson wants a Tutor for his small boys – two very young, 7 and 8, but *very* nice little chaps.

You would like him much and adore her, and be very happy. You would live in the house but be very free – the freer you were the more they would like it.

They can't pay much – not more I should fear than from £100 to £120.

They could have paid a great deal more, but the amount was the equivalent of £5,000 or so and with board and lodging and a good deal of free time it was not too bad a bargain. It was an attractive if rather intimidating prospect for a young man to live at such close quarters with the Poet Laureate, the poet he most 'worshipped'. Marian Bradley, who knew Tennyson well by now, wrote in her diary that month that his 'talk has wondrous charms. I long to catch some of the gems out of it and write them down, but I am generally over-dazzled by their rich abundance.' Dakyns, sharing Tennyson's own distaste for 'the ghouls', refused to write anything down at the time and regretted it later; he would remember Tennyson's humour, 'far deeper and wilder than most people would have guessed', and the sort of 'Rabelaisian' talk Edward Lear hated and which neither Marian Bradley nor Emily probably ever heard.

Two other remarkably consistent views of Tennyson in January 1861 suggest vividly the man Emily loved – spontaneous, warm, maddening. Sydney Dobell wrote:

Nothing could be kinder than both Mr and Mrs Tennyson – he in his great blind superhuman manner, like a colossal child – and his often repeated disappointment that we could not stay longer near them was evidently as unfeigned and straight-spoken as everything, large and little, that comes out of that mouth, with which he rather seems to think aloud than, in the ordinary acceptance, to speak. When E. told him, in the morning, that we were going to bring an authoress, his horror at 'writing women' was grotesque to behold.

Remembering Tennyson's respect for Jane Austen and Elizabeth Barrett Browning, it is reasonable to suppose his reaction in this case was largely play-acting – but Emily perhaps never did tell him of the stories she seems to have been writing at this time. In any case, not a single one was ever finished.

Benjamin Jowett's report that month was that of a closer friend, one whose 'heresy', as Emily said, continued to alarm the neighbours. Of Tennyson, Jowett wrote:

This year he has written nothing but a short piece . . . He has been ill and greatly suffering and depressed, I fear. The more I see of him the more I respect his character, not withstanding a superficial irritability and uneasiness about all things . . . No-one is more honest, truthful, manly or a warmer friend; but he is as open as the day, and, like a child, tells any chance comer what is passing in his mind . . . He is the shyest person I ever knew, feeling sympathy and needing it to a degree quite painful.

Graham Dakyns arrived in Freshwater on 20 February. Emily had proposed putting him off until the autumn, 'for I should like to lift Lionel a little more out of the baby before he is troubled with him.' He was not seven until the following month. 'But Ally is so kind he thinks I ought to have help sooner.' Lionel prepared a welcome for the new tutor, 'which he means to sing, flag in hand', but his courage failed 'and he only puts snowdrops into Dakyns' room.' When the young man was shown into the drawing room he saw a scene he described exactly fifty years later for Hallam. It appealed, Graham Dakyns said, 'not only to the eye, but to the heart':

Your mother, as I think I have often told you, was seated half-reclining on the sofa which stood with its back to the window, with that wonderful view of capes and sea beyond. And you two stood leaning against her, one on either side. She was, and always remained, supremely beautiful, not only in feature and the bodily frame, but still more from the look in her eyes, the motion of her lips, and the deep clear music of her voice. Such a combination of grace and dignity with simplicity and frankness and friendliness of accost as never was.

Graham Dakyns became, until her life's end, one of Emily Tennyson's most devoted admirers. He was another who called her 'equally great', knowing so well from the day to day association with her, in every sort of circumstance, the calm sweetness and strength of her character, and how much Tennyson depended on her. Emily was happy with her first impressions of Dakyns. He 'promises very well,' she wrote to Alfred Gatty next day, 'as far as one can judge him by the praises of those who have known him at Trinity and Rugby and as far as a pleasant face and

a kind simple manner enable one to judge in a one day's acquaintance.'
Emily had proposed that Dakyns should teach the boys only 'from
eleven to one in the morning'. 'If he would take the Latin and arithmetic,' she had suggested to Bradley, 'I might do the things not so
imperative'. 'We are well aware that we have asked a great favour,
asking you to help us with such little boys.'

Emily naturally had some mixed feelings about Dakyns's arrival.
Nothing would be quite the same again. 'I cannot but miss "the life in
life" we have hitherto had, however good I hope the change is in some
ways. He makes the change as little hard as may be to me by joining
heartily in our out of door work and drawing my carriage and in reading.' A week after the young man's arrival, she describes them all rushing 'along the road with me, a wild party to call on the Cloughs.'

Arthur Hugh Clough, whose poetry Dakyns admired almost as much
as Tennyson's, was staying with his family in Freshwater that February
and March. He had been to the Isle of Wight before; how well Emily
knew him at this point it is difficult to say, but the year before he had
given her a copy of his own edition of Plutarch. Jane Brookfield said
Clough had 'the most peculiar manner I almost ever saw'; she found
him 'ununderstandable'. Jowett, whose pupil he had been, thought him
a man of genius; he had resigned a fellowship at Oriel rather than pay
lip-service to the Thirty-nine Articles and practised a sort of 'faithful
scepticism'. Like Jowett, he was devoted to Florence Nightingale, that
national heroine, who was his wife's cousin, and became deeply involved in her work – to such an extent that when he died she could say,
'I am his true widow'.

Poor Blanche, his wife, was pregnant in 1861 and Clough himself
was ill; he would be dead by the end of the year. Everyone seemed to be
ill. Emily herself was not at all well and the boys were still coughing – a
year after what might have been whooping cough. Edward Lear's sister
Ann died that March. 'You must come to us when you are equal to it,'
Emily said. A week later, when he was on the Island, she wrote again:
'Yes, you must come please today certainly and tomorrow if you can
and will. It grieves me to think that you do not feel even a little better
but it does not surprise . . . These are wounds that heal slowly slowly'.
She knew when writing letters of sympathy (so many over the years)
that she should be thinking of the joy of heaven for those who had died
but 'the blank they leave is so terrible.'

Remembering how he had felt about Alfred on his last visit, thinking of how he felt now in his wounded bereaved state, Lear had decided to take rooms at the hotel on the bay. 'Cold and sad,' he wrote in his diary. 'He dines with us', Emily wrote in hers, 'but too sad at the loss of the sister, who has brought him up from his birth, to stay with us altogether.' He could work at the hotel and he needed to work. He 'began to colour the last Mt Athos views.' 'O dreary dreadful terrible days!!' he wrote, marking the pages with the X he always used to indicate his epileptic fits. He felt as if he could never laugh again and even Emily could not help him. There is a lot of Greek in the diary as he spent two evenings at Farringford which 'vexed and worried' him. Tennyson's conversation he found very ugly after dinner – he was talking of being poor and finished as a poet, it seems. Tennyson had always drunk a lot and now his talk was ugly, Lear said. He twice used that same Greek word – *askhemos*. As for Emily, 'hers is a sad, tho' a beautiful and true life'. He could not bear it. Next day Lear wrote to tell Emily he was off. 'It was difficult to go without seeing her again, but the drawbacks and chances of staying are too painful.'

In his diary he had written that, on the day of his arrival in the Isle of Wight, he had a long talk with 'dear good E.T.', and added: 'The paragraph in the Court journal it seems *did* relate to C. and Anne Weld.' Three days later he wrote that the talk was again of the Welds – 'CW is a bore', he wrote, but Charles Weld, Emily's brother-in-law, the one who had been so helpful over the trouble with Moxon's brother and the Illustrated Edition, was more than a bore. He was an unfaithful husband who had lost his job and his family home through his behaviour. Some of Emily's letters to Lear which referred to the affair have been destroyed; his letters to her have had paragraphs cut out of them. Emily's grandson Charles would refer only to 'serious trouble' and no-one seemed to know what it was – one recent biographer of Tennyson even guessing that Weld's 'mysterious disgrace' was because he was homosexual. But the evidence is easily available in the files of the Royal Society. And other evidence remains of what must have been one of the most painful and challenging episodes in Emily's life.

In Louisa's diary (which is so unreadable that few have tried to read it) on 14 March 1861 there is the entry: 'Day great anxiety and distress. C.W.' Louisa was thinking of her sister Anne. Next day she wrote: 'Unhappy A. So every morn. Let C.W. tell her – not yet come home. Vex Pa. Pa confess distress aft. hear C.W.' Charles Weld had had to resign from his post as Assistant Secretary and Librarian of the Royal Society because he had 'introduced a lady' in his wife's absence into their apartments. He was given six months' salary and asked to leave immediately. General Sabine, Treasurer and Śenior Vice President, told the Secretary of 'the relief which all who have business to transact at Burlington House and who are acquainted with the facts recently made known, will feel when he has quitted his office. In my last interview with Mr Weld he seemed anxious to explain to me that the Lady in question was a Lady of independent fortune! I think that in such case her introduction into the apartments at Burlington House, whether those of the Society or into Mrs Weld's, was if anything still less excusable than if she had no home of her own.' Weld was obviously wanting to make it clear that the 'lady' was not a prostitute, but he could not retrieve his reputation. After over seventeen years, in which he had not only served the Royal Society but written its history, he had to leave. There is no evidence of his wife's reaction, but it seems likely that the whole business had a good deal to do with his daughter's subsequent problems; Agnes had just had her twelfth birthday when the scandal broke.

Emily wrote to Lear on 15 April: 'The offence is of the nature we believed it to be, but we have had no particulars. Continual threats of self-destruction come to one, and all in that quarter is dreary and dark. The only hope of improvement is in occupation and that under the circumstances is not easy to find.'

Emily had always been very fond of Charles Weld since those days so long ago when they had all been young together and he had saved her from losing money in the Matthew Allen scheme. She had travelled with him and Anne and their father in France in the 1840s and when in 1859, just two years before, he had written a book on *The Pyrenees*, he had dedicated it to her. She had written to him, 'Your affectionate dedication took me so pleasantly by surprise that I must confess to having been moved to tears by it and I feel now so shaky I am not well able to write, but you will believe how much I value this proof of your affection.' The book's printed dedication read: 'To Mrs Alfred Tennyson this volume is affectionately inscribed by her brother-in-law Charles Richard Weld, Burlington House, May 1859.' Someone less trusting than Emily might have suspected that he wanted to draw attention to his connection with the Poet Laureate. In his own hand he had written, 'Emily Tennyson, with C.R.Weld's affectionate love.'

Now Charles Weld needed all the affectionate love and family loyalty the Tennysons could offer. Emily was certainly concerned primarily with saving her sister Anne's marriage, as she had been in the case of her other sister, Louisa, and *her* Charles, during their long years of separation. The Welds had led rather separate lives for years and now they would come close to breaking point. Weld had a notorious temper, which was obviously not improved by the guilt he felt at losing his job and the family's home. Emily's relationship with Anne was no easier than it was with Louisa, devoted as she was to both of them. She worried constantly about her sisters, both of them so much less fortunate than she was herself. She would long to make life happier for her 'poor Nanny', as she called her. 'Anne has put up the old hurdles again,' Emily would tell Hallam years later. Not everyone found it easy to be as open with Emily as she wanted them to be. Anne seems to have wanted to hide from Emily some of the worst of her problems over the years.

On 22 April Emily told Lear that 'poor CRW was so ill owing to want of sleep thro' his troubles that his doctor orders him immediately to leave Town. He is to come here tomorrow. I forgot to tell you that the reasons assigned to the council for giving up the office are simply "family reasons".' Emily asked Lear not to talk about the affair, 'more than you can help'. Everything was being hushed up and the three Welds were welcomed at Farringford, though the house was full with Horatio and his wife and their two tiny girls and two nurses. Already on the 10th Emily had told Woolner she was 'very much oppressed with guests.' It was not that the guests themselves were oppressive, far from it – but she needed some leisure for 'reading and thinking to restore the elasticity of one's mind, now too like a bow spoilt by long bending.' It was a relief that she had Graham Daykns in the house; he had turned out 'very simple and kindly and intelligent and most conscientiously anxious about the boys.' 'Simple' was always one of Emily's favourite words of praise.

Tennyson had been very fond of Charles Weld too. 'You know that whenever you wish to shake off London smut you are welcome here,' Tennyson had written from Farringford six years earlier. Tennyson had often turned to Weld for advice, legal or financial. Burlington House had been his favourite place to stay in London in recent years – central, 'quiet and agreeable'. Tennyson was not yet himself a member of the Royal Society. (He was not a scientist after all.) But he had spent a lot of time there and had become friends with Walter White, Weld's assistant who would succeed him. In November 1861 White would write in his journal that they had walked down Piccadilly together and Tennyson had said that he 'could not yet muster courage to come to Burlington House after what had taken place.'

It had been an embarrassing business at the least. At Farringford in April Tennyson pleased Emily enormously by taking her into the conservatory out of earshot of their guests and encouraging her to ask the Welds to stay on until their new home was ready to move into. She wrote in her journal: 'A moment not to be forgotten since I know that he longs to be alone.' For once, in this extreme situation, Emily was putting other people's needs before Alfred's.

The new home, to which the Welds moved in October, was a house in Lansdowne Crescent, Notting Hill, which they took for three years. Emily wrote: 'God grant that it may be a happier home than she has had before since leaving our father's!' Emily was talking about a period of nearly twenty years. Weld would get some temporary work later in the year as a superintendent for the International Exhibition of 1862, and general manager of the Exhibition's 'philosophical department'. The Tennyson connection must certainly have helped; it was for this exhibition that Tennyson wrote an ode which caused him a great deal of trouble, not least because it had to be capable of being sung by four thousand voices. It was certainly written partly as a token of support for Weld, who would eventually bring to Farringford a 'beautiful urn and salver graceful in form and design' in acknowledgment of the Ode.

Not every relationship survived Charles Weld's behaviour. Lady Franklin, the sisters' aunt, who had reason to be grateful for all the help he had given her in planning her Arctic search expeditions (Polar exploration was a subject he would lecture on), wrote in her journal in October 1865:

Anne adds that 'Charles' has been interesting them very much with an account of his Normandy adventures. Is it possible that poor Anne says this to make us regret the pleasure we have lost in refusing to meet him? It rather makes us rejoice to think what jovial familiarity we might thus have been brought into with a man whom we desire to ignore.

In the summer of 1861 Francis Palgrave suggested to Arthur Clough that 'the Tennysons appear to have been fairly worried out of their house by floods of visitors. They have fled in the direction of Auvergne, carrying with them tutor and children.' They also carried with them Anne and Agnes Weld – but not Charles – and their servant, Elisabeth

Andrews. They left the Isle of Wight on the 27 June. Elisabeth Andrews is described in the Census that spring as thirty years old and employed as a 'nurse'. On their travels, she was a great deal more – companion, cook, lady's maid, messenger. She was such an excellent servant that a Russian family in Pau tried to seduce her away from the Tennysons. Emily called her 'good and clever' but there are few references to her in Emily's revised journals. From Hallam's nine-year-old travel diary – a lengthy, laborious, ill-written but admirable achievement – it is obvious that Elisabeth was treated as someone who had just as much right as anyone else to see things and enjoy the expeditions.

Elisabeth was the older sister of Joanna Andrews, who spent almost her entire life as a cook-housekeeper in the Tennysons' service. Elisabeth herself was married the following March and received as one of her wedding presents a fair copy of Hallam's journal of the journey to the Pyrenees. It was a task, the copying out, which proved rather more tedious than he expected and the finished present has some sections in Emily's hand and some in Dakyns's – a combined effort, which the recipient must have treasured all her life. Hallam would end with a French proverb: 'Qui bien veut avec Dieu peut' – which could have been Emily's own motto.

Hallam's diary is delightful, although the examples he gives of his parents' conversation are less than illuminating: 'Mamma remarked in the carriage how short the cows and sheep and horses were here and Papa said People too and Mamma said Yes.' He says that the Welds left them on 10 July in the Auvergne, and that 'they had lost nearly all their luggage'. Emily said they went no further 'as neither was well'. The whole expedition – the three months away – was 'haunted' by illness. 'The perpetual illness of most of the party made the time a very anxious and harassing one for me,' Emily would write. But it began well enough with the drive from Clermont Ferrand to Mont Dore, 'one of the things Ally and I most enjoyed'. 'The air was delicious' and Emily's strength in mid July was pleasing her older son, as we saw in his diary.

Hallam gives a good idea of the strain and stresses of the journey:

There was a cook here and she was thought to be insane and she brought in a chicken and we said it was bony and Mr Dakyns said Why it is the back is it not? and Mamma said Surely not but Mamma turned it over and found it was.

Mrs Ganne our landlady here charged more than she had agreed and so Papa went to the juge de paix and so Mrs Ganne came tramping up and teazed Mamma and then I fetched Mrs Wynne a very kind lady and at last she got away.

Mrs Wynne, an 'English lady', was the fortunate possessor of a canary and a little white dog called Daisy. With her Brussels education, she was apparently a match for the landlady as Emily evidently was not. What Tennyson himself was doing after his visit to the justice of the peace, Hallam does not say. The chicken by the way was edible; other food was not. Hallam notes: 'Mamma bought us some biscuits . . . because they had only sour bread and horrid butter.'

It was soon after this that 'Papa went out for a walk as usual before breakfast. He came in and said "Mr Clough's come" and cried out "Clough come upstairs" and so Clough had some of our English tea,' preferable apparently to the French coffee. 'Whom should I see but Tennyson?' Clough wrote to his wife, 'They go to the Pyrenees and I am to follow them.' The uncertainty of the Tennysons' plans would cause endless problems; both letters and Clough himself would travel back and forth across the mountains as he tried to find them and pin them down. 'I make no plans till I hear from you,' he wrote from Luz, in a letter that carried the news of the terrible death in a fire of Longfellow's wife. Eventually Clough went on horseback from Luz to Arreau and then on to Luchon the following day – a rough ride of fourteen hours in all, which he liked well enough to 'go back à cheval' a few days later, 'by the way I came' – the Tennysons themselves travelling in a diligence.

Arthur Hugh Clough was on leave from 'the Education Committee of the Privy Council' in London. He had been advised to go abroad for his health, in spite of the fact that his wife was expecting their third child early in August. He would never see that child. His activity that summer with the Tennysons seems hardly appropriate for an invalid. Did Emily reflect on that, years later, when she said that 'independent of all liking for herself, Mrs Clough and her children have for his sake a kind of sacredness in our eyes.'

Clough would put himself out for the Tennysons; Emily wrote of him: 'There could not have been a kinder or more unselfish or more thoughtful companion than he.' The two of them, Clough and Dakyns, 'were always doing kind, helpful work for us, looking after houses and carriages.' Clough told his wife, 'AT is but helpless by himself and thinks himself even more so than he is.' Emily's primary worry was the boys. When they eventually rented a pleasant house among maize fields just outside Luchon, she stayed there (while the others walked and rode) 'to amuse my sick boys and to watch over them, for in such young creatures perpetual diarrhoea, even when not bad, makes one very anxious.' 'I was continually doubtful and anxious', she told Lear after their return, 'as to whether the whole was not nearly a failure'; at times it had seemed more sensible to return than to go on. And yet, looking back, she agreed that all their minds had been refreshed, however much their bodies had suffered, and the boys were eager to return to the mountains. She herself remembered with most pleasure the Col d'Aspin, the high pass between Luchon and Bagnères de Bigorre, with glorious views in every direction of stony hills and far blue mountains, with heather, harebells and scabious at their feet, and silky black goats foraging in the scrubby undergrowth.

Hallam's diary hardly reflects Emily's anxieties. It is full of the excitement of travel. One day Dakyns's portmanteau was very nearly stolen. 'A robber was going to carry' it off – but fortunately a man in a cart told them and the robber pretended that it had dropped off the diligence and that he had picked it up. 'Our coachman fired up at him and he ran away like a coward and we saw a glacier.' The boys also enjoyed the railway journeys. On one they met a 'count who was exceedingly like Sir John Simeon, his face and his beard and his watch-chain was and his shawl was. Perhaps he was Sir John Simeon talking French and pretended that he did not know us.' On another journey, later, Emily records their meeting a General, who had been aide de camp to Marshal Ney. 'He seemed amused by the boys' dinner and their fight with newspaper swords against a bundle of cloaks.' There was never any question of those boys being seen and not heard.

Clough had not expected that the Tennysons would like Luchon. Indeed Palgrave had suggested to Clough that the Pyrenees would not suit them at all. ('I always thought they would find themselves ill placed in the Pyrenees on many accounts.') They had left the Isle of Wight to escape the tourists. They had no intention of returning home (Far-ringford was let) until the end of September when the 'Cockneys' went home again to London. But the Pyrenean villages were full of the Parisian equivalent – 'People flaunt about and wear strange Parisian mountain-costumes' and hats that resembled Tennyson's, a fashion he had adopted thirty-one years before on his first visit to the Pyrenees with Arthur Hallam.

Emily must have been well aware of the importance of Tennyson's return to the valley of Cauterets. 'It had always lived in my recollections as a sort of Paradise,' he said. She records that he wished to go on the old road which he had walked all those years before with Arthur Hallam. On Wednesday, 4 September Clough wrote: 'Tennyson and Dakyns have walked on to Cauterets and I and the family follow in a calèche.' Dakyns too realized the significance of the valley. 'I being the young man of the company was the great man's walking stick. When we came to the valley – I knew it was a sacred place – I dropped behind to let him go through it alone. Clough told me afterwards I had done well.' Tennyson said, 'Dakyns isn't a fool.' They were in Cauterets a week, Emily rejoicing in the view from their windows of the Gave, edged by dark pines, rushing in its rocky bed from far away among the mountains and falling in a cataract.

Emily thought 'It was seemingly fuller of life than any river I have ever seen.' It still is. 'Cauterets is overhung by mountains which almost meet, leaving only a small triangular piece of ground on which the houses are built,' Charles Weld had written in the travel book he dedicated to Emily. Tennyson was 'quite glad to be here again,' Clough said. He is 'very fond of this place evidently' – but Cauterets was changed. One day they could hardly see it: there was a heavy 'brouillard' down to 'the ankles of the hills'. When the sun shone and the holidaymakers came out, it was just another 'rather odious watering-place', Tennyson considered, with dozens of carriages lined up and ponies for hire with their owners soliciting for customers at the tops of their voices. The streets were full of 'touters for hotels' and 'Spaniards crying chocolate'.

Hallam recorded that, on Sunday 8 September, 'Papa and Mr Clough and Mr Dakyns escaped to Lac de Gaube and had a pint of port and rowed across the Lake.' 'The hills wore their old green,' Tennyson said, 'and the roaring stream had the same echoes as of old.' That night Tennyson wrote down the lines that had first begun forming in his mind as he walked along the valley ahead of Graham Dakyns. He read them to Emily but she does not record what she thought as she listened, beyond commenting that they had noticed together the deepening of the river's voice at night.

> All along the valley, stream that flashest white,
> Deepening thy voice with the deepening of the night . . .

The first version did not contain the phrase with the most direct reference to the painful past. They all knew the arithmetic was wrong. It had been in 1830, thirty-*one* years ago that Tennyson had first walked there with Arthur Hallam:

> All along the valley, where thy waters flow,
> I walked with one I loved two and thirty years ago.

'Altogether I like the little piece as well as anything I have written,' Tennyson would say. Emily seems to have underestimated its importance. Back at Farringford, she would write to John Simeon: 'Ally has not been doing anything except just a few lines.'

They were all just about well enough to enjoy Pau, where they said goodbye to Clough. Dakyns had already left them – to spend a month studying French at Tarbes. Sending him love and kisses, Lionel said encouragingly: 'I dare say you will be able to chatter like a Frenchman when you come home.' The boys' own French was coming on. 'If there are little French children in the house we are staying in, I generally play with them,' young Hallam wrote. Emily had been reading the boys *The Swiss Family Robinson* in French, though Hallam said Papa laughed at them for liking it.

Pau was a favourite place with Victorian travellers. Caroline Jebb would call it 'one of the most beautiful spots on the earth's surface.' The Tennysons walked through every room of the castle of Henri de Navarre. 'Mamma is delighted,' Hallam reported. Emily herself wrote, 'One feels that it would not be unpleasant to live in the old castle, looking over the river to the wooded hills and the noble range of mountains beyond.' It is tempting to suppose the castle at Pau influenced them a few years later when they were planning the house at Aldworth.

'Alfred turned so unwell', Emily told Dakyns, 'that his one wish was to get home'. By an extraordinary chance, travelling on the same train from Amiens to Boulogne, were Robert Browning and his son, Pen. Elizabeth Barrett Browning had died in Florence three months earlier; the sad father and son were on their way back to England. Pen, the boy his mother had so wished would meet and play with the Tennyson boys, was twelve. Robert Browning saw the complete family on the quay – the Folkestone boat about to leave – and, understandably, could not bring himself to speak to them. The Tennysons did not know of his wife's death; she had died after they left England. He could not bring himself to tell them. Meanwhile Arthur Hugh Clough was on his way to Italy, where he would be buried that November near the grave of Elizabeth Barrett Browning in Florence.

The Tennysons returned to Farringford at the end of September in rather poor health. But Alfred told Emily that just one sunset he had seen 'on the Port de Picade' had 'repaid him for all the discomfort and illness of the journey,' and after that Emily declared she was content. 'I cannot count our journey lost since Alfred has seen things which delight him and which he will remember with joy, I hope, when he is better,' she told Thomas Woolner. But it was 'delightful' to be home. It was on this occasion that Emily said she felt 'lost in a perfect ecstasy' –

'the ecstasy of being at home and in such a beautiful home; for indeed much as you may be disposed to laugh at me, I have seen no place in our wanderings where I should so much like to live.' After all, one could not *live* on the Col d'Aspin. She continued to Dakyns: 'The boys were wild with delight. I fear you will say they have done very little during your absence; but, as you know, we have not been settled anywhere on the road as to do much.' Lionel was 'as fantastic as ever', but weeping for his poor mouse, who had died while they were away.

There had been a letter from Graham Dakyns waiting for them on their return in a pile of seventy or eighty other letters – 'a cruel bondage'. It is significant that Emily should write an extremely long letter to Dakyns a few days after their return, when there were so many others to be answered – and he would be back with them very soon. It was a measure of how much she had become attached to him, how much he had become one of the family. She knew he would soon have to go and start his real work in life, but it would be difficult to find 'one who will fit so well into our home as you have done.' She said how much she appreciated 'the rest I have had whilst you have been here and have felt by no means so worn out as I used to do.'

One of the other letters waiting for them was from Lord Dufferin in Ireland. He had built a tower in memory of his mother and was asking Tennyson to write some verses ('some little gem') for his small 'Palace of Art'. Dufferin was an interesting character who will come into Emily's life again. Now she was involved in the decision as to which version was preferable of the three Tennyson sent. 'This my wife likes best: she is most likely right,' Tennyson wrote, knowing she often was. It was good of him to oblige Dufferin so promptly when he was still not feeling at all well, complications, he thought, of a chill he had caught at Cauterets.

Tennyson was in London for nearly four weeks for all sorts of peculiar treatments prescribed by Mrs Cameron's brother-in-law, Dr Jackson: chlorine baths, nitric acid and mustard plasters. Although it could be 'dreary' without him, there were times when Emily was actually relieved when he was away. When he was at home she said, 'it exposes him to so much worry.' Emily detected other reasons than what he called the 'foul ways and unhappy diet' of the French for his 'torpid liver', and for his 'not having much pleasure in anything'. He was not engaged in a major poem; he had not enough to do and too much time to think about the things that worried him. He was very bothered by what was happening to their part of the Isle of Wight. Emily shared his concern about that. As early as January 1860 she had written:

Our beautiful views will be spoilt before long. People are seized with a building mania . . . We are obliged to buy land at the rate of a thousand pounds an acre nearly, to prevent more of the bay being hidden by ugly brick houses . . . We begin to say perhaps we shall be driven from our home by press of people. If our down were no longer lonely, we could not stay. We could only be here in the winter when it is too stormy for visitors.

Now in November 1861 Tennyson saw Freshwater, where he had 'pitched his tent, taken with its solitariness', threatened by development. 'They talk of laying out streets and crescents and I oscillate between my desire of purchasing land at a ruinous price in order to keep my views open, and my wish to fly the place altogether. Is there no millionaire', he asked, 'who will take pity on the wholesome hillside and buy it all up?' It seems particularly happy that one of the founders of the National Trust, who did just that, was the son of their great friends Kate and Drummond Rawnsley. The Tennysons would undoubtedly find it difficult to believe how little the Downs have changed in over a hundred and thirty years.

In 1861 there was plenty of cause for alarm. 'More and more lodging houses spring up and more strangers come with introductions so that we have already begun to feel sure that we shall have to look for another home.' Even so they were still making improvements to the house and grounds – pulling down the stables which were too near the house, for instance – and in October, soon after their return from France, they took over the management of the Farringford farm, which had previously been run by a 'very slovenly' tenant, Isaac Merwood, the same poor fellow who had tried to sell them bits of carpet five years earlier. Now they put in Charles Heard, their gardener, as manager or bailiff, and intended to be a great deal more involved themselves. 'I cannot help hoping that Alfred will be better for this new source of interest,' Emily wrote to Lear. And to Simeon: 'I trust when Merwood is gone on the 11th he will find an inducement in the farm to get out more.' Merwood had been a constant source of annoyance – 'very niggard of manure in the fields' and always setting up 'little odd jobs' to offset his rent so that at the end of the year the Tennysons got almost nothing, in spite of their own hard work, helping with the marling of the fields, and the haymaking.

The new arrangement was much more satisfactory and Emily would delight in their own stock (the new lambs, the cart-horses which the boys rode whenever they could) and their own produce (the butter, the five hogsheads of cider). She would take a professional interest in everything, noting for instance, when they were in Normandy three years later, 'the cattle have very few roots and only beet, when they have any.' In January 1863 the Tennysons' wheat won a prize at the International Exhibition. Emily loved to see 'the reapers reaping winter barley and oats at Middleton, those pleasant breezy fields of ours', and the horses 'drilling and harrowing' the turnips 'in the withy field'. It *was* a source of interest for Alfred, but it was not until 1867 that 'the farm has paid for itself'. The boys were much involved over the years, 'riding home on the farm horses after their day's work and driving home the cows and milking them.' 'Alas alas our hay. What a day for our poor hay,' eight-year-old Lionel exclaimed on one miserable summer day.

Tennyson did like to hear that only the Duke of Richmond's sheep could rival his, but there would come a time – in just eight years, with the boys away at school – when it would all get too much for them. 'The Farm is not the source of out of doors interest to A. which I had hoped it might have been', Emily would write in her journal in November 1869, 'and the accounts proved too hard for me with our many letters.' They fixed an agreement with Charles Heard 'as tenant of the Farm, the land having improved so much under him as our Bailiff.' Emily continued to take a passionate interest in agriculture in general and in the Farringford farm in particular. In the back of a late address book she has jotted down: 'Yellow Aberdeen Turnips grow best here. The Barley famous over the island. The mixture of clay and chalk has succeeded well.'

Although he was her Poet Laureate and had attended a royal soirée soon after his appointment, Tennyson had never actually met the Queen. There had been more than one occasion when it had seemed she might call at Farringford, but she never did. It was the Prince Consort's death in December 1861 that brought about some sort of relationship, though Emily herself met Victoria on only one occasion.

The family, all four of them, called at Osborne – fifteen miles away – on Christmas Eve to sign the visitors' book as a gesture of sympathy. On 5 January Victoria wrote in her diary 'Much soothed and pleased with Tennyson's "In Memoriam". Only those who have suffered as I do, can understand these beautiful poems.' Soon there would be more lines to soothe 'her aching, bleeding heart'. Tennyson had managed to write a dedication, in memory of the Prince, for the new edition of the *Idylls of the King*, poems which the Prince himself had told Tennyson he valued.

Emily Tennyson's devotion to the Royal Family was largely a result, it seems, of their appreciation of her beloved Alfred and his poetry. If Victoria had not always been so 'kind and gracious' to her Poet Laureate, Emily would never have written, as she did extravagantly after she had met her in 1863: 'One feels that the Queen is a woman to live and die for.' It was extraordinarily moving that she had annotated her copy of *In Memoriam* and could say to Tennyson, 'I am like your Mariana now.' ('"He cometh not," she said . . . "I am aweary, aweary, I would that I were dead."') Even so, Emily kept things in proportion; it was the poetry itself that mattered.

On 24 February 1862 she recorded the arrival of letters from the Duke of Argyll (with a message from the Queen) and from the Princess Royal. But the day was really memorable because she had read 'what A. has written of "Enoch Arden".' She had already heard him read it; indeed the Bradleys and their visitors had heard it too. Now, for the first time, she could read it to herself. T.S. Eliot would think Tennyson had 'no gift at all' for narrative; Emily thought the use Tennyson had made of Woolner's story was one of the best things he had ever done – and Matthew Arnold, not easily pleased, was inclined to agree with her. 'Very fine and very beautiful it seems to me,' Emily had written in her journal when she first heard it. She felt particularly responsible, having so much encouraged Woolner to suggest stories for Tennyson. She had also been plying FitzGerald in Suffolk with 'fishing questions' to help with the poem. He had answered late and possibly uselessly, as he said himself, reminding Emily, who did not really need reminding, how tricky the whole poetic process was. FitzGerald suggested she should introduce his information 'at the good moment, when the Stars are right for Pegasus to come to his Corn bin.' He also urged Emily to send 'the old wretch' to Woodbridge, 'where nobody scarce knows his name. (Don't be angry, Mrs A.T.)'

It would be another fourteen years before Tennyson would get to Suffolk, by which time even Woodbridge had heard of him. At a Lincolnshire railway station, Barnetby, in 1862, Emily was sending off a package containing Alfred's mackintosh, which he had, rather typically, left behind. When the clerk saw the name he said, 'What! the great poet Alfred Tennyson?' This sort of thing did indeed give Emily pleasure as Fitz had realized – however much it seemed to bother Tennyson himself. Long after this, Julia Cameron's great-niece Virginia Woolf would satirize the effect of Tennyson's increasing fame in her play *Freshwater*:

Twenty earnest youths from Clerkenwell are in the shrubbery; six American professors are in the summer house; the bathroom is occupied by the Ladies Poetry Circle of Ohio. The son of man has nowhere to lay his head.

It was not quite as bad as that, but the accessibility of Farringford, in spite of that Solent crossing, was really beginning to bother Tennyson. There was one particular occasion when Emily and Alfred were walking in the garden and noticed what appeared to be a gentleman (his clothes suggested he was), 'squatting on the top of the bank and peering down into our lawn.' Tennyson went up to him and asked him to come down, saying 'It's not pretty – your listening to the talk between my wife and myself.' 'I hope you will forgive me, Mr Tennyson,' the man said. His remark was included in Emily's journal, but it did not form part of the story when Tennyson told it to Allingham a few months later, together with a grumble about being 'pursued full cry along the road by two fat women and sixteen children.'

Enoch Arden was not published until the summer of 1864. Emily was, as always, concerned with the title of the new book. She was worried when she saw it announced in a magazine as *Idylls of the Hearth*. 'Will not *Enoch Arden and other Poems* be more in thy usual simple style?' The next day she wrote again to Tennyson in London:

I am anxious about the title, dearest, wilt this do? *In Memoriam* has proved a good title so perhaps I may be right in this too. *Idylls of the King* too ... Perhaps it would be giving it undue pre-eminence to call the book *Enoch Arden and other Poems*. If not, perhaps this is the best, not *Idylls of the Hearth*. This was not thy name I am sure ...

The book, which did indeed appear as *Enoch Arden,* was particularly important to Emily for Alfred dedicated it to her in a verse, which, judging by the many drafts, he found very difficult to write.

Dear, near and true – no truer Time himself
Can prove you, though he make you evermore
Dearer and nearer, as the rapid of life
Shoots to the fall – take this and pray that he
Who wrote it, honouring your sweet faith in him,
May trust himself; and after praise and scorn,
As one who feels the immeasurable world,
Attain the wise indifference of the wise;
And after Autumn past – if left to pass
His autumn into seeming-leafless days –
Draw toward the long frost and longest night,
Wearing his wisdom lightly, like the fruit
Which in our winter woodland looks a flower.

Robert Browning wrote to Julia Wedgwood on 2 September 1864: 'I have not read this book yet – and know nothing of the "dedication" – except that I rejoice at it, loving Mrs Tennyson singularly.' Julia Wedgwood replied saying she liked the dedication 'less on a 2nd reading, there is a little too much about himself in it and not enough about his wife.' It is a good point, but not one that would have struck Emily herself.

By November that year, 1864, Tennyson told Walter White that 'he had sold more than 40,000 of *Enoch Arden* and cleared more than £5000, that he had abusive letters from people who blame him for accepting so much profit.' He also told Walter White that the sixpenny selections, to be published the following year, were expected to sell 50,000 copies and make perhaps £10,000. In fact, this was overoptimistic. Emily would say that at least 'One has the satisfaction of feeling one has done what is right in this small respect.' There was a great deal of money coming in, all the same, and the Tennysons knew exactly what they wanted to do with it. They wanted to find a place where they could escape, not just from the increasing crowds of holidaymakers, but from the horrendous building development that was threatening Farringford's peace and quiet. They had been worrying about it for years.

Edward Lear described the situation as he saw it in October 1864.

I found all that quiet part of the Island fast spoiling and how they can stay there I can't imagine. Not only is there an enormous monster Hotel growing up in sight – but a tracing of the foundations of 300 houses – a vast new road – and finally a proposed railway, cutting through John Simeon and AT's grounds from end to end. Add to this Pattledom has taken entire possession of the place –

Camerons and Prinseps building everywhere. Watts in a cottage (not Mrs W) and . . . myriads more buzzing everywhere.

The proposed railway across Tennyson's land was never built, and 'Pattledom' – Julia Margaret Cameron and her sisters (née Pattle) and their families – could be a blessing as well as a menace. Emily had much warmer feelings about Mrs Cameron than Lear did. She was delighted when 'good Mrs Cameron' would join them in the evening to help to entertain Benjamin Jowett, even though she had only just returned from 'an expedition to Alum Bay'.

We should look back over the three years since Emily had first heard *Enoch Arden*. Watts's wife, young Ellen Terry, had come and gone. She had been at Freshwater just long enough to describe Emily, poised on a library ladder, cataloguing books. She saw her as a 'slender-stalked tea-rose', but wearing 'thick gloves' against the dust. John Simeon, that close friend, had married again, only just over a year after his first wife's death. This was difficult for Emily who, believing in some sort of reunion after death, was always uneasy with second marriages, though she understood how much the bereaved children needed another parent. She had actually written to Simeon on his wife's death about 'the never-ending oneness of a real marriage'. Now her letter of congratulation on this new marriage was a tactful triumph.

I think we can understand it all very well and I am sure we heartily say May God bless you and give you all the good and happiness in your marriage that heart can desire. We feel that we cannot but learn to love one all in all to you, being sure she must be worthy of all love. Thankyou that you can still feel in these first moments of the full enjoyment of such an affection that ours is not less to you. It is my theory (I suppose most other people's too) that the more one loves one the more one can love all, that love grows by loving.

In January 1862 Emily told Dakyns: 'We have got over the first meeting with the new Lady Simeon, which is a relief.' To Woolner in March she said that they had also got over the first visit to Swainston under the new regime. 'The little children seem happy. It must of course need time to make the elder ones too.' Louisa, 'almost a daughter' to Emily, was by now eighteen: this was the time when she thought of becoming a nun, to Emily's distress.

It was also in January 1862 that Franklin Lushington married – a wedding that gave Emily a less mixed pleasure, though Tennyson wished 'the lady had more money'. Emily had first met Kate Morgan many years before; she had been brought up with Frank's sisters at Park House. 'I trust you will find Frank's home a comfort and a pleasure to you,' Emily wrote to Edward Lear, worrying that he would not. Both Lear and Emily would be godparents to Frank's children. Before long, Emily would write to Lear of yet another death: 'Poor Frank and Katie, you know of course of their loss. A kind of awful doom seems to hang over that family.'

Graham Dakyns, the first tutor, left Farringford in April 1862, amidst 'passionate tears' from Lionel and regret from all of them. By April 1867 the then fourteen-year-old Hallam would write a letter beginning 'dear, dearer, dearest Graham'. Dakyns would often return to visit them; he would be a hard act to follow. His replacement was a young man called Francis Atkinson, taller and less relaxed. Emily's assessment of Dakyns's character, in a letter to him when he told her he had decided to make teaching his career, shows she knew his weaknesses as well as his strengths, though she can hardly have realized how sympathetic Dakyns was to John Addington Symonds's homo-erotic confidences. Dakyns found it difficult to make firm and calm decisions, Emily felt, seeing all sides of a question. He was a little too diffident. 'When you are in a place of authority you had better be sometimes wrong than encourage in yourself and others a habit of mind fatal to all action.' Yet it was his very diffidence, his lack of dogmatism, that had made them all love him so much. He had treated the boys undoubtedly as younger brothers rather than pupils, enjoying their company.

Lionel's eight-year-old remark about Jowett, which struck Emily so much that she liked to quote it (as others have done since), suggests how entirely the boys were at ease in adult company. The boy was 'quite indignant' with his aunt Anne, when she spoke of Mr Jowett's 'pupils' – the undergraduates he had with him on a reading party in Freshwater. For some reason, Lionel said: 'They are not his pupils at all. Mr Jowett is a young lad. They are all just the same, just entering life together.' Jowett – like Dakyns, like Woolner, like Charles Dodgson, like so many of the Tennysons' friends – treated the boys as if they were all 'young lads' together. Francis Atkinson found this impossible. He would find the boys impossible, bright and lovely as they were.

Everything started well. Atkinson had recently graduated from Caius College, Cambridge. He was twenty-two and found Farringford 'a pleasant and happy place'. By the end of April he was teaching the boys in the summerhouse on Maiden's Croft and helping them to make model boats (Emily made the sails) and collect fossils. In July an embarrassed Francis Atkinson wrote to Dakyns asking, 'To whom has one to apply for one's quarter's salary! It is a delicate but still, for me, a necessary question.' Emily had evidently forgotten to pay him. In this same letter Atkinson told Dakyns that he got 'on very well with the boys, though I find they want a deal of disciplining and require to be much urged to keeping regular time for working.' He agreed with Dakyns in theory that you could not be too kind to young boys – but he felt '*real kindness* consists in punishing sometimes'. His employers never saw any need for it. The boys' work was fine – they would 'take a good place in any public school', but they were, it seems (he did not actually say so), hopelessly cheeky and talkative, unpunctual, untidy and self-indulgent.

Lionel's piano playing, which Emily loved, was typical of the generally permissive atmosphere at Farringford. 'Almost every spare moment Lionel flies to the Piano now and really, though he has never learned a single air, his harmony is generally good; and often there is a wild kind of melody in the notes.' It was altogether more delightful than the dutiful scales and little party pieces most eight-year-olds played – and Lionel would grow up into a fine musician. The only discipline the boys sustained and enjoyed was being drilled by a 'master gunner' from the Fort with the Cameron boys. Hallam signed a letter to Dakyns, 'Your affectionate Captain Tennyson' and Emily found they enjoyed their drilling so much they were staying out late on the summer evenings and sometimes not in bed until nine o'clock.

Francis Atkinson was teaching the Cameron boys as well. Charlie and Henry were not so bright, in fact they were 'rather rough colts'. Atkinson thought it was time for them all to go to school. He would resign – but not for over a year and only after, in April 1863, the Tennysons had tried the experiment of housing the tutor in Orchard Cottage near by. Emily had then breathed a sigh of relief at having occasional evenings alone again with Alfred, when she could once more 'share his thoughts and works'. Part of the trouble had been Atkinson's awe of 'the Noble Poet and His noble wife'. Emily said Lionel, in particular, found Atkinson's attitude irksome and had 'turned quite rebellious'. Atkinson resigned, he told Dakyns, because he could not 'eradicate their really serious faults,' largely because he was not 'backed up' by the parents, who apparently saw nothing wrong with the beloved boys.

Charles Dodgson (not yet Lewis Carroll) visited Farringford in the spring of 1862 and his account of a bargain he struck with Lionel suggests the sort of behaviour Atkinson found so trying. Dodgson was persuading Lionel to give him 'some MS of his verses' (Lionel would always write poetry – not an easy thing to do as Tennyson's son).

It was a very difficult bargain to make; I almost despaired of it at first, he put in so many conditions – first, I was to play a game of chess with him; this, with much difficulty we reduced to twelve moves on each side; but this made little difference, as I checkmated him at the sixth move. Second, he was to be allowed to give me one blow on the head with a mallet (this he at last consented to give up). I forget if there were others, but it ended in my getting the verses, for which I have written out 'The Lonely Moor' for him.

It was on this visit that Hallam and Lionel signed the photographs in an album of Dodgson's work now at Princeton, so that the 1857 portraits carry the date April 1862 and the eight-and nine-year-old signatures. Emily must have looked at the young clergyman a little dubiously after his curious letter to Hallam three months before, encouraging him to cut himself – and Lionel – with the knife he had given him for Christmas – a knife which in any case Emily had put away 'till he was older'.

It may have been on this April visit too that Dodgson took his third photo of Emily's niece Agnes, now thirteen and enjoying dressing up with her cousins. 'She and the boys are great friends,' Emily had told Lear. In her journal for 21 April she wrote:

Nanny and Agnes arrived while the boys are walking with Mr Jowett. Infinite joy at the meeting. The three young creatures give us Tableaux Vivants from Shakespeare and The Sleeping Beauty and Hallam gives up his part to Lionel in the sleepwalking scene in Macbeth. Mr Atkinson taking one part

– although he had only been in the house four days. 'Really very pretty and good,' Emily told Woolner, adding that she was 'very poorly from my cough.'

Emily's health was, on the whole, rather good in 1862. She was riding the boys' pony Fanny regularly, walking again on the downs occasionally and even helping a little with the haymaking. But Anne Weld ('poor Anne' as her sister would now always call her) persuaded Jowett, on his return to Oxford, to write a letter suggesting she should take more care of herself.

Mrs Weld said that I was to 'write and scold you' . . . Do you ever look forward ten years, dear Mrs Tennyson? Nothing can be more important than that you should see your two boys fairly into manhood; it may make every earthly difference to them. As for Alfred, if he was deprived of you he could hardly have any more happiness or power left in life. I want you to think about these considerations and then to draw the inference that the first of religious duties is the care of health . . . It grieves me to see you, who care for the most trifling of wants of other people, so helpless about yourself . . . Mr Atkinson could answer all the letters that need to be answered equally well. Do not throw away your life in the performance of imaginary duties which are really un-important . . . Ever since I have known you I have noticed that you overwork . . . It is not the letter writing but your life and presence that do the real good and blessing in the home. Your unselfishness really passes into a sort of apathy or indolence about self which is quite wrong.

Jowett ended with soothing noises, but it was still hard for Emily to be told that all her manifold tasks were imaginary and unimportant. In her journal she notes 'a letter from Mr Jowett full of affectionate warn-ing about my health to which A. bids me attend,' but she seems to have taken little notice of the warning, as Jowett expected. Was she con-stantly driven by a feeling that she needed to justify her position as the wife of the great poet? She wanted to do more not less, and more important things, certainly, than the routine acknowledgment of the fan letters and volumes of unreadable verse that arrived every day by the penny post.

In the summer of 1862 an attempt to *do* something Emily Tennyson considered important failed miserably. After what Coventry Patmore called 'the long preparation of fear', his wife Emily, that other 'Angel in the House', finally died, leaving six motherless children, one of them the godson, Tennyson Patmore, who had been born in the summer of the Tennysons' own honeymoon. Henry, the youngest, was only two.

When their mother died, some of the children were being looked after by Maria Jackson, Julia Margaret Cameron's sister and the wife of Dr Jackson, who continued to take an interest in Tennyson's own health. Emily was particularly conscious of the children's situation. Coventry Patmore, still working in the British Museum, obviously needed financial help and Emily determined to get it for him, so he could rent a house, bring his family together again and employ suitable people to look after them. She wrote to the Royal Literary Fund. What happened next Emily could hardly have foreseen. It was the end of the friendship between Tennyson and Patmore.

Twenty years later Patmore described to Tennyson how 'when my wife Emily was lying dead in my house, I received a letter from Mrs Tennyson enclosing for my signature a memorial which had been made and presented by you to the Committee of the Literary Fund for my advantage.' She must have acted extremely quickly. He was a proud man. He could not admit that he needed help. He wrote immediately to the Fund, asking the Secretary to ignore the application by 'Mr and Mrs Tennyson'. He wrote to Emily, so he said, declining their help, but inviting them to come and see him. She never replied. Neither she nor Tennyson ever wrote a letter of sympathy. There was no communication until 1881 when Thomas Woolner attempted some sort of bridge building which failed – again, it would seem, from Tennyson's horror of letter writing. He wrote regretting 'this long estrangement', but the letter was too brief to heal a twenty-year-old wound.

Did Patmore's letter of invitation soon after his wife's death really get lost in the post as the Tennysons asserted twenty years later ('I am perfectly certain I never received any such letter . . .')? Or rather was it not somehow overlooked in the piles of trivial and unwelcome mail that arrived every day? Perhaps Emily assumed Alfred had written that important letter of sympathy and he assumed that she had. She had certainly written to Woolner about the death. Letters dominated Emily's life; in this instance the failure to write one had even more of an effect than the ill-received attempt to help. They never saw Coventry Patmore again.

Emily's letters are full of a frustrated concern for other people and for the world. She was excited about what was going on in Italy. Already in September 1862 Lionel was suggesting they invite Garibaldi to Farringford – an amazing idea that somehow worked out. Emily was also passionately concerned with the situation in Schleswig-Holstein, wishing she had asked Tennyson in London to send her a telegram about the result of the vote of censure in the House of Commons when Palmerston narrowly escaped defeat for his policy of non-intervention on behalf of Denmark. Emily would also worry constantly about the Empire. It became increasingly her hope that England would unite with her colonies 'body and soul', instead of 'casting them off'. She always saw the Empire as a commonwealth of nations, a group working 'conscientiously and harmoniously for the common good'. But what could *she* do to help that? Or indeed anything else. 'Surely we should do something for the Poles,' she wrote to Dakyns as they rose against the Russians early in 1863. 'Alfred feels so strongly for them and so should I, only I have grown so unfeeling, I think. One's feelings get so snuffed one cannot do the good one would and so one almost ceases to try.'

If one could not do anything abroad, one might at least try to do some good at home. In October 1862 Emily persuaded Tennyson to write to Gladstone. They did not know each other very well at this stage, but there was that shared love of Arthur Hallam – and they had spent the weekend at Cliveden together the previous May as guests of the Duchess of Sutherland, seeing, as Emily said, 'a good deal of each other'. It helped of course that Gladstone, who had had some mixed feelings about *In Memoriam*, had no reservations about his admiration for *Maud* and the *Idylls*. The admiration was mutual except, as it would always be, on the vexed question of Home Rule for Ireland.

Now Tennyson wrote tentatively to Gladstone as Chancellor of the Exchequer:

To you, as our great financier, I send the enclosed. You are not requested to answer, only to read it (there is not much to read) and see if there be anything in it.

They are my wife's notions, and she, though much afraid of seeming presumptuous, is yet so anxious on these matters that I told her I would transmit them to you in confidence.

In fact, there was a good deal to read. There are seven pages in Emily's handwriting lodged in the Gladstone papers at the British Library. They show her concern for the unemployed, the poor, the elderly. She had some idea of an old age pension – years before it came about. If Jowett said, as he did, that her wishes went further than 'Political Economy can truly allow,' and she could easily be dismissed with the sort of 'sentimental paternalism characteristic of his letters to women on politics', yet Gladstone was moved by her concerns, which he shared. The sums involved – even translated to their current value – seem pitifully, even ridiculously, small.

After some complex suggestions about how the cotton manufacturers, affected by the American Civil War, might be subsidized by the government in order to keep the mills working, Emily went on:

A fund to be raised by subscription and donation, right royal let it be, worthy of England. Let it be called the Victoria and Albert Fund. Let it replace part of the National Debt in the funds.

In connection with it let each government Savings Bank become a bank for the receipt of the poor mans 'Old-age Savings'.

Let him save, say 10s a year. Let him, if he can, find a patron who will double the sum after the manner of the clothing clubs.

Let the interest of his yearly £1 accumulate and when old age comes let him be entitled to the interest of the accumulated sum and a share of the interest arising from the 'Victoria and Albert Fund' proportioned, not to the sum he has laid by, but in an inverse ratio to the wages he had received, so that the poorest shall have the largest claim on the fund.

Let the interest of the sum he has placed in the Savings bank and its accumulation be not only for himself in old age but also an inheritance for his children (the interest not the principal).

These however shall not be entitled to his share of the interest from the Victoria and Albert Fund. They must earn a share in this as their father did by their own Savings placed in the Savings' banks.

In some such way, it seems to me, the poor man may be saved from the justly dreaded work-house and the whole tone of the working classes be raised.

It seems unlikely that Emily had any real effect on the government's policies, but she may have encouraged Gladstone to move in directions he already had in mind. She would make her own arrangements for her own long-employed servants, so that none of them would spend their old age in the workhouse. And she would not give up her concern for the wider issue. Eighteen months after her letter, Gladstone would introduce the Government Annuities and Assurances Bill – designed to introduce a new era of self-help for the poor. When the Bill, against stiff opposition, finally became law and the annuity tables were published in *The Times*, Emily wrote to Thomas Woolner: 'I should like to set all the bells in England ringing, so much do I rejoice over this first gleam of hope for our labouring class.'

She wished Gladstone could be 'compelled to steal a little of his surplus every year to make a fund to augment the small annuities of the labouring class. I prophesy that this would swallow up the poor-rate, rendering it soon almost a forgotten name and I think it could not fail to raise proportionately the tone of the people . . .' When the boys were eventually at Cambridge, she proposed that the subject of old age pensions should be debated at the Union and that Hallam and Lionel should pledge themselves to the cause.

*

In 1862, when Tennyson first visited Osborne and was received by his Queen as Poet Laureate, she had asked him whether there was anything that she could do for him. He said: 'Nothing, Madam, but shake my two boys by the hand. It may keep them loyal in the troublous times to come.' There was a great deal of shaking hands when the whole family was eventually summoned to Osborne in May 1863, but when the Queen gave Emily her hand 'I found myself on my knee, kissing it but I don't exactly know how I got there.' Hallam described it like this:

We saw the pet donkey 13
which used to draw the Queen carriage
We drove back to Osborne
we went into one of the drawing
-room's The Queen came & made
a very low bow Her Majesty
shook hands with mamma
& mamma very courteously went down
on one knee & kissed the
Queen's hand & the Queen shook
hands with Lionel & myself
& we shook hands with all
the Prince & Princess's except
Princess Louisa she only shook
hands with mamma I had
a chat with Prince Leopold
about the south of France
& Paris he said he did not
like Boulogne The Princess
Louisa asked one whether I
could draw I told her I could not

Emily, writing to Alfred's mother about their visit to Osborne and their meeting with the Queen, remarked that 'I believe it is not etiquette for her to shake hands with gentlemen.' Fortunately for Alfred's promise to the boys, they were not yet gentlemen.

The modest Hallam, who admitted he could not draw (as surviving evidence confirms), passed no adverse comments on the Queen's appearance. He would never have said, as Effie Ruskin did, some years earlier: 'The Queen looked immensely stout and red but very calm.' He had been encouraged in admiration; both his parents thought her appearance far superior to her portraits. Hallam said: 'The Queen is not stout. Her Majesty has a large mind and a small body to contain it therein.' He ended his account:

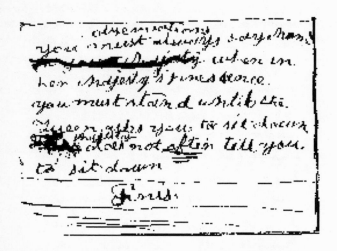

Emily said she found the Queen's face full of intelligence and thought and feeling, 'ineffably sweet and of a vast sympathy'. She felt they had got on extremely well. 'We talked of all things in heaven and earth it seemed to me.' They talked of Huxley, of the stars, of the Millennium and of Jowett. 'I never felt it so easy to talk with any stranger before,' Emily told Jowett. Sadly Victoria, in her diary, makes no reference to Emily whatsoever, apart from naming her:

Saw Mr and Mrs Tennyson and their 2 sons. Had some interesting conversation with him and was struck with the greatness and largeness of his mind, under a certainly rough exterior.

Speaking of the immortality of the soul and of all the scientific discoveries in no way interfering with that, he said, 'If there be no immortality of the soul, one does not see why there should be any God . . .'

Benjamin Jowett, who had accompanied Tennyson to Osborne on that earlier occasion when Emily could not go, told Emily he thought all the benefits were on the Queen's side. It is 'good for her to see people who come from the fresh air of the outer world.' She never saw the Queen again. She was invited but was not well enough to go.

In a conversation a few years later Emily apparently gave the misleading impression that she was a regular visitor to Osborne. Anne Gilchrist, who will soon come into this story, described 'a luncheon which the Tennysons gave . . . Mrs Tennyson talked to us; told us that Tennyson likes and admires the Queen personally much, enjoys conversation with her. Mrs Tennyson generally goes too, and says the Queen's manner towards him is child-like and charming, and they both give their opinions freely, even when they differ from the Queen's, which she takes with perfect good humour . . .'

This is odd. In her letters about Tennyson's visits to Osborne Emily would always add something of this sort: 'I know you will not mention what I have said. Things get so repeated.' And yet here she was in Surrey apparently gossiping and giving a wrong impression herself. The explanation surely is not any wish for personal aggrandizement, as Anne Gilchrist would suggest, but her total identification with Alfred. She lived so much through him; she reported immediately on his return exactly what had happened – for the record. They were (she felt they were) as one, in that 'never-ending oneness of a real marriage'. And she had obviously felt, on that one visit in May 1863, that she had been, not a timid bystander or silent observer, but an equal sharer in the conversation. 'We both agree in any rank she would be a remarkable woman.' In talking of Alfred, Emily would often use the pronoun 'We' – no sort of 'royal we', but an expression of their unity. Queen Victoria never realized that Emily Tennyson was another remarkable woman.

Whatever Frederick her brother-in-law might say in the future, there is very little evidence that rank meant much to Emily. In this year, 1863,

Lady Franklin, who was yet another remarkable woman, recorded in her diary a visit from her niece, Emily's sister Anne Weld.

She spoke a little of her sister's way of life at Farringford, acting incessantly the hostess, the house being always full. The Duke and Duchess of Argyll have been among her guests. She makes no difference in her establishment for anyone. They keep six indoor servants, of whom only one is a man or boy, and two are in the kitchen, for her table is always a handsome one and her cook first-rate, she says . . .

The following year Lady Franklin herself visited Farringford with her companion, Emily's cousin, Sophie Cracroft. 'In the evening A. reads her "The Grandmother", which is a great favourite of hers and she of his.' They would all see a good deal of each other over the years, when she was not in some distant part of the world.

Religion and politics were often discussed at Farringford, but prosody could be even more dominating a subject. There is a glimpse of Emily in William Allingham's diary for late December 1863. It is the only time anyone ever reports her as bored. Her feelings about the tedious talk of 'classic metres' are echoed both by Allingham himself, and by Marian Bradley in their journals. (Such a feeling, even if recorded at the time, did not survive into the copy of Emily's own journal.) The real problem seems to have been the presence of Montagu Butler, at this time the young headmaster of Harrow, who was staying near by with his wife. Marian Bradley would note: 'When Mr Butler is at Farringford the conversation always becomes more shoppy – all classical – and we do not have those old charming evenings we used to.' 'Evenings there always pleasant but a tendency to discuss the meanings of Greek words makes conversation duller when Mr Butler is there. ET more sweet and charming than ever.' This was one of the times when Mrs Bradley remarked on how Emily had 'laid a good foundation and made her mind very rich in the days before marriage', whereas she herself was too young 'and find it hard work now'.

William Allingham reported on three days he spent in the house, with walks on the Downs with Tennyson, Palgrave and the boys. The evening he arrived, the talk was all about 'Classic Metres, to which I naturally have little to contribute.' The second evening there was after dinner more talk of 'Classic Metres' with Tennyson standing on the hearthrug repeating 'with emphasis' (perhaps apropos of metres):

Higgledy-piggledy, silver and gold
There's – (*it's nothing very dreadful*!)
There's a louse on my back
Seven years old.
He inches, he pinches,
In every part,
And if I could catch him
I'd *tearr* out his *hearrt*!

'The last line he gave with tragic fury. Prose often runs into rhyme. T. imitated the waiter in some old-fashioned tavern calling down to the kitchen – "Three gravies, two mocks and a *pea*"! (soup understood). On "pea" he raised the tone and prolonged it very comically.' This was hardly boring, but Montagu Butler was not there.

The next night he *was*. In the drawing room, Tennyson, Palgrave 'and the two Bs' – Bradley and Butler – 'all on "Classic Metres".' Allingham had 'the ladies all to myself and we discoursed profoundly on "poets and practical people", "benevolence true and false", "the gulf between certain people and others", etc. Mrs T. confessed herself tired of hearing about "Classic Metres".' 'I can sometimes scarcely hear her low tones,' Allingham said on one occasion, but he heard her clearly this time.

Marian Bradley suggests in *her* diary the sort of intimacy she and Emily enjoyed that winter. 'Dear Emily T.' and the boys had met the Bradleys off the boat at Yarmouth when they arrived just before Christmas. The beautiful baby in the party was Emily's god-daughter: Emily Tennyson Bradley, now fourteen months. Emily Tennyson was not well enough to join Marian and the men on a 'bitterly cold' walk towards the Needles on New Year's Day 1864. Marian herself found the cold too much.

Turned back alone and ran to Farringford. Tucked my dearest Emily up under her furs on the sofa and chatted for three quarters of an hour. What a difference there is between people ... A few bright stars help you miles along towards heaven ... My darling Emily T is my brightest heavenliest star.

Two days later she wrote:

Sat two hours with Emily T – talked as I never quite talk with anyone else – she said she felt it also – that we understand each other heart and soul. Spoke much of the deadness of personal feelings of love to Christ, now of the danger of losing hold of *Him*, our life our love, in an abstract kind of religion. She has a more devoted personal love for Christ than anyone I ever met with.

They did not talk much of literature. Marian Bradley knew herself to be ill educated and ill read. Her taste in Tennyson's poetry was for the more sentimental lines. She loved the description in 'Aylmer's Field' of the child's feet: 'the tender pink five-beaded baby-soles'. 'Emily laughed and said "I knew you'd be charmed with that".'

While the two mothers were talking, the Bradley and Tennyson children would be playing together. Edith, who was almost exactly Hallam's age, later described some of the delights of Farringford as she remembered them, 'the happiest hours of her childhood', with Tennyson himself the only worry. She described how 'loving and considerate' the boys were to their mother, and the games they had together all over the rambling house. There was one occasion when they were playing hide-and-seek and Tennyson himself came across her and swept her up in his arms and 'pretended to smother me in the folds of his huge cloak.' When the children were staying there, she hated his goodnight kisses, with 'the odor of tobacco in his raggedy beard. My hair was very long and heavy, and he used to take hold of it by the extreme end, throw that end round my neck and then turn and turn until he'd wound himself close enough to my face for what he called an "osculation"'. Did Emily realize how much the child disliked this?

One day Edith's father, Granville Bradley, greeted Tennyson joyfully, having just arrived on the island for the holidays. 'Hello! How are you?' he asked. 'Tired of life,' was the reply. The boys more than made up for their father's gloom. Allingham described Lionel as 'odd, shy, sweet and, as his mother says, *daimonisch*. Hallam has something of a shrewd satirical turn, but with great good nature.' Edith Bradley said Lionel was full 'of pranks and mischief' and they were both full of high spirits and stories and ideas for games. There was a splendid rocking horse *not* in the nursery, but in the stone-floored hall. The four children could all ride on him – 'two on his sorrel back and one in each of the seats at the ends of his rockers – weaving imaginary tales and singing long, loud songs.'

Edward Lear was at Farringford this year for his first visit since the one just after his sister's death. 'It is very pleasant to see Mr Lear so well and cheerful,' Emily's journal reads, but in his he writes sadly: 'I sup-

pose it is the anomaly of high souled and philosophical writings combined with slovenliness, selfishness and morbid folly that prevents my
being happy there.' At dinner Tennyson was 'far from overwise', raving
about England: 'Best thing God can do is to squash the planet flat'.
Even when Tennyson was completely sober Lear thought Alfred's
manner 'assuredly odious at times'. He never saw any sign that it
distressed Emily, but he wrote: 'I believe no other woman in all
this world could live with him for a month. It always wrings me to
leave Farringford, yet I doubt – as once before – whether I can go
again.'

Lear knew Emily much better than Edward FitzGerald did. Indeed
Fitz had not been at Farringford since the time of Lionel's christening
and 'I have scarce seen the original Man for Ten Years,' he told
Emily regretfully. It was not long after that that Fitz made his
famous suggestions that Alfred might have done better to have married 'a jolly woman who would have laughed and cried without any
reason why.' ('Foolish and wicked talking,' as he said.) According to
Lear, any such jolly woman would have walked out on Tennyson
long before.

At church the day after the 'Classic Metres' evening, Emily had given
to Marian Bradley 'some splendid photographs of the four of them'.
These were a set taken by the Swedish photographer Oscar Rejlander,
who had been at Farringford in May. They are the only photographs
that survive of the four of them together and one forms the jacket of
this book. But there are many other images of the Tennysons dating
from this time. Emily never felt that photographers did justice to them:
'I am always rather hopeless about photographs of any of us. I don't
think we photograph well.' Three years later, when both boys were
finally away at school, Emily wrote in her journal: 'What would I give
for faithful portraits of my boys and their Father – their beautiful
smiles. No artist who ever was could give them.'

In London in the summer of 1862 William Jeffrey of Great Russell
Street took photographs of them all, but not all together. Emily looks
solid and not frail at all in her voluminous street dress, with a boy on
either side, Lionel's hand in hers. No smiles at all. They were on their
way to Grasby to look after Henry Sellwood while Louisa and Charles
had a holiday. There are splendid photos of Hallam at this time by both
Rejlander and Mayall; he is an extremely handsome boy. But only
Rejlander was able to capture Lionel's striking looks – looks which

made even the Bradley children feel marked him out as someone special. Emily loved the one of both of them with Lionel leaning against a pillar, a book in his hand. He is only nine but looks extraordinarily mature. It is a photo which makes Watts's painting of the long-haired boys two years later look insipid and sentimental. Of the painting Emily would say: 'Very beautiful but not so beautiful as they. Like them but not their very selves. How should it be?'

Julia Margaret Cameron's photograph of the boys together must have been taken in 1864, when she first started making her mark as a photographer, after her daughter's gift of a camera the year before. It is remarkably natural, with the boys' hair untidy and the two of them looking as if, just that minute, they had reluctantly come in from playing with Charlie and Henry – those 'rough colts'. There is no photograph of Emily by Mrs Cameron. Did she not once say that no woman should be photographed between the ages of eighteen and eighty? Henry Cameron, the youngest son, would take Emily when she was indeed nearly eighty, with Hallam and Alfred, but it would not be a success.

Watts's well-known portrait of Emily was also painted at this time. Emily sat for him in November 1862, 'to surprise A.'. Watts was so pleasant that sittings did not seem tedious, and the boys were so interested in what he was up to that they begged to be allowed to stay and watch. When he was working on the portrait subsequently, Watts wrote to ask Emily to send by the messenger 'the lace veil you wore and the collar if it is not a fixture. The face of the picture is not dry enough to work upon, but I can put in all the rest before I bring it for the last sitting, or rather another sitting.' When the portrait eventually arrived at Farringford, the Argylls were there and exclaimed enthusiastically that it was equal to Gainsborough, that it was 'one of the great pictures that future generations will look at.' Someone else 'almost felt in sitting near it that I could speak to her.'

Emily herself, with her habitual self-deprecation, was inclined to think that Watts had spent far too much time and thought on her. 'I do not know how such a beautiful picture has come, but you are a subtle alchemist, a great magician, that I do know.' It was *not* apparently a very good likeness. Edmund Lushington, seeing a representation of Emily in the *Illustrated London News* the following year, marvelled that 'it is possible to make a picture of you unliker than Watts has done.' (It would be interesting to know what Edmund Lushington thought of the Millais portrait, apparently so undervalued by the family.)

The *Illustrated London News* picture appeared on 23 April 1864 and it commemorated a remarkable occasion: the visit of the Italian patriot Giuseppe Garibaldi to Farringford, the visit Lionel had wished for two years before, hearing stirring tales of what was going on. The Tennysons had always taken a close interest in Italian freedom and unification. In 1860 Tennyson had written of 'the gleam of light' from Italy and of Garibaldi – 'we shall hear of him again'. Now he was in England. The revolutionary had a potent appeal to the British public, as the champion of an Italy liberated from an external oppressor. The British government was uneasy about Garibaldi's visit – the huge demonstrations of democratic fervour, the invitations from radicals and socialists. When Garibaldi arrived at Charing Cross Station, one hundred thousand people flocked to welcome him. A few days later he stood for five hours at Nine Elms, as crowds marched past to honour him. Queen Victoria had been extremely perturbed at the Prince of Wales attending a reception in Garibaldi's honour; she spoke of his 'incredible folly and imprudence'. Did she realize her Poet Laureate had actually invited the Italian to his own home?

On 5 April 1864 Emily wrote to Tennyson's sister Matilda to tell her they had just come back from seeing Garibaldi on his arrival in the Isle of Wight. 'Such a noble looking man, a grand high square forehead like the great men of the Elizabethan days, strong and sweet with kindly simple manners. He stroked Hallam's head and said it was a good thing the boys lived in the country, that his had grown up strong in the free air of Caprera.' 'I expected to see a hero and I was not disappointed,' Tennyson said, after Garibaldi had come to Farringford itself a few days later on a day of glorious sunshine and cold wind. Flags flew, crowds gathered and the hero planted a Wellingtonia, raised from a Californian cone, a tree that survived, growing ever a sadder sight, until very recently. It was Emily who recorded the much-repeated story of Mrs Cameron's rebuff: 'Mrs Cameron wanted to photograph Garibaldi, and dropped down on her knees before him, and held up her black hands, covered with chemicals. He evidently thought she was a beggar and turned away, until we explained who she was.' But she did not get her photograph and we have to rely on the feeble sketch in the *Illustrated London News* for an impression of what Emily called 'a most striking figure in his picturesque white Poncha lined with red, his embroidered red shirt and coloured tie.'

Emily still wanted to return to Italy, which she persisted throughout her life in preferring to France. But it seemed too far away for a family expedition. Moreover Brittany had Arthurian associations and Emily was longing for Tennyson to get back to the 'Idylls', after the 'Northern Farmer' and his narrative poems based on the stories Thomas Woolner

had provided. 'I hope you think he has given your stories well,' Emily wrote to Woolner in July 1864. 'I wish he would give mine now and do the "San Graal" for me.' In this same letter she said she hoped that Woolner, now engaged, would not delay his marriage later than September. She would often think of the years she and Alfred had wasted in separation. 'The months of our short life are precious. Why should they drag wearily with absence, when they might go winged with presence' – and then mocked herself for a sentence 'I take to be worthy of Queen

Elizabeth herself in its elaborateness, or whatever else it might be called.'

Emily was determined the family would cross the Channel together again in 1864 after a particularly sad English summer the year before. Tennyson had then had terrible problems with his leg, with 'a gouty affliction' and a sort of eczema he could not help attributing to the vaccinations they had all endured. One doctor had suggested he tried Harrogate for a cure. The family was at Clifton House in Queen's Parade for six weeks, none of them liking it, which was not surprising as Tennyson himself was actually 'in bed for a fortnight'. Moreover 'the summer was no summer,' 'stormy and sunless and to me often hopeless besides,' Emily wrote, 'for he seemed so much worse'. Lionel called Harrogate 'a horrid dull place'. The only redeeming features of August 1863 had been outings to Knaresborough and Fountains Abbey – and the company of a fair-haired temporary tutor called Butterworth, who unfortunately could only stay for the vacation.

After Butterworth's departure, the Tennysons were without a tutor for seven weeks. 'I am happy teaching them. What a pity this cannot last,' Emily wrote in late October, but by 17 November she was tired, and grateful for Alfred's help with Virgil and Horace. By the end of the month she was pleased to welcome Thomas Wilson. Wilson's temperament was rather like Alfred's – he was the tutor to whom Tennyson once said (Wilson himself recorded it): 'If you wish to kill yourself, don't do it here: go to Yarmouth and do it decently.' Emily knew just how to handle his 'fits of melancholy' and he would always stay in touch. There are letters surviving which suggest what good friends the boys were with Wilson, and how helpful he was to Emily. When he became engaged in the spring of 1866, Hallam (by then thirteen) would write, reflecting the Farringford view of marriage, that he hoped to meet 'your wife to be, your evermore delight'.

In March 1864 Wilson was roped in to play 'a very poetical Wall' alongside the boys in a birthday rendering of the Pyramus and Thisbe scene from *A Midsummer Night's Dream*; 'besides ourselves only Mrs Cameron and the servants' in the audience. Lionel was ten years old and had woken up in the middle of the night to look at his presents. In the morning 'he rides with his gifts to different cottages and on the down, his cap blows off and frightens Fanny and he is thrown and dragged in the stirrup but not hurt, Thank God,' Emily wrote in her journal. The summer before, on the way back from that disastrous holiday in Harrogate, they had been in a cab that had overturned in London. 'The poor horse was perfectly quiet or we must have been smashed to pieces.' In November Lionel would have another fall, jumping. 'I bandage him and sleep in his room,' Emily records. But he had not even broken an arm. Alfred had been playing football with the boys and the fall meant Lionel missed some games. That was all. They seemed to lead charmed lives, the four of them.

In August 1864 they set off for Boulogne, 'on Papa's birthday' as Lionel said, for the sort of holiday mixture of fun and improvement familiar to many parents. In the Boulogne hotel one of the *femmes de chambre* recognized them and so did someone who had seen them on Rouen station, though it was three years since they had been in France. They were a memorable family, seldom, as Emily said, 'taken for English when on the continent'.

The cathedral at Chartres was a place Emily had seen before on her one French tour with her father and the Welds twenty years earlier. They saw it on Hallam's twelfth birthday. Lionel was keeping a diary full of explosive comments on terrible lodgings and cheating restaurants, which sound as if they may have echoed Alfred's. By the 18th they were setting out for Carnac and Emily was feeling excited at 'being so near the fulfilment of the chief object of our journey.' At one of the inns Emily was very much moved by a woman who spoke of the boys as angels. 'Tears came into her eyes while I was speaking. I felt she had some great sorrow in [her] heart which . . . she had fain have told me.' 'Carnac disappointed us,' Hallam wrote to Dakyns; Alfred growled that it was 'not nearly so fine as Stonehenge'.

Emily's journal describes in detail an intensive tour in Brittany. She told Francis Palgrave that they had not seen 'as much as we ought to have done of the western and northern coasts . . . having foolishly omitted to get a good map in Paris, and not having been able to find one afterwards. The people we found very uncommunicative, and, as far as we could discover, totally ignorant of the past history of their country, and of the Arthurian legends. We went to Lannion on purpose to see Keldthuen (where Arthur is said to have held his court) and Avalon: but Keldthuen we found a moated and not ancient chateau and, tho' our driver showed us Avalon, the sailors declared it was not.' Emily admitted that she had told the hostess at one inn that Tennyson had written about Arthur. Hallam would say: 'She proclaimed everywhere that he was the poet of "notre grand roi, Arthur".'

The family's health bore up extremely well during the month they were away from England. Emily saw most of the things the others did. But on 31 August Lionel records: 'Get quinine and sal volatile for Mama'; she was too tired to go over Mont St Michel herself. 'But I begged [she had crossed out 'insisted'] that we might drive there and very glad I was that A. and the boys saw what interested them so much, ascending the Mount while I rested below.'

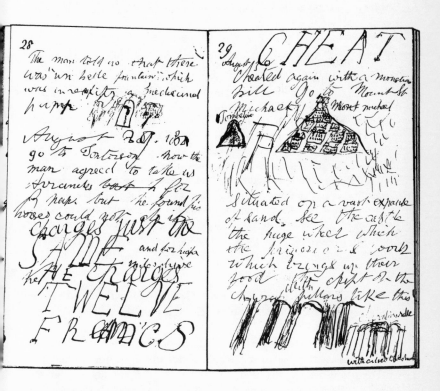

Lionel's journal is more fun to look at than Emily's – traces of her writing can be spotted amidst the exuberance of his. Her comment on the Bayeux tapestry in her own journal is interesting: 'It gives one a feeling of perfect truthfulness. The object of the piece seemed to us the justification of William. A good wife's deed.'

In November 1864 a friend of Graham Dakyns called in at Farringford on his honeymoon tour. It was John Addington Symonds about whom Dakyns knew – and we know – a great deal more than Emily ever knew. The Victorians it has been said were 'extremely skilful at pushing skeletons into closets'. The Tennysons would know Symonds's father, a distinguished Bristol doctor, in difficult circumstances. The son, even more than 'Lewis Carroll' (who had already called Lionel the most beautiful boy he had ever seen), was a connoisseur of young male beauty. To Dakyns he wrote:

I have been today to Farringford. I only saw the setting. Tennyson was in London. But as the Play of Hamlet even if given without Hamlet's part, leaves Ophelia Polonius and Laertes, the terrace at Elsinore and the Ghost, – so of Farringford. Mrs Tennyson and the boys I saw, and the rooms full of works of Art intense. She is a strange woman: I love her from the little I have seen, almost monastic in her shy retirement, plain drapery, and worn heavenly face. But those boys: . . . My heart bled and my soul yearned to them. They filled me with a love sadly deep even at first sight. It seems folly to say so. Yet I am not in a vein of sentimentality. I felt as if I knew them. And I know that if I saw them daily they would find in me strong sympathy. I touched their hands and I looked at them and I spoke three or four words. That was all. But there was something in the light that ran over Hallam's face, in Lionel's grace, and in the delicate fibre of both felt through their fingertips, wh. revealed them to me. You say they have 'la maladie du Siècle' already. But good God! do you know what form this will take with one or both of them? I see it. In this I am not apt to be mistaken. But the bitterest cup may be kept from them. Would I could die for you, my brothers.

Next day he added a note to Dakyns. 'This letter is rather wild, written in a style to be avoided. But I felt it last night and you do not misunderstand.'

Dakyns understood perfectly that Symonds feared the Tennyson boys, 'one or both of them', would suffer the same homosexual pre-occupations which obsessed the two friends. Symonds was at that moment dangerously trying to subdue his own inclinations by marriage. Dakyns too would marry and have children, but not until 1872. The same day he added his note, Symonds wrote very differently to his sister, who did not know Emily or her sons:

We found Mrs Tennyson in a large gloomy room, fitted up in Gothic style, a drawingroom and a study with a big bow window all in one. She greeted us kindly, softly, and a little shyly. She was dressed in what Catherine calls 'Drapery', of grey, with no crinoline; and looked altogether monastic, worn in face, with white features and a calm expression. She seemed to suit the room and to have come out of a chapter of past history. So did her boy, Lionel, whom we saw first, a splendid creature, tall and lithe, with long curls and a pear shaped face extremely beautiful. He was curled up in an oak arm chair hanging his red legs over its side. Some hurt had kept him in the house. Mrs Tennyson talked a good deal about Jowett and Mr Bradley: she asked after Papa, and said she had once received a very kind letter from him and that many people had talked to her about us. While we were discussing Mr Jowett's salary, the other boy, Hallam, came in, also medieval, but not so handsome as his brother. Those are remarkable children. They will be great some day, if they are not spoiled, and if their obviously over irritable nerves and delicate sensibilities allow them to expand and harden in the world. Now they are growing in a hothouse, and are pale, feminine, and full of upward striving, accordingly. The eldest seemed, nevertheless, frank, and had a boy's voice. They are more noticeable than any thing else at Farringford. Mrs Tennyson is too shy to be known at once, though she left on both of us an impression of an indefinite charm and sweetness. She was very kind – sorry that her husband was away and anxious to be of use to us if we stayed here.

The boys were 'growing in a hot house'. Symonds was not the only one who saw it was time the boys were allowed to 'expand and harden in the world'. It was time they went over the water to school. Eighteen months before, in May 1863, Benjamin Jowett had begun urging the step on Emily: 'I think they want more discipline and "bullying" (do not be alarmed at the word).' Emily *was* alarmed, remembering perhaps one night when Hallam was not at all well. He had told Dakyns:

I was ill last night and I went to bed at about half-past five and Mamma read to me while Lionel made his ship. Mamma had her dinner upstairs with me whilst I had my tea in bed. Lionel waited so nicely on Mamma and me. I had the night-mare and then I asked Matilda to bring the candle and stitch, and so by degrees it went off and I went to sleep.

What would happen if the boys were ill and had nightmares at school? Who would read to them in bed or sit by them and sew by candlelight?

Jowett continued to encourage Emily; the boys were getting 'too old for the matriarchal form of government'. On two occasions, seeing Tennyson in London, Gladstone had expressed concern that Hallam had not yet started school. Tennyson seems to have had just as mixed feelings about sending the boys away as Emily had. He himself had come home from Louth School at twelve, hardened by some knocks and with more domestic ones in store.

In July 1863 Emily had told Edward Lear that both boys were entered for Marlborough, where their friend George Granville Bradley was headmaster. 'We put ourselves pretty much in his hands, thinking we cannot go far wrong trusting thus to his knowledge of boys in general and ours in particular.' He 'does not wish that they should go before they are twelve,' she said. Now in August 1864 Hallam *was* twelve but they did not think he was ready to go straight into the maw of Marlborough, even with the Bradleys at hand. Mrs Henry Taylor wrote to recommend a preliminary step:

What should you think of sending them to a Mr Paul who has a few pupils at a place (said to be very healthy) about four miles from Wimborne? He is a friend of Mr Maurice and of Mr Kingsley, to both of whom he refers. He is married to a very nice little person . . . clever, observant and very refined. They would both greatly like to have your boys.

The Pauls were indeed keen to have the Tennyson boys and on 14 October suggested a starting date at 'the end of this month or the beginning of next', at fees of '250 guineas for the two'. Emily had sent a photograph of the boys, probably one of the ones taken by Oscar Rejlander, and Charles Kegan Paul had suggested that it would be 'for your boys' advantage' if they should look more like the other boys in a plain 'jacket and waistcoat' and with their hair cut. Tennyson cheerfully told the Duchess of Argyll that it was the haircuts that delayed the boys starting. 'My wife . . . asked whether they could come in their long hair and he said they couldn't and she did not like to cut it off in midwinter for fear they should take cold as they have worn it long all their lives – and the result was, that they do not go till Easter which for their sakes I trust may be a warm one.'

Emily told Margaret Gatty: 'Mr Paul does not wish to have the boys till Easter and has undertaken to provide a Tutor meanwhile.' Frederick Lipscombe, the tutor who began in November 1864, was so good that Emily would tell Woolner the following March that 'Ally says had he known Mr Lipscombe would have stayed another year he would have kept Hallam and Lionel at home, but I fear their doom is sealed now and that they could not be kept at home without ill-treating Mr Paul.'

As it turned out, the boys did not start at Easter 1865 as had been arranged. Emily told Edward Lear on the 12 May: 'We have been in a distressed condition about the boys. Three times we have begun preparation, expecting to go at once with them to Mr Paul and three times whooping cough there has prevented us from going. It is very unsettling . . .' The boys had been painted by Watts – without fee – in April and then on 9 May Emily had braced herself, and had herself 'cut off part of the boys' beautiful golden hair'. On the 18th, with the Thackeray girls, who were there for lunch, watching, the boys had proper haircuts, 'the first time that a barber's scissors' had been near them. 'The boys are sadly spoilt,' Emily wrote to Lear, by their 'ugly dress', as well as by the haircuts.

Both parents took the boys to school. They said goodbye to them apparently at the station. 'A sorrowful sight to us both, our two boys, on the Bailie platform, alone, for the first time in their lives as our train left.' The Tennysons had been observed crossing the water to Lymington in 'dirty weather'. The observer, A.J. Munby, did not bother to describe the woman: '(I suppose) his wife'. Of Alfred he reported not only his extraordinary clothes – 'odd careless dress, tall wideawake, camlet cloak, loose blue trousers, frock coat and open shirt front – no gloves', – but also his physical appearance: his 'long, wild curling hair', his beard, his lips, his complexion, his aquiline nose, his whole face 'supreme in manliness and mental power', among the fat parsons, the tourists and sailors. With a father like that to live up to, it was no wonder Emily worried about the boys and what would happen to them now. 'Our darlings leave us,' she wrote in her journal.

CHAPTER TWELVE

Searching for escape

At the end of 1864, Emily Tennyson had written from Farringford to Margaret Gatty – always more important as a correspondent than close as a friend:

We are talking of 'Devil's Jumps', not far from a home I had and lived in with my father in Surrey, only one talks in such a way as not believing, not daring to believe, we shall ever be driven from this that has grown so dear, in spite of ever-increasing vexations of land to be bought to keep away or shut out brick boxes . . .

Walter White, who had been Charles Weld's assistant at the Royal Society and had succeeded him after his ignominious departure, remained in touch with Weld's brother-in-law. It was he who told Tennyson about the Devil's Jumps – ninety acres of dramatic landscape near Hindhead and the Devil's Punchbowl – available for only £1500. 'What an address,' Tennyson said. It seemed the sort of place where a poet should live. 'Land I should think poor enough,' he reported to Emily, 'but scenery he says splendid'.

There was an encouraging letter from Anne Gilchrist, who lived in the area. She was the widow of Blake's biographer, a friend of many of the Tennysons' friends, and a devoted admirer of the Laureate's poetry. She confirmed that that district (where Surrey, Sussex and Hampshire meet), although so much nearer London, held the possibilities of the solitude they felt was disappearing from Freshwater each spring and summer, as more and more holidaymakers flocked to the island, some of them (too many of them) 'eternal sight-seers', intent on Tennyson-spotting.

Anne Gilchrist got the impression that Emily was quite happy *not* to buy land and build, but 'I think the Laureate is rather tired of that Cockneys' Paradise, the Isle of Wight. *She* would like to retain Farringford, and add some room to a farmhouse in this neighbourhood, but *he* has an idea of giving Farringford up, and building a large house on one of these Devil's Jumps.' Nothing would come of such plans until much later, but throughout 1865 and 1866 the Tennysons watched the new roads and hideous houses being built on the Isle of Wight with ever-increasing alarm. It was not only the tourists but the new inhabitants they feared. In February 1865 Emily wrote to Edward Lear that they were 'threatened with several large villas on the new road between Alum and Colwell Bays and sit shivering at thought of all the people that will live in them.' They were also distressed by the 'deep cutting across beautiful Afton Down where the military road gashes its sides.' Even Queen Victoria would hear from Tennyson – on one of his rare visits to Osborne – about the worries over the intruding hordes. Emily told her father and Anne that the Queen said they were not much troubled at Osborne and Ally said to Her Majesty: 'Perhaps I should not be either if I could stick a sentry at *my* gates.'

When Anne Gilchrist wrote about the Tennysons' plans, she had just been reading Arthur Hallam's *Remains*, the collection put together by his father, who had himself died in 1859. She had read the book, she said, 'with some eagerness for the sake of *In Memoriam*', but apart from some of 'the love poems addressed to Tennyson's sister, which I like much from their sweetness and earnestness of feeling, there is not much that strikes one.' Many people wondered, reading the *Remains*, whether Arthur Hallam had really been as remarkable as Tennyson and Gladstone and so many of his friends had thought him. Emily, constantly using the beloved name Hallam for their son, must have felt the splendid living boy had laid to rest at last the splendid dead man whose name he bore. Tennyson himself would say that Arthur Hallam had left nothing behind him worth naming: 'His poems are worthless' but he 'would have achieved great fame, if he had lived.' Guests at Farringford rarely heard Tennyson speak of Arthur Hallam, but once to Emily Ritchie, one of Thackeray's nieces (with their cousins often at Farringford), he said simply over his port: 'How you would have loved him!'

Marian Bradley, Emily's devoted friend, worried about her that winter. She thought Emily 'more delicate with her cough and more worn and worried even than usual.' She wished she would not 'be always buying and troubling about land. I think her nature requires leisure and repose to blossom fully – this sort of life deteriorates her. It is a pity for such a lofty, lovely nature not to have room to blossom in.' While Emily was busying herself with business, Tennyson having rejected Jowett's idea that he should try writing about Galileo, was tinkering with his translation of parts of the *Odyssey*. He would read it to Emily in the evenings.

'I hope that he has got a subject,' Jowett said to Emily in May 1865, going on to try to cheer her in the boys' absence with the thought that it was good for them to get among other boys. He supposed that she was 'refusing to be comforted'. Emily wrote to Alice Woolner, Thomas's new wife, 'The house seems very sad and still without the boys.' She must have been rather surprised by Hallam's first letter, which sounded as if it came from a holiday camp, not a school. There had been a trip to buy fishing rods in Blandford, swimming in the river Stour among the water lilies and an 'all night' fishing expedition as the highlight. 'I would not have my boys coddled,' she wrote. Above all she wanted them to be happy, but was this what they needed to harden them for the real world, or at least to prepare them for life in a public school?

More comforting than Hallam's letter was one from their headmaster – if one can call Charles Kegan Paul a headmaster, with the small crowd of boys in his large thatched vicarage known as the Bailie House. At least he mentioned the boys' *work*. 'In no way', he wrote to Emily, 'would one think them first launched into so new a life ... Hallam is very watchful and tender over Lionel and they are both thoroughly nice boys. It is too early to give any decided opinion about their work, but they seem to me above the average, Lionel the more brilliant, Hallam by far the more accurate.' This was perceptive; it would always be so, in all sorts of ways. It had been so that spring, before they left home, when the boys had put aside their usual passions (football and chess) and become obsessed by 'battledore' – the bats and shuttlecock a present from Mrs Cameron. Lionel would make some brilliant shots, but he was not 'steady enough' to keep up the rallies Hallam and his father enjoyed. Emily told her sister Anne: 'Ally and Hallam kept up two thousand four hundred and even then the shuttle cock did not fall.' Tennyson's notoriously poor eyesight does not seem to have handicapped him in this engagingly useless feat.

It was a year of deaths and family upheavals. In February 1865 Tennyson's mother, Eliza died, full of years and piety. When he was in

London, Tennyson had been in the habit of paying brief visits to the household at Rosemount in Hampstead. His mother had lived latterly with her sister, Mary Anne Fytche, and a changing cast of her children – often Cecilia Lushington (retreating from the problems of Glasgow and Park House), as well as the unmarried Matilda and Septimus, the Jesses and sometimes Arthur and Horatio and their wives. Emily had never been particularly close to her mother-in-law, and she naturally could not entirely subscribe to Alfred's once stated view that his mother was 'the beautifullest thing God Almighty ever did make,' however much she admired her blameless life.

On the Isle of Wight Emily sent the boys to Cowes to be measured for mourning suits, and the tailor said they were the tallest of their age he had ever measured. 'They ought to be,' Emily considered, facing the fact that they were no longer little boys. 'Both their grandfathers about six feet two and their Father six feet.' On the day of the funeral, 'by a touching chance', Lionel put snowdrops into the crimson glass his grandmother had given Emily and Alfred when they were married. The weather was severe and there was no question of Emily going to the funeral. Alfred 'wished for the country churchyard' that he would also be denied. Emily's sister Louisa, another daughter-in-law, did go, and her 'memoranda book' is as usual full of obscure sad thoughts.

Louisa felt the correct Christian joy, knowing Eliza Tennyson was dying in the sure and certain hope of eternal life. 'Feel her spirit sing with me,' she wrote on the day of her mother-in-law's death. On the funeral day she wrote: 'Arthur and Cis behave ill. Want go home feel ought.' The next day: 'neglect Miss Fytche. Vex CW. Cis naughty . . . calm her. Wish praise, feel no-one cares for me.' There are all the ingredients of a family drama, but we shall never know exactly what went on. Kate Rawnsley long after would write: 'All her sons then in England attended the funeral. The clergyman said it was a remarkable sight. 6 I think there were.' There were indeed six: Frederick, Charles, Alfred, Arthur, Septimus, Horatio. But the one who was missing was the unmentionable Edward, not abroad but still incarcerated in York.

Alfred wrote to Emily that 'the departure of so blessed a being . . . seems to have no sting in it.' 'We are all *pretty* cheerful,' he thought, unaware of what Louisa was writing in her diary. Not long afterwards Emily would tell Edward Lear that Tennyson was 'much depressed and no wise himself.' Less than three weeks later Mary Anne Fytche also died. 'How soon did the sisters follow each other. They were not to be separated for long. I think it is often ordered so by providence,' Charles wrote to a cousin. 'They were indeed the dearest conceivable mother and aunt, both pure and generous, with those shades of difference in likeness which members of the same family necessarily must have.' Years before, Arthur Hallam had called Aunt Mary Anne 'the life of the family'. Emily saw in her 'a delightful proof that a single woman may keep her heart open and loving, free from all old-maidism, and her spirit ardent.' Now she too had gone, and in the wake of her death came the break-up of the household in Hampstead and the problem of another 'old maid', Matilda, and *her* maid Cole, who would from this time on 'make their home with us,' as Emily said.

Emily of course put a brave face on the situation. It was as well that, as things turned out, Matilda obliged by spending a good deal of time with her sister Cecilia, mainly in these years in Edinburgh or in Eastbourne. Twelve years later Matilda would exasperate George Eliot by her 'nonsense and ignorance'. Matilda and Cecilia would end up at Park House with Zilly, the one survivor of Cecilia's four children, and live well into the twentieth century.

Emily told Graham Dakyns cheerfully in October 1865 that 'Our sister Matilda . . . is a dear noble creature and no-one could have found a third person more easy to live with'. Alfred said, 'She settles here as well as can be expected, considering the recent past.' Matilda herself wrote of two 'such heavy shocks' – though as her mother and aunt were both in their eighties, their deaths can hardly have been entirely un-expected. For Emily the problem was that, when they did not have visitors, the last thing she wanted, in the boys' absence, was the con-stant presence of a 'third person', least of all one who was always 'so nervous about herself' as Matilda was.

Lionel would complain to his mother that Aunt Tilly's 'sonorous roar' made reading difficult and later, as a young man, he would com-pare his aunt with Uncle Toby in *Tristram Shandy*, 'with an externality of "naturalness", which in rustic phraseology means idiocy.' She was, it seems, a 'character' and characters can be difficult to live with. There are nice stories of her unconcernedly putting up her umbrella in church to protect herself from draughts and trying out a bath at Maples by climbing into it, button boots and all.

Matilda Tennyson could put her foot into things metaphorically as well. As Tennyson once put it, 'blowing up' his sister after dinner one day: 'Relations step in where Angels fear to tread.' The angelic Emily, who was rarely afraid to step in, if it were necessary, would write to Hallam: 'Poor Aunt Tilly is so very good – she has got to understand that we might wish to say a word to each other sometimes. I love her more and more and I think I feel her rather less of a barrier between us than I did.' It was only to her sister Louisa that Emily admitted how trying she had found it to have Tilly 'always complaining' about Far-ringford and what a relief it was when she decided she liked it, so long as the boys were at home to entertain her. Visitors now were welcome not just for Alfred's sake or their own, but because they could divert Matilda.

Emily was brooding on family relationships that year. At least twice she wrote to people she thought might know to ask for the origin of a Norse story about a king who was told that 'to avert some evil to his people', 'he must sacrifice his dearest. He consents. The priest lifts the axe over his son as dearest. The wife rushes in and receives the blow.' Emily makes no comment on this story but it obviously intrigued her. As the years went on Hallam would become extremely close to his father, travelling with him and working for him as Emily was still doing in the late 1860s. At this point, with the absent boys always in her mind, she must from time to time have wondered whether *she* was putting them before their father, devoted as she remained to him.

The older generation was fast disappearing. Tennyson's father's three siblings all died around this time. Emily went with Tennyson to visit Aunt Russell in Cheltenham where she was in 'a precarious state' after a stroke – paralysed, but still mentally alert. 'A and I have each had long talks with her,' Emily wrote in her journal. She had been his favourite aunt. Years later, Emily Jesse, her niece, would sum her up neatly: 'So here goes,' she wrote to Alfred, 'as Aunt Russell vivaciously expressed herself as she plunged into some water while in Scotland . . . to cross out of the reach of a drove of wild bullocks.' As for Mary Bourne and Charles Tennyson d'Eyncourt (the builder of Bayons), 'the grave is only a deeper hiding'. There was a death in their own generation too – Septimus, that sad brother (he who had told Rossetti that he was 'the most morbid of the Tennysons'), died the year after his mother.

Henry Sellwood, Emily's father, still survived. For years he had lived mainly at Grasby with his daughter Louisa and her husband, Tennyson's brother Charles. He had been active and useful, while disagreeing from time to time with Charles about such things as pruning (Charles, like Alfred, liked a luxuriant garden). Louisa appears to have kept some of her angry feelings confined to her diary – though 'vex Pa' may well mean he was entirely aware of them. In 1861 Henry Sellwood had noticed errors in Charles's agent's accounts and put an attorney on to the matter. The agent, J.T. Burkinshaw, turned out to owe Charles the remarkable sum (multiply by fifty or sixty for today's value) of £4,337, money which, once reclaimed, was used to restore the church at Grasby. One of the new bells would be dedicated to the memory of Charles's mother, the other to Henry Sellwood. But that year poor Louisa's diary suggests her relations with her father had deteriorated further. She wrote on the last day of that year in her crabbed code: 'Pa's presents to sisters feel grudge.'

That was the year of Charles Weld's disgrace and dismissal from the Royal Society. The Welds had lived in London while Weld was working for the International Exhibition, but Emily was disturbed by her sister's situation. In 1863 Emily became involved in purchasing some land near Farringford for Anne Weld. Reporting the end of her successful negotiation, Emily wrote 'HURRAH AUNTY NANNY! as the boys would say.' Two fields were secured for £600. Jane Franklin wrote in her diary:

Anne has been lately at Farringford where, I was pleased to hear, she has been buying five acres of land with her own money and is going to build a house on it. It is near her sister, on high ground, commanding a charming view . . . She also added of her own accord, for we asked no questions about him, that Mr Weld would not live there the whole year round, but would travel a good deal.

That seemed a good idea; but in fact, Charles Weld would refuse to live there at all, and would insist on a house on the mainland. Emily wrote to Anne:

I am continually thinking of you and I cannot help feeling anxious when I do not hear. I cannot help thinking that things might be managed so as that you should live here in peace and comfort. If Charles could be content to keep aloof at present, saying he does not mean to visit at present, or something of that sort. I have such a longing to try and make life somewhat happier to you, my poor Nanny . . . I am very anxious too to know how Charles takes my note. People quite expect you here . . .

When Charles Weld published, nearly two years later, another of his travel books, *Last Winter in Rome*, he wrote in it: 'Emily Tennyson with CR Weld's affectionate love,' apparently not having resented her 'note'. His winter in Rome meant that the whole burden of finding and buying a house on the mainland fell on Anne. Aubrey House at Keyhaven near Milford in Hampshire, just across the water, was found and approved, with the help and advice of both Margaret Gatty and William Allingham. Emily explained to Mrs Gatty that her sister had been 'commissioned to get a country residence somewhere during his absence. Rather a serious undertaking, I should say.' Emily trusted Charles Weld would consent to the purchase, and 'that all will be satisfactorily arranged.'

In the end, presumably because Weld did not agree and because Henry Sellwood was happy to leave Grasby (and his problems with Louisa), Aubrey House was bought by Sellwood not Weld. Emily was delighted to have her father so much closer, so that she could get to him quickly if he were ill. He would also, when he was living with the Welds at Aubrey House, spend a good deal more time at Farringford. Emily would enjoy playing the piano and singing 'the old airs' they had loved at Horncastle and Farnham when she was young. Most of all it delighted her 'to hear my A. say of him that he is the model of an old gentleman, though I know it so well.' He was getting tired and deaf, but to Emily 'he grows more dear and beautiful in all ways.' Seeing him off on the boat one day at Yarmouth, she wrote in her journal, 'I see him seated on deck in his great coat, looking like a pale king. The boat looks majestic as it moves away. I never saw it look so before.' Was she, unconsciously, comparing her father's sanguine temperament with the more difficult moods of that other 'kingly' man in her life, Alfred Tennyson?

Anne Weld's problems were by no means over. Emily scrawled a postcript to a letter to Alfred after Charles Weld's return from Rome. 'CRW has taken strongly against Aubrey, but don't say so. Poor Nanny!' 'He loves gay cities better. Eternal winters in the eternal city would be more to his taste, I suppose, for he seems to have been gayest of the gay this last winter when there,' Emily told Margaret Gatty. Two years later she told Lear: 'CRW was so discontented at Aubrey that my Father has been persuaded to sell it. A sad pity it seems to us.'

The Welds would be at Aubrey House for only two and a half years, until a further move to Weston, just outside Bath, taking Henry Sellwood with them. Agnes, by then aged seventeen, would approve of the move, telling Lionel: 'I hope to meet with some young people that I like better than the Milford set – they are so *fast* and *vulgar* in their words and manners.' Agnes also considered Aubrey House's proximity to Hurst Castle and a prospective garrison of six hundred soldiers was 'by no means agreeable'. (Was Lydia Bennett's behaviour somewhere in the back of her mind? Her uncle must certainly have recommended Jane Austen's novels to her.) Emily would write to her sister, as she had written several times before, 'May the next home be happier.'

Henry Sellwood, returning on the boat one evening in June 1865, reported a fellow traveller who, having no idea who he was, wanted to talk about the Tennysons. Was it, the lady asked, because Tennyson was 'high' – presumably she meant arrogant – that he refused to see people or was it just that 'he likes to be quiet'. Emily commented in her journal: 'No need to give his answer. Then she asks questions about me, but of course he keeps his counsel as to who he is.' Emily could never be accused of arrogance and indeed would sympathetically wring the hands of total strangers who really wanted to wring Alfred's, or kiss a child presenting a 'nosegay' to the poet, to cheer it up when the poet himself had turned away.

The boys came home from their first term with the Reverend Charles Kegan Paul in July. Their parents both went to Yarmouth to meet the boat, with Tennyson peering 'through the glass to try and see the boys'.

Emily wrote extravagantly in her journal: 'I don't know whether I have had such a moment since I first welcomed my little Hallam into this world as this moment when I have them again.'

The four of them went abroad together in August. Effie Millais, travelling on the Continent in that summer of 1865, found just the sort of people the Tennysons were trying to escape from in the Isle of Wight. She commented on 'plenty of English of the most vulgar description who don't know a word of a European tongue and are always calling for Allsops Pale Ale.' The family managed to avoid such people at Waterloo, where they spent a week. (FitzGerald, hearing of it, hoped something would come of it.) The plain, Emily wrote, was 'beautiful with waving cornfields and many different crops. The villages in the distance are clear in a golden light but the wind raves wildly . . .' Alfred said it was as if 'the dead were lamenting'. The sergeant who showed them round had himself fought at Waterloo fifty years before; he remembered sitting all night on horseback in rain and thunder and lightning, without anything to eat for twenty-four hours, 'yet so great was the excitement that he felt neither wet nor hunger,' and 'the whole time seemed to him five minutes'.

The Tennysons travelled on to Luxembourg and Trèves – and then to Mulheim, where they were rowed down the Moselle to Koblenz, and journeyed on to Weimar. 'The people there,' Emily wrote, 'seemed to be rather stupid about Goethe and Schiller, and in vain we tried to impress upon our driver that we wanted to see all which concerned them.' There is a paradox about the Tennysons visiting the houses of these dead German poets they so much admired, while in England so many people distressed Tennyson himself by peering curiously at Farringford, the home of the poet *they* so much admired.

The Tennysons saw three rooms of Schiller's house, 'pleasant enough in spite of their bareness'. Emily noticed his wife's guitar lying near his bed and they were both struck by the peace of the place. In Goethe's town house, Tennyson was touched by the sight of the writer's old boots at the entrance. Emily told Thomas Woolner that a friend of Carlyle's had managed to get them 'a sight of the forbidden study'. They had stolen stealthily in 'lest others, excluded ones, should hear our steps and be jealous. This was, as you will believe, an immense gratification to him.' In her journal, Emily described in detail all the little things that struck her – the boxes for manuscripts, 'visiting cards strung like bills together' and Goethe's old empty wine bottles. In his bedroom, she noticed on the washing stand 'some of the last medicine he took'. Did Tennyson reflect that his own deep interest in these things contradicted his famous abhorrence of biographical curiosity? He would say he was glad Shakespeare had left no letters – but if he was so gratified by Goethe's narrow study, would he not also have wished to have seen Shakespeare's, if that had been possible?

Hallam, Emily told Woolner, had taken a very lively interest in everything they saw; Lionel – perhaps inevitably for an eleven-year-old – was most interested in Waterloo. Emily's own highlight was a Raphael Madonna and Child in the art gallery in Dresden. She had known and loved a print of it for years. It hung on the drawing-room wall at Farringford and Emily had once told Woolner of baby Lionel's delight in 'the pretty baby and the lady'. He had practised his first words on them. It was the painting known as the Sistine Madonna – with Mary standing with a large and very real child in her arms and those two marvellously bored-looking boy cherubs leaning over the frame of the painting at her feet. In the revision of her journal she wrote that the child 'made A. "marvel at His majesty".' To Woolner, she wrote: 'I don't think he cares for it so much as I do.' He certainly told the Duchess of Argyll he would have preferred not to have seen Mary's feet. They returned to England via Aix-la-Chapelle, where they saw Mass going on in the ancient church where Charlemagne himself had been crowned; then there was a trying journey to Ostend, the carriages so packed, but a calm crossing, and so home to the usual 'alarming' mounds of letters.

By an odd chance, there survives in Lincoln, retrieved from Emily's own desk, a pile of letters from this period, apparently unanswered. Emily continued to write huge numbers of letters. If not an entirely efficient secretary, she was a very conscientious one. This surviving packet indicates the kind of letter that occasionally defeated her. One imagines her reading them and sighing and putting them back in the desk, not in the wastepaper basket, with perhaps some vain hope that that was less unkind. The letters are nearly all addressed to Tennyson himself and presumably handed over by him to her to be dealt with – or not, as she felt inclined.

One which was certainly waiting when they returned to Farringford in September 1865 was from an Irishman living in western Canada – a man called Thomas Fenton. He complained he had sent a poem of his to Tennyson for his opinion and was amazed not to have had a reply.

Surely, Fenton considered, Tennyson was above 'the littleness of common natures and can afford, when solicited, to patronize the poet yearning for notice, with a grace and condescension becoming your position in the ranks of literary men.' It was one of hundreds of such letters, some answered, some not, which caused Emily untold agonies. Edward Lear would encourage her to give up 'answering fooly people's pain provoking pages' but it was difficult for her to take his advice. Tennyson would say one reason he went away was to escape letters – but they would always be waiting when they got back.

More easily ignored (why was it kept?) was a letter from a woman who was obsessed with Gladstone: 'Why did Mr Gladstone become a eunuch if he did not love me . . . I offered love: I asked for love. I believe Mr Gladstone loved me . . .' There were many mad letters and others not quite so mad which yet were difficult to answer. One 'To the Poet of the Age' from Henrietta Caroline Pumfrey: 'So often have I tried to get to know the actual spot of earth, which is distinguished on the world's map, as the Home of "Tennyson", tho' your home is everywhere and in every true heart.'

Tennyson's objections to curious sightseers, people like Miss Pumfrey who longed to gaze at the 'actual spot on earth', continued. He was always grumbling about intrusions on his privacy, on being unable to take a walk on the Downs without being stared at, of having to look for a refuge from the 'cockney' hordes who 'come trampling over my grounds and staring into the windows.'

The word 'cockney', much used, is curious. It did not always have overtones of class distinction. Its undertones were purely urban. In Cintra in 1859 Tennyson had lamented that 'The place is cockney . . . crammed with Lisbon fashionables and Portuguese nobility.' There was the Cockney School of poetry, of course, earlier in the century – with poor dead admired Keats tarred by the connection. The beloved Arthur Hallam had used it of himself; he wrote of his own 'cockney raptures' to Tennyson's sister, not long before his death. Frederick Locker, the author of the best-selling *London Lyrics*, who would become very close to Tennyson, called himself a Cockney. These tourists Tennyson so much resented were simply townspeople, city folk, of every class and kind, people Tennyson despised because they did not know the difference between the fruit of the arbutus and a strawberry, between the nightingale and the rook. 'Pooh, you Cockney, they were rooks,' he said of the birds in the high Hall-garden, which were calling to Maud.

Mainly he hated the trippers simply because they *came*, so many of them, and often enjoyed themselves in a noisy way, 'without reference to the scenery', as A. J. Munby put it in his diary that summer, after walking on the Downs and seeing 'a gentleman's servants' dancing to a 'German concertina'.

Emily would usually call the intruders simply 'tourists' and regret that they curtailed Alfred's walks. A 'country man' he met on the road would tell Munby that they never saw Tennyson. 'He does his poetry work at night on the downs.' It was certainly time he found somewhere where he could walk without needing the cover of darkness, but in the autumn of 1865 he did walk on the Downs with an important visitor to Farringford. The boys had hardly gone back to Paul's before they were home again. Emily had asked permission for them to come and meet an exotic monarch – Dowager Queen Emma of the Sandwich Islands, who had come from the Pacific to raise money for a new Anglican cathedral. 'I confess I have not much spirit for receiving the Queen,' Emily wrote to her father and sister, 'but I must do my best'. Queen Emma's visit had been encouraged by Emily's aunt, Lady Franklin, who had recently visited Hawaii – and it had the sanction of that more glorious Queen, who had never yet visited Farringford, but would receive the young black widow at Osborne.

It was a problem fitting everyone in. Emily often had to exercise ingenuity over her hospitality before Farringford was enlarged in 1871 – and even then, from time to time. Now she told the boys their rooms would be needed for the royal party and Aunty Nanny and cousin Agnes would have 'the Tutor's room' and she would have two beds put up for the boys in the Lodge. 'I am very grateful to Papa for letting you come at all . . . after lessons on Friday.' Alfred thought they should do their preparation on the Friday evening and had proposed Saturday morning for their crossing; 'But you would learn your lessons at home, would you not?' Emily added optimistically.

One unexpected uninvited visitor found himself lodged at the Freshwater Gate Hotel. This was Charles Hopkins, uncle of the more famous Gerard Manley, who had lived in Hawaii since 1844, enjoyed a productive *menage à trois* on Oahu with a local couple and became well known for his attacks on the rigid sexual morality of the local missionaries. His brother, Gerard's father, had actually reviewed *In Memoriam* in *The Times*, lamenting its tone of 'amatory tenderness'. None of this was known to the Tennysons, but Lady Franklin had warned Emily of the problems attached to entertaining Queen Emma. The poor woman had in fact arrived at Upper Gore Lodge, Lady Franklin's house in London, in tears. She was someone much given to weeping, 'but not warm and cordial in her manner, for this is not her habit . . . I believe she does not know exactly what to say, so says nothing.'

Queen Emma seemed to prefer to use Charles Hopkins as her aide-de-camp, rather than the gentleman provided 'by command of Her Majesty, Queen Victoria'. Lady Franklin felt bound to suggest Hopkins was not someone who could be introduced to Osborne, even if the Tennysons had to put up with him. He seemed to be 'a loose unmarried man addicted to drunkenness'. Emily Tennyson would meditate on how this 'calm and sweetly dignified lady is so near the days of Captain Cook' – who had been killed in her homeland only eighty-six years before. Lady Franklin was more worried by the possibility of her step-grandchildren (the children of Emily's cousin Eleanor) overhearing talk about strange Hawaiian customs. Queen Emma, unmentionably, was the widow of her own half-brother. Queen Victoria, who thought her 'peculiarly civilised', though 'a savage' in appearance, perhaps was not aware of her incestuous marital history.

The Hoapilis, Queen Emma's Hawaiian companions, also had their drawbacks, but they spoke English 'with sweet voices in the pleasantest possible manner'. In London Queen Emma often seemed to be 'ex-hausted' and disappeared into her room at every possible opportunity. At Farringford it was different. She obviously found the Tennysons delightful hosts. They made her feel welcome with an ALOHA woven out of 'small dahlias on a background of ivy' over the portico and the Hawaiian flag waving near the Queen's bedroom. Emily totally under-stood her liking for the simple pleasures of hiding from the crowds of visitors in the summerhouse in the kitchen garden ('among the cab-bages' Emily said she said) and running about 'like a child with delight on the downs'. Agnes Weld and the boys had gathered bryony berries and made a wreath for Mrs Hoapili's head – the effect spoilt only by her unfortunate facial hair – 'something very like a black moustache', noted by Lady Franklin in her diary, but kindly omitted by Emily from hers.

The Hoapilis sang 'wild melodies' together, culminating in an ode to the young Prince, the Queen's son, who had died as a child. The mother was overcome by passionate weeping, which went to Emily's heart. 'She has an affectionate nature,' Emily wrote. There was 'something very pathetic about her'. Lionel's soft hazel eyes had reminded the Queen of her own dead boy.

'It all went off admirably,' Lady Franklin said afterwards, noting in her diary that Queen Emma had 'naively' observed 'her unworthiness to have been in intimate intercourse' with the Poet Laureate in his own house – 'observations so unlike her general reserve', as was her 'affectionate parting from the boys'. Her kiss for Hallam had so delayed him, as the steamer was about to depart, that he was too late to step on to the pier and had 'to take a boat – happy boy!' The Queen had been sad to leave Farringford. 'Only think of her shedding tears all the way to the boat!' Lady Franklin wrote to her niece, Emily.

Tennyson had worried about them all after the departure. He wanted 'to try and protect Hoapili against Lincolnshire . . . and even talked of going himself for this purpose.' His 'ludicrous foreshadowings of the Lincolnshire visit seem likely enough to clothe themselves with too too solid flesh,' Emily considered – but in the event Hoapili, staying with another of Emily's cousins, the Reverend Richard Wright in Wrangle, gave an 'excellent speech, without notes, astonishing Richard and all who were present.' Tennyson called on Queen Emma in London, just before she left England, and found her sad and suffering from a cough, 'which she said she caught that morning when she went with Hallam up the down before breakfast.'

By this time the boys – congratulated by their mother on their exemplary behaviour – were back at Mr Paul's near Wimborne. 'A sad blank they leave you will not doubt,' she wrote to Annie Fields in America. Emily believed Charles Kegan Paul to be 'a good and able man in his way – but his way is scarcely ours. He cannot in the least estimate Lionel – Hallam's dear strong sense and conscientiousness impress him'. She felt let down by what the boys had told her of their fellow pupils – even the 'young men' Paul was coaching were behind the Tennyson boys and the other boys in the summer had been 'a stupid set'. She hoped they might have 'more advanced companions this year'. Paul had complained of Lionel as 'apt to be idle'. Emily could not resist reminding the boys that 'idleness is the root of all evil' and that, as their father's sons, they had a particular duty to make the best possible use of their talents. At the end of November Emily was writing to them from their 'own little room' because the drawing-room fire smoked so much. The one in their room was smoking too, she added: one must wonder whether these smoky fires exacerbated the coughs she so regularly suffered from.

'I cannot help hoping that my boys will do some good service in the world and to do so they must work hard from the first,' she wrote to them. She bombarded them with advice about all manner of things – they were always to consider 'other people's feelings' and not to overexert themselves with walks that were too long for their strength. When they sang they were to remember:

Fill your chest with air and give it out slowly – Every long note should begin softly, swell out and die away thus.

She drew a little diagram and reminded them that the loudest singer is not generally the best. She begged them not to think her 'over-anxious and fanciful'. She feared she was.

Lionel told her Mr Paul wanted to invite his parents to hear him sing an anthem solo 'which I *certainly* will not do before the whole church and choir besides. But when the invitation comes after Christmas you must find some nice excuse to get me off.' He was confident that she would. When Emily apologized for a dull letter, he sweetly told her that 'on the contrary' while reading it he had said to himself, 'It is the most interesting letter I've had yet'. In the same letter on 10 December he said: 'On the 15th we break up. Hurrah! Old home is the jolliest place on earth.' The same day Hallam wrote to Emily: he found it difficult to make his point, crossing out and repeating himself.

You will have had a letter from Mr Paul to say Lionel's stammering has increased and that he thinks he is tired from the long half, which he is rather and offering to send him home a week before me. As it is on the 15th we break up Lionel says as it is so soon and he does not want to be at home without me, because he would feel it dull he does not want to. Mr Paul says that Lionel is a very clever little fellow and that we have both been very good and got on very well . . . He is merely a good deal stammering because he is tired.

From London, Tennyson wrote to Emily as if it was the first he had heard of it: 'I am very sorry to hear about Lionel stammering. I hope it is only work and weather.' Lionel arrived home –'quite knocked up' – on the 11th, in spite of the boys wish to come home together. Tennyson had escaped from the quietness of Farringford where, he told Allingham, 'Sunday touches Sunday' at that time of the year. Emily wrote bravely in her journal that he 'writes to me every day. I am very glad that he is seeing those he loves to see.' But she was sorry he was not there when the boys returned. Ten days later Emily told Margaret Gatty he was 'wonderfully better for the change'. There were two ponies now and the boys spent the holidays riding together. Lionel never went back to Paul's. He was saved from singing his solo, but the stammer persisted and Emily would spend the next two years hoping for a cure.

There were a great many suggestions about what should be done for Lionel. Graham Dakyns hoped that Dr Symonds would treat the boy in Bristol, and that he might live with his old tutor. 'I do not think that I could make up my mind to part from Lionel to anyone except yourself now,' Emily wrote to Dakyns. Dr Symonds said he would be 'really glad and proud to do my best for your son, and if I fail to remove or lessen his infirmity it will not be for want of effort on my part.' But the scheme came to nothing. It was Dr Symonds who changed his mind; did he suddenly wonder whether Dakyns – his unreliable son's friend – was after all a suitable host for Lionel? Did he find Dakyns's interest in the boy disturbing? Or was it simply that he realized his own lack of expertise? 'We must believe that it is all for the best,' Emily wrote to Dakyns. It was the belief she lived by. 'We make immediate arrangements for taking our Lionel to Town with us.'

After some vacillations – Emily reported Alfred 'frightened by the idea of moving the household' – the Tennysons had agreed to rent Lady Franklin's house, Upper Gore Lodge in Kensington, while Emily's aunt and her cousin, Sophie Cracroft, spent the winter in India and Ceylon, indefatigable travellers as they were. In London the Tennysons would take the opportunity of consulting James Paget about Lionel's stammering. As Surgeon-Extraordinary to the Queen, he was hardly the expert they needed; various other people were also consulted. 'Dr Flower's Exercises' were suggested and tried. Lady de Grey, encountered at the Gladstones', strongly recommended Dr James Hunt of Ore House in Hastings, the author of a compelling publication on the *Management of Stammering and Stuttering Children*. Hunt had treated both Charles Kingsley and Charles Lutwidge Dodgson, though Dodgson does not seem to have had a very high opinion of his character. Hunt's main appeal to Emily was that his regime was based on kindness and the 'systematic training and strengthening of the voice and articulating organs', while not neglecting 'the cultivation of the intellect'. Dr Hunt entirely rejected the 'absurd and cruel treatment to which stammering children are often subjected . . .' Lionel would start at Ore House the following August.

Hallam returned to the Reverend Charles Kegan Paul at Bailie House that January. 'Get me into Marlborough this Easter if you possibly can,' he wrote to his mother. The main event of his last term at Paul's, as far as Emily was concerned, was his confirmation in Sherborne Abbey. Paul assured Mrs Tennyson that Hallam's religious feelings were 'deep and real, manly and free from superstition,' though, in a typically English way, he felt it important not 'to dig too deep about the roots'. To his mother, Hallam observed sensibly of the Holy Communion, 'I suppose you would not take it if Christ had not commanded it.' He told her that *her* explanation of confirmation had told him much more than had his headmaster's preparation classes. Hallam was also extremely pleased with the presents she had bought for his fellow pupils at his request, 'as a little remembrance of me'. 'Those presents are the very thing and they are liked exceedingly,' he told her.

Mrs Cameron had sent Hallam a photograph of his brother. 'One thing is nice,' Hallam told Emily. 'It does not make him a fool as some photographs do.' Lionel had, indeed, a habit of looking foolish in photographs, but he would go on to be Mrs Cameron's 'star performer among the children,' according to Edith Bradley. 'Indeed', she said, 'he was artistic enough to satisfy anyone.'

Hallam was rather envious of the idle life he thought his brother was leading in London in the February and March of 1866. 'I should like to swim if I went to London and see Mr Gladstone and Mr Browning,' he wrote. Lionel did not swim but he did meet both Gladstone and Browning and enjoyed a giddy round of London pleasures: Madame Tussauds, the Zoo, a 'secret' passage at Westminster, fencing and boxing and 'broad sword exercise'. He even saw the Queen on her way to open Parliament. All this in spite of the fact that both his parents were struck down by 'a bad influenza that many had more or less'.

When they were up and about, they took the boy everywhere with them; he was twelve that March. They took him to the Deanery at Westminster for luncheon one day. It was a place that would become very familiar to all of them over the years. Arthur Stanley was now the Dean. He was one of the liberal churchmen who had supported both Jowett and Maurice. In 1863 he had made a late marriage, celebrated by the boys at Farringford with 'the waving of red flags and salvos of percussion-caps'. His bride was Lady Augusta Bruce, whom the

Tennysons had got to know when, as a lady-in-waiting to Queen Victoria, she had made the arrangements for the Osborne visits. Her sister Lady Charlotte (they were daughters of the Earl of Elgin) was married to Frederick Locker and they had one daughter, Eleanor, just a little younger than Lionel. The two children met for the first time at Upper Gore Lodge that winter.

Robert Browning, seeing Emily for the first time since the encounter in Paris fifteen years before, 'asks if he may be excused if he looks at me a little more,' Emily wrote in her journal. He wrote, 'She is just what she was, and always will be, very sweet and dear.' Inveterate diner out, he had enjoyed that evening more than most. Browning's situation was so much worse than Tennyson's – his wife dead, his poetry unpopular. But he rarely growled; he had a different temperament. Jowett saw him as likely to write 'more or less unintelligible verses for thirty years longer – I think he has a great enjoyment of life; he is a fine fellow.' Lionel thought so too; twelve years later Browning would agree to be the godfather of his son, the first Tennyson grandchild.

Lionel had met Browning. Now Emily could not resist letting him stay up to dine with Gladstone, the second great man both boys wanted to meet. Emily did not mention Lionel's presence in her letter about the dinner party to her father and Anne – perhaps she felt they would not have approved. Gladstone, she told them, had spent nearly the whole meal talking to her 'most eloquently'. In his diary Gladstone wrote, 'He shows so well as host, and in her there is a great charm.' One wishes he had said more. 'I am delighted to have seen him,' Emily wrote, 'for, fine as his speeches are when one reads them, they give one but a faint idea of the power and intensity of the man. He is quite affectionate in his manner to us. Mrs Gladstone said to me, "Doesn't he look happy?" when he was talking with Ally.'

Tennyson and Gladstone were obviously *not* talking at that point about Home Rule for Ireland nor about the case of Governor Eyre. It was just ten weeks since the evening at Thomas Woolner's house, recorded in such detail by John Addington Symonds, son of the Bristol doctor, who was also present. Gladstone and Tennyson, 'both with their strong provincial accent', had clashed over 'the Jamaica business – Gladstone bearing hard on Eyre, Tennyson excusing any cruelty in the case of putting down a savage mob.' Symonds recorded Tennyson's terrible murmurings, as he 'kept drinking glasses of port'. 'Niggers are tigers; niggers are tigers', he said, *sotto voce*. 'I could not kill a cat, not the tomcat who scratches and miaows over his disgusting amours and keeps me awake.' Tennyson went on to talk of his own lack of courage: 'I could not wait six hours in a square expecting a battery's fire.'

The conversation that night, in young Symonds's compelling account, seems to teem with strong feelings of anger and prejudice, and Tennyson's ugly words about niggers have often been quoted out of context. One has to remember the word 'nigger' was a more neutral word in a Victorian ear. If they were tigers, they had the courage Tennyson felt he himself lacked. Tennyson might well have used the word 'nigger', without prejudice, of Queen Emma, who had stayed in their house so happily two months before. Symonds saw the two great men in their argument as 'both of them humorous, but the one polished and delicate in repartee, the other broad and coarse and grotesque' – and undoubtedly rather drunk.

Was it all just talk? Symonds sensed, somewhere in Tennyson, his 'profound moral earnestness'. Gladstone, as they said goodnight, declared he always slept well – that only twice had he been kept awake, and both times by the recollection of a misquotation in a speech in the House. Next day Tennyson had written to Emily of meeting at Woolner's Dr Symonds, the 'famous physician of Bristol who had come all the way to dine with Gladstone and myself. I liked him much. The great man was infinitely agreeable ... and seems, though he suspends his judgement, to think that Eyre has been so terribly in the wrong that he may have to be tried for his life.'

Emily had been unaware of all that 'tipsy' male talk at Woolner's, but it was not very different from the sort of talk that often went on at her own dinner table. She was well used to Tennyson muttering and declaiming as he got through his bottles of port. Sometimes his 'shocking' behaviour had undertones of seriousness; sometimes it was just for diversion. Jowett, writing to Florence Nightingale just at this point – when he, too, had been 'quarrelling tonight with Tennyson about Governor Eyre' – said how low the poet was. He 'has the feeling that his life is past and that he will never do anything more; the *Quarterly* killed his great Poem thirty years ago and the retrospect of life and all things in it is sad to him.' 'His is a very pained and melancholy nature with many troubles and few if any pleasures,' Jowett considered. But it was wonderful the way his wife sustained him. 'She is a saint – a really good woman, with hardly enough of self in her to keep herself alive.' It was something he would often say.

Tennyson had now apparently abandoned Arthur for a poem on Lucretius. Emily had praised Hallam for copying out a 'long rather difficult article on Lucretius' for his father so correctly. Evidently the boy was already being trained to take over some of his mother's tasks. Several times at this period – he was fourteen in that summer of 1866 – Hallam wrote letters for her when she was not well. He was becoming very protective of Emily, constantly solicitous about her well-being in his letters home: 'Do bundle the Lushingtons out soon or else I shall have to write to them myself and say they tire you.' 'TAKE REST WHEN WITH GRANDPAPA.' 'You have written too much this week to me.' 'Lionel is not to get into scrapes and vex you while so unwell.'

After the influenza in London, Emily had considerable trouble with her teeth in the early summer of 1866. She went up to London to see the dentist by herself. 'Remember to send for me if at all wanted,' Tennyson wrote to her from Farringford where he had been left unexpectedly to keep an eye on Lionel and to entertain Alice Woolner. That was not difficult ('I take my book after dinner and she hers'), but Lionel was helpless without Emily. 'I had to put on an unclean shirt and my clothes unbrushed this morning,' he wrote to his mother. Observers of his father thought that Tennyson quite often did just that; Emily found it difficult to keep a servant up to the mark when Alfred cared so little what his clothes looked like.

Emily told Margaret Gatty that May that there was, besides her trouble with her teeth, 'another sort of illness which has still more incapacitated me'. Could this have been a veiled reference to gynaecological problems, to a prolapse of the womb? It was just at this time that Julia Margaret Cameron's sister, the previously tireless and hospitable Sarah Prinsep, took to her sofa. Hallam could hardly believe it when his mother told him. 'Is it really true,' he asked, 'that Mrs Prinsep is on the sofa for her life – that active and energetic Mrs Cameronic woman?'

In 1866 Emily was still far from taking to the sofa. Richard Chenevix Trench, Archbishop of Dublin, visiting Farringford at the end of June, described Emily Tennyson as 'a most gentle lady, in evident feeble health, with remains of rare beauty.' The poet's sister he described simply as 'an old maid'. Emily might not be strong, but she provided an 'excellent but simple' meal –'soups, salmon, roast mutton, ducks, peas, tarts, puddings, strawberries and cherries'. The recipes may have been simple; the quantity sounds excessive. Next morning at nine it was Emily who conducted family prayers for the Archbishop. Trench had been at Cambridge with Tennyson, who remembered him as stately enough for an Archbishop even in those days. He used to tell a story of Arthur Buller pulling on Trench's coat tails in the Cambridge Union when he was saying solemnly, 'I do indeed believe, Sir, there is a God in the Universe.' Trench turned round and said in the same solemn voice for all to hear: 'If you do that again, Buller, I'll poke your eye out.' Looking at Trench now, Tennyson laughed to think of it and Emily knew why.

Tennyson certainly did not care what the Archbishop, or anyone else, thought of him. Again and again people remarked on how he always behaved just as he felt like behaving and said just what he felt like saying. He would criticize a friend, 'much the best scholar in the company': 'You never open your mouth without making a grammatical blunder.' He abused the tea at the Palgraves' and the soup and mint sauce at the Bradleys. He once told Marian Bradley she looked like a 'Scotch fish wife'. Another day, overhearing someone say 'Mr Tennyson is delighted to make your acquaintance', he said: 'What made you say that? I never said I was ... Your voice sounds like the piping of a little bird in the storm.'

Tennyson could get away with behaviour that would not have been tolerated in anyone else. Emily told with relish the story of how at Osborne he defied 'one great official' after another who tried to make him take his cloak off before seeing the Queen. 'Thank you. I have a cold and had rather keep it on,' he repeated politely, 'to their great dismay'. 'The Queen laughed heartily when she heard of it. So goes the story at all events and I hope you may smile at least,' Emily said to her father and Anne.

So often all she could do was smile. Once when given a bunch of grapes by one of his neighbours, who told him they would do him good, Tennyson said 'he thought they would more likely give him belly ache.' What could a wife do with such a man except smile and enjoy his bluntness, his honesty, his unconventional behaviour? Edward Lear, visiting in October 1864, had again been horrified at what Emily had to put up with. He was intensely irritated by the contrast between Tennyson's writing and his behaviour, his self-absorption and 'slovenliness'. Lear hated Tennyson's drinking and deplored his lack of 'self-respect'.

Emily's concern about Alfred's smoking and drinking has been largely eliminated from the surviving papers – but one comment of Woolner's, writing to Emily from the Cornish tour he took with Alfred, suggests she constantly worried about it. Woolner wrote to reassure her that Alfred was 'not smoking much, and drinking scarcely any wine. So you may consider all this as flourishing.'

At home his habits were generally very different. Later Edward Lear would even talk of Tennyson being 'violent' as well as contrary after an evening's drinking – but the violence was verbal rather than physical and only, it seems, in male company. Certainly Tennyson would always say that he could 'never wrong a woman,' and Emily's utter devotion suggests she believed that this was true, however embarrassing to its young female recipients some of his behaviour might be. There was that extraordinary quality to him that made him seem to live outside normal rules. Marian Bradley had written in her diary: 'There is a look in his face like a brightly burning light, like an inward fire consuming his life.' 'He is the only person I ever saw', Allingham considered, 'who can do the most ludicrous things without any loss of dignity.' He had watched him jumping around 'most comically, like a cock-pigeon', as he read the verses of his song-cycle 'The Window', cheerfully telling Allingham, 'They're quite silly.'

The story of the evening when Tennyson pulled down the girls' hair at his own dinner table, has often been told. What is most interesting, as far as Emily is concerned, is that she was happy enough to copy out the story in full, just as Emily Ritchie had told it. It was Hallam – many years later – who censored it. First he changed 'pull' to 'take' and then he cut out three and a half lines after 'trying the effect at once'. On the next page is the passage as copied by Emily.

Without those few lines, a vivid incident is tamed. Was it because Hallam feared it sounded as if his father had had too much to drink? In fact, it is almost impossible writing about Tennyson (even for Hallam so many years later) to convey him as other than someone always himself, 'not chipped to the smooth pattern of the times' (as Emily Ritchie's cousin Anne Thackeray wrote), but 'a poet leading a poet's life'.

Less well known is Comyn Carr's story of when he was staying with Mrs Cameron as a boy and often occupied 'very earnestly in private theatricals' with Henry Cameron and the Tennyson boys.

One evening at Farringford Tennyson was suddenly seized with the idea that he would like to dress up one of Mrs Cameron's nieces in the garb of a man. He got one of his own long coats from the hall, and with a burnt cork himself disfigured her pretty face, daubing upon it a heavy black moustache and imperial, and then retreating to the other side of the room to gaze with manifest delight upon the result of his own handiwork.

'He said [of] the most becoming fashion was
wearing it flowing without being put
up at all and beg[an] to wish that they would
let it hang down their backs. He suggested
our trying the effect at once and proceeded
to take our my hair (I was sitting near
him) and then to make my sister
and the other young ladies do the same
We all sat round the desert table with
our hair down and he approved of us very

Carr does not mention Emily; but another boy who visited at this period – Arthur Brookfield, son of Tennyson's old friends William and Jane Brookfield – gives a glimpse of Emily one evening at Farringford. Arthur at fifteen was a precocious and maddening boy, who had been sent to stay with Mrs Cameron to improve his behaviour by a plot to treat him on every occasion as a child. Julia Cameron's nieces, the Prinsep girls, were very active in keeping the boy in his proper place – but were defeated by the Tennysons' appreciation of his boyish appetite, in the absence of their own sons, away at school.

Arthur Brookfield tells the story:

I was received with particular kindness, and at dinner had the good luck to please Mrs Tennyson by showing a wholesome appetite for some sheep's trotters. They were placed on the table in a silver entrée dish and it appeared that our host was usually left to patronize this kind of delicacy alone ... They established a certain bond between us that night, and . . . when the ladies rose in order to retire, I took no notice of their signals that I was to retire also; but shutting them out with my own hands, returned to the Poet Laureate's table, and at his invitation filled myself a glass of port.

He asked me what I had been reading lately; upon which, instead of saying that I was deep in *Enoch Arden*, I told him I was reading a novel of Mrs Braddon's. Fortunately he had not yet come to *The Trail of the Serpent* and the account I gave him of the work made him laugh so loud, that one of my enemies, who had tried to prevent my amusing him at all, put her head in at the door for just a moment, to see what could possibly be the matter . . . Just as we were taking our leave, and Mrs Tennyson was saying that she was afraid Alfred had gone off to smoke, he suddenly came into the hall, shouting 'Not so! Not so!'

It had been a triumph for the boy, as he claimed. Mrs Cameron was not usually so easily defeated. This was now the heyday of her photographic adventures and Emily's letters are full of her friend's triumphs. 'Mrs Cameron is making endless Madonnas and May Queens and Foolish Virgins and Wise Virgins and I know not what besides. It is really wonderful how she puts her spirit into people,' Emily told Edward Lear, who was not one of Mrs Cameron's warmest admirers. Tennyson exclaimed to one of the Cameron boys, 'All your mother's geese are swans and all her Taylors are Gods!' Certainly Henry Taylor looked godlike or at least kingly in the photographs. Emily described to the boys an occasion when their devoted cook Andrews was 'caught' by Mrs Cameron, 'when I sent her with the coffee', and dressed up in flowing robe and scarf and coronet and made into either Goneril or Regan – with Mary Hillier, Mrs Cameron's favourite maid and model, as Cordelia, and Henry Taylor as King Lear. 'The picture would have been a splendid one' but someone 'moved and came out with many noses. Andrews has to go again.' Tennyson's relationship with Henry Taylor was always ambivalent. If Mrs Cameron made him a king or a god, how was it that Tennyson himself emerged as a 'dirty monk'?

When Tennyson took Hallam to Marlborough for his first term at his public school, Emily wrote to Thomas Woolner: 'It was grievous to me that I was too ill to go'. The father and son were extremely considerate, telegraphing Emily from Reading station en route, 'because we thought we should be too late for the post here,' as Hallam wrote in his first letter, the moment he arrived at his Headmaster's house. Tennyson had sent his son, he said, to Bradley rather than to Marlborough, and the boy would always enjoy a special position in the school.

'Hallam is sure to do well in the best sense', her friend Marian Bradley wrote to Emily, commiserating with her over 'the trying business' of her teeth, and sending a recipe for the scones Tennyson had enjoyed for breakfast. She preserved the 'blue and rose Breakfast cup' he had used as 'henceforth sacred'. Tennyson stayed a few days, judging the school's prize poems, writing a ballad and being altogether 'very jolly and happy'. It would not be long before he would use that cup again in less happy circumstances.

Hallam *did* do well. When he went back after the summer holidays he wrote to his mother: 'I have been top of my form since I have been here. I hope to keep so. Thanks to you for making me work in the holidays.' Lionel was by now at Ore House with Dr Hunt, the specialist in stammers. They had said goodbye to him on the 20 August – another of those sad partings they all found so hard. Emily had watched from the Hastings hotel Lionel walking with Alfred along the road to Ore House – until all she could see was 'the top of the hat, that dreadful chimneypot'. The tender father had 'walked twice back along the road with him to comfort him'. Lionel would give them – nearly always – much more cause for concern than Hallam. Hallam from Marlborough reminded his mother to 'write to him more than to me . . . because it is the first time he has been separated from everybody.' He urged Lionel himself to sit down and read a novel 'as thy mother does' if he ever felt the urge to 'rabbit-nose' as he confessed he did himself when first alone at school. 'Rabbit-nosing' was apparently the family phrase for that first twitching of the nose and prickling behind the eyes, which *can* be stopped from turning into tears.

Lionel told them that the Hastings garden sounded as if it was full of wild animals as the boys practised the exercises Dr Hunt had set them. 'It feels very lonely here without Hallam, but I suppose it is all for my good and the harder I work the sooner I shall get away,' he wrote a little pathetically. He encouraged Emily not to write 'except once a week or praps just send a line in an envelope for I am sure your arm ought to have *rest*, or anything just to hear how you are and Papa is. I am very very sorry that he is not well . . . Any word is delightful but *don't tire your arm*.' He told Emily the boys were not allowed to drink water and 'half a glass of beer is not enough for anybody for blazing holidays like this, so I have to buy some generally.' He had to eat meat three times a day (for 'Breakfast at 8, Dinner at 2½ and Tea at 8') and considered that was the reason he had a small boil on his leg. It was rather worrying, even when he assured his mother, only four days after they left him, 'I am very happy here now.'

Emily wrote to Lionel nearly every day, bombarding him with questions and suggestions. Could he not have an egg for breakfast instead of meat? Could he not drink soda water instead of beer? (Lionel calmed her down by saying he had not been visiting all the taverns but buying 'very harmless' ginger beer from a little shop.) 'What lessons do you learn?' She hoped he was keeping up his Ovid and Homer; 'it would be a pity to lose what has been gained with such trouble.' ('Homer is not used here till the Sixth Form,' Hallam wrote from Marlborough, and hoped 'Dr Hunt is not an outrageously fierce fellow.') Both boys were pressed for their famous father's autograph. Hallam wrote in tiny writing to thank Emily for sending some: 'I don't like writing it – because they bother Papa.' He was cross with Lionel for asking for so many, and suggested they should 'send him two or three or *none*, because when Lionel goes to school he will be wanting autographs for all the 800 boys.'

Of course, all three of them worried about Lionel's stammer. Emily recalled the boys climbing on chairs and making speeches when they were little. She probably never made a speech in her life, but she had always encouraged the boys to express themselves clearly. What *had* gone wrong? She said she would 'never cease to thank God and Dr Hunt if that great and trying hindrance to happiness and usefulness is removed.' 'Does he improve, do you know?' Hallam asked his parents in September. In October he wrote to Lionel: 'Do you feel that you can speak better, in fact as well as I do, to a stranger?' Soon after asking Emily how to make 'jam so as to keep' with the blackberries he had picked (needed to disguise the taste of the horrible Marlborough butter), he could say, 'What a joyful way Lionel writes. I suppose he has told you about what he says, "Hurrah I am nearly cured".' Hallam could hardly bear to complain even about the butter – he was so eager for Lionel to be sent to join him at Marlborough. Emily told her father, 'The boys seem to be fonder of each other than ever. Hallam's longing for Lionel at Marlborough is so great.'

By November the boys' letters were going to 'Mrs Newman's, Stoatley Farm, Haslemere, Surrey.' Lionel wrote: 'I am exceedingly well, my chest is broad, my appetite good, my stammering better and my health's perfect.' His parents had been alarmed earlier when he spent a week in bed – 'a thing which never in his life happened before.' Now he said: 'I eat like an Ogre, and roar like a Lion.' He was encouraging his parents to let him leave Ore House. 'I know you will say yes.' But Dr Hunt (who obviously knew the value of his pupil) would not let him go. Lionel wrote sadly, 'I am not yet cured enough to go home because I have been speaking worse than usual lately.' Dr Hunt's methods remain clouded in mystery, partly because of Lionel's impossible handwriting. 'It is against rules telling Hunt's system, it seems,' Hallam wrote, but Lionel tried to explain that he had to shout out 'A as long as you can thumping your breast and next all the vowels in the same way.' It seemed, too, he had to sleep with his tongue at the bottom of his mouth, a difficult injunction to obey. Lionel would be home for Christmas, but return to Ore House in the New Year.

The main preoccupation of his parents in the last months of 1866 had been the search for a summer refuge. There had been earlier house-hunting disappointments, but it was not until September 1866 that they had finally got round to investigating the possibilities of the Haslemere area. Emily was still reluctant to make any sort of major commitment, but of all counties it was Surrey that 'suited her best'. She told Margaret Gatty, 'The breath of Pines and Heather is an elixir for me.' She had her happy memories of her 'Hale Paradise' before her marriage.

Anne Gilchrist, who had written to Emily nearly two years earlier, inviting the Tennysons to stay with her when they were in the area, was surprised when on 5 September 1866 her maidservant brought her Tennyson's card. They had called, after a night in an inn, to ask the way to the Devil's Jumps.

He looks older than I expected, because of course the portraits one was early familiar with have stood still in one's mind as the image to be associated with that great name. But he is to my thinking far nobler looking now; every inch a king; features are massive, eyes very grave and penetrating, hair long, still very dark and, though getting thin, falls in such a way as to give a peculiar beauty to the mystic head. Mrs Tennyson a sweet graceful woman with singularly win-ning gentle manners, but she looks *painfully* fragile and wan.

It was on this occasion that Tennyson kissed Mrs Gilchrist's seven-year-old daughter, 'stroked her sturdy legs and made Mrs Tennyson feel them.' How uninhibited a pre-Freudian could be. He also checked on the number of Mrs Gilchrist's children. 'Four?' 'Quite enough! Quite enough!'

Mrs Gilchrist reported that Tennyson was by no means impressed with the Devil's Jumps and 'indeed it struck me', she wrote to a friend, 'as one of the barest, most desolate looking spots to be found here-abouts, though not without a certain wild bleak grandeur.' Emily was more enthusiastic. 'A grand view. If it were not looking north, we should buy the place forthwith. . . A. no longer laughs at me for my love of this wild region.' This land was never built on and today one can see the wild region looking very much as it did when the Tennysons looked at it in September 1866. They would look further in the same area in November, spending two days with Anne Gilchrist at Shot-termill and then taking lodgings at Stoatley Farm, where sadly 'the rooms were smokey and the fires obstinately bent on not burning' but Mrs Newman was such a good cook that Tennyson annoyingly ex-claimed: 'I do not eat in this way at home.'

While at Stoatley, they decided to rent Greyshott – variously called Hall and Farm, 'high up on a brown moorland' (as Tennyson told Longfellow). Hallam, very much his father's son, thought that it would be 'nice to be able to spend summer away from cockneys. I hope it is a place where you can roam over heaths.' Emily felt only relief at the return from Stoatley to Farringford, to be back in her own 'delightful home' – though there was as usual a huge pile of mail, and among it the proofs of 'Elaine', over which Emily would spend 'so many hours', only to find the publishers going ahead without waiting for the proofs' return. 'Vexatious,' Emily said.

Anne Gilchrist would put her 'hero-worship into a very practical shape this winter' and do 'some real hard work for Tennyson' getting Greyshott ready for occupation and trying to make sure that the poet's plans were kept out of the papers. 'A paragraph in the Athenaeum would disgust him with the whole project.' Tennyson would not tell Palgrave the name of the place 'because I wish it to be kept secret'. He thought it would be safe from intruders for 'the house is quite solitary and five miles from town or village'.

Hallam wrote from Marlborough that he proposed to spend a night in Bath seeing his grandfather's new home and the Welds before return-ing for the Christmas holidays. He was now fourteen and feeling very independent. 'Persuaded, Papa, you must be,' he wrote, 'because it seems a pity not to see them when I am so near. You must send about three pounds to get me through my journey.' His parents turned down this idea – it was too complicated a journey; the trains did not allow it.

'With their lazy servants I am quite willing not to go,' the boy said cryptically, putting into practice his mother's philosophy that all set-backs could be seen to be for the best.

On the last day of the year, Emily wrote happily in her journal: 'How thankful I ought to be for such a Father and sisters and husband and sons as I have, the boys wonderfully tender and thoughtful, so different from what one often hears of boys.' Tennyson, however, could not feel happy. He was, Jowett said, 'doing nothing'. 'How unmanageable these strong creatures are!' Emily, as so often, felt he needed a change and some new stimulus. She urged him to go to Rome with Thomas Woolner. She hoped, she said to Woolner, that he might not be able to 'resist going with you', but admitted: 'I dare not urge Ally too strongly to go lest any ill should come of it, but I do very much regret that he should miss such an opportunity. He had, as I think I told you, talked before of going with me in the spring – but I cannot tell whether he will go, either with you or me.' As so often in the past, Tennyson could not make up his mind. Neither of them ever got to Rome.

In February 1867 Tennyson told Allingham he was 'very unhappy' – not from the general daily problems that afflict everybody – though there were plenty of those – but from 'his uncertainty regarding the condition and destiny of man' and from his inability to write the poems he wanted to write. Allingham recorded him as saying exactly what Jowett had reported him saying the previous April about his Arthurian epic. 'I had it all in my mind,' he said, when struck down by the *Quarterly* reviewer. When his sister Tilly asked him, 'Where are you going?' as he rose to go off after dinner, abandoning the company, Tennyson said, 'To read the Scriptures'. Allingham would say Tennyson was 'the most delightful man in the world to converse with, even when he disagrees,' but he did not always want to talk.

There was a more memorable evening later the same month when the American Bayard Taylor and his wife ('a charming German lady' who grumbled about American servants) stayed overnight. He had been welcomed to Farringford ten years before as a friend of Thackeray. Now he told Tennyson that he thought the idyll of Guinevere was 'perhaps his finest poem'. Taylor said he could not read it aloud without his voice breaking down at certain passages. When Emily had first heard Tennyson read the parting of King Arthur and Guinevere, she had found it 'grand and gigantic and awe-inspiring'. It was a poem that meant a great deal to her. Four years later it would make George Eliot weep. Tennyson boasted to Taylor, after some fine drinking, 'Why, I can read it and keep my voice!'

Tennyson read in his strange, monotonous chant, with the unexpected falling inflections. 'Finally, when King Arthur forgives the Queen, Tennyson's voice fairly broke.' Taylor found tears on his cheeks and his wife and Emily were crying, one on either side of him. Tennyson made an effort and went on to the end, closing grandly. Taylor said, 'This poem will only die with the language in which it is written.' Emily Tennyson started up from her couch. 'It is true!' she exclaimed. 'I have told Alfred the same thing.'

'My things are ready for packing that I may come to you when you want me', Emily had written to Lionel when he was in bed at Ore House in Hastings the previous October. 'We are to be telegraphed for if wanted.' 'Small is my pleasure in anything until I know that you are well.' But it was Hallam not Lionel who brought his parents rushing to his bedside in bitter weather on 1 March 1867. 'Hallam is very happy at Marlborough', Emily had written more than once. Now he was desperately ill. The telegram from the Bradleys was a terrible shock. He had been so well, considering his daily cold bath 'a sure steel sheath' against illness. It was only three weeks since they had all sung round the piano on the last night at home and 'Ally made a bowl of weak punch and gave them a little.' Now it seemed that his life was in danger. He was 'perilously ill with pneumonia and low feverish symptoms.'

It was 'a terrible time'. Marian Bradley recorded in her diary that 'the first week of Hallam's illness was very anxious – he was nearly gone once or twice.' Tennyson told John Simeon on 3 March: 'Yesterday we thought he was going for the pulse stopt ... We telegraphed for Dr Symonds.' He came immediately from Bristol, arriving in the evening but having to leave again at seven in the morning. He gave them hope that the worst was over. Emily added to Simeon's letter: 'We may hope that he will be restored to us now.'

Emily accepted the objections of the school doctor and matron to her constant presence. 'They are so kind and attentive one feels bound to yield to their wishes', though 'Dr Symonds would evidently have let me be with him as much as I liked.' There was another crisis and she lay awake in bed at the Bradleys' all through the night until the house-clock struck six and then got up and went to the boy 'without asking anyone'. 'The separation is too much for me,' she told Lionel, 'being sure that it is not good for him either'. Hallam was very weak; Dr Symonds prescribed brandy every hour and a spoonful of 'essence of meat' every fifteen minutes. The school sanatorium was at some distance from the Headmaster's house. She travelled 'in a shut-up Bath chair' wrapped in 'duvets' with a hotwater bottle on her knee. On two occasions a snow plough had to clear the path for her before she could get through.

Marian Bradley wrote in her diary: 'AT was very touching about H. when we were despairing of his recovery. He said with his face white and quivering and tears running down his cheeks: "I have made up my mind to lose him, God will take him pure and good from his mother's lessons. He is very simple and religious and surely it would be better for him than to grow up such an one as I am" – but he is wrapped up in the boy and God has spared him, I trust and pray, for his father's good, as well as for a noble and Christian life in the future. AT made me remark how his hair and beard had some white streaks in, the first white hairs; they came when H. was at his worst.'

The Bradleys had been through a similar crisis themselves, less than four years before, when the life of their small daughter Mabel, their fourth child, had flickered in the balance for days on end. They sympathized perfectly. 'No friends could be nearer to us,' Emily recognized. 'We are all bound to them forever.' Marian Bradley, as she welcomed the Tennysons in their distress into her home, was herself dreading her seventh confinement. The 'days were full of pain and fear and the dread of death,' she wrote in her diary as she struggled to make sure the Tennysons were comfortable in a house not only crowded with children, but with a stranded visitor who had broken his leg.

It was Emily, not Tennyson, who seemed to Marian Bradley to be calm. She did not draw attention to the colour of *her* hair, or groan and lament as she prayed quietly to God for acquiescence to His will. 'It is all for the best,' she wrote to Lionel, preparing him for the worst. 'It was very sad and anxious work at first,' Marian Bradley wrote. 'We almost feared her fragile frame would sink under it. Thank God she was so strengthened, "in patience possessing her soul" always, that she leaves us looking less worn and weak than I have seen her for a long while. Never was a sweeter soul – a more lovely Christian. I feel that the daily communion with her, when we talked unreservedly, has refreshed my soul unspeakably.'

In his illness, Hallam showed over and over again the sweet thoughtfulness he had indeed learnt at his mother's knee. The nurse in charge of him reported that when he was at his worst one night he opened his eyes and saw her sitting beside him. He asked her if she were not going to bed. 'Not tonight,' she said. He replied: 'It is hard for you to have to sit there.' On a particularly bitter day, the boy sent his mother a message telling her not to come, though nothing would keep her away.

Emily wrote to Lionel every day, to her father and the Welds in Bath and to her sister Louisa too. She wrote letters whenever Hallam was asleep. Alfred worried at her giving the same distressing news over and over again. The boys longed to be together. Again and again Lionel asked if he could come and Hallam begged that he should be allowed to. Lionel wrote: 'Whenever you want me, you have only just to write to Mrs Hunt and I can come at any time.' To stop him coming Emily suggested Hallam's illness was infectious. There was, in any case, no room to spare at the Bradleys', though 'it would be a great comfort', she told him, to have him with them. She was worried about him travelling all the way from Sussex in the bitter weather. She was worried about his reports of paper chases, which Dr Hunt thought were 'good for stammering'. 'We think nothing of going 20 miles,' Lionel wrote, which was enough to stir his father into writing one of his rare letters. ('You must not do it.') Most of all, Emily was worried about Lionel exciting Hallam.

'Never mind if it's infectious,' Lionel wrote. 'If it's God's will I should have it, he would send it me anyhow . . . I am ready to go at any time,' he said ambiguously. This fatalism was *not* learnt at his mother's knee. Of course you have the free will to go out without an overcoat or forget to take off wet clothes, Emily would say sensibly to Hallam, when later he showed a carelessness about such things. It's no good thinking with your 'strong fatalistic feeling' that if you are fated to get ill you will anyway. All that is certain is that it is 'pre-ordained that I am thy Mother and that thy Father is not less anxious than I am about thee . . . Take care of thyself.'

'Write very cheerfully to Hallam,' Emily asked Lionel, who wrote accordingly: 'I am afraid it is not in my line to write very amusing letters but I do my best.' He told Emily a story about a drunken groom to amuse Hallam. 'It's I sir, rolling rapidly,' the bibulous fellow told his master. The worst of the worry was over by the day of Lionel's thirteenth birthday. Emily could write of Hallam's 'merciful recovery'. 'This is a kind of epoch in thy life, the passing into "the teens",' Emily wrote to Lionel, telling him that they had all three drunk his health in some of Hallam's port-wine. His brother was 'as merry as a bird', lying on a sofa in a red and white 'poncha' and a pair of loose, 'eastern-like, purple and gold-coloured trousers', a present from Mrs Cameron, nibbling delicious grapes supplied by her sister, Mrs Prinsep. Lionel must have gritted his teeth as he settled down to read one of the books Mr Payne at Moxon's had been asked to put in the post, and shared with his stammering fellow pupils the cakes Andrews had sent from Farringford. 'It is thy first birthday away from us, own darling,' Emily wrote. He knew it well.

Emily was weary, but wrote to her sister Anne in Bath, 'What a blessing I have got through so far.' She said several times how she wished she could 'cut herself in two' and 'be with our Daddy and help you'. Henry Sellwood had had a stroke six weeks before and seemed to be making a slow recovery, though he was nearly blind. Now he sent Emily a ring with her mother's gold hair in it. He was getting ready to go. Emily felt sad and guilty that she had not seen him, but she had not 'the strength to bear so long a journey as to Bath in this cold.' Anne had been urging both Emily and Hallam to drink Fortnum and Mason's Concentrated Beef Tea 'and all the strengthening things you possibly can'. She added, 'I cannot persuade Agnes to take care of herself.' Agnes had just had her eighteenth birthday and Emily had sent her niece, rather strangely, 'a beautifully embroidered skirt of mine done with wreaths copied from Tasmanian plants and a pretty low body to wear with it.' It was not the sort of thing Emily herself normally wore, preferring nearly always a Quakerish grey. Would Agnes wear it? Anne's words about her daughter were ominous, foreshadowing problems to come.

The Bradleys had done their best to make Tennyson comfortable at Marlborough, setting aside a room for him to read and smoke in (writing was perhaps too much to hope for). He used to walk with Granville Bradley in the afternoons, when the weather allowed. Not long before they left, Bradley had even found time for a game of battledore with his guest. Both Emily and Marian considered it an extremely good thing for Tennyson to have seen the Headmaster's busy daily life of 'active goodness'. Tennyson said to Bradley: 'I envy your life of hard, regular, useful, important work.' 'All the same', Marian Bradley considered realistically, 'his nature wouldn't fit into suchlike work.' Marian Bradley wrote in her diary: 'He has never realized such a life before and the men he is intimate with are not such good simple Christians' . . . Emily

'has often spoken to me with great sadness of the low tone of Christianity in their circle' – of their Vicar's terrible sermons, of the neighbours
who dutifully attended church services (and, she feared, criticized
Tennyson for not doing so) – but never thought of what Christ's love
should mean in their lives.

Lionel had been having trouble with the sermons in Hastings. Emily
proudly quoted to her father the boy's dismay at a 'frightfully ranting
sermon' abusing Roman Catholics, holding himself the belief (another
of his mother's lessons) that everyone 'has a right to worship God in his
own way'. Emily had herself just been reading a speech by an 'un-
converted Brahmin', who seemed to have a far better understanding of
Christ than many Christians.

Emily said, optimistically, on their return to Farringford (the con-
valescent Hallam carried by their dear servant William from train to
train), that Alfred was glad to get back to the 'old home ways', but, in
fact, as soon as the Easter holidaymakers arrived on the island, he was
eager to be off again. Emily would happily have remained at home now
that she could 'see the cowslips glittering in the Park', but the farm-
house lodgings they had rented at Greyshott near Haslemere were
ready for them and she would not complain.

Emily hoped for a time of 'peace and joy after all this sad unrest of
anxiety', but Tennyson was finding plenty to grumble about. 'He is very
much plagued by our publisher', Emily said, the 'our' suggesting, as so
often, how closely she identified with Alfred. There was also an American 'hanging over our heads who wants to come and read the charge of
the 600 to Ally.' They left Farringford on 29 April, as soon as Hallam
was strong enough. She and Hallam went to meet Lionel – at last re-
leased from Ore House 'much improved in speech' – at Guildford. 'We
have forgotten to bring any luncheon but get some slight thing at the
station and in about half an hour have the delight of welcoming our
Lionel.'

They were all four together again. Hallam would say, 'We must not
complain of anything as long as we four are left to each other'. It would
be an important summer, but the Greyshott lodgings were not a success. 'It was not wholesome enough for me to like to keep indoors', she
said. There were problems with the drains. She shivered until they got
'the water pumped from the cellars under the drawing-room'. There
was snow, incredibly, as late as 22 May, which prevented them 'finding
anything about land here'. The boys were kept busy helping to draw

buckets from a well two hundred feet deep. They were always making themselves useful. Emily's 'daily chit-chat', as she called it, to her father suggests she sometimes felt their efforts misdirected. She went out to the kitchen 'having an inkling that there was a design' on the washing-up

and found Hallam, towel in hand, prepared to wash the tea things in a hand basin! I remonstrated and he replied Oh it was only his face towel. However I convinced him that 'only a face towel' would not do by way of drying tea-things and it was replaced by a clean one and I was assured that the basin had been well washed.

She was worrying about the lack of a piano and a larger library for the boys at Greyshott. 'One feels that even this little time may have a large influence.' She was herself reading the Duke of Argyll's book *The Reign of Law* and finding particularly interesting the chapter on Law in Politics. The book contained so many Tennyson quotations that it renewed Emily's interest in a 'half formed purpose' of her own. Would she herself be justified in 'making a book of the great thoughts and sayings' of Tennyson? Perhaps not, for 'great thoughts and sayings lose so much of their life when riven from their natural place', when read out of context.

Tennyson was glad to escape the crowds on the Isle of Wight but he was not really, as Julia Cameron wrote to John Simeon, 'a Timon in heart; and if he had the utter solitude he aspires after I think he would sing his own song I am aweary, aweary etc etc!! And as for *her* there is too much of the Divine in her, for her not to bless her fellow creatures and be blessed.'

They had certainly not taken Greyshott in order to escape their friends and Emily was grateful to those who found their way there. Benjamin Jowett rather regretted he had made the effort, even though, as he would tell Emily, 'I know that a poet is an inspired person who is not to be judged by ordinary rules'. He wrote to Florence Nightingale on 22 June 1867:

I spent yesterday with Tennyson, not without regret. I doubt whether he will do much more; he seems to me to have lost his energy for writing. He is also so utterly unpractical and (not altogether from selfishness) so intensely egotistical, as at times to be insupportable; you feel at the same time that there is a noble element in him. She is a saint, a sacred person, who can never be spoken of as highly as she deserves, but she has not self-love to keep herself alive.

Jowett compared Emily to Eve in Jeremy Bentham's condemnation of 'pure benevolence'. 'Eve in like manner has no regard for herself: the whole of her regard has for its object Adam.' 'Well, that is her case. She is living in a house utterly uninhabitable in the worst sanitary state because Tennyson has such a dislike to the house in the Isle of Wight and she is consequently always ill.' In fact she had got up at quarter to six to see him off, hardly the behaviour of an entire invalid. The boys had joined them 'half-dressed', just as he was finishing his breakfast. Lionel had written to his grandfather as if he were Emily ('Dear Daddy') with this news and the sad story of a missed expedition to Hale because of the weather. Emily, taking over the pen, wrote: 'Excuse this waggish son of mine.'

Jowett's letter was a gross distortion of the situation as Emily herself saw it – but it has to be remembered that he was one of their closest friends, who probably saw as much of them over the years as anyone else outside the family. Though a clergyman, he was certainly not the sort of good simple Christian Marian Bradley felt Tennyson needed.

Later that year, at Farringford, Edward Lear would record an unhappy dinner. 'AT snubs the boys in a brutal manner and is too sadly selfish sensual. I wonder how they are so respectful as they are, to a father so utterly wanting in self-respect as AT is.' It makes chilling reading until we remember how much evidence there is of other happier evenings, of close companionship between the boys and their father. Both Emily and the boys tolerated the poet's moods, his drinking, his occasional harshness, in a way that Lear found impossible. But this passage does perhaps explain how *much* closer the boys were to Emily than to their father, so that she sometimes had to remind them, when they wrote from school, to include Papa in their salutations.

It has to be remarked that the friends who complained most of Tennyson were Emily's most devoted admirers. Others meeting him for the first time at this period would find the poet as delightful as so many people always had. Richard Jebb – who would later succeed Edmund Lushington in the Chair of Greek in Glasgow – said: 'It is impossible not to like him, and not to understand that he is a man of genius.' George Grove of Macmillan found Tennyson's conversation quite different from Jowett's and Lear's description. He told Bradley, 'He did not say a word I wished unsaid; and he said a great many I would fain remember . . . Moreover he was very religious and Christian in all his talk about life and politics . . .' It must have been all the more surprising to Grove when he came to read 'Lucretius', which Tennyson had agreed to submit to *Macmillan's Magazine*. As Emily copied the poem, Tennyson wrote, '*She* says she does not think it will shock people' – but Tennyson eventually had to omit some of the more erotic details.

Anne Gilchrist had worked so hard on their behalf that Emily found it difficult to complain about Greyshott, though the drains were 'persistently bad'. She was fascinated by the widowed Mrs Gilchrist, seeing her as 'beautifully contented under her great sorrow', and 'so really convinced apparently of the good of poverty'. In the neighbourhood, Emily reported, the widow was known as 'Lady Gilchrist', though the only servant she had was 'but a rough-looking girl of all work. It shows that they measure people by themselves not by their wealth, does it not?' It might well prove to be the right place to build if that was what Alfred wanted to do. 'Surely never were there kinder people than we have met here.' There were not too many of them, and the railway from Haslemere seemed to be taking people to London and back rather than bringing Londoners to disport themselves amidst the scenery.

Tennyson was in a delightful mood when Anne Gilchrist visited Greyshott. She wrote to a friend that he was 'comfortable and cheerful, chiefly jocose indeed, at dinner – says when he ceases to sell as a poet he shall start the Tennyson biscuit, an invention of Mrs T's which he considers surpassingly excellent.' Emily told Mrs Gilchrist tactfully that 'notwithstanding the drawbacks of Greyshott, she regarded the coming here as a great success'. Tennyson 'likes the country and the people and enjoys his walks, and is anxious to buy . . .'

James Simmons was at Greyshott as well that day and it was he, a landowner and magistrate, and a neighbour of Anne Gilchrist, who would negotiate the purchase of the land, known either as Greenhill or Blackdown Copse, which the Tennysons saw first on 5 June 1867.

Emily wrote to her father and her sisters on the day before their seventeenth wedding anniversary, adding the postscript that 'You will be amused to hear the boys ordered a knife-cleaner as a gift on our wedding day.' There was a great deal to celebrate.

I must tell you about Greenhill as I hope we have a good chance of getting it tho' at present there can scarcely be said to be a road to it. The last part I achieved on a donkey and the very last on my feet half sliding half stepping down an exceeding steep bit. Two miles the road passes over a bowery lane used only at present for wagons from the stone quarries. I was alone in the carriage and needful enough that I should be you will say when I tell you that at one time the rut was as deep as the axle of the wheel. However this would easily be mended and the parish would be bound to keep it in repair and to help repair it.

When you get there, these perils past, you find yourself some 8 or 900 feet high, on a ledge in the hillside overlooking perhaps a hundred miles of plain and wood and hill. Lovely fox-gloves and underwood clothe the hill and a few trees; a wooded promontory juts out and protects it somewhat from the south-west winds. There is also some protection from the east for Blackdown curves round the little estate and is rather above it but not enough to make too high a wall behind. The land is, of course, worth little enough. There are a farm-house and building below but the 35 acres are only let for £19 a year altogether. We should be about 2½ miles from Haslemere. We flatter ourselves that Mr Simmons will get it for about £35 an acre.

Anne Gilchrist said she could see 'the sea distinctly from what will be their lawn and three ships on it through the gap in the downs by Littlehampton.' It was an extraordinary view, far below them, over 'Surrey, Sussex and parts of Hampshire and I suppose part of Kent'. There was no possibility that it would ever be spoiled by 'doleful brick boxes' or anything else. The only thing lacking was 'a great river looping along through the midst of it,' Tennyson considered. Mrs Gilchrist said: 'I do think if ever there was a place made for a poet to live in this Green Hill, as it is called, is the spot . . . Tennyson was so pleased; a sort of child-like glee that is beautiful; contrasting curiously enough with his saturnine moods.'

Emily had underestimated the problems of access. It was not the parish but Lord Egmont who was responsible for that rutted lane and 'it took years of negotiation and trouble to obtain a practicable road to it . . .' The initial purchase of the land was rapid, the agreement concluded less than a fortnight after the family expedition to see it. It was Emily who wrote to Simmons with the final cheque on 1 August 1867.

Before that, by what seems an odd chance, Tennyson ran into James Knowles at Haslemere station. Knowles is an important character in Tennyson's story; he would soon become one of his closest friends. Emily's feelings about him at the end of her life were influenced not only by what he wrote in his magazine the *Nineteenth Century*, but also by the increasing animosity over the years between Knowles and Hallam. It was far in the future that Knowles would write, in a paper found after his death, of Hallam's jealousy. In 1867 the ambitious

Knowles (at a point in his life when he wanted to be much more than an architect) immediately accepted Tennyson's casual suggestion that he should build him a house. They had first met the year before when, after sending Tennyson a copy of his Arthurian stories for children, he had called at Farringford. Tennyson had said, as he often said, 'I am so short-sighted that I shall not know you if I meet you unless you speak to me.'

Knowles spoke to Tennyson at the station and was able to give him a lift to Shottermill and tell him he would accept the commission without a fee, 'only paying the journeys'. It was very much in James Knowles's interest that the house – for which he would always be known – should be a splendid one, but Tennyson was naturally nervous of the cost of building it, even if the architect gave his services free in return for the pleasure, so he said, that Tennyson's poetry had given him.

The account of the planning of Aldworth has always been largely based on James Knowles's own account, written long afterwards, and the brief entries in the epitome of Emily's journal. He said that the plans for 'a four-roomed cottage gave way somewhat as I talked the matter over with Mr and Mrs Tennyson, the latter giving me certain rough ideas which she could not quite express by drawing, but which I under-stood enough to put into shape; and presently I went to Farringford with designs for a less unimportant dwelling. It grew and grew as it was talked over and considered, the details being all discussed with Mrs Tennyson, while he contented himself by pretending to protest against any addition and improvement.'

Emily's letters to Thomas Woolner in July 1867, around the time of Knowles's visit to Farringford, suggest a rather more complex story. Tennyson had apparently remembered Woolner telling him of an excellent house designed by Alfred Waterhouse, costing a great deal less than Knowles was estimating. Knowles had told the Tennysons they would have 'such a very tiny and imperfect house for three thousand or more' – nothing but a four-roomed cottage, in fact. That was *not* what they wanted. They were, of course, interested to see Waterhouse's 'plan of a perfect gentleman's house costing only £2000'. Emily wrote to Wool-ner: 'We only mean to have two sitting-rooms in our new house instead of four as we have here, but we should like to have two good ones. Also we only mean to have two stories in our house. I made a plan that pleased Ally and the boys and the idea of which the architect applauded, but his differs so widely that have it we will not.' Woolner immediately suggested Waterhouse should be asked if he could achieve

Emily's own plan for £2000. Next day Emily said it was too late: 'On no account let Mr Waterhouse trouble himself for us.' She had simply asked if they might see the plan of the house already built – but 'we are already pledged to Mr Knowles who has taken infinite pains for us and now I think understands what we want, at all events says that he had entirely misunderstood.'

The foundation stone of the new house was laid on Shakespeare's birthday in 1868. It was a block of local sandstone with their linked initials Æ on one side. That the house that was eventually built shows no signs of Emily's original wishes suggests the power of James Knowles's personality. 'This fellow makes me have all this,' Tennyson would say, showing a neighbour round in Knowles's company. 'He is the cleverest man we any of us have known,' Emily would say. It was not a compliment. But she would see the man's value as far as Tennyson's poetry was concerned. 'His active nature, I think, sometimes spurs A. on to work when he is flagging.' Tennyson needed such a friend.

The 'very handsome country house' would one day become accepted as 'designed by Lady Tennyson and built by Knowles' – but its grandeur owed very little to Emily's original conception. It was Knowles who planned a house fit for a Poet Laureate and persuaded Tennyson he could afford it. The final cost was around £8000. The architect's free services had cost them very dear but certainly, in spite of his joke about possibly needing to market a Tennyson biscuit, the poet was financially secure enough to build a substantial house with every modern comfort, however much he might grumble at the time. In Emily's mind would grow the feeling that they would one day be able to leave one large house to each son. In December 1869 she wrote to Hallam, regretting the winter weather on that Blackdown ledge: 'A pity for our Lionel if he is to have this place . . . Perhaps he will be a rich man, who will have another place to go to in the winter.' She always preferred Farringford and thought of that as their real home. Throughout their lives Emily and Alfred continued to spend most of the winter and the spring at Farringford.

Walter White would describe the new house aptly as 'a palatial-looking house on a small scale', even if the scale was hardly as small as Emily had first imagined. With its regularity and solidarity, its shields and inscriptions and steep-roofed skyline (recalling that French castle at Pau which Emily had so much admired) Aldworth, as it would become, was very different from Farringford, but equally remarkable.

It was Emily who chose the words for the splendid carved frieze that runs across the southern face of the house: GLORIA IN EXCELSIS DEO ET IN TERRA , and so on round the side. The surviving pencil sketches (inscribed 'for Aldworth by A & ET') already show the three storeys and the arched portico at the east front of the house.

After the initial misunderstandings, Emily certainly remained closely involved in the planning. A chance comment in a letter to FitzGerald about 'doubting whether to tile or slate', brought forth a passionate paean to the virtues of tile. How could a Poet hesitate for a moment. Yet they chose slate.

Jowett would say the Tennysons now possessed 'two of the prettiest places in England' and Emily would tell Alfred: 'Thou couldst not well have given me two more delightful homes . . .' She considered 'The different character of the two houses made the change from one to the other very good for us all,' however arduous that changeover might be. Tennyson himself would naturally have mixed feelings. Allingham, at one point, listening to him lament the dullness of country life, could see him with 'two big houses tied to his legs, like cannon balls'.

It was not until May 1870 that the house was called Aldworth, after the Berkshire village where Emily's father had grown up. Anne Gilchrist would always find it difficult to give up the old name Green Hill and for years it came naturally to Tennyson to talk of Blackdown not Aldworth. For Emily, Tennyson's agreement that the house should be called Aldworth was an important recognition of her own family background and the fact that the boys, with whose inheritance she was always so concerned, were as much hers as his, carrying her father's blood into the future, though the Sellwood name was dying out.

Henry Sellwood was much in Emily's mind in that crowded spring and summer of 1867. It seems she had not seen her father since his stroke in January though she had been in constant contact. On 19 September came the telegram she had often expected, summoning her to Bath. By a wonderful chance, Hallam happened to pick up the telegram the moment it arrived in Yarmouth, rushed home with it and then drove his parents to the boat. If it had not been so 'we should have been too late'. When he got back to Farringford, Hallam at once sat down and wrote to his mother, a letter which reached her after her father's death and is worth quoting in full.

If Grandpapa die do not fret, for he will go to heaven better surely than earth with his poor blind eyes, he must only feel himself a burden. If he die be happy that God has taken him out of this world of sorrows.

Bear up for you have all three of us to live for. And think of this

'He gave thee, he took thee and he will restore thee,
'And death has no sting for the Saviour has died.

440

Copy Papa's example, how nobly he bore up against the sorrows of death.

He ended, 'God help you. Your loving son, Hallam Tennyson.' Certainly Emily had much to be thankful for, and she knew it.

Emily and Alfred arrived in time for Henry Sellwood to know them and seem pleased that they were there. They reached the Welds' house at Weston outside Bath at a quarter past ten. Just over an hour later the dying man began to have difficulty in breathing. Emily was persuaded to go to bed as the doctor said it could go on for days. She slept a little but at the first glimmering of light she could not rest, having heard that 'the spirit so often departs as night and morning meet'. She sat up with her sister Anne, with Agnes and the nurse and at about six her father died peacefully in his sleep, just as the birds began to sing. Louisa and Charles were on their way but arrived too late.

In her diary on their father's funeral day Louisa wrote her usual unintelligible but suggestive notes. 'Feel worthy Lamb and attend service but think of unbelief and at grave all at last feel desp. Give up bad life . . .' Eleven years later on her father's birthday, the last before her own death, Louisa wrote a clearer message in a letter to a friend: 'I wish my most worthy father could, from Paradise, see his daughter even the least in the Kingdom of Heaven. This is his birthday so I think of him. I treated him shamefully and he gave up his life for us.'

Emily put Farringford roses on her father's coffin, 'he having so often spoken of the last roses of summer which he had placed on our mother's' in the house in Horncastle over fifty years earlier. Emily was full of joy that she had seen her father's 'beloved face once more in life'. She reflected on the interest her father had taken in 'all that was great and good' and the way that from their early days 'he strove to inspire his children. One of the great blessings of my life is that he and A. have cared so much for each other.' She read, over and over again, the last part of the seventh chapter of Revelation, thinking that her beloved father was among that 'great multitude' who 'hunger no more, neither thirst any more . . . for the Lamb which is in the midst of the throne shall feed them, and shall lead them unto living fountains of waters: and God shall wipe away all tears from their eyes.' Emily felt close not only to her father but to God.

Tennyson put it into words:

> Speak to Him thou for He hears, and Spirit with Spirit can meet –
> Closer is He than breathing, and nearer than hands and feet.

Swinburne might make the poem the subject of one of his funniest parodies, but to Emily it was comforting. 'Depend on it, the spiritual is the real,' Tennyson would say to Marian Bradley. 'It belongs to one more than this hand or foot.'

Returning to Farringford, Emily wrote to her dearest sisters and Agnes: 'Truly may I say that tho' I returned to my own boys, I missed you more than I can say. The unearthly peace of the last week had to be broken, it could not be otherwise, but it is sweet to look back upon and inexpressibly precious to remember the love that ... soothed our common grief. It seemed hard yesterday to be with those comparatively indifferent,' – though she told them that both the new tutor (the boys 'not strong enough for school' were being taught at home again) and Tennyson had put on mourning for Henry Sellwood and 'Tilly has bought a new silk dress.'

In reply to Sir John Simeon's letter of sympathy, Emily wrote: 'You do indeed truly divine what my Father was. Life can never be the same to his children now that he is gone.' His peaceful death made her say: 'Having had this great mercy I ought never in my life to murmur at anything.' She could not know how much harder a death she would one day have to bear.

Henry Sellwood had given his seals to the boys and his watch to his son-in-law Charles Tennyson Turner. In his will he left one third of the residue of his estate equally to each daughter for life 'which shall not be subject to the debts or control of her husband'. It was a clause entirely typical of that father of daughters who had tried his best to bring them up to be strong and independent women.

Hallam recorded in a school exercise book in which he jotted down some of his father's talk: 'After marriage it is scandalous that a woman is not allowed to keep her money. If she has a £5 note in a savings bank now, her husband can draw it and spend it on drink.' Both Tennyson and Emily supported the Married Woman's Property Act, which was passed just three years later. Tennyson could see many things 'that would be bettered by women's enfranchisement'. He also thought that if women then lost their vote on marriage it might make them 'more wary about marrying,' an important consideration before the passing of the Property Act. Tennyson would reiterate his earlier views: 'What I said in the "Princess" years ago, I say now, I do not say men and women are unequal powers but equal, made to fit into each other, to supply each other's deficiencies. All this *fighting* for

Rights is very unnatural, and against all the laws of our Being. No one ever seems to realize this harmony and fitness, in discussions on Women's Rights.'

Emily was wearing mourning for her father when Henry Wadsworth Longfellow visited the Isle of Wight in July 1868. Sending a note to his hotel by the boys, Emily said: 'We are all at your command (as all England is for that matter judging from our little corner).' Longfellow's sister thought Emily 'a very lovely and attractive lady' 'dressed in black silk deeply trimmed with crape'. Matilda came off less well, being described as 'dyspeptic and angular . . . not so attractive'. As many as forty people were invited to take tea with the great American poet under the shady trees on the Farringford lawn. Tiny Cotton from the neighbouring estate of Afton described 'the angelic Mrs Tennyson' floating among the assembled throng 'in her most etherial manner' and delighted to hand over to her the task of pouring tea from a silver urn. There came a point when the young women present felt annoyed that the men were totally monopolizing Longfellow, keeping all his 'wit and wisdom to themselves'.

So, Tennyson passing by, we hailed him with acclamations of displeasure. He was charming and so delightfully shy and naive with it! protesting it wasn't his fault and held out his hand to me saying 'Come, I'll introduce you to him or anybody who wishes!' *I* hung fire (of course) but a moment after Mrs Tennyson in the most beautiful manner made it all right by putting her arm within Longfellow's and telling him 'the ladies were dying to shake hands with him' . . . and she took him round the lawn with an appropriate word to each.

Emily said afterwards she 'could not possibly have done it to an Englishman but to an American it would not be objectionable'. She was right; Longfellow certainly did not object. Miss Cotton would reflect on how Emily's relaxed and natural behaviour 'entirely obliterated the faintest idea of stuffiness'. 'There certainly is an angelic halo about her.'

It was Miss Cotton who had been so taken with Edward Lear's singing a dozen years before. And it was her brother Henry who had married Mary Ryan the previous summer – a wedding that had fascinated Emily as much as everyone else in Freshwater. Emily's letters are full of the romantic story of Mrs Cameron's protégée, the beautiful Irish child she had plucked from Putney Heath where she had been begging with her mother, and trained to help her with her photography as well as to act as a model. 'This beggarmaid shall be my Queen!' Tennyson had written many years before. He had also written of a marriage across classes in 'The Lord of Burleigh' – the problems of the village maiden whose 'landscape painter' lover turns out to be a noble lord. It was no wonder Emily was particularly fascinated by this real-life love affair, the 'Pygmalion' story. She assured her sister, yes, Mary Ryan really and truly was 'a beggar girl taken out of the Putney lanes, educated, clothed and fed by Mrs Cameron.' Emily lent her new landau to take the bride to church. It was a splendid vehicle, her birthday present just three years before. Emily had felt it inappropriately luxurious when it first arrived – 'I am perversely more ready to cry than laugh over it,' she had told Marian Bradley, who would understand her feelings. Now it was coming into its own. 'Lionel dons his new grey suit and borrows white gloves from me and mounts the carriage as page.' 'The bride was brought here afterwards,' Emily wrote, 'and very pretty she looked in her wreath and veil with golden hair glimmering through. It is said the beggar mother does not like the marriage, but she was there.' Later Emily's landau took the bride and groom to the boat. Henry Taylor had worried when the girl was first taken up by Mrs Cameron, his impulsive friend: 'What will become of her?' It was a story with a happy ending. The beggarmaid eventually became Lady Cotton, a devoted wife and mother of three sons, one of whom was in his turn knighted for his services in India.

Hallam had first gone back to Marlborough in the August after his March illness – but Emily had been alarmed by an outbreak of 'scarletina' and had had him home again with Lionel – who still stammered when he was 'over-tired' – and tutors, over the winter of 1867–8. In February he went back happily and cheered Emily with his ebullient letters. 'Never fear about my being despondent,' he once wrote. 'I am blessed generally with a superabundance of spirits.' ('Very few fellows could be much merrier than I am,' he once told Lionel.) By August 1868 he was captain of his dormitory and setting himself up as an agent for Mrs Cameron's photographs. Her 'rose-bud garden of girls' (Mary Fraser-Tytler and her sisters looking extremely soulful) was 'much admired by the fellows who have seen it' and he suggested his mother should get Mrs Cameron to send him a few 'Dirty Monks', Carlyles and so on. He was full of advice for Emily, begging her not to tax her strength ('You have got to reserve it for us'), telling her to get out for regular drives, and wrap herself up well, and fearing she would 'knock herself up' if she had 'too many parties' in the evenings.

There had been much debate over whether Lionel should join Hallam at Marlborough. Emily had very much wanted them to be together and so had the boys themselves. But in the end it was decided that Eton would suit Lionel better. It was something to do with that disastrous March when Hallam had been taken ill, with icy winds sweeping across Salisbury Plain.

Lionel took 'a good place' in the entrance examination in September 1868. Eton had strong associations for Tennyson, of course. His brother Frederick had been there and so, more importantly, had Arthur Hallam. Tennyson would ask to be allowed to sit alone in the garden of the house which had once been Hallam's, smoking his pipe in silence, remembering his friend. Lionel's grandson, many years later, would say that it was better at Eton to have the name of Tennyson than to be the son of a Duke – and that must have been just as true in 1868.

Emily went with Alfred to take Lionel for his first term. It was as hard a parting for all of them as it had been in Hastings two years before. Emily wrote in her diary: 'It is desolating to see our poor boy weeping alone in his garret.'

Hallam sent Lionel all sorts of good advice in his first letter to Eton:

Make them understand you have read Hecuba, Homer, Livy, Virgil, Horace etc . . . Pick out your friends among the unbeastly and the pure in speech . . . Do not be shy in dormitory, undressing or praying etc. Do what you see other fellows do. If you enter into things vigorously your thoughts do not dwell on home so much . . .

He ended up: 'May God bless you and keep up Mamma's and your spirits.' Then he added that he was going to a Ball on the Tuesday with the Bradleys, borrowing their son Arthur's dress clothes. He was sixteen and five foot ten and a half. It seemed at last that the boys' childhood was over. 'Well, it is no use pining for the past,' Emily wrote.

CHAPTER THIRTEEN

'Beset by work of many kinds'

Leaving Lionel, Emily and Alfred spent the night in Reading. Emily was in such a state that she ordered the carriage to meet them at Yarmouth from the wrong boat, which meant Alfred had to telegraph, something he hated doing because it meant he had to give his name. Emily was very penitent. It was 'doubly provoking as an impertinent woman came up to him yesterday and asked . . . "Is your name Tennyson?" "Why what matter?"' Tennyson growled. It was the sort of encounter he loathed, as Emily knew very well even if she could not wholly sympathize. His face was now almost as recognizable as his name, 'by reason of your confounded photographs', he told Mrs Cameron. (Hotels charged him double, he said.)

When they got back to Farringford in a storm their farm workers were 'feasting at the harvest home supper in the servants' hall' – but the 'distant sounds of mirth and revelry could not take away the heart stillness of the house.' 'I feel the want of the voices,' Alfred said. He missed the boys 'as much as I do,' Emily wrote in her journal. A few days later she added, 'A. so very good. We have delightful talks, still he thinks I may be dull. One's heart cannot but yearn towards one's boys but surely I, if anyone, ought to be thankful for my lot.'

'It always seems to me that you are the most overworked person I know,' Benjamin Jowett wrote from Oxford. 'Do you think this is quite right?' There was indeed always a great deal to do. In October, as well as coping with the usual letters and household matters, she was hard at work on the proofs of a French translation of *Lancelot and Elaine*, which had been submitted to Tennyson for his approval. Emily was full of suggested alterations. 'She seems to me to have improved them,' Tennyson wrote to the translator in France. 'I hope you will agree with me.' He was aware that some of Emily's changes 'may not be perfect French,' though she had always kept up the language, not only from her travels there, but also from teaching the boys. Lionel would pay tribute to her 'perseverance in teaching me' one Easter holiday, which meant he was one of the few boys in his division who did not have to redo his Holiday Task.

In that autumn of 1868 Emily was receiving some rather miserable letters from Lionel at Eton and a very long consoling one from Marian Bradley, recognizing the 'fires that the poor dear child must pass through ... I can quite fancy a high-mettled imaginative boy like Lionel, used to much personal attention, feeling bitterly the ... want of appreciation he would get in the character of a new boy.' He had complained that he was having to go over work that he had done long ago and was learning nothing new. Mrs Bradley had had to comfort Hallam in his distress at Lionel's letters. But very soon the younger boy had settled down, cheered by hampers packed by Annie Andrews, the cook at Farringford, full of strawberry jam and sponge cakes and mutton pies – supplies to bridge the gap between nine and two. A month after his arrival, Lionel wrote a typical letter:

Money runs away very fast here, frying pans and saucepans and so on and eggs between the hampers. If you have, next week, any eggs or sausages to spare I shall be very glad of them. I am getting quite accomplished as a cook if I am learning nothing else here (that is one comfort). For if every other resource failed I could go out in the world as a man cook.

He asked his mother not to send Hallam's letters on to Eton 'because being of a careless nature I am sure to lose them.' Careless he might be, but loving he certainly was and his advice to Emily was as frequent as Hallam's: 'Do take care of yourself and not overwork yourself.'

It was impossible advice for Emily to heed. At the end of October, Emily's sister-in-law – Horatio Tennyson's wife – died suddenly, leaving five small children. They would become a major concern of Emily's for the next few years until Horatio married again. It was she who would arrange for them to rent one of Mrs Cameron's cottages, until the Terrace, a house belonging to the Tennysons, was available for them. It was she who found a nurse and governess for the bereaved children. (Hallam was interested enough to ask his housemaster if he knew of any suitable candidates for the jobs.) 'Too much occupied with letter-writing and the poor little children to have time for my journal,' Emily wrote briefly on 7 November 1868. Horatio himself is 'very good in trying to talk and looks better since he came,' she reported to Lear. 'There is something tragic in the perfect happiness and great merriment of the children. They were merry even when planting things' on their mother's grave. They did not yet know what it meant to be motherless, as Emily did.

Farringford was full of children. Tennyson escaped, leaving Emily to cope. After seeing him in London on his way to Paris with Frederick Locker, Lear exploded elliptically: 'How queer is the smallness and egotism of such a man. It is so melancholy at Farringford now that Horatio and his children are there (as if E. were *not*!).' Emily understood perfectly, even if Lear did not. 'There is so little possibility of quiet here,' she wrote to Alfred, 'that it is really better to be obliged to be away a little.' Alfred had escaped, not only his brother's grief, but an outbreak of typhoid fever at Farringford, which meant that the house might have to be evacuated. A new maid was delirious; there was doubt about the drains. One of the tenants came in to help with the nursing, but it was an anxious time. Emily kept a close eye on the girl's pulse rate and saw Dr Hollis regularly.

'Do not worry, be philosophical,' Hallam wrote from Marlborough. 'I quite think it proper to have stayed in the house (to set the servants a good example) and very Christian.' He was grateful to Lady Augusta Stanley for a Christmas holiday invitation to the Deanery at Westminster. 'But home is home and parents are parents and holidays are holidays ... The only thing I am the least afraid of is your anxiety. As for people not coming to you, so much the better, I say. Why should it be in our house at all, why cannot she have brought it with her? ... I hope Papa still enjoys himself.' Lionel from Eton begged his mother not to go into the sick servant's room. 'If you can, let other people do your work for you.'

In the midst of all this Emily had been cheered by seeing *The Holy Grail* in print at last, although it was only a trial edition. She had always felt particularly close to it – 'I doubt whether the San Graal would have been written but for my endeavour.' 'It is my treasure to myself now and I can pore over it at will' – but she did not have much time for poring. 'I have often so much to do that I scarcely know what I do,' she wrote to Edward Lear. 'Our poor good doleful Andrews', the cook who had been with them for many years, 'is still resolved on going' – to help her parents with a shop they had bought. (Did Emily ever think of her grandfather's little shop in Spilsby, where her mother had been born?) Fifteen months later Annie Andrews returned to the Tennysons – and stayed with them almost until the end – but that winter the search for a new cook was another of Emily's worries.

The decision was made to move into Headon Hall, on the cliffs high above Alum Bay, while Farringford was thoroughly examined. Emily had found lodgings for the maid Anne, who was now much better, with a woman who was immune to the infection. Tilly had gone to Edinburgh. Lionel arrived from Eton 'without a great coat', 'rosy and dear and tall and stronger-looking'. Emily went to great trouble to make the bare billiard room in the rented house comfortable for Alfred, bringing up curtains and 'a turkey carpet and books' from Farringford, but still he found it dreary and said 'he must go home'. Emily managed to persuade him to stay and, although he had a cold, he 'slept well, thanks to an embrocation of Squills Paregoric, almond oil and rosemary leaves and salvolatile', which Emily prepared for him.

On the day of Hallam's return from Marlborough, the clerk of works arrived from the building site at Blackdown and pronounced the Farringford drains perfectly safe. Four days later, they heard from Edmund Lushington that their niece, his adored daughter Emily, had died of typhoid fever at Park House on Christmas Day. She was nineteen.

The next death affected the Tennysons even more closely. Emily would write to her aunt, Jane Franklin, 'One is so in the midst of death, it seems difficult to think of life. I have seldom been out of mourning since Queen Emma was with us. I sometimes think that our very gloomy garb makes us think rather of the grave than the resurrection from it.' So many gone: in these three months Emily's sister-in-law, her niece, and now, on 15 January 1869, her brother-in-law Charles Weld, about whom they had had over the years so many mixed feelings. He was nearly fifty-six; he had been born in the same year as Emily. They remembered his 'energetic kindness' at the time of the financial negotiations after Moxon's death. They had always found his travel books – one of them dedicated to Emily – 'pleasant, picturesque and graceful'. He had been good company. But they knew too what a totally unsatisfactory husband he had been, what unhappiness both Anne and Agnes had endured.

There is, however, joy in heaven over one sinner who repents and Emily was able to feel comforted by what Anne now told her and hope

that Anne would be able to find her own peace. She wrote to Edward
Lear, in whom she had always confided about her sister's problems:

Is it not a blessing that the last year was so much the happiest that has been for
many a year. He was quite changed. Never once lost his temper the whole year.
At the communion on Christmas day not only Nanny but the officials noticed
his extreme devotion. It was only a few days before that Friday that we learnt
that the doctor had pronounced this pain in the side and shortness of breathing
from which he was suffering to be from enlargement of the heart.

All day the Friday he had been well and extremely kind. They went to bed
about ten, about eleven he rang, my sister who was in his study close by was
with him in a moment, Agnes too. One quarter of an hour of terrible agony and
he died in Nanny's arms having begged their forgiveness and granted his and
blessed them both.

Emily encouraged Anne and Agnes to come to the Isle of Wight. They
would have to stay initially at Farringford, since Horatio and his family
were now in the Terrace, the house the Tennysons owned near by.
'Come to us very quickly,' Emily wrote. She wanted to remove them
'from the scene of so much sorrow'. 'All words seem so cold but you
know that my heart is not cold but that scarcely anything in the world
would be such a pleasure to me as being any comfort to you.' There
were dry stables and rooms over the coach house where they could
store their furniture. 'I will do my best I need not say to keep it properly
aired and cared for.'

There were some misunderstandings and problems about where the
Welds were to live permanently. Should Anne build on those fields
Emily had helped her buy in 1863, should she and Agnes go into lodgings, should they live at Blackdown in the winter and Farringford in the
summer or should they live with the Tennysons all the time? Alfred
said, after Anne and Agnes had been in the house for a month, that he
was 'very happy' with them 'and even proposes their living with us'.
Emily felt that such a major decision should be a family one. She wrote
to both boys in May, rejoicing in having had a few days alone with
Alfred before more visitors arrived. 'The cares of this life engross me so
much, what with our own affairs and Uncle Horatio's and Aunt
Nanny's.' She knew 'the anxious risk' in trying to blend 'so many very
strong individualities' into one household. Lionel's reply is interesting.
He was now fifteen.

As to Aunty Nanny and Agnes living with us, I have no objection with regard to myself, which am but nobody; but as to you Mama, you know whenever Aunt Tilly is at Farringford in the evening the study resounds with the sonorous roar of a pair of bellows, so what will it be when there are 2 because 2 = twice 1, so there will be 3 pr of bellows, and reading will be impracticable . . . I think you will require a little loneliness in the evenings sometimes, which you will not be able to get . . . and another thing you know how Agnes's manner towards Aunty Nanny vexes you so sometimes – an everlasting repetition of that would be anything but pleasant to you, I know.

Lionel had put into words Emily's own fears. Agnes was indeed often 'quick and sharp' with her mother – in sad contrast to the way Emily's boys talked to *her*. Eventually Anne would see Emily's decision ('in opposing their living with us') as the right one, but it was a difficult time. Emily had always taken a very close interest in her sister's life and had tried to make it easier for her. Anne had a good deal to put up with from poor Agnes, the child of that unhappy marriage. As early as 1865, when she was sixteen, Agnes was showing signs of the sort of eating disorders we would now call anorexia nervosa and Emily was tenderly urging her to 'take porter and port and all that is good for you' and to 'take care of yourself so that you may have the strength to fulfil your appointed task in life.' Ominously, Louisa Turner, her aunt in Grasby, with whom Agnes spent a good deal of time over the years, wrote in her diary something about 'eating and drinking against God'. Emily had told the girl's mother: 'Mrs Cameron says she was in a similar state to Agnes when a girl. There is good hope for Agnes if she is to grow as strong.' In January 1868 Agnes had been causing her mother such worry that Emily wrote: 'If you will have all business papers sent here' (Charles Weld, that 'geographically restless' man, had of course been away) 'I will try to do all the business for you when you are equal to telling me what has to be done.'

Now in 1869 Charles Weld was dead and both Anne and Agnes were fit for very little. As usual, the burden fell on Emily. It was eventually decided that Anne would build her own house on her Freshwater fields, just a mile from Farringford. Hawkridge was finished in 1870 after endless problems with the builder. Tennyson gave the stone for the house from their own quarries. 'What a rascal Kennet is,' Lionel would write to Emily about the builder. 'And how completely he bamboozled poor Aunty Nanny, who thought him a perfect angel, despite our cautions.'

Emily's mind was never wholly on domestic matters, though Lionel thought she worried about her sons so much that, when he reported a headache from Eton, he sent her a picture of herself to encourage her to smile:

Although, as usual with the boys' letters, it was also addressed to his father and Hallam (who had not yet gone back to school), the whole thing is really aimed at Emily. He was scornful about her suggestion he should wear a scarf in chapel to protect against sore throats, as he had said it was so cold: 'No-one wears them.' Lionel was finding Eton a little dull after the theatricals and other pleasures of the Christmas holidays. He cheered them by quoting Horace, but he was pining for Farringford, sending his love to 'old Paul', the shepherd (whom they all loved), and asking, 'How many lambs have we now?'

The letter with Emily's portrait arrived just as she was worrying, not about the boys' health but about politics. Gladstone was now Prime Minister and Emily decided it was worth, once again, writing to him directly about her ideas. She had now come up with a new system of taxation, which would entirely abolish the two separate systems of income tax and rates. Rates still cause problems, whether they are called Poll Tax, Community Charge or whatever else. Emily Tennyson in February 1869 suggested that every form of wealth – including money and land – should be thrown into one great mass and 'taxed and rated and tithed equally'. The whole country, she thought, should be divided into districts under a 'steward' 'who shall register, collect and administer somewhat after the theory of some native Indian administration.' 'Perhaps my thoughts have been often before thought,' she wrote, and begged Gladstone not to 'waste one moment' in answering her letter. But of course he did, remembering their dinner party three years earlier. He wrote a prompt and tactful reply, saying how glad he was he was no longer Chancellor of the Exchequer but looking forward to discussing her ideas next time she was in London.

Emily was in London in April, glad to escape from all the problems on the Isle of Wight – 'the daily pressure of three separate families' – their own, the Welds and that of Tennyson's brother Horatio. Emily found Horatio's harshness to the excellent governess she had engaged for him particularly difficult to bear, with the children white-faced from overhearing their father's anger. (Alfred was protected from knowledge of such things; it was Hallam at school she confided in.) In London Emily did not see Gladstone; she was concerned almost entirely with the furnishing of the new house on Blackdown. James Knowles was making himself very useful going with the Tennysons to look at grates and tiles – and taking them to the Deanery at Westminster to see if they would like him to copy 'a certain stone mantel-piece which he admires.'

Tennyson was not an enthusiastic shopper. It made him 'half dead of fatigue'. On 23 April Emily wrote in her journal: 'I tell Ally that I will not take him out shopping today.' But the following day he is back on the job – looking at Eastern carpets and carved furniture. They were staying with the Knowleses at the Hollies on Clapham Common; their own house was progressing, but not as fast as they hoped. It was still covered in scaffolding. Emily's maid, Mathilda Williams, was making curtains (with 'peacocks on them') for Tennyson's new study, and helping with the 'anxious work of furnishing' in all sorts of ways. 'No work seems too much for her.' Emily was 'half-way through my French proofs of *Enid*,' on the day she wrote that in her diary.

Emily Tennyson would be constantly aware of how much their complicated way of life and the smooth running of two large houses depended on loyal servants. She would often think up treats and outings to reward them. She appreciated they had families of their own and would often pay their fares so they could rush home to ill or dying parents. When William Knight, the devoted Farringford coachman, spent his first summer with his family at Aldworth, living over the new stables, she spotted them out for a walk one Sunday and gave them a guided tour of the house – everything except the servants' quarters. William was the one who, according to Charles Tennyson (knowing him well long after this), 'had an immense contempt for the female sex with the exception of my grandmother.' It was William who characterized the indoor servants as 'the donkey drawing-room'. In 1871 Jowett would find a better-paid opening for William Knight in Oxford. Emily felt bound to pass on the offer but was delighted when he refused it. He was so good with animals that no vet was ever needed.

The acquisition of Aldworth obviously added enormously to the complications of the Tennysons' lives. Annie Andrews, the cook/housekeeper, would sometimes have to make special journeys from Haslemere to Farringford to oversee the handover of the house to a new lot of tenants, and whenever she was absent Emily would have to add some of her duties to her own. Emily would from time to time refuse short-term tenants for the houses, because of the extra work it gave her servants.

At the time of the 1871 Census, the Tennysons had five living-in servants at Farringford. Annie Andrews, thirty-seven, was back after her period helping in her parents' shop. Mathilda Williams, Emily's own 'lady's maid', was thirty, and came from the same Lincolnshire village, Rigsby, as Annie. Then there were a kitchenmaid, a housemaid and a parlourmaid. The other member of the household, apart from the family, was described as a 'boarder'. This was another William, William Seaton, now aged twenty-five, who had worked as a 'page' in the house as a boy and then gone to sea with Emily's encouragement. He had returned in 1867, desperately ill, and, as he was an orphan, Emily had taken him in. He was thought to be dying at the time of Emily's own father's death, but with loving care he had recovered and continued to live in the house while apprenticed, with Emily's help, to a local carpenter.

In the summer of 1869 Emily encouraged Tennyson to go off to Switzerland until the new house was ready. He went with Frederick Locker and a clergyman called Stenton Eardley, an acquaintance of Mrs Cameron, who had called in May full of plans for going to Murren. Emily wrote to John Simeon, now once again MP for the Isle of Wight, on the day Tennyson left. She said she felt he needed to get away: 'He has been depressed and nervous of late, suffering a good deal from that internal trembling which is so hard to bear. These disagreeable hits continually recurring in different newspapers and periodicals are thought more of here than they will be in the throng of men or amongst the great mountains.' As for Stenton Eardley –'His chief credentials to me are that he once carried a drunken woman on his back thro' a hooting London crowd and then reclaimed her and her husband from drunkenness!' Did this mean, she wondered, that he 'has tact and management enough for Ally?'

Locker would send an objective view of Tennyson's state of mind and health from Switzerland to reassure Emily. 'I think he is quite well and he has not complained in any way.' Locker was justifiably proud of that fact. Tennyson wrote to Emily 'nearly every day'. On one day four letters arrived together for Emily from Alfred; none of them survive. On 16 June Emily wrote to Alfred: 'I am recovering from my fatigue.' It was just as well, for on his return in July Farringford was overflowing.

At one stage that month, Emily told Lear, there were '18 or 20 souls in the house', while half of Emily's mind was concerned with furnishing the new place. Emily had even encouraged Hallam to invite a suicidal boy who was in trouble at Marlborough for 'billiards and drinking'. 'With thy leave', Emily had written to Alfred in Switzerland, 'I would have him here for two or three days should Hallam think this would be of use to him.'

Emily had asked the Lockers to Farringford – Frederick, Lady Charlotte and Eleanor, who was nearly fifteen (just five months younger than Lionel). Could she really manage it, Locker had asked, 'moving as you are from one home to another?' Emily could, and found Lady Charlotte 'quite delightful, her delicate wit which never wounds and her loving heart ready to do the humblest service for any suffering human being.'

It was at this time that Emily was also involved in a charitable plan, about which very little is now known. Indeed it is extremely difficult to find evidence of any of Emily's good works. She might in theory subscribe to the idea that her light should shine before men that they might see her good works and glorify her Father which is in Heaven – but in fact she rarely wrote about what she was doing. Certainly she burned to do something useful for her fellow women and would have moments of revulsion from society. In London three years before she had written to her father and her sister: 'I wish people could meet to do some good work which would give real pleasure instead of meeting to look for pleasure and finding none.'

After their father's death at the end of 1863, Anne Thackeray and her sister Minny had spent a good deal of time at Freshwater and Anne, who had inherited some of her father's genius, became one of the family's closest friends. Emily loved her 'good heart' and her 'great wit'. Leslie Stephen, her brother-in-law, called her 'the most sympathetic and social of beings that ever lived.' Anne had called Freshwater 'the funniest place in the world' where 'everybody is either a genius, or a poet, or a painter or peculiar in some way.' But she, like Emily Tennyson, was well aware of another kind of person altogether, who needed help.

'She is very delightful and we agree in our notions of how to do good in the world,' Emily had said in October 1868 when she and Anne Thackeray met a number of times to discuss a plan. Anne told a friend how excited she was 'about this little dream of Mrs Tennyson's and mine, a sort of living club for single women. I think it would cheer up some of the forlorn ones very much to have nice little apartments and a cook's shop on the ground floor.' Emily wrote in her journal: 'We have both been thinking about what could be done for this pitiable class of beings.' Tennyson might write 'comical lines' on the subject, but it was a serious concern.

Years before, Frank Lushington had chided Emily for her 'immoral wish to be always doing work and sacrificing' herself, and teased her that individuals who have 'a very distinct turn for doing no work at all are the wisest and least troublesome'. Emily took no notice of such talk and was never content to restrict her good works to her family, friends and servants. There are occasional mentions in her letters and journal of typical Victorian 'treats' – of Alfred and Emily at Aldworth, for instance, distributing 'frocks and buns and gingerbread to eight little girls from the Infant school' while the little boys wept at not being invited. But there were much more ambitious dreams and plans over the years, however difficult it may be to discover what became of them.

Even Emily Tennyson's work for Dr Barnardo's, to which warm tribute would be paid in her obituaries, has left no written record beyond them. There is one sad reference in her journal (8 March 1870): 'We give up the soup kitchen for poor people. So few come owing to jealousy, we hear, of those very poor for whom we pay.'

Certainly the fate of 'poor gentlewomen' ('some dying in workhouses') remained one of her concerns. Nearly twenty years later, she was suggesting that some of the Queen's Jubilee money (from a national collection) would be better spent on homes for such desolate people, rather than on 'an Equestrian Statue' of Prince Albert. Behind everything Emily did was Christ's example and His teaching. He was more important to her than 'metaphysical speculations' about God, much as she enjoyed such conversation. It was 'the living, loving Christ Himself', as 'the perfect realization of all that is highest within us', who inspired her. Jowett called Emily 'a lover of the poor'. Agnes Weld said she had been 'chosen of God to do many a good work for Him'. But the good is oft interred with people's bones, and much of it seems to be in Emily's case.

Emily spent her first night on Blackdown, in the house they would call Aldworth, on 30 July 1869. The wide terrace in front of the house was a 'small Sahara' and the whole place full of workmen; it was 'touching to see their gratitude' when Emily gave them some beer as they worked in the summer heat. The boys helped the men while Alfred watched them and worried about his new study. 'Though we keep it quiet for him, the windows and the ceiling are as displeasing to him as at first.' It was difficult to keep things quiet as there were 'wheelbarrows continually coming and going and sometimes carts', and the sounds of joiners and stonemasons and a blacksmith at work.

Hallam had to go back to school in the middle of August. 'I never had so little enjoyment of his holidays because of having been so beset by work of many kinds', Emily said. Hallam wrote from Marlborough hoping his father was taking long walks with Lionel (the Eton term started a month later), reading poetry to him at night and improving him generally. It was Hallam who 'entirely suits his father as a companion', Emily told Lear. 'He is so very cheerful and so devoted in his attention. As Lionel gets older he will be less shy, I hope, and more able to shew himself to his father.' He was *not* shy at school and was enthusiastically involved in various scrapes and japes he attempted to justify to his mother. They were 'childish pranks', she suggested, and it was time he grew out of them. She thought him still 'the same dear innocent child as ever.' But Lionel, at fifteen, was already having difficulties with girls, worrying to Hallam about flirtatious Nelly Ritchie – one of the Thackeray cousins – when he was not at Farringford to 'see after my own interests'.

Hallam's letters from school at this period were amusing (talk of 'Chinese conjurors threading needles with their toes over their shoulders') but also challenging, as he pressed Emily to help him with his essays by sharing her views on Cabinet Government or the House of Lords, comparing Seneca and St Paul, or defining the difference between a parable and an allegory. 'Hints if you please', he would say, and she would take all his questions very seriously and object, when reading the results, to his occasional lapses into 'journalism'.

Emily's own views on all sorts of things come out in her notes for Hallam's essays. When he had to write on Milton, she took down his prose works from the shelf and came up with some useful quotations – and chided Milton gently for speaking so much about the freedom of the soul but not speaking out for the freedom of the slave. 'I cannot help thinking that' his soul 'might have been wanting somewhat in tenderness and sympathy. I suppose it is next to impossible that so strong and soaring and absorbed a nature should have them. He would have been almost more than human if he had.' She must have been thinking of her own poet, because she added, 'I fear he had only one wife who understood him and she died after a year of marriage'. Great poets need understanding wives; there was no question of that.

Tennyson was delighted with the new house at first, especially the running hot water which they had not had before. 'Nothing in it pleases me more than the bath, a perennial stream which falls through the house and where I take three baths a day.' Emily called it 'an innocent sight', seeing him afterwards 'running up and down stair with his two pitchers of bath-water' or even pouring it out of the window on the hard thirsty grass beneath. The turf was brought from the Isle of Wight – seven wagon-loads of it. Emily felt 'rather compunctious at taking so much thence, however much I like to have it here'. As the procession of wagons arrived, Emily wrote to Hallam, 'I tell Papa people will call him the mad poet on the hill.' On 8 October she said, 'Papa and I helped to lay the first turf from dear old Farringford down yesterday and we have been very busy superintending the planting.'

They planted trees along the edge of the lawn and on the slope below: cypresses, Douglas firs and cedars. When the sun shone, the terrace would remind them of Tuscany, with its low stone wall, urns, steps down the hillside and paths into the woods that 'should never be explored' but left to the imagination. So Tennyson said; Emily was glad to be drawn in her wheeled chair by Lionel into the more accessible woods, each evening during that first summer on Blackdown. Walking for any distance remained a problem.

Emily tried hard to fit in some serious reading among all her domestic pre-occupations –'a great refreshment I need not say'. It was a refreshment she always needed. Emily was worried about the boys' reading and wrote an encouraging argument in favour of their working through a list of the greatest writers available:

The intellect grows to what it feeds on. Ten years hence it will make comparatively little difference to you whether or not you now read all the newspapers, reviews, magazines, exciting novels and other ephemeral productions of the day, but it will make the greatest difference to you whether or not you have accustomed yourselves to know and love great books.

After a lifetime's diet of 'great books' (she said she knew Homer's voice 'as I know the voice of a friend'), Emily was in 1869 very interested in Renan's *Vie de Jésus* and was now reading Edmund de Pressensés reply to that book, as well as reviews of Renan's *Life of St Paul*. She was also reading at this time W.E.H. Lecky's *History of European Morals* and James Martineau's new book, *Essays Philosophical and Theological*. Martineau was someone who, like the Tennysons, never saw any conflict between Christianity and Darwin's theories of evolution – though Emily would say lightly of Darwin that she was not entirely convinced by his hypotheses and would prefer it 'if it tended to make us out angelborn'. 'We are already too much of the brute.' They would talk a lot about it. 'How can Evolution account for the ant?' Tennyson would wonder. When he told his new neighbour, James Mangles, that he rather believed in Darwin's theory, he added that he had not read Chambers' *Vestiges of Creation* – published fifteen years earlier – when he wrote *In Memoriam*, though everyone 'accused him of having copied from it'. It was a 'great relief' to Emily when she could have time to herself, time to read, away from visitors and builders and the problems of the Welds and of Horatio Tennyson.

By 22 October Emily was telling Hallam: 'The work gets on very badly.' Some would have to be done again, 'the terrace squints so'. Emily was anxious to get everything done 'so as to return to a comfortable place in the spring – Papa begins to talk of the possibility of never returning here.' It was not just the problems of the house and grounds. Delighted at the prospect of an illustrious new acquaintance, the neighbours were beginning to leave cards. 'Poor Papa,' Emily wrote to Hallam. 'What will he do with all the people?' She herself, when the road allowed her to take 'lovely drives', did not mind the occasional call on General Yaldwyn and his wife at Blackdown Cottage, the Mangles family at Valewood, and a few other houses in the neighbourhood. 'So much done,' Emily wrote, after one of these outings.

Their invited guests could be more of a problem. Tennyson had apparently asked Dr James Acworth and his wife in October 1869. Emily had not really wanted any guests – apart from Edward Lear – until the house was finished. What made it worse was that Mrs Acworth was a medium, a spiritualist, 'and I dread her,' Emily told Lionel. In her journal Emily recorded: 'A. and Tilly much amazed by raps on the table in the middle-room. In A's study a table heaves like the sea.' Emily would think 'something there must be in it', but she found it deeply disturbing, considering it 'a power more liable to abuse than others, more like sorcery when abused than anything else.' The Tennysons in general and particularly Frederick, Mary Ker and Emily Jesse, were all disciples of Swedenborg and obsessed by spiritualism. James Mangles said how curious Alfred was about it. Hallam, after his father's death, told Henry Sidgwick that Tennyson was 'in uncertainty as to what to think of it: altho' he was anxious to believe in it,' as he believed so passionately in some sort of life after death. Mary Brotherton, Frederick's spiritualist friend on the Isle of Wight, said Alfred 'had a strong objection to being announced as a Spiritualist . . . partly, as he told me . . . because it would have pained his wife – and the tenderness and chivalry of his nature (the Tennyson nature where women are concerned!) would not permit him to pain her where there was no necessity.' Mrs Brotherton analysed Emily's objections like this: 'Mrs A.T. is a good woman and a sincerely religious one in the narrow orthodox way; and a few mistaken texts of the Bible scare her from all attempts to lift the veil . . . It is curious how many excellent persons are frightened from the half-opened gate by their superstitious scruples.' Emily would of course have denied that her own religion was narrow and felt that it was the spiritualists themselves who were superstitious. Caroline Jebb,

Lionel and Hallam Tennyson, aged three and five, by 'Lewis Carroll', 1857.

15 Lionel and Hallam by Julia Margaret Cameron, c.1864.

16 Julia Margaret Cameron and her sons, Charlie and Henry, c.1859.

17 Edward Lear by Holman Hunt.

18 Benjamin Jowett by George Richmond.

19 Emily and Alfred Tennyson by Jeffrey, 31 July 1862, from a family album recently acquired by the Tennyson Research Centre.

20 Farringford, after Waterhouse's 1871 alterations.

21 Aldworth from a photograph by Poulton.

23 Lionel and Hallam shorn and transformed into ordinary schoolboys, 1865: 'sadly spoilt by their ugly dress', as Emily wrote to Lear.

22 Hallam and Lionel Tennyson by O. G. Rejlander, Spring 1863.

The whole family by O. G. Rejlander, Farringford, Spring 1863. Anne Thackeray Ritchie said: 'There is a
photograph I have always liked, in which it seems to me the history of this home is written . . . The father and
mother and children, hand in hand, come advancing towards us.'

25 Agnes Weld by 'Lewis Carroll', probably 1859, when Emily's niece was ten.

26 Tennyson by Julia Margaret Cameron, 186[
He himself dubbed it 'the Dirty Monk'.

27 Emily with the boys, 1862, by Jeffrey.

Lionel Tennyson, Emily's younger son, c.1884, ken by Henry Cameron. His mother ordered ve copies after his death, but Lear thought it did e justice to him – 'the whole expression sleepy instead of what his really was'.

29 Eleanor Locker, Lionel's wife around the time of their marriage.

30 Mary Gladstone by Edward Burne-Jones.

31 Audrey Boyle, Hallam's wife.

32 Emily, Hallam and Alfred at Aldworth by Henry Cameron, late 1889. Henry called it 'one of my ge Hallam said it made his mother look like the Witch of Endor.

33 The first grandsons, Alfred and Charles Tennyson (aged four and three), finished in July 1883. Elea wrote to Emily: 'I do not in the least expect that Mrs Merritt will succeed in doing what Watts and Mil have failed to do – that is to please you.'

that cool American observer, was amazed that the 'great genius' Henry Sidgwick seemed 'as easy to delude and as anxious to believe as any infant'. He was not the only one. But 'all my friends are sceptics and scoffers', Mary Brotherton said, seeking comfort from Frederick Tennyson in her isolation on the Isle of Wight. Frederick would deny Alfred's wish to believe, but Mrs Brotherton insisted that, in one mood anyway, he had certainly said he did – though he was 'sceptical by nature'.

The problems with Aldworth, the new house, continued for years. There were burst pipes that winter and in the summer of 1870 Emily was saying to Hallam, 'Papa does not settle here one bit, so that things are altogether rather embarrassing.' They had men at work on the drains, rather spoiling Kate and Drummond Rawnsley's first visit to the new place. Emily said her nose had guided her to the seat of the evil. She admired the men's toil to put things right: 'Admirably they have worked, even on one Sunday after having been at work till twelve the night before, and once they get up at three or four, Mr Knowles thinking it important. No traps where traps are marked and altogether a disgraceful state of things'. Yet the Tennysons do not seem to have blamed Knowles for his lack of supervision at the time. It would have been hard to do so under the generous terms of the original agreement.

The following summer Tennyson was talking of 'that beast the Builder' – not the architect, though he had used the same word more lightly of Knowles, as the encourager of so much spending. It was the beastly 'Builder, who had built his house so badly, and with a fall of eight hundred feet to the sea, had laid the drains in quite flat.'

Tennyson's study was another nightmare. The floor between his room and the drawing room below has 'three layers – pounded shells and concrete and what not and yet he heard distinctly the sound of dice below'. He would also hear the sound of Emily's beautiful new piano from the downstairs library. She was playing a lot, in any brief pauses there were in the streams of visitors, as the simplest way to entertain Tilly, 'poor soul', who was with them, as so often. Tilly would always grumble at how dull it was when there were no visitors, but she fortunately loved music. In the December of 1872 Tennyson's study was totally emptied so 'that the floor may be once more taken up. We have such difficulty in keeping the room quiet,' Emily wrote, not quite in despair. Two years later Emily was still thinking the whole business of building Aldworth might have been a mistake. Tennyson, travelling up to town from Haslemere with Mangles and Knowles, said he was 'growing weary of his Blackdown house. Of the two, would prefer living in the Isle of Wight.' 'So Aldworth doesn't do?' Edward FitzGerald wrote to Emily. 'It is a comfort to find that others miscalculate as well as oneself, you know.'

The inaccessibility of the magnificent site, which had been part of the attraction, was part of the initial problem. It was after many letters from Emily and several years that the question of the access road was resolved. Richard Monckton Milnes, by now Lord Houghton, would say that 'the Bard' 'has built himself a very handsome and commodious home in a most inaccessible site, with every comfort he can require, and every discomfort to all who approach him. What can be more poetical?' Tennyson was still grumbling about Lord Egmont and the old access problem when Edmund Gosse visited Aldworth in 1888.

Early on, Tennyson had grumbled to Gladstone about the lack of a postal delivery on their 'top of a mountain'. Emily worried about how difficult it was to get to church. The extraordinary views – with storm clouds and mists sweeping over the landscape – could be overpowering at times, and the birds, Tennyson said, 'don't seem to care to come so high'. Emily wished they had been told of the cold mists 'before we built here'. The Tennysons would always miss the 'home views, cattle, green fields and water' they enjoyed at Farringford. 'I must have nooks,' Tennyson said in September 1870. 'I have not had time to make them yet.' Anne Thackeray agreed: 'I like a cock and a hen and a kitchen garden, and some lilies and lavender quite as much as these great dream worlds and cloud-capped lands . . . I can never appropriate a horizon as one does a haycock, or a bunch of river weeds, or the branches of a tree.' For Emily, Farringford would always be home, although she appreciated Aldworth's nearness to London, which meant people could visit them who would never travel as far as the Isle of Wight – Gladstone, for instance. She knew how important such contacts were for Tennyson, how they revived and stimulated him.

One observer felt very critical of the luxurious social life she saw at Aldworth. It is worth giving Anne Gilchrist's letter in full, for it is so rare to have evidence of anyone considering Emily's strategies wrong-headed or ill-advised. Mrs Gilchrist had, as she said, 'unusual opportunities for obtaining insight into her character,' after so much contact over the house and land hunting. She wrote to William Rossetti in the spring of 1871:

Underneath that soft, languid manner there lurks a clear-headed, acute, energetic, strong-willed character. She devotes herself with the most unwearied zeal (spite of fragile health) to realizing in her husband's home her ideal of what a Poet Laureate's home should be. And though I think her ideal a factitious, miserably delusive one (fanatical believer that I am in a tranquil sequestered mode of life, with much solitude and no luxury in it), it is impossible not to admire and respect the devotedness with which she pursues her aim. She really goes through an amount of hard work and nervous strain incredible to any one who has only seen her in society: and I believe that languid, invalid manner is a wise and necessary precaution against the nervous exhaustion that would certainly ensue if she put much briskness and animation into that perpetual 'playing the agreeable' to the streams of guests that flow through their hospitable home from one year's end to another; in addition to her other labours. For she it is who writes almost all letters for him, manages all business matters, saves him everywhere from all fatigue and worry, besides what goes to managing a large establishment and providing for the luxurious entertainment of that tormenting stream of admirers and fashionables.

But no-one can see Tennyson's profoundly *ennuyé* air and utter lack of the power of enjoyment without realizing what a mistake it all is. Mrs Tennyson, watching him with anxious, affectionate solicitude, endeavours to find a remedy in the very things that cause it – surrounds him ever closer and closer with the sultry, perfumed atmosphere of luxury and homage in which his great soul – and indeed any soul would – droops and sickens. But there does not breathe a more devoted or a sweeter tempered wife, I am persuaded. . .

William Rossetti, who knew little about the situation, thought it must appear to be the fact 'that she attaches to position and appearances a certain value beyond what you do: and I can most cordially say in this matter I agree with you and not with her. The phrase "High thinking and plain living" has been rather run to death of late years; but it is a true and high ideal wherein I humbly acquiesce.'

Rossetti did not realize how much 'high thinking' went on in Mrs Tennyson's head. She actually uses that phrase in a letter to Hallam the following year, encouraging him not to be too lavish in his hospitality at Cambridge. 'Thou must return hospitalities liberally. I quite approve of thy giving good but not too recherché things, for I have a great notion that "high thinking and plain living" have more real connection than people are apt to believe now.' She had always been in favour of 'plain-living' for herself, whatever Anne Gilchrist thought – apart from her beloved champagne. Emily always ate very little and very simply herself. And it was in the very year that Mrs Gilchrist wrote to William Rossetti that Tennyson himself gave up meat and wine for luncheon and began a regime of cold milk and bread and butter, thinking it suited him better. Emily also mentions in her journal Tennyson eating vegetarian food – 'agaric steaks', which Emily said he enjoyed, 'for one of his Fast Day dishes'. Edward FitzGerald was a vegetarian and in Tennyson's poem written for him, he celebrates Fitz's diet of 'milk and meal and grass' and recalls how he tried such a diet himself:

> And once for ten long weeks I tried
> Your table of Pythagoras,
>   And seemed at first 'a thing enskied'
> (As Shakespeare has it) airy-light
>   To float above the ways of men,
> Then fell from that half-spiritual height
>   Chilled, till I tasted flesh again . . .

Guests were always offered a lavish menu, though some of them (like Archbishop Trench) had thought Emily's dinner 'excellent but simple', and had written of the 'simplicity of the household' or the 'simple and homely atmosphere'. 'Simple' was always Emily's own favourite word of praise.

More important than the question of luxury is Anne Gilchrist's observation of Tennyson's mood. If she saw him in company as profoundly bored, as showing 'an utter lack of the power of enjoyment,' others saw differently. At Farringford, in January the year before, Marian Bradley had particularly noticed that Tennyson was 'in the happiest state I have ever known him in – in spite of vexatious publishing matters . . . He mellows and grows sweeter . . . he is very affectionate and jolly to us . . . I feel a sense of entire freedom that I never quite experienced before.'

The truth was that Tennyson was entirely unpredictable. He would be delightful one day, curmudgeonly the day after, lively one moment and sunk in gloom the next. One day he longed for company; another he was 'tired of guests and does not feel in spirits for them'. Emily would watch his state of mind, as Anne Gilchrist saw, with an 'anxious solicitude' and report on it to the boys in her letters. James Mangles, their new neighbour at Aldworth, recorded in his diary every mood. He reports Tennyson saying, 'It is a great mistake to fill a country house with people. One goes into the country for quiet and peace, not for a crowd.' That was one mood. Tennyson could also lament 'the dullness of the country' when there were no guests. Emily had seen, over and over again, how company stimulated and cheered him, particularly when it consisted of people happy to listen to the poet reading 'Maud'.

Mangles recorded Tennyson attacking his sister, Emily Jesse, 'in a joking way'. He *never* attacked his wife, Emily, in a joking way or otherwise (Knowles said he was always saying, 'My wife is the most wonderful woman in the world'). Tennyson accused his sister of being 'tipsy' the day before and having 'to be helped home'. Another day he grumbled at his sister Tilly for failing to draw down the blinds and allowing his 'velvets' to fade in the bright sunshine. Many of the guests at Aldworth were not the 'admirers and fashionables' of Anne Gilchrist's letter but relations and old friends.

Mangles's lively diary records only one remark of Emily Tennyson's which might distress us as much as Anne Gilchrist, that worshipper at the shrine of Walt Whitman. He says that, when asked whether she had read *Leaves of Grass*, Emily said: 'Of course not – it is one of the most disgusting books ever written'. This does not sound like Emily, particularly at a moment when Tennyson was himself writing warmly to Whitman about his 'large and lovable nature' and asking him to visit them. One remembers that Mangles was writing his diary several hours later, or even the next day. Perhaps Emily said simply, 'No, I haven't – people say it is one of the most disgusting books ever written,' echoing the unknown remark of her unknown namesake, Emily Dickinson, who had written to Colonel Higginson nine years earlier: 'You speak of Mr Whitman – I never read his Book – but was told that he was disgraceful.' It would be unlike Emily Tennyson to condemn something without reading it.

James Mangles in another diary entry shows how clever Emily could be at defusing a potentially embarrassing situation. Mangles was talking about slang and said he was always trying to laugh his sisters out of using such words as 'awful, fearful, stunning etc'. Tennyson said: 'I was surprized to hear you use such an expression as "*Like* a snake goes." It is common enough, I know, but clearly wrong.' Emily said swiftly, 'Oh no doubt, you caught it from your sisters!' At which everyone could smile and relax.

*

Edward Lear went abroad to live permanently in 1870. He would build a villa in San Remo and call it Villa Emily – a name that inevitably commemorated Emily Tennyson, though he was reported as saying once that it was after his great-niece in New Zealand, whom he had never met but had named as his heir. This house he eventually had to abandon as a hotel was built just below it, blocking his light and his view of the sea. His second San Remo house, the house where he died, he called the Villa Tennyson. Lear remained entirely loyal to Tennyson's poetry and cherished to the end his plan for an edition of the poems with his own lavish illustrations. But his visit to the Tennysons in September 1869 – his first visit to Aldworth – was not a happy one, and was at least partly responsible for his decision to leave England.

Everything went well on the first day and he thought Emily 'better than she has been for some time, the Poet so so.' Lear spent that Sunday afternoon looking at land near Haslemere. He had been considering settling in the area since his visit to the Tennysons at Greyshott two years before. 'No part of England is lovelier than this,' and there was a delightful field for sale. 'But it by no means follows that I could live "happily" – even if I built a house there.' By the next evening he was sure he could not. Tennyson had behaved appallingly by any standards. Lear had been showing Emily and Alfred some of his work which was for sale. It was indeed the way he made his living. Tennyson himself had chosen two pencil drawings of Corsica and then decided – after Lear had packed everything up – to change his mind and take a painting. Then he 'vacillated' again and started muttering about the cost and that he might spend the same £10 on the carving on the outside of the house and how could he 'meet such expense' anyway; Tennyson said that if it had been carpets Lear had been selling that would have been different, the suggestion being that they needed carpets and no-one needed Lear's pictures. Then he said that it was Emily who really wanted the drawings, not he, 'in that if he had them he would afterwards worry and regret and bother her'.

So Edward Lear got into a rage. He said it was 'like Madame D'Arblay's young lady who cried to order', but surely a spontaneous rage would have been well justified. Lear said Tennyson was 'given to worry and everyone knew that'. Of course he would not expect Tennyson to buy if that was the way he felt. Lear stormed off and packed his things, but when he came down Emily calmed him, poured oil, insisted on giving him a cheque for ten guineas for 'Morn broaden'd' – a splendid picture of the Rock of Civitella di Subiaco in Italy, inspired by a line from Tennyson's 'A Dream of Fair Women'. Emily persuaded Lear not to rush away, and somehow things were patched up. 'Talk with ET', Lear wrote in his diary, 'who is never less than delightful'. Alfred appeared at dinner with no signs of temper and 'less violent' in his conversation over the meal 'than often'. Lear told Tennyson he was sorry he had spoken so angrily. Tennyson admitted no fault of his own and simply said ('How characteristic!' Lear thought) that the only thing that had upset him was Lear saying that 'everybody' thought him given to worry.

London seemed to be exerting more and more of a pull on Tennyson. At the end of 1869 he had made the decision to take 'chambers in Victoria Street' on a three-year lease. No. 16 Albert Mansions was on the fourth floor, at the top of the building, 'second door to the left at the top of the stairs'. A letter to James Spedding suggests Tennyson wanted to regain the 'comeatable, runupableto, smokeable' relationships he had enjoyed before his marriage. Emily had nothing to do with furnishing the flat. The Lockers, with their daughter, Eleanor, lived conveniently close by at 91 Victoria Street and Lady Charlotte helped to set up the little establishment. It *did* make some sense. Tennyson had been begging London beds from friends for years – from Spedding, from the Welds (his favourite place when they were at the Royal Society), from Woolner, from Palgrave and most recently – but rather inconveniently – from James Knowles at Clapham (necessitating a cab from Vauxhall). Knowles had been the architect for the Albert Mansions development and he shared the use of the flat with Tennyson.

It was nevertheless an odd time to rent such a place, with Aldworth only an hour and a half from London. In fact once Tennyson had signed the lease, he decided, typically, he did not much like it. One foggy day he called Victoria Street 'a street in hell'. He wrote a plaintive letter to Emily at Farringford from 16 Albert Mansions (supposed to be a *service* flat) saying he rang 'the bell twenty times and nobody comes'. Emily could not bear to think of him 'being there alone with no-one to supply' his 'very few and simple wants'. Knowles had suggested hiring a boy 'to sit at the top of stairs and run up and down at 1/6 a week.' Emily thought it might be more sensible for her to send Frank, one of their own servants. 'We can manage very well without him.' She sent Tennyson sheets, tablecloths, eggs, wine, seltzer water, biscuits and butter – 'all in a black box' which she hoped he would take care of, because it was her 'bonnet-box when we married'. She told him she had packed plates and knives 'in thy portmanteau'. How could he have overlooked them? She longed to hear if he were comfortable in his rooms. Was there some restaurant that would send up meals? It seemed a bit ridiculous to cook things on the Isle of Wight and send them 'to have them recooked there'.

It was not only a 'comeatable' social life Tennyson occasionally craved, but the flat, Emily agreed, would be useful for his professional visits – his endless publishing confrontations and his recurring consultations with doctor and dentist. In spite of the huge amount of time she had needed to spend on problems concerning the new house and the usual long hours on the poet's mail (sometimes seven hours a day, she told James Mangles at this period), Emily had been much involved in the stresses and strains of Tennyson finally leaving his publisher and his quarrels with Bertrand Payne, who had taken over Moxon's firm and become transformed in Tennyson's iconography into Ancient Pistol, 'the foul-mouth'dst rogue in England'. Much of the correspondence in the next few years with the competing publishers and with Arnold White, the Tennysons' solicitor, involved Emily and it was always she who made the copies for their files. She had shared Tennyson's annoyance over an unauthorized concordance and said the engraving on the front made Tennyson look 'very like an Irish beggar'.

Emily also naturally shared Tennyson's worries about his new publisher, Alexander Strachan. Strachan had published Knowles's own *Legends of King Arthur* but it was apparently F. D. Maurice who introduced Strachan to Tennyson. Strachan had published two books for Tennyson at Christmas 1869: *The Holy Grail and Other Poems* for those who already had the earlier Idylls, and a volume containing all eight called *Idylls of the King*. Already a month before publication, Emily had told Hallam that 26,000 of one and 31,000 of the other had been ordered. But somehow Strachan failed to provide on time the huge sum (£4,300) they considered was due on publication and which they had counted on to cover all sorts of extraordinary bills for the new house – 'Maples for instance charging £150 for putting up blinds'. (Could it really have been so much?) 'I am so weary of publishers,' Tennyson said.

Emily was particularly concerned at this period to prevent periodical publication of Tennyson's precious poems and also the circulation of poems in manuscript. It was in 1870 that poor Charles Lutwidge Dodgson got a rather undeserved rap over the knuckles from Emily after asking if he might copy 'The Window', which had already been privately printed with the subtitle 'The Song of the Wrens'. It was very important, she felt, to keep as much unfamiliar material as possible for the next volume, however much editors might try to persuade Tennyson otherwise. If you gave in to one, it made it much more difficult to refuse others. 'Make a stand at once,' she wrote urgently to Tennyson in London when he was about to accept an offer from *Good Words*. 'Put it on me if thou wilt, for I do entirely object.' Tennyson seems to have taken her advice, until Knowles persuaded him otherwise when he was editing the *Contemporary Review*.

Emily worried constantly about Alfred when he was in London, though the last thing she wanted was to be there with him among the 'talking-machines' with their 'hollow brilliant clatter'. She always insisted that she never 'in the smallest degree' grudged his absence and that her heart rejoiced at what London could do for him, 'in the way of seeing people' who might interest him. She told him she saw that the point of his visits was for him to be 'refreshed by the society of many of the best and greatest men of the day, to say nothing of the women.' She provided him with lists of people who would welcome his calling upon them: Venables, Frank Lushington and Anne Thackeray and Aunt Franklin, the Gladstones and the Argylls, the Brookfields, the people at Little Holland House. She suggested he should call on the Tennyson d'Eyncourts in Cornwall Gardens and many more. 'The drive in a brougham with a glass front will be good for Eleanor, I think, if she and Mr Locker will go with thee and good for thee I am sure.' Tennyson, as usual, had mixed feelings about the whole enterprise. Ignoring Aldworth, he would tell Thomas Hardy he was 'compelled to come to London for a month or two every year, though he hated it, because they all "got so rusty" down in the Isle of Wight.'

Emily did her best to encourage him to enjoy himself: 'I think it would be interesting for thee to go once to Lord's' she suggested, and told him Louy Simeon would be 'charmed to be thy companion when thou art in want of one to go anywhere.' (But did he really want to be seen with that 'distressingly plain' girl, fond as he was of her?) When he had problems with his leg again and was laid up in July 1870, Emily regretted his doctor's wish to keep an eye on him in London: 'For myself thou knowest I have more faith in lying up on our lawn with the down breezes around thee', than in bed in stuffy Albert Mansions – and indeed in *not* lying up, 'considering his nature and the slightness of the ailment in the leg'.

If he really had to stay in Town, Emily wrote, 'Let me come and sleep in the dressing room. I can bring a bed.' In his reply, Tennyson made no reference to this suggestion. In her next letter she pressed her point: 'If I can be of any use or comfort telegraph me of course. Thine own loving wife . . .' 'I cannot bear the thought of thy being in bed and shut up in those dreary rooms and no-one with thee.' She hated the idea of his bed 'all tumbled and forlorn.'

By 18 July she was accepting that she could be of no use to him and that she needed to stay at Aldworth 'to receive the guests and look after workmen.' 'I hear of Papa lying on the sofa at no. 16, cheerful and surrounded by guests,' she wrote to Hallam. It was not as she had imagined. And there was plenty for her to do. After the road agreement, she was having the new line marked out 'that it may be ready for thy approval,' she told Tennyson, and inviting Lord Egmont's agent and his wife to luncheon. She was supervising the drawing-room cornice. 'How I wish thou wert here to look after the tinting of the cornice – I cannot get my ideal realized.' But she would do her best. 'The man is very obliging and anxious to get it right.' Then there were the decisions to be made about the number of urns for the balustrade. At least the drains problem seemed to be resolved. But 'home is not home without thee,' she said; it was something she usually schooled herself *not* to say. Marian Bradley wrote, full of sympathy, aware that Emily was 'low' and 'overdone in many ways that I know all about.'

At last, on 24 July, Tennyson did ask for her to come to him and she hurried to do so. Hallam was home from school and would help her up the steps. 'It will indeed be delightful to bring thee back.' Tennyson's leg was much better, but he would make it worse on his return to Aldworth – he would walk too much, tired of so much lying down. It was still not better on 10 October: 'He has seen a homeopathic doctor with no result,' Lionel told Dakyns, with whom they were all still in touch. It had been a difficult summer, with many disappointments 'owing to his not having been well,' Emily told James Spedding, wishing they might have seen him.

In October Emily and Alfred were at last alone (except for Aunt Tilly); Emily told Hallam that she and his father had had a 'divinely happy talk' on Sunday while Matilda Tennyson was sleeping in the drawing room. It was a talk, she wrote in her journal, 'to be remembered as long as I live.' Again Emily shows how well she realizes the links between mental and physical health, writing to Hallam:

This is the happiest time I have ever had here and I know that thou wilt thank God for it as I do; but for this I believe I should have been quite ill for I have not been well enough to sleep properly, but I am stronger as to walking notwithstanding. So here is a great deal about myself . . .

In her journal she wrote: 'I am indeed thankful for this improvement in strength since I had the rest and refreshment of being alone with him sometimes.'

Emily attributed Tennyson's own slow recovery from what had seemed so slight an ailment to the effect upon him of the death of Sir John Simeon. Simeon had died abroad, having just completed his fifty-fifth year. According to *The Times*, he had 'sat as M.P. for the Isle of White [sic] in the Moderate Liberal interest', 'the only Roman Catholic member for an English constituency'. He had been for years Tennyson's closest friend, and Tennyson went all the way to the Isle of Wight from Aldworth and back on the same day for the funeral. It 'shocked' Emily to hear there was a newspaper reporter there, taking everything down. 'Such is modern life,' she said to Lionel.

Nine months after Simeon's death, Emily told Edward Lear that Tennyson was 'much more languid than I like to see him. He has never got over our loss in May. Knowing Sir John, you may know something of what he was to us. So much sympathy, tact and knowledge of the world joined to so tender a friendship we are scarcely likely to meet again.' Simeon had left a widow, his second wife, with a young child; she would be another of the 'forlorn ones' whom Emily would need to cherish in the years ahead. Emily never felt as much at ease with her, that second wife, as she did with the bereaved daughter, Louisa. When Louy stayed at Aldworth soon after her father's death, Emily felt again that complete relaxation she had always felt 'for I can only talk when I may say just what I like, and to her I can'. It was the feeling she had otherwise, outside the family, only with Edward Lear and Marian Bradley.

Lionel greeted the news of Simeon's death with a dismaying comment on the new fourth baronet, aged twenty. 'Poor Louy,' he wrote from Eton. 'From what I hear about Jack, he is not very fit at present to have very much money under his care; I am afraid he is very wild.'

Lionel's comment on Dickens's death two weeks later was more self-centred. 'Of course you have seen that Charles Dickens is dead, a great blow to those who were wishing to finish *Edwin Drood*.' Emily told Hallam that at Dickens's funeral on 14 June: 'The whole congregation' tried 'to catch a glimpse of Papa. Ladies climbing on the benches and parents holding up their children that they might see too. Be thou, as I believe thou wilt by God's help, a worthy son.' That last sentence looks so solemn and oppressive in cold print – but, in the original, scribbled impulsively and lovingly along the margin of a letter, the words perhaps did not seem too daunting.

Emily was already worrying about the boys' careers. What were they going to do with their lives? They were both writing poetry, but that was hardly to be thought of as a way of earning a living for their father's sons. Emily asked Alfred 'to talk to people about work likely to be suitable for the boys.' Lionel, now sixteen, was still stammering when he was tired. In November 1870 he was sent home from Eton suffering from 'exhaustion'; Emily found him very good company, capable of translating Virgil and Homer 'admirably' to his mother at night, before they rounded off the evenings with backgammon. Emily told Lear that both boys had the same deeply loving natures they had always had. Lionel was now also six feet tall, but Emily said his 'sweetness and simplicity' were still touching, though he was inclined to worry her by running out of money. He would give lists of his expenses to suggest he was not wasting it, but more than once admitted to fines (once for 'spiking' the scorebook) and sweepstakes.

Everyone continued to find Hallam delightful. 'I do love that boy,' one of their Isle of Wight neighbours said one day. He was at home for the first part of 1870 because of illness and deaths at Marlborough. School was a hazardous place. Bradley's move to be Master of University College, Oxford, would come as a relief to him and his family after the succession of illnesses at the school had led him to threaten his resignation unless the governors did something to prevent such devastation. 'This long break is very trying,' for Hallam, his mother told his father that March. 'It is not that he does not work but that he has – I think from the over-work at school – apparently no love for work tho', of course, a pleasure in reading . . . I think Browning would be charmed with the way he reads his things. He makes them sweetest music. Gruff as his voice still is in speaking it has something of the old ringing birdlike sweetness of his childhood when he reads lyrics.'

When Hallam returned to school that summer, not only was his eye 'nearly put out by a cricket ball', but a boy in his room developed scarlet fever and was calmed in his delirium by Hallam, with no thought of his own safety. Hallam was relishing Marlborough all the same. He was 'applauded immensely' for his playing of Hastings in *She Stoops to Conquer* (with some hints from his mother as to 'action and speech') and on the cricket field he caught out 'the best batter in the eleven'. He was eighteen in that August of 1870, but in no hurry to leave school.

Hallam was becoming more and more interested in poetry. There is an interesting exchange of letters – as so often he was asking for his mother's help with his essays – when he sent her a copy of a piece he had written about Matthew Arnold's recently published poems. His father read his paper too. Emily suggested an alteration which would avoid 'the implication that Matt Arnold is the crown of poets in these days.' She did not say it, but she obviously felt it was important that Hallam should not be thought to be undervaluing his own father.

There continued to be a great deal of discussion at this time about the boys' futures. Emily was rather keen for Hallam to join the Bradleys at Oxford. She liked the idea of a smaller college. Moreover, 'We are afraid that for want of mathematics neither of you will do at Cambridge.' After the years at different schools, with different holiday patterns, she was keen for them to be together again, wherever it was. Fortunately their mathematics was not as poor as Emily feared and eventually both boys would follow their father to Trinity College, Cambridge. A letter he wrote to the Master, three years or so earlier, saying he would feel more 'blown out with glory' from spending a night in the Master's Lodge at Trinity than from a week in Buckingham Palace, makes it impossible to imagine Tennyson accepting anything else for his sons. Fortunately the examiners were 'easily satisfied'. Trinity at this period had a quarter of the University's total number of undergraduates. It was, in every sense, 'the greatest college in England'.

Emily suggested to Hallam that, without the Bradleys to turn to,

You might grow up stronger by being forced to rely more on yourself in God. Strength is that in which the age is pre-eminently deficient. We would fain see a greater measure of it in our boys than we see in others.

Emily so wanted Hallam and Lionel to be free and independent and capable of thinking for themselves. But could they ever be wholly independent after all those loving years of anxiety and concern? In a letter to Hallam she mentioned a speech she had read in *The Times* about 'the codifying of the English law. Now this is the work in which I should delight for thee and Lionel.' She suggested to him, in the same letter, that 'originality consists in thinking for oneself, not in thoughts being unlike those of other people'. Was she worrying that their upbringing had been too unconventional?

In February 1871, with the main problems of Aldworth behind her, Emily was planning major alterations at Farringford. She loved the place so much that it was extremely important to her to make it as comfortable and attractive as possible for Tennyson and the boys. Tennyson, for all his difficulties in settling down at Aldworth, would often be reluctant to fix a date for their return to the Isle of Wight – though it was on Emily that all the associated organization fell. One deterrent had been his study at Farringford.

'Ally's poor eyes suffer so much from the winter darkness of the dear old study,' Emily wrote. It had been locked up in 1870 while tenants had been in the house and, on their return in December, Emily had found the sofa and chair 'a mass of moth's eggs'. She had to have all the coverings and stuffing burnt and also the tablecloths. There would always be problems, over the next twenty years, as they moved back and forth between the two houses, but she was determined that they should not abandon Farringford.

Tennyson said, 'Though I am grown no bigger the room has got to be too small for me and I am building another larger one at the far side of the greenhouse.' Mrs Cameron came up with her own 'clerk of works' to talk about the new rooms. There were prolonged discussions. There had been recent alterations at Dimbola, the Camerons' place. 'Wonderful improvements they are,' Emily said. Mrs Cameron had 'joined her two houses by a tower so that her mansion now has quite an imposing air'.

At Farringford they decided to knock down part of the old greenhouse. Tennyson's large new study would be over a ground-floor family room. There would be an arched doorway linking the new room with the remaining part of the conservatory. The downstairs room would give space, not only for dances and theatricals, but also for 'battledore and shuttlecock' and 'children's romps'. This time they would indeed use Alfred Waterhouse as architect – but his plans were as far from

474

Emily's intentions as those of James Knowles had been for Aldworth. On 3 March 1871 she wrote to Hallam: 'We have brought Mr Waterhouse's vagrant imagination back to the original idea. Now the hesitation is as to how much of the greenhouse must be sacrificed.' She hated to lose any of the 'lovely green gloom' they enjoyed as it was 'roofed in its whole length with vines'. The builder, the 'rascal' Kennet, apparently forgiven, estimated the cost of the new rooms at £386 'and some shillings and pence'. 'They always amuse me, the s and d, in such estimates'. How *could* they know? The promise was that the work was to be quite done in four months' time. There was a penalty clause; Kennet agreed to forfeit five shillings per day for every day beyond four months. In May, Emily was telling Hallam that 'the only chance for it being done is that we should watch it daily'. The house was to be let to Lord Dalkeith while they were at Aldworth, so it was important everything should be straight as soon as possible.

There is a lot of political talk in Emily's letters at this period. She reports on a speech by W.E.H. Lecky on the Federation of Europe and seems to have approved of his idea of an intimate federation such as that of the United States and 'only one Army and that an European one, not national armies'. If this sounds familiar, a preview of the EEC and NATO, Emily's ideas on Empire certainly sound more like an ideal Commonwealth than Victorian Imperialism. Emily wanted to have England and her colonies as closely related as the counties, with one great multiracial council with representatives from all over the world originating legislative measures 'which should, I hope, decide how best to give most to each other, not how to keep most, each for himself or his colony or island.' She was keen on 'colonists' being eligible for office throughout the whole Empire – a sort of mobility of labour for civil servants, which would strengthen the ties between England and the colonies. She was also telling Hallam she still believed strongly in her scheme for taxing land with income 'for the good of the community' and that the 'government should purchase what land it can for the poor, selling it to a cooperative company of small proprietors.'

'How alarming the Paris news is,' Emily wrote to Hallam in March 1871. 'Those National Guards entrenching themselves with cannon on Montmartre.' She was glad the boys had seen the city before 'these disastrous days'. Jowett wrote to Emily: 'Are these really the worst times for Europe or do all times seem to be the worst?' Emily read *The Times* every day and frequently commented on the news. But there were also problems closer to home. Horatio had married again the previous December, Catherine West, the sister of Arthur Tennyson's wife.

Emily was involved in a practical way. ('I have many letters to write because of a difficulty in Horatio's marriage settlement.') But she was also emotionally involved. She found it extremely sad that the five children, who had lost their mother two years before, now had to lose 'the care of one who has done so much for them' – of Miss Vernon, the excellent governess Emily had found for them. When Emily called at the Terrace, she saw the poor stepmother 'looking, I thought, ill and worn'. Though his new wife seemed 'entirely devoted to him', she was something of a problem. Emily was grateful to Mrs Cameron ('I never knew her more amusing') for helping them through one evening when 'Mrs Horatio' dined at Farringford.

In March 1871 Farringford was overrun with builders and Tennyson wanted to escape. 'He has so much palpitation of the heart and fluttering of the nerves that he resolves on going to Aldworth,' Emily wrote in her journal. He was in such a state that she hardly liked to let him go on his own, but Lionel was due home to be confirmed at Freshwater Church on 29 March, so she went only as far as the boat. Tennyson found Aldworth in a more 'dreadful muddle' than Farringford: floors up, pipes displaced, the porch smashed by the fall of part of the parapet. Emily wrote to thank Isabella Mangles at Valewood for rescuing him from the mess.

At Valewood Tennyson worried about the state of his shirt. He had apparently packed only socks and had 'to sleep in and wear again his yesterday's shirt'. He had done his own packing. Emily was not blamed. Indeed it was on this visit that Tennyson told his host how clever his wife was, that she had planned the house and 'could do almost anything'. It seems slightly ironical with the state Aldworth was in at that moment – but it was certainly not Emily's fault that Knowles had employed so 'beastly' a builder.

There was an even more worrying household at Freshwater than Horatio's. Emily's sister Anne and her daughter Agnes – who was now just twenty-two – moved into their new house, Hawkridge, in February though they were still having problems and 'the road is not yet passable for the carriage'. Jowett wrote in April that he would not come to Farringford as usual that spring 'as you are in trouble'. He wrote:

I am very sorry about poor Miss Weld's illness. She was a very interesting and good child and I hope that her life may be spared . . . Tell her that she ought to make an effort to get well and not to run away and desert you all so young. I am afraid her illness entails a great deal of trouble and anxiety upon you. Did you ever consider that if you continue to overwork you will never live to see your boys settled in life?

He had told her that before. But Emily did not think of herself; she thought of Agnes and of her own poor sister, a distraught mother as the girl got thinner and thinner.

Emily's worries over Agnes, her increasing fragility and mental disturbance, continued for another eighteen months. The doctors found it difficult to describe what was wrong with her. The phrases 'cerebral anaemia', 'inflammation of the brain' and 'an hysterical affection of the lungs' were used at different times, but there seems no doubt that Agnes's problems were caused by a failure to eat and would today be diagnosed as anorexia nervosa with all the associated emotional and mental disturbance that implies.

The problem was not new. The year before she had seemed desperately ill, but turned out to have been over-dosing with cod liver oil. Somewhere in the background – how could it not have been so after her mother's experience with her father – there were fears of men and of the flesh, which may well have been encouraged by her aunt Louisa on the girl's many visits to Grasby.

Emily wrote to Hallam on 6 April 1871, 'Poor Agnes makes me very sad': she had eaten quite 'as little for what was her dinner as she used to do for luncheon. One thanks God that Dr Jackson having accidentally (as we say) met her in the Camerons' garden, said to Mrs Cameron "That girl is in a fearful state. She ought without the least delay to have a medical opinion." Mrs Cameron sent a messenger after her and her mother who brought them back. He examined her and said there was nothing the matter, but that she was exactly in the state in which children were brought to him after the Indian famine. Her tongue half its proper size and her frame dried up. She must eat or she must die. Is it not sad? He ordered her to be rubbed with oil. To this she consents. God grant she may eat also!'

The girl's condition fluctuated. One moment she was worse; a few days later 'much better'. She must have been eating something, but by September she was in 'a terrible state of thinness'. By the following spring she was violent and talking like Ophelia: 'You know I am not quite in my senses'. Ten days later she 'asked for milk', 'the first thing she has asked for for I know not how long.' She began playing the piano again and doing needlework. When Emily went to see her niece, Agnes said her aunt was Mahommed. 'But she sounded as if she knew better' Emily thought. Did she not pick up the poor girl's identification with the mountain? Soon after, Anne Weld was 'in the depths again about Agnes who had relapsed yesterday after having said the Lord's Prayer quite correctly the day before.' Hallam would worry about the effect of Agnes's illness on Emily. 'Do not stay too long at Hawkridge when you go,' he wrote.

Mrs Cameron wrote to Hallam of his cousin, 'that poor Child – for I always think of her as still a child in the same dark misery. This life closing round her in dark shades and no ray of the real eternal life visible to her troubled soul . . .' Emily would try to cheer her sister's despair: 'I know no-one I think – who has borne up against so much so bravely as thyself.'

A 'very clever' new doctor, Dr Dabbs, 'lately come from Newport', who would remain with the family from now until the end, took 'infinite pains' but also believed in plain speaking. Emily thought Agnes might be 'frightened into being cured now'. Dabbs said that if she persisted 'in the life she now leads paralysis is what she has to fear' – a fate much worse than death for a girl who saw death as the gateway to eternal life. By October of the following year Emily was saying that Agnes's recovery was 'little short of a miracle'. The following year and for many years after, she walked regularly on the Downs with her uncle, Alfred Tennyson.

By March 1873 Emily could write: 'Papa has grown to like Agnes very much, I think. She is so full of information – chock full of all sorts of reading, as he says.' She was now 'only too fat and as merry as a bird'. Tennyson described her case to Walt Whitman. 'She lost her mind and no-one who saw her believed she could live; but under the superintendence of a good doctor she has perfectly recovered and looks plumper and fresher than ever she did before.'

But Agnes would never marry and her aunt would always 'feel a boundless kind of pity for her as well as admiration' as she dedicated her life to Christian charity, giving away nearly all that she had. After Tennyson's death Agnes wrote about her uncle in the *Contemporary Review*, and the Duke of Argyll wrote to Emily:

I do not recollect having heard of her before. Your husband seems to have spoken very freely to her in former days – and I suppose we may trust her account for accuracy?

Hallam's copy of her book *Glimpses of Tennyson* is splattered with his annotations, mainly exclamation marks and the repeated cry 'No!' To T.J. Wise he wrote that her account was 'much spoilt throughout by words she *imagined* my Father to have said. It is most untrustworthy.'

Yet perhaps Tennyson did quote one day to Agnes as he rubbed rosemary leaves between his fingers in the kitchen garden, 'Where rosemary flourishes, there the woman of the house bears rule', adding that 'if all women bore rule as his wife did, he could wish every garden in the land to be filled with rosemary.'

One result of her sister's sadness was that Emily thanked God even more fervently for her own happiness. An entry in her journal in the spring of 1871 reads: 'Surely love as one grows older has the tenderness of the eve of parting – the long parting. A. never seemed to me so beautiful and touching and I never had moments of the same sort of happiness. Thank God for ever for this time alone with him and our boys.'

Emily found it hard to leave Anne and Agnes in Freshwater when her own family moved to Aldworth in June 1871. (It would be even harder the following year.) Tennyson himself, Emily told Hallam, 'clings to old Farringford again. I don't think he would leave it at all if we were not obliged, or only for a little while'. They were obliged as Farringford had been let. It was not a time to be visiting the Continent; Hallam and his father went no further than Wales that August. On Hallam's nineteenth birthday, the first he had ever spent away from his mother, Tennyson sent her some hexameters about a noisy hotel and swimming in a pool near Pont Aberglaslyn. 'Then we returned. What a day! Many more if fate will allow it.' He was worried only by a creaking boot. He called it Mrs Creak and thought he had cured her on one long walk, but she got her irritating voice back on his return to Aldworth, as he told James Mangles, grumbling funnily, as he did so often.

'The tormenting stream' of visitors reported by Anne Gilchrist rarely merited her description of them as 'fashionable', though it did in the summer of 1871 include the Gladstones. Emily's letter of invitation was typically attractive, encouraging them to bring any members of the family they wished: 'We have room for more of you, both in house and heart, if more would care to come, for he thought you would like a little rest better than company.' There was never any need to say who 'he' was. Emily took the opportunity to press some of her favourite schemes for local government and the Empire on Gladstone ('O that Gladstone would give ear!' she said later), but he obviously did not resent it. He wrote in his diary:

This is a characteristic and delightful abode. In him are singularly mixed true greatness, genuine simplicity and some eccentricity. But the latter is from habit and circumstance, the former is his nature. His wife is excellent and in her adaptation to him wonderful. His son Hallam is most attractive.

It was the first time Hallam had met the Gladstones; he would become deeply involved with Mary, a daughter he had not yet met. A couple of weeks earlier there had been some suggestion that Hallam should join his father in London and be introduced to the Prime Minister at a garden party. Tennyson left the decision to his son, who told Emily he was afraid 'Mr Gladstone will only say in his heart, "What an ugly boy" and turn his back and think no more about him.' Hallam felt he was at 'the least favourable period of his life', gawky and 'shy and shaggy'. Gladstone obviously saw beyond the shaggy exterior to the attractive boy within. There was no doubt that both boys were less comely than they had been as children, but they remained lovely in their parents' eyes. Fortunately Emily never knew that another observer, Algernon Swinburne, lamented that the adolescent Lionel (about whom he had enthused seven years earlier) had 'shot up into a tall loutish common-featured youth'. It was around this same time that Tennyson called Lionel 'my handsome son'.

Another visitor at Aldworth that summer was Lionel's friend from Eton, Henry Cator. Mangles noted how very put out Tennyson was at waiting dinner for him. 'Absurd, waiting for an Eton boy.' Emily thought this Henry a great improvement on Henry Cameron and enjoyed his piano playing. When they did eat on that night of the boys' arrival, Tennyson took very little notice of the guest. 'Was very silent at dinner – abused the joint of Beef he was carving.' At least he *was* carving; often Emily did it. She said that at one point it was the only exercise she got, but it did not suit her weak arm.

Most of their guests were relations eager to enjoy the new house and make the most of Tennyson's hospitality. They poured in, most of them proposing themselves. At one point there were three of Tennyson's sisters in the house: Mary, Emily and Tilly. Horatio and his new wife, the Lushingtons (steeped in sadness) and Charles and Louisa came too. Charles looked so fragile she feared they would soon lose him; it was a relief, Emily wrote, that 'the theological discussions are not stormy now.' Tennyson's brother-in-law Captain Jesse, his sister Emily's husband, was as always a problem. Emily wrote to Hallam: 'I must try to stop Papa's return or send him on to Farringford. The Captain's chatter will drive him wild.' When she could not prevent Tennyson's return, she was 'in constant fear lest his talk should over-pass the measure of Papa's patience.' Ten days later she considered, 'Papa gets on pretty well, I am thankful to say.' But, in her absence, James Mangles observed the two men sparring and realized Tennyson 'clearly disliked' his brother-in-law. 'Sometimes they were quite abu-sive to one another.' Was Jesse not amused one night, as Mangles was, by Tennyson's story of the Irish waiter who reassured a guest that the mouse that was playing round his feet was a real one and not *delirium tremens*?

Emily found the house-party difficult herself, but she could hardly prevent Tennyson's own family from visiting them. 'I strive against flutter and fluster,' she told Hallam, "tho it is a hard struggle with weary body and nerves sometimes.' The weather was wretched and 'Days pass so slowly when one has to talk a great deal.' She would have preferred to read, but she felt the duty of hospitality. Had not Christ encouraged us to feed the hungry, give drink to the thirsty and cheer the lonely and broken-hearted, amongst whom could be numbered most of their relations? It was certainly not just a matter of distracting Alfred and providing him with an audience for his poems.

It was this summer that George Henry Lewes and 'George Eliot', living as man and wife, rented Anne Gilchrist's cottage, not far from Aldworth, so that the novelist could concentrate on *Middlemarch*. George Eliot told a friend that Tennyson had 'found us out', 'so that we have lost the utmost perfection of our solitude – the impossibility of a caller.' But it was Lewes, who had less interest in avoiding society, who met Tennyson on the train to Haslemere and took him to Brookbank. He had called him the 'greatest living poet' more than twenty years earlier in his review of *In Memoriam* and was delighted with his catch. There was a good deal of mutual admiration – but Tennyson told Man-gles on 25 August that 'ladies would not allow her to come to his house'. It was 'very hard' for 'she had done nothing morally wrong –

Lewes could not get a divorce tho' his wife had eloped'. Had there been some sort of argument with Tilly about the impropriety of receiving the technically unmarried novelist? Emily herself had no qualms about calling on her on 26 August and telling Hallam that she had done so. 'I called there and stayed some time and then left him and he read some of *Maud*. Mrs Lewes said that his reading ought to be taken down in notes – recitative-wise – but that will not give his magnificent voice with its delicate intonations.' Emily said the distinguished writer was 'delightful in a tête à tête'. She apparently managed to disguise the fact that she was anxious to get on with *Middlemarch*. Emily said, 'She speaks in a soft soprano voice, which almost sounds like a fine falsetto with her strong, masculine face.' Emily did not mention her 'big nose', but Tennyson did – though he felt it was wrong that society should make life difficult for her. 'She had been the making of Lewes and the making of his family.' Jane Carlyle had said: 'Poor soul! there never was a more absurd miscalculation than *her* constituting herself an improper woman. She looks Propriety personified.' Years later, when George Eliot lived in the same area at Witley, she wrote to Emily regretting she had been out when the Tennysons called. 'I cannot bear to seem unmindful of any friendly sign made by you and yours.'

Benjamin Jowett entertained the agnostic novelist in Oxford and was one of her warmest admirers. 'Almost anything worth writing must provide a good deal of resentment in antipathetic minds, which is very often the measure of its excellence and success.' It is a reminder that Victorian objections to George Eliot were not simply on the conventional ground that she had flouted society. But it was surely because of that that Hallam would omit from the *Memoir* any reference to Emily's contact with the unmarried couple. George Eliot's only reference to Emily herself is in 1875 when she wrote to Frederick Locker: 'I am grieved to hear that gentle Mrs Tennyson is an invalid. She must be very precious to both husband and sons.'

This is interesting because it shows how little Emily seemed an invalid in 1871. For all her talk to Hallam of 'flutter and fluster', Emily was still, as she said herself, 'pretty well'. She had even on one occasion walked so far in to the wood with Hallam that the parlourmaid could not find them when Mrs Mangles called. Emily thought that something of a 'triumph', though she was sorry her neighbour had missed a cup of tea. At nearly sixty she was also, as usual, burning with mental energy. 'It is so delightful', she wrote not long after this, 'to feel still the enthusiasm of one's youth in reading of great men and great deeds. I often think no-one has had more in life than I in this way. My want and my trial have been that I have been, as a woman, debarred from action, but then, being a woman, I consider this a lesser evil than being unwomanly.'

Emily's feeling of frustration at being 'debarred from action' fluctuated. The new outlet for her energies was a plan for a chapel at Aldworth; the nearest church was so far away. 'This beast,' Tennyson said, pointing to Knowles, 'says it will cost only £1000; I know it will cost at least £2000.' It would also have meant cutting down an oak tree. It was never built, though the money was undoubtedly there. An American magazine had just paid Tennyson £1000 for three stanzas he had had lying around for years. Also, though Jowett might grumble to Florence Nightingale about Tennyson's obsession with Arthurian legend (all those 'prodigious tales of Knights'), the *Idylls* sold extremely well. The public loved them, however much his friends and the critics might wish he were doing something else.

After both Emily and Alfred had made a long-wished-for visit to Oxford in November 1871, Jowett wrote, 'Another Idyll and another and another. He is caught in the vicious circle of the Arthur legend and seems as if he could only think or feel through this.' Jowett had asked Emily six months earlier: 'Is it worth doing so many poems of the same kind? This ought to be positively the last.'

'This' was 'The Last Tournament', the Tristram Idyll. (Emily and Alfred had talked over the corrections together at Aldworth that October.) But it was *not* the last. It was followed by 'Gareth and Lynette', the one which he said ('jokingly', Emily recorded) was 'to describe a pattern youth for his boys'. Tennyson found it more difficult than most and it was not published by Strachan until the summer of 1872, together with 'The Last Tournament'. It was Emily who had proposed the epilogue 'To the Queen', which appeared in 1873 in Strachan's Library Edition of the complete *Idylls* – Tennyson's favourite of all the editions of his poems. There are two pages at Lincoln addressed to 'Victoria, the beloved', which Hallam later annotated: 'My mother's proposed end to the Idylls of the King'. Tennyson's version, fortunately for it, bears little resemblance to Emily's plodding lines, but he does inevitably refer, as she did, to the dedication to the Prince Consort , and it was surely this poem that revived the Queen's interest in her Poet Laureate, whom she had not seen for six years. It led not only to an invitation to visit

Windsor but also to a proposal that he should accept a baronetcy.

After a good deal of vacillation, Tennyson wrote to Gladstone to say: 'I had rather we should remain plain Mr and Mrs, and that, if it were possible, the title should first be assumed by our son.' This was a rather extraordinary thing to ask and Tennyson realized it was probably 'against all precedent and could not be managed'. The correspondence was complicated and the subject would come up again. Hallam certainly said he would not want 'to wear the honour' while his father was alive. But what the odd suggestion indicates is how much in 1873, the year Hallam came of age, his parents were already concerned that it might be difficult for him to make anything of his *own* life.

Emily was voiceless and almost incapacitated for several weeks in the Christmas holidays of 1871–2. It was a foretaste of things to come: 'My Hallam is a perfect nurse. One day he writes fifteen letters for me and my Lionel tucks me under in his arm in his own dear fashion' (presumably helping her to walk rather than carrying her) 'and writes for me too sometimes.' 'A. says, "I leave you to your sons," but he does not. Watches over me as affectionately as ever.' Tennyson had just turned down a suggestion from the Camerons that he should take a voyage to Ceylon. He refused on the grounds that he would miss Hallam's holidays, which Emily reported to the boy himself (still at Marlborough), knowing how much it would please him. Emily was glad Tennyson had decided not to go and wrote: 'I would he had not this restless longing for the tropics.' But it was not the tropics themselves that worried her, but that deep restlessness itself, which meant that, so often, wherever he was, he wished he were somewhere else.

Emily had always made it clear how much she hated Hallam being away. Her first letter after one return to school in 1871 had included the words: 'It is all very sad and strange without thee, but we must try and make good use of our time all of us till we meet again and then we shall meet all the more joyfully.' A month later she wrote: 'I yearn for thy bright companionship even more than usual.' When Tennyson was in London that July (it was the time young Edmund Gosse first met him at the British Museum), Emily had written to him: 'Our Hallam sings to me, reads to me, walks with me and is as thou knowest excellent company – still the house without thee is empty for both.' Hallam had become his mother's closest friend and confidant. When he was away she wrote to him, often several times a week, and with great frankness.

'It is so sweet to me,' she wrote once, 'to be able to speak the thoughts and feelings of my heart to thee who understandest them so well that perhaps I say too much.' She hoped she did not weary him and there is no evidence that she ever did.

Already it seems hard not to believe that Emily was envisaging an ideal future when, having encouraged Lionel to go out into the world, she and Tennyson would live happily ever after with the perpetual bright company and help of their beloved Hallam. One source of this impression is undoubtedly that Lionel was much less careful in preserving Emily's letters. His letters to her suggest an almost equally close relationship – open, honest, confessional – but his accounts of his scrapes, his requests for money, his schoolboy jokes and extravagances also suggest that he is not someone on whom she can entirely rely. Certainly, at this stage, both of his parents were worried by how little Lionel read, how lazy he was about serious practice at the piano and by his 'sporting propensities'.

In March 1872 he sent his parents 'a really admirable essay' from Eton and told them he had gained 'the highest mark for his verses three times this half'. Emily hoped that at last 'the poor old laddy has aroused himself from his H.H.H.C. stupor or torpor'. Lionel's friendship with Henry Cameron had always concerned Emily. Henry was hoping to follow his sister on the stage. His theatrical mother had always encouraged the children, including the Tennyson boys, to play parts of one sort and another. Emily liked 'theatricals' herself – it was she who started her own boys acting in the nursery and the new big room under Tennyson's study was an ideal place for them – but to make the stage a career, that was another matter. At one point Lionel himself would come very close to doing so.

There has been a tendency to fix Lionel as a playboy, in contrast to a stolid worthy older brother. But for all the 'sweetness and loftiness of his character', there was nothing stolid or dull about the young Hallam. Both boys were lively lads, with that 'elasticity of spirit' Emily found so lacking in Frederick's daughter Emilia, who worried her aunt by being 'nearly bored to death' on a wet holiday at Aldworth. It was Hallam's 'merriness' they all needed to cheer them up, Emily said. As for Lionel, his examination results at Cambridge, his poems, his later journal, his serious interests as an adult, all suggest he was cast in a very different mould from his namesake nephew, with whom he is sometimes confused. Hallam would be saddened by and alienated from this son, whose habits he deplored. He would remain completely devoted to his brother, the essential fourth side of a dove-tailed square.

This was the period of a particularly close relationship between the Camerons and the Tennysons. Julia Margaret Cameron continued her obsessive taking of photographs, seizing models wherever she could. Lionel was still one of her favourite subjects as well as one of her star actors. She was producing plays at every opportunity, as well as embracing all the 'desolate creatures' she could receive under her roof. 'Surely never was there a larger heart,' Emily wrote. No-one could refuse her any request, although Marian Bradley grumbled in her diary that 'Arthur had to spend all his time learning stupid parts for Mrs C.'s theatricals.' Mrs Cameron was 'as severely exacting as a director as a photographer. At one rehearsal she cried out in horror at her son's performance, "Oh heavens, Henry! do you call *that* making love? Here let *me* show you how to do it."' The scene is hard to imagine, even if we remember she was talking merely about flirting. Lionel was not always an amenable actor. Edith Bradley remembered the boy on one occasion turning his back on the audience, which included his parents, and 'twisting his face with horrible grimaces for the encouragement of the fellow-sufferers.' But he did not stammer on the stage and Emily rejoiced at his clear intonation.

Hallam had gone back to Marlborough for a final term at the beginning of 1872. His father had at one point hoped he might start then at Cambridge. He had not begun in October, at the normal time, apparently because he himself could not bear to desert his housemaster whose wife had just died, a reason even more unusual than Emily's reason, seven years before, for delaying the boys first going to school. The Master of Trinity, keen not to lose Tennyson's son, said he would 'waive the custom of the college' and accept him in January, but Emily wrote to Hallam, 'We feel it best on consideration that rules should not be broken for thee.'

Hallam should have ended his time at Marlborough in a blaze of glory, winning the Cup for the quarter-mile in the school sports for the second year running, but it would have meant his missing a major event at Freshwater, the marriage of one of Julia Margaret Cameron's nieces, Louisa Prinsep. 'I think it would be taken as a great unkindness if thou wert not at the wedding,' Emily said more than once, suggesting how much Lou and everyone else wanted him to get home in time.

That was undoubtedly true, but it was Emily herself who wanted him most of all. 'When one is suffering one longs to be together with one's very own.' She had had a terrible time in those first months of 1872, a time almost as hard as the March five years before when Hallam himself had nearly died. The surviving journal gives no idea of what was going on. The extremely distressing illness of her niece Agnes was at its worst and Emily's difficulties with her sister, the girl's mother, 'grow instead of lessen'. Then in March came a devastating letter from Lionel's housemaster at Eton. At the same time, fortunately, there arrived a telegram from Lionel himself: 'ALL IS PROVED A LIE'. Without the telegram the suffering, Emily said, would have been greater, though 'of course we believed him innocent'. If the telegram had not come, they would both have gone straight to Eton. Emily burnt a number of letters, allowing Lionel's side of the story to survive. It makes a difference in reading it to know, as Emily did not perhaps, that John Probyn was only thirteen years old and in his first half at Eton. His brother had died at the school the previous year and this may have been the reason he was officially 'withdrawn by his parents' rather than expelled. Lionel's letter is undated and written with some confusion and a not entirely justified exuberance. He was understandably relieved that his tutor believed his denial that he was involved in any sexual philandering, but his explanation sounds priggish.

My dear Papa and Mama, What a fearful business this has been! and thank Heaven it has come to such a glorious end: and thank Heaven too that I have such a character that will bear me through I trust without a blemish. My tutor knew me too well to suspect me, I am thankful to say . . . I hope you were not alarmed by the telegram but I thought it was the only way to prevent your coming down. What a boy this Probyn is! and what motive he can have for giving up my name I cannot conceive unless, as I told my tutor, it be that I would not conform to his wishes. Don't imagine that I am in the habit of going to these places. I saw a friend of mine going in there and I particularly wished to talk to him, so I went in there too and there I met *him*, Probyn, in company with two other fellows: I did not check his advances at once: I am quite aware that we boys do not look down upon and abhor this familiarity of smaller with bigger fellows enough: though I think I can confidently state that the number of fellows who commit the actual sin is *very*, *very* small: I laid myself open by not checking him at once: and when I did, he took advantage of the occasion of his being found out with some-one else to give my name out of spite. I need not tell you that I am 'innocent of the great offence'. This is a sad check on my endeavours to improve: but I trust that my character will not be tarnished by this: indeed it cannot as I am proved innocent. The feeling of the school about me and other fellows is tremendous: fast verging to a rebellion: and the master who caused all this trouble is in danger of an assault, almost I fear, the feeling is so strong. He promised that if this fellow would give up four names, that no measures would be taken: he gives them up: this – I can't call him a man – Luxmore gives up all the names and screens the only fellow who was his pupil: and takes violent measures against the rest. Two other fellows were given up by Probyn as a last act of spite when he left. I need hardly say that I trust I am as spotless in your eyes as before and I deeply regret my indecision in not cutting him at once. Many thanks for the hamper which was excellent. I can't write about anything else, my mind is so full of this horrid business.

For all Lionel's optimism, and however hard his parents tried to put the 'horrid business' out of their minds when he came home, it was not the end of the matter. Emily said to Hallam – to whom Lionel had asked them to send on the letter – that 'poor Lionel' had been 'subjected to a terrible ordeal. He may have to thank God that this great lesson of life has been branded on his very soul with fire. So I tell him. How I long to have my boys with me again!' She would have Lionel with her rather longer than she expected, for, in spite of his assertion that he had been 'proved innocent', he was apparently suspended from Eton, presumably for going into one of 'these places' which were out of bounds. 'Papa is quite ill with flutterings of the nerves from Eton troubles,' Emily told Hallam. Tennyson was probably extremely worried that it would get into the newspapers. He refused to write any letters himself. 'Thankful shall I be when the writing is over,' Emily said. On 23 May she wrote to Hallam, who was staying with Leslie Stephen – through the family's great friendship with Anne Thackeray, Stephen's sister-in-law – to hope that he would take the opportunity of asking Lionel's housemaster 'if thou canst and ascertain what he thinks best as to his returning. We had thought he would be expected to return but Mr Cornish's words rather make me doubt.' Francis Warre-Cornish was conveniently married to Blanche Ritchie, one of Anne Thackeray's cousins. He was a master at Eton and would eventually be Vice-Provost and Librarian. Lionel *did* return soon after, but it had been an anxious time.

The wedding of Louisa Prinsep that Easter had also caused a certain amount of anguish for Emily. There was more anger and this time it was Horatio who was sending the telegrams. Lou Prinsep had told

Emily that she would very much like to have Cecilia and Maud, two of Horatio's young daughters, Tennyson's nieces, among her bridesmaids. 'Did I think Horatio would let them come?' Emily was pretty sure that it would be best *not* to ask Horatio, who was away from the island and had been for months. She told the bride: 'I have leave to give them leave to do things and I will give them leave for this and I will provide their dresses.' When Horatio heard, he was furious; he said that 'being one of twelve bridesmaids would make Cecy vain.' He absolutely forbade it and insisted they should leave Freshwater before the wedding. Emily took the blame. 'I said that the fault, if fault there were, was wholly and solely mine.' She did not tell him they thought his scruples 'perfectly ludicrous'. But it was no good. Cecilia and Maud, weeping, left on the early boat a fortnight before the wedding.

'I am very sorry for Papa has quite taken to them,' Emily told Hallam, 'now that he finds they have grown into simple children loving primroses and daffodils.' In his brother's absence, he had been reading to them 'amusing stories out of the Jest Book and took them to the farm to be weighed.' The children kept saying, 'Do you think we shall come back?' Their brother, Bertram Tennyson ('our little Bertie' Emily called him), was apparently not in danger of having his head turned. He was allowed to follow the bride with Archie Cameron, Julia Margaret's grandson. Emily and Tennyson both attended the breakfast. Emily thought the bride (the bridegroom is never mentioned) and her twelve bridesmaids (there were still twelve, even without the Tennyson girls) looked charming with bunches of primroses in their hair and on their white serge dresses. 'Altogether it is like a scene in a fairy story,' Emily thought. John Addington Symonds, who happened to get involved, told Graham Dakyns that he found the whole thing 'a racketing and junketing', but wrote to Emily of 'the charming Idyll' the wedding week had been. Julia Margaret Cameron said she was herself an 'honorary hostess' and bore the expense only of the music. 'The richer relatives of the Prinseps' supplied the breakfast.

Mrs Cameron told Emily she had no idea what she would do with the guests the following evening so the Tennysons offered a general invitation, the boys polished the floor, and the 'ball-room' under Tennyson's new study was used for the first time. 'The dance is pronounced most successful.' A fortnight later there was another one, 'also got up in a hurry'.

Soon after, the news came of the death of Lady Charlotte Locker. Her sister, Lady Augusta Stanley, wife of the Dean of Westminster, said, 'She literally fell asleep, without a pang or a groan.' It was Lady Charlotte who had helped Tennyson equip his flat in Albert Mansions. Her father was the Earl of Elgin, of 'Marbles' fame; her mother had been remarkable for her intellect – a first-class classical scholar and mathematician. Her sister had been part of the Queen's household before marrying Dean Stanley. Her only daughter, eighteen this year (the same age as Lionel), had always been a favourite with Emily.

When the girl had been to the Crystal Palace with Tennyson, Knowles and her father the year before, Emily had commented how glad she was that they had 'the bright young thing' with them. They would see a great deal more of the girl now she was motherless. When she stayed at Aldworth that November, Emily wrote in her journal: 'Dear little Eleanor very lovable.' To Hallam she wrote, 'Eleanor has grown such a charming girl, not brilliant, not beautiful, but so good and wise and sympathetic, with a sweet, touching, picturesque face. Poor child she is very sad.' It was just seven months after her mother's death and Emily took her to her heart.

The following year when the Tennysons were in London, Eleanor's father, Frederick Locker, joined them 'most evenings and is brotherly in his kindness.' Dearer than most of his own brothers, Tennyson certainly found him. Locker had always been affectionate and helpful. In 1869, when Emily had been particularly pressed that first summer at Aldworth, he had written a number of letters for her and offered to help her regularly. Now he and Eleanor were becoming almost part of the family.

That summer of 1872, after about six weeks at Aldworth, the Tennysons set off for the Continent with Mary Ker, Tennyson's sister. She was next in the family to him, just thirteen months younger. They had seen very little of her since she and her husband Alan Ker had gone off to the West Indies twenty years before. She was the sister who had once been described as 'something like what Alfred would be if he were a woman, and washed.' She was the one who had written gloomy letters at the time of Alfred's marriage. He had told his Aunt Russell he wished she knew her niece better; but he had never made much effort to go on knowing her himself, hating to write letters as he did. Mary wrote poetry herself and had strong feelings about men. Most men, she thought, 'are given to very shifty ways; not half so good and upright as women.'

Mary Ker was particularly close to her sister Emily Jesse, who called her 'the spiritual sun of the family'. They shared a house at one point (28 Clifton Terrace, Margate) and an obsession with Swedenborg and séances. It is tantalizing not to know much about how she and her sister-in-law got on during that travelling summer on the Continent. There is only one revealing glimpse in Emily's journal, written in Grenoble: 'Fortunately for me Mary loves travelling and can get on without English maids. One night here she dines in the room with thirty or forty priests' – this apparently when Emily was eating in her own room and Lionel and Alfred out on the town. They had left Hallam on the way at Fontainebleau to improve his French in the household of a Pastor Braud. Emily missed him a great deal, particularly on what Tennyson called 'the best day' when they drove from Valence to Grenoble along the valley of the Isère. They had stayed in Valence, Emily told Hallam, because 'Papa was slightly deranged yesterday by a hot walk and vin ordinaire' and it seemed better to take a shorter journey from Vienne. It was in Vienne that Emily saw the sarcophagus with 'two places in and two skulls side by side' and thought that one day that was how she would like 'A. and myself to lie in our grave'.

Lionel had to write to Hallam to discourage him from addressing his poste-restante letters to Emily, as he always did. She was usually too tired when they arrived anywhere to make an extra journey to the post office. In Grenoble he and his father had been refused the letter when they called in and had had to come back to the hotel and get a carriage so they could all go together. Emily thought Hallam's letter gave 'a very good idea of the life at Fontainebleau, but does not say quite so much about thyself as we could have wished.' However much Hallam told her, it would never be enough. Lionel was winning praise in Hallam's absence by looking after his parents: 'He finds out everything which will interest us to see and does everything that has to be done admirably.' Moreover 'his father got to know more of him', which pleased Emily. At the meeting of the Rhône and Aisne they heard, as the night deepened, how the rushing of the river grew louder and louder – as they had noticed at Cauterets eleven years before. There were memories too, at several places, of that first continental journey they had made together in 1851.

There was a terrible muddle over meeting Hallam on the way home. A letter of Emily's had gone astray and he had misunderstood the telegram and waited for them on the Mélun platform at Fontainebleau station, rather than at Mélun itself, as they had meant. The poor boy had walked around the station for five hours 'until the station master set a gendarme to watch him, thinking that he meant to throw himself under a train.' The eventual reunion was even more joyous than usual. It had been a good tour, in spite of some dirty hotels and noisy fêtes, but altogether it was pleasant to get back to Aldworth. James Mangles reported Tennyson boasting that he had climbed a mountain and that the guide had said 'he did it better than he had ever seen a man of his age do.' Emily thought that on the whole the holiday had been good for Alfred – but as for Hallam's month at Fontainebleau, six months later she lamented to Edward Lear that he had probably lost everything he had gained, 'never having opened a French book, I should think.' Hallam was by then at Cambridge, with other things on his mind.

In September Hallam wrote to his schoolfriend Francis Jenkinson to tell him he had heard they had two sets of rooms in the same lodgings. They would turn out to be overlooking the Market Place, a 'lively' view. He said: 'My father and mother say that if it is any convenience to you, you must come and stay one or two or any number of nights here', on his way from his home to Cambridge. Jenkinson was just the sort of friend the Tennysons wanted for Hallam. His 'work as a lad in the Trinity scholarship examinations' had been the wonder of the examiners. At Marlborough he had been known as an expert on moths; he knew every bird's song. He was as good a mathematician as a classicist, and became a first-rate naturalist, palaeographer, bibliographer, antiquary and gardener, with an amazing knowledge of both music and art. When he got his Fellowship at Cambridge in 1878 Hallam would write, 'What a picture of complacent ease and learned luxury,' envying him a little his independence, his career for life.

In 1872 the new undergraduate was 'trotting about seeing tutors' and trying on various gowns and surplices. His cousin Walter Ker, Mary's son, was beginning at Trinity with him. 'When Walter and I got into our surplices we mutually agreed that both of us looked like overgrown babies in long clothes'. His mother longed, as she always did, for 'a history of thy day from morning till night'. When Hallam sent her an article he had written, she could not resist writing, in less than exemplary fashion: 'Be very careful about thy language, old darling – no slipshod above all things. Go as far as possible into the innermost depths of thy being. What comes there expresses itself naturally in clear forceful language.' Emily always believed in writing straight from the heart, but the result could sometimes be clumsy, if not slipshod.

His mother continued to take a close interest in Hallam's work. Of one German History essay she wrote: 'Gustavus Adolphus will come into it and all the thirty years war and the seven years war, to say nothing of the war of succession. It looks rather a gigantic undertaking' – but one it seems Emily might well have undertaken herself, if she had ever had the chance. More than twenty years later, not long before her death, it is sad to see Emily accepting Oxford's defeat (on 3 March 1896) of the proposal to allow women to have full degrees. The reason she gave to her niece Agnes is worth considering at this point.

Emily Tennyson felt women *had* to accept St Paul's pronouncement that just as the head of every man is Christ, so 'the head of the woman *is* the man.' (The Weld women had always entirely differed with the Tennysons on the subject.) 'We would have both developed to the utmost,' Emily wrote. 'Let women be as educated as possible.' Indeed there was no reason why 'they should not have those bits of paper as *Honorary* BAs', but it would apparently make life more difficult for women if they did not accept society's opinion of their situation. If they were married, they had promised to 'obey'. 'It would be hard indeed to have to obey from the beginning to the end of life were not man as a *whole* intellectually greater than woman as a *whole*. Of course individual women, and many of them, are superior in intellect to many men.' The disastrous thing was if women married men who were their inferiors. 'Let women take care that they mate wisely with those to whom they are to be helpmates. Here is a lecture for you!! I am sure that the order of the world gives women more power than ever so much self-assertion.' There had never been any question of the power Emily herself held.

'No son could well be more missed by his parents or more deserve it,' Emily wrote, not long after Hallam started at Cambridge. Edward Fitz-Gerald in Woodbridge soon heard a good report of the boy – whom he had not seen since he was two – from the wife of the Master of Trinity. He told Emily 'she, and others, were much pleased with your son, Hallam, whom they thought to be like the Paltry Poet – poor fellow.' He was worrying about the Laurence portrait of the poet: 'I talk to it sometimes, and everyone likes to see it. It is clumsy enough, to be sure: but it still recalls the old Man to me better than the bearded portraits which are now the fashion.' (Tennyson had had a beard for fifteen years.) 'But oughtn't your Hallam to have it over his Mantelpiece at Trinity?' It was FitzGerald who had persuaded the young poet to sit for Samuel Laurence and it has become one of the most famous images of Tennyson, though apparently retouched by Burne-Jones after FitzGerald had finally given it to Emily in 1876. Surely it was not, as has been suggested, to romanticize the image but to restore a flaking oil, that Hallam and Emily approached Burne-Jones after Tennyson's death?

Emily was busy that autumn sending out copies of Tennyson's new volume, *Gareth and Lynette*, and worrying about the reviews. She told Hallam that his father was pleased with the one in *The Times*. 'It is certainly meant to be complimentary though I cannot consider it altogether appreciative.' Tennyson was enjoying the letters that were coming in from their friends. 'I am low spirited and I like a little wholesome flattery,' he said. He was in London and reported to Emily that Lady Strangford had said *she* was worth twenty Poets Laureate. That was hardly flattery, but in some moods he was inclined to agree.

At Farringford in February 1873 a sudden thaw brought rain through the roof of the house. 'I am glad Papa is not here to be vexed by it,' Emily wrote to Hallam. Tennyson was staying with Frederick Locker and Eleanor in London. Emily was glad because she thought he needed a change; he had been at Farringford more than two months and, after various departures, he had had 'not a soul to speak to', though Emily said she did her best to entertain him. She was herself glad enough to stay quietly at home and give some support to Julia Margaret Cameron. Mrs Cameron always said – as she told Hallam – that when Tennyson was at home she did not often go up. 'But when she is alone I go to *fill* my soul with light and love – to get that which tastes of Heaven in its purity and depth: . . . "a living sparkling stream of Love whose fount is never dry".' Julia Cameron needed that light and love in the spring of 1873. Emily said she seemed to be 'dying of anxiety'. She had come up to see Emily one day, arriving at six ('dear soul'), rather than at the one o'clock that had been suggested. Emily had just begun her own lonely meal but Mrs Cameron would take nothing except some bread and champagne. She was just telling Emily 'an interesting story when she was seized with one of her giddy fits. It was not much . . . but the state of alarm it threw her into was most pitiable. Her poor nerves are thoroughly shattered.' Not long before, her son Charlie had

had 'a dreadful operation' 'to remove part of his jawbone', after a long illness. Now she was equally worried about Henry's future.

In February Emily had told Julia 'plainly, that I feared Henry had not the energy to do great things on the stage nor to prevent himself from being dragged down by his associates.' Now in March she had come round to saying she would see if Tennyson would be willing to help Henry with money for a year so that he could try his luck on the stage. The only alternative seemed to be for Henry to go out to Ceylon to join his brothers, and Emily (obviously imagining herself in the same situation) thought it would 'kill her outright' to part from Henry. 'Henry soothes and manages her beautifully', Emily said, whereas 'Charlie is such a sorrow to her.' Emily's idea was that Henry and his mother should go up to Town together and rent an airy apartment, letting Dimbola to pay for it. Henry Taylor declared that these two 'rough colts', who had once shared the Tennyson boys' lessons were now 'as refined and tender as girls', but someone in the family said that Henry Cameron was 'given to every sort of vice'.

Certainly Emily still saw him as a bad influence on Lionel, at home that spring between Eton and Cambridge. It is 'a great boon to have Henry away at his theatricals', she wrote. 'His success' (with or without Tennyson's help) 'seems to have been very great'. Emily had encouraged Julia Margaret Cameron to improve the family's financial position by selling her photographs; she wrote a good many letters on her behalf. Late in 1873 Mary Brotherton reported to Frederick Tennyson that Mrs Cameron had opened a gallery in London, 'but I fear it is not a successful speculation – as to money. She is not likely to make money as a photographer, or indeed in any way. She is too orientally magnificent and generous in her ideas. I wish the Laureate would let her make another study of him – it would be of use to her financially, no doubt, but he objects to her portraits – which are full of power but hardly as flattering as a man once so handsome as the Laureate may wish his likeness to be. Nevertheless I would rather, were I him, go down to posterity in one of Mrs Cameron's grand Rembrandtesque photos, than in the "glorified-footman", dying duck Mayall vulgarities which he, strange to say, prefers. He looks at Mrs C.'s portraits and says with grim displeasure –"lines are not ditches".' In November that year Lionel went with Mrs Cameron to Southampton to see Henry off to Ceylon. Emily wrote to Lionel: 'I will not bemoan thy absence in the face of this great parting . . . Thou wilt have comfort in feeling that thou had used thy influence with Henry for good – one of the greatest comforts we can have in this world.'

Tennyson returned from London in March 1873 'very cheerful, thank God', but Aldworth was continuing to be a terrible worry. There were builders there replacing the drawing-room ceiling (that tint so carefully chosen). The 'cotton', put in as sound insulation for Tennyson's study above, had become damp and made the beams rotten. A comment of Emily's shows how much the whole point of Aldworth was not simply to be a retreat from the trippers on the Isle of Wight, but to make Tennyson more accessible to visitors from London during the season. The work at Aldworth that summer meant they would be kept at Farringford, Emily told Lear, 'until after he will much care to go, until after people have left London that is.'

There was now a plan to share the costs of Lady Franklin's delightful new house in Seamore Place, Mayfair and Hallam wrote from Cambridge: 'You must let Aldworth on a lease of ten years or so if you take houses in London.' He thought a London house was a good idea, as he would need 'somewhere to lay my head' as 'a barrister at the Inner Temple'. It would be much cheaper in the long run than if he lived at the Temple, and he could keep the house aired for them while they were at Farringford.

In the results of the Second Previous Examination that spring, Tennyson of Trinity was placed in the First Class ('Those who have passed this Examination with credit'). It was sufficient qualification for the Inner Temple, which would admit him on 24 April 1877. It was the Inn of Court of which two of his great-uncles, Charles Tennyson d'Eyncourt and Willingham Franklin, his uncle Edmund Lushington, and Arthur Hallam had all been members. His sponsors would be Franklin Lushington and George Venables. Clearly Hallam was set on a career long after the time he himself suggests in the *Memoir*. Once admitted to the Inn, students remained lifetime members, though they did not of course become members of the Bar until they had passed further examinations.

Emily would get enormous vicarious pleasure from Hallam's time at Cambridge. She told him not to worry about writing, much as she loved to hear from him, but he was good about it. He would generally tell them the sorts of things they loved to hear. 'A man on seeing me the other day said "What a cheerful merry fellow!" I also work very tolerably hard.' But he did not hesitate to write home in the middle of a difficult trigonometry exam he couldn't do or to tell them a story about teasing a girl who, not knowing who he was, asked him whether he knew Tennyson's son, who she had heard was up at Cambridge? 'She supposed he was stupid, was not he, like all sons of great men?' Hallam told her he did not know him, but had indeed heard he was 'rather a fool', and then talked to her ('such is the good I have derived from theatricals') for half an hour before she found out who he was. 'Fancy her horror!'

Emily became closely involved with a magazine Hallam revived with a friend: the *Undergraduates' Journal*. It was not a literary magazine but an opportunity to exchange information and 'air grievances'. Emily was as usual burning with ideas. She wrote to Hallam, 'I wish everyone had the wild delight I have in every new suggestion on social questions.' She was still hoping some national insurance scheme would come into operation. There should be 'part-payment of wages in the form of payment for annuities' and a grand central fund from compulsory taxation to replace 'the present poor law arrangements'. She wanted Hallam to write about it in his journal and debate it in the Union.

Dismayed by the first issue, she begged to be allowed to correct his proofs next time. She was so experienced at correcting proofs and she longed to be of use. 'Excuse my presumption,' she wrote . . . 'There is so much that is good marred by want of a few obvious corrections – obvious for one who has been accustomed to look pretty strictly at the construction of sentences and their correction . . .' 'I am so sorry the printers should spoil thy work,' she said tactfully. Lionel, after he had left Eton, submitted an article for the journal which Hallam sent back with the suggestion that 'if Mamma could revise it and make the Idealism more clear I think it might do; it does not do as it is. But metaphysics are too ambitious – only high class men try and write them here.' It was a tribute to his mother that he thought she might, all the same, make something of the piece. Lionel's reaction is not recorded.

Emily was as usual overwhelmed by visitors that spring and summer of 1873. She would say how fatiguing life had become, how much she was 'knocked up' by all the talking, but she could not resist telling people to get in touch if they were ever in the neighbourhood and she could not refuse the friends who proposed themselves, or turn away the callers. After all, they might entertain Tennyson. And often they did. The main problem that spring was 'eight or nine weeks' of Emily Jesse, who appears not to have entertained any of the family, though visitors could be fascinated to meet the woman who had once so long ago been betrothed to Arthur Hallam.

Emily lamented 'the fret on the nerves of the constant guest and her attendant goblins'. A letter from Lionel to Anne Thackeray exults in the fact that he and his father had managed a walk 'marred by no intruding Jesse or Jesse demon' and then facetiously ends the letter with a lot of exclamation marks and 'Mrs Jesse's love, Crow's love, Pluto's love'. Pluto was his Aunt Emily's appalling dog who was fed on bread and butter. Crow appeared at luncheon daily on his owner's wrist, eating only raw meat, 'cut up in her presence'. Tennyson's solution was to take his walks at night and to be hardly seen during the day. His wife could not escape so easily. She missed the chance to talk to Alfred – either other people were there too, or he was not. She told Hallam it calmed her irritable nerves 'to write to thee or talk to Lionel and rests me more than anything except prayer and helps me to bear the want of talks to Papa'. As soon as Emily Jesse left, Tilly returned. Arthur Tennyson and his wife were there too and then moved on to Hawkridge 'to take care of servants etc' while Anne Weld and Agnes were at Grasby. Fortunately Tennyson 'gets on quite well with them,' his brother and his sister-in-law.

Tennyson went to Switzerland and Italy with Hallam that summer while Emily stayed at Aldworth, trying to get hold of some sheep to keep the grass down and renting a cow to provide some decent milk. She wrote to Hallam in Pontresina: 'Beloved, No, I do not expect Papa to write now thou art there to write and I am very glad he has a real holiday both in having thee and having thee to write for him.' Emily was glad to be quiet, but gladder still when Lionel was there too. At one point he was at a house-party where, he told his mother, he had – exhausted by all the late nights – gone to sleep on the stairs at a dance and cut half his partners in consequence. In his absence Emily rejoiced that 'we have at least the added wealth of a baby – a little girl born to William,' the coachman and his wife in the flat above the stable. Nine days later she said: 'Mrs Knight and the baby go on well, but poor William's arm does not get well. A gathering from the bite of an insect he thinks it is.' Emily's letters are full of this sort of comment; she took an intense interest in the servants. She had lost one, Frank, earlier in the summer – the man who was supposed to keep Tennyson's clothes clean.

It seems Emily was not very observant (her eyes had been bad, so perhaps that was some excuse); by the time she commented the clothes were 'in a very disgraceful state', though Frank had put them out for Tennyson to wear. She asked him to clean them again and they came back, as far as she could see, in the same state. 'In the evening Frank expressed his sorrow that he could not suit me about the clothes, that he did his best' and perhaps he had better go. Emily then resolved on trying what her 'own weak hand could do. The clothes are presentable now in spite of long neglect.' The point of this story is perhaps that neither Alfred nor Emily really noticed what state Alfred's clothes were in. There were other more important things to think about. Other people would notice. But it is also interesting that Frank was busy helping with the new wallpaper in the Farringford drawing room a few weeks later, having been taken on by the Freshwater builder and decorator.

In the autumn of 1873 Lionel joined Hallam at Cambridge. Emily had worried whether Oxford (with less emphasis on mathematics) might suit Lionel better and whether, if both boys were at Trinity, their 'different tastes may create difficulties'. But she was certain that Hallam's influence would be good for Lionel and indeed that his 'view of things' had changed so much recently that the brothers could 'work and live happily together'. And so it proved. Missing them, Emily thought, 'May we be kept to each other yet and two of the four through life and may the shorter partings prepare us for the long one.' It seemed sad to her that 'having my A.' she should still feel 'dumb in heart and brain losing the boys,' but so it was. And in fact, as their father felt the same, she decided it brought them closer together. 'We have surely grown and developed a new love for the old, not less but larger I trust in some ways than it was even at first.'

Lionel told Emily that Hallam was 'goodness itself in feeding him and introducing him to all his friends', and Emily was happy that the boys 'delighted in each other', which was 'one of the dearest desires of my life, as thou knowest'. She kept them closely in touch with developments at Aldworth. 'Papa inclines to letting the house for the summer months only. I tell him we had better let it altogether' on a long lease. Then they would not have the expense of the gardeners, of continually having to get the house ready for new tenants, which was what they had been doing at Farringford each summer. In spite of all the problems there is never any suggestion of any arguments between Alfred and Emily. She would grumble to Hallam, she would certainly give her own view, but in the end she accepted Alfred's decisions, should he be inclined to make any. 'We must of course conform to Papa's wishes,' she said on this occasion. 'I fear that we shall not be able to persuade Papa to let us have a piano,' she would say when they took on Lady Franklin's house in Mayfair.

Aldworth was put in the hands of an estate agent. The man from Gouldsmiths looked all over the house on 21 October and then, poor man, trudged down the hill in the rain 'to see the gardens etc.'. Emily told him they did not want an excessive rent but someone who would take care of the place and feel an interest in it.

They moved into the Mayfair house on 28 October – a beautifully sunny day at Aldworth, but thick fog when they got into London. It was not a good omen. Lady Franklin had 'set her heart on our going there' during her absence, but Tennyson was protesting that even if they found tenants for Aldworth they could not afford the Seamore Place house in the season.

Emily told Lear in November:

People are very kind and we see a good many of them, but for my own personal liking nothing short of the Premiership and the modest confidence of genius befitting could make me happy in London, I think, unless it were the fact that our boys had found work suited to them here and that their home was with us, or that I saw my Ally really the better and happier for being here. On the contrary he has been but poorly here and out of spirits and at Aldworth he was well and cheerful. However or notwithstanding he is convinced that it is good for him to be here. I suppose it is and so here I am content to be, though glad to think he wishes to go home to Farringford for Christmas.

Hallam entertained his father in Cambridge that November. James Knowles went with him, which did not please Emily very much. She said to Hallam she hoped it had not spoiled the visit for him. She had admitted to Lady Franklin that she was 'jealous' of Knowles's influence over Tennyson, and Hallam seemed to share her feeling. Richard Jebb, of whom Hallam had become very fond, sat on Tennyson's right hand at dinner in Hallam's rooms and heard the poet read, including the two 'Northern Farmers' – 'I like Hallam Tennyson thoroughly; he has a beautiful nature,' Jebb wrote to his fiancée in America, 'And now that I know him well, I wish more than ever to know his mother. Everyone says that she is perfection.'

The following month he had the chance in London. He wrote:

Well, on December 17th I went to town to spend two days with the Tennysons, and very delightful days they were. I had long looked forward to meeting Mrs Tennyson. She is tall, slight, with the traces, they must be called so now, of a sweet serene beauty; she is as stately as consists with a grace which has nothing of rigour; gentle, of perfect courtesy; with a sympathetic insight which made those whom she admits to the friend-circle feel at once at home by assuring them of being understood. Two people, independently of each other, described her to me by saying that she was a *châtelaine*; and the description is really happy, expressing as it does something of the sweet queenliness of a French mistress of the manor of the old régime, helped by some quaint felicity in her dress which would evaporate under male analysis . . .

Kate Rawnsley, staying with her cousin Emily at this time, found her looking 'fragile and worn'. She was not feeling at all well and indeed had consulted the doctor who said she was 'perfectly healthy, only I want strengthening'. She did not feel perfectly healthy. She was feeling tired and inadequate. Sending her love to the boys in a letter, she wrote, for I think the only time: 'I only wish it were from one worthier.' Tennyson, too, was 'languid'. Browning came to dinner and noticed it, though he enjoyed himself all the same.

The Christmas holidays at Farringford were comparatively quiet after all the visitors in London. 'I am more happy than I can say and more thankful to be at home alone with my three,' Emily wrote in her journal on 8 January 1874. Lionel had refused 'a great many invitations' to house-parties and Balls all over the country; 'Hallam still more'. But they were out of the house a good deal, with the usual Freshwater 'theatricals'. The relationship between the boys was particularly close, as it had been when they were little, before they went to separate schools. Tennyson brought Emily the first snowdrops of the year and she heard on a splendid frosty morning the sad notes of a bird – was it a storm thrush? It reminded her of 'the saddest notes of that nightingale I heard so long ago at Hale'.

The poet was groaning over the lines he had felt obliged to write to welcome to England Marie Alexandrovna, the new Duchess of Edinburgh, who had married Queen Victoria's second son. But he seemed to have rediscovered the pleasure of quiet evenings reading aloud to Emily. 'He does not want any company,' she told the boys in February just after another visit from the Rawnsleys. They were reading Holinshed and Froude on Queen Mary. Tennyson was planning a play about her and had already sketched two or three scenes. But his contentment did not last for long and Emily encouraged him to go to town to witness the procession for the new Duchess. 'The change will be good for him.' In his absence, she said: 'I have been rather hard at work over Papa's books and am somewhat tired and stupid in consequence.' She was doing one of her periodical re-arrangements and cataloguings in a vain attempt to help Tennyson find the book he wanted when he wanted it, a problem much complicated by the frequent moves between houses. In the process she came across a book 'on the Sewage Question'. She was always a natural 'looker up' and now, as she said, without really intending it, she was able to supply Hallam with some useful information about the use of peat for 'filtration'; he had been complaining of his Cambridge drains.

The boys came home for the Easter vacation at the end of March. Tennyson was back at Farringford too. 'So now, thank God, I have all my three best beloved at home once more.' She was certainly realizing that this blessed state of affairs was not likely to go on much longer. There were the usual crowds of visitors that April, culminating in a dance on the 17th. 'The boys write all my invitations for me and spare me all they can.' Then it was time for them to return to Cambridge. In the surviving epitome of her journal under 20 April 1874 are the words: 'They leave us two or three days after my illness came and I could write no more.'

Weddings

——

In one of her stories, Emily wrote of a husband's anguish at his wife's mysterious illness: 'Her strength, which had been so long failing, at last quite gave way and days and nights I passed beside her almost in despair.' It was typical of Emily to imagine herself in Alfred's position rather than her own. She could 'write no more', but so much of her writing had been for him. He would now be the one to suffer, and not only from seeing his wife, who had always been his strength (even in her own weakness), now helpless and in pain.

There was no dramatic collapse with Hallam rushing back from Cambridge to take his mother's place, as has often been suggested. At first Emily did not seem any worse than she had been on other occasions in the past. On 28 May 1874 Hallam wrote from Cambridge: 'I am so glad Papa is really better, but you *must* get well, Mamma. Do take care of yourself.' The following month, when his parents were at Aldworth, Lionel wrote to Anne Thackeray: 'Owing to the present iciness, Mama does not get well half so quickly as she ought to do – but when the summer *does* come we will hope for better things.'

Warmth and sunshine seemed at this point likely to be the best treatment. On 6 August, the whole family set off for France. Aldworth had at last been let after various delays which made Emily think the agent had set the rent too high. Plans to let it on a long lease had apparently been abandoned, though Hallam remained attached to the idea of giving it up entirely and taking a London house. 'London spurts me up marvellously,' he said; he still had every intention of reading for the Bar.

'Mamma must travel comfortably,' Hallam wrote in his diary, which involved paying the porters a good deal. In Paris the boys lay upon the floor in the evening listening to their father read Shakespeare to the three of them. Paris was no warmer than Aldworth, and nor was Tours, where they stayed shivering for several weeks. Alfred and Hallam escaped for a few days to the Pyrenees, leaving Emily in Lionel's care. It had not been much of a tour, Tennyson told Palgrave. And yet Emily seemed to have benefited. Hallam, writing Emily's usual letter to Fitz that Christmas, told him inaccurately that his mother had not been able to hold a pen 'since last April'. 'We all went to Tours to make her better and I think on the whole our journey was successful.'

'Wrap up well, Mrs T,' Hallam wrote from Cambridge in October, as he had so often written before. 'Take care of yourself. I am so glad you feel better.' The suggestion was certainly that she was *not* taking proper care of herself, though she said she had 'less pain than I have had lately'. Lionel had to tell her to get the servants to fetch and carry for her. She was still writing too much to her sons and he told her: 'I shan't punish you this time by writing on a postcard, but next time you transgress rules I shall.' Tennyson told Sophie Cracroft that young Dr Dabbs from Newport was treating Emily with 'phosphorous', which seemed to be doing some good, but five days later Lionel wrote sternly: 'We are not pleased with the account you give of yourself, Mama: you should see Dr Dabbs oftener and tell him *everything* and take his *advice*.' By the end of the year she seemed to be getting worse, not better.

If only we could know what Emily told Dr Dabbs. There has been a suggestion that Emily had become 'mysteriously, probably psychosomatically, perhaps self-protectively, and in any case permanently ill.' Could her problems in fact have been purely physical? Or was it that her physical problems were complicated by what used to be called loosely 'a nervous breakdown'? Her few surviving letters from this period do not suggest that, though there is an odd one, written on 3 November 1874, where she packs every inch of the front of the folded sheet of paper (about Thomas Gray and Wycliffe, for Hallam's benefit) and ignores entirely the blank inside.

It can hardly have been a coincidence that James Paget, who was one of Tennyson's doctors and may well have attended Emily in London in November 1873, had just at this time given a lecture on 'the nervous mimicry of organic diseases' in which his description of 'spinal neuromimesis' accords very neatly in some respects with Emily's case. The patient is 'painfully fatigued by slight exertion' and complains of 'pains in the limbs, especially in the lower limbs; . . . a sense of constriction of the chest . . . a sense of weakness in the lower limbs, so they are scarcely capable of supporting the weight of the body.' In a second lecture, Paget said that, 'The brain is often wearied and rendered powerless by overwork; and the physician meets, daily, cases in which there is no disease, as the phrase so glibly runs, but in which there is, very obviously, the greatest distress. Inaptitude for work or rest, depression of spirits, with irritability of temper; a sense of weariness and hopelessness; frequent disturbance of general health; the digestion fails, the secretions are disturbed, and the man "breaks down", he is "tired", and what he wants is a "rest".'

Tennyson's own diagnosis depressed him. Was it partly his fault that his wife was so ill? Surely he could not be blamed. He wrote to Knowles:

She has overwrought herself with the multifarious correspondence of many years, and is now suffering for it. I trust that with perfect quiet she will recover; but it will never again do for her to insist upon answering every idle fellow who writes to me. I always prayed her not to do so but she did not like the unanswered (she used to say) to feel wroth and unsatisfied with me.

He told the Duchess of Argyll that he would never again let Emily 'write letters for five hours a-day', that she had been prescribed 'perfect rest', that she could 'neither write nor read, being obliged from spinal weakness resulting from overwork of the brain to lie all her length.'

In all her comments on her health over the past years, Emily had only once mentioned her spine. In 1867 she had said she was 'very unwell from the pain in the head and spine etc.' This would seem to suggest a general feeling of achiness rather than that it was a spinal weakness that had caused her frailty. I still think it possible that it was the unmentionable uterus that was the reason for her continual ill health, and uterine prolapse that made her doctor encourage her to 'lie all her length' in 1874 and 1875. Binding and horizontal rest was the only cure known for prolapse at this period. It is curious to reflect that if it were indeed the uterus, the womb, that caused Emily's problems, her condition could accurately then be described as 'hysterical', however calm her acceptance of her situation.

Benjamin Jowett had always said Emily overworked, that she had not enough self-love to keep herself alive. It was extremely hard for her to obey her doctors' orders, to be utterly selfish – to preserve her own health by ignoring the needs of others and lying quietly day by day. Yet once she had accepted the medical advice she had the patience to be a good patient. Years later, she told her niece Agnes, warning *her* against overwork, that in her own case it had ended 'in not being able to do anything but be patient, which I tried to be.' She had always enjoyed solitude, quiet, the life of the mind. She had the self-knowledge and inner resources to keep her going. She did not depend on others to nourish her well-stocked mind or her soul, though of course she was always happy when Tennyson read to her, as he so often did.

Not long before she was ill, she had written to Hallam about 'meekness', because he had asked about it. It is a word many have found difficult and it is naturally banished from most modern translations of the Bible. Oddly, it now suggests not just a submissive spirit but spinelessness. Emily tried to accept 'meekly' what she saw as the will of God. 'Blessed are the meek for they shall inherit the earth.' Meekness, she told her son, is 'the root of gentleness', but it 'by no means implies want of spirit'. The meek inherit the earth because 'they do not fret as others do for lack of what they think their due and so can enjoy and be thankful for what God gives them,' however hard it might seem.

Lying on her sofa, day after day, she schooled herself not to be restless or discontented. It helped surely that she could seek the kingdom of God and his righteousness as easily, perhaps more easily, on a sofa as in the world. Her faith was firm and the frustrations and deprivations of these years could do nothing to shake it. (There was a much more testing time to come.) Jowett joined in the chorus urging her to do nothing. 'The only prescription which I can offer is that you should do nothing for the rest of your life and *you* may do so much good in doing nothing.' It was rather difficult to feel like that in the Christmas holidays of 1874–5 when she was forbidden by her doctors to write, or even to talk. It was a hard prescription for all of them. It was now that Hallam said he had taken over as the 'family-secretary'. But it was only a temporary appointment and he returned to Cambridge with Lionel in January.

The boys said that they had had the best Christmas holidays they could ever remember, even though their mother was so 'weak'. Lionel's diary is full of happy goings-on – rehearsals, parties, billiards, driving out with the horses. There are mentions of the cousins, Horatio's children, of I Spy at Mrs Cameron's house – and many mentions of Eleanor Locker, who spent the holidays at Farringford. Emily was not well enough to receive guests, but Eleanor was different. She seemed almost to be one of the family. Lionel was nearly twenty-one and now realized he was falling in love with Eleanor, whom he had first met when they were children in London in 1866. Was her own childhood memory of Tennyson in the Market Square at Horncastle one of the factors that would make Emily so happy about this romance? It was impossible for *her*, having suffered as she had, to make things difficult for the young.

In the previous March, when Tennyson went to London for the Duchess of Edinburgh's procession, Emily had encouraged him to call on Frederick Locker, who had been so 'ill and low'. By July he was transformed; Tennyson attended Locker's wedding to Jane Lampson, the daughter of an American millionaire. The new Mrs Locker (soon the two names would be linked) was not an easy stepmother, though a perfectly kindly one. She was an immensely pious Evangelical, who would not open her Sunday post until Monday morning, drank nothing, had no interest in the arts and indeed never entered a theatre. By Christmas 1874 she was expecting a child. Eleanor had always been fond of the Tennysons and now she spent more and more time with them. Lionel went back to Cambridge, writing poems for Eleanor in his notebook:

> When we talked last night together
> And the busy world was still
> Were we something to each other?
> Friends or lovers? What you will?
> Did you speak in love or earnest?
> Did I feel a precious tear?
> Was I dreaming? did you like me?
> Did you love me? Tell me, dear.

At home at Farringford, without the boys, Tennyson was becoming more and more depressed. It was a fearfully trying winter. Even in March the snow – unusual in the Isle of Wight – still lay 'in ragged patches about the gardens and roofs' of Freshwater, and the violets were shrivelled and nipped in the bud. The death of his Cambridge friend William Brookfield was much in Tennyson's mind and his mood was not helped by Mrs Cameron's photographs of the *Idylls*, an extraordinary scheme he had encouraged and then regretted. Both he and Emily were also deeply saddened by the death of their niece Lucy Lushington, who was the same age as Lionel. She was the third of Cecilia and Edmund's children to die, leaving only Cecilia's namesake, known as Zilly, who sadly was 'not the child of her affections'.

If Emily's illness was not life-threatening, it certainly threatened Tennyson's way of life. 'I cannot laud this life, it looks so dark,' he wrote in his sonnet for Brookfield. Emily had written to Venables in March 1874, after Lady Houghton's death: 'Well, as the circle grows smaller, may it grow stronger.' But without her letters to their old friends, the circle could only grow weaker. James Spedding was with them, however, in February 1875. When Emily apologized to him for not having anyone in the house to meet him, 'he said he had all he could desire'. Emily found his conversation very agreeable, but she was trying to obey her doctor's rules and callers were 'staved off' day after day.

Tennyson had been impatient with Knowles in January. He had already told him, he said, that he could not leave his wife at present. He could not accept any invitations. Perhaps 'in a week or two' he might get up to London, but he could not promise. That Emily's mind and spirit were lively, even though her body was not, is suggested by the fact that with this same letter early in 1875 Tennyson enclosed Emily's plan for a 'fog-excluder'. Tennyson wrote:

My wife sends you what she deems her invention – which (if it be her invention) – she trusts will make our fortune and yours, more than the biscuits which they patented. You are to look at it. It is so simple that it has no doubt been tried before. She requests you to have it put – by Act of Parliament – in every house in London before we come thither again, that we mayn't die of fog.

There is another vivid glimpse of Emily in 1875, which shows she remained entirely herself, however passive she was supposed to be. In June Tennyson had sent Robert Browning a copy of his new book – the play *Queen Mary*. Browning's acknowledgment was so enthusiastic that Emily felt he deserved to be thanked for it, and said so. Tennyson turned the conversation into a letter.

After-dinner talk between husband and wife.

W. Why don't you write and thank Mr Browning for his letter?
H. Why should I. I sent him my book and he acknowledged it.
W. But such a great and generous acknowledgement.
H. That's true.
W. Then you should write: he has given you your crown of violets.
H. He is the greatest-brained poet in England. Violets fade: he has given me a crown of gold.
W. Well I meant the Troubadour crown of golden violets: pray write: you know

I would if I could; but I am lying here helpless and horizontal and can neither write nor read.

H. Then I'll go up and smoke my pipe and write to him.

W. You'll go up and concoct an imaginary letter over your pipe, which you'll never send.

H. Yes I will. I'll report our talk.

He goes up and smokes, and spite of pipe writes and signs himself

A. Tennyson

Browning's sister was so delighted with this letter that she learnt it off by heart and would recite the dialogue to her friends.

Tennyson's depressed feeling that Emily's illness had been going on far too long is well indicated in his letters. In March 1875 he told his old friend Sophy Elmhirst (Kate Rawnsley's sister-in-law) that Emily had been 'very unwell for upwards of a year, not able to write or read except for a minute or two at a time.' Three months later, in June, in his description of her condition to the Duchess of Argyll, Tennyson thought she had 'been for two years in this state'. He also told her that, 'Hallam has been at home all this Cambridge term and acting as secretary for us both – hard upon him, I fear, however good for us.' So Hallam had missed what should have been his last term at Cambridge, the term when he should have taken his final examinations. He had been called home just as his father had been, forty-four years before.

In 1875 Hallam took a far less gloomy view of his mother's situation than his father did. He had every intention of returning to Cambridge, and indeed did so that October. He told Lionel in May that at Aldworth Anne Thackeray was playing 'lawn tennis with Papa – to which game he is so attached that no coaxing can induce him to walk.' It was the new game. (It is unlikely that James Joyce, who would long afterwards sneer at the titled poet as Alfred Lawn Tennyson, knew that he loved playing.) Hallam also reported that 'the new medicine seems to revive Mamma'. When it was sunny she was able to sit outside on the lawn in her 'sofa-chair' and watch the game or listen to Alfred reading to her the 'daily papers or some book'. Even when it rained and there were visitors, she did not seem too much 'knocked up'.

In June they heard from Frederick Locker that Dean Stanley liked the epitaph Tennyson had written for the memorial to Emily's uncle, Sir John Franklin, in Westminster Abbey. It was thirty years since he had said to her that if he were lost, she should always remember his firm belief in a north-west passage. And now, just two weeks before the memorial was unveiled, his widow, who had tried so hard to find where in 'the white North' lay his bones, died herself in London. Kate Rawnsley, another niece, wrote in her diary: 'An indomitable woman and cleverer than her husband.' Others would say the same of Emily.

Now Tennyson wrote to Locker to congratulate the middle-aged new father on the birth of his son and heir. 'Peace and health to you both and the new-born,' Tennyson wrote; 'And to Eleanor whom you do not mention.' It seemed poor Eleanor was likely to be feeling rather in the way after the joyous birth of her half-brother. The Tennysons invited her to go to France with them.

They had talked of Italy; in the end, however, the route and the holiday plan was much the same as the year before. But, for Lionel, Eleanor's presence changed everything. Lionel had himself probably suggested that Eleanor should go with them. In his diary there is an underlined '*Walk with Papa*' at Aldworth soon after his return from Cambridge, which obviously had some special significance. On 26 July he wrote: 'Enter Papa with Eleanor,' and there were days of talking and visiting before she returned home to get ready for the tour. On 3 September they were in Pau, with Emily able to feast her eyes on that amazing view – the distant prospect of the Pyrenees, snowcapped even in high summer. In Lionel's diary there is the bold word 'YES'; he had obviously proposed to Eleanor. The day before, Hallam and Tennyson had gone off for a couple of days walking in the Pyrenees. The ring was bought ten days later in Tours. On their return to England Lionel went almost straight away to see Frederick Locker. In his notebook he wrote:

> Man was not made to live alone:
> There is no joy but what is shared:
> Then grant the prayer that I have dared
> And let us, dear, at last be one.

To Henry Cameron in Ceylon he wrote of 'the greatest event that has ever happened to me in my short little life . . . I am engaged to Eleanor Locker: it is at present a dead secret, though of course I have told Mrs Cameron . . . We are not to be married naturally enough until I find a profession which I hope to do in a year when I leave Cambridge.' He told Henry the Lockers had been 'as kind and affectionate as possible'. He says nothing, unfortunately, about his parents' reactions or Hallam's, at this first intrusion into that dove-tailed square.

Hallam had written a good deal to Emily about girls in his letters

from Cambridge. He had danced at Girton that February and had lamented that the men and 'lady undergraduates' so rarely mixed. Then he
decided that it was perhaps a good thing, as 'men and women before
marriage do not appear to have the power of being friends; what with
an English girl's ideas of early marriage and the world's babble.' It was
an odd thing for him to say when he had a good many women friends
himself, particularly Anne Thackeray and her Ritchie cousins – but
Anne, at least at this point, seemed almost middle-aged and unmar-
riageable; and he had been well trained by his father to suspect 'the
world's babble'.

Now it seems he may have regretted Lionel's decision to commit
himself so early. But it was, of course, in their situation at that time, the
only way in which Lionel and Eleanor could, in any sense, 'be one'.
Eleanor's first letter to Emily after the return home was everything she
could have wished. 'I shall be so happy trying to be useful to you and
Mr Tennyson and though I cannot expect in any way to fill the boys'
place, I shall do my very best to be a daughter to you. I can never repay
you for all your and Mr Tennyson's kindness to me.' She was twenty-
one years old that summer, just a few months younger than Lionel. At
the time Emily said she welcomed her into the family with joy.

The account in the *Memoir* is closely based on one written by Emily
herself, though she had romantically suggested that the three of them,
Eleanor, Lionel and Hallam, had 'as children' 'danced about the fields
at Farringford'. Hallam writes more soberly of Eleanor 'whom as a
child we had known well and who was like one of our own family.'
Emily, nearly twenty years later, wrote that though the engagement had
not been foreseen it was 'as welcome as so anxious an event can be to
those whose life has been with their children and for their children.'
Was that really how she saw her life, as one not entirely dedicated to
Alfred and the promotion of his poetry, but as one devoted to her sons?
Certainly, in some moods that was so, and again and again in her
journals and letters one feels the power of the bond between devoted
mother and devoted sons. Edward Lear, who loved Emily himself, was
only one of many who noticed how the boys responded to her love:
'The affection of the boys to her was beyond all idea,' he would write in
his diary on his next visit. Alfred and his needs would always come first,
but it was still going to be hard to let her two tall sons go. Had she ever
really wanted a daughter? Tennyson certainly had and now he insisted
upon being called not 'Mr Tennyson' by his future daughter-in-law, but

Pate, 'as short for Pater'. He called her 'half a Bruce and half a "London Lyric".' (*London Lyrics* was the title of Frederick Locker's best-known book.) 'We have known her from a child and approve of her heartily. But as he is only twenty-one they must wait till he get some employment, of which at present I see small prospect.'

Life at Farringford that autumn seemed almost to have returned to normal, though Tennyson told Gladstone that Emily was only 'slowly recovering from a long illness' and that he was 'accordingly homebound'. It was a better word than housebound for he walked daily on the Downs and played tennis in 'a beautiful clearing in the high wood', which was now a tennis court, reached by a glade from the garden-door of the house. His eyesight, what he could and could not see, seemed more curious than ever. Blanche Warre-Cornish remembered 'a perfect holiday-time', listening to a reading of *Queen Mary* and watching Tennyson play tennis. She caught his speaking voice: 'I like the play, but hate the game,' he said. 'Fifteen love, thirty love, deuce . . . I never could count.'

Tennyson might be pessimistic about Lionel's career prospects, but Hallam, back at Cambridge that autumn, was already being given the chance of some work. On 24 November he wrote to his parents:

I have been offered a lectureship in Liverpool and Hackney by Stuart on behalf of the University of Cambridge. I am to address monster meetings if I take it. I should like it immensely – but I must consult you about it first when I come home. They would like me either to lecture on Nature-poets, owing to my having got a Declamation prize on Gray as a nature-poet. Or more than all they would like me to lecture on you, Papa – you being, they say, far the most popular poet among the unwashed. If you could help me – I should like to lecture on the Idylls of the King and on your Ballad poetry – and on your nature poetry and on In Memoriam. It would be such a grand thing for me to educate the masses on you – and to make them know and appreciate you. I should try and bring in History and Politics too.

For all his slangy superior reference to the 'unwashed', Hallam shared with Lionel a real concern for popular education and the work of the University Extension department. Lionel once said 'the only test of genuine merit is the applause of an artizan audience'.

Hallam left Cambridge that Christmas, after the usual nine terms. He had no degree certainly, but he did have his qualification for the Inner Temple, as well as the promise of this extension lecturing. Emily was reasonably well. Lionel wrote to her: 'I heard from Dabbs . . . you were decidedly better for which I am very thankful for to be better in this weather is to be better indeed.' And there survives one business letter, dated 27 October, entirely (even Alfred's signature) in Emily's hand, which suggests that at least occasionally she was back at her old tasks.

Hallam's health was proposed at 'a big end of term dinner' at Trinity – 'coupled with Macaulay's', his fellow editor of the *Undergraduates' Journal*. 'I shirked my return speech and Macaulay spoke for both of us . . . and they sang the Charge of the Light Brigade in your (and my?) honour. I will telegraph if I want the carriage to meet me at Yarmouth on Saturday.'

Was it only in his middle age, working on the *Memoir* of his father, regretting his own lost chances, reflecting on his own career (undistinguished at that point), that Hallam, with Emily's willing acceptance, slightly rewrote history? There are a few lines at Lincoln which reveal how it seemed to him, looking back. 'My mother was seriously ill in 1875. I was summoned home from Cambridge. I became my father's secretary, and hardly left home again for a single night until his death.' Reading the last part of the second sentence through, he must have realized what nonsense it was and how easily disproved. He crossed it out for a milder variation, 'and stayed with him continuously until his death.' It must have felt that that was the way it was. In April 1878 Emily gave her own inaccurate version: 'Hallam did not return after the Long Vacation, giving up all chance of honours, but worthy of far higher for his devotion to his parents. Nothing could have exceeded the goodness of A. and our boys to me.'

'I did not return to Cambridge after the Christmas of 1875,' is Hallam's own published statement in the *Memoir*, and the Trinity Residence Book seems to confirm it. Why then was he writing to Knowles on 13 January 1876: 'I go back late in this month to Cambridge'? Perhaps he was merely visiting Lionel. Certainly on 8 February Aunt Tilly, returned to Farringford from mournful Park House for the first time in two years, wrote to her friend Mrs Craik: 'Lionel . . . has gone back to Cambridge. Hallam stays at home to help his mother. She is very weak but she is better than she was last winter.' It is interesting it should be his *mother*, not his father, that Matilda Tennyson sees Hallam as helping. At this period, he would write the letters, order the port, pay the servants and so on. But she would usually decide what went into the letters, how much wine to buy, how much the servants were paid.

Tennyson's letter to the Master of Trinity (regretting that 'our absolute need of Hallam at home has prevented him from accomplishing his university career') was not written until 29 March 1876. Tennyson trusted 'the Master would not think the worse' of Hallam for not taking his degree. There was, as has been suggested, the definite feeling that Tennyson hoped the Master would not think the worse of Tennyson himself. He added: 'I need not say that it is very pleasant to his mother and myself that Hallam's Shoreditch lectures have been so successful.'

Emily, like any proud mother, had been sending lecture programmes to all sorts of friends and relations. Hallam gave a series of lectures in the spring of 1876. 'Which do you advise me to come up for?' Lionel asked on 23 February. In the end he found himself involved on one occasion, duly reported to Emily by Eleanor, who would so often write over the years to keep Emily in touch with at least some parts of Lionel's life. Of Hallam's second lecture on 'Shakespeare and his Humour' in the Town Hall, Shoreditch (Admission 1d, A Few Front Seats 3d) on 20 March, Eleanor wrote:

The lecture it seemed to me could not have been a greater success. Mr Gordon told Lionel it was even a greater success than the last. It lasted from 8 till ¼ to 10 and the interest of the audience never flagged. There was not a large audience owing (they said) to the cold, but they calculated over 700 were there, which is 300 more than generally attend the Science lectures. His voice never failed. 'Maud' was most enthusiastically received and Lionel was so applauded and 'bravo-ed' that he had to come forward two or three times to bow.

Lionel had recited 'the mad scene in Maud'. Reading through her letter to Emily, Eleanor crossed out 'two or three times' and substituted 'once or twice'. She did not want to exaggerate, but it had been an exciting evening. She did not attempt to explain why Lionel was reading from 'Maud' at a lecture on Shakespeare's humour. The *Hackney Express* on 18 March had reported Lionel's presence on the platform the previous week, as well as 'a brilliant solo on the pianoforte' by the boys' friend Charles Stanford, the young organist of Trinity College, who had written the music for *Queen Mary*, Tennyson's play, which caused them all such problems that winter. Hallam was billed as 'the Son of the Poet Laureate'. At least some of the audience in the Town

Hall may have been the very same 'Cockneys' whom Tennyson had accused of making his life a misery by peering at him curiously through the trees and across the downs at Freshwater.

Hallam had certainly taken the lectures extremely seriously. Each week everyone who came to them was given a paper, which included a list of books for recommended reading and a series of essay subjects. ('To what extent is cowardice part of Falstaff's character?' 'Sketch the character of a man about your own age whom you would like for a friend', etc.) On the paper: 'Mr Tennyson hopes that anyone who can answer any *one* of his questions will do it. All answers to be sent on Saturday to H.T., Farringford, Freshwater, Isle of Wight.' It is one of those tantalizing stories with no ending. There is no evidence of how many people sent essays to Farringford, adding to that huge mail that poured in each day, or whether Hallam ever gave the series in Liverpool or lectured again – on his father, or on anything else. What is certain is that Emily would have talked over the questions with Hallam and discussed the submitted essays with him, if there were any. What is also certain is that neither of Emily's sons would ever be able to escape that label 'Son of the Poet Laureate'.

Nothing is recorded of Emily's feelings about the production of *Queen Mary*, Tennyson's first play to be performed, which dominated all their lives at this period. It is possible she shared her neighbour Mary Brotherton's feelings. *She* told Frederick Tennyson she feared it would be 'a fiasco', 'which would greatly pain and annoy him, and perhaps reduce him to silence for the rest of his life! He could never join in hissing his own play as Charles Lamb did!' Nor could she imagine him 'in a front box with his hand on his heart, bowing and sweetly smiling, the kind of thing old Lytton gloried in!' In this same letter she describes poor Emily in 'a fright', not so much because of an alarming drawing-room chimney fire, but because of Hallam's attempts to put it out while balanced precariously on the Farringford roof.

Lionel was becoming more and more obsessed by the theatre. He told Henry Cameron he was looking forward to the day when Henry would 'regenerate the British Stage' and he himself would 'look up longingly and perhaps jealously from the position of a "super"' – in other words an extra or bit-part player. Did he talk to his mother – knowing her feelings – about going on the stage himself? In a letter home, he described *Queen Mary* as not exactly a fiasco but 'more of a domestic tragedy than a historical drama: the mounting is tasteful but by no means splendid: and how anyone unacquainted with the whole play could make out the story in the acted play, I can't conceive.' Emily never saw the play. It ran for only twenty-three performances, but far from turning Tennyson away from the drama it seemed to spur him on so that the following years saw him writing almost entirely for the theatre: *Harold, Becket, The Falcon, The Cup, The Foresters, The Promise of May*. Emily's special interest was to put some of the lyrics in the plays to music. It is the moment to look again at Emily's skills as a composer.

It has been said that Emily Tennyson's 'harmonic vocabulary rarely extended beyond the three basic chords'. She was, presumably, self-taught as a composer, if not as a pianist. Nothing is known of her music lessons long ago in Horncastle. A twentieth-century musician has asserted that elementary errors are to be found 'both in her melodic lines and their accompaniments'. Emily was always very modest about her own achievement. Hallam suggested the main interest in her settings of Tennyson's poems was that they 'were made mostly after she had first heard them read by him, and give the impression of my Father's reading'. And she herself told Woolner how important it was for the music to follow the metre of the poem. She would never have called herself a composer. 'Handel is to my mind the Archangel of composers,' she said in 1873, knowing some people at this period would think her a 'benighted creature for saying so'. She longed to hear the *Messiah* 'grandly performed' and never did. She also loved Bach, Schubert, Beethoven. She knew her own achievement was not to be taken very seriously. But her music gave her great pleasure and it went on in her head with so much other consolation in the hours when she was confined to a sofa.

Tennyson has often been said to have had little interest in music, but one should set against James Knowles's late assertion that he cared so little for it, Venables's early suggestion that Tennyson, with his 'love of music and tobacco', should try living in Prague. He certainly, in spite of his reluctance to spend money on pianos, encouraged Emily to set his poems and valued her settings, as we have seen, above those of others. Emily must have hated it when Knowles wrote that Tennyson did not care 'for any "setting" of his own songs, which he justly felt had already their own music'. At the end of his life, Tennyson encouraged Emily to copy out her settings of his poems and was delighted when they were arranged and played in public.

*

As Lionel approached the end of his time at Cambridge, his parents were busily trying to find an opening to some sort of career for him. He had done well in his earlier examinations, being placed in the first class both times, in spite of what Emily called 'the hideous Algebra'. In 1875 he had been one of only eight firsts out of an entry of about sixty. It must have been a disappointment when, in the summer of 1876, he took only a second in history. Lionel himself thought he had every reason to be gloomy about his employment prospects. In January he had written to Venables to tell him that his father had tried in vain to secure him a clerkship in the House of Lords and was writing to Sir Erskine May about the prospects in the Commons. 'My father bids me say that, as he is very ignorant of these matters, he would be grateful if you would give him a little advice as to which offices it would be well to seek a nomination in; my mother inclines to the Colonial.' This was not surprising considering her passionate feelings about the Empire and the importance of a close relationship between England and her colonies as a force for good and justice throughout the world.

In February Lionel reported that he had had a letter from his future father-in-law Frederick Locker, 'saying that he learns from William Rossetti there is a deadlock in the Civil Service, the Foreign Office and Education Office excepted, that trying for the House of Commons is useless, that Sir E. M.'s letter was tantamount to a civil refusal: that the FO is the only thing to be tried for and failing that Commerce or some vague scheme of going up to the Bar. It doesn't sound lively, does it?'

Emily asked Benjamin Jowett if he would nominate Lionel. ('You are most welcome to use my name (or to forge it) ... He will find no difficulty in getting a nomination.') But the nomination was generally only a right to sit an examination and the competition was always very stiff. Edward Lear, who had been lamenting in letters to his friends from the Villa Emily, San Remo, the illness of 'that nearly angel-woman Emily Tennyson', now wrote to congratulate Lionel on his engagement. Everyone was talking and writing to him about it. It was certainly not a secret. Lear told Emily he had known 'the young lady's mother in Palermo years ago and am glad to know the young couple are likely to be so happy. But I hope he will *do* something by way of profession and not dawdle into idleness. If I had sons, I would make them Fishmongers or Letter carriers, – or Coal heavers rather than nothing'.

He added a picture of himself and Foss, his cat, showing the state he was in himself. The drawing must have gone to Emily's heart.

View in Villa Emily. Sanremo.

Emily and Alfred absolutely agreed with Lear, as he knew, about the value of work. Hallam would remember his father saying to him, as they looked over a ploughed field: 'The needless charlock grows if we be idle and chokes the crop.' Tennyson had always said how much better he felt when he was working on a long poem. Emily still needed to feel she had some work in life, that she could be of some use to her husband and her sons. In March, when perhaps she had gone through an essay of Lionel's for him, she wrote, 'I have done my best and I am grieved that I cannot do better. (No, I ought to thank God I can do this.)' That was her constant thought. She would say to Agnes towards the end of her life, 'how hard this is to bear' if we have no scope for our energies. Carlyle had put it neatly: 'Blessed is he who has found his work; let him ask no other blessing.'

Emily actually wrote at some point a sort of hymn to the delights of work, beginning: 'Brothers, sing we all the joy of labour!' It was, one supposes, a 'subject' for Tennyson, something to inspire him to write his own superior version. He never did. Emily's paean of praise for work ends with the words: 'No task so weary as idleness.'

Hallam travelled with his father that autumn. There was a tour of East Anglia, which culminated in the long-postponed visit to FitzGerald in Woodbridge, with 'Papa and his Fitz telling one another stories of their youth.' Hallam kept his mother closely in touch with each day's doings. She was certainly dealing with some of the post again. He told her not to answer Charles Kegan Paul, his old teacher, now, in his new role as a publisher, embroiled in a row with Tennyson over an anno-tated edition of the poems. 'Merely say we are away,' he suggested. 'I am glad Eleanor is taking good care of you.'

Eleanor spent a lot of time with Emily that year. In March his mother had told Lionel in Cambridge: 'Eleanor is as good as can be to us. It is such a blessing to have one who enters so enthusiastically into all that interests us.' She was a particular help with poor Aunt Tilly, whose nerves – never very reliable – were now shattered by those two years at Park House. Eleanor had become so much a part of the family that when she was at Farringford she shared in the general family letter rather than having one of her own from Lionel; that cannot have pleased her.

Lionel went to France to improve his French. For the next year he would spend his time either abroad or at Scoones, the crammer in London, preparing for his Foreign Office examination. From one of Eleanor's letters to him in Paris, it seems clear that he had been ser-iously thinking of taking up the stage as a career. She had been to the Briary, the house near Farringford where the painter G.F. Watts was now living with the Prinseps.

What pleased me most was a conversation I had with Mr Watts. He began to talk of your acting. He said he was perfectly astonished when he saw you in *Rivals* . . . He spoke a great deal of what a position he thought you would take and how you would raise the stage if you had adopted it as a profession and he spoke in such genuine, sincere admiration that I was very delighted . . . Mr Watts says you would restore the English Stage to what it was in Garrick's time . . . *We* are too sure of this to need telling, but I like to hear other people say so, especially as it confirms what your Father has so often said.

It sounds very much as if Lionel, Eleanor and Tennyson himself were all united in thinking Lionel should go on the stage – and that it was Emily who had encouraged him to have a more respectable profession and remain an amateur actor and singer. She loved his singing; she enjoyed watching him act. When he was seven years old Emily had written to Woolner in delight about the little harmonium he had given the boy: 'He goes fluting about on the fairy flute and is as wild and fantastic as ever', but fifteen years later she was glad he had calmed down. She could hardly believe it when Lionel quoted the Chaplain of the Savoy Chapel declaring 'there was no more moral class' 'than the actresses of London'. She certainly could not bear the thought of seeing him go through what Henry Cameron had gone through before he gave it up and left for Ceylon. Failure would be hard to take, but success might prove even more difficult to accept.

Lionel failed in his attempt to get into the Foreign Office in May 1877. He apparently fell ill in the middle of the examination and was 'obliged to come out'. Perhaps he had been struck down by the measles, which Eleanor had at just that time. She was at Farringford as usual and Dr Dabbs pronounced it a very mild case. Tennyson, writing to reassure her father, said: 'Lionel is a very good nurse and reads to her' and sleeps 'close by'. Emily does not seem to have been too attentive a chaperone. 'Miss Locker is enjoying the measles', Lionel wrote to a friend in America.

Hallam had been to Hawarden with his father in November 1876. Tennyson had every hope that that might lead to some sort of work. Mary Gladstone observed the boy – as she called him; she was five years older – while his father read on and on relentlessly for two and a half hours, right through his new play *Harold*, taking every part. The boy was motionless, she said, 'but now and then referred to by his father and having to fill in a word or passage, actually knowing it all by heart.' It was, Mary thought, 'a great thing to see and hear. We were forced to take no heed of such earthly things as luncheon.' At dinner she sat next to Hallam and talked about poetry. It was the beginning of what would become more than friendship.

Hallam made the arrangements that winter for renting a house at 7 Upper Wimpole Street. It was the sort of thing Emily had always done in the past. There was plenty for Hallam to do, but there are a number of indications that the intention at this stage was that Hallam should have a career of his own. He became his father's permanent secretary and companion only when various other possible careers had failed to materialize. For Hallam – and for his mother – there must always have been some feeling of failure, of talents unused, of potential unfulfilled.

On 24 April 1877 Hallam was admitted to the Inner Temple and seems to have kept his first term in the way Arthur Hallam had done exactly forty-five years earlier. *He* had told *his* Emily Tennyson it was 'a process performed by eating – very agreeable do you think? – very disagreeable, I know, for one is surrounded by hideous students in gowns and red whiskers, chatting about entails and mortgages.' His namesake, Hallam Tennyson, went on eating dinners for years. In May Edmund Lushington advised Lionel to consult 'Lawyer Hallam' on a question of evidence. Hallam was living in lodgings in Hanover Street (with Lionel, back from France) and rowing on the Thames. But he certainly was not committed to the Bar. On 19 June he told his parents that he had heard 'nothing more of Inspectorships'.

Lionel, having failed to get into the Foreign Office, was now nominated for the India Office by Lord Salisbury, at his father's request. In the materials for the *Memoir*, Emily would write that Lionel 'passed well into the India Office'. Hallam omitted the 'well'. The fact was that Lionel entered without an examination, unlike his friend Richmond Ritchie (Anne Thackeray's cousin), who had been at Eton and Trinity with him and joined the India Office just a few months before Lionel did. Lionel was appointed to a junior clerkship in the Political Department of the India Office on 24 August 1877, though he did not actually start work until 8 October. 'Nominees' had a very different status from those who entered by examination at this time and Lionel's career, in spite of a good deal of grinding and a genuine interest in India, did not flourish. He never earned more than £250 a year. It was Richmond Ritchie who enjoyed the sort of career Emily had dreamed of for Lionel, ending up as Permanent Under-Secretary for India, knighted for his services to his country and the Empire.

On the day that Hallam had heard nothing about 'Inspectorships', there is a glimpse of the brothers in Regent Street. Edward Lear, just back from Italy, had gone out to get something from a stationer's when 'two big fellows rushed after me and one took me by the hand – they were *Hallam* and *Lionel* Tennyson!!' They had grown out of all recognition. They went back to Lear's rooms with him – 'very delightful lads evidently'. It made him think sadly of Farringford and the days that had gone, never to return. Soon after, on 7 July, he was at Aldworth, the trees much changed, like the boys, since his visit nearly eight years before. The view was still 'amazingly fine', and so too, to his delight, was Emily. He had expected her to be 'aged and altered' after her illness, but she appeared 'younger, and handsomer, and diviner than ever'. Even Tennyson seemed 'more genial than of old, though of course he had his growl about his publisher after dinner'. As he always did, Lear commemorated the evening with a sketch of the dinner-table placement. It had been his happiest evening for a long time – 'such is the fascination of this lot of intellectual coves'. Lear said they 'drank (as usual) too much wine – though not knowing at the time that I did so'. Emily had by then gone to bed. It was a pleasure 'to see her so well'.

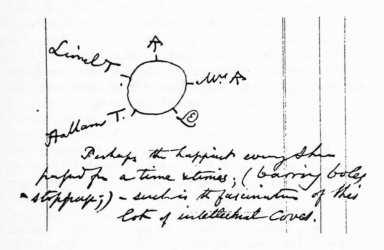

In May while at Freshwater Anne Thackeray had received a telegram from Richmond Ritchie saying he had got into the India Office and that they could be married. She went straight round to Farringford to tell Emily. The marriage of two close friends should be an occasion for undiluted joy, but there were inevitably some gasps and mixed feelings, for Anne was thirty-nine, seventeen years older than Richmond, and they were first cousins. Hallam said, 'C'est magnifique mais ce n'est pas le mariage.' Anne herself said that happiness 'has come like a sort of miracle.' The wedding was described by Richmond's sister Emily in a letter to Emily Tennyson. She noted the contrast between impressive Lionel, the best man, and 'Anny's supporters on her left', poor Leslie Stephen (her sad, 'deplorable' brother-in-law), and Julia Duckworth, Mrs Cameron's niece, who would marry Stephen not long afterwards, but was then still in mourning for her first husband.

Lionel wrote lively letters to his mother that October on his first experiences of employment. Emily had always been interested in India, since those far-off days when her uncle Sir Willingham Franklin and most of his family had died in Madras, leaving her cousin Kate an orphan. Over the years she had recorded her interest in her journal, and had followed Lear's journeys there as the guest of Lord Northbrook, the Viceroy, that 'amiable brick', as Lear called him.

Emily was particularly interested in the question of caste; she would point out to Lionel an account in *The Times* of a meeting in India where only one person present wished the system to continue. 'The highest class Brahmin said he would gladly give up all its privileges to have it abolished.'

On his first evening home from the India Office, Lionel wrote Emily just the sort of detailed letter she loved, though he said he was dealing with 'secret dispatches' and 'dreadful, awful mysteries' he would never be able to tell her about. The dealing with them mainly involved simply learning 'how to index them'. But he had, on that first day, communicated with the Governor of Bombay and edited a dispatch, sanctioning the draft with his initials. 'It promises very well altogether,' Lionel said of his new job, though he regretted 'he would not be able to get away until 2 on Saturdays.'

At first, his mother thought, Lionel 'devoted himself quite passionately to all studies likely to make him a better public servant.' He pored over a great map of India and studied Indian history. His intellectual energy was such that he would also learn Russian to add to the French, German and Italian he already had. But over the next few years his work failed to yield the rewards he had hoped. A great deal of it was immensely tedious and he was sometimes working to deadlines which meant long dreary days. He remained deeply interested in India itself.

There is plenty of evidence that Lionel possessed none of the feelings of racial superiority so common at the time. Palgrave would write: 'With the natives of India themselves he was popular and his house was always open to those who happened to be in England.' He joined the Northbrook Indian Club 'formed to promote intercourse between natives and English.' He would take Indian friends down to Aldworth. There must have been some occasions when Lionel arrived there alone on a Saturday, his tired mind full of Indian affairs, to find himself involved in one of those bibulous after-dinner conversations which had so often distressed Edward Lear. Any record Lionel himself may have made has been destroyed, but one of Mary Brotherton's revealing letters to Frederick Tennyson in 1879 gives an idea of the sort of thing Emily and her sons had to put up with from time to time.

Emily had not heard Tennyson's talk at Thomas Woolner's dinner party at the time of the Governor Eyre affair over ten years before. But she was almost certainly present at Farringford when Mary Brotherton challenged his unChristian views during the second Afghan War, a time when Tennyson was writing 'The Defence of Lucknow'.

Mrs Brotherton wrote:

He and I often have quarrels over public matters. I cannot approve his warlike spirit, and tendency of his poetry. It seems to me so far below the divine mission of a Great Poet to foster the sanguinary passions of men and to fall into the commonplace of dignifying patriotism as a first-class virtue – instead of part of the vanity and weakness of human nature . . . Your brother disdainfully asks if I would make war with rose-water; and declares that 300 barbarians (the Indian highlanders) had better be killed than 3 Englishmen . . . I say . . . unless war can be made with rosewater, that is brotherly and loving words and deeds, it is indefensible from a Christian point of view, and that I hold the 3 Englishmen more guilty of barbarity than the 300 barbarians, who 'know not what they do' in the bloody raids and revenges – rapine and treachery.

Although she would sometimes try to calm Tennyson down, Emily was never inclined to quarrel with him (or indeed with anyone else) and there had been times when she was happy enough to join him in stirring up feelings of national pride. She had set Tennyson's patriotic songs to music ('Who says that wars are over?'). But 'she was peace herself,' Jowett said. On her sofa, she spent a lot of time and mental energy on the problem of whether war was ever just, and in trying to imagine what Christ would have us do in any given situation. Mary Brotherton said she once heard an honest clergyman 'shout from a London pulpit: "They talk of Christianity as if it were established – *It has never been tried*".' Emily would echo that shout, would imagine a world where swords had been beaten into ploughshares. She was relieved when Tennyson wrote his epilogue 'To the Charge of the Heavy Brigade':

> And who loves War for War's own sake
> Is fool, or crazed, or worse;
> But let the patriot-soldier take
> His meed of fame in verse.

The early months of 1878, when the Tennysons took a London house in Eaton Square, were overshadowed by dire news of Charles and Louisa. Charles was extremely weak and ill; it was, he said, as if he had 'toothache all over the body'. Louisa was increasingly unstable. On 14 January Lionel wrote to Emily: 'Don't fret yourself, Mama. I dare say things aren't so bad as they appear.' He went down to Bristol where they were in lodgings (near Arthur Tennyson and his helpful wife Harriet) to sort out some of the problems. The doctor was very urgent about 'Louy going at once' into some sort of care. Charles was still able 'to write sonnets occasionally' and read; he was always 'so patient and gentle'. Louisa's self-loathing and despair simmered now closer to the surface and sometimes overflowed.

There was one further short period when Charles and Louisa lived together at Shanklin on the Isle of Wight, later that year, when they were 'under the care of Dr Dabbs', that very 'skilful man', in whom Emily had such faith. But in October 1878 Charles went to Cheltenham, where it was hoped his sister Mary's brother-in-law, Dr Ker, a homeopath, might be able to help him. Louisa was admitted to an asylum called Laverstock House in Wiltshire, 'by consent of the commissioners in lunacy'. She was sixty-one. The application had been signed by her nephew, Hallam Tennyson.

Her sister Emily wrote to her every two or three days, an endless loving stream of little bits of news that might cheer and divert her for a few minutes. She sent her wool and encouraged her to knit blankets and scarves. Her nephews visited her, but neither Alfred nor Emily ever did. From Aldworth, which seemed so far away, Emily wrote, 'If thou wert but at the top of this hill so that we might see thee every day, that would indeed be a comfort . . . Say every day to thyself for my sake "God is love".' 'Take all the nourishment thou canst and then the poor brain, which has been so long exhausted and overworked, will recover by degrees, please God, and become an honest servant to the soul. Remember Louy what a joy and blessing it would be to Charlie and to us to have thee well and try thy best to be.'

Emily tried to help Louisa ('my darling, my sweetie') by understanding that she had always tried to do 'what seemed to thee right', that there was no good reason for her 'self-accusation'. 'Who among the sons of men is worthy?' she wrote, protesting how little worthy she was herself. 'Forgive me for presuming to advise thee'. 'My darling, try to think always that our sins are blotted out. Try to forget those things that are behind and to reach forward to those which are before . . .' But for Louisa, childless, separated from her husband, lonely among strangers and deeply despondent, there was nothing to which she could look forward.

*

On 28 February 1878 Lionel Tennyson was married to Eleanor Locker in Westminster Abbey. It was the *place* that gave rise to almost the only harsh comments about Emily that anyone ever made in the course of her long life. Inevitably, such is our need for clay feet, it is these remarks that have been picked up and remain in some people's minds as the thing that they 'know' about the poet's wife, together with FitzGerald's suggestion that Alfred's poetry might have benefited if he had married a jolly woman without a thought in her head, or remained single in Lincolnshire with 'an old Housekeeper like Molière's.'

It was in his letters to Edward FitzGerald that Frederick Tennyson declared that the choice of the Abbey was an 'ambitious flight' of Emily's – so FitzGerald told his friends. 'He does not like her on that account,' FitzGerald said, adding that '*I* never saw any sign of it in her'. He reiterated this to Frederick himself and thought that Lionel 'may be a very good Fellow and his Match a very promising one, though inaugurated in Westminster Abbey. I remember your notion of Mrs AT's ambition: I had never noticed any symptom of it in her: but you say you have rather a "microscopic" Eye for Human Character'. Certainly Emily had no *personal* ambition, but she longed for the boys to make their mark in the world and she may indeed have thought that an Abbey wedding would start Lionel off on the right path. The really nasty remark came from young Alfred Tennyson, the jealous, hopelessly unsatisfactory son of Frederick, who – not knowing his aunt himself – had been well indoctrinated by his father. He wrote of 'the "great gun" at Farringford, whose wife desires to monopolise everything and to put every member of the family, save herself and hers, into the shade.'

The choice of Westminster Abbey was a perfectly natural one. The Dean – and the Dean was of course in charge of the place – was Arthur Stanley, Eleanor's uncle by his marriage to Lady Augusta Bruce, who had died just a short time before. Emily wrote that, as it happened, 'The dear Dean was ill and could not officiate, but he sent for the young bride and bridegroom to his room and talked lovingly, gave them his blessing, as a Father to them ... In after years he said that one of his great pleasures was to spend an afternoon with them and their little ones in Sussex Place.' Dean Stanley was part of the family. When he eventually died, it was a relief that his replacement was Granville Bradley, so that the Deanery at Westminster always remained to the Tennysons a place where they felt at home.

The marriage service was actually taken by Canon Farrar (later Dean of Canterbury) who had been Hallam's headmaster briefly at Marlborough after Granville Bradley had gone on to Oxford. Farrar described what was almost a disaster, how nearly Emily came to missing the entire ceremony:

As the throng was very large, the Dean arranged that places should be reserved to the Poet Laureate, Mrs Tennyson, and their son Hallam . . . and that they should come in at the last moment by the little side-door in the north transept of the nave – a door which is scarcely ever used . . . The door was to have been left unfastened for the entrance of Mr and Mrs Tennyson, but by some accident this had been overlooked. The bride and bridegroom, the best-man, the bridesmaids, were all standing ready; the choir was densely thronged. I did not see the father, mother, and brother of the bridegroom; but they might be easily overlooked in such a multitude, and I naturally assumed that they were present. The service began, and it was only when I came to the sentence, 'I pronounce that they be man and wife together,' that I noticed the Tennysons entering the choir. Finding the door locked by which they were to have been admitted, they were under great difficulties, since it is not easy for strangers to find their way about the Precincts. They came, I suppose, through the Deanery, round by Dean's yard, and so by the Abbot's private entrance; and I was particularly glad that they came in just in time to hear the blessings pronounced upon the wedded pair. Mrs Tennyson was a great invalid; and it was a touching sight to see her enter, supported by the Poet Laureate and her son, upon whose arms she leaned.

Mary Gladstone, who was seeing a good deal of Hallam ('tongues wagged,' she wrote in her diary two days before), said that, 'Mrs Tennyson came in late, half carried by Hallam'. This was hardly surprising after the worrying rush across unknown territory. Mary Gladstone also commented 'many bigwigs there'. There were indeed. Tennyson in the dim light failed to recognize George Eliot. The only witnesses who signed the register besides the parents were Browning, the Duke of Argyll and Gladstone. Alfred Domett wrote in his diary: 'Tennyson had chosen them, I suppose (though Browning did not of course say so), as it was pleasant to leave on the register on such an occasion, the names of the most famous poet, next himself, the most literary and perhaps most talented member of the House of Lords and the celebrated Prime Minister.' It was just as well the 'great gun's' disgruntled namesake nephew did not see the register.

Agnes Weld wrote an account of the wedding to her uncle Charles, still in Bristol at this stage, and asked him to pass it on to his sister-in-law 'Mrs Arthur'. Lionel, she said, wore 'a bunch of violets in his button-hole that was thrown into the carriage by a poor man, quite a stranger to him. He prizes such things,' she said, knowing Lionel, and how little he was likely to be seduced by 'society'. His choice of Henry Cameron as best man confirmed this. 'Aunt Emmie did not go to the breakfast but bore up wonderfully' during that part of the service she did not miss. It was just as well Emily had decided not to try to go to the breakfast. It was such a crush, Agnes said, that neither Uncle Alfred 'nor ourselves nor the Lushingtons and Tilly could get in until after the speeches were over.' In fact the whole thing was a shambles; Alfred was not likely to change his feeling that that quiet wedding in the village on the Thames twenty-eight years before was the nicest one he had ever attended. ('We want to go to Shiplake but we don't know where it is,' Lionel would write that spring.)

The 'fantastic and ridiculous' Sabine Greville (the description is from Henry James) leaves a happier image of the day. 'What *most* impressed, was your Mother's saint-like grace and more than pathetic beauty. I always have said that she is the most graceful Angel out of Heaven – and perfectly dressed . . . Naturally Lionel and Eleanor looked like the Prince and Princess in a fairy tale.' George Gissing, deliberately there to catch a glimpse of 'no less a person than *Alfred Tennyson*', said how 'unmistakable' the poet was. 'I knew him in a moment. He wore precisely the same cape-coat which you see in his portraits. His son was remarkably like him.'

Dean Farrar, writing about the occasion years later, called Lionel 'the Poet Laureate's brilliant son', but there was not much call for brilliance as a clerk in the India Office and life was already beginning to conspire against him. The honeymoon seems to have been a testing time as honeymoons often used to be. Eleanor conceived immediately ('A honeymoon child' Emily would call her grandson when he arrived nine months later). Eleanor spent a great deal of the six weeks they were away feeling ill. The weather was often 'damned'. The English were 'a great bore in Seville'. There were inferior meals, including a dreadful dish which resembled 'fledged tadpoles or untimely ducklings'.

It was a relief for Lionel to see James Russell Lowell in Madrid and have some interesting talk about Calderón, Spanish drama having become one of his special interests. Eleanor wrote of being shut up in hotel rooms – finding a mouse in their bed one night – of reading

French and Spanish novels and 'quarrelling'. To *say* you are quarrelling is at once to defuse the situation but it seems rather an odd joke to tell your new husband's family that 'Lionel has fallen dreadfully in love with a Miss Bard, an American young lady, daughter of a friend of the Fields and to whom they very imprudently gave us an introduction.' Lionel and Eleanor had always joked in their letters about 'flirtations'. 'Choose a more worthy object,' Lionel had once written from Paris. They were a very unconventional 'modern' young couple; the joking only sounds ominous in the light of the way that things went. Years later Caroline Jebb would say of Eleanor: 'She used to flirt tremendously . . . When she and Lionel stayed with us, she did exactly what she pleased, and he went his own way.'

There was a muddle on their return to England in April. Emily wrote: 'They were later in returning than they expected and the term for which we had taken the house expired so that our two trains drew up' – perhaps at Basingstoke – 'on opposite platforms, but a kind guard procured us the sight of him.' She does not mention Eleanor, though she would now ask her to call her 'Mama'.

'Dearest Mama', Eleanor wrote in June from their temporary home – Thames Bank House, Mortlake. 'It is only difficult to begin calling you this, because I went on for so long calling you "Mrs Tennyson" that I kept falling back into it, but now "Mrs Tennyson" is banished for good and all.' There would come a time when she could no longer call her 'Mama' though she remained devoted to her, however unwelcome Emily's intense interest in her family's lives could sometimes be.

Was it partly because she knew how much Tennyson himself needed so often to be left alone to his thoughts, which *might* come to poems, that Emily found it so difficult, though aware of the dangers, not to involve herself so deeply in her sons' lives? She could not let them go. That intense interest which had sustained them as boys at school, and which had never seemed to bother them at Cambridge, must now at times have seemed oppressive. 'I shall remember all I do each day to tell you,' Eleanor said kindly – while protesting that it was impossible to put it all in a letter. But there was no doubt that Eleanor and Lionel needed her. They were always short of money and welcomed hampers of food – chickens and ducks and vegetables – even if Eleanor often forgot to return the hampers themselves until Emily reminded her. 'Lionel is satisfied with the plainest dinners,' Eleanor told Emily, not wanting to sound extravagant, but assuring her that he always had a good break-fast, and not only porridge, before he went off to the office in the morning. They welcomed Lionel's Cambridge towels and cutlery 'which would do beautifully for the nursery' and furniture from the Terrace, now apparently sold, for the house they would rent in Sussex Place, Regent's Park that summer. (In 1881 they needed financial help with buying the lease.) They even needed the loan of Andrews, the Tennysons' housekeeper, to help them through the problems of moving. Eleanor would stay with Emily at Aldworth that September when Tennyson was in Ireland with his sons.

The two women sorted out the family baby clothes. Emily told Louisa:

We are having Hallam's and Lionel's christening robe washed for the new Lionel or Lionella, but I am so greedy over it that I only lend it. The rest of the things I have divided having given some to Eleanor, kept some for Hallam's Eleanor – whoever she may be. He seems in no hurry to choose her and we cannot be very sorry that he is not, dear old darling, tho' God forbid we should stand in the way of his marrying when he does wish it.

These were years of disappointment for Hallam. He had passed his Roman law and eaten a great many Temple dinners. He was now 'read-ing English law' but really 'law is not to his taste as it appears in law books, however reverently he regards it in practice'. What was he going to do with his life? He must – it would have been only natural – have been a little jealous of Lionel with his lively wife, his fine house at Regent's Park, his career (which still, at this point, seemed promising) and, on 20 November 1878, his first-born son.

The first grandson was called Alfred Browning Stanley Tennyson, with the names of his two godfathers, the poet and the dean, sand-wiched between the names of his grandfather. Emily thought that 'the poor little laddy has a heavy burden of names imposed on him'. 'Stanley has been a very kind friend and relative and Browning, I pro-nounce, the most brotherly of poets. He takes such hearty pleasure in Ally's fame, I do believe, and has never shown one touch of jealousy,' Emily wrote to Edward Lear. The godmothers were Janie Locker (Eleanor's stepmother – a very tactful gesture) and Agnes Weld. 'Rather an odd mixture of sponsors,' Emily thought, 'each as unlike to the other as can well be imagined, tho' all very good in their way.' Lionel had first suggested his son should be called Wilfrid, because they liked it, 'being honest and Saxon'; '"Alfred" is Hallam's birthright.' Perhaps Hallam himself, wondering whether he ever would have a son, encouraged them to use it.

Emily described her grandson to her sister Anne in Freshwater, who told Mary Brotherton, who reported it to Frederick: 'Of course there never was a baby before – to signify – and there are daily reports of its habits and manners from Grandmama to the Welds. It has, I hear, Lionel's nails, its mother's eyebrows, very large hands, feet and appetite.' Eleanor was not able to feed the baby herself which gave Lionel every chance to be a 'new man'. His aunt Tilly would confirm this view of him, writing to Emily after a visit to Sussex Place when she had found Lionel alone: 'Lionel was so kind; he is as good as a lady in the house'. Emily must have smiled, remembering the little boys and the tea towels at Greyshott and how she had trained them. Lionel had always been good with children (Horatio's, for instance), but he had not had much experience with babies. All the same Eleanor reported: 'Lionel nurses Alfred as if he had been brought up to it and gives him his bottle in such a masterly manner that even the nurse approves.' 'I wish you could see Lionel feeding baby and baby sucking away and grunting with satisfaction.'

Eleanor had hoped Emily would get to Sussex Place, but she went straight from Aldworth to Farringford that December and was ready with 'bassinette' and extra milk ('a pint and a half of milk in the morning and the same in the evening') to welcome the child on Boxing Day. It gladdened Emily's heart 'to see such a happy three'. The baby was five weeks old and 'excessively wide awake'. 'The two things he won't stand are being kept waiting an instant for his food' – an instant beyond the proper three hours apparently – 'and being laid in his Bassinette awake – he roars then so as to be heard all over the house'. He was, in fact, a perfectly normal baby.

This was the 'golden-haired Ally' his grandfather would celebrate:

Gold-head curlyhead little grandson of mine.
Shall the name in the front of my book be thine

What will come to the earth in the days that are thine?
What will come to thee too, little Grandson of mine!

A later version would become the dedication to *Ballads and other poems*, when he was eighteen months old. Tennyson had just finished his new play *Becket* and was 'extremely cheerful' on the child's first visit to Farringford, but he could not help fearing, even as he enjoyed him, what lay in store for his grandson as he sketched these lines. Tennyson hoped his name would never be, as Emily feared, a heavy burden for the boy to bear. 'Mayst thou never be harmed by this name of mine.'

Edward Lear wrote from the Villa Emily in San Remo:

I am immensely pleased by hearing from Frank that you are a grandmother and AT a grandfather and moreover I believe the event will very probably do your health good, by giving you one more interest in life. The next thing I hope to hear is that Hallam has followed his brother's example in marrying . . .. My ancient cat Foss is not a bad companion.

Lear ended: 'I shall stop, as the un-wound-up watch said to his self. Believe me, O glorious grandmama, yours affectionately . . .' Replying, a little late, Emily asked him to make allowance 'for the infirmities of the Grandmother – poor old thing!' It was a role she would enjoy for the rest of her life.

In January 1879 'dear old Julia Cameron' (as Tennyson would think of her) died far away in Ceylon where she had travelled – with her own coffin – in 1875. She had been back in England briefly the year before, but they had already accepted she had gone from their lives, which diminished the pain. 'We shall never see her like again,' Lionel wrote to her son, Henry. Mary Brotherton thought 'the whole world feels the colder and darker for her leaving it'. Surely Emily must have remembered Julia as she had seen her in 1862 coming 'across the Park looking gorgeous in her violet dress and red cloak, walking over the newly mown grass' and acknowledging the cheers of the working men. Other people wrote of her ugliness; Emily never did. She was 'so loving and strong in her woman's way and so childlike in her faith'.

Just at this moment, Charles Tennyson Turner in Cheltenham wrote to his wife, Louisa, a tiny painful letter in response to her long agonized screeds.

God bless you. Look to Christ alone, not to your sins. I am, the Dr. says, getting better.

Louisa continued to brood on her sins in spite of the letters from Charles and Emily which attempted to sustain her. Marooned in the asylum near Salisbury, knitting an endless scarf for Hallam Tennyson, she saw this final separation (repeating the long separation at the beginning of their marriage) as a just punishment. She had written to a friend:

Now another, a sister, has to minister to him, not because I am not strong enough, but from the depths of my iniquity; the corruption of a long life of sowing to the flesh ... Latterly I have become so much worse that I have no trace of what a Christian ought to have or to be – I could never, for one moment, have conceived the things I have said thought done felt towards God, myself, my neighbour this last year or more ... So many took my strugglings to be real sanctity. To return to poor Charles ... I grieve to say he came to me in Shanklin as sea air was recommended. I did not tell him how much worse I had become whilst I had been there – my horrible ways there shocked his nerves so that his old pain returned and he grew worse. For his life's sake I was obliged to ask the doctor to remove me once more from him ... The help you so kindly thought I was to him I am not but am here in the *most awful* condition yet not feeling it.

Emily must have received dozens of letters from Louisa on this theme; the only consolation was that she said she was 'not feeling it'. But Charles was not, as he thought, getting better. There was some sort of seizure and on 25 April 1879 he was dead. Emily sent from Farringford 'a box of primroses and forget-me-nots' she 'knew he would have liked'. 'How gloriously Mary did her duty by him,' Arthur Tennyson wrote to their brother Frederick. She had been with him through those last months in Cheltenham, the sister to whom he had been closest long ago in Somersby. Charles was buried beside Septimus. Emily wrote to the widowed Louisa, feeling both the pain and the joy, the sorrow and the relief:

Thy beloved one has gone to the rest he so much desired and thou wilt joyfully follow him in God's own good time.

Three days later (can she *really* have meant it?) Emily wrote:

Thou hast been ever a perfect sister to me and let it not be forgotten that that true loving simple Christian soul ... called thee his 'Guardian Angel' and that to thee has been granted this exceeding blessing that through thy help he came out of a state, brought on chiefly by illness, from which scarcely any other human being has been known to be freed into that state of patience and faith and love and hope which has been an example and a delight for all.

This was a clear acknowledgment that she felt Louisa had saved Charles from his addiction to opium, though there had certainly been times when Emily had felt that Louisa and their incompatibility (sexual? religious? both?) had exacerbated rather than alleviated his problems.

For her birthday – her sixty-third – Alfred wrote to Louisa probably the only letter (no more than a note) he ever wrote to her, adding it to one of Emily's.

Keep your heart up, my dear. He is waiting for you yonder. I send you a brother's kiss.

Did Louisa have the chance to read it? She died that day, on 20 May 1879, less than a month after Charles, following him where sorrow and sighing flee away.

Emily, who had always loved her motherless, childless younger sister, through all the madness, the sadness, the accusations (so well suppressed for so many years), must have felt that Tennyson spoke for her own separate, different grief, as he mourned his brother in that grey summer:

> And through this midnight breaks the sun
> Of sixty years away,
> The light of days when life begun,
> The days that seem today . . .

Anne Thackeray Ritchie wrote to Emily on 27 May.

I was dreaming of you all last night, and I feel as if I must tell you how I think of you, and send you my faithful love. Richmond told me the sad peaceful news as we were starting. Your sorrows and your realities seem only to make me know more and more how much I owe you, and how much my life seems to belong to you and yours.

The Ritchies were seeing a great deal of Lionel and Eleanor at this time. Richmond had been their first guest at Mortlake; Anne was the first to see the baby Alfred, apart from the Lockers. Their children would play together; the adults dine together. But at the India Office the relationship of the two men was difficult.

*

534

The burden of sorting out Charles and Louisa's estate fell mainly on Franklin Lushington, that stalwart lawyer who was the Turners' trustee. Frank wrote to Hallam about 'an old Japanese writing table of your aunt Louy's in the drawing-room, with a locked drawer ... Had I better get it picked and the papers and contents made into a parcel and sent direct to you or your mother at Aldworth?' These are the Turner papers that survive at Lincoln. Did Emily open the parcel, attempt to read those cryptic unconnected words and pile them away in a cupboard, unread because they are almost unreadable? Surely if Hallam or Emily *had* read them, they would have been destroyed. Surviving, they help to make us realize how fortunate Emily, that eldest sister, must have felt in her own marriage, knowing how entirely different had been the experience of both Anne and Louisa, fond as Emily herself had been of both her brothers-in-law, Charles Weld and Charles Turner.

'Blessed as I am in my Ally and our boys, none can be to me exactly what thou art' – Emily had written to Louisa – the clearest indication that Anne, since they had seen so much of each other at Freshwater, had become rather *less* close to her over the years. Once, delaying their return to Farringford one early winter, because Tennyson's Aldworth study was so much less draughty, Emily had said she did not think Anne and Agnes would miss them, having so many other friends now on the Island. The following winter the Welds would take off for the Holy Land and Cairo where Agnes would become engaged to a clergyman – an engagement that ended in tears, not a wedding. By 1886 the Welds had moved to Oxford ('much more congenial to their tastes') and it would only be after Anne's death that Emily would resume a really close relationship with her only niece.

Agnes inherited some of Louisa's money, and gave a great deal of it away, believing that Christianity really was something to be practised not preached – and constantly reminding her beloved aunt of the way Christ asks us to live. The Turner money caused some dissension in the family, as money so often does. Harriet Tennyson, Arthur's wife, felt Charles should have left his money ('as we have such hard work to get on') to Arthur, Horatio and Tilly. 'He has left a little more to Horatio which I am so glad of.' 'It's not needed by half the family,' Harriet said. One person who benefited, who was very glad of it, was Lionel, with his miserable clerk's salary at the India Office, which had always needed to be supplemented by his parents as well as Eleanor's own money. There is an interesting letter from Eleanor to Emily, showing how much she was needed as a calming intermediary, even between the two loving brothers. Hallam, worried about the next generation's education, wanted the Turner money to go directly into an 'Education Fund'. Lionel, Eleanor explained to Emily, did not want the money paid straight away in the children's name and 'not subject to his own control.' It was by then 1881 and golden-haired Ally had been joined by his brother Charlie.

Charles Bruce Locker Tennyson (the names Frederick and Turner were both considered) was born on 8 November 1879, when 'the veteran baby', not quite a year old, was 'still without available legs of his own'. Hallam took little Alfred down to his grandparents on the day that Charles arrived and he was returned after a month 'in most splendid condition'. Eleanor told Emily that Alfred stroked his new brother's 'head so gently'. The two boys would grow up together as inseparable and devoted as their father and his brother had been. The whole family was at Farringford at Christmas and, when their parents returned to London fog, they left the babies there with their nurses in the good sea air.

In the six quiet years between Lionel's marriage and Hallam's, the grandchildren, 'our little boys', became Emily's great interest, as Lear had predicted; she seemed to thrive on their presence. They would be with their grandparents for weeks on end. Over and over again Eleanor had reason to write: 'A thousand thousand thanks' for being so good to the children, for taking such great care of them. If it should be thought that Emily was simply lying on a sofa and reading them a quiet story, there is plenty of evidence to the contrary. 'Don't write too much and tire yourself about the children, Mama,' Eleanor would have to write. Emily would help to feed and dress them and drive out with them. She would play the piano to them, including her settings of Tennyson's old 'Child Songs', which would appear in the American children's magazine *St Nicholas* just at this time.

In February 1880, Eleanor was distressed to learn from Jane, the boys' nurse, that Emily had had a fall 'running after Alfred', who, at fifteen months, had just begun to run himself. On another occasion – was she really sitting on a wall? – Lionel told her, 'You really must take care, Mama. Humpty Dumpty is an example not worthy of imitation.' The children were the delight of their grandfather, too; he was reported to be 'more easy and softened than of old'. He had always been good with children; now he blew bubbles for his grandsons and would also drive out with them in the carriage. William Allingham told the story of being collected by Tennyson, calmly wearing his grandson's tiny straw hat, while, beside him, the three-year-old was proudly swamped by the poet's huge sombrero. It was the day Helen Allingham sketched Don, 'the handsome old setter'. Later she would draw Emily too.

When they were at home, Eleanor told Emily, Lionel and the boys were such allies that she felt quite out of it. But there was never any sexual stereotyping in the house. Eleanor bought Charlie, with his birthday money, 'a wee wax baby in a cradle which is kept in tremendous order by Alfred.' She was saving up to buy a rocking horse. For his fourth birthday Charlie bought himself 'a perambulator for his two dolls, which has made him completely blissful.' Alfred's ritual every morning was to climb into his parents' bed and brush their hair 'with his own little hairbrush'. Eleanor said to Emily: 'I believe he thinks we wouldn't get through the day unless this ceremony is duly performed.' Alfred would ride down to breakfast on his father's shoulders and Lionel would rush back from the office whenever he could in time for nursery tea.

Lionel and Eleanor were both reviewing books for James Knowles, who had moved on a long way from being the Tennysons' attentive architect and was now the powerful editor of the *Nineteenth Century*. Eleanor wrote: 'I never dreamt of your not knowing about the reviewing for Knowles. I do the novels and Lionel poetry and all sorts.' Tennyson was worried that Lionel 'will draw down enemies upon him and do no good to his career.' But Eleanor assured Emily that 'Lionel will only be one of half a dozen, so he cannot well make enemies . . . In any case Knowles's theory is to ignore unworthy books and not to abuse them.'

One of Eleanor's neighbours – she knew Emily would be interested – was a Miss Harrison, living alone. She had taken 'a 1st class at Cambridge', was writing a book on archaeology, takes people round the British Museum and 'teaches Working Men and Women in the College.' Jane Harrison, already a remarkable woman, was one of the audience when, in December 1880, 'Mrs Lionel Tennyson's Private Theatricals' took place in a little theatre which cost only £4 a night, 'including scenery, gas, attendance and stage managing' and avoided 'the whole nuisance of turning the house upside down'. There were two performances and the actors included Eleanor herself as well, of course, as Lionel and Henry Cameron, with more professional ambitions still lingering in their hearts. Lionel was having singing lessons and his voice was much praised. Depressed by his failure to gain promotion, to secure a secretaryship, Lionel was putting more and more energy into his activities outside the India Office.

Emily provided an endlessly sympathetic ear for Eleanor's constant problems with the servants. They were always leaving, for one reason or another – the work was too heavy or they were getting married or they were found helping themselves to something that was not theirs. One cook had only been there two days and 'her Mother is dying at Brighton'. Emily would often provide not just sympathy, but temporary assistance from her own staff. She was also always ready to have the children to stay at Aldworth or at Farringford. Little Alfred, not yet two in the summer of 1880, was thought to have admirable manners; he would never pass a gardener or another servant without saying, 'Morning!'

The following summer, Mary Brotherton, seeing the 'two sweet little boys' at Farringford, reported to their great-uncle Frederick that the elder was 'a noble child, whose protecting love for his little flaxen brother is very pretty to see.' 'They are very dear little fellows', Emily told Lear in 1881, when they had been with her for two months. 'Very affectionate and obedient and full of fun.' She wished Lear might see them and be 'as good to them as you used to be to their father and uncle.' Emily must often have felt happily that history was repeating itself as she watched the two little boys. The problems and the heartache would come with the third brother, Michael, born in December 1883 when Alfred was five and Charlie four – the year of Emily's own seventieth birthday.

Before that, there are from time to time glimpses of Emily in London, in one of the houses the Tennysons rented for a couple of months in the late winters of these years. People who did not know Emily – Henry James, for instance, and Thomas Hardy – might find her extremely pale and frail. She might cough and lose her voice, and walk very little, but she was a good deal better than she had been. She did find the regular journeys between Farringford and Aldworth and London something of a strain and was content to avoid any other travelling. But in December 1880 she told her cousin Kate Rawnsley that she had borne the journey from Aldworth to Farringford better than any 'since my illness began'.

Henry James tells the story of arriving for lunch in Eaton Place, at the house the Tennysons were renting from the widowed Lady Simeon, and meeting on the doorstep his compatriot the diplomat and poet James Russell Lowell. They found 'Mrs Tennyson's luncheon table an open feast' with places available for any number of guests who might or might not turn up. Emily suggested Lowell should sit at the far end, where Tennyson would eventually arrive, as indeed he did. Henry James and Emily, separated from the two poets by 'an unpeopled waste', were both more interested in the poets' conversation than in their own. It murmured on until the moment when Tennyson growled, 'Do you know anything about *Lowell*?' At which point Emily interrupted anxiously, from the other end of the table, 'Why, my dear, this *is* Mr Lowell!'

It was also at this period that Thomas Hardy made his chilling remark that Emily was, on his arrival, 'lying as if in a coffin', although she got up to welcome him. Did she look so deathly pale? He never saw her again and regretted that he had never taken up their warm invitation to visit them at Freshwater. They were giving out these invitations again and life was very much as it had been – except that Hallam was now attending to all the routine mail. Emily was still deeply concerned with what Alfred was writing or not writing. She would tell Kate Rawnsley she hoped they would keep a lookout for 'any stories that will do for Poems'. She was worried by all the research involved in the plays – *Harold*, *Becket* and so on. They 'require much reading,' which was not good for Tennyson's weak eyes.

When Hallam and Tennyson were away in Germany and Italy in the summer of 1880, Hallam chided Emily for her return to her old habits. She was 'slaving away at the accounts', and writing to them every day on their travels. Tennyson never wrote to her now, but Hallam would pass on messages: 'Papa sends his love and says you are to get out every fine day and whirl about the island as much as you can and not overdo yourself.' Hallam considered Emily was writing far too much. He had begun to feel that some matters were best left to him. He told her not to answer letters from anywhere, especially not from Glasgow: 'They know we are away.' Tennyson had become embarrassed by his nomination as Rector of Glasgow University. There had been a misunderstanding. It was Emily who wrote to Edmund Lushington, who as Professor of Greek at Glasgow had been deeply involved, on this as on previous occasions, in hoping to lure Tennyson to honour his university. Alfred had a right, Emily said, 'to make his own conditions and has also a right to withdraw, they not having been observed.' Tennyson had found to his horror that he had been nominated by the university Conservative Club and Emily said he had spent a lifetime refusing to range himself with either political party. (Surely he *had* supported the Liberal John Simeon, but perhaps only secretly.) Emily ended her letter to Lushington 'with kindest love and a hope that you will see Ally is in no way to blame.' That was always her dearest wish.

It would have been particularly difficult at this point for Tennyson to have had the support of a Conservative Club, however conservative some of his views might be. This was the period (before Gladstone's commitment in 1885 to Irish Home Rule, which would split his party) of the Tennysons' increasing friendship with the Gladstones. In fact, the year before, Hallam Tennyson had fallen in love with Mary Gladstone. The evidence is clear. Though Hallam destroyed all Mary's letters to him, only a few of his to her have disappeared and, with the help of her diary (obliquely phrased as it is), it is not too difficult to piece together the story from the Gladstone papers in the British Library. What seems certain is that the Tennysons approved of the relationship and that they harboured a hope that these devoted offspring would unite the families of the 'two greatest living Englishmen'.

Mary, the fifth of Gladstone's eight children, was a striking, clever girl with fluffy hair and a fair skin. With her strong faith, her music, her devotion to her parents and her father's work, her liveliness and un-conventionality and her unfashionable clothes, Mary was just the sort of girl to appeal to Emily. It would be hard for Emily to believe that Mary did not love Hallam, so entirely lovable did Emily think her son. Emily would never have written in her diary the sort of thing Mary wrote in hers, but she would certainly have sympathized with her dis-like of the 'ceaseless chaff and chatter' she found in London. Mary wrote: 'London society gives me such a dreadful uncomfortable feeling of superiority and I like being humbled so much better, as I am every day by the poorer and simpler lives I live among.'

The extraordinary account in Mary's diary of her visit to Farringford in June 1879 has been used to illustrate Tennyson's curious and some-times embarrassing behaviour with young women, when the emotion in the account has in reality far more to do with Hallam than with his father.

'Farringford did me one good turn,' Mary wrote. 'It was a test and it showed me more clearly the real nature of what I felt . . .' The visit, which seems to have been expressly designed to give Hallam the opportunity to propose, ended in Hallam's despair, and Mary's anguish. Mary had been invited with her friend Maggie Warren. It seems Mary must have had some idea of what was in store for her. She was nervous enough on the crossing from Lymington and was alarmed to see Hallam waiting on the pier. 'We had counted on the quiet drive for gathering ourselves together.' Through a week of summer pleasures – of walking on the Downs ('looking sheer down gleaming cliffs into the green blue waves below, the wind all scented with gorse, and seagulls floating majestically in the sunny air'), of 'jumping' into the sea, feeling 'glowing and delicious and salt', of driving through the 'loveliest lanes' and sitting reading Henry James in the 'peaceful-birdsinging-green-garden' – Emily is only mentioned twice in Mary's diary. Her sofa in the drawing room, with the lovely view through a frame of green branches, seemed to Mary 'ungracefully placed' – but when Mary found some of Tennyson's talk 'daunting' and hard to take, it was Mrs Tennyson who said, 'It is a Palace of Truth'. He is not teasing, he is not flirting; he means what he says when he calls your eyes 'wonderful' and your face 'remarkable'. Hallam had to hold up a rug to shield Mary's blushing face from his father's appreciative gaze. 'Hallam has a great respect for that young woman,' Tennyson said to Maggie Warren.

On Monday 9 June, when Maggie had been dispatched elsewhere, Hallam took Mary out on her own in a dogcart. They walked along the sands and were cut off by the tide and had to climb a steep cliff. It must have been sitting there, 'entranced with the panorama', the Needles across the brilliant silver water and, ahead, the distant view of Hampshire, that Hallam told her how much he loved her, and she told him that she loved him only as a friend. 'The sun withdrew from the Island, leaving us in shadow and chilly wind.' They both had 'unspeakably wretched' nights. They had breakfast alone together and he gave her a letter and an account of the dream he had dreamt. In the garden that morning with both father and son, Mary listened to Hallam reading Plato and saw him weeping at the death of Socrates, and not only at that. Tennyson called her a 'hard little thing' for not weeping too. When she left, he gave her a copy of *The Lover's Tale*, the poem he had written as a boy, which had just been published. 'Coals of fire', Mary wrote in her diary. 'Everything around was too beautiful for words. Yet never was anything so like a funeral and worse ... Such is life. Oh dear.'

That they salvaged a deep and continuing friendship from this crisis seems a credit to them both. A year later, on 9 June 1880, Mary noted in her diary: 'An anniversary. Received a MS poem of Tennyson's in memory. A beautiful thing . . .' Their friendship sustained them through the difficult years until they eventually both married other people – Hallam not for another five years and Mary not until nearly two years later than that. When she was already thirty-eight she married the curate at Hawarden, Harry Drew, a marriage that would allow her to continue with her role as secretary to her parents – for she, like Hallam, had become indispensable at home. 'What will your parents do without you?' Emily would ask. 'But . . . they will be happy in your happiness.'

That both Mary and Hallam kept quiet about what had really happened on that summer Monday is suggested by a letter Lionel wrote home ten days later, saying he had seen 'Mary the fascinating'. 'She seems to have enjoyed Farringford muchly; Mr Palgrave says he never met anyone who enjoyed anything so much before' – proving yet again that one should not believe everything one reads. But I think Hallam confided in his mother; he always had, and his intimate unsigned letters to Mary in the years until his marriage nearly always include 'my mother's love'. Fearing that Mary was overworking, he once told her: 'Do, do remember my mother and take warning.'

In March 1881, when the Tennysons were at 9 Upper Belgrave Street, Hallam gave Mary reasons 'why you should come in as often as possible'. They include:

1) Because my father and mother like to have you and are disappointed that you do not drop in as you used to do . . .
2) Because it is good for you. Your life ought *not* to be *all* politics . . .
3) Because it is really good for me . . . You said 'Let us be real friends.' My answer was 'Yes – trust me.'

Mary's own advice on marriage accorded with that of Hallam's parents: that he should actively look for someone and, above all, that he should marry for love and not for money. He assured her he was looking for 'the most unworldly and penniless lady that I can find.' It was in August 1883 that Hallam, writing to Mary Gladstone, first mentioned Audrey Boyle, the niece of lively Mary Boyle, who had got to know his parents the year before. 'You would like her,' he said. He signed off the letter, after his mother's love, with his name – unusually – as if he knew that their long intimacy was coming to an end but he hoped their friendship would continue. 'Throughout life we must *always* be true to one another and try to help one another – because you say that I help you and I know that your sisterly affection . . . helps to purify me and make me a better man.'

Mary showed 'sisterly affection' for Lionel too. She loved 'his extra-ordinarily bright delicious smile' and the way 'it flashes so suddenly into his odd, lank, languid, absent face' – the languid face of so many photographs, which one realizes must always have been far more at-tractive than the photographs suggest – even now when he was becom-ing more and more like his father, with 'an untidy appearance, a black beard and no manners,' as his friend Margot Tennant put it. Mary found herself involved in trying to help the careers of both the Tennyson brothers. The whole question of what her sons were going to do with their lives was Emily's main concern at this period. Tennyson was now over seventy. He had critics, certainly, but his influence and immortality (on earth and in heaven) seemed permanently assured and he was still writing.

Did their father's fame make life easier or more difficult for Hallam and Lionel? In 1881 Emily was beginning to feel strongly that it was time Hallam 'should have a career of his own'. It seems he had finally given up the Bar, though he would certainly continue to describe him-self as a student of the Inner Temple. In the *Memoir*, Hallam would write, describing how he had spent so many years as his father's sec-retary, 'Yet he would willingly have set me free for a more definite career; and at one time he consulted Mr Gladstone as to my taking up a political life.' The trouble was no-one seemed to want his services. In December 1881 Emily wrote to Gladstone that she had heard there was 'likely to be a vacancy among your secretaries'. She said she knew he knew 'a little of all that Hallam has been to his Father and myself'. If Gladstone would take him on, 'we should thankfully give him up to you and take a secretary ourselves, being very sure that he would loy-ally and zealously serve you to the best of his ability.' Emily's use here of 'ourselves' is typical. She would still see herself as deeply involved in all Tennyson's affairs and not only the running of the households. *She* needed secretarial assistance, just as much as Tennyson himself did. It is typical that when Hallam writes to Tennyson's new publisher Macmil-lan about the new seven-volume edition, which eventually came out in

1884, he says: 'My father and mother would like as big a print as you can allow ... They think that the Author's edition print is too small and faint ...'

Gladstone was extremely fond of the Tennysons. 'Among the things I covet most is the desire to see more of you and your husband,' he had written that March, wishing the cares of office did not make that impossible, but he did not need a secretary when Emily wrote in December 1881. In any case, it would hardly be a long-term appointment if he did find he had a vacancy; and he was 'rather a ferocious master'. Should they not consider other possible openings? Lionel's own experience just at this moment was demonstrating what a thorny path they were considering for Hallam. Lionel had become more and more disillusioned with the India Office. He was convinced that sarcasm was what you need to get on in the Civil Service. It was not a quality he valued. Devoted theatregoer that he was himself, his opinion of his fellow workers seems to be summed up by his comment that *even* the people from the India Office had gone to see *The Cup*, Tennyson's new play at the Lyceum starring Ellen Terry and Henry Irving.

Emily herself did not see any of Tennyson's plays, but there is a glimpse of her at dinner the night Tennyson went to *The Cup* with Hallam and young Albert Baillie, the sixteen-year-old son of Eleanor's Aunt Fanny (who had been Lady Frances Bruce). Baillie described 'gentle' Emily and Hallam in one of their most frequent roles as pacifiers and encouragers of the poet, trying to divert him from his growls about his publishers. Baillie also described Tennyson's behaviour at the play. It was no wonder Emily preferred to stay at home.

He drew the curtains of the box around him, fussing about not wanting to be seen, and then behaved in a way to draw the utmost measure of attention to the box. He thundered applause when there was silence, and was silent when there was applause. It was an awful evening.

There was an even worse one to follow when *The Promise of May* was produced late in 1882 and a brutal gallery and pit jeered and hissed and laughed in all the wrong places. It was particularly painful for Eleanor who was sitting with Mr and Mrs Gladstone, while Hallam and Lionel were with Mary Gladstone and Maggie Warren in another box. *The Times* suggested that as 'a play the best fate to be hoped for it is that it may be speedily forgotten,' and surely that must have been Emily's feeling, though she liked to remember how Lionel had stood up for his father. On 16 November the *Daily News* published his anonymous and illuminating defence of the central character, Philip Edgar – after the atheist Lord Queensberry's startling attack on him in the middle of a performance – an attack as ludicrous as if a Moor of Venice had risen up from the stalls in *Othello* and shouted that *he* had never murdered his wife.

Lionel had made a number of efforts to get away from the routine drudgery at the India Office. In December 1881, just at the time Emily was writing to Gladstone on Hallam's behalf, Lionel was involved in 'cadging' for an appointment as private Secretary to Lord Enfield, the Parliamentary Under-Secretary of State for India. A letter from Eleanor to Emily describes the agonizing process of lobbying that had gone on. Mary Gladstone had encouraged them to get everyone to write to Lord Enfield. 'She says it is *the only way to get anything*.' One of the problems was that Richmond Ritchie, one of Lionel's closest friends (Anne Thackeray's husband), was also in for the appointment and 'Lionel says Richmond is a much better clerk than himself!' 'I really *long* for the change of work and prospect of a career that it would open out to L.,' Eleanor wrote. On the 17 December Lionel was able to write to Henry Cameron that he had secured the appointment, 'a good thing pecuniarily and prospectively'.

But the appointment was only for a year and in January 1883 Tennyson was writing to the Permanent Under-Secretary, Sir Louis Mallet, about his worries over Lionel's future.

Perhaps I have done not altogether wisely in permitting one of so much originality and refinement of intellect, and so sensitive to his surroundings, and so dependent upon his interest in his work for his highest continued power of working, to place himself among the subordinates of a Public Office. Be this as it may, it is so great a misfortune for a young man to be without regular work that I cannot but recommend him to stay where he is, and I feel sure that sooner or later he will find employment as congenial as that which he has lost.

Lionel was obviously considering giving up the India Office altogether when he had failed to secure a post as Private Secretary to Lord Derby. This time it had indeed gone to Richmond Ritchie. Lionel told his family: 'He has behaved very well about it and I am glad for his sake . . . When you write to the Gladstones, will you make it clear to them that it was through no fault of my own that I did not get the appointment.' He was to be tried in the Statistics Department for two months; it was not an enticing prospect and he put more and more energies into his singing and his charity work. He was singing 'Alma River' and 'Drink to me only' at Woolwich to a crowd of 'mechanic engineers'; he sang at Holloway College and 'at Chelsea for Octavia Hill'. He was singing with a choir as well as, sometimes, as a soloist. They were nearly always 'People's Entertainments' of one sort or another: 'Music for the People'. He was on various committees, including that of the York Road Lying-in Hospital. He had plenty to occupy himself, a thriving social life (with lots of lawn tennis in the summer), but his career seemed to be going nowhere.

Hallam had continued throughout these years to work devotedly for his parents, but he seems also to have been keen, probably at Gladstone's suggestion and with Mary's encouragement, to get himself selected for a parliamentary seat. Lear had suggested in his diary the problems that this might present. If Hallam acquired a seat as Gladstone's nominee, what would happen when he wanted to vote the way his parents would certainly expect him to vote – on such issues as Ireland and the extension of the Franchise, where the Liberals were divided, and becoming more so? 'Politically, I hate him like the devil,' Tennyson would say of Gladstone in December 1885 and Emily, that same winter, would accuse him of fanaticism. 'A statesman who is just is just to all or can be just to none.'

There are two surviving records of Hallam's parliamentary aspirations. He had considered standing for the Glasgow and Aberdeen University seat – but was put off because it looked unwinnable for the Liberals and the election expenses seemed likely to be twice the £2000 he said he could afford. He also sought nomination in May 1883 for one of the Leeds seats, as a surviving telegram at Lincoln to Herbert Gladstone (the Prime Minister's son, who had himself taken over his father's old seat) makes clear.

Nothing had turned up in the way of work for Hallam when in October 1883 he wrote to Mary Gladstone from Aldworth.

Your advice has been followed and a penniless one has been found – I want you to keep it a *profound* secret till Xmas for her brothers do not even know it. I did not think of marrying at all but circumstances which I will one day explain to you have brought this about. She is a noble-hearted girl . . . It all came to pass over 'In Memoriam' – and I want you for my sake as well as for her own *always* to help her and be loving to her.

Her name is 'Audrey Boyle' . . .

We shall have hardly anything to live upon so I must work. If you hear of a political crossing-sweeper's place for me, let me know. I should like to go up from here every day . . . and live in the country, for she loves the country.

God bless you, Mary. Ever your affectionate brother,

Hallam Tennyson.

Please do not tell *anyone*.

Hallam and Mary had, at her insistence, been as brother and sister for four years – and it was surely because Mary had rejected his different kind of love that Hallam had at one point decided not to marry at all. What had made him change his mind? Not apparently the simple fact of meeting Audrey, or he would have said so. Could it have been anything to do with pressure from his parents? They were already seriously worried about what would happen to him after their deaths.

It was in the wake of Hallam's unsuccessful attempts to find a new career for himself that Tennyson finally accepted a peerage. That he should henceforward become known as Alfred, Lord Tennyson (a strange sort of title anyway) was entirely his publisher's wish. 'Would *Alfred Tennyson's Works* or *The Works of Alfred Tennyson* do, thus evading the Lord and Mr?' Hallam wrote in January 1884.

Some sort of honour had been suggested many times in the past. 'He is not so much against the thing as I am,' Emily had written to her father nearly twenty years earlier, of a proffered baronetcy. Tennyson had always made it clear that it was only for Hallam's sake that he would ever accept. And now he felt the House of Lords would give their son the chance of a career in public life after his father's death. That this eventually led to Hallam becoming Governor-General of Australia would have seemed to his parents the perfect justification.

Benjamin Jowett, who knew Emily so well, guessed exactly how she would feel. He wrote: 'I am afraid that you may be rather indifferent to the sound of a title, but at any rate some of your friends will like to address you by it. I have no doubt the new honour will be a great advantage to Hallam: and no-one is more worthy to wear it.' 'Some will carp,' he said, but she should not let that worry her. They did carp, of course. There were verses in the *Pall Mall Gazette* which ended:

> Pray Heaven for a noble heart
> And let the foolish title go

and the *Spectator* said, 'the Peerage will be at best an ill-fitting Court costume,' which must have made Emily smile, thinking of Alfred going to his first (and perhaps only) levée in Samuel Rogers's trousers more than thirty years before.

Emily wrote to Edward Lear: 'It seems to me a solemn thing to enroll oneself and one's heirs as long as the race lasts among the legislators of England, but no-one could do so with more hope than my Ally looking at our Hallam. It is a delight to us that yourself and all the friends we most value recognise this for surely never parents owed more to a child than we do to him.'

Emily had been rather ill in the early part of that year, 1883, and, as she said, Hallam had become more and more necessary to them: 'I still lose my voice and such strength as I have with a very little talking, so the care of our numerous guests devolves on Hallam.' Lionel said, 'If you would only eat $^1/_{10}$th part as much as a flea you would be all right,' which suggests a certain loving exasperation. 'I hope you will eat like a pig,' he said on another occasion, a rather inappropriate suggestion. Emily certainly shared some of the revulsion Louisa and Agnes had showed towards over indulgence. But Emily's lack of appetite seemed to be an effect rather than a cause of her weakness.

Hallam, whenever he was away, would send instructions: 'DON'T TALK', 'DRIVE OUT', even once 'DO NOT SEE MUCH OF LAURA TENNANTS etc' – naming one of the bright young things who had sailed on the Pembroke Castle that autumn, when Horatio's daughters, Maud and Violet, had been at Aldworth with Emily. Even when he was away, Emily knew, Hallam thought constantly of her welfare.

When he was at home, they still worked together to protect and spare Tennyson, sometimes with unwarranted enthusiasm. Knowing that Tennyson had written to Gladstone to try to persuade him not to let Knowles publish some of Arthur Hallam's letters in the Nineteenth Century, they withheld from Tennyson the copy of Records of an Eton Schoolboy sent to him by the editor Charles Milnes Gaskell. Emily wrote to Julia Lennard, Arthur Hallam's only surviving sibling:

Certainly fresh and pleasant and thoughtful as these youthful letters are, one cannot but feel that Mr Milnes Gaskell has done well in printing them for private circulation only, lest the public ideal of your brother should in any way be disturbed. For the same reason, but on infinitely stronger grounds, we have withheld the book from my Ally and I hope that in this you also agree with us. One has to be very careful with so very sensitive a nature, as you know.

Hallam Tennyson was endlessly busy on his sensitive father's behalf, but one day he would no longer be needed. Emily told Lear: 'It is a new source of thankfulness to me that he should have an honourable career marked out for him when his work for his Father has ceased. Not that I am insensible to the fresh mark of respect for his Father, only, you see, I have been used to have homage paid to him, so, like a child, I think of my new toy, no toy but a very real thing of great importance to the child.' There seems to be a little confusion about who was the child. Emily was now identifying with Hallam, as she had so often identified with Alfred.

To Gladstone, Emily had written: 'That Hallam should inherit the duties belonging to this distinction is cause of deep thankfulness to me, they being among those for which I believe him most fitted as they certainly are among those in which he is most interested.'

The most carping voice of all, and one that has been reported over the years as if it had some truth in it, was that of Frederick Tennyson, who had spoken before of Emily's ambition at the time of Lionel's wedding. Now we hear it most vehemently from a bitter father writing to his disappointing second son, Alfred, who had so often hurt not only his father but his older illegitimate brother:

As to the Peerage which is the crowning honour at least so considered – of a literary life – I do not believe that the desire to obtain it originated in your Uncle's mind. Mrs – Baroness T of Aldworth and Freshwater – has not been laid upon her back most of her life without nursing ambitious dreams, now realised. She, of course, will plead the advantages accruing to her children and theirs . . .

Frederick thought his brother had been induced by his 'wife's worldliness' to accept the empty honour to an 'already illustrious name'. 'As for Hallam,' he added: 'What earthly justification can there be of his succeeding to the title – Hereditary peerages should be done away with.' However much one agrees with *that*, it was an ugly outburst, perhaps excused by the contrast between Frederick's worthy nephew and his own profligate son, who had now, after years of loafing about in Gray's Inn and North America (and incidentally contracting a venereal disease in New York), decided to take to the stage. 'What you say,' his father grumbled in this same letter, 'about turning actor, and beginning with elephant's legs – is simply ridiculous.' It would hardly be, Frederick suggested, 'any sort of introduction to the higher departments of the histrionic profession – it is simply a miserable refuge for the destitute, the vulgar and probably the dissolute' – a description which he hoped did not fit his son and heir.

Emily, not knowing anything of Frederick's feelings (as of course he knew nothing of hers), wrote a sympathetic letter soon after this, on the occasion of the death of Maria, Frederick's Italian wife, whom she remembered as having been so good to them in Florence in 1851. She offered him a 'loving welcome' at Farringford as soon as he felt equal to the change. It was perhaps unsurprising that he did not accept the invitation.

It was a good time for Emily, the winter of 1883–4. The peerage had secured Hallam's future but his prospects had been more immediately brightened by his engagement to Audrey Boyle, which delighted and relieved his mother. 'It all came to pass over *In Memoriam*,' he had said to Mary Gladstone. He told Browning that they had read some of his *Men and Women* together. Poetry had certainly had something to do with it. Years later Audrey would write: 'I have a very happy nature and so has my Hallam and we somehow are always able to enjoy the circumstances of the moment even when they are not of our choice.' It was just as well. Hallam gave up his search for work and Tennyson increased his allowance. Audrey accepted Hallam knowing what her life would be; she understood perfectly that he would always put his parents' needs first, that that was his *work*, not just his inclination. Audrey herself had 'been a devoted daughter and nursed her sick father for sixteen years,' a long time for someone who was not yet thirty. She was the only surviving daughter of her parents (together with six brothers) and they inevitably had some problems with the transfer of her devotions to the Tennysons. Audrey would endure many migraines and much anxiety in the five years until her first child was born – but Hallam had undoubtedly made an excellent choice.

'She is a great darling,' he wrote, 'very self-denying and sympathetic and sweet'. In the letters announcing his engagement, he quoted, over and over again, his father's assessment that Audrey was 'royal in her sweetness and innocence'. Audrey had a good deal in common with Emily, although her interests – in spite of a father who had been a Fellow of All Souls – were far less intellectual. That Hallam considered Audrey had a bright intellect is obvious from a number of letters and, at the time of Mary's engagement, he wrote to her: 'I do trust that, however deeply buried, there is an intellect on which to rest.' (What had she said about the handsome curate Harry Drew?) 'In marriage this is *absolutely* necessary for the higher sort of happiness and especially for you.'

One important thing about Audrey was that she shared Hallam's total devotion to Tennyson's poetry. But even so it seems that Mary Gladstone was the 'great love' of Hallam's life. When he writes to congratulate Mary on her marriage, he says he is glad she has found *her* 'great love' and then crosses it out and substitutes the simple 'him'. 'I hope that he will like me ... Always your friend, Hallam Tennyson.' He hoped she would be 'as happy as I have been in my marriage,' he wrote, sending Farringford snowdrops he wanted her to wear on her wedding day.

Hallam's marriage would never give his mother the sort of worry that Lionel and Eleanor would give her over the next two years. In December 1883 everything seemed still set fair, though Emily had been disappointed that Eleanor had decided to send the little boys to her cousin in Hertfordshire while she was confined for the birth of her third child. Emily had wanted to have them at Farringford and had been feeling energetic enough to be looking forward to teaching little Ally, who was now five.

The new grandchild was born on 10 December 1883. Ally wrote to his Grandmama with the help of Jane, their nurse: 'I call him Jack, Nanny says it is not pretty for our baby so I think I shall leave it for Father and Mother to choose ... We wish very much it had been a little sister but we shall love it all the same.' They were both, he and Charlie, 'disappointed at not coming to see you and dear Grandpa'. Emily conducted a vigorous correspondence with her grandsons over the following years and masses of childish letters survive to their dearest Grandmama.

The child was christened Michael Sellwood Tennyson – a name that made Emily feel particularly close to him. The 'delicacy' and backwardness of the 'dear affectionate boy' would always be a major subject in the letters exchanged between Emily and Eleanor, as 'poor little Michael' failed to measure up to his extremely clever older brothers. It is sad to realize that if he *had* been a girl, as they had all hoped, his inability to read until he was seven (at an age when Ally and Charlie were learning French and about to begin Latin) would probably have caused no problems and the child might well have led a normal life, instead of spending nearly sixty years confined in institutions, for (it would seem) far less reason than his great-uncle Edward. He was almost entirely wiped out of the record, not only by his uncle Hallam but by his own brother, Charles.

What was wrong with Michael it is very difficult to know. His photograph bears out Emily's description of him as 'a fine strong boy with a beautiful face,' and the most like his father. She always attributed his problems to a severe illness – inflammation of the lungs – he had just before his first birthday. When he was nearly three, she told her American friends the Fields that 'he talks but very little yet. He however delights in singing and really catches an air tho' he cannot sing many words.' By the time he was seven he was able to write to his grandmother – 'Quite nicely,' she told her sister Anne, though, as his mother said, 'he is still very different from an ordinary child' of his age.

This was all in the future. In January 1884 Michael seemed a perfect baby and Eleanor felt free – in the extraordinary fashion of the time, which might not be entirely unconnected with what happened later – to obey her doctor's suggestion, leave the new bottle-fed infant in London with his father, his nurse and little Charlie (who was perfectly 'wrapped up' in his new brother) and spend three weeks at Brighton with five-year-old Alfred and a nurse. The sea air would do her a world of good, it was thought, though she herself had at first jibbed at the idea of Brighton in January and had suggested Aldworth instead.

Lionel had at last got some work at the India Office which really interested him. He had been chosen to write the annual (eighteenth) report on *The Moral and Material Progress of India,* covering the years 1881–2. To Lionel the job was totally absorbing and whetted his appetite to visit India. To *The Times* reviewer it was a routine 'official history', of interest to only a few. 'It will be conceded to the compiler of the present report, Mr Lionel Tennyson, that in clearness of style and arrangement, his volume does not fall behind the work of any of its immediate predecessors.' Faint praise indeed. Lionel told Emily, who had eagerly awaited the reviews, that it was inevitable that the papers would be interested in the facts and not in the author.

In February, when the report was finished, Lionel again felt convinced that he should leave the India Office. The regulations assured that he was unlikely to be promoted. 'I have written to Mary Gladstone to ask her to do something for me if possible. Anything would be better than this red-tape bondage.' Four days later he assured Hallam that he would not resign 'unless I got an equivalent,' but no-one could 'give an opinion worth hearing, unless they knew the inner workings of the office'. Perhaps the regulations would be changed, 'but I don't feel inclined to waste my life on a probability'.

Lionel was also worrying about money. The Turner inheritance from the Grasby rents seemed to be taken up on repairs, before they saw any of it. Should not someone check what was going on? Something more devastating also seems to have been going on – unless there was some further agreement of which we know nothing. Did Lionel have any idea that in this year, 1884 (indeed the day before Hallam's wedding), Tennyson signed his last will and testament, making Emily and Hallam not only his executors, but his sole beneficiaries? There is no mention whatsoever of Lionel in the will – though certainly Emily had imagined, years before, that he would inherit Aldworth and Hallam Farringford. Whether Lionel knew the terms of the will or not, he was certainly not happy, as the time approached for his brother's wedding.

In the spring of 1884 Mary Brotherton as usual reported to Frederick Tennyson the news from Farringford: it was sometimes from a misreading of her letters that Frederick had got ammunition for his dislike of Emily. 'Hallam', she told him, 'has sprained his ankle badly . . . It was late at night and he fainted with pain . . . and as he is, I believe, to be married in June, it is to be hoped he will not limp to the altar. His sweetheart is a very nice little thing . . . She seems to have every recommendation except money, of which she does not possess a farthing! . . .They are to live together [with his parents] – which is an arrangement not frequently successful – but I trust this may be one of the exceptional cases.'

Emily had hoped that Hallam and Audrey would be married from Audrey's family home at Hawkhurst in Kent. She wrote to Edward Lear: 'We long to have a quiet country wedding but Mr Boyle is too confirmed an invalid to have it from his house, so it is to be from that of his cousin Lady Sarah Spencer (in St James's Square) and in Henry VII's chapel quietly in the afternoon. Ally and I if all be well go up for the ceremony from Aldworth and return at once.' They remembered with some distress the crush at Lionel's wedding and hoped for something less grand, but – as the papers recorded – it was an extremely smart wedding in Westminster Abbey that Wednesday afternoon, 25 June 1884, with the new Mrs Tennyson looking 'strikingly handsome in her dress of white satin, trimmed with rare and costly Brussels lace or point de gaze,' and a large number of distinguished guests including Mr and Mrs Gladstone. William Allingham recorded that Browning caught his

eye 'and gave a friendly wink'. Mary Brotherton, writing her usual
report to Frederick after the ceremony decided it was a 'raree-show'
and thought it would be a good idea 'to *civilise* marriage pomps and
vanities into a purer and simpler festivity'. Hallam himself, she said,
had 'a great dislike of the parade, which was insisted on by his wife's
family' – in other words, by the Boyles. It was certainly just the sort of
thing Zacyntha Boyle wanted for her only daughter.

It was a brief enough service, as Emily had wished, and not in the
nave but in the chapel, 'under the tattered banners of the old knights'.
There were only two hymns, one of them 'composed by my mother,'
Hallam told their American friend John Field, 'and very tender and
pathetic it was'. She had set to music the words of an eighteenth-
century poet James Merrick: 'Eternal God we look to thee.' The tune
was called 'Farringford' and 'everyone was so much struck by the
beauty of it'. There was a large congregation. Hallam thought perhaps
'at no time has there been gathered in the place . . . so many great, good
and famous men – and all in honour of my Father'. He does not mention the women, and certainly George Eliot was dead, but his mother
was there. Edmund Lushington regretted that they did not get a chance
to speak to the parents of the groom. He wrote to Tennyson:

It was hard to bear – not to be able to see and speak to you and Emmy on
Wednesday, tho' of course unavoidable – see *you* indeed I did, and the two
little boys in front of you, but I never could catch a glimpse of her. Cissy says
she did, as Emmy past down the chapel after the wedding . . .

Edmund told them how, during the solemn service, he had remembered 'quiet Shiplake', and hoped the strain of the day would not be too
much for Emily. During the service, *she* was not thinking of herself, of
course, but of how 'noble and beautiful' the young couple looked 'and
as if', she told them, 'you ought to do good work for the world and by
God's help you will'.

Emily did not go to the reception; Lionel took her into the Deanery to
rest and enjoy the company of her dear friend Marian Bradley, whose
husband was now the Dean of Westminster. 'There not only herself but
all our servants were hospitably entertained.' Emily was distressed that
'poor old William', their coachman, 'was not very well and could not
come to supper'. The cost of the servants' train tickets from Haslemere
is entered in Emily's account book (£4.15s), together with the cost of
the little boxes for sending out pieces of wedding cake (3s 9d). Lionel

took 'most tender care' of his parents on the way home. Emily told Hallam he had even 'gathered up my dress that it might not be injured by the wheels of his chair and he seemed very pleased that people in the crowd said as we went along, what a beautiful dress. I only repeat this because you will know how much it means in him.' In Hallam's absence, Lionel was behaving more like Hallam.

Emily sat in the 'desolate house', feeding crumbs of wedding cake to Lufra, the wolfhound. 'She raised her nostrils in the air and insisted on having a bit.' It is the only time she ever mentions the dog in her letters, as if she had never felt the need of the dog's companionship before. She wrote to Audrey:

My Darling,

We shall be true Mother and Daughter thro' life – please God.
May you be happy as I desire and happier far than I know how to desire.
Your loving Mother,   Emily Tennyson.

Was that last enigmatic sentence a suggestion that she was aware of how limited her own experience of love and of life had been? Could it have been that she realized she had suppressed her own needs to accept only the sort of happiness she was offered?

Hallam wrote from Ashridge to say how glad Audrey was to have Emily's tender little note. 'She likes being read to immensely. That is a grand thing. She is wonderfully gentle and *tremendously* happy.' They left for the Continent on 29 June, visiting Antwerp, Bruges and Ghent. Although Hallam's letters are addressed to 'Papa and Mamma', it is always Emily he is thinking of. Eleanor and the three children were now at Aldworth, with Lionel coming down at the weekends. Hallam is full of suggestions for his own absence and praises Eleanor for her 'dragon-ship'. They finished the honeymoon with ten days at Farringford, before going to Aldworth to begin 'the real life of marriage'. He wrote to ask that there should be no fuss on their return after the four weeks away. 'Pray do not let any decorations be arranged at the gate' as there had always been when they came back for the holidays as boys.

Two days later on 26 July William Allingham recorded in his diary on arriving at Aldworth: 'Found an arch in Avenue, "Welcome Home" – so the Bride and Bridegroom are back.' Hallam wrote to his American friend: 'My mother has of course been much tired by the excitement of the last months, but is growing stronger and better than she has been owing to the warmth of the weather and the peace of mind.'

CHAPTER FIFTEEN

'The deepest cloud of human sorrow'

That peace of mind was not to last. It was Lionel who would disturb it, in more ways than one. Tennyson himself would say at this time: 'To me the paths leading into the Future seem somewhat gloomy, and (as our Shakespeare says in his *Julius Caesar*) "crave wary walking".' No wariness would save them from what lay ahead.

Emily was determined that something should be done to release Lionel from that 'red tape bondage' at the India Office and give him a career more suited to his talents. When he was a boy, she had told him how much she hoped he would do 'some good service in the world' – 'as your Father's son'. The Bradley children had even thought Lionel had inherited 'a touch of his father's genius'. Jowett, who had so much experience of the bright young at Oxford, had thought so too. Had Lionel Tennyson been crippled by expectations, by the fact of being his father's son?

In the autumn of 1884 Emily wrote to the Marquis of Dufferin and Ava, who had just been appointed Viceroy of India and for whom, more than twenty years before, Tennyson had written the lines 'Helen's Tower'. She thought how delightful it would be if there were a chance of Lionel serving on the Viceroy's personal staff; she would not suggest it, she said, if she were not sure that Lionel was capable of 'a true personal devotion and a great enthusiasm for hard work'. Lionel was at this point in Scotland, on long leave from the India Office, but he would immediately return to London if there were a chance of Lord Dufferin being able to 'relieve him from this drudgery,' which was all that seemed to lie ahead for him.

A fortnight later Emily wrote again. She said Lionel himself knew 'that all appointments in India, except purely personal ones, belong to the Indian Civil Service and that it would only create commotions to have them given elsewhere.' Had Lionel been embarrassed by his mother's intervention? Dufferin kindly assured Emily before he left England: 'I am very very anxious to be of service to him though until I go to India I am not able to judge to what degree or in what respects I can promote your own and Lord Tennyson's wishes.' In a further letter he added, 'It will be hard if, between us, we do not hit out some way for me to be useful to him.' It was a determination which would have fatal consequences.

The winter of 1884–5 was a bad one for Emily's own health. It was also the time of a great deal of anxiety over Michael, the youngest grandson, whose first birthday was that December and who was suffering from an 'inflammation of the lungs', to which Emily would attribute many of his later problems. The Tennysons stayed at Aldworth that winter, the only time they ever did. Emily was not well enough to travel. Yet she would usually appear for meals when there were guests. There is a glimpse of her in William Allingham's diary when he dined with them that December. She was very pale and spoke very little. After the meal, she 'went upstairs again, almost carried by Hallam. A dear, almost angelic woman,' he added. Francis Palgrave was there in January. He saw little of Emily, 'but there was always the old bright intelligence and indescribable gracious charm'.

That month, Palgrave dedicated his selection of Tennyson's lyrical poetry to Emily, recalling that he had dedicated his *Golden Treasury* to Tennyson himself 'when Hallam and Lionel were hardly older than "golden-hair'd Ally"' was now.

You have allowed me, in this Dedication, to grace it with a name honoured, wherever Lord Tennyson's is known, as that of the one –
Dear, near, and true
to him from youth to age, – the counsellor to whom he has never looked in vain for aid and comfort, – the Wife whose perfect love has blessed him through these many years with large and faithful sympathy.

Emily, thanking him for the dedication, modestly saw it as 'a reminder to myself of what I ought to be'.

There was another dedication to Emily in 1885. Edward Lear, lonely in San Remo, was drafting a long dedication to her of the *Landscape Illustrations* of Tennyson's poems, on which he had been working for forty years. They had become something of an obsession and his inability to find a satisfactory means of reproducing the drawings was to become part of the general sadness of these last years of Lear's life, a sadness of which Emily was always acutely aware and which she could do nothing to alleviate.

Emily was herself struggling that winter, with an illness that threatened to kill her. Anyone who considers Emily's ill health was largely psychosomatic, should read this letter from Hallam to Mary Gladstone:

I have been most frightfully anxious about my mother ... She became unconscious for one and a half hours the other day and we were greatly alarmed – but she has taken the turn for the better – tho' she will never be able to see much of her friends again – I fear – for her strength is only just up to being able to live. When she goes, one of the most gifted and angelic souls in this world – will be lost to us – (tho' she is my mother). Audrey has been the greatest help and comfort to my Father and myself.

They had been reading the Chinese philosopher Lao Tse. Jowett had originally put them on to him. 'I shall consider myself fortunate if I have succeeded in finding a subject for Alfred,' he wrote to Emily. Hallam had quoted to Mary Gladstone Lao Tse's 'three great virtues': Compassion, Humility and Thrift. But it was also his faith and optimism that appealed to Emily. Tennyson put it like this:

> Cleave ever to the sunnier side of doubt,
> And cling to Faith beyond the forms of Faith!
> She reels not in the storm of warring words,
> She brightens at the clash of 'Yes' and 'No'.
> She sees the Best that glimmers through the Worst,
> She feels the Sun is hid but for a night,
> She spies the summer through the winter bud,
> She tastes the fruit before the blossom falls,
> She hears the lark within the songless egg,
> She finds the fountain where they wailed 'Mirage'!

For Lionel, Emily felt the sun was hid but for a night; just how dark the night was perhaps Emily did not fully realize. His letters had become scrappier and scrappier, his visits less frequent. Emily must have known, for Eleanor tried to keep her in touch with their activities, what separate lives Eleanor and Lionel were leading. It is no wonder that, when he came down to Aldworth with Margot Tennant in February 1885, Emily did not appear at dinner, and might well not have done even if she had felt better.

Lionel had asked his friend Margot (who would one day marry Herbert Asquith and be a rather unconventional Prime Minister's wife) what she wanted for her twenty-first birthday. On the day itself he had given her a poem:

> Think of me as you will, dear girl, if you will let me be
> Somewhere enshrined within the fane of your pure memory;
> Think of your poet as of one who only thinks of you,
> That you *are* all his thought, that he were happy if he knew –
> You did receive his gift, and say
> (Ma bayadère aux yeux de jais)
> 'He thinks of me today.'

But the gift the dear girl wanted was the real poet – the chance to meet his father. She asked Lionel if he would take her down to Aldworth for the weekend.

In his diary that winter (a diary in which Eleanor is never mentioned by name) Lionel meditates on the nature of woman, quoting Lord Chesterfield who said that her two passions are 'vanity and love'. 'Of course, the former is the consequence of the latter . . . she only thinks of what others think of her.' Was this true of Eleanor as well as Margot? Lionel could hardly have believed in such a generalization about women, having been brought up by a mother whose lack of self-love Benjamin Jowett, in particular, had often remarked.

Lionel wrote in his journal: 'Why is it that I have so furious a desire to do people good? I cannot see a fault without desiring to correct it. It is not because I think myself better than the rest of the world. Far from it.' It seemed, and there was something of his mother in this, that he wanted to help people to direct their energies to worthwhile ends. Of Margot Tennant, he wrote: 'I have seldom talked so freely with any woman. "Talking of love is making it" says somebody, but not in this case. I want to give her a higher idea of life. Something beyond amusement. Her amusement by the way is by no means a harmless one. It is not, I think, strictly flirtation, it is *better* and *worse* than that. I want to teach her that she has no right to play with human happiness as she does: but how? What can a woman do that will give her a serious interest in life?' His mother – the poet's wife – had been lucky. Her poet's life had been her life and 'his necessity her great opportunity'. Lionel wished he could direct Margot's 'clever little brains to search for something worth having.' As for his own marriage, 'the difficulty of married life, at least to sensitive people, is to soften down their angles which cause constant irritation and destroy the health and peace of love. It is not so much that married people get tired of each other, but often they become uneasy in each other's presence.'

Emily had undoubtedly sensed that uneasiness. It was probably one reason that she was so keen for Lionel and Eleanor to break the pattern of their London life and travel abroad together. In May – by which time she was feeling much better – Emily was delighted to get a letter from Lord Dufferin.

I hope you won't think that I have forgotten Lionel. Ever since I have been in India, I have been on the lookout for some post which would suit him and which he would be entitled to fill, but the Civil Service in this country is so constructed that there is scarcely any situation of importance that could be offered to an outsider.

Dufferin went on to suggest that if Lionel could get leave from the India Office, it would undoubtedly be of service to him to 'take a little tour round India'. He said he and his wife would 'welcome them with open arms'. In July Lionel was able to tell his parents he had five months' leave for India. He was excited, imagining the chance to visit 'hill tribes and the Afghan border'. He had always been deeply concerned with a peaceful solution to the Afghan question. It had been the reason for his Russian lessons. He eventually left Aldworth on 12 October and in his first letter he said: 'I cannot say that I am not somewhat melancholy at going, but I suppose it is all for the best, and that I shall enjoy it when once I get there. In the meantime, I feel parting with you all very much, as you know.' He was going further away than any of them had ever travelled.

In India he covered vast distances, received inevitably as his father's son, not just as himself. There were Three Cheers for him and Eleanor and 'Three for the Poet Laureate'. 'At Lucknow they hoisted the old flag in my father's honour . . . because of my father's poem' – 'flying at top of the roofs in the ghastly siege of Lucknow'. Lionel was 'rather disgusted with the mutual intolerance' between the races, which was worse than he expected. But he had many Indian friends from his years in the India Office. In Bombay he was a guest at a Parsee Club, though normally Europeans were 'excluded in revenge for our excluding natives'. In that city inevitably he recorded the vultures, 'the great indecent, melancholy birds, sitting in the tower waiting for the next funeral.' Much that he saw entranced him: the minarets, the tombs and temples and palaces, buffalo fights, a torchlight procession of elephants, the orange trees, the dancing girls, the bands. Eleanor is hardly mentioned. The first comment of hers is perhaps revealing. 'Beautiful bungalows and compounds on the Hooghly banks. "Rather like the Thames," Eleanor says.'

The first indication that anything was wrong with Lionel took a long time to reach England. Eleanor did not want to alarm them with telegrams. There *would* be telegrams, some comforting, some alarming, but first there were letters telling them Lionel had a fever, but they were not to be worried. On 15 February from Barrackpore, Eleanor wrote a long letter to Hallam marked 'PRIVATE', telling the full story. Lionel had 'malarial fever complicated with congestion of the liver and pleuro-neumonia' – pain which had originally been misdiagnosed. Their return to England, she feared, would now not be until the middle of May, long after Lionel's leave ended. Hallam would need to get in touch with the India Office, and new arrangements would have to be made for the three boys –'such good children . . . full of spirit, intelligence and individuality', as Emily proudly told her sister. They had spent the winter in Scotland with Eleanor's aunt Lady Frances Baillie. 'I will try to write Mama a separate letter . . . Tell her as much or as little as you think best.' Before those letters reached Farringford, the first 'serious telegram from India' reached them.

By 9 March Lionel and Eleanor were at Government House, Calcutta and Eleanor decided she must send a wire to Farringford where they all were. She addressed it to Annie Andrews, the housekeeper, 'which it seems to me will be the most likely way to prevent its falling into the hands of your Father or Mother,' she told Hallam in a letter written on the same day. There had been an operation on an abscess on Lionel's liver; when his fever remained they operated again, discovering more abscesses, again on the liver and on his lung. He had been removed from Barrackpore to Calcutta on his bed by steam launch down the river. Lord Dufferin had been in Burma and was distressed to find what had happened to Lionel since he had last seen him. He had told them at the beginning: 'This is a feverish place. Promise me to take a quinine pill every day,' and had asked to look at their tongues. Now he wrote to Emily in England, 'I shall await with the greatest anxiety the news of Lionel's safe arrival home. Nothing can exceed his courage and his patience and his goodness to us all. He is never irritable, and is so grateful for any little thing . . .' It was essential that he left without delay 'as the heat in Calcutta is becoming fearful.' There was every hope, as Lionel started on the long voyage 'that the change of air and the fresh sea breezes would save his life.'

Emily was insistent that she should be kept in touch with what was going on, though they tried to protect her. 'I would not on any account not have known the real state of things,' she told her sister Anne. She had been 'wonderfully well' that winter – so much better than the year before, but as her anxiety over Lionel increased, she was 'prostrate' and unable to see anyone. She had always been intelligently aware of the relationship between mind and body and wrote to the Welds on 5 April: 'It is not to be wondered at that I should have felt very ill for the last month.' It was Hallam who wrote to thank Edward Lear for his picture of Pentedatelo in Calabria, which illustrated a few lines from 'Mariana in the South'. Telling Lear of the telegram about Lionel, Hallam said, 'I have not told people yet for the world will begin to write and condole – only I know that you will sorrow with us . . . We should like to see you again and shake your hand for we all love you, as you know.' They would none of them ever see him again either.

A few days later Emily wrote to Bombay a letter Lionel would never read. It was eventually returned with the words 'GONE TO ENGLAND' on the back in pencil. 'Pray God you may be nearly home before this reaches Bombay, but I write nevertheless . . . You know how our thoughts and our prayers have been with you day and night. God grant us speedily the exceeding happiness of seeing you both.' Emily hoped they had not been 'quite overpowered' by all they had gone through. 'Suffering together, bonds closer.' On 13 April, Hallam wrote to the Welds: '*I fear the worst.*' On 20 April Lionel's suffering ended. A telegram that day read: 'SINKING NO SUFFERING UNCONSCIOUS TENNYSON'. They had to wait five days for the confirmation that it was all over.

On the last morning lying on a chaise longue on the deck (escaping the stifling heat of their cabin), Lionel suddenly raised his head and began to sing 'Our blest Redeemer ere he breathed his – last farewell.' He could not remember the word and Eleanor had to tell him: 'tender' was the word he wanted. Then he kept repeating 'tender last farewell'.

Eleanor read the hymn to him and 'Lead, kindly light', which he had always loved. At the words 'far from home', he said 'Yes, far from home'. It was Farringford he thought of, Emily felt sure when she heard. And he must have thought of her as Eleanor read the last two lines of the hymn:

> And with the morn those Angel faces smile,
> Which I have loved long since, and lost awhile.

His breathing got slower and slower 'and then it ceased at 4 o'clock (Ap. 20th). The (burial) service was at nine that same evening, with a great silver, solemn moon. The ship stopped and then all was over.' He had died between Aden and Perim and his body was committed to the Red Sea. On Easter Day from Suez Eleanor wired: 'HE PASSED AWAY VERY PEACEFULLY ON APRIL TWENTIETH ALL POSSIBLE DONE.' Emily must have thought of that other terrible Easter Day thirty-five years before and the death of her first-born son. 'Christ is risen,' Horatio wrote. 'How the great words thrill with light the deepest cloud of human sorrow.' 'Such sorrows are beyond words,' Emily wrote to Edmund Lushington. 'There are no words for such a loss.' But Tennyson would eventually find words, even for this:

> Not there to bid my boy farewell,
> When that within the coffin fell,
> Fell – and flashed into the Red Sea,
>
> Beneath a hard Arabian moon
> And alien stars. To question, why
> The sons before the fathers die,
> Not mine! and I may meet him soon.

That was their great comfort, that they might meet him soon, never to part. Over and over again they had written words of sympathy on the deaths of others and now what Emily had called 'poor rags of comfort' came to them. Years before, when *her* son died, Tennyson had written to Sophy Elmhirst, his old friend: 'I myself have always felt that letters of condolence when the grief is yet raw and painful are like vain voices in the ears of the deaf, not heard or only half-heard.' He had urged her even so to hear him saying that the son 'whom you so loved is not really what we called dead, but more actually living than when alive here. You cannot catch the voice or feel the hands or kiss the cheek – that is all – a separation for an hour, not an eternal farewell.'

As the sympathetic voices clamoured to be heard (the letters of condolence arriving by the basketload) and were not heard or only half-
heard, they all three tried to believe in what they had so often said they
believed. 'It is an estimable blessing to be a Christian.' 'You have a
strong faith to light you thro' the dark hour.' 'All sadness,' Emily wrote
to the Fields in Washington, '*should* be lost in the light of the for-ever to
come', 'but alas it is not so, or only for some moments'. When, the
following year, the son of Emily's dear cousin Kate Rawnsley seemed to
be dying, Emily apologized sadly for not writing sooner: 'This world's
hope had gone from me too much to give you any comfort in it and for
the hope of the next I knew that you had that which I could not give,
tho' I hope' – she crossed out the word and wrote instead 'tho' I *might*
share it and I do according to my measure, share it, thank God.' It was
a tentative statement, very different from the words Alfred had used
nearly twenty years before when Hallam had seemed to be dying as a
boy at Marlborough. 'God will take him pure and good,' his father had
said. Was it that Emily was not at all sure how 'pure and good' Lionel
had been?

It was Lionel's grandson, another Hallam Tennyson, who published
a letter from Eleanor to her son Charles which underlines the unhappiness of the marriage. In 1909, when he himself was about to marry,
Eleanor wrote to Charles, wondering why she had told him so little
about his father. 'It seemed impossible to speak without disloyalty to
the Dead and without giving you pain ... I should like you to know
that I dearly loved your father, and of course for a long time that always
made me hope, and my suffering was so acute, and the effort after self-
control so great ... that in after life it was almost impossible to speak.'

Certainly it would have been impossible for Eleanor to speak to
Emily about Lionel's emotional infidelity either before or after his
death, but Emily, described over and over again as so perceptive and
sympathetic, must have realized the situation. As I said, it may well
have been one reason Emily had been so keen for them to go together to
India. At least there had been no open scandal. Now there would be
rumours, which probably did not reach Emily's ears, of Eleanor dancing through the night on board ship while Lionel lay dying. The 'spiteful gossip', as Lionel's grandson called it, probably originated from the
Ritchies, for, not long after Eleanor's return to England, there was a
devastating development.

Anne Thackeray Ritchie was ill that summer and autumn, taking the waters at Aix. She suggested that Richmond, her young husband, should in her absence, help Eleanor, their widowed friend. Lionel had been *her* friend since he was a child; he had been Richmond's best man at their wedding; she was little Charlie's godmother. The two men had been colleagues and rivals at the India Office. It was obvious that Richmond was the person to help Eleanor as she tried to sort out her life, finding tenants to take over the lease of the Sussex Place house, finding more suitable accommodation for a widow (a 'mansion' flat overlooking Kensington Gardens with the security of a resident porter) and sorting out her changed financial position and the problems of Probate. What could not have been foreseen was that Eleanor and Richmond would fall in love.

The Ritchies' marriage withstood the threat. Richmond chose to stay with his wife. It may well have been of this crisis that Emily spoke when she wrote to Hallam in 1889 of how difficult it was to be just to Eleanor. It is impossible to know what Emily knew, how much she suffered from, not only Lionel's death, but from Eleanor's behaviour, which suggested so clearly (in Emily's naturally prejudiced opinion) how much she had failed as Lionel's wife.

The tributes to Lionel were full of the words 'love' and 'lovable'. 'What a fine lovable fellow he was,' Roden Noel wrote. Francis Palgrave remembered 'that almost imploring look of appeal for love which (to me) marked him through life.' Edward Lear wrote to Audrey: 'The loss to your Hallam is indeed most terrible – they were such brothers! – For God never created a human being more delightful and lovable – as baby, child, boy or man – than dear Lionel.' Lionel needed love, attracted love, but Eleanor, trying to explain the unhappiness of her first marriage to Caroline Jebb when staying with her years later, said that she 'never could understand Lionel. She could not feel that he cared for her or the children.' 'Sympathy and affection are the food she lives on,' Mrs Jebb told her sister. It was Caroline Jebb who recorded that during her marriage to Lionel 'and after it' Eleanor used to 'flirt tremendously' and 'did exactly what she pleased'. Hallam certainly must have known for he had seen a great deal of them and had often stayed with them in Sussex Place.

Caroline Jebb's immediate reaction to the news of Lionel's death was: 'His mother will be broken-hearted,' but was there not a possibility that he had broken her heart already, 'that strong, tall young man of thirty-two who was born to live as long and be as vigorous as his father?' If only he had been more like his father he need never have gone to India. Did that line from 'The Holy Grail', the poem that meant so much to Emily, come into her mind? 'In the great sea wash away my sin.'

There is a wild note in Emily's hand recording the visit of an Indian who had travelled to England on the same ship: 'Mr Dittmor said if ever a young man had gone to Heaven our Lionel had.' Emily seized eagerly on such crumbs, on every record of how nobly he had borne his suffering, how well he had died. These reports filled her with 'the blessed hope that he is happy'.

Over and over again Hallam, replying to the letters of condolence ('Words weaker than your grief would make grief more,'), repeated Lord Dufferin's words describing Lionel in Calcutta. Dufferin was now overwhelmed with grief himself. He told Emily, 'It seems almost as if I had been the instrument through which all this misery has been occasioned, for if I had not asked your poor Lionel to India he might have been still with you.' Emily knew that this was true, but that behind Dufferin's invitation had been her own plea that he should find some work for Lionel. How fortunate it was that they could both say, and really feel it, 'It was all in God's hands.'

Hallam wrote:

It is all like a terrible nightmare. He was a noble gentle fellow. Lord Dufferin wrote that in his last terrible and painful relapse 'nothing can exceed his courage and his patience and his goodness to us all.' My Father's grief is somewhat mitigated by his tender anxiety about my mother. She, angel as she is, bears up wonderfully, tho' she is physically crushed. I never saw such wonderful courage and faith as hers. I loved him and he me, as much as anyone could love . . . We have lived our lives together from babyhood. I can only say 'May all of us that loved him, feel (as Audrey and my mother do) God looking down upon us and blessing us!' Once Lionel said 'In the midst of joy I always feel a sadness – and perhaps in the midst of sorrow one may find joy in like manner.' Perhaps we may, when the first shock has lessened by time.

The small glimmer of joy, in the midst of grief, came not only from some hope of eternal life, but from the fact that Lionel was now safe from the voices of gossip and rumour and from all the temptations and tedium and disappointments of this earthly life. The India Office papers record the death of the Hon. L. Tennyson, Junior Clerk in the Correspondence Department on a salary of just £245 a year. The

Athenaeum called him 'the beloved son of the most beloved English-man of our time', praising his knowledge of world drama and saying how worthy he was 'of the great name he bore'. When a schoolboy friend of Hallam's had died in 1873 Emily had rejoiced that he was 'as we hope, safe', 'remembering the thousand snares of life'. Now Lionel was safe. 'They are wonderfully calm and resigned,' Eleanor said. 'It is not resignation. It is bliss,' the spiritualist Mary Brotherton said, looking at the expression on Emily's face.

Tennyson's words, so often quoted, are in Emily's handwriting: 'The thought of Lionel tears me to pieces – he was so full of promise and so young.' If Emily was herself torn to pieces, she was strong enough not to show it. She had the consolation that she had always shown her love for Lionel. For Tennyson there was a further cause for grief. He wrote on the cover of Froude's *Oceana*, which he had been reading on the day of Lionel's death, 'There is anguish in the recollection that we have not appreciated the affection of those whom we have loved and lost.'

Eleanor reported that her mother-in-law has 'had strength to support the blow'. Emily could even tell their Aldworth neighbour James Man-gles that if only we can trust in God, even such a loss may be 'in some way, we know not how, good for all of us.' 'All this woe is to work our highest weal,' she had written to Lear when his dear servant Giorgio had died. Now, of Lionel, she wrote, 'The loss to us is indeed unspeak-able, but infinite Love and Wisdom have ordained it.' Her faith in God's wisdom and mercy seemed to be unshakeable. 'My mother's marvellous faith and courage carries her through it all triumphantly.' Hallam said they filled him with amazement. 'It is a source of strength to us all.' 'May you be the peace and comfort of others,' Benjamin Jowett wrote, knowing her faith and courage would not fail.

Emily grieved for her surviving son as well as for the one who was dead. 'They were such brothers,' as Lear said. Hallam had lost not only his brother but his closest friend. In September Emily wrote to their American friends John and Eliza Field: 'We look about for friends and companions to our boy. He has none who in the very least takes our Lionel's place', but she thanked God Hallam 'has such a good wife' and that Audrey 'gets on admirably with his Father'. 'Audrey is the greatest comfort and blessing to us all,' Hallam confirmed.

To Francis Jenkinson, his friend from school and Cambridge, whom he so rarely saw, Hallam wrote: 'I felt and feel that half my life has gone – but still one must struggle on and do one's best in hope.' He told

Mary Gladstone who was now, he felt, 'sundered from him', married and far away, 'I have lost one whom I loved with all my heart and strength.' Going through Lionel's papers for Eleanor, Hallam must have read with anguish the very first poem his brother had copied out – on 14 October 1873 – in that handsome thick notebook marked PRIVATE he had started at Cambridge. It is Shakespeare's sonnet which begins:

> No longer mourn for me when I am dead
> Than you shall hear the surly sullen bell
> Give warning to the world that I am fled
> From this vile world with vilest worms to dwell.
> Nay, if you read this line, remember not
> The hand that writ it, for I love you so
> That I in your sweet thoughts would be forgot
> If thinking on me then should make you woe.

Lionel had also copied out his father's poem 'The Sailor Boy'. Had he, had Emily, feared the devil rising in his heart? ('Far worse than any death to me.')

Lionel had escaped the vilest worms; his bones were washed clean in the Red Sea. They could remember him, not with woe, but with joy and thanksgiving. Long before Emily had written to Hallam:

Sweet – how can it be selfish to be cheerful when God has given thee so many blessings and even when the time comes that some must be taken away I hope thou wilt rejoice in the midst of thy sorrow. Should it not be so with one who believes that God does all in love and wisdom.

She had been thinking when she wrote that letter, more than a dozen years earlier, that she and Tennyson would be the ones to be 'taken away'. In her Bible, the one her cousin Kate Rawnsley had given her on her wedding day, Emily had written, 'For my Lionel when I am gone.' It was much harder when a son, a brother, died first.

Even so, three months after Lionel's death, Hallam was able to report to his mother that Tennyson was 'in excellent spirits' after Sir Andrew Clark, his London doctor, had pronounced him 'absolutely sound' and he had enjoyed a performance of some scenes from his play *Becket*. If they were still officially in mourning (as they must have been), that did not stop them seeing *Faust* at the Lyceum and visiting the Colonial Exhibition.

In these difficult months after Lionel's death, Emily had been comforted and cheered by Lionel's boys, who spent much of their time with their grandmother. She read to them Hallam's version of *Jack and the Beanstalk* in English hexameters, which he had dedicated to his nephews. It was supposed to be a sumptuous picture book, in full colour, illustrated by Randolph Caldecott, but had appeared with only some preliminary sketches, for Caldecott had died that winter, aged thirty-nine, just two months before Lionel.

The boys would continue to come for holidays over the years, regularly visiting both Farringford and Aldworth, though Eleanor would always tell Emily how very hard she found it to 'spare' the boys and was 'very grateful to you for writing so constantly while they were with you.' Eleanor would veer between trusting Emily entirely ('Give them as much rope as *you* think wise') and wanting to lay down exact rules for the older boys' behaviour, diet and sleeping patterns. 'Please insist on smooth hair and clean hands at meal-times.' 'They go to bed at 8.30 and consequently I think should not have tea earlier than 6.30.'

If you can wait long enough, the past sometimes has a way of returning, and the two bright older boys, Ally and Charlie, were a constant reminder of her own sons. They delighted in Emily's tales of 'the young days of their dear Father and Uncle'. Their progress and that of their difficult young brother (and later their cousins) would be a major interest for Emily in the years that remained. It was not only a 'great pleasure' but a privilege too, Emily thought, to have the grandsons to stay so often. One of their joys, she told the Welds, was 'to put on an apron and cook!' One day Charlie ('the delightful boy') cooked their dinner and her luncheon on an open fire, 'even my pudding, which would have been very good had he not unfortunately got hold of a very oniony saucepan.' 'They have made a garden too and the paths were swept two or three times over to make them clean for me.' When they were ten and eleven, Ally and Charlie rode twenty miles from Aldworth all over the Devil's Jumps and returned for a game of cricket – telling Emily they were 'not the least tired'. They set up 'a sort of manufactory of spears' and would rush about the garden 'sticking them into the flowerpots and the trees, pretending that they are giants and knights.'

Emily was also deeply interested in other less privileged boys. The year before, the whole Tennyson family had become involved in a plan to establish the Gordon Boys' Home, in memory of General Gordon, killed at Khartoum. Once the first Home was open, it was Emily – not

Tennyson himself – who wrote the hymns the boys sang every day, one in the morning, one in the evening. They are included with five of Tennyson's own poems (and others by his brothers, Frederick and Charles) in Palgrave's *Treasury of Sacred Song*, which was published in 1889. It is impossible not to think of Lionel, when reading the second stanza of Emily's Morning Hymn:

> Thy servants pray, O hear us, Lord!
> Be Thou our shield, be Thou our sword,
> Be Thou our guard against all sin,
> From foes without, from foes within.
>
> O make us loving brothers all,
> Forgetting self at duty's call:
> Bless Thou the guardians of our land,
> And keep our dear ones in Thy hand.

The Gordon Home was obviously a Christian enterprise, but Emily had a wider view of its importance as 'something of a model for all National schools, for all sects and denominations, and faiths – I may say – looking to our Buddhist and Mohammedan fellow men of the Empire.' Emily always recognized and appreciated the multi-racial, multi-cultural nature of the British Empire – seeing it as its strength, not a weakness. The important thing was the relationship between the in-dividual man or woman 'toward the order of the world and towards God'.

Many letters reflecting Eleanor's difficult relationship with the Tenny-sons over the next few years have been destroyed, but it is possible to piece together a picture of understandable misunderstandings and problems as the Tennysons continually sought to keep Lionel's sons at the centre of their lives and Eleanor struggled to achieve independence and a new life for herself and her 'poor little Fatherless boys'. On her return from India, Eleanor had found all three boys 'the very picture of health and strength', 'both in mind and body'. There seemed to be no particular worry at this stage about Michael – as there soon would be. There survives an inscription from Emily to Michael on 'his most dear Father's photograph' in which she prayed that her grandson, 'my dar-ling', might be 'ever patient and courageous, unworldly, diligent, truth-ful, forgiving, loving and constant as he was.' At two and a half, Michael's only problem seemed to be that he was 'much in need of discipline', as Eleanor told Emily in a letter beginning 'Dearest Mother'. It would not be long before her letters would begin 'My Dearest Lady Tennyson'.

As early as July 1886, Hallam wrote to his mother telling her that Eleanor's aunt, Lady Frances Baillie, 'said that Eleanor had entirely altered in the last few days and entirely trusted us and no-one else really (except herself, Lady F., of course).' There is a disturbing letter from Eleanor which seems to be pleading that she may be allowed to return to Aldworth, even though 'Father is not well'. 'Besides wanting to see the children', she can only get breakfast at the house where she is staying in London, and she hates to have to go into restaurants alone. There is another letter which suggests how hard the Tennysons found it to cope with *her* loss as well as their own – or was it that they feared her loss was *not* as great as their own? Eleanor was anxious for Emily's approval and eager to be helpful. 'I am almost glad to hear that Papa and Hallam and Audrey may be away part of August,' she wrote to Emily from London, 'as I shall feel that I am being of a little use to you. It is most good of you to think of my having a friend, but I shall not want anyone with you and the children.' She was busy with negotiations and acquisitions for the Albert Hall Mansions flat, but was 'longing to get back'. When she is away, she is grateful to Emily for 'writing such delightful accounts' of the children. Emily told Lear that the new flat was almost on the site of Gore Lodge, Lady Franklin's house, by then demolished – 'where Ally and I were with our Lionel more than twenty years ago.'

When finally they were settled in the London flat, Eleanor told Emily: 'I will write very often so that you may be quite au courant of all we do.' Young Ally also became 'a pretty constant correspondent of mine,' Emily wrote when he was still only eight. She could never rely on a swift reply from Eleanor who was 'always in a whirl'. But she did confide in Emily and the fact that so many of her letters from this period have been destroyed suggests the fact that it may have been her dangerous relationship with Richmond Ritchie, as much as her subsequent marriage to Augustine Birrell, which led Emily to write that 'poor Eleanor' had indeed 'deeply wronged us'.

In November 1887 Eleanor was anxious about young Ally, by then at day school in London. One day he had 'slipt away' and walked home alone across the Park instead of waiting for the maid. 'He said he wanted to prove to his Mother that he knew his way about London!'

Emily told her sister, with no suggestion of disapproval. Eleanor told Emily: 'A certain amount of turbulence and roughness results from the intercourse with the other boys and this makes him overbearing with Charlie. Charlie is so yielding by nature, so much weaker physically and so adoring of Alfred that he cannot stand up against him in the least. It is rather a worrying state of things. I know my nerves are sensitive and from having been an only child I am unaccustomed to boys ... If they had a Father ...'

Eleanor was ill earlier that year, an illness which caused Emily to make some interesting critical remarks about the medical practices of the day. They had gone to Brighton: 'Eleanor was ordered there after the lowering of the severe discipline of rest to which she has been subjected – a treatment which seems to me too much the fashion now. For nine weeks she was kept eighteen hours out of the twenty-four in bed – I hope the weather will allow her to walk before she finally settles' in London. Emily obviously made a distinction between the sofa and bed itself and she always recognized the value of walking. Alfred's health was measured by his ability to take his regular walks and Emily's grandson Charles saw as crucial that declaration she had made to the great physicist John Tyndall thirty years before. When the conversation turned on the relation between mind and matter, Emily had declared quietly, 'You can at all events walk till you die' – a remark which it makes no sense at all for Charles Tennyson to have quoted unless he himself, who knew her until he was nearly seventeen, had seen her doing exactly that, making the effort each day to walk a little.

By the summer of 1888 Eleanor was married to Augustine Birrell, a lawyer (a QC in 1894) who would be, after Emily's death, President of the Board of Education in Campbell Bannerman's Government and Chief Secretary of State for Ireland. He had himself been widowed long before, after only thirteen months of marriage. He had made his name four years earlier with a volume of essays, *Obiter Dicta*, which Lionel had torn to pieces in his journal – 'clever and shallow' he called it. If the book was a success, 'it only shows how inartistic a public is who can swallow so much nonsense for the sake of sensation.' Probably the other Tennysons felt the same, but Emily's sadness and bewilderment that summer was not primarily to do with Birrell's writing, his radical politics, or his background – though Eleanor's new husband was the eighth of nine children of a Baptist Minister in a drab suburb of Liverpool, 'at a time when non-conformity, like Offa's Dyke, marked a boundary hard to jump over.' It was from a basic dislike of second marriages, a result of her belief in some sort of re-meeting ('Das Wiedersehen') after death. (She did not like the word 'reunion'.) Over and over again Emily had stressed her belief in the 'high and holy fact of the never-ending oneness of real marriage,' and the fact that 'two spirits bound on earth by union so close and holy can know no severance, even in that world where there is neither marrying nor giving in marriage.'

In 1861 Emily had written that she could take little interest in second marriages – and yet she had often had to accept them among their friends. So many husbands dead, so many wives – and she had admitted how good a stepmother the second Lady Simeon, for instance, had been. That had been at the time of Coventry Patmore's second marriage. She was never totally intolerant, even of divorce; her sympathy embraced everyone. But she was 'bewildered'. It was the word she used writing to her sister Anne in June. 'You must forgive me, my Nanny, for I am very sorry not to have done anything for the bazaar, but since the beginning of April I have been in such a bewildered state from Eleanor's engagement and marriage and all the attendant troubles that I seem to have forgotten most things.' It was just over two years after Lionel's death. She was thankful that the wedding was in the parish church (not in a Baptist chapel). 'There were no invitations issued' and just twenty people in the church, including the servants. Afterwards 'they went off in a Brougham to lunch somewhere and then to Dover for Venice.' Emily knew this from a friend of Eleanor's who 'found out the hour and went to the church and she wrote us this account.'

It was an extremely happy marriage. Caroline Jebb noticed Eleanor was 'a changed being'. Augustine Birrell was not only a devoted husband, but a 'perfect stepfather to her three Tennyson children who all worship him.' They would eventually have two more sons of their own. Birrell could even cope with Tennyson's harsh initial greeting (reported by the stepson and grandson Charles): 'Why do you want to force an entry into my family?' Tennyson, saying exactly what he was thinking (as he nearly always did), came to realize Birrell's value. Emily was genuinely glad of Eleanor's happiness and of her grandsons' love for their stepfather, though she knew how hard Hallam found it to be fair to her. She herself longed for her old close relationship with Eleanor. In May 1890 she wrote to the Welds: 'I had hoped to have seen Eleanor often and to have become acquainted with Mr Birrell. We have had perpetual nurses and sickness ever since their marriage. Eleanor is very good in writing about our Darlings, but I wish that she wrote more about herself as well.' It must have comforted Emily that Eleanor could still write: 'I do indeed feel for you as if I were your daughter.'

When Eleanor eventually took the older boys away from the Rawnsleys' school, Park Hill, to send them to Summerfield in Oxford, where she had been told they would have a better chance of obtaining the Eton scholarships they did eventually both win, Emily found it painful that she had not been consulted or even informed. 'We have no influence,' she told her sister. Willingham Rawnsley himself had had to tell her. She felt as sad about the move as they did; the boys were so happy at Park Hill, and the family connection and their nearness to Farringford meant much to their grandmother.

These last years were inevitably dominated by illness and deaths – and not only the illness of the older generation. Audrey, still childless after several years of marriage, suffered crippling headaches. Hallam alarmed them with a 'dangerous illness' in the spring of 1887 and Emily took over his secretarial duties again while he was 'a prisoner upstairs'. Benjamin Jowett, visiting, suggested that illness had its compensations, in self-knowledge and an increased awareness of 'the affection and helpfulness of others'. It was something Emily had always known. Jowett found 'the old poet softens with years, his powers otherwise are unchanged. He and Lady Tennyson – that sweet and aged saint,' as he described her to Florence Nightingale – 'were extremely well'. Hallam was ill again in 1889; he was operated on after a longstanding wound from a cricket ball mysteriously resulted in a 'crater' in his thigh. The Duke of Argyll would then write to Emily – she was acquiring a new role – 'You have been the strong one of the family of late and you must not lose your character.' She had always been the strong one in the most important sense. She was made 'of far sterner stuff than poor Hallam' as Mary Brotherton put it four years later. But both parents depended a great deal on the remaining son.

When Emily Jesse died in January 1887 – a death that 'shook' her brother – Emily Tennyson reported it, even after all these years, as the death of 'the sister who was to have been Arthur Hallam's wife.' The Jesses were devoted spiritualists, but when told she would be reunited with Arthur in the next world, Emily Jesse is reported to have told her husband Richard that she considered that an extremely unfair arrangement: 'We have been through bad times together in this world and

I consider it only decent to share our good times, presuming we have them, in the next.' For the Tennysons, Arthur Hallam remained a central presence in their lives and not only because of the son who had proved so worthy to carry his name. Visitors to Farringford and Aldworth, when he was well, continued to comment on the son's 'quite unostentatious but devoted care of his Father and Mother.' One said, 'I really do not think that anything ever impressed me more in my life.'

In the autumn of 1888 Tennyson himself became gravely ill. It proved to be a rehearsal for his death four years later, helping them all to cope so admirably when the time came at last for him to go. That winter they all thought that he was dying at seventy-nine. There was a perilous fever, described as 'rheumatic gout'. Sometimes as he lay on his sofa near the south window in his study at Aldworth, with the great landscape spread out before him, he felt as if he were already 'looking into the other world'.

They took him to Farringford as soon as he was able to travel. It was 'the old beloved home', as Emily had called it in her last letter to Edward Lear, just before *his* death, far off in San Remo. Farringford was the place where both Tennyson and Emily hoped to die – though neither of them did. Travelling there in 1888, Tennyson was well enough to enjoy guessing people's characters from their legs, which was all he could see of them from his invalid carriage on Yarmouth quay. Hallam kept a diary during this illness, thinking it would be the last months. He said that his father 'liked my mother to be in the room with him even when he slept.' The diary gives a vivid sense of the closeness of the three of them in those dark winter days of 1888–9, as their hopes rose and fell of Tennyson's recovery. He was a distressing sight; he could scarcely move his limbs and his hands were tied with bandages. He was 'as near death as a man could be without dying.' It was now that Hallam recorded Tennyson saying: 'No man could have had two better sons than I have had' and 'before this': 'No man could have had a better and truer wife.' They seemed like last words, like deathbed statements, and comforted both Emily and Hallam over the years in which they laboured on the *Memoir*.

Hallam's diary this winter tells us more about Emily than Audrey's diary of Tennyson's later and final illness. Hallam records that his mother 'is brave but very anxious'. She is aware 'how awfully ill he is. He has lost a great deal of weight, as much as three stone.' (Emily herself, weighed at the same time, is only '6½ stone, although she is tall'.) She contrives all sorts of 'delicate dishes' to tempt his appetite. At one point, Hallam says, Tennyson 'chaffs my mother', quoting 'Rejoicing in the wreck of her good man' – 'and then he speaks to her lovingly'. Emily had always had to cope with both 'chaff' and love, but most of the chaff is not recorded. What we do know is that nothing apparently ruffled her serenity. Another day – on 5 December – Hallam writes of his parents having 'a good talk' – 'she trying to cheer him as he was depressed.' It was something she had attempted over and over again, down the years and often with success. Tennyson in that winter of illness, begged Hallam 'not to let her distress herself'.

Benjamin Jowett, as always, was sure of Emily's strength. He wrote to Hallam when he thought Tennyson was dying: 'Your mother does not require words of consolation, nor could I venture to offer them – I always look up to her as blessed in her whole life. She will not give way in this hour. There are some things still remaining for her to do.' They were already thinking of the *Memoir*, the great tribute which was to fix (they hoped for ever) their version of Tennyson's life. Emily would survive with Hallam's help to accomplish the memorial.

Hallam was extraordinary. Edith Bradley remembered his devotion to Emily as much as to Alfred: 'No daughter could have done more for a mother than Hallam did; nor all daughters would have done as much.' Emily's love for Hallam, matched only by her love for Alfred, seems entirely natural. But was not there something a little unnatural about his devotion to his parents, passing it seemed his love for his wife? Emily was well aware (how could she not have been?) that the Bible tells us that 'a man shall leave his father and his mother and shall cleave unto his wife.' We expect a child's love for the parents to fade over the years as the colour of a well-loved garment fades with use and cleaning. But, until their deaths, Hallam would live their lives rather than his own.

'Our best help and comfort next to God,' Emily called him to his uncle, Edmund Lushington. 'Dear, contented Hallam' – as if she was surprised that he were so. Yet understandably she had come to rely entirely on his devotion. There is a revealing letter to Agnes Weld, when her mother is ill, showing that Emily expected *her* to sacrifice her mathematics class (in her middle age she was studying with Charles Dodgson, who had taken her photograph when she was child), if it was in her mother's interest. Even so, Emily thought continually of Hallam's life *after* his parents' deaths. That was why she had been in favour of Tennyson accepting a peerage. That was why she thought about money ('It is only for Hallamee we are concerned,' she told her sister. 'The books make all easy for us now.') And in the December of 1888 (when Tennyson seemed to be dying), Hallam went to Winchester to take the oaths as a magistrate, a justice of the peace, because his parents wished it. He sat on the bench for the first time on 22 December, and would continue to serve on the Newport bench for many years.

'Poor fellow, all the burdens are on his shoulders and he is, as ever, the most unselfishly devoted of sons,' Mary Brotherton wrote to Frederick on Boxing Day, not realizing – she never did – how painful the contrast was for Frederick with his own son, Alfred Tennyson. The third Alfred Tennyson, the once 'golden-haired Ally', was still with Charlie at Willingham Rawnsley's school at Park Hill, near Lyndhurst, not far from the Isle of Wight – not yet removed to Summerfield. Hallam saw his nephews (and Wordsworth's grandson who was one of their masters) the day he went to take his oaths. Both Tennyson boys were top of their forms in classics and also doing very well in French. Eleanor sent on to Emily the boys' weekly letters and reports from school and they often wrote to her themselves. Ally had written to his mother: 'You need not send us any tuck for Grandmama has sent us plenty which will last us all the term.' Matron was 'an awful stinge' and made sure they did not make themselves sick from eating too much of it at once. Ally cheered them all by reporting that he had had a fight with a boy called Bambridge, because he was bullying Charlie. 'I gave him a punch in the eye with one hand while with the other I broke the fern with which he was whacking Charlie.' Even Emily, hating violence as she did, could only admire this evidence of brotherly love. The grandsons were very dear to her. One day in the summer of 1889 it tore her heart to overhear them singing in the hut they had built at Aldworth. 'There is no parting there . . .'

That winter, with his mother expecting her first Birrell child, Michael was sent to Scotland again, where he had been as a tiny boy when his parents were in India. His mother's cousin wrote to Farringford cheeringly about the child's progress 'and his likeness to his dear father', whom he could not remember. Did Tennyson still feel, as he had fifty-five years before, writing to his cousin Emma when *her* son was born? 'I hope, for his own peace of mind, that he will have as little of the Tennyson about him as possible.' It does not seem so. His own life's work – his poetry and his sons – had, thanks to Emily, lifted the curse there had seemed to be on the name of Tennyson. In the diary he was keeping Hallam recorded his father's pleasure at this comment on Michael.

Michael was now five years old. Little in his short life had given him confidence or security. Was it any wonder he grew up disturbed and aggressive? Emily's concern increased over Michael Sellwood Tennyson. In November 1890 she would write to her sister: 'Dear little Michael, it makes me very sad to think of him and I cannot help wishing that I could have him with me, but God knows what is best we know and does it.' In this case, there was a harmful passivity. If God knew what was best, Eleanor herself certainly did not and some early grandmotherly interference might have saved the child.

It is interesting to discover that Frederick Locker, his other grandfather, had been as late as Michael in learning to read. (In 1829 he could not 'read even tolerably, though almost eight'.) By the time, largely through Emily's intervention, that Michael was taken on, aged eleven, by the Rawnsleys at Park Hill, with special privileges 'for the poor delicate boy', it was really too late. A dozen moves, a dozen opinions and he was labelled as unfit for normal society – but it was only after Emily's death that he was finally confined to one of the institutions in which he would spend the rest of his long life. While Emily was alive, he was her 'dear little Michael'. He stayed with his grandmother almost as much as the other boys and she would record his sweetness and his affection for his cousins. 'Michael said so prettily last night when we wished him "pleasant dreams", "I hope I shall dream of you all. You have all been so kind to me."' Four months later she said, still optimistic in the year before her death: 'The great brain doctor considers it only delicacy from which he suffers.' They did not speak of the black blood. Emily never allowed Michael to be pushed out of the picture, as he would be finally by the rest of his family. When Tennyson signed copies of *Demeter* for his grandsons, Ally and Charlie, Emily told her sister, 'Another day I hope to get one for my poor little Michael.' His mother thought he had plenty of abilities, but 'his peculiarities hinder him making use of them'. She did not know how much it sounded like his Tennyson great-great-grandfather's description of his great-uncle Arthur, but Emily must have thought of those 'peculiar' young brothers of Alfred's at Somersby sixty years before.

By March of 1889 Tennyson had recovered sufficiently from his illness to take his first walk in the sunshine. By the autumn Richard Jebb was able to say that: 'The poet, who was 80 in August, is wonderfully well.' Emily had asked George Craik of Macmillan to organize a 'good solid old-fashioned wooden desk to stand on his writing-table' and to address it to Mrs Andrews, the housekeeper, so it did not 'fall into his hands before the 6th,' his birthday.

There would be one more worrying illness before the final one. They kept on Nurse Durham – to whom Emily taught French when there was little nursing for her to do. This gave pleasure to both of them, though Emily was grieved how out of practice she was. 'It is so long since I taught French'; it was so long since her boys were young.

Tennyson was able to express, over and over again, in these last years, just what Emily meant to him. In 1886 he had dedicated to her the volume *Locksley Hall Sixty Years After*. He stressed the poem itself was a 'dramatic monologue' but it contained the words that have inevitably been associated with Emily: 'She that linked again the broken chain that bound me to my kind.' It was her tenderness that he most loved. He had said to Anne Thackeray Ritchie: 'She is almost too delicate and tender for this world.' And one night he said to the Duke of Argyll, just after Hallam had taken his mother off to bed: 'It is a tender, spiritual face, is it not?'

It was a face to which no justice was done at all in her final photograph, one taken by Henry Cameron at Aldworth with Hallam leaning over the sofa on which his parents are sitting. Henry in the *Pall Mall Budget* called it 'one of my gems'. Hallam had arranged for him to take it, to help him, for the sake of their long family friendship, but he wrote to Craik: 'Did you see the awful group of us all? My poor mother looks like the witch of Endor.' Mary Brotherton seeing it in the magazine wrote to Frederick: 'Your brother seems turning with a very uncharacteristic smirk to Lady Tennyson, who looks stern and unpropitious; Hallam leaning over the sofa-back casts up his eyes piously, and looks unpicturesquely fat.' The other image of Emily from this last period of her life, is a painting by Helen Allingham, who visited them over and over again at both Farringford and Aldworth, both before and after her husband's death in November 1889. Helen made some charming pictures of the houses and their grounds and a fine late portrait of Tennyson in the study at Farringford – but her water-colour sketch of Emily is of a pale almost blank mask which gives little idea of a real person.

Emily and Alfred had now come through together, in spite of Lionel's death, to what Marian Bradley described as the 'calm sunshine of his old age'. Mrs Bradley was happy for Emily that Tennyson's 'self-absorption and melancholy of his earlier years' had largely passed away, that he was growing 'more and more unselfish and thoughtful for others'. He was naturally extremely pleased to have survived an illness which his doctor said 'would have made an end of nine men out of ten' of his age.

Alfred's tenderness had always been one of the things that Emily most valued. When she gave Audrey one Christmas Frances Hodgson Burnett's autobiography, *The One I Knew the Best of All*, Emily must have remembered Tennyson weeping, as he had more than once, over her story 'Surly Tim', the tears rolling down his cheeks. His own poems had often moved him to tears. Now many remarked on his greater tolerance and willingness to listen. Theresa Melville Lee, meeting him for the first time in the summer before his death, said, 'It did not matter to him that I was no-one of importance. He cared to make me happy and give me his best, listening to my remarks and caring for my appreciation.' This conjures up the same Tennyson admirers had always known. He made her happy by reading 'Maud'; he listened attentively to her praise of him. But he remained also interested in what she could tell him, asking many questions about the Passion Play at Oberammergau, which she had seen. 'I think women must have always found him sympathetic,' she said. 'There was a playfulness, considerateness, and chivalry in his manner which were very attractive.'

It had always been there for Emily as well as for the numerous women who flocked to admire the Laureate. As Willingham Rawnsley said, 'though he was called brusque, sometimes he could say very pretty things.' None of the women now heard the sort of talk John Addington Symonds had not been able to repeat in a letter to his sister: 'too grotesque (to say the least) for me to record here.' It was a long time since he had thought nothing of shocking the young women listeners with tales of an African woman who asked to be breakfasted upon (by white men) or told his schoolboy sons of a chieftain who had 'killed young girls to warm his feet in their bowels'. If he was tamer these days, he was certainly much more comfortable to live with.

Emily and Hallam continued to protect Tennyson from most of the ordinary problems of life. There is a typical remark in a letter from Emily to her sister Anne in the summer of 1889, after the illness of a housemaid. 'Our nice Bessy is obliged to go.' The girl had had pains in her side and needed hospital treatment. 'We are all very sorry that Bessy must go – all I mean who know about her. Ally of course does not.' There were all sorts of problems with servants at this period, but Emily saw no reason for Alfred to bother about them. It was extremely difficult to keep a kitchenmaid. 'As soon as they can cook a little they want to go into cook's places,' which was understandable. Emily imagined a time would soon come when everyone would prefer to be 'clerks or schoolmasters and mistresses or dressmakers' or part of 'the honourable army of nurses'. She hoped there would soon be some sort of robot or automaton to help in the house. 'Flesh and blood it appears we shall have none.'

But there was another problem which disturbed Emily in the summer of 1889 far more than the problem of finding new servants. It is important not only because it grieved Emily that Robert Browning was so hurt in that last summer of his life (as it turned out to be). It also strengthened Emily's resolve to make sure no-one could be hurt when the time came – as she knew it was coming – for the *Memoir* of Alfred's life to be written – though she assured Browning that nothing could really harm 'your wife and my husband . . . We must leave them to the ages.' She was confident of posterity's judgment.

Would Emily herself have been hurt if she had known, as we know, that Elizabeth Barrett Browning had once told Annie Fields that she thought Emily was too much Tennyson's 'second self', with the suggestion that his poetry might have benefited from less devotion and more criticism? Emily would have said, quite rightly, that Mrs Browning knew absolutely nothing about it. Was not enthusiasm as necessary for a poet as criticism? It was indeed *more* necessary for one so easily wounded by 'puny darts' and stings. And what did Mrs Browning know of their relationship? She had seen them together only once in Paris in 1851. She had died when the Tennysons had been married only eleven years. Yet her opinion – like that of FitzGerald (who again never saw them together after the 1850s) – has been quoted as authoritative evidence of Emily's deleterious effect on Tennyson's poetry. That was something Tennyson would strongly have denied, and for which there is really no evidence, however much the British public loves best the early 'Lady of Shalott', and *In Memoriam* remains his most important poem. 'She has been my life-long and truest critic,' Tennyson told Hardwick Rawnsley. Jowett, too, thought Emily 'probably her husband's best critic, and certainly the one whose authority he would most willingly have recognized.'

Emily found herself in the position of defending Edward FitzGerald in 1889, six years after his death. ('FitzGerald is FitzGerald to me after all.') His friend Aldis Wright of Trinity College, Cambridge, editing his letters, had included his callous, casual, sexist remark, which obviously Fitz himself had imagined no-one but W.H. Thompson – to whom he wrote – would ever see. He seemed to rejoice in the death of Elizabeth Barrett Browning. The passage in the letter was indefensible:

Mrs Browning's Death is rather a relief to me, I must say: no more Aurora Leighs, thank God! A Woman of real Genius, I know: but what is the upshot of it all? She and her Sex had better mind the Kitchen and their Children; and perhaps the Poor: except in such things as little Novels, they only devote themselves to what men do much better, leaving that which Men do worse or not at all.

Where would Alfred have been if Emily had restricted herself to Kitchen, Children and 'perhaps the Poor'? Emily made no comment on FitzGerald's remarks about women, or indeed specifically about the vilest joking word – Fitz's 'relief' at Elizabeth Barrett Browning's death. She wrote to Anne Thackeray Ritchie after reading both the published letter and Browning's furious devastated response in the *Athenaeum*. Emily could write that she knew the words should not be taken seriously. She was trying to imagine herself, the poet's wife, in Browning's position.

Yes indeed Edward FitzGerald's friends perfectly understand the spirit in which those unhappy words were written. He would have laid down his own life to save hers, I think, all unknown personally tho' she was to him. I suppose I must be more self-confident than other people. It does not hurt me that dear old Fitz does not care – even for 'In Memoriam' and The Idylls of the King. I feel it was a want in him that he did not, that is all . . . I wish Aldis Wright had not only omitted those words we speak of, but I wish that he had told that old FitzGerald lived for a time in a house in his Father's park on five shillings a week that he might give the rest of what he had to the poor. A man so kind never would have written those words had he thought they would be made public . . .

Anne Thackeray Ritchie sent the letter on to Browning who found it 'most sympathetic as it was sure to be' – but missing the point. 'His contempt of her works was wholly out of my mind: I only thought of the woman my wife.' In a long letter, Browning told Emily he could put up with any amount of abuse about his own poems – even of his wife's – but *nothing* could excuse FitzGerald's phrase. 'You, dear Lady Tennyson, could hardly realize the effect of all this on me – from your utter inability to perpetrate ugliness in thought, word or deed. How I remember your goodness to her, and how she appreciated it!' But how would Emily have felt if a writer had been pleased that Tennyson was too ill to write any more *In Memoriams*? '(The exact parallel is too abhorrent for me to think out and write down.)' He told Emily not to reply to his dismal letter, but she did: 'It has been cruel work and we grieve deeply for you and your son and FitzGerald's family.' As usual, she was seeing everyone's side of the problem. Alfred's comfort was even less helpful: 'Ally bids me to say with his love that Fitz never meant what you take him to mean.'

CHAPTER SIXTEEN

'The dead are not dead but alive'

Though they sometimes seemed 'shadowy' and unreal, on the whole they were good years, the nearly four years between Emily's facing up entirely to the likelihood of Tennyson's death in the winter of 1888–9 and his actual death late in 1892. The great joy was that Audrey after a difficult early pregnancy (which may well have followed earlier miscarriages) produced a son in November 1889. Hallam borrowed a house in London for the event, 7 Grosvenor Crescent, and in fact it was not until March 1890 that the new baby, Lionel Hallam Tennyson, arrived at Farringford. From Christmas on he and Audrey were at Wimbledon with her brother's family and Hallam spent a good deal of time with his parents, *wanted*, Emily knew he was, by all of them: 'He cannot be in two places, dear old darling and his first duty has been in London,' she told Anne Ritchie, knowing too (as she told the Welds) what a good thing it was for him 'seeing people' and 'feeling the footing he has among them'.

Over the run-up to the publication of Tennyson's new book *Demeter and Other Poems* (on the very day, 12 December, that Robert Browning died in Venice), Emily was back in her old position, writing to George Craik at Macmillan, dealing with the final proofs. It was indeed her idea that the collection should take the name *Demeter*; Tennyson had suggested *Scraps*. Emily's eye remained keen, picking up, for instance, 'whispers' as a misprint for 'whimpers'. She sent Craik 'a new reading in the Leper's Bride' – 'such great exception having been taken to the old', though Tennyson thought he might 'reinstate the old line' in a second edition. This was in the poem 'Happy', triggered off apparently by an article in the *Isle of Wight County Press* that recalled how lepers were followed into banishment by their faithful wives. It is spoken in the voice of a leper and includes the lines, that have, perversely, been used to suggest that Tennyson himself undervalued sexual love:

> I loved you first when young and fair, but now I love you most;
> The fairest flesh at last is filth on which the worm will feast.

On 6 November 1889 Emily wrote to Hallam, 'I quite agree about Katherine,' as she spelt it. 'Mabel robs the ballad of half its fire. Papa acquiesces, I think. He only remonstrated "Mabel is softer," but when I spoke of the loss of fire he said no more.' This was in an old poem 'Forlorn' which was to be published for the first time. Tennyson had changed 'Catherine' to 'Mabel' in the proofs, but reverted with Emily's encouragement. How could 'Mabel' be softer than 'Catherine'?

Emily told her sister Anne that 'I have been quite overtasked and knocked up. Of course it was useless saying anything about it. What had to be done must be done as long as I could do it . . . 18 or 20 letters in a morning as I have had some mornings to read before I could let Ally see them are in themselves hard work for an old and far from strong old woman, are they not?' She was now seventy-six. To Hallam she said, 'Papa has been most touching in his care of me.' He took over tasks that had lately been Hallam's. At night Tennyson said, 'Hallam's last words were that I should read to you. If you want very much that I should read, I will.' It sounds a little grudging, but he helped her up the stairs each night, 'exactly at ten'. When Hallam was away, sometimes they played backgammon together 'in old Darby and Joan fashion'.

Hallam scolded her for doing too much in his absence. 'Even a loving scolding is sweet,' she wrote to him, 'tho' it does give me a small choking fit at breakfast'. She had written large numbers of letters about the new baby, for instance, to Sarah Prinsep: 'I do hope that our little Lionel Hallam may be a blessing to all. He is a splendid fellow and looks very pretty, I hear, in Hallam's clothes – and that he is like him.' 'You may think how I long to see him,' she wrote to Hallam. Later, she promised him she would write less, and only regularly to 'thyself and the boys and Eleanor' and the Welds. Even so, she had to read all the letters that came in and sort them out before sending some on to Hallam. And, as usual, she was 'busy with bankers' books'. She remained entirely in charge of the family accounts and of running the household when she was over eighty, indeed until not long before her death. There are accounts and wine lists in her writing, and letters concerning the hiring of new servants, after Tennyson's death, in which she says all communications should be addressed to Emily, Lady Tennyson, not Lady Tennyson, lest they should be sent on to her daughter-in-law, 'wherever she may be'.

Emily's relationship with Audrey was sometimes, inevitably, a little difficult, though she was constantly saying how happy she was that Hallam had such a devoted wife. There are only glimpses of impatience with her; Emily was used to having her own way. Audrey had told her she could not tell anyone about her pregnancy until the last weeks. ('I would have told you months ago' Emily wrote to Agnes, 'but had to promise silence'.) Audrey had chosen her nurseries; 'I should prefer the sunny side for baby,' Emily said. Who indeed would not? Emily did get her way over the baby's name, not wanting him to be burdened with 'Alfred' and 'Charles' ('both names are already in our branch of the family'), as well as the simple 'Lionel Hallam' she loved.

The good news, which certainly suggests difficulties in the past, was the effect on Audrey of having produced the 'splendid fellow'. Emily wrote to her sister in April 1890, just a few weeks after the new mother and child were established at Farringford: 'Do not say anything but she is really quite a different person since her baby was given to us.' Jowett, realizing just what Hallam's son meant to Emily, said: 'You must live a few more years for the sake of your family and to see the young heir of the house grow up, and therefore I wish you a few more Christmases.' 'I hope you are well,' he wrote. 'I know that you are always at peace.'

That Christmas they were also rejoicing in the reception of *Demeter and Other Poems*, which had sold 20,000 copies before publication. Tennyson's reputation was such now that the reviews did not actually matter. F.W.H. Myers had written in the *Nineteenth Century* earlier that year of 'The persistence of Lord Tennyson's gift in all its glory – a persistence scarcely rivalled since Sophocles . . .' W. E. Henley would describe his late poetry as 'far more plangent and affecting'. He considered Tennyson now a sculptor where before he had been a jeweller. The huge sales of Tennyson's books would continue long after his death. In that year, 1892, the receipts from Macmillan were over £10,000. Emily's comments on *Demeter* include: 'The little poem of "The Moaning of the Bar", it seems to me must be one of the loveliest ever written.' (Under the title 'Crossing the Bar' it would be sung not only at Tennyson's funeral, but at her own.) 'Even "The Ring", of which I was rather doubtful somehow seems all right.' Emily made no comment on 'The Roses on the Terrace', Tennyson's delightful lyric which undoubtedly ends on the terrace at Aldworth.

> Rose, on this terrace fifty years ago,
>   When I was in my June, you in your May,
> Two words, '*My* Rose' set all your face aglow,
>   And now that I am white, and you are gray,
> That blush of fifty years ago, my dear,
>   Blooms in the Past, but close to me today
> As this red rose, which on our terrace here
>   Glows in the blue of fifty miles away.

There are commentators who say firmly, because it is addressed to 'Rose', that the lyric 'is to Rosa Baring'. Others, among them her grandson Lionel and Harold Nicolson, say it was addressed to Emily herself. It seems highly unlikely that Tennyson would have offered up such a tempting morsel to the ghouls by addressing it to 'Rose', if he did indeed have Rosa Baring in mind. 'It is curious how little credit people give to the Imagination of a Poet,' Emily said, telling her sister Tennyson had had no particular 'Bar' in mind in 'Crossing the Bar', however much it might seem he had been crossing to the Isle of Wight when he first thought of it.

The Tennysons were so maddened by 'the localising craze', by people trying to identify the Moated Grange and so on, Emily suggested it would be better to have no notes at all: 'Let the poems speak for themselves.' But Tennyson's own comment on 'Locksley Hall Sixty Years After' is worth reading at this point. 'There is not one touch of autobiography in it from beginning to end,' he wrote in a letter. 'I am not even white-haired, I never had a gray hair in my head.' And again, a few months before his death, he wrote: 'If by "wintry hair" you allude to a tree whose leaves are half gone, you are right, but if you mean "white", you are wrong, for I never had a gray hair on my head.' This was not strictly true, but Tennyson would never have said of himself, 'Now that I am white . . .' 'My father almost always writes from a dramatic point of view,' Hallam said, however unsuccessful he was as a dramatist. How could anyone suppose he was speaking in his own voice? Tennyson would, perhaps a little disingenuously, protest.

There was one poem that is unquestionably in his own voice and unquestionably for Emily. It is the dedication to Tennyson's last book of poems: *The Death of Œnone*, which was published just after Tennyson's own death.

> There on the top of the down,
> The wild heather round me and over me June's high blue,
> When I looked at the bracken so bright and the heather so brown,
> I thought to myself I would offer this book to you,
> This, and my love together,
> To you that are seventy-seven,
> With a faith as clear as the heights of the June-blue heaven,
> And a fancy as summer-new
> As the green of the bracken amid the gloom of the heather.

Together with 'Dear, near and true', the dedication Tennyson had written nearly thirty years earlier, 'June Bracken and Heather' is a deeply satisfying expression of what Emily, the poet's wife, meant to him. This lyric captures Emily's special quality, that 'fancy as summer-new' she kept right to the end of her life, with her clear faith. She wrote to her sister in October 1890 at seventy-seven, 'I do not find that age cools passionate feeling', and the letters of her last years (particularly those to her niece, Agnes,) teem with strong feelings, ideas and the energy of mind Emily Tennyson showed until her last hour. Her serenity came from her faith, from an assurance (for all her lack of 'self-love') that, with God's help, she knew what was right and could live with her own particular adaptation of Christ's teaching.

If Christ said it was more difficult for a rich man to enter the kingdom of heaven than for a camel to go through the eye of a needle, she believed there were ways for a rich man to use his wealth that were as acceptable to God as literally giving away all that you have and distributing it among the poor. She was proud of the fact that Tennyson provided work for a great many people. Although their income was huge, the regular outgoings were as well. Their wages bill each year was at least £1,300: 'Well!' Emily said. 'It is a useful way of spending money and one is thankful to have it to spend.'

Emily made sure the Welds realized that there was not much money to spare. 'Expenses are so heavy that I do without all I can. Two bedroom carpets I had to get for the Bishop, which I should not have got probably for ourselves.' They were still letting Farringford for the summer, whenever they could find bishops or other respectable tenants. She gave what she could to charity, but it always seemed embarrassingly little and Agnes sometimes did not scruple to embarrass her.

'How overpoweringly much remains to be done. Courage Faith and Love – how much are needed!' 'One might spend millions, much to one's satisfaction', helping those in need. They were trying a soup kitchen again at the Farringford farm. Emily would write to Agnes, 'We had a hundred and twenty-six applications for soup and loaves yesterday, so you may think that there is great distress here.' Audrey was Chairman of the Workhouse Committee at Newport. Not many elderly women have to defend their records, as Agnes expected Emily to do. 'I wish I could help you in your work,' Emily wrote to Agnes, not long before her death. 'My lot has seemed to be quite differently cast. God forgive my failures in it.' Had she been right to devote her life almost entirely to her family, to her poet? She put up a spirited defence of their way of life. 'It is they who *trust* in riches, not they who employ them according to the order of God's world, whom He reproves.' She made the point that single people, such as Agnes, can be much more free to take no thought for the morrow, and she rejoiced in Agnes 'having had the heart given you to do so much for others'. But Emily warned Agnes of the danger of getting into debt, from obeying too enthusiastically Christ's injunction to give away all that we have to follow him. 'You must not ruin yourself. Money slips away very rapidly.' Her aunt begged Agnes to listen to the Holy Ghost to guide her through 'the emotions and circumstances of our life'. Fortunately Emily never knew how little Agnes heeded her warnings.

Emily was still writing music. She set several of the songs in Tennyson's play *The Foresters*, but they were not used in the final production. 'Sullivan is to write the music for the songs, with which he is delighted,' Emily told Jowett. Her 'wifely mind', she said, had a rather higher opinion of Tennyson's plays 'than is as yet generally granted to them,' but she knew nothing about the theatre. I 'have never seen a play acted since I was seventeen, I believe, except by our boys, the ante-room being stage, the corner of the drawing-room boxes! Of course Ally also lacks all critical knowledge of the stage and his plays have to be adapted by those who have it.'

Emily had never had any personal ambition; she was also delighted Sir Arthur Sullivan was to write the music for this last play, even if Tennyson knew so much less about stagecraft than W.S. Gilbert, and

Emily herself knew very little about contemporary music. When Hallam and Audrey had gone to hear Stanford's setting of 'The Revenge' in the Albert Hall, Emily had commented that their report of the reception ('a slight flapping of small wings') must have been rather 'deadening to those who need applause by way of stimulant'. Emily herself never needed applause. But she must surely have had some satisfaction from the public acknowledgment of her own small talent as a composer, which culminated in the use of one of her own settings at Tennyson's funeral and a number of recitals in the period immediately before.

These recitals were the result of the admiration of Natalie Janotha, a famously exuberant Polish pianist who was much in demand. Janotha, as she was always known, was 'a wild genius', according to Emily. Hallam eventually pronounced her completely 'cracky' and Jowett thought her 'really a little mad'. But everyone agreed she was an excellent pianist. Mary Gladstone had described her as a 'curious little passionate being', who played the Moonlight Sonata to Gladstone, 'drank one teaspoonful of tea and then vanished again like a flash of lightning into the gloom.'

Janotha had first come to Aldworth in September 1890, arriving for tea ('as we thought') but staying the night. Her object was to get Emily's agreement that she should play some of Emily's settings of Tennyson's poems in future concerts. That August Hallam had written in his diary that Tennyson 'always has tea with my mother, who is copying her settings of his songs, mostly made after his first reading of them to her, for his Notes, as he has asked her to do.' Emily emphasized that her settings were always made at Tennyson's own request. Even her music, both Hallam and Emily seemed determined to suggest, was only part of her devotion to Tennyson himself, her wish to make his poems even better known and understood, as he desired. Emily had been writing music for Tennyson's poems all their married life, and some had been published. But it was only now near the end of it, that a considerable number were published together (with both their names attached) and given professional performance at several recitals.

Emily described Janotha's versions of her settings as 'fine sonatas made on the airs rather than accompaniments'. Janotha's own account of her relationship with the Tennysons, which appeared in the *Pall Mall Gazette* in May 1891, may be 'really a little mad', but it is worth reading:

In my opinion the accompaniments were worthy of the beautiful songs; the melodies seem to me to be in the sweetest harmony with the words. It is a mistake to suppose Lady Tennyson wrote the accompaniments quite recently, one after the other. Several were written thirty or forty years ago; sometimes when I have been invited to 'smoke a pipe' – that is how he puts it – with Lord and Lady Tennyson at Aldworth, we have sung them together. It is wonderful to hear Lord Tennyson sing; he manages to take all the notes, tenor, baritone etc. In all, Lady Tennyson has written the music of fifteen songs at different times and I arranged seven of them for my concert. But only one 'To sleep, To sleep,' was set to music for the concert . . . Her Majesty the Queen has expressed a desire to hear the songs so they will probably be given at Windsor.

Janotha's letters to Emily are full of the most extravagant language. For example, in March 1891, she sent, with Chappell's contract, the words: 'I am sure the great gift of the works of the immortal holy genius, – is given to me, by your angelic order and hands, which I kiss in gratitude and quiet worship!! –' Everyone was asking, she said, 'Are the Songs of Lady T. out?' She wrote: 'I have a presentiment that my dearest Lady Tennyson will be very very celebrated as a "unique composer".' Harsher critics might think that if she had not been the wife of the Poet Laureate her music would never have been published.

Even so, when seven of the songs were performed in St James's Hall on 13 March 1891 the critics seem to have been largely respectful, though there was a feeling 'that Janotha's very Schumannesque accompaniments were too elaborate a foil' to Lady Tennyson's simple melodies. Hallam felt that something needed to be done and seems to have discussed the matter with his composer friend Charles Stanford who had arranged Emily's setting of 'Hands All Around' sung all over the Empire on the Queen's Birthday nine years before. Hallam also talked to both Hubert Parry and Charles Wood. After all sorts of disagreements, Janotha wrote to Emily in May 1892 to say the songs were at Chappell's. 'We worked finally with Dr Wood . . . We all are quite an army devoted to our sweetest melodious leader, but no-one surrounds your dearest self and each note of your musical thought with such devotion and attachement as your Grateful and true Janotha.' Hallam had done the quarrelling; Emily had remained 'my heroic angel whom I do adore'. The songs were not actually published until the end of October 1892, just after Tennyson's death. On the copy of 'The Silent Voices', brought home to Emily by Hallam from Tennyson's funeral,

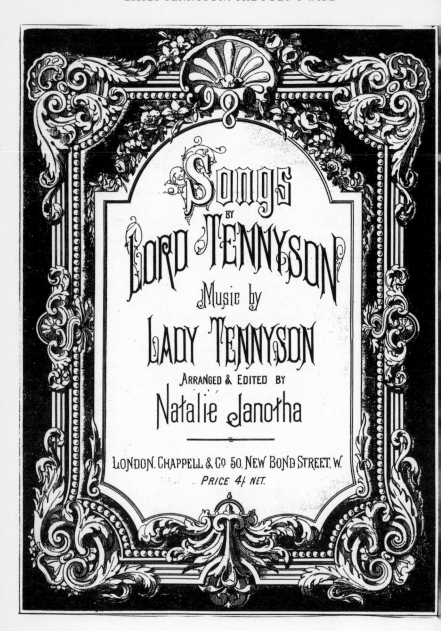

Emily would write in her own hand the words 'at his desire set to' after the printed words 'MUSIC BY LADY TENNYSON'.

The year 1891 was also notable for the birth of 'a fine boy', Alfred Aubrey Tennyson on 2 May at the Briary, not far from Farringford. Hallam had borrowed the house from G.F. Watts so that the event disturbed his parents as little as possible. Emily rejoiced at the arrival of Hallam's second son. She had always felt that 'an only son is a perilous gift, both for his own sake and his parents.' His parents got their way and added the name Alfred to Aubrey, the name by which the boy was always known, but it is interesting that when Emily had some silver pencil cases engraved for her grandsons, the wording was 'Lionel Hallam Tennyson from E.T.' and simply 'Aubrey Tennyson from E.T.' (Aubrey de Vere was 'the godfather from whom he took his name'). Emily was already worrying about the effect of his name on the career of the first grandson, Lionel's son Alfred. They asked his mother Eleanor to be one of Aubrey's godmothers. It seems an attempt to bind the family closer together. The new Tennyson babies were much the same age as the two little Birrell boys, Francis and Tony. The cousins (Lionel's and Hallam's boys) got on very well together, to Emily's delight, in spite of the age gap. Charlie, in particular, always made a great fuss over little Lionel, feeding him and giving him his bath.

A few days before Hallam's birthday that year, 1891, Emily drafted a clumsy, ill-expressed prose version of what she hoped might become a poem for Hallam who – deserving as he was – had never had a poem written for him by his father. 'Blessing to parents rare in this our age', Emily began, and eventually went on: 'Blessing to us without alloy save in the fear that dreams of noble doing and daring haunting thine earlier years surrendered, may not have been to thee all gain. Yet, no idler hast thou been within our walls. With loving devotion hast thou rendered help, wherever and whenever help could be. A day must come which brings to thee work of wider range. God's blessing ever on thee and thine! . . .' At the bottom of the page Emily wrote: 'Ally mine I want you to write something of this sort to our Hallam on his birthday. Begin it today I beg of thee.' Finding it on his desk, Tennyson must have sighed and picked up his pen and inevitably put it down again.

Certainly Hallam had 'slaved' for his parents, but he was never simply an unquestioning attendant and, even as a boy, he had often called the tune, had been bossy, not meekly dutiful. He was always telling his parents how they should behave: 'Be philosophical.' 'Wrap up warmly.' And William Allingham caught the true note of the relationship between father and son. When Tennyson was talking of Chelsea Embankment once, as 'a charming place – I could live there all the year,' Hallam commented (*sotto voce*), 'He always gets tired of London in a fortnight.'

Hallam Tennyson had a marvellous temperament and 'an amazing charm', as Marian Bradley, his headmaster's wife, had noted when he was a boy of sixteen – not always a charming age. His mother constantly commented on his bright spirits. He hardly deserves the image that seems to prevail of a dour 'unsmiling' guardian of the shrine. If Emily protested a little too often at how 'contented' he seemed, there was no denying the impression he gave to everyone. Even when he was not well 'he always manages to be cheery himself and to cheer others.' 'Hallamee is as of old our Joy,' Emily wrote to her sister, using the pet name she used so often.

There were deaths, of course, as well as birthdays. Inevitably the survivors of Emily's own generation were going down, one by one. Kate Rawnsley, her dear cousin, died in May 1892, and, not long after Alfred's own death, three more of those closest to Emily: Edmund Lushington, Benjamin Jowett and her sister, Anne Weld. Anne died in a peaceful sleep, as Emily had prayed she might. At her funeral they played a hymn which, long before, Anne had played for the cousins, Lionel, Hallam and Agnes, to sing together.

> He gave thee; He took thee, and He will restore thee;
> And death has no sting, for the Saviour has died.

Alfred Tennyson's death, when it came in October 1892, was also without sting. The sheaf was fully ripe to be garnered, as Hallam said when Emily's own time came. Emily wrote: 'We would not have had' him 'live the suffering life he has done of late. We who love him best know that he has never been the same since his bad illness four years ago and from last February there was, we fear, no enjoyment of life.' It was two years since he had been in 'capital spirits', enjoying shouting 'The Charge of the Light Brigade' and 'The Bugle Song' and laughing with his baby grandson at the mysteries of Edison's phonograph. It was eighteen months or so since he had demonstrated his agility by rising quickly twenty times from a low chair without touching the arms. It was as long since he had danced 'a graceful chassé' in the ballroom at Farringford with May Hichens. The time had come for him to go and Emily could accept it was so, with the hope of that other life to come, the life eternal which Christ had promised. She could not wish things otherwise. The days leading up to Tennyson's death, the impressive funeral, the aftermath and the work on the *Memoir* have all been explored at the beginning of this book.

It was Emily who decided on the wording of the tablet in Freshwater church:

In loving Memory
of
Alfred Lord Tennyson
Poet Laureate
Whose happiest days were passed at Farringford in this parish
Born Augst 6th 1809
Died Oct 6th 1892
Buried in Westminster Abbey 12th 1892
Speak living Voice! With thee death is not death
Thy life outlives the life of dust and breath.

It was not until the end of October 1894 that Emily told Agnes, 'Our tablet was put up last week. It is like our Lionel's and over it.' Under the ten lines commemorating 'Alfred Lord Tennyson', there was a space leaving room for Emily herself. It was indeed 'our tablet'. Emily's own inscription carries Tennyson's own words about her:

DEAR, NEAR AND TRUE – NO TRUER TIME HIMSELF
CAN PROVE YOU, THO' HE MAKE YOU EVERMORE
DEARER AND NEARER.

However much Emily had thought of a quiet funeral, the country churchyard, the two graves side by side in the green grass by the river Yar, she admitted that the huge crowds and the Abbey ceremony were the fitting farewell for the great poet. Emily had given so much to Tennyson and had gained so much from him, from being the poet's wife. Jowett had imagined what thoughts she must have had lying on her sofa, 'some sad, others bright': 'You have shared the life of one of the noblest and most distinguished men of his time and have been able to support and comfort him in a way that no other woman could have done . . .' 'He could never have been what he was without her,' Jowett said. Only a few casual comments of her own ('Of course, it was useless saying anything about it.') and Edward Lear's diary, suggesting so strongly that *only* Emily could have stayed married to Tennyson for more than a month, survive to indicate how hard the road must sometimes have been, how much her devotion must often have been tested.

Emily felt near to Tennyson as she worked on the *Memoir* of his life, of their life together. At the same time, Emily was corresponding with Dean Bradley about the gravestone and the bust in Westminster Abbey. 'Our old Clerk of Works, a Lincolnshire man, has taken infinite pains,' Bradley told her. There were some problems about acquiring the Woolner bust they wanted.

When the *Memoir*, their joint work, in many ways as much Emily's book as his, was finally published, fourteen months after her death, Hallam wrote to the Queen: 'The great comfort that I have in my work is that it was a comfort to my Mother in her loneliness.'

It was the book that kept Emily going for nearly four years after Alfred's death until the time when she was almost exactly the age he was at his death. Her health did not allow her to do much else. She couldn't eat much, but she could at least take Liebig's or Brand's Essence and 'chicken soup with a tiny bit of chicken.' She continued to believe her beloved champagne was the best medicine in the world, except for the times when she decided she preferred Vouvray. She rubbed eau de cologne on her forehead and had a tablespoonful of brandy 'in a large tea-cup of arrowroot at bed time'.

Daisy Bradley, the Dean's daughter, described Emily Tennyson in old age without the trappings of invalidism: 'Her silky auburn-brown hair, partly hidden by lace lappets, was untouched with grey and her complexion kept its rose-leaf delicacy, just as her strong and cultivated intellect kept its alertness to the last days of her life.' Annie Fields said

Lady Tennyson 'stepped with the same spirited sweep' as she had more than thirty years earlier when the Fields had arrived at Farringford with a letter of introduction from Longfellow. And one of Jowett's last acts before his death was to record that in her old age Emily Tennyson 'had not lost the freshness or elasticity of youth, or the step and gait of youth' – utterly refuting those who see her permanently stretched out on that sofa.

It was her grandson Charles who wrote of Emily's 'wonderful serenity that nothing seemed to disturb'. It was the serenity which comes from a lifetime of prayer and meditation, from an awareness that it is the life of the spirit that really matters and that all things work together for good. Emily had once rashly told Tennyson that when she prayed, 'I see the face of God smiling upon me.' We would not know that if Alfred had not told Jowett ('as indeed he told some things to everybody, which others keep to themselves') and Jowett wrote it down for the *Memoir* just before his own death. Emily had protested that it was impossible to publish this, but she was in no position to get her way by the time it appeared. And it was, after all, but an echo of a favourite Cowper hymn: 'God moves in a mysterious way'.

> Judge not the Lord by feeble sense,
> But trust Him for His grace;
> Behind a frowning providence
> He hides a smiling face.

Emily Tennyson had never been one for judging, either God or man, and certainly not Alfred. Love had been the word she lived by. 'If we love one another thou dwellest in us, and thy love is perfected in us,' she had written in her prayer book. 'And the Lord make us to increase and abound in love one toward another and toward all men . . . '

For Alfred she had shown an unchanging love since the Somersby days. Her love for God was similarly unswerving, 'free and faithful, strong as death'. 'The Lord is loving; his mercy is always with us.' ('One can beat this into one's brain when one is too dull for anything else, cannot one, my sweetie?' she had once written to Hallam.) Jowett had written: 'There is no-one who seems to me to have a stronger faith or a more real love of God than you have and I know that they will not fail you at the time when you most need them.'

After Tennyson's death there were still some periods when, as Emily said, 'our house keeps its old character of an hotel.' (One week Emily counted nineteen 'closely packed' at Aldworth.) There were always people coming and going, but Emily herself concentrated on the book. She wrote to Agnes at the end of 1892, less than three months after Tennyson's death: 'I see no one, therefore I do not know much of people's doings. I cannot manage the writing and seeing people. The writing takes all my strength and at my age this is a duty which must not be trifled with, must it?' She was determined to live until she had done all that she could do to help Hallam with the *Memoir*, which was to add to Tennyson's reputation and confirm his claim to a place among the immortals. It was always 'our work' when she referred to it, a joint enterprise. Emily's wish to influence things, 'according to what I believe to be right', was more passionate than ever. 'If it were not so, it would be hard indeed to go on living.' Working on the *Memoir* was hard enough.

Emily had often heard Tennyson expressing himself strongly on the subject of memoirs and biographies – 'betraying a serious terror' of those which would be sure to appear the moment he slipped this mortal coil. 'It seems that Chaucer did something wrong five hundred years ago, and they are now raking it up and publishing it.' When the Laureate had told Mary Brotherton this, years before, she had observed, '"Well – but – depend on it, Chaucer don't mind . . ." "How do you know he doesn't?" growled Great A. –' to Mrs Brotherton's delight, as she, a convinced spiritualist, felt it showed Tennyson was not the sceptic he sometimes seemed to be, having decided that if spirits *were* trying to contact us, it would be unlikely to be through table rattlings.

Tennyson's growls about biographers must often have sounded in Emily's and Hallam's ears as they worked on the *Memoir*. It was the work he had left them to do – to counteract many of the things that had appeared in the press: 'LIES, LIES, LIES'. He had hated fulsome praise as much as criticism. He had been inclined, he said, 'to vomit morally'. He had been 'driven mad' by inaccuracy. Their friends tried to encourage them in their task. 'How people do love and feel his greatness and how they will prize anything of him you and Hallam give to the world,' Anne Ritchie wrote soothingly. 'There is so much that only Hallam and I can do,' Emily told Agnes, who had wanted to help.

'I am thankful for what is left of me,' Emily wrote to Mary Watts, continuing to count her blessings, 'for there is something I have to do, I think. I wonder at all I have had in life.' Again, to another friend she wrote at this time: 'I can but feel my unworthiness of all I have had in this world.' 'No-one has had more delightful nearest belongings than myself: Father, Husband, Sons . . . and my very dear Sisters besides.' But not to have known a mother's love – that was an important loss.

Emily was now eighty, but it did not seem a time to give up on her devotion to Tennyson's reputation, though she was preparing for the possibility of incompetence, an incompetence that never came. On the anniversary of her marriage, 13 June 1894, Emily wrote out for Hallam a sort of power of attorney.

My Hallam,

I wish that we agreeing as we do, you should act for me and sign with your own signature, omitting mine.

Emily Tennyson.

But she was not yet letting go. Two weeks later the proofs arrived of the Printed Materials, a sort of trial copy of the *Memoir*, but bearing much less resemblance to the final book than Tennyson's trial copies had done. Emily read with intense concentration one set of four volumes. She had trained her eye over forty years of correcting proofs, but these were obviously very different from the volumes of poems she was accustomed to. She picked up a number of slips, mistranscriptions in the prose or in the poems included, but she also constantly made intelligent suggestions for omissions (the material was to be reduced by about half) and the reordering of material. She was, it seems, quite often less inclined to suppress things than Hallam was.

Emily probably did not think that the story of pulling down the girls' hair, which she had copied out in full herself from Emily Ritchie's letter, suggested that Tennyson had had too much to drink. She was less nervous too than Hallam, it seems, about the references to Charles's opium taking. She had been brought up in a Lincolnshire where the drug was far from unmentionable and indeed where, in her youth, country people grew poppies in their gardens to obtain it.

Emily, too, may well have realized that there was no point in trying to hide anything. She probably knew that her close, observant friend, Edward Lear, had kept a diary, and that many others did the same and that those diaries and many letters would reveal much that the *Memoir* chose to hide. Only once did Emily write in the margin of a bound proof: 'IS IT WISE TO PUBLISH THIS?' It was the early unpublished poem, 'Life of the Life within my blood,' which Hallam did publish in the *Memoir*, ignoring Emily's hesitation. It is the erotic song of Sir Launcelot, rejoicing in the life of the body:

> Bathe with me in the fiery flood,
> And mingle kisses, tears, and sighs,
> Life of the Life within my blood,
> Light of the Light within mine eyes.

It was the young passionate Alfred speaking from sixty years earlier – the sort of thing that might well have brought a blush to the young Emily's cheek. Tennyson's friend, John Kemble, writing it down in 1833, said that 'for the sake of my future clerical views and Alfred's and Sir L.'s character, I must request that it be kept as quiet as possible.' Sensibly, Hallam assured his mother there was nothing objectionable about it. After all, he made it clear it was Sir Launcelot who was speaking.

'Time is so short with me,' Emily said to Agnes in November 1894, sorry that her reading was uncharacteristically limited. 'I must confine myself to reading (or listening and reading further) that which touches on present work, public and private.' In the first year after Tennyson's death, there had been a feeling of urgency, as Hallam originally intended to publish for Christmas 1893. But as the scale of the work involved became apparent, Hallam decided he must take longer. 'There's no hurry now,' he said in September 1893, just before Benjamin Jowett died, leaving 'rough notes' which were 'much better than the polished sentences of other people'.

Writing briefly to Francis Palgrave in November that year, Emily said, 'I will not add more to the 23,000 letters than this.' Hallam himself dealt with 'as many more'. Thousands of letters were destroyed, sometimes apparently without the permission of the recipients, who had kindly returned them to help with the book. And hundreds were copied, mostly by Audrey.

Emily would tell Agnes not to feel anxious about her. She was only doing what she had to do. Sometimes she would write one day and say it might be a week or two before Agnes heard again. 'I may have too much to do to write again immediately. You will understand how it is if I do not write.' The suggestion was definitely that she would be too busy, rather than too ill: too busy with the *Memoir* or with visitors. She was constantly having to juggle rooms or have people put up in the village. To release a room for a guest, she had to ask her maid Mary at one point to share with the cook, reliable old Andrews, 'which is a pity but I cannot help it'. She liked Hallam and Audrey to see people; she did not want life to be dull for them. Hallam would need all the friends he had after she was gone and the *Memoir* published.

Emily's interest in both history and contemporary events continued. 'I am more thankful than I can say still to keep my interest in the life of my friends and of the world, tho' with a kind of stranger feeling'. When her eyes were tired, Hallam read aloud to her, but the *Memoir* continued to take precedence over everything else. In August 1895 Emily told Agnes: 'I am quite riveted by the Canadian Parkin's book on Imperial Federation ... We are behindhand with books having had so much to do and myself able to do little except write and for a year not much of this.' But it was during this year she had read and commented on so acutely the four volumes of proofs of the Printed Materials of the *Memoir*.

In the summer of 1895 when she had finished correcting the proofs, Emily wrote to Agnes, 'I am afraid, dear child, that my life is not a very useful one now – You must pray God that I may struggle to the end and make it the best I can.' Hallam gave her a brass trivet for her eighty-second birthday 'not liking to see me stoop to pick up my coffee from the hearth where it was put to keep warm.' The trivet was in the shape of a winged dragon and was thought to be about three hundred years old. On hearing its age, five-year-old Lionel asked: 'Is Grandmother three hundred years old?' She sometimes felt as if she were, but visitors continued to remark on her youthful appearance – the unfaded hair, the unlined face. She rejoiced in Hallam's work at the House of Lords, encouraging him to take part in votes and even writing speeches for him that she hoped he might deliver. She had written to Agnes: 'I cannot tell you what a joy it is to me to see his dear face so bright and happy when he came home ... Had he allowed himself a career of his own, he could not have found one so well suited to him.' As well as the Lords, he sat on the committees of the Gordon Boys' Homes and the Marlborough Old Boys – and presided regularly as a magistrate in the court at Newport. It was a great relief to Emily that he had such occupations, though work on the *Memoir* was by no means finished.

In the months before Emily's death, Hallam was brooding over structure. Would it be sensible to take out most of the reminiscences and other people's letters and keep them for a later volume? The whole book, which he had intended to be short, had got out of hand. In spite of all the burning and elimination, there was still far too much un-absorbed material. Henry Sidgwick suggested the *Memoir* would be more striking and impressive if it contained nothing but Tennyson's own letters, Emily's recollections and a linking narrative, with every-thing else kept for later volumes. But Craik at Macmillan thought the great demand would be for the *Memoir* itself and held out no hope for subsequent books. (It would be 1911 before *Tennyson and his Friends* was published.) In the end there would be a compromise, but in 1896, the last year of Emily's life, nothing had really been decided about the final form of the *Memoir* – there would be no proofs of that until 1897.

When the new edition of *The Works of Alfred Lord Tennyson* came out in 1895, Emily was pleased to see that the poem 'De Profundis' now at last carried, under the title of the poem Tennyson had written at the time of Hallam's birth, the dedication 'To H.T. August 11, 1852.' Emily had asked George Craik to add Hallam's name, wanting it 'to appear among *His* poems', though she realized it was perhaps 'a foolish thought'. Emily's own copy of the 1895 edition has her name in Hal-lam's hand, followed by the words: 'She cut through all the leaves of this book just before her death.' The dedication continued to appear in subsequent volumes of the Works, obviously produced from the same type, but Hallam took it out in the Eversley edition, after his mother's death.

The children continued to give their grandmother pleasure. They made her look at the present and into the future rather than entirely back at the past, as her work on the *Memoir* had encouraged her to do. When they were five and nearly four, Emily overheard Hallam's boys 'discuss-ing who wrote the Bible'. Aubrey, the smaller one, said 'Baba wrote it'. It was their name for the Poet Laureate, the grandfather he could not remember, though Tennyson still dominated their lives. 'No,' small Lionel corrected his brother, 'God wrote it'. Aubrey was not the only one who was occasionally confused.

When, in April 1896, the sixth grandson, Hallam's third child, was born, Emily captured exactly the small brothers' reaction to the new baby. In typically Victorian fashion, the children had apparently not had any idea what was going on. Hallam said to them 'There is a great surprise for you.' Emily wrote to her niece, Agnes:

Aubrey guessed guinea pigs, and when they stood before the baby they both crammed fingers into their mouths and burst out into uproarious laughter, asking whether it was a baby and their brother or a girl, and Aubrey decided that it was better than guinea pigs and both burst again into laughter when they had touched him and kissed him. Lila met me and asked if I had heard the news and seen the boy and he was a brother and a baby.

Emily reported Harold's birth to Frederick, 'Patriarch of the race' – still completely unaware of how he felt about her.

Three months later Emily wrote, on 4 August 1896, her last letter to Agnes. She was at Aldworth and told her niece that 'the beloved boys', Ally and Charlie (Lionel's two older sons, now nearly eighteen and seventeen), were with them for their holidays 'to our delight'. Emily liked the noise of the boys, their laughter and talk. Alfred's talk was much missed. ('He was, taken all in all, the best talker I have ever known,' Palgrave said.) The house was full of family. Indeed little Lionel's governess had had to go on holiday, so that her room could be used for guests. Emily admitted she was not feeling at all well. There was some sort of 'inflammation of the cranial membrane' with 'a good deal of pain and exhaustion,' but Dr Dabbs did not consider the attacks dangerous.

Tennyson's words in 'The Grandmother' may have gone through Emily's head: 'I seem to be tired a little, that's all, and long for rest.' Was it not time for her to move from this room into the next? 'I shall go in a minute.' She was less and less inclined to write letters. Letter writing had dominated her life. She had found it as natural to write letters as to speak, and often easier. There had been hard times when she had been forbidden by doctors to do either. Now she was ready to put down her pen for the last time. Hallam was reading to her as he had done so much over the last few years, to spare her eyes. She had always been interested in history since the days when Henry Sellwood had read aloud to the three girls in Horncastle. W.E.H. Lecky's *History of European Morals from Augustus to Charlemagne* had made a profound impact on her when she read it in 1869, the year after she had met Lecky himself and had had hours of interesting conversation with him; discussing, for instance, whether it is possible for someone to find his 'highest pleasure in sacrificing himself for the good of others.' At the beginning of that book Lecky had written: 'Our moral sentiments do not flow from but long precede our ethical systems.' She had written about it to Hallam when he was a boy at school, saying how much she agreed with Lecky about 'the intuitiveness of conscience'. She might call it the Holy Ghost, but her recognition of its primary importance over forms and conventions, edicts and rituals meant that she recognized entirely what was natural for her to call the brotherhood of man, the love for our fellow human beings that transcends differences of race, religion or gender. Now as she lay in her final illness the book she turned to was Lecky's *Democracy and Liberty*, which had just been published. Hallam told Lecky:

Almost to the last I was reading aloud to her (and she was reading it to herself) your *Democracy and Liberty* – discussing every subject with me eagerly. We had just begun the second volume.

Right at the end her intellectual energy did not fail her. Nor did her concern for her grandsons.

Charles and Ally were in the house as she lay dying. Almost the last thing she did, Charles recalled long afterwards, was 'to send us her blessing and enjoin my uncle to be sure on no account to forget our two golden sovereigns.' The boys had always left their grandparents' houses with that splendid coin in their pockets. By the time they left on 10 August 1896 Emily Tennyson was dead.

Dr Dabbs told Hallam on Sunday 9 August that she would not recover. Hallam wrote down the things she was saying: 'I have tried to be a good wife.' When her son assured her no one could have been a better wife, she said, 'I might have done more.'

These were not her last words. She went on to thank Hallam: 'Thank you my darling for all your great goodness to me.' Then she asked to see Lionel and Aubrey and when the little boys had gone, she said: 'I hope I am not impatient.' Last of all she said, 'Great and small sins are the same in the sight of God, in that he forgives them all.'

We cannot always believe everything that Hallam wants us to believe. In his notes on 'My mother's last words' he had originally changed the order as if he wanted his mother to end thinking of Tennyson: 'I might have done more.' But then, presumably for accuracy, he puts a balloon round the paragraph and reverses the order, making the words read as I have used them. It is curious, considering how much emphasis his mother always put on truth, how little regard Hallam had for accuracy. One can never be sure that anything was exactly as he said it was, even to those words on his mother's deathbed.

In the bulletin he sent out to the newspapers he gave the impression that before her death Emily had corrected the final proofs of the *Memoir* for the press, and he repeats this in the *Memoir* itself. It was far from the case, though she may well have thought the proofs of the four-volume Materials she *had* corrected were much closer to the final *Memoir* than was actually so. What matters was his acknowledgment of how closely involved she had been, how intellectually active, right up to the end of her life. If, in the *Memoir* itself, Hallam tends to push his mother out of the picture, in writing replies to the letters of praise and sympathy that poured in he acknowledged entirely her crucial import-ance to him, even saying to one friend 'Many times I have been held back from doing evil and urged to do good from thought of her.' That it is so difficult to imagine Hallam 'doing evil' is perhaps because of the power of his mother's belief in his utter goodness, and an image of him which is disturbed only by James Knowles's surviving diatribe about his jealousy and smallmindedness. James Knowles was inclined to find fault – even, Dean Bradley had told Emily, with the insufficiency of Tennyson's bust in Westminster Abbey. '*Of course*, he found some faults,' Bradley had said.

Eleanor knew of Emily's death from the boys when she met them at Waterloo station on the day she died.

Charlie's face as he stepped out of the train told me there was something wrong . . . Dear Hallam, I think I can understand what this loss is to you – who have witnessed, through so many many years of intimate companionship, your un-tiring and unfailing devotion to your Mother and her absorbing love for you. Nearly everyone feels at such times bitter pangs of self-reproach for things left undone and loving words left unsaid – you are one of the very few who can truly feel that your relation with your Mother was perfect, that you *never* failed her, and that there is no single thing you can reproach yourself with. This takes some of the bitterness from sorrow – but perhaps the loss is almost the more felt.

Eleanor, who had known such bitterness and such self-reproach when Lionel died, went on to say: 'Your mother was unvaryingly good to me from the very first to the very last . . .' Emily Tennyson was, it seems, exactly that: 'unvaryingly good.'

Agnes Weld travelled from Oxford to the funeral with a wary eye. She crossed to the Isle of Wight by the last boat and stayed the night in a quiet cottage close to the church. 'I felt that living all alone as I do I must never if possible go to Farringford again, but try and keep it in my thoughts with her dear presence ever in it,' she told Hardwick

Rawnsley, who was not able to get there. Emily's body travelled from Aldworth by train. and boat and was met by 'William, the faithful coachman' at Yarmouth. Agnes was waiting alone by the church when the coffin arrived in Freshwater, under the same white embroidered pall that had covered Tennyson's coffin on its way to Westminster Abbey. Agnes waited while the organist played 'I know that my Redeemer liveth':

Hallam and Audrey and the other relations did not arrive till half an hour afterwards. As soon as they were seated the choir sang the 'Silent Voices' and afterwards 'Crossing the Bar', at the grave 'Holy, Holy, Holy'. Hallam joined in all these, I tried to do so but in vain for I was too much overcome by all I had gone through.

Hallam bore up wonderfully till he kissed me and said 'God bless you' at parting. I could see his wife was in no way sharing his sorrow, but on *no account betray that I have told you this*, which makes me feel all the more for poor Hallam. It pained me to see her in fancy black instead of proper plain mourning. I do not mind about crape but I do not like to see lace and finery on such an occasion. I think she feels sorry for Hallam's grief, but she does not grieve the least herself and being a very truthful person thinks it right not to pretend a grief for Auntie's death she does not feel. To me her loss is irreparable for, though we saw little of each other, her precious letters caused a constant intercession of soul with soul and almost all our interests were held in common.

Audrey's relief at Emily's death must seem understandable to any objective observer, whatever one feels about 'fancy' clothes.

Agnes told Rawnsley it was a comfort to travel back on the boat with 'Henry Cameron, my childhood's friend, and still more your two brothers'. 'They all tried so hard to get me interested in the passing yachts, the cormorants and herons.' It was forty-three years since the Tennysons had crossed that stretch of water together in a rowing boat and seen one dark heron flying over the Solent backed by a daffodil sky.

Hallam wrote to George Craik, their faithful editor at Macmillan:

Yes, you were one of the few people in the world that realized the complete union between Father Mother and Sons – then between Father, Mother and Son, then between Mother and Son. No-one but myself will ever know what a great and good woman she has been.

Hallam felt that he alone knew his mother's true worth, though others had also spoken of her greatness and thousands would read in her obituaries of her goodness, of the devotion of her life as the poet's wife. Only Tennyson himself can provide words for the end of the life of Emily Tennyson which might have been Emily's own. The manuscript note (the sort of note that even Emily had approved) for the poem 'Vastness' is: 'What matters anything in this world without full faith in the Immortality of the Soul and of Love?'

What is it all, if we all of us end but in being our own corpse-coffins at last,
Swallowed in Vastness, lost in Silence, drowned in the deeps of a meaningless Past?
What but a murmur of gnats in the gloom, or a moment's anger of bees in their hive? –
Peace, let it be! for I loved him, and love him for ever: the dead are not dead but alive.

FRANKLINS, RAWNSLEYS and SELLWOODS

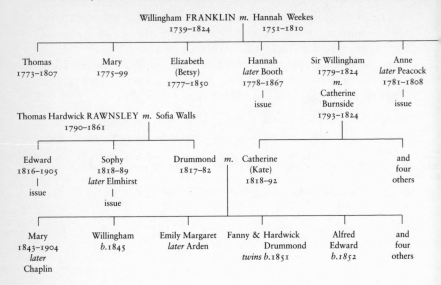

Willingham FRANKLIN *m.* Hannah Weekes
1739–1824   1751–1810

| Thomas 1773–1807 | Mary 1775–99 | Elizabeth (Betsy) 1777–1850 | Hannah *later* Booth 1778–1867 | Sir Willingham 1779–1824 *m.* Catherine Burnside 1793–1824 | Anne *later* Peacock 1781–1808 |

issue   issue

Thomas Hardwick RAWNSLEY *m.* Sofia Walls
1790–1861

| Edward 1816–1905 | Sophy 1818–89 *later* Elmhirst | Drummond 1817–82 | *m.* Catherine (Kate) 1818–92 | and four others |

issue   issue

| Mary 1843–1904 *later* Chaplin | Willingham b.1845 | Emily Margaret *later* Arden | Fanny & Hardwick Drummond *twins b.*1851 | Alfred Edward b.1852 | and four others |

TENNYSONS

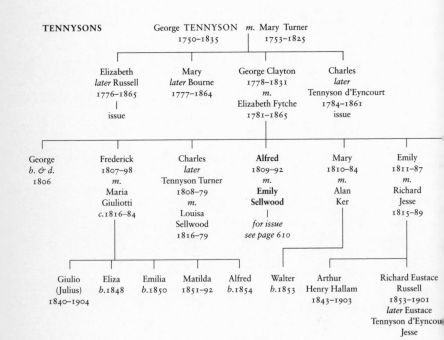

George TENNYSON *m.* Mary Turner
1750–1835   1753–1825

| Elizabeth *later* Russell 1776–1865 | Mary *later* Bourne 1777–1864 | George Clayton 1778–1831 *m.* Elizabeth Fytche 1781–1865 | Charles *later* Tennyson d'Eyncourt 1784–1861 |

issue   issue

| George b. & d. 1806 | Frederick 1807–98 *m.* Maria Giuliotti c.1816–84 | Charles *later* Tennyson Turner 1808–79 *m.* Louisa Sellwood 1816–79 | Alfred **1809–92** *m.* **Emily Sellwood** *for issue see page 610* | Mary 1810–84 *m.* Alan Ker | Emily 1811–87 *m.* Richard Jesse 1815–89 |

| Giulio (Julius) 1840–1904 | Eliza b.1848 | Emilia b.1850 | Matilda 1851–92 | Alfred b.1854 | Walter b.1853 | Arthur Henry Hallam 1843–1903 | Richard Eustace Russell 1853–1901 *later* Eustace Tennyson d'Eyncourt Jesse |

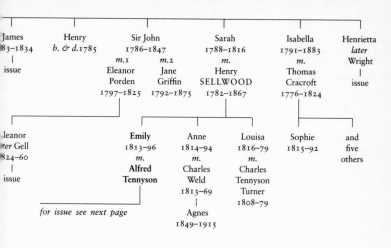

James
83–1834
|
issue

Henry
b. & d.1785

Sir John
1786–1847
m.1
Eleanor
Porden
1797–1825

m.2
Jane
Griffin
1792–1875

Sarah
1788–1816
m.
Henry
SELLWOOD
1782–1867

Isabella
1791–1883
m.
Thomas
Cracroft
1776–1824

Henrietta
later
Wright
|
issue

leanor
er Gell
824–60
|
issue

Emily
1813–96
m.
**Alfred
Tennyson**

Anne
1814–94
m.
Charles
Weld
1813–69
|
Agnes
1849–1915

Louisa
1816–79
m.
Charles
Tennyson
Turner
1808–79

Sophie
1815–92

and
five
others

for issue see next page

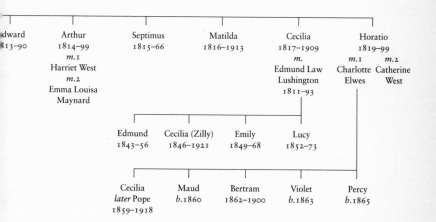

dward
13–90

Arthur
1814–99
m.1
Harriet West
m.2
Emma Louisa
Maynard

Septimus
1815–66

Matilda
1816–1913

Cecilia
1817–1909
m.
Edmund Law
Lushington
1811–93

Horatio
1819–99
m.1
Charlotte
Elwes

m.2
Catherine
West

Edmund
1843–56

Cecilia (Zilly)
1846–1921

Emily
1849–68

Lucy
1852–73

Cecilia
later Pope
1859–1918

Maud
b.1860

Bertram
1862–1900

Violet
b.1863

Percy
b.1865

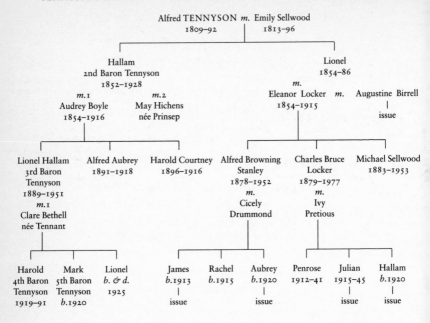

Alfred TENNYSON *m.* Emily Sellwood
1809–92   1813–96

Hallam
2nd Baron Tennyson
1852–1928
m.1   *m.2*
Audrey Boyle   May Hichens
1854–1916   née Prinsep

Lionel
1854–86
m.
Eleanor Locker   *m.*   Augustine Birrell
1854–1915
issue

Lionel Hallam
3rd Baron
Tennyson
1889–1951
m.1
Clare Bethell
née Tennant

Alfred Aubrey
1891–1918

Harold Courtney
1896–1916

Alfred Browning
Stanley
1878–1952
m.
Cicely
Drummond

Charles Bruce
Locker
1879–1977
m.
Ivy
Pretious

Michael Sellwood
1883–1953

Harold
4th Baron
Tennyson
1919–91

Mark
5th Baron
Tennyson
*b.*1920

Lionel
b. & d.
1925

James
*b.*1913
|
issue

Rachel
*b.*1915

Aubrey
*b.*1920
|
issue

Penrose
1912–41

Julian
1915–45
|
issue

Hallam
*b.*1920
|
issue

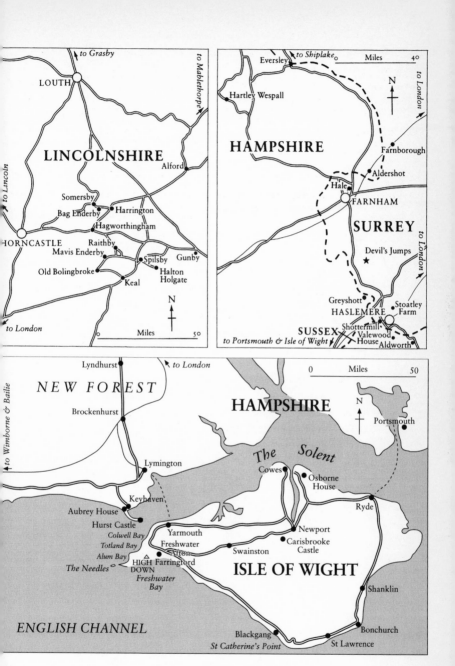

Acknowledgments and Sources

As can be seen from the repetitive abbreviations in the Notes, I owe a great deal to TRC and L&S. I spent many months at the Tennyson Research Centre at Lincoln, over a period of nearly six years, and was constantly refreshed and excited by its contents. It is a remarkable archive, not least because it belongs to Lincolnshire County Council. I am grateful to the Council for the free access to this collection, without which this book would not exist, and I am particularly grateful to the librarian in charge, Sue Gates, who shares deservedly in my dedication. Her patience, sympathy and knowledge made enjoyable what at home sometimes seemed an overwhelming task. The collection includes not only several thousand of Emily Tennyson's own letters, but a great many letters to her, including both sides of the important family correspondences and the letters she exchanged with Edward Lear. Some letters to her, for instance from James Spedding, should have been returned to the family who had lent them for possible use in the *Memoir*. I sympathize with today's Speddings of Mirehouse and take this opportunity to thank them for two pleasant visits to the house and for their encouragement.

TRC holds not only letters but many other things in ET's hand which have never before been properly examined, including an address book (on which a whole essay could be written), all sorts of household notes and lists, her prayers, her accounts, drafts of subjects for poems, lectures and speeches (which she did not consider using herself) and even a number of unfinished stories, which seem highly autobiographical. It was excellent to be able to work at TRC surrounded by the Tennysons' own books and to be able to take them down from the shelves to check an inscription or a quotation. Most important of all TRC possesses ET's own 'Narratives' and the epitome of her many journals (abbreviated as 'Journal') she kept throughout her married life with Tennyson's encouragement. I have *not* given references to the printed editions of parts of the Journal as they are unreliable, nor, for the same reason, to the American selection from her letters.

This seems to be the place to comment on the occasional extreme difficulty of ET's handwriting, best illustrated by the fact that, at one stage, I thought I was reading that Emily was saying in March 1891 that they had had seven glasses of port the night before – when I realized she was actually writing about 'degrees of frost'. HT's writing is also difficult. Is he writing of 'pathetic' or 'patriotic' songs? I criticize in my Notes some errors of transcription, where I know I am right. There will undoubtedly be some cases where I have myself fallen into error, and not only in transcription. This is also the place to mention I have occasionally omitted random capital letters and amended punctuation for clarity.

L&S is my abbreviation for the great three-volume edition of Tennyson's letters, edited by Cecil Lang and Edgar Shannon. It includes a great deal besides AT's own letters. I have given

L&S references for the reader's convenience, even when in many cases (and always with ET's own letters) I have looked at the original or (occasionally) a photocopy. I am grateful to both editors and particularly to Cecil Lang, who entertained me very well in Charlottesville and afterwards packed up a large parcel of useful material, including *Tennyson Research Bulletins* *(TRB)* he no longer needed.

Another important debt is to Alistair Elliot and Michael Millgate, both of whom read the first printout of my text and made many useful suggestions. The book is undoubtedly much better than it would have been without their generous attention and sometimes alarming honesty. They know how grateful I am. Michael also passed on to me material he had gathered when writing the Tennyson section of his *Testamentary Acts* (1992). I must also thank warmly Christopher Ricks, for all sorts of comments and reactions. My own interest in Tennyson I trace, not to my father's regular quotations from him, but to staying in the Ricks's cottage in Lasborough at the time Christopher was working on the first edition of *The Poems of Tennyson* (1969). His three 1987 volumes have been constantly read and consulted over the last few years.

I am also indebted to Robert Bernard Martin, whose biography of Tennyson often stimulated and guided me, however much I disagree with some of his conclusions and generalizations. He has also been a helpful correspondent. I am grateful to Roger Evans of the British Library, who shared with me the results of his research into the lives of Charles and Louisa Tennyson Turner, and to Christopher Sturman, whose knowledge of the Lincolnshire Archives (LAO) enabled him to put me on to much useful material, in particular the Tweed and Peacock papers and Kate Rawnsley's diary. I much appreciated his willingness to share with me his own painstaking research, including work on the Bousfields, not yet published.

It is a pleasure to thank Rosalind Rawnsley for her trust in lending to me for a long period what I have called the 'Rawnsley papers' – more than a hundred letters, almost all unpublished, most of them sent to H.D.Rawnsley when he was working on his *Memories of the Tennysons* more than a hundred years ago. My own doctor, Stephen Bamber, was extremely helpful in answering all sorts of medical questions and, above all, in analysing the detailed information I gave him on the subject of Emily Tennyson's health, taken from her own words in letters and her journal. David McKitterick at Trinity College Library was particularly assiduous in helping me to trace the careers of ET's sons at Cambridge. Richard Jefferies, of the Watts Gallery, identified beyond all reasonable doubt a previously unknown portrait.

Another portrait, that by Millais, I first saw in the home of James Tennyson, ET's great-grandson in Wellington, New Zealand. It was delightful to find him living close to my own old friends Barbara and John Yaldwyn, as John's family had been the Tennysons' neighbours at Aldworth. I am grateful too for a copy of a long letter from A.B.S.Tennyson to Hester Ritchie, Thackeray's grand-daughter, 'with an account of the poet's wife'. The present Hallam Tennyson has also been encouraging and helpful and quite prepared for me to dispute his published view of his great-grandmother.

Many individuals have helped me in different ways. I hope they will forgive me for naming them only in a long list. I am really grateful for all sorts of assistance and kindness:

Brian Alderson, Ann Baer, Andrew Belsey, Susan and Thomas Chitty, Christopher Curtis, Frances Dann (grand-daughter of ET's last cook/housekeeper, Clara Redfern), Hunter Davies, Oliver Davies, Angus Easson, Barbara Elliot, Marie and Ronald Ewart, Gill Frayn, William Gladstone, Steve Gooch, Sheila Gooddie, Sue Harrop, Brian Hinton, David Holmes, Elizabeth Hutchings, John Irving (great-grandson of both Henry Irving and Thomas Woolner), Roy Jenkins, Hermione Lee, Peter Levi, Penelope and Jack Lively, Katharine Macdonald, Jan Marsh, Colin Matthew, Vivien Noakes (Edward Lear), Iona Opie, Alyson Price, Dick Rampell, J.P. Rudman, Peter Scupham, Hilary Spurling, Wendy and Brian Talfourd-Cook (Holmwood), Desmond Taylor, Ina Taylor, Karen and Pete Townshend (of 'The Who' and

Tennyson House, once Chapel House), Ellen and Arthur Wagner, Jane Wates (Shiplake Old Vicarage), Frances Woodward (for her index to the Franklin diaries).

I must also list gratefully a number of very helpful local historians and Tennysonians in both Lincolnshire and the Farnham/Aldworth area: Eileen and the late C.L.Anderson, Colette and David Ardagh, Michael Blower, Norman Clarke, Ray Elliott, Sue Farrow, Elsie Fidling, A.S.Lancaster, the late Terence Leach, Douglas Mitchell, Jim Murray, Marshall Scarborough, Fred Shaw, W.R.Trotter.

The libraries and institutions that follow also deserve my gratitude, particularly those which are still able to offer information without asking for a fee. If all libraries charged the fees some now do, it would be impossible for such a book as this to be written by someone without a university salary. I have used all the following and many of the people mentioned have taken a particular interest in my project, for which I thank them.

Balliol College Library, Oxford; Barnardos; Berg Collection (New York Public Library); Berkshire County Reference Library; Berkshire Record Office; Bodleian Library (Judith Priestman); Boston Public Library (Massachusetts); Bristol University Library (N.A.Lee); British Library (BL); Brotherton Library, University of Leeds (C.D.W. Sheppard); Cambridge University Library (CUL, Godfrey Waller); Christ Church Library, Oxford; Crawley Library (Charles Kay – Warninglid research); East Sussex Library Service; Eton College (Michael Meredith); Farnham Museum; Farringford Hotel; Houghton Library, Harvard (Susan Halpert); Huntington Library, San Marino, California; India Office Library (Ian Baxter); Inner Temple (I.G.Murray); Isle of Wight County Record Office and County Reference Library; Keats Fearn (estate agents, Farnham); Library of Periodical and Eclectic Literature (Falls Church, Virginia); Lilly Library, University of Indiana; Lincolnshire Archives Office (LAO); Lincolnshire County Library Service (Angela Child, as well as Sue Gates); Location Register of Eng.Lit. MSS and Letters, Reading (David Sutton); the London Library; John Rylands Library, Manchester University; Marlborough College (David Ives); Massachusetts Historical Association; National Library of Scotland (Elspeth Yeo); National Library of Wales; National Portrait Gallery (Terence Pepper); Newcastle University Library; North Devon Library (Jamie Campbell); Norwich City Reference Library; Ohio University Library, Athens, Ohio; Pierpont Morgan Library, NY; Princeton University Library; Rochester University Library; Rocklands Hotel, St Laurence, I.O.W.; Royal Commission on Historical MSS; Royal Society Library; Scott Polar Research Institute (SPRI, Robert Headland); Swainston Manor Hotel; Syracuse University Library; Trinity College Library, Cambridge (Diane Chardin, as well as David McKitterick); University of Texas at Austin (H.Ransom Research Center, Cathy Henderson); University of Virginia Library, Charlottesville; the Watts Gallery; Wellesley College (Jill Triplett); Beinecke Library, Yale University (Vincent Giroud).

I was extremely grateful for a Churchill Fellowship, which covered the expenses of a long tour of American university libraries and also some travel in France and Italy in the steps of the Tennysons. The Authors Foundation returned to me £1,000 I had rashly returned to them after my success with A.A.Milne. It had by then become obvious that this book was making no financial sense and I am grateful to the Foundation.

My outstanding debt is, as always, to my husband, Anthony Thwaite, without whose practical and loving support (I have to say yet again) this book could not have been written. I must end, also as usual, by thanking my devoted typist, Hilary Tulloch, whose technological expertise and patient intelligence continue to impress me. This time round I have a particular reason to be grateful to her and her husband Dick. They know how much I appreciate all they have done at a difficult time. Robert McCrum, my editor at Faber, has also been having a difficult time. I am particularly grateful for his keen eye, and for that of my copy editor, Gillian Bate.

Ann Thwaite, Low Tharston, Norfolk. March 1996

Abbreviations

PEOPLE

Tennysons:

AT	Alfred Tennyson, the poet, husband
Audrey	Audrey Boyle, later Tennyson, daughter-in-law
CT	Charles Tennyson, grandson
CTDE	Charles Tennyson, later d'Eyncourt, AT's uncle
CTT	Charles Tennyson Turner, brother-in-law
Eleanor	Eleanor Locker, later Tennyson, later Birrell, daughter-in-law
Eliza T	Elizabeth Tennyson, mother-in-law
ET	Emily Sellwood, later Tennyson
ETJ	Emily Tennyson, later Jesse, sister-in-law
FT	Frederick Tennyson, brother-in-law
GCT	George Clayton Tennyson, father-in-law
GT	George Tennyson, AT's grandfather
HT	Hallam Tennyson, son
LT	Lionel Tennyson, son
LTT	Louisa Sellwood, later Tennyson Turner, sister
Mary T	Mary Tennyson, later Ker, sister-in-law
MT	Matilda (Tilly) Tennyson, sister-in-law

Others:

AG	Anne Gilchrist
Agnes	Agnes Weld, niece
AHC	Arthur Hugh Clough
AHH	Arthur Henry Hallam
Argyll	8th Duke of Argyll
ATR	Anne Thackeray, later Ritchie
AW	Anne Sellwood, later Weld, sister
BJ	Benjamin Jowett
BW-C	Blanche Warre-Cornish
CLD	Charles Lutwidge Dodgson (Lewis Carroll)
CP	Coventry Patmore
CR	Catherine (Kate) Franklin, later Rawnsley, cousin

ABBREVIATIONS

Craik	George Craik
Dufferin	1st Marquis of Dufferin and Ava
EBB	Elizabeth Barrett Browning
EL	Edward Lear
ELL	Edmund Law Lushington, brother-in-law
EP	Emily Patmore
Fitz	Edward FitzGerald
FLo	Frederick Locker, daughter-in-law's father
FLu	Franklin Lushington
FN	Florence Nightingale
FP	Francis Palgrave
GD	Graham Dakyns
GSV	George Stovin Venables
HDR	Hardwick Rawnsley
HS	Henry Sellwood, father
JAS	John Addington Symonds
JF	John Franklin, uncle
JMC	Julia Margaret Cameron
JS	James Spedding
MBrad	Marian Bradley
MBro	Mary Brotherton
MGa	Margaret Gatty
Mary G	Mary Gladstone
RB	Robert Browning
SRE	Sophy Rawnsley, later Elmhirst
THR	Thomas Hardwick Rawnsley
TW	Thomas Woolner
WA	William Allingham
WEG	William Ewart Gladstone
WFR	Willingham Franklin Rawnsley

BOOKS

A Child's Recollections	*A Child's Recollections of Tennyson*, Edith Nicoll Ellison (1907)
Anne Gilchrist	*Anne Gilchrist: Life and Writings*, ed. H.H. Gilchrist (1887)
ATR Records	*Records of Tennyson, Ruskin, Browning*, Anne Thackeray Ritchie (1892)
Background	*The Tennysons: Background to Genius*, Charles Tennyson and Hope Dyson (1974)
Brookfield	*Mrs Brookfield and her Circle*, C. and F. Brookfield (1906)
Champneys	*Memoirs and Correspondence of Coventry Patmore*, ed. Basil Champneys, 2 vols. (1900)
Circle	*A Circle of Friends: The Tennysons and the Lushingtons of Park House*, John O. Waller (1986)
Critical Heritage	*Tennyson: The Critical Heritage*, ed. John D. Jump (1967)
CTAT	*Alfred Tennyson*, by his grandson Charles Tennyson (1949)
Dakyns	*Letters to a Tutor: the Tennysons to H.G. Dakyns*, ed. R. Peters and Janine Dakyns (1988)
Dear and Honoured	*Dear and Honoured Lady: Correspondence between Queen*

617

	Victoria and Alfred Tennyson, ed. Hope Dyson and Charles Tennyson (1969)
Dearest Love to All	*With Dearest Love to All: The Life and Letters of Lady Jebb*, M.R. Bobbitt (1960)
Domett *Diary*	*The Diary of Alfred Domett*, ed. E.A. Horsman (1953)
From Friend to Friend	*From Friend to Friend*, Anne Thackeray Ritchie (1919)
From Verse to Worse	*From Verse to Worse*, Lionel Tennyson (1933)
Glimpses	*Glimpses of Tennyson and of some of his Relations and Friends*, Agnes Grace Weld (1903)
Hoge *J*	*Lady Tennyson's Journal*, ed. J.O. Hoge (1981)
Hoge *L*	*The Letters of Emily Lady Tennyson*, ed. J.O. Hoge (1974)
IM	*In Memoriam A.H.H.*, Alfred Tennyson (1850)
Interviews	*Tennyson: Interviews and Recollections*, ed. Norman Page (1983)
Kolb	*The Letters of Arthur Henry Hallam*, ed. Jack Kolb (1981)
L&S	*The Letters of Alfred Lord Tennyson*, Cecil Y. Lang and Edgar F. Shannon, 3 vols. (1982, 1987, 1990)
Letters to FT	*Letters to Frederick Tennyson*, ed. Hugh J. Schonfield (1930)
Mangles	*Tennyson at Aldworth: The Diary of J.H. Mangles*, ed. E.A. Knies (1984)
Memoir	*Tennyson: A Memoir*, Hallam Tennyson, 2 vols. (1897)
Metcalf	*James Knowles: Victorian Editor and Architect*, Priscilla Metcalf (1980)
Palgrave	*Francis Turner Palgrave, Journals and Memories*, G.F. Palgrave (1899)
Pinion	*A Tennyson Chronology*, F.B. Pinion (1990)
Rader	*Tennyson's Maud: The Biographical Genesis*, R.W. Rader (1963)
Rawnsley *Memories*	*Memories of the Tennysons*, H.D. Rawnsley, with Reminiscences by W.F. Rawnsley (1900)
RBM	*Tennyson: The Unquiet Heart*, Robert Bernard Martin (1980)
Ricks	*The Poems of Tennyson*, ed. Christopher Ricks, 3 vols. (1987)
Ricks *T*	*Tennyson*, Christopher Ricks (1972)
Stars and Markets	*Stars and Markets*, Charles Tennyson (1957)
Sturman	*Poems by Two Brothers: The Lives, Work and Influence of G.C. Tennyson and Charles Tennyson d'Eyncourt*, Christopher Sturman and Valerie Purton (1993)
Talks and Walks	Unpublished conversations between Alfred Tennyson and Audrey in the Tennyson Research Centre at Lincoln
T and his Friends	*Tennyson and his Friends*, ed. Hallam Tennyson (1911)
Terhune	*Letters of Edward FitzGerald*, ed. A.M. and A.B.Terhune, 4 vols. (1980)
WA *Diary*	William Allingham, *A Diary 1824–1889*, ed. H. Allingham and D. Radford. Introduction by J.J. Norwich (1985)
Vice-Regal Days	*Audrey Tennyson's Vice-Regal Days*, ed. Alexandra Hasluck (1978)

Further Reading

═══

RBM (pp. 616–24) provides a lengthy bibliography. I have consulted most of the books on it and many others. My briefer list here includes many published since *RBM* (1980).

Allingham, Helen and Arthur Paterson,*The Homes of Tennyson* (1905).
  Helen Allingham's England Ina Taylor (1990).
Anon, *The Wives of England – their relative duties, domestic influence and obligations* (1843).
Asquith, Margot, *The Autobiography*, 2 vols. (1920, 1922).
Birrell, Augustine, *Things Past Redress* (1937).
Brookfield, Frances M., *The Cambridge Apostles* (1906).
Browning, Elizabeth Barrett and Robert: *The Brownings to the Tennysons: Letters from EBB and RB to AT, ET, HT*, ed. Thomas J. Collins, Waco, Texas (1971). *Robert Browning and Julia Wedgwood*, ed. Richard Curle (1937). *The Brownings' Correspondence*, ed. Philip Kelley and Ronald Hudson (1984–95).
Cameron, Julia Margaret: *JMC: Victorian Photographs of Famous Men and Fair Women*, introduced by V. Woolf and R. Fry (1926, 1973). *JMC: A Victorian Family Portrait*, Brian Hill (1973). *Whisper of the Muse: The World of JMC* (Colnaghi catalogue), Jeremy Howard (1990). *Immortal Faces: JMC on the Isle of Wight*, Brian Hinton (1992).
Campbell, Nancie, ed., *Tennyson in Lincoln* (a catalogue), 2 vols. (1971, 1973).
Carlyle, Thomas and Jane Welsh, *Collected Letters*, ed. Sanders and Fielding (1970–93).
'Carroll, Lewis': *Letters*, ed. Morton N. Cohen, 2 vols. (1979). *Lewis Carroll: A biography*, Morton N. Cohen (1995).
Clarke, J.N., *Education in a Market Town: Horncastle* (1976).
Clough, A.H., *Letters and Remains* (1865).
Colley, Ann C., *Tennyson and Madness* (1983).
Elliot, Philip, *The Making of the Memoir*, Tennyson Society (1978, 1993).
Fields, Annie, *Authors and Friends* (1896).
Franklins: *Life of Sir John Franklin*, H.D. Traill (1896). *The Life, Diaries and Correspondence of Jane Lady Franklin*, ed. W.F. Rawnsley (1923). *John Franklin's Bride: Eleanor Anne Porden*, E.M. Gell (1930). *Portrait of Jane, a life of Lady Franklin*, Frances Woodward (1951). *The Fate of Franklin*, Roderic Owen (1978).
Gladstone, Mary, *Diaries and Letters*, ed. Lucy Masterman (1930).
Gladstone, W.E., *The Gladstone Diaries*, ed. H.C.G. Matthew etc. (1968–94).
Gosse, Edmund, *EG: A Literary Landscape*, Ann Thwaite (1984). *Portraits from Life*, ed. Ann Thwaite (1991).

Grove, Valerie (as Valerie Jenkins), *Where I was Young*, CT's Regent's Park (1976).

Guedalla, Philip, *Bonnet and Shawl: an album*, section on ET (1928).

Hagen, June Steffensen, *Tennyson and his Publishers* (1979).

Hutchings, Richard J., *A and ET: A Marriage of True Minds* (1991).

Hutchings, Richard J., ed. with Brian Hinton, *The Farringford Journal of ET* (1986).

Jowett, Benjamin: *Letters*, ed. Abbott and Campbell (1899). *Jowett, a portrait with background*, Geoffrey Faber (1958). *Jowett to Florence Nightingale*, ed. Quinn and Priest (1987).

Lear, Edward: *Letters of EL to Chichester Fortescue*, ed. Lady Strachey (1907). *Later Letters of EL*, ed. Lady Strachey (1911). *EL: Landscape Painter and Nonsense Poet*, Angus Davidson (1938). *EL: the life of a wanderer*, Vivien Noakes (1968). *EL's Tennyson*, Ruth Pitman (1988).

Levi, Peter, *Tennyson* (1993).

Locker, Frederick, *My Confidences* (1896).

Martin, R.B., *The Dust of Combat: a life of Charles Kingsley* (1959). *With Friends possessed: a life of Edward FitzGerald* (1985).

Maurice, Frederic, ed., *The Life of F.D.Maurice in his own letters*, 2 vols. (1884).

Merriam, H.G., *Edward Moxon, Publisher of Poets* (1939).

Millgate, Michael, *Testamentary Acts, Browning, Tennyson, James, Hardy* (1992).

Murray, Jim, *Tealby Gleanings* (1995).

Napier, George G., *The Homes and Haunts of Tennyson* (1892).

Nicolson, Harold, *Tennyson* (1923).

Palgrave, F.T., ed., *The Lyrical Poems of Alfred Tennyson* (1885). *The Treasury of Sacred Song* (1889).

Richardson, Joanna, *The Pre-Eminent Victorian: a study of Tennyson* (1962).

Ricks, Christopher, *Tennyson and His Friends*, Catalogue of an Exhibition at Harvard (1992).

Shatto, Susan, and Marion Shaw, ed., *Tennyson In Memoriam* (1982).

Shaw, Marion, *Alfred Lord Tennyson*, Feminist Readings (1988).

Symonds, John Addington: *JAS: A Biography*, Phyllis Grosskurth (1964). *The Memoirs of JAS*, ed. Phyllis Grosskurth (1983).

Taylor, Ina, *Helen Allingham's England* (1990).

Tennyson, Hallam, ed., *Studies in Tennyson* (1981). *The Haunted Mind* (1984).

Thackeray Ritchie, Anne: *From Friend to Friend* (1919). *Letters*, ed. Hester Ritchie (1924). *Thackeray's Daughter*, H.T. Fuller and V. Hammersley (1951). *ATR: A Biography*, Winifred Gérin (1981). *ATR: Journals and Letters*, ed. Shankman, Bloom and Maynard (1994).

Thorn, Michael, *Tennyson* (1992).

Turner, Charles Tennyson, *Collected Sonnets*, introd. J. Spedding (1880). *A Hundred Sonnets*, ed. CT and John Betjeman (1960). *Secret Rooms: the life and work of CTT*, Roger Evans (unpublished Ph.D. thesis,1994, at TRC).

University of Rochester, *The Rowland L. Collins Collection of AT*, exhibition catalogue, Library Bulletin xxxxiii (1993).

Wakefield, Priscilla, *The Female Sex: reflections on the present condition* (1817).

Ward, Wilfrid, *Aubrey de Vere* (1904).

Waugh, Arthur, *Tennyson* (1892). *One Man's Road* (1931).

Wheatcroft, Andrew, *The Tennyson Album: a biography in photographs* (1980).

White, Walter, *The Journals of Walter White* (1898).

Woof, Robert, *Tennyson 1809–1892: A Centenary Celebration*, exhibition catalogue (1992).

Woolner, Amy, *Thomas Woolner, RA: Sculptor and Poet. His life in letters* (1917).

Notes

═══

PREFACE

p. xv 'Emily jump?' from 2 versions of V. Woolf's play *Freshwater, a Comedy*, ed. Lucio P. Ruotolo, NY (1976), pp. 13 and 62. VW diary, 2 Dec. 1934: 'I will write the play for Xmas: Freshwater a farce – for a joke.' It had been first thought of in 1919 (VW diary, 30 Jan. 1919) and was performed 18 Jan. 1935 – 'an unbuttoned laughing evening'.

'Philip Larkin's verse' 'The Literary World', *Collected Poems*, ed. Anthony Thwaite (1988), p. 38. (Unpublished at the time.)

xvi 'my first biography' *Waiting for the Party: the life of Frances Hodgson Burnett* (1974; 1994).

'planting their own happiness' Leibnitz quoted by Theodore Watts-Dunton in his obituary of ET in the *Athenaeum*, 15 Aug. 1896.

'structure our view' Rosie Jackson in *Mothers Who Leave* (1994), p. 133, on Elaine Feinstein's *Lawrence's Women*.

'Tory MP's wife' Anita Townsend, wife of M.P. for Bexleyheath, in 'Tory Wives', film directed by Rebecca Frayn, 1995.

'hidden lives' 'unvisited tombs' George Eliot, *Middlemarch*, last page.

'painfully conscious' FLo, *Memoir* 2.80.

xviii 'My want and my trial' ET to HT, 27 Feb. 1872, TRC.

'the head of the woman' 1 Corinthians 11:3.

St Paul and 'no competition' ET to AW, 27 March 1892, TRC.

'order of the world' ET to Agnes, 7 March 1896, TRC.

'his necessity' Annie Fields, *Authors and Friends* (1896).

'true marriage' 'two celled heart' etc. AT in *The Princess* VII, Ricks 2.290–1.

'Biographers of Tennyson' But Michael Thorn in his *Tennyson* (1992) does acknowledge (p. 363) that ET was 'a much more spirited and gritty woman than the saintly character so often depicted.'

'to his wife's perpetual . . .' James Knowles, 'Aspects of Tennyson', *Nineteenth Century* 33 (Jan. 1893), p. 188.

'with little worsted strands' Harold Nicolson in *Tennyson*, p. 156.

'what was most wild' 'wistful lady' Nicolson himself suspected the picture was not 'wholly fair', p. 157.

'the prick of a thorn' ET to HT, 25 Oct. 1870, TRC.

'deeply conventional' *RBM*, p. 327. Cf. *Memoir* 1.279 where AT says he is 'always shy with false or *conventional* people'.

xvii 'worldly ambition' FT to his son Alfred, 4 Jan. 1884, Lilly.
'an old Housekeeper' Fitz to Milnes, 12 April 1874, Terhune 3.487.

xviii 'second self' etc. EBB in Annie Fields, *Authors and Friends* (1896), pp. 352–3.
'people are only influenced' C. Ricks to me, 29 March 1995.
Emily's sons In the introduction to Tennyson's letters (xxi) L&S say: 'One does not think of HT as ever having been young.' I hope I can at least overthrow this perception of him.
'Parents are formed' C. Ricks on the *Memoir, Essays in Appreciation* (1996).
'Blessed is he' Carlyle, quoted as epigraph to *Anne Gilchrist* (1887).
'after so many years of trial' Aubrey de Vere to Isabella Fenwick, 24 Sept. 1854, L&S 2.97.
'Poets' wives' Eileen Simpson (first wife of John Berryman) in *Poets in their Youth* (1982), p. 198.
'My mother thinks' HT to EL, 17 Dec. 1885, TRC.

xix 'Words in enigmas' Green journal, Feb. 1867, TRC.
'What drops, and sticks,' from 'Nescit vox missa reverti' in *The Dust of the World* by Anthony Thwaite (1994), p. 39.

PROLOGUE Beginning near the end

1 Audrey's notes at TRC, published in *Dakyns* as 'The Death-Bed Diary', p. 129.
'self-love' BJ to FN, 22 June 1867, Balliol.
'as great as he was' 'Should this remark . . .' *Memoir* 2.467.
'as if from a coffin' (March 1880) *Thomas Hardy: Life and Work*, ed. Michael Millgate, p. 140.
'lying flat on her back' Edmund Gosse, 6 Aug. 1887, Ashley, BL.

2 'computing moderately' EL to Fortescue, 12 June 1859, *Letters of EL*, p. 138.
'sickness had gone on' etc. 'The Death-Bed Diary', TRC, *Dakyns*, p. 129.
sarcophagus Journal, Aug. 1872, TRC.
'Two graves grass-green' 'Circumstance', Ricks 1.274.
'think over the blessings' BJ to ET, 4 Oct. 1892, TRC.
'I am grieved' BJ to ET, 5 Oct. 1892, TRC.

3 'own book of prayers' TRC. The stanza (the 4th of the Prologue) is quite different in the final version. See Ricks 2.316.
'there was no hope' 'The Death-Bed Diary', TRC, *Dakyns*, p. 134.
'the only tolerable view' 'Two things . . .' AT in WA *Diary*, 25 Nov. 1887, p. 368 and 27 July 1884, p. 329.
'If thou shouldst never . . .' 'Morte d'Arthur', Ricks 2.117.

4 'Why should we expect a hereafter?' ATR to HT, 11 Dec. 1895, Eton.
fearing the grave as little as the bed. ET to HT, 15 July 1870, TRC.
'as calmly as to a future day' AHH to AT, 4 Sept. 1832, copy TRC, Kolb p. 638.
'O, that Press will get hold of it now' AT's remark (recorded in Mat. 9.95) at the moment the Queen's telegram arrived, refers surely to the fact that the news of his illness would now be public. It was altered by HT (*Memoir* 2.426) to 'O, that Press will get hold of me now!' suggesting AT was fearing what the press would say about him after his death. Arthur Waugh, *One Man's Road*, p. 208.
Bequests to Eleanor née Locker, then Tennyson, then Birrell. Anne Weld. Cecy was Cecilia Pope, Horatio's daughter.
'blessing to thee and thine' This use, which is normally associated with Quakers, was

natural to ET throughout her life and not only in writing. *Stars and Markets*, p. 15: 'It was characteristic (and perhaps commoner in their generation than is generally realized) that she and my grandfather often used the pronoun "thou" and "thee" when talking to one another.'

4 'joyful in the hope' ET to Welds, 11 Oct. 1892, TRC.
'eternal reunion' ET to Fields, 14 Sept. 1886, Pierpont Morgan.

6 'Cymbeline' in Johnson and Stevens edn. (1785) vol. 9, p. 355, at TRC.
'dearest brother Charles' AT was particularly close to CTT, but *Dakyns* (p. 11) recorded on 18 June 1861 a dream where AT spoke of Septimus as his 'favourite brother'.
'This must have been' HT to Victoria, 13 Oct. 1892, *Dear and Honoured* p. 142.
'My mother is crushed' HT to Victoria, 5 Oct. 1892, *Dear and Honoured*, p. 139.
'Take no opium' AT to Brookfield, mid-March 1832, L&S 1.70.
'God bless you, my joy' HT to Argyll, 24 Oct. 1892; also to Victoria, Royal Archives, Windsor, *Dear and Honoured*, p. 140.
'those words of Emmie's' MT to HT, 12 Jan. 1893, TRC.

7 'one of the finest' Carlyle to Emerson, 5 Aug. 1844, L&S 1.228.
Rembrandt *Illustrated London News*, 15 Oct. 1892.
'last heat' 'The Two Voices' (lines omitted as 'too dismal'), Ricks 1.587, see *Memoir* 1.109.
'not grey' 'one gray glimpse of sea': 'Prologue to General Hamley', Ricks 3.92.
'at the gates of Death' AT to FT, 25 Jan. 1884, Lilly, L&S 3.279.

8 'grand eyelids' ET to Boyd Carpenter (Bishop of Ripon), 18 Oct. 1892, BL.
death certificate TRC, Gout (Rheumatic) 4 years, syncope, 15 hours.
'for fear there should' 'The Death-Bed Diary', TRC, *Dakyns*, p. 139.
'without pain' W. T. Stead, Nov. 1892, *Review of Reviews*.
'May my end' AT to CTDE, 15 March 1831, LAO, L&S 1.53.
Letter in *The Times* 30 June 1892, p. 6, see L&S 3.446.
'No Home Rulers' Macmillan archives, BL.
'made an excuse' Roy Jenkins letter to me, 11 Feb. 1995: Gladstone devoted 'a ridiculous amount of time' to his lecture; 'perhaps . . . he did not like funerals'. (He also missed Peel's forty years before.) WEG to HT, 8 Oct. 1892, TRC.
Mary Drew's telegram Hawarden, 9.35, 10 Oct. 1892, TRC.

9 'laid up' Watts to HT, Oct. 1892, NPG.
'other inaccuracies' e.g. *Illustrated London News*, 15 Oct. 1892, had Lionel, the grandson, as 'a graceful little girl' and said that 'Silent Voices' was 'her husband's last poem dictated to her shortly before his death'.
'bearing up wonderfully' Audrey to Lady Boyne, 15 Oct. 1892, Yale.
'basket on gate' picture in *Daily Graphic*, 12 Oct. 1892.
'old friends' ET to EL, 25 Sept. 1855, TRC.
'his study is my room' ET to Welds, 18 Oct. 1892, TRC.
Dakyns 'one of us' Audrey to GD, 6 March 1901, *Dakyns*, p. 184.
letter to Lushingtons Ackn. by ELL to HT, 7 Nov. 1892, TRC.
'excuse the paper' 'dislikes dowager' ET to Welds, 18 Oct. 1892, TRC.

10 'Audrey has slaved' ET to Welds, 13 Oct. 1892, TRC. (Hoge *L* misreads as 'shared'.)
Audrey on her mother-in-law's health to Henry Van Dyke, 18 Nov. 1892, Princeton.
'sterner stuff' MBro's letters to ATR, Eton, to FT, Lilly, 10 Oct. and 18 Oct. 1892.
'buoyed her up' HT to FLo, 17 Oct. 1892, Rochester.
Tilly wrote 13 Jan. 1893, Rochester.
funeral arrangements Macmillan archive, BL.

10 'more of our loss' ET to S. Browning, 18 Oct. 1892, Baylor University, Waco, Texas.
11 'giving him to a grave' MBrad to ET, 14 Oct. 1892, TRC.
    'If it is thought better . . .' draft for ET's telegram (5142) and Bradley's telegram
    (3345), 7 Oct. 1892, TRC. It is possible that Emily's draft was actually made in the
    winter of 1888–9 when AT seemed to be dying. Her omitted words refer to the Flag
    of England on his coffin written presumably before she knew of Rawnsley's pall. She
    uses the present tense in a further sentence as if AT were still alive: 'the beloved Queen
    and the Nation [and the] Empire he loves so truly.'
    'We all of us hate' AT to ET, 27 Feb. 1865, L&S 2.394, TRC.
    local roadworker Rawnsley, pp. 156 and 158.
    'Sunset and evening star' ' Crossing the Bar', Ricks 3.253.
    Emily's description of procession from Aldworth etc. TRC (5141).
    'our Lionel left' ET to Welds, 15 Oct. 1892, TRC.
12 the pall TRC has a letter from HDR to ET and AT, 10 Oct. 1892 which stresses the
    link between the two Laureates, as the pall came from Wordsworth's Lakes. The roses
    also stand for the Arthurian poems being 'the flower of chivalry'. Nothing about
    when the work ('a labour of real love') started or how long it took. It is now in
    Carisbrooke Castle on the Isle of Wight, where it was taken for ET's own funeral.
    Renan's funeral comment and 11,000 wanting tickets Rawnsley *Memories*,
    pp. 175–6.
    Frederick Bridge, 1844–1924, not to be confused with Frank Bridge.
    'Lady T's own music' *Daily News*, n.d., cutting at TRC.
13 'The sun . . . filled Poets' Corner' *Daily Graphic*, 12 Oct. 1892.
    'little white-frocked thing' FP to HT, 14 Oct. 1892, TRC.
    'carrying his hat' Audrey, 'The Death-Bed Diary', TRC, *Dakyns*, p. 145.
    'golden-haired Ally' AT's poem 'To Alfred Tennyson My Grandson', Ricks 3.70.
    'seedy waiter' A.B.S. Tennyson to Eleanor, Sept. 1892, TRC.
    'I was very good to him' ET to Welds, 1 Nov. 1892, TRC.
    'The child was wonderful' MBrad to ET, 14 Oct. 1892, TRC.
14 'kind to dear Aunt Tilly' HT to FT's son AT, 15 Oct. 1892, Lilly.
    MT's description from ELL to ATR, 23 Oct. 1892, Eton.
    'void unendurable' ET to AW, 15 Oct. 1892, TRC.
    'no man dies less . . .' Hall Caine in *Daily News*, n.d., cutting, TRC.
    'Thy life outlives . . .' Line on AT's memorial in Freshwater church.
    'no particular Bar' ET to AW, 30 Dec. 1892, TRC.
15 'I never was at any . . .' FLu to ET, 25 Oct. 1892, TRC.
    Gosse on funeral BL. See 'After the Funeral' in *Portraits from Life* by Edmund Gosse,
    ed. Ann Thwaite, p. 53.
    Hardy on funeral from *Life and Work*, ed. Michael Millgate, p. 265, and *Collected
    Letters* ed. Purdy and Millgate, 1.287.
    'only men can go' ET to Agnes, 11 Oct. 1892, TRC.
    Henry James from Leon Edel, *Life of HJ* 2.38 (Penguin edn.).
    Swinburne 'no longer a Red' *Illustrated London News*, n.d., cutting, TRC.
    Swinburne on funerals to Burne Jones, 15 Oct. 1892, *Letters*, ed. Lang, 6.36.
16 'splendid tribute' ET to Swinburne, 19 Dec. 1892, BL.
    Swinburne visit AT to R.J. Mann, 3 Feb. 1858, TRC (Mat. ii. 142–3), L&S, 2.194.
    'letters of condolence' AT to SRE, 26 June 1871, L&S, 3.6.
    'He told a story' BW-C in *London Mercury Interviews*, p. 116.
    bathchair pushing J.M.F. Ludlow to ET, draft CUL.
    'Kindness to the young' A.G. Butler to ET, 13 Oct. 1892, TRC.

16 'I can hear him still' ATR to ET, 25 Nov. 1892, TRC.
   undertaker's letter J. Raston of Ryde, *Dakyns*, p. 125.
17 draft statement TRC (8104).
   'our greatest poet of intimate bereavement' Ricks, *Essays in Appreciation* (1996).
18 'energetic temperament' TW to ET, 22 Oct. 1864, TRC.
   'Energetic people' JS to ET, 26 May 1860, TRC.
   'but the prick of a thorn' ET to HT, 25 Oct. 1870, TRC.
   'some sat upstairs' ET to Welds, 22 Oct. 1892, TRC.
   drafts of replies to letters of condolence and lists, all at TRC.
19 'weak sentence' ET to TW, 24 Dec. 1856, TRC.
   'How thankful we are' MBrad to ET, 14 Oct. 1892, TRC.
   ' "To HT" should be added' ET to Craik, 24 Sept. 1893, BL (See p.602.)
20 help with *Memoir* FP to HT, 9 Oct. 1892, TRC.
   publishing for Christmas HT to BJ, 15 Sept. 1893, Balliol.
21 Argyll 'worried' to ET, 2 Nov. 1892, TRC.
   'lovely boys' Argyll to ET, 27 Oct. 1895, TRC.
   'Farringford . . . home' Journal 2.259, TRC.
   'dearest spot' ET to EL, 25 Dec. 1887, TRC.
   'perfect ecstacy' ET to GD, 3 Oct. 1861, *Dakyns*, p. 15.
   'live in the past' ET to Mary Watts, 23 Jan. 1893, NPG.
   'May God comfort' Mary Watts to ET, 9 Nov. 1892, TRC.
   'I am thankful' ET to Mary Watts, 29 May 1894, NPG.
   'The longer we are' EL to ET, 1 June 1884, TRC.
22 'Hallam is right' Emily Lushington to ET, 25 Oct. 1892, TRC.
   'Jowett encouraging' BJ to HT, 25 Oct. 1892, TRC. Jowett thought the work should
   'be completed in six months'. He didn't want it to 'drag on like Stanley's Life' and
   encouraged HT to read Boswell.
   'I can be a help' ET to Welds, 11 Oct. 1892, TRC.
   'Fain would we leave' ET to Mary Watts, 23 Jan. 1893, NPG.
   E's version of Preface to *Memoir* TRC (5143).
   'I loathe to hear' Gissing to Clodd, 6 Nov. 1897, *Letters of G. Gissing* 6.376 (1995).
23 James Knowles's reminiscences in the *Nineteenth Century*, Jan. 1893, partly in
   Interviews, p. 87.
   'speak out plainly' Argyll to HT, 4 Jan. 1893, TRC.
   Knowles's 'treachery' ET to AW, 15 Feb. 1893, TRC.
   'Non ragioniam' correctly Dante *Inferno* 3.51. cf. *Memoir* 1.227.
   'melancholy, long, withdrawing roar' 'Dover Beach', Matthew Arnold.
   'grave groping' Acton to Mary G, 21 June 1880, *Letters of Lord Acton to Mary G*, p.
   16.
   'the torrent of babies . . . Yet God is love' *Memoir* 1.314.
   'A warmth within the heart . . .' *Memoir* 1.315; *IM* CXXIV, Ricks 2.444.
   hated biographies AT to WA, 25 Nov. 1887, WA *Diary*, p. 368.
24 'rollicking' talk 'ripped open' etc. JMC to Henry Taylor, [c. 29 Nov. 1862], L&S
   2.319, AT to Taylor, 23 March 1885, L&S 3.312, *The Times*, 24 March 1885; 'he
   knew nothing, of Shakespeare, etc. also in Talks and Walks (Audrey's hand), TRC.
   There are of course many letters by Jane Austen surviving.
   'pigs' AT's pig-slaughtering imagery (cf. AT preferring to kill a pig rather than write a
   letter) reminds us they had a pigsty at Somersby Rectory.
   'Modern fame' WA *Diary*, 4 Oct. 1863, *Memoir* 1.513.
   Henry Sidgwick encouraging to HT, 14 Sept. 1895, TRC.

24 'eliminate any "praising"' HT to Sidgwick, 10 May 1897, TRC.
'How his name' H. Hallam to ETJ, 7 Nov. 1853, TRC.
25 'What a strange thing fame is' ELL to HT, n.d. 1879, TRC.
'stains of ink' *Leaves from the Notebooks of Lady Dorothy Nevill* (1907), p. 68.
'When I am dead' AT in 1889 to M. Rawnsley Arden reported in M. Arden to HDR,
Jan. 1893, Rawnsley papers.
'In my youth the growls!' Rawnsley *Memories*, p. 113, *Memoir* 11.74, Ricks 3.12.
'My mother and I' HT to HDR, 17 Jan. 1893, Rawnsley papers.
26 'You little know' HT to J. Knowles, 20 Dec. 1896, copy at Yale.
'final and full enough' *Memoir* 1. xii.
keep out 'penny-a-liner lies' HT to ATR, 30 Oct. 1892, Eton.
AT encouraged ET MS Mat. 7.
'the authority for a good deal' ET to Welds, 2 Nov. 1892, TRC.
'they kept journals' HT to ATR, 30 Oct. 1892, Eton.
'annotated edition' known as the Eversley edn. 1908. (One vol. with memoir 1913.)
'stirred his lemonade' *Memoir* 1.202.
27 'The worth of a biography' *Memoir* 2.165.
'doubtless an arduous task' *Memoir* 1.165.
'Thus the priesthood . . .' E. Gosse, *Edinburgh Review*, Oct. 1918, in *Portraits from
Life*, ed. Ann Thwaite, p. 58.
'the true and full picture' HT to H. Sidgwick, 29 Aug. 1895, TRC.
Alfred Lyall in *Edinburgh Review* ccclxxxii; *T and his Friends*, p. 344.
28 'not chipped to the smooth pattern' ATR *Records*, p. 60.
Ricks, *T*, p. viii, calls *Memoir* 'capacious and honorable' if inaccurate and reticent –
'at its best in breathing a sense of what it was like in the immediate vicinity of T.
during the second half of his life.'
Waugh remembered later Arthur Waugh, *One Man's Road*, p. 208. Cf. note to p. 4.
29 Iachimo the villain in Shakespeare's *Cymbeline*.
the Lushingtons like many of these people will play a large part in the biography.
Cecilia Tennyson, one of AT's sisters, was married to ELL.
30 'I am going to write a short life' HT to Sophie Tennyson, Oct. 1892, Lilly.
Frederick and Somersby In *Stars and Markets* (p. 168) CT suggests AT had told HT
very little of life at Somersby.
'in the jugular vein' Eliza T to GT, 27 Feb. 1829, LAO, L&S 1.29.
Browning/Aldis Wright/FitzGerald affair See this book Ch. 15, pp. 581–3.
RB loved ET 'singularly' RB to Julia Wedgwood, 2 Sept. 1864, *RB and Julia
Wedgwood Letters*, p. 75.
31 'some caprice' etc. Emily in Narrative, first version, 4, TRC. I shall not distinguish
between the different versions of the Narrative (all at TRC) in these Notes. Hoge's
inaccurate publication of them (*Texas Studies in Lit. and Lang.* XIV.1. Spring 1972) is
convenient but sometimes misleading. It would appear that everything except the
short (2,600 words) narrative on blue paper, dated 9 Dec. 1869, was written after
AT's death. The 1869 version begins: 'My Boys I was thinking in bed last night . . .' It
is similar in appearance to some of Emily's own stories and ends at Beech Hill (c.
1840). There is also a black notebook with a narrative of twice that length, but which
is identical in some parts to it. This dates from the 1890s and was obviously designed
specifically to help HT with the *Memoir*. It begins: 'A friend of the Somersby days
writes' – starts with Somersby and continues to 1851 and the end of the Italian
holiday. Although at the top of the pages bound in the green volumes with Emily's
epitome of her journals, she writes 'in black covered book', they actually follow on

from the blue (uncovered) pages and end soon after Park House in the 1840s. There are also at TRC two short typewritten versions of the Narrative, one with changes and annotations in Hallam's hand. Hoge's unreliable edition of *Lady Tennyson's Journal* (1981) starts with part of the Narrative but entirely ignores the material after 1874 except to say (p. 371): 'There is an addendum of Hallam Tennyson's penned in at the end of her Journal book. This addendum, which offers sketchy coverage of major events between 1874 and 1892, is entirely in Hallam's hand.' This is nonsense. It is *all* in Emily's hand.

31 Hallam's version *Memoir* 1.15.
'It will be a long time' AT to Duchess of Argyll, 12 July 1875, TRC, L&S 3.107.
looking for journals ET to Welds, 1 Nov. 1892, TRC.
reducing journals to an epitome e.g. ET adds 'the bailiff' after a mention of Heard and changes 'the children at the Terrace' to 'Horatio's children' to make the story more intelligible to strangers.

32 'old calamity' *T and his Friends*, p. 186. Yet some of BJ's letters to HT just after AT's death suggest he had no idea of the tragedy of the 'simple home' at Somersby.
'serene and unblemished life' A. Waugh, *Tennyson* p. 301.

33 'It is very difficult . . .' ET to Welds, 9 Nov. 1892.
Alfred, A, AT In Emily's original he was consistently, I feel sure, 'Ally'.
ET's version of preface to *Memoir*, 5143 at TRC.
'The picture . . .' HT Preface to *Memoir*, p. xv.

35 'two moderate-sized volumes . . .' H. Sidgwick to HT, 14 Sept. 1895, TRC.
'in Ally's study' ET to AW, 4 Aug. 1893, TRC.
condensing her journals There is a note by Hallam in the epitome Journal at TRC: 'Resumé journal corrected here and there by my mother and me for publication in Memoir. Passages have been cut out for my Memoir and pasted in my MS book [i.e. MS Materials]. Also see various additions and corrections in original diary and Memoir.' So at this time presumably HT did not mean to destroy original. In writing out the Journal ET occasionally makes slips caused by introducing later knowledge. For instance, in April/May 1871 she describes Margaret Rawnsley as Margaret Arden, though she is not married until the following year. Obviously there was no surname at all in the original journal and she adds the wrong one.
her own handwriting ET to AW, 2 Nov. 1893, TRC.
'essays' for HT by ET, 5148, 5158, at TRC.

36 1834 scene *Memoir* 1.148.

37 'I was thinking in bed' This is the first version of the narrative 'For My Sons' at TRC.
'her own story' Recollections in *T and his Friends*, MS in Hallam's hand at TRC.

CHAPTER I The girl at the Market Place window

39 'passing the window' and following quotations from ET Recollections in *T and his Friends*, pp. 3–7. MS in HT's hand, TRC, 'a fragment written in 1896', slightly different, e.g. MS has 'private' where printed has 'favourite' of theatricals. No MS in ET's hand apparently survives.
Anne born 27 Oct. 1814, Louisa, 20 May 1816.
Bertrand Russell, *Autobiography* 2.38 (1968).

40 Alfred Tennyson and Anne and Louisa Sellwood were also baptized within two days of birth; it was not uncommon for the sacrament to be performed almost immediately – but then infant death was also not uncommon.
Clitherows Law lists show Sellwood joining in 1809. As he was then twenty-seven, he

may already have been articled in Berkshire. No formal examinations or qualifications existed until 1831; the separate profession of attorney (lawyers who combined the work of solicitors and barristers) was abolished in 1875. Information from I.G. Murray, archivist, Inner Temple.

40 'road to ruin' *Memoir* 1.329.
'he would be slain' Agnes Weld, *Contemporary Rev.* , Nov. 1897.
grandparents Martha Sellwood died in 1827, aged seventy, Henry in 1832, aged eighty-two (graves at Aldworth).

41 Hewett's *History and Antiquities of the Hundred of Compton, Berks.* confirms that the Sellwoods once owned land which had belonged to the De La Beche and Langford families and that the Pibworth estate had come to the Sellwoods through marriage to a Rowland. The giant knights were *not* ancestors of Emily's. They are said to date from 1300–50. The mutilation apparently occurred in the seventeenth century. A leaflet in the church at Aldworth incorrectly says that Pibworth was ET's home as a girl and that the Sellwood tombs in the churchyard are of her parents and grandparents. Her grandparents (Henry and Martha) are there but the others are an uncle and aunt, Richard and Maria, and an uncle who died at three. The family tomb was in a very bad state when I saw it in 1994.

41 John de Selwode was elected Abbot of Glastonbury 15 Nov. 1457. See *Memoir* 1.332.
Trev's Franklin House Bakery seen by me, looking rather dilapidated, in 1994. It carries a plaque showing it was the birthplace of Sir John Franklin.

43 'what sort of person Sarah . . .' There seem to be no surviving letters either to or from her. One indexed at SPRI as to her from JF is more likely to be to Betsy.
Spilsby bank 'Old Private Bankers of N. Lincolnshire.' H. Porter, *Lincs. Mag.*, March/April 1936.

44 Franklin: his statue by Charles Bacon, 1861.
'heroic Franklin blood' ET to Lady Richardson, 2 Oct. 1871, Rochester.
Sellwood 'kindly, cultivated . . .' *Memoir* 1.329.
'the model of an English gentleman' 25 June 1865, e.g. 'gentlemanly', Robert Roberts in Nicolls & Wise, *Literary Anecdotes of the Nineteenth Century*, W.T. Page to Macmillan, 9 Oct. 1892, BL.
On general standing of solicitors. See John Frere to FT (in *Letters to FT*) writing from Suffolk, 22 Nov. 1834: 'Our parish is rather a singular one. The Farmers and Tradesmen make the aristocracy – there being not a single gentleman above two Solicitors and two general practitioners.'

45 'Whoever would think . . .' from Weston Cracroft diary. See *TRB* 3.1 (1977) pp. 26–9.
'the education of the poor . . .' and subscription list See J.N. Clarke, *Education in a Market Town: Horncastle* (1976).
'a later report' 6 Feb. 1836.

46 Sellwood's integrity AT draft Mat. 11.39, L&S 1.172.
Sellwood's 'real estate . . .' from will at TRC.
famous for its fairs Pigot, Directory, 1830.
the Sellwoods' own house now demolished and replaced by a Woolworths, one of the worst buildings in Lincolnshire. A plaque without dates was fixed in 1996.

47 'Horncastle and its vicinity' 'urns, coins' White's 1826 Directory.

48 ET's earliest surviving French book at TRC is *L'Enfant Aveugle: historie amusante et morale, à l'usage de la jeunesse*, Paris, 1822, though she may not have acquired it in the year of publication, of course.
Education at Home by E.W. Benson (1824), TRC.

48 Harrington Hall ET to AW, 30 June 1890 and 17 Aug. 1889, TRC.

49 'destined from birth' T. Watts-Dunton, Obituary, *Athenaeum*, 15 Aug. 1896.
   one feminist Jean Strouse, *Alice James: a biography* (1981). See also M. Shaw, *Alfred Lord Tennyson*, pp. 14–15
   description of AT at thirteen ET to Alexander Macmillan, 15 May 1884, BL.

50 owl and monkey *Memoir* 1.19.
   the Grammar School at Louth AT's copy of the *Iliad* at TRC contains an annotation ending 'In the little Louth school C. and I learnt – well – I should say – absolutely nothing.'
   AT with the children *Memoir* 1.5.
   'a kind of waking trance' AT to B.P. Blood, 7 May 1874, Harvard, L&S 2.78.

51 GCT to his father 14 Aug. 1820, LAO, Sturman, pp. 20–21.
   'the old brute' AHH to Brookfield, 12/14 Aug. 1832, Kolb, p. 619.
   'disinherited' used in *Memoir* 1.13, comes from ET's Narrative. The family's inheritance is complex and as this is primarily Emily's story I do not go into it in detail. See Sturman and 'The Disinheritance Tradition Reconsidered', Francis Hill, *TRB*, 3.2, Nov. 1979.

52 'not yet a schirrus' 15 April 1822, GCT to Mary Tennyson sen., LAO, Sturman, p. 21.
   Mary Tennyson sen. to CTDE 'noise of his children' 22 Jan. 1823, LAO, Sturman, p. 23.
   'So many boys' Fanny to CTDE, 3 Feb. 1823, LAO, Sturman, p. 23.
   'Phoenix like' GCT to CTDE, 1 Feb. 1824, LAO, Sturman p. 25.
   'crippling inertia' GCT to CTDE, 21 Jan. 1824, LAO.

53 Eleanor Porden and JF letters Franklin history H.D. Traill, *The Life of Sir John Franklin RN* (1896) and E.M. Gell, *John Franklin's Bride* (1930). Letters at SPRI. *The Fate of Franklin* (1978) by Roderic Owen, great-grandson of CR, is also interesting. He writes of 'Rawnsley papers', 'which my late aunt Susan Rawnsley . . . contrived to destroy.' The 'Rawnsley papers' I refer to (over 100 letters, largely to HDR for *Memories*) are in the possession of Rosalind Rawnsley. Other Rawnsley papers are at LAO and Harvard.

54 'find room in your heart' JF to E. Porden, 10 June 1823, SPRI. Members of the Booth, Cracroft and Wright families – at this point at Ingoldmells, Keal near Bolingbroke, and Wrangle – would remain in touch with Emily Tennyson all her life.

56 'Tell me all about' W. Franklin to HS, 14 Nov. 1822, LAO.
   Kate Franklin, born 21 Dec. 1818. The Lincolnshire Pedigree for the Franklins gives the death dates of two of the children: Emily b. 13 June 1820, died 17 Sept. 1822, and Willingham, b. 19 Nov. 1821, died 2 Oct. 1822. But the death dates are really not possible as their father writes from Madras to say they 'arrived all safe and well' on 18 Oct. 1822. Willingham possibly died (aged eleven months) in Oct. 1823 as another son born later that month was given the same name. He and Catherine aged five and three-quarters were the only members of the family to survive. Sir Willingham himself, 31 May 1824, his wife 22 Sept. 1824, Emily (I assume) 17 Sept. 1824 and Elizabeth 17 Nov. 1824, all perished from cholera. The news must have chilled the Sellwood family in Horncastle. Catherine (Kate) – so important in this story – spent the years immediately after 1824 with her mother's family in Nottinghamshire. The Pedigree also has Willingham Franklin senior's death as 1822; in fact it was 3 April 1824, not long before his son far off in Madras.

57 Brackenburys I am not sure how the Brackenburys fit into the Franklin family picture. All the Bousfields – Dr William B. and his teacher sisters – carry Brackenbury as a middle name, which suggests their mother was one. In 1813 GCT writing about lodgings at Mablethorpe damns the 'lousy race of Brackenburys thro all its branches

and from end to side' for having a prior claim to a house he wanted to rent. There were Brackenburys all over Lincolnshire. Two were Rectors of Halton before the Rawnsleys and others crop up in an 1849 extract from the Cracroft diary (L&S 1.310). There was an attorney in Spilsby of the name.

58 Stuff Ball to encourage the textile trade, mistakenly rendered as Staff Ball in *John Franklin's Bride*.
'Your Aunt Mary . . .' Narrative, TRC. Harps were often conveyed around the county. Cf. ETJ to E. Hallam, 24 March 1833, TRC, 'They have not a harp. Ours is therefore to be conveyed . . .'
Rate sheets in Lincoln City local history reference library.
Bousfield on GCT in Mary Tennyson sen. to CTDE, 31 March 1816, LAO, Sturman, p. 16; Eliza T to CTDE, 5 March 1825, LAO, Sturman, p. 26.

59 'a fund' *Stamford Mercury*, 28 Oct. 1836, 1.2.

60 'My dear Dulcinea' AT to Miss Bousfield, n.d., Yale, L&S 1.3.
'I am dying' Eliza T to CTDE, 5 March 1825, LAO, Sturman, p. 26.
'one of the grandfather's friends' J.H. Vane, 14 May 1825, LAO.

61 W. Chaplin to CTDE 'He will not allow them.', 10 Oct. 1827, LAO, Sturman, p. 28.
'malt liquor' Bousfield to CTDE, 17 Oct. 1827, LAO, Sturman, p. 29.
'to the caprice' M.A. Fytche to GCT 24 Oct. 1827, LAO, Sturman, p. 30.
'I am glad Mr Sellwood' JF to 'My dear sister' (identified wrongly as Sarah), SPRI, n.d.

62 For Ingilby's relations with CTDE see *Tealby Gleanings* by Jim Murray (1995). Election comments from 'The Poll', Lincoln, 1824. Parliamentary Election Papers. Ingilby was returned unopposed in 1826 and 1830, so did not need Sellwood's services.

63 death of Thomas Cracroft E's uncle, described as 'cousin' in Recollections, *T & his Friends*, p. 4, TRC. There were six children born to Thomas and Isabella Cracroft. Henry (bapt. 1818) must have been already dead and Catherine (bapt. 1823) not yet born when their new aunt visited in 1823 as she records four. The youngest children were presumably too small to go to the sheepshearing (Thomas b. 1819, Emma b. 1821 and Catherine).

66 'It is very extraordinary' GT to E. Russell, 1 Jan. 1828, Yale.
schools My enquiries to try and discover more about the schools Emily went to in Brighton and London came to nothing, e.g. Brighton has no records relating to the 1820s. Emily's own memories in Recollections, TRC.

67 Kate on Lady Franklin diary, 18 July 1875, copy at LAO.

68 Lady F. 'a great favourite' Journal, 22 Sept. 1864.
'a letter from America' from H.K. Atkinson. When it arrived in Nov. 1873, AT would have 'flung it aside', thinking, from the American stamp, it was a request for an autograph, but ET said 'Here is a letter which is delightful'. The original letter was apparently destroyed in the San Francisco earthquake, but there is a draft at TRC (Mat. 3. 244–5) longer than the version in L&S 3.67.

69 Horlins' words *Memoir* 1.14.
AT to his grandfather 12 July 1829, LAO, L&S 1.41.
Chaplin to CTDE 10 Oct. 1827, LAO, Sturman, p. 28.
Bousfield to CTDE 17 Oct. 1827, LAO, Sturman, p. 29.
Elizabeth Russell 'for spirits like ours' 28 July 1825, LAO, Sturman, p. 31.

70 AT to Aunt Russell 18 April [1828], L&S 1.22.
'died a few weeks old' *CTAT*, p. 16, Rawnsley *Memories*, p. 40, 'one died a babby'.
'under the most deplorable state' THR to CTDE, 12 March 1829, LAO, L&S 1.31.

71 'Those three boys' GT to CTDE, 26 Jan. 1829, LAO, L&S 1.25.
'I mean to be famous' *Memoir* 1.17.
'I see so many little natures' Fitz to FT of Septimus, Terhune 1.67.
'I consider Tennyson . . .' AHH to WEG, 14 Sept. 1829, Kolb, p. 319.
'a void in his heart' GCT to THR, 1 Jan. 1830, LAO, Sturman, p. 34.
Alfred's music lessons What evidence? See *CTAT*, p. 102.

72 shops from Horncastle town directories of the period.
'almost as clever as their brothers' Rawnsley *Memories*, p. 49. HDR enthusiastically
embroidered with dialect people's memories reported to him. I have made the words
plainer.
the Husks *CTAT*, p. 164.
friendships 'not very lasting' AHH to ET, 12 Oct. 1832, Kolb, p. 664.
'All country booksellers . . .' GCT to CTDE, Dec. 1812, Sturman, p. 12.

73 'How they could have all got in . . .' HT to AT and ET, 13 Sept. 1892, TRC.
'though he burns and shines' AHH to Eliza T, 20/30 June 1830, TRC, Kolb, p. 365.
'much-praised book of poems' See *RBM*, p. 105.
'far too good to be popular' AHH to W.B. Donne, 31 May 1830, Kolb, p. 363.
'Poems are good things . . .' AHH to AT, 31 Oct. –3 Nov. 1832, Kolb, p. 679.
'When I think what he was' Narrative for my sons and Recollections, TRC.

74 'I used to feel moods of misery . . .' Talks and Walks, TRC.
'leafiness and luxury' AHH to ETJ, 26 May 1832, Kolb, p. 582.
'I cannot be happy' 'My life here has been . . .' AHH to Blakesley, 13 April 1830,
Kolb, p. 360.

75 'Mary's noble countenance' Blakesley to Trench, 1 April 1833, Kolb, p. 746.
'something like Alfred' Blakesley to Thompson, 16 April 1833, Kolb, p. 749.
'chippy and unmanageable' GCT to GT, 27 Feb. 1829, LAO, L&S 1.29.
'idle as a foal' etc. GT to CTDE, [18 June 1831], LAO, L&S 1.61.
Emily writes about 'The Emperor of Morocco' in Narrative, TRC. Further
information kindly supplied by Iona Opie.

76 AHH on Undine to ETJ, 30 Oct. 1832, Kolb, p. 675.

CHAPTER 2 'The sharp desire of knowledge'

77 'meeting' story by HT *Memoir* 1.148.
Of this visit to Somersby in April 1830, Willingham Rawnsley foolishly said in his
1909 Centenary lecture (offprint at TRC) that Emily Sellwood had 'driven over with
her parents', apparently unaware that her mother had died when she was three.
Oddly, Sir Charles in *CTAT* (p. 103) repeats this error, although he knew his
grandmother well. It confirms how little AT's biographers have been interested in the
Sellwoods. In L&S the editors want this visit to be in the autumn of 1830 because ET
says (L&S 3.291) that AT 'had the hue of southern France in his complexion as he had
always after'. Certainly AT had been in the Pyrenees that summer, but the colouring
was permanent, not temporary. In her Narrative ET says that AT's sister E. had 'the
colouring of the south of France inherited I suppose from a member of Madame de
Maintenon's family.' She said AT himself was 'never thought to be an Englishman on
the continent'.
'My native village . . .' AT to William Howitt for his *Homes and Haunts*, see L&S
1.254, 'distinction' is mistranscribed possibly by their source, Amice Lee.

78 drawing by Anne Sellwood at TRC. *RBM* says, p. 105, that this drawing 'hung over
T's fireplace the rest of his life,' based on *Glimpses*, p. 52. In fact, on her mother's

death Agnes Weld gave ET the picture of AHH, which pleased her. See ET to Agnes, 27 Sept. 1894, TRC. There could have been *two* drawings by Anne Sellwood of AHH, but if there was already one in the Tennysons' possession, it is unlikely ET would have been so pleased, and only one survives.

78 'My maxims of conduct . . .' AHH to CTT, 12 Sept. 1830, Kolb, p. 374.

79 'I do feel rather mad' AHH to Blakesley, 13 April 1830, Kolb, p. 360.
'by nature sanguine' AHH to Brookfield, 12–14 Aug. 1832, Kolb, p. 618.
'a very delicate . . .' Jessie Harden Clay, Rawnsley *Memories*, pp. 85–6.
'wild bustling time' AHH to Trench, 2 Dec. 1830, Kolb, p. 387.
'as near perfection . . .' ATR *Records*, p. 21.
'the sweetest and justest' AT to SRE, 22 Feb. 1851, L&S 2.4.
'teeming with talent' Henry Elton to AHH, 19 Feb. 1832, Ch. Ch., Kolb, p. 528.
'O bliss, when all in circle drawn' IM lxxxix. 21, Ricks 2.406.
'all in love with him' Journal, 29 Nov. 1869, TRC.
'Dearest dear Emmie' ET to ETJ, ? July 1839. This letter (Wellesley College), wrongly dated and badly transcribed, in Hoge *L* p. 43. The misdating of this letter means Hoge (*L*. p. 10) says 'not a word' survives from this period.
AHH's letters are available in a one-volume edition by Jack Kolb (see Abbreviations: Books).

80 For information on balls from *Stamford Mercury*, I am indebted to Christopher Sturman.
'the Clergeman so strange' Eliza Massingberd to F.C. Massingberd, 7 Feb. 1831, LAO. See Rader, *Notes and Queries*, Dec. 1963, pp. 447–8.
AT in his father's bed *Memoir* 1.72.
'All his life . . .' FT to John Frere, 23 March 1831, L&S 1.56.
'a thousand kind and good' CTDE to his father GT, 18 March 1831, LAO, see Sturman, p. 36.

81 'poor Dr Tennison' 'What is to become' Eliza Massingberd to F.C. Massingberd, 28 March 1831, LAO, L&S 1.57.
'put their great Talents' THR to GT, 4 April 1831, LAO, L&S 1.58.
'Poor Alfred' AHH to FT, 8 July 1831, Kolb, p. 431.
'consolation and hope' AHH to AT, 17–24 April 1831, copy TRC, Kolb, p. 423.
'all our unhappiness . . .' AHH to ETJ, 22 Jan. 1832, Kolb, pp. 508–9.

82 'an article of mine' AHH to Moxon, 15 July 1831, Kolb p. 438. AHH's article appeared in the *Englishman's Magazine*, Aug. 1831, pp. 616–28.
'easy about your MSS' AHH to AT, 10 April 1832, Kolb, p. 549.

83 'They sung . . .' 'try to reform' AHH to Brookfield, 4 March 1832, Kolb, p. 537.
'lazy loons' AHH to ETJ, 21 April 1832, Kolb, p. 555.
'listlessness' GCT uses the word to *his* father, 21 Nov. 1827, LAO, L&S 1.16.
'too magnificent . . .' of Monteith and Garden, FT to Frere, 18 April 1832, Kolb, p. 538.
'outward circumstance' Even 'The Two Voices', a poem, with its talk of suicide, once assumed to owe a good deal to AHH's death, was written earlier. See Ricks 1.570.
'howls and growls' AHH to Kemble, July 1832, Kolb p. 607, L&S 1.77.
'complains constantly' AHH to Milnes, 8 May 1832, Kolb, p. 572.
'spoiling the young man' AHH to ET, 12 Oct. 1832, Kolb, p. 663.
'O Alfred' etc. Kemble, Spring-Rice and Tennant, AHH to Kemble, 14 June 1832, Kolb, p. 597.
'the only desirable place' AHH quoting ETJ to her, 17 April 1831, Kolb, p. 420.
'overwrought sensibility' AHH to ETJ, 16 Feb. 1833, Kolb, p. 725.

84 on Septimus 'going the way of us all', AHH to ETJ, 26 May 1832, Kolb, p. 583.
    'at an age' AHH to ETJ, 18 May 1833, copy TRC, Kolb, p. 761.
    'the most morbid' *CTAT*, p. 199, quoting D.G. Rossetti, quoting Septimus.
    on Frederick GT to CTDE, 27 July 1832, LAO, Sturman, p. 40.
    'the old brute' AHH to Brookfield, 12–14 Aug. 1832, Kolb, p. 619.
    'his relationship' AHH to Gaskell, 8 Sept. 1832, *Records of an Eton Schoolboy*
    (1883) pp. 170–2, Kolb, p. 639.
85 loving Charles Brookfield to AT, 15 Aug. 1832, L&S 1.78. JMC to CTT, 10 Oct.
    1874, TRC. AT to WEG, 3 Nov. 1880, BL, L&S 3.197.
    'All my griefs . . .' AT 'Prefatory Poem to my Brother's Sonnets', Ricks 3.45.
    describing CTT *WA Diary*, 16 Aug. 1865, p. 121.
    Coleridge on sonnets in CTT, *Collected Sonnets: Old and New*, ed. HT (1898).
    Frederick on CTT to MBro, 21 March 1872, Lilly.
    'books with indecent titles' 'pure and good' JS to Thompson, 4 March 1833, Kolb, p.
    733.
    prescribed for . . . some complaint *CTAT*, p. 128.
    'drops of laudanum' AT to JS, 7 Feb. 1833, now at Rochester, L&S 1.86.
    'denies laudanum' JS to Thompson, 4 March 1833, Kolb, p. 733.
    'nothing but stupefaction' AT to Brookfield, [mid-March 1832], L&S 1.71.
    'relief in dissipation' AHH to Brookfield, 13 Feb. 1832, Kolb, p. 525.
86 'unmanageable etc.' GCT to GT, 27 Feb. 1829, LAO, L&S 1.29.
    'so unnotched' Eliza T to CTDE, 8 Nov. 1832, LAO, L&S 1.81.
    called in a colleague Thos. Probart to GT, 31 Oct. 1832, TRC, L&S 1.81.
    'as a Pupil' CTDE to H.B. Hodgson?, 13 Nov. 1832, draft at LAO, L&S 1.83. In the
    Rawnsley papers there is some evidence that the fiction was not just for Edward
    himself. M. Staniland of Harrington Hall wrote to HDR (n.d.) when he was gathering
    material for *Memories* that local gossip had it that Edward 'went to be a doctor and
    died, poor thing'. That was presumably what the servants were encouraged to think
    and pass on.
    survives in a sonnet A number of other poems by Edward survive at TRC; only one
    was published in his lifetime.
    'Despondency and madness' AHH quotes Wordsworth ('Resolution and
    Independence', l. 49) to AT, 12–19 March 1831, TRC, Kolb, p. 413.
    1837 report on Acomb House, York. See Christopher Daniel, *Notes and Queries*,
    March 1987, Sept. 1988.
87 'And ever when the moon was low' 'Mariana' first published in 1830, Ricks 1.205.
    Speculation is always dangerous and I have tried to avoid any direct identifications.
    As early as April 1831 (Kolb p. 418), AHH was writing to Alfred's sister Emily:
    'Many years perhaps . . . after we have all been laid in dust, young lovers of the
    beautiful & the true may seek in faithful pilgrimage the spot where Alfred's mind
    was moulded . . . Some Mariana, it will be said, lived wretched and alone in a dreary
    house . . .' The identifications of the moated grange have been enthusiastic. See, for
    instance, George G. Napier (1892), pp. 84–7.
    'The Lady of Shalott' published 1832, much revised 1842 ('came from' became 'went
    to'), Ricks 1.387.
88 'still best known' A poll to find the most popular poem in Britain in October 1995
    was conducted by the BBC. 7,500 people voted by phone. 'The Lady of Shalott' came
    second only to Kipling's 'If'. In 1996 Orion published a 60p pocket selection of AT's
    poems called the *Lady of Shalott*, with the Waterhouse painting on the cover.
    'dowered with the hate of hate . . .' 'The Poet', published 1830, Ricks 1.243.

88 John Bourne on GT's attitude *Background* p. 86.
   frail and faithless Charlotte etc. ETJ to E. Hallam, 11–15 May 1835, Trinity.
   'that vixen' AHH to ETJ, 20–27 Feb. 1833, TRC, Kolb, p. 728.
   Catherine (Kitty) Burton Bapt. at Somersby, 3 Aug. 1811. Kolb identifies the 'Miss Burton' Charles loved as Charlotte, but there is not one who fits. Charlotte Burton was a Hale who married Langhorne Burton in 1837.
   'decidedly to blame' AHH to ETJ, 15 March 1833, Kolb, p. 737.
   Horatio 'a good lad' R.J. Tennant, Oct. 1834, draft Mat. 1.230–1, L&S 1.126.
   The close connections of these Lincolnshire families (in which we can include the Sellwoods through the Franklin/Rawnsley connection) is emphasised by the fact that Charlotte Bellingham, who jilted FT, was a cousin of Drummond Rawnsley. Mrs Rawnsley's sister Elizabeth was married to Sir Alan Bellingham. See L&S 1.143.
   Mary T and John Heath ETJ to E. Hallam, 11 March 1835, TRC, 'I suppose Julie Heath has told you that Mary is engaged to her brother.'
89 outsider Robert Roberts whose memories of the Sellwoods are in *Tennysoniana* by W.R. Nicoll and T.J. Wise in *Literary Anecdotes of the Nineteenth Century* (1895–6). Roberts later became a printer in Boston.
   Emily tall HT in 1888 diary, TRC. Emily weighed only 6½ stone 'although she is tall'.
90 'Tennysonian whims' AHH, 25 May 1833, Kolb, p. 763.
   'We spent rather' Recollections, TRC. Pearson, the odd name out in this list, was presumably John Pearson (1613–86), theologian, whose lectures, *Exposition of the Creed* (1659), were still much read in the nineteenth century.
   Coleridge died in 1834, Scott in 1832 and Wordsworth in 1850.
   'Here the people are all Radicals' Eliza Massingberd to F.C. Massingberd, 28 March 1831, LAO, L&S 1.57.
91 'I dare say' JF to his sister E. Franklin, 17 Jan. 1835, SPRI.
   AHH on AT in the *Englishman's Magazine*, Aug. 1831, i, 616–28. (See *Critical Heritage* pp. 41–2 and 49.)
92 Christopher North and J.W. Croker, quoted in *Critical Heritage*, pp. 50–83.
   'one spark of genius' AT to John Wilson, 26 April 1834, L&S 1.110. Byron famously accused Croker of killing Keats with his review of *Endymion. Memoir* 1.93–4 and *CTAT*, pp. 136–7 suggest his effect on Tennyson was almost as bad. Both FT and AHH thought the 'filthy thing' (FT, L&S 1.104) would arouse interest in the book. See Kolb, pp. 754–5.
   'I am so glad' ET to HT, 7 March 1871, TRC.
   Schiller's *Werke* At TRC (3378), ET from ETJ, Oct. 1837.
   Tasso *Jerusalem Delivered* was first translated into English in 1594. Emily's edition in Italian carries the signature 'ATennyson' after her father's birthday inscription. AT quite often appropriated E's books in this way.
   AHH quotes Tasso to ETJ, Dec. 1832/Jan. 1833, Kolb, p. 711.
   'Do not give way . . .' AHH to ETJ, 16 Feb. 1833, Kolb, p. 725.
   'influenza fever . . .' AHH to ETJ, 27 April 1833, Kolb, p. 792.
   'His Spirit' Henry Elton to AT, 1 Oct. 1833, Kolb p. 792.
93 'always feared' John Kemble to Fanny K., 13 Oct. 1833, Rawnsley papers (copy).
   'more than Brother' FT to John Frere, 10 Feb. 1834, L&S 1.107.
   'more than my brothers' *IM* IX. 20 and LXXIX, Ricks 2.328 and 392.
   'the affliction' FT to G.H. Tennyson, 18 Dec. 1833, LAO, L&S 1.104.
   'one white rose . . .' 'unspeakable loss' Narrative, *Memoir* 1.109, cf. Prologue.
   'Give as little' H. Hallam to AT, 30 Dec. 1833, TRC, L&S 1.105.
   'Vienna, September 1833 . . .' BW-C, *London Mercury*, Dec. 1921.

93   'I suffered' AT to Princess Alice, *c*. 23 Dec. 1861, draft at TRC, L&S 2, 290.
     'just the same' AT to MBro, quoted by BW-C, *London Mercury*, Dec. 1921.
     Francis Garden to AT 14 Dec. 1833, draft Mat. 1.198–9 (in ET's hand), L&S
     1.102.

94   'more written' of 'Ulysses' AT to James Knowles, *Nineteenth Century*, Jan. 1893,
     Interviews, p. 96.
     'Some work of noble note' Ricks 1.619.
     'fearful cloud from Vienna' Narrative, TRC.
     18 June 1834 Rashdall diary (quoted Rader, p. 18), Bodleian.
     'several dances' Recollections, TRC.
     ET loving dancing 26 Jan. 1863, to Drummond Rawnsley, TRC.
     'Louy and I disliked . . .' 'Byron's Mary Chaworth' Recollections. ET had
     undoubtedly read *Byron's Life* by Thomas Moore (1830). In the one-vol. edn. (1838)
     Mary is identified in the Index as 'afterwards Mrs Musters'.

95   'fond of dancing . . .' Narrative. 'Waltzing' may refer to a slightly later time. Alfred's
     sister Emily learnt to waltz in the winter of 1834–5 in London and perhaps introduced
     it to their circle. See *RBM*, p. 195.
     'sometimes in the midst' and gout SRE on AT, Rawnsley *Memories* pp. 67–8.

96   'denunciation' WA *Diary*, Dec. 1884, p. 340.
     AT at Somersby see letter to Moxon, 13 Oct. 1832, L&S 1.80. This letter incidentally
     was first sold at Sothebys in 1878 and resold in 1880 for 26/- (unidentified newspaper
     cutting n.d.).
     Mary Tennyson 'astonished' AHH to ETJ, 12 Oct. 1832, Kolb, p. 664.
     John Rashdall's diary Nov. 1834, Bodleian.

97   'Thy rosy lips' 'Sweet, ask me not' Rawnsley *Memories*, pp. 63–4, Ricks 2.60–2.
     'whole family quitted' THR to CTDE, 12 March 1829, LAO, L&S 1.31.
     'the lightest . . . dancer' ETJ to E. Hallam, 14 April 1835, Trinity, L&S 1.130.

98   'All the Rawnsleys' AT to Mary Rawnsley, ?25 Nov. 1849, Mat. 1.365, L&S 3.460.
     'with greater pleasure' AT to S.W. Rawnsley, n.d., Harvard, L&S 1.105.
     'not to put feet on sofa' Weston Cracroft diary, 18 Nov. 1849, L&S 1.311.
     'never kissed a woman' Laura Gurney Troubridge, *Memories and Reflections* (1925),
     p. 30.
     'stupid Gallery of Beauties' *RBM*, p. 164.
     'sufficiently distinct' AHH to ETJ, 12 Oct. 1832, Kolb, p. 665.
     'None are bold enough' 'Kate' Ricks 1.497.

99   'seriously in love with Rosa' CT 'AT and Somersby', *The Tennyson Chronicle* X,
     Aug. 1959. This is a more extreme statement than in *CTAT* (1949), when he writes
     only of 'affection'. In 1974, after Rader's work, the relationship is described in
     Background as a 'frustrated love affair'.
     'Early Verses of Compliment' Ricks 2.61.
     'Kisses sweeter' *Maud* part II, l. 149–50 ('Oh! that 'twere possible').
     quoting to Palgrave See Ricks 2.60. The text is in FP's hand at BL. See also L&S 2.92.
     'shamed' 'Locksley Hall', l. 148, Ricks 2.128.
     AT to SRE, 8 June 1854, L&S 2.92. I am satisfied the Rosa is *not* Rosa Chawner. L&S
     plant the suggestion which Thorn takes up (p. 281) that AT's walks (Hoge *J*, p. 35)
     that summer were to see Rosa Baring Shafto. ET's gnomic comment arouses
     suspicions in the suspicious.

100 'Rosa Baring, I only knew . . .' Rawnsley *Memories*, p. 62.
     'my whole heart is vassal' 'To Rosa, 1836', Ricks 2.76.
     'given to my mother' W.F. Rawnsley, Tennyson Centenary Lecture, offprint, TRC.

101 'An advantageous settlement . . .' Priscilla Wakefield, *Reflections on the Present Condition of the Female Sex*, 2nd edn. 1817, Chapter IV, p. 30.
'The woods decay' 'Tithonus' Ricks 2.605.

102 'Why suffers human life?' Ricks 1.321.

CHAPTER 3 'Learning to love and weep'

103 Clara to George Tennyson [d'Eyncourt], 27 April 1834, LAO, Sturman, p. 41.
'He has not woo'd . . .' 'A Country Dance' CTT, *Collected Sonnets Old and New*, ed. HT (1898), p. 377, ded. to ELL, introd. by JS.

104 'the loveliest girl' Narrative (1869), crossed out in later version, TRC.
'sudden dissolution' ETJ to E. Hallam, 16/18 March 1835, Trinity.
Information on Samuel Turner from Roger Evans, PhD thesis at TRC.
'self-indulgence' Horatio to FT's son Alfred, quoted *Background*, p. 131, 'Yours is a nature, as once was my own, very prone to self-indulgence, and every gratification of the senses nails a man down to the earth, more and more . . . There are certain natures whose upward development is sadly hindered by a certain indolence . . .'
'surviving letters' ETJ to E. Hallam, Trinity and TRC.
ETJ's relationship with Ellen seems to have been almost as close as that with Ellen's brother. Her 1842 letter, about missing letters after death, to her uncle Charles (*Background* p. 146) would certainly have held memories of Ellen as well as Arthur.
'truly parental kindness' ETJ to E. Hallam, 29 May 1835, Trinity.
'All that remains' H. Hallam to AT, 10 Oct. 1833, TRC.
'Darling that thou art!' ETJ to E. Hallam, 30 April/7 May 1835, Trinity.

105 Horncastle Book Club Weir's *Horncastle* (1820) states that 'A Literary Society has formed a permanent library . . .'
'harmless life' THR to CTDE, 6 April 1835, LAO, *RBM*, p. 197.
'Tennysons are apt to do . . .' ET to Ellen, 4 March 1835, Trinity; Coleridge was in fact dead which emphasizes how cut off they were in Lincolnshire.
T grumbling about Lincs. e.g. to Fitz, 10 June 1835 (?), TRC, L&S 1.132.
'wretched market town' AT to Brookfield, May 1835, L&S 1.131.

106 'courting' HT diary 1890, reporting his father's talk, TRC.
'The sooner I see thee' AT to Fitz, 10 June 1835 (?), TRC, L&S 1.132.
'James's great Lion' Phyllis Spedding, 9 May 1835, *RBM*, p. 201.
Lady Mary Vivian See *Brookfield*, p. 26.
Jane Franklin's diary (Franklins at Friskney, 15 June 1835) SPRI. For drawing my attention to this entry, I am grateful to Christopher Sturman, *Lincs. History and Archaeology* vol. 26, 1991, pp. 4–18. This Booth baby b. 26 Dec. 1834 died without issue.

107 'excellent friend' JF to E. Franklin, 26 March 1835, SPRI.
'two small and respectable' 'daughters still absent' Jane Franklin diary, SPRI.
'There is nothing to equal' 'Talk' notebook at TRC.
'I should certainly' JF to E. Franklin, 26 March 1835, SPRI.

108 'we three young creatures' ET to AW, 22 Jan. 1894, TRC.
'I used to sing duets' Recollections, *T and his Friends*, p. 5.
Mercury report, 17 July 1835 The newspaper's full title was *The Lincolnshire, Rutland and Stamford Mercury*.
'done what he always' CTDE to his son George, 1 Sept. 1835, LAO, L&S 1.139.
'as Emily would put it' Narrative. Mrs T's jointure came from Frederick's new income from a life interest in the Clayton estate at Grimsby.

109 'It would hurt' GT to CTDE, 1 Feb. 1833, LAO, Sturman, p. 44.
'I am very glad' Edwin Tennyson [d'Eyncourt] to his brother George, 30 July [1835], LAO, Sturman, p. 45, Ricks *T*, p. 289.
porcine insults these included 'What can you expect from a pig but a grunt?' CTDE to G.T. d'Eyncourt, 3 Sept. 1835, LAO.
'a tribe' Clara Tennyson [d'Eyncourt] on Somersby people, LAO, *Background*, p. 82.
inscriptions It is just possible that the neat inscriptions are in Louisa's hand not Charles's; they remain interesting.
'travelling . . . taking a wife' AT to Brookfield, May 1835, L&S 1.121.

110 'more frenzied than ever' 'old pain in my side' etc. TRC holds copies of the letters from ETJ to E. Hallam which are at Trinity.
'these grievances' ET to E. Hallam.
'well established' Priscilla Wakefield, *Reflections of the Present Condition of the Female Sex* (1817), p. 19.

111 Emily Sellwood ETJ to E. Hallam, 1 March 1835, Trinity/TRC.
'on the little yellow sofa' Narrative, TRC.
'I saw from the high road' AT to ET, Mat. 1.209. L&S 1.159 has this as [March or April] 1838, following *Memoir* 1.167. I would date it 1839, looking back to 1836. Margaret Bourne of Alford dined at Somersby on 30 March 1836 and might well have received that invitation on the occasion AT refers to.
'a man always discontented' Frances Brookfield, *The Cambridge Apostles* (1906), p. 168.

113 'elasticity of mind' ETJ to E. Hallam, 1 March 1836, TRC.

114 'As soon as we descended' CTT to Louisa Sellwood, March 1836, TRC.
'They had rarely' *Memoir* 1.148.

115 'for fourteen years' AT to Ludovic Colquhoun, 10 July 1850, TRC, L&S 1.329.
'How thought you . . .' Ricks 2.79.
'True feeling' AT to E. Russell, 10 March 1833, L&S 1.89.
'O Bridesmaid' Ricks 2.90.

116 'just twenty' Louisa had her twentieth birthday four days before the wedding.
opium I can find no evidence for *RBM*'s statement (p. 222) that CTT took opium on his wedding day. *CTAT* (p. 179) has him 'almost immediately giving way once more to opium taking'. Pinion and Roger Evans follow this.
'Poor Charles' ET to AT, 26 March 1859, TRC, L&S 2.220.
Sellwood–Tennyson marriage disastrous The introduction (by Sir Charles Tennyson and Betjeman) to their edition of CTT's sonnets suggests that C & L were 'happy in each other and in their work'. *RBM* (p. 223) suggests C & L 'were totally devoted to each other'. I find little evidence to support this. Sir Charles's sad lack of interest in the Sellwoods is confirmed in the sonnets' introduction; he calls Louisa, 'the *elder* sister of his brother Alfred's future wife Emily'.

117 crossing out Tennyson ET to J. Mangles, 1871, Ohio.
'the loveliest bride' 'Aunt Louy's loss . . .' Narrative, TRC.
Emily reading 'Comus'. Arthur Tennyson remembered this occasion, nearly sixty years later, as the 'first' time he saw Emily Sellwood (*Memoir* 1.148) but that seems highly unlikely.
'Lycidas' 'a test' *Memoir* 1.152.
'The bride and bridegroom' Narrative, TRC.

118 'Farewell! It is my parting hour' This sonnet by CTT is addressed 'To a Lady' and could be for either Emily or Anne Sellwood. It was published in 1837 in *The Tribute* and does not appear in CTT's *Collected Sonnets*. It was republished with slight

changes under the title 'A Bridal Farewell' in 1873. I am indebted to Roger Evans for this information.

118 Van Diemen's Land Sir John and Lady Franklin took with them JF's daughter by his first marriage, thirteen-year-old Eleanor, and another cousin of Emily's, Sophie Cracroft, who would be the devoted companion of Lady F. for the rest of her life. Eleanor met her future husband, Rev. J.P. Gell, in the colony. Lady F. established there a High School for girls, which may well have had something to do with 'The Princess'.

'examination paper' 30 March 1892, Rawnsley papers.

119 that evening in June 1836 RBM dates the dinner party at 11 June, based on the 7 June letter where AT says (L&S 1.144, Yale) he will be happy to dine on Saturday. This may be so. But CR (to HDR, 30 March 1892, Rawnsley papers) said that at the time of the dinner 'Louie had been married only a week or ten days previously'. It is not certain AT's letter (no year date) refers to this occasion; if it did, why does he write in the singular and not on behalf of the others who came from Somersby too to Horncastle in early June 1836?

120 'Zobeide' In the Arabian Nights she married the caliph Haroun-al-Raschid.
'Woman of noble form' Memoir 1.147, Ricks 2.80.

121 'dreadful departure' Narrative, TRC.
'huddle and confusion' AT to Leigh Hunt, 13 July 1837, BL, L&S 1.154.
'nerves shattered' HT in typed version of Narrative described the nerves as 'sensitive' rather than 'shattered'. This is used in Hoge's version, Texas Studies in Literature and Language XIV. 1 (Spring 1972), an unreliable text.
'greenhouse' etc. Cecilia Tennyson to Susan Haddelsey, June 1837, TRC, L&S 1.151.
'muddy pond' AT to ET, Memoir 1.168, L&S 1.157.
'One gets up to London' AT to S.W. Rawnsley, 28 Jan. 1838, Harvard, L&S 1.157.

122 'naturally met' Narrative, TRC.
'smokes the strongest' J.W. Blakesley to R.M. Milnes, 19 March 1838, L&S 1.159.
'magic music' 'The Princess', Prologue l. 192, Ricks 2.194, Cf. Fitz to Bernard Barton, April 1838 (Terhune 1.211): 'magic music' 'between growling and smoking'. Jane Carlyle's tribute from Collected Letters of Thomas and Jane Welsh Carlyle, ed. Sanders & Fielding (1970), p. 85.

123 'Trust in me always' AT to ET, 24 Oct. [1839], TRC, L&S 1.175.
The Tribute Sept. 1837. See Ricks 2.20 and 2.571, for its place in 'Maud'.

124 'I have been at this place . . .' Memoir 1.168, L&S 1.157.
turns down £60 letter to G.T. d'Eyncourt, LAO. See RBM, p. 244.
Camden Town RBM (p. 229) calls Mornington Crescent, Hampstead, which gives rather the wrong impression.
'My mother is afraid' Draft Mat. ii. 39, L&S 1.171.
'These days are always' ET to AT, 30 April 1857, TRC, Hoge L, p. 109.
Far from the Madding Crowd though not published until 1874 is set at around this period.

125 'If I build at Grasby . . .' CTT to Susan Haddelsey, 12 Feb. 1837, LAO. I am indebted to Roger Evans for drawing my attention to this letter.
'rough and illiterate' Background, p. 109.

126 'I feel quite melancholy' Cecilia Tennyson to Susan Haddelsey, 23 March 1839, TRC, L&S 1.169.
'And, while she hid' 'Letty's Globe' by CTT, p. 73 in A Hundred Sonnets(1960).
'She could not dream' 'It was her first sweet child . . .' p. 76 in A Hundred Sonnets.

126 'very well, only Charles' *Memoir* 1.352.
'Within three years' *CTAT*, p. 179.

127 'a late letter' ET to LTT, 30 April 1879, TRC, Hoge *L*, p. 317.
'Look to Christ alone' ET to LTT, Feb. 1879, TRC.
Louisa's diaries and papers TRC. See p. 535.

128 'a saint' ETJ to Eustace Jesse on Charles's death, in Eustace's scrapbook, TRC.
'Louisa's lachrymosity' CTT diary, 27 Dec. 1866, TRC.
'No tears for me' See AT's poem, my p. 115.
Cecilia Tennyson to Susan Haddelsey, 11 April 1838, TRC, L&S 1.159.

129 'Yet less of sorrow' *IM* cxvi, 13–16, Ricks 2.437.
'The current of his mind' *Memoir* 1.165.
'Do not continue' GSV to AT, Aug. or Sept. 1838, Mat. 1.206–7, TRC, L&S 1.162.
'My friends have long ceased' AT to ET, *Memoir* 1.174, L&S 1.176.
'In letters, words too often' fragment, n.d., TRC, L&S 1.173.
'How hast thou come to me' fragment, n.d., TRC, L&S 1.186.
'I will not speak' fragment, n.d., TRC, L&S 1.168.
'A good woman' fragment, n.d., TRC, L&S 1.185.

130 'There is heredity . . .' W. Boyd Carpenter, *Some Pages of my Life* (1911), p. 268.
'discussions are not stormy' ET to HT, 15 March 1872, TRC.
'The thought of annual infants' EL to Fortescue, 23 Jan. 1853, EL, *Later Letters*, pp. 29–30.
'Come as soon after the birth' AT to Patmore, [July 1850], Champneys 2.302, L&S 1.333 (not from Tent Lodge, but from the Miss Burtons, Keswick).
'I require quiet' fragment, n.d., TRC, L&S 1.172.

131 'I need thy assurances' AT to ET, fragment, n.d., TRC, L&S 1.182.
'separating from his family' E. Barrett to Miss Mitford, *Letters*, ed. Miller (1954), p. 44. It was not until June 1845 that EB heard a report of AT's marriage, see ibid. p. 245.
'Alfred is dreadfully embarrassed' men 'adapting their conversation' Jane Carlyle to Helen Welsh, 31 Jan. 1845, *Jane Welsh Carlyle: Letters to her Family*, ed. L. Huxley, p. 230, L&S 1.233.
'probably on this visit' HT (*Memoir* 1.248) puts their discussion in 1839. Nov. 1838 seems more likely to me.
the Husks Our knowledge of this 'group' is very sketchy. *CTAT* (pp. 164–5, 174–5) picks up several references in family letters, e.g. Cecilia to Susan Haddelsey. See L&S 1.152. Mary Massingberd had married William Neville.
'O I wish' 'The Princess' Prologue, l. 133, Ricks 2.192.

132 'Our home circle' ETJ to Julia Hallam, 12 Dec. 1838, Ch. Ch. (Hallam papers).
Mary Neville as weak as Emily Sellwood Cecilia to Susan Haddelsey, 23 March 1839, TRC, L&S 1.169.

133 considerable annual allowance £300, perhaps as much as £15,000 in today's terms.
'Dearest dear Emmie' ET to ETJ, n.d., see note to p.79. Hoge *L*, p. 43 mysteriously leaves out the extremely interesting last paragraph.

134 'provincial pianos' HT renders this in *Memoir* 1.173 'pre-historic' pianos, and this is followed by L&S 1.172. If one looks at the only manuscript surviving, in MS Mat. 2, it is obvious that HT (whose own MS copy of his father's letter it was) guessed wildly, unable to read his own handwriting. It looks much more like 'provincial'. The book that dates this letter also causes handwriting problems. AT had inscribed it 'Penrhyn Arms, Bangor, July 21, 1839' – the name of the inn where he stayed. L&S have 'Ains'.

134   Mrs Branchs Branch is still a local name in Linton. L&S 1.174, transcribes incorrectly 'Blanche'.
    'Daddy's sojourn' 'stale sort of letter' AT to ET, 24 Oct. [1834], TRC, L&S 1.174.

135   'That truth can never' *Pericles* v. 1.203–4.
    'Take a cup' ET to AW, 23 May 1892, TRC.

136   'I heard a few days ago' HS to J. Booth, 4 Nov. 1839, LAO.
    'I was sorry to hear' Robert Cracroft to HS, 27 Nov. 1839, LAO.

137   a great deal better HS to J. Booth, 4 Dec. 1839, LAO.
    'extraordinary brood' See *Background*, p. 100.
    'God made the country' 'Papa told the proverb' HT to ET, 26 Aug. 1873, TRC.
    'Of all horrors' AT to ET, fragment, n.d., TRC, L&S 1.171.
    'Poor Louy' HS to J. Booth, 2 Jan. 1840, LAO.

138   'I send thee' 'I murmured' L&S have both these undated parts of letters at 1 Jan. 1839. I think Jan. 1840 is more likely. The first fragment is postmarked JA9 from Waltham Cross; the Tennysons were still at nearby Beech Hill in Jan. 1840, about to move. The reference to sisters in the plural suggests AT is thinking of Louisa as well as Anne being with Emily. In Jan. 1839 Louisa had not left Charles; in Jan. 1840 she had just returned to him, but AT would not know this.
    R.H. Paterson to the Bishop 29 Jan. 1840, LAO. I am grateful to Dr Roger Evans for drawing my attention to this correspondence.
    Jane Franklin diary 20 Aug. 1840, SPRI.

139   'a widower virtually' CTT to Bishop Kaye, 24 April 1843, LAO.
    Cotterill at Grasby Mary Anne Fytche to Susan Haddelsey, April 1843, TRC.
    'I cannot but say . . .' CTT to Bishop Kaye, 24 April 1843, LAO.
    'bound by the golden cord' 'The Ring', l. 393, Ricks 3.185 ('*their* first love').

140   To go on loving It was also Anne Elliot's. See *Persuasion* ch. 11.
    'I had, as I suppose' ET to HT, Oct. 1868, TRC.
    echoing Alfred AT (24 Oct. 1839): 'The happiness resulting from power well exercised', TRC, L&S 1.175.
    'mists of weakness' *Memoir* 1.172, L&S 1.174.
    'other worldliness' *CTAT*, p. 125. Fitz to FT, 10 Dec. 1843, Terhune 1.408: 'rather unused to the planet'. Horatio would be back from Tasmania by June 1843, having lost most of his money.
    Julio, Giulio, Julius illegitimate A letter from MBro to HT at Yale (8 May n.y. but perhaps 1898) makes it quite clear that FT and Maria lived together unmarried, contrary to what CT says in *Background* (p. 100). MBro had no time for Maria, but is a frank and reliable witness. MBro wrote 'BURN THIS' on the letter but HT evidently did not. Julio's brother Alfred exploited his situation as the only legitimate son.

141   'Never was any thing' Matthew Allen to AT, ? Nov. 1841, TRC, L&S 1.197.
    'I lent you all I had' 'my honourable poverty' AT to MA, ? mid-July 1842, TRC, L&S 1.205.
    'an entire loss of property' Narrative, TRC.
    'Men of genius' Jane Carlyle quoted, *Memoir* 1.188.

143   'streaming eyes' 'Love and Duty', l. 2, Ricks 2.167.
    'Days of affliction' etc. Narrative, TRC.

CHAPTER 4 'Living so long unmarried . . .'

144   'The far future has been' April 1840, *Memoir* 1.168, L&S 1.179.

144 'Love and Duty' Ricks 2.166, first published 14 May 1842.
two-volume *Poems* one volume of earlier poems revised, one of new poems.
'hated the book' AT to Fitz, ? July 1842, TRC, L&S 1.204.
'forgot praise and remembered' Oct. 1881, WA *Diary*, p. 315 – variants on this throughout AT's life.
'by far the most eminent' Henry Crabb Robinson to Thomas Robinson, 31 Jan. 1845, L&S 1.232.
'on everyone's lips' Bradley in *Memoir* 1.205.
'bitter personal experience' *CTAT,* p. 182.
'I was surprised' JS to W.H. Thompson, 14 Oct. 1840, Trinity. It is not certain it was 'Love and Duty' JS was discussing, but Ricks (2.167) makes a plausible case.
no evidence AT discussed e.g. when JS gives A de Vere the news of AT's marriage in 1850 de Vere does not recognize Emily's name.

146 'revolving in itself' Fitz to Milnes, 12 April 1874: 'I used to tell T thirty years ago.' Terhune 3.487.
'thin and ill' Fitz to B. Barton, 7 May 1847, Terhune 1.560.
'cursed watering place' 'rusting in ignorance' AT to Tom Taylor, 10 Nov. 1846, L&S 1.363.

147 'every night for months' Emerson's Notebook, quoting Carlyle on AT, L&S 1.285.
'talking like an angel' Jane Carlyle to Helen Welsh, 31 Jan. 1845, L&S 1.233.
'refused to dine' AT to Matilda Jesse, 14 Jan. 1849, L&S 1.296.
'eighteen lemons' 'miserably imbecile' AT to Carlyle, 7 Aug. 1844, L&S 1.229.
'heart so large' Savile Morton to MBro, quoted in L&S 1.229.
wine and hard biscuits AT to Fitz, 12 Nov. 1846, TRC, L&S 1.264.
Dickens story Dickens to Forster, 24 Aug. 1846, L&S 1.260.
'That is the way we do' Brookfield to Emerson, quoted in Emerson's Notebook, 5–6 May 1848, L&S 1.285.
'a long, hazy kind of man' RB to EBB, 12 May 1846, *Letters of RB and EBB* 2. 701, ed. Kintner (1969).
'verge of going to Italy' Fitz to Barton, 11 Nov. 1848, Terhune 1.622.
'thinking far more of his bowels' Fitz to Cowell, [Nov. 1848], Terhune 1.623, L&S 1.296.

148 'foul with the rust' AT to GSV, 16 July 1844, L&S 1.226.
'wise men say . . .' AT to Charlotte Burton, 4 Jan. 1847, *Memoir* 1.235, L&S 1.270.
forbidden composition, reading AT to A.M. Hall, Brotherton, 23 Feb. 1844, L&S 1.223 (and similarly to E. Russell, L&S 1.224).
'The Two Voices' Ricks 1.569.
'restored to courage' *CTAT,* p. 193.
'We must bear' 'to endure whatever may chance' AT to ET, ?July or Aug. 1840, fragment at TRC, L&S 1.183.
'killed with sadness' AT to ET, 9 Jan. ?1840, TRC, L&S 1.169.
'so much stronger' AT to ET, TRC, L&S 1.183.

149 'Memory's darkest hold' 'Love and Duty', Ricks 2.166.
'all life is a school' *Memoir* 1.171.
'too old to begin' ETJ to E. Hallam, 1835, Trinity.
'who so lovingly trained me' 'lived by her own choice' Narrative, TRC. In her Recollections (1869) ET wrongly remembers CR's stay as *before* Louisa and Charles's marriage, but she went to the Horncastle house for the first time in June 1836, just after the wedding, and did not live there until 1840, when she was twenty-one. In Narrative, ET says CR ('a rather wealthy orphan') lived with them by her own

wish for two years before her own marriage – which was Sept. 1842. CT and HDR have given circulation to the idea that CR lived with Emily when they were children.

150 'same long letter' 'old man of the sea' CR to HDR, 30 March n.y. (1877?), Rawnsley papers. The date is suggested by the sentence: 'Mrs T. died in Hampstead some 12 years ago.'

'one of the finest looking men in the world' Carlyle to Emerson, 5 Aug. 1844, L&S 1.228.

'torches of flame' 'Oenone', Ricks 1.419.

151 'in your little study' AT to THR, ?17 March 1841, Harvard, L&S 1.189.

'I think his wife' FT to THR, Feb. 1843, Lilly.

'no truer or more devoted friend' CR to HDR, 30 March n.y., Rawnsley papers.

'Dost thou remember thy pink silk' ET to LTT, 25 Jan. 1879, TRC.

152 'I do not think I ever' LTT to AW, 1842, TRC. Keble's hymn correctly 'The trivial round, the common task, Will furnish all . . .'

'What a disgrace to womanhood!' EB to George Barrett, *Letters of Brownings to GB* ed. Landis, p. 99.

153 'second attachment' ETJ to E. Hallam, 4 March 1835, Trinity.

'Is it not extraordinary' Jane Elton to Brookfield, 7 Oct. 1841, *Brookfield*, p. 102. When the Jesse family in 1906 complained at what appeared in the book, Charles Brookfield wrote to Eustace Jesse: 'If you only knew what, and how much I have left out' (note in Jesse scrapbook at TRC).

'perpetual maidenhood' *IM* VI. 43, Ricks 2.325.

'clearly disliked' *Mangles*, 1 Oct. 1871, p. 107.

'When girls marry' ETJ to Mrs Allport, 10 July n.y., TRC.

'Thou sayest they are' Horatio to Eliza T, 7 Aug. 1842, TRC.

154 'her grand-daughter suggested' Fryn Tennyson Jesse quoted by Kolb, p. 802.

'which seems a funny plan' Jane Brookfield, *Brookfield*, p. 118.

'to Scarborough' 'good for all parties' Mary T to Mrs Allen, 25 July 1842, Yale (copy), L&S 1.207.

'to feel like a stoän' BW-C, *London Mercury*, Dec. 1921.

14 October 1842 Date correctly given by ELL in Mat. 1.249 and in *CTAT*, p. 185, as confirmed by Boxley Parish Register. Incorrect in L&S 1.212 and Ricks 2.452 (see *Circle*, note p. 269). In *Memoir* 1.203 (Ricks 2.452) HT quotes AT as saying in 1845, 'I have brought in your marriage at the end of *In Memoriam*' but elsewhere we are led to believe Emily 'chose' the title from various alternatives in 1849/50 (see p. 191).

'a mere mouse-trap' AT to ET, ?Jan. 1840, *Memoir* 1.171, L&S 1.177.

'only an hour and a half' AT to THR, 16 April 1847, L&S 1.274.

Emily's visit Journal, Aug. 1866, TRC. This presumably when she was staying at Park House.

155 letter of praise copied by ETJ, *Memoir* 1.213–14 (AT 'lost the letter' *Memoir* 2.73).

Lushington brothers at Cambridge *Circle*, p. 51: 'Contrary to assumptions occasionally published as fact, it was not at Cambridge that either Edmund or Henry began their close friendships with AT.'

'He drank my wine' AHH to E. Hallam, 3 Dec. 1828, Kolb, p. 249.

156 detested Glasgow ELL to AT, 25 Dec. 1874 'as much as ever', TRC.

'the losers' *Circle*, p. 128.

Lushingtons' biographer John O. Waller, *A Circle of Friends* (1986).

description of wedding ETJ to Julia Hallam, 17 Oct. 1842, in *Philological Quarterly* Winter 1985, pp. 140–1, J. Kolb on 'Tennyson's Epithalamium', Iowa.

156 'no more reviews' He had just read Leigh Hunt's in the *Church of England Quarterly Review*, Oct. 1842, 'very unhappy in its want of insight'.
'head vertiginous' AT to Moxon, 15 Oct. 1842, L&S 1.212.

157 'Nor have I felt so much of bliss' *IM* [Epilogue] l. 5–8, Ricks 2.452.
'O when her life was yet' *IM* [Epilogue] l. 33–6, Ricks 2.453. Cecilia had been twelve at the time of AHH's first visit to Somersby. The rose is more evidence against the assumption that roses refer to Rosa Baring.
'I rather avoid weddings' AT to Millicent Knowles, 2 Jan. 1888, L&S 3.364.
'Thy blood, my friend . . .' *IM* LXXXIV.10, Ricks 2.396. 'The mingled blood' in this case was to be that of AHH and AT's sister Emily.
woodcarving scheme see pp. 140–141.
'a poor forlorn body' AT to Fitz, 2 Feb. 1844, TRC, L&S 1.222.

158 'fidgets himself to death' Mary T to Mrs Allen, 5 July 1842, Yale, L&S 1.207.
'sensation' 'ruin in the distance' AT to ELL, 8 Sept. 1842, L&S 1.210.
'Altho' I am not entirely ignorant' HS to CTDE, 1 Nov. 1841, LAO. There are further letters in LAO showing the situation clearly. With one later letter Sellwood encloses a letter signed by Septimus as well as the four Tennyson girls. It asks their uncle (3 Nov. 1841) to place the deeds in 'Mr Sellwood's hands in consideration of his having undertaken to raise the £1900 for us and as his friend who lends him the money will not be satisfied unless they are in the hands of Mr Sellwood.'
'the prudence of the speculation' CTT to CTDE, 24 Oct. 1841, LAO, L&S 1.196.
'your distressed nieces' M, E, M and C Tennyson to CTDE, 5 Nov. 1841, LAO, L&S 1.198.

159 'Orders are flowing in' Matthew Allen to AT, ? Nov. 1841, TRC, L&S 1.197.
'Lecture at Royal Society' where Charles Weld was working. M.A. Fytche to Susan Haddelsey, n.d., TRC.
'I give my little Nanny' ET to AW, n.d. 1843?, TRC.

160 'In twelve months your share' M. Allen to FT, 6 Nov. 1841, *Letters to FT*, p. 55.
Henry Sellwood is also mentioned in this letter as holding Deeds.
'utterly ruined' M. Allen to FT, 4 March 1843, *Letters to FT*, p. 55, Yale, L&S 1.216.
'Do not hunt after high' ET to Agnes, 31 Oct. 1894, TRC.
insurance on Allen's life M. Allen to AT, 23 Nov. 1840, TRC, L&S 1.186. Cf. Ricks T, p. 181. The mistake arises from *Memoir* 1.221 repeated in *Background*, p. 159. In the 1890s ET could not remember, if she ever knew, the exact arrangement. *Circle* refers to AT's 30 Nov. 1843 letter (L&S 1.222), which makes the matter clear. Ricks had suggested that the arrangement, as it was then perceived, 'might have attracted the attention of the police'. He also plays on words 'A stroke. A stroke of good fortune.' Sadly Allen died of 'heart disease' (Fitz to FT, 6 Feb. 1845, Terhune 1.479).
'a tragic end, is it not' Journal, TRC.

161 'Mr Sellwood writes to me' M. Allen to FT, 6 Nov. 1841, *Letters to FT*, p. 56.
Haddelsey/Burkinshaw/Turner I am indebted to Roger Evans's thesis on Charles Tennyson Turner at TRC for directing me to letters at LAO, e.g. CTT to CTDE, 21 Sept. 1843.
'poorer than a church mouse' AT to H.G. Adams, 1 May 1843, Yale, L&S 1.218.
plea for AT to be Laureate F. Egerton to Peel, 27 March 1843, BL
influential friends H. Hallam to Peel, 23 Feb. 1845, BL. WEG to Peel, 24 Feb. 1845, BL.

162 'Your scruples' H. Hallam to AT, 2 Oct. 1845, Yale, L&S 1.243.
'He is not here' *IM* VII. 9–12, Ricks 2.326.

162 'Of the Poems' H. Hallam to AT, n.d., Yale.
'Poor Alfred' *New Letters of T. Carlyle*, ed. A. Carlyle (1904), 2.6.
'unlikely to marry' Duffy's *Conversations with Carlyle*, p. 5.

163 'quadrilling at Horncastle' 'crones' AT to THR [mid-Oct. 1845], Harvard, L&S 1.246.
'The days are awa'' Burns, 'Lady Mary Ann', l. 18.
'mountain glories' ET to AW, watermarked 1843, TRC.
'disappointed with mountains' *Edward Moxon* by Harold Merriam, p. 176. 'Moxon reported to Kenyon, who gave the news to Elizabeth Barrett, who sent it to Browning, that Tennyson was "disappointed".' EB's comment then follows. The trouble was partly cloud over Mont Blanc. AT to Fitz, 12 Nov. 1846, TRC, L&S 1.264.
The Friend at TRC, as are all inscribed volumes mentioned. It had originally been a weekly paper that ran for twenty-eight issues in 1809–10. The 3rd edn. added Coleridge's 'Treatise on Method'.

164 'unspotted from the world' 'visiting fatherless' Epistle of James 1:27 – the definition of 'pure religion'.
'bearing tribulation' see Paul's Epistle to the Romans 5:3.
Venables diary National Library of Wales. *Circle* drew my attention to this and much else.
'depends on character' ET to HT, 3 March 1873, TRC.

165 'This comfort is mine own' from Christina Rossetti's poem 'By way of remembrance' in W. Rossetti's edition, p. 385, not written until *c.* 1870.
'never kissed' Laura Gurney Troubridge, *Memories and Reflections* (1925), p. 30. See *RBM*, p. 286, and my p. 98.
chastity see *Mangles*, 28 Oct. 1872, p. 128 and *Memoir* 1.250. *Guinevere*: 'To love one maiden only . . .', l. 472, Ricks 3.542. That 'the world's ills' T had in mind seemed to be overpopulation as much as adultery and fornication does not alter the power of the central statement.
'scratching beats fornication' *Mangles*, 29 March 1871, p. 72.
'paid a visit to Tennyson' De Vere diary, 16 July 1845, ed. Wilfrid Ward (1904), p. 87.

166 'must have a woman' Jane Carlyle to Thomas Carlyle, 5 Oct. 1845, *New Letters and Memorials* ed. A. Carlyle (1903).
'If I am lost' Franklin to ET, *Memoir* 1.382.
'just the same as ever' Jane Franklin diary, 18 June 1844, SPRI.

167 'search after search' from 1850 to 1857. WFR, *The Life, Diaries and Correspondence of Jane Lady Franklin*, Roderic Owen, *The Fate of Franklin*.
'narrow provincial society' Eleanor Porden later Franklin, quoted in Gell, *John Franklin's Bride*.
'simple, noble, devout' 'heroic Franklin blood' 'simple' was always one of ET's favourite words of praise. She also used it of AT. ET to Lady Richardson, 2 Oct. 1871, Rochester.
St Lawrence Journal, 15 April 1857.

168 Dymoke funeral ET to AW, 28 March 1845, TRC.

169 'worst piece of news' Cracroft to HS, 21 Sept. 1846, LAO (Tweed and Peacock papers).
sixty-fourth birthday HS born 10 Nov. 1782.
Sellwood's partnership with J.W. Conington, which had existed since 1842, was dissolved in Dec. 1846.

169 'a consumption' 'Lincolnshire climate' 'at Hale' ' Paradise' Recollections MS, TRC
and *T and his Friends*, p. 7, and to TW, 20 March 1865, TRC.

170 Hale near Farnham, Surrey. Local tradition (acc. to Farnham Museum) was that the
Sellwoods lived at Hale Place, now destroyed for a housing estate, for no other reason
perhaps than that it was the biggest house in the village. It seems certain however that,
from 1847 to 1849, they lived at Hale House, then the name of the still surviving house
opposite the church, then just built, and now by the traffic lights. Yale has a number of
empty envelopes addressed to Emily Sellwood at Hale. The latest date is 19 May 1849.
'happy to be godfather' AT to Charlotte Burton, July 1847, Yale, L&S 1.277.
'Tennyson habit of coming unwashed' *RBM* (p. 309) suggests a Lushington said it to
Brookfield and CT in *Background* has Jane Brookfield saying it (p. 168). The source is
Brookfield (p. 213) where it actually comes in a letter from Harry Hallam to JB
(whom he calls 'Linda') reporting on a remark by FLu. It definitely refers to T's
siblings rather than T himself. See also *Circle*, pp. 153–4.

171 'furiously honest things' Arthur Tennyson to ELL, see *Circle*, p. 211.
'poetic' penchant AHH to CTT, Yale, 12 Sept. 1830, Kolb, p. 374.
'met unexpectedly' Narrative, TRC.
Venables diary National Library of Wales, see *Circle*, p. 154.

172 two books (Fichte and Venables and Lushington poems) at TRC. John Waller (*Circle*,
p. 165) thinks Emily received the poems at the time of publication, which may be so.
In fact, the surviving copy has 'Emily Tennyson' in it, not 'Emily Sellwood' and some
late verses by FLu. Michael Thorn (*Tennyson*, p. 216) dates the renewed relationship
from the names in a Bible dated by Emily in Jan. 1847. Alfred adds his name later.
There is no indication that he gave it to her in 1847 and in fact it looks clear that he
did not.
'Well, I can't help it' AT to THR, 16 April 1847, Mat. 1.315–6, L&S 1.273.

173 'offered to give up horses' Narrative (ET in 3rd person, N. 13), TRC.
Vestiges of Creation It has sometimes been said that the book had a profound effect
on *IM*. On 28 March 1871, *Mangles* (p. 63) reported that AT said he 'had written *IM*
without having seen *Vestiges of Creation*, was quite excited when he read it. Others
accused him of having copied from it.' Basil Willey in *More Nineteenth Century
Studies* (1956) said AT anticipated both Chambers and Darwin.
'many speculations' MS Mat. 11.141, 15 Nov. 1844, L&S 1.230.
'had even definitely refused' W. F. Rawnsley, Tennyson Centenary lecture first given
at Ambleside, Sept. 1909, offprint at TRC. WFR gave the lecture many times. At some
point he added '2 years back' after the printed 'refused', to make things clearer, i.e.
that from Emily's letters to CR, he gathered Emily refused AT in 1847, two years
before they finally agreed, late in 1849, that they would marry.
'for seven years 'etc. Rawnsley *Memories* p. 71.

174 existing letter WFR to HDR in Rawnsley papers (unpublished), n.d. from Shamley
Green, Guildford. He said he had similar letters from Mary T to Mrs Burton. These
are quoted in my Chapter 5 from his quotations; the letters themselves seem also to
have disappeared. WFR's letter also comments on HT's use of the letters to CR in
Memoir 1.330, which are at Harvard (L&S 1.327). I am still optimistic the other
letters will turn up. The Rawnsley brothers are not always to be relied on, but I think
we must follow them on the reference to AT's 1847 proposal as they had seen letters
we cannot see.
The Princess inscribed TRC, quotations from Ricks 2.291 and 290.
quote that image ET to Willie Ritchie and Magdalene Brookfield in 1873, seeing the
marriage as 'an exceeding happy thing for both'.

175 'simple as a child' A. de Vere to Mrs Villiers, *Aubrey de Vere* (1848), p. 146, Ward, L&S 1.283.
'I would pluck' *Memoir* 1.250.
'Now sleeps the crimson petal' 'The Princess', Ricks 2.284.

CHAPTER 5 'Round my true heart thine arms entwine'

176 'My Book is out' AT to Fitz, late Dec. 1847, Yale, L&S 1.281.
Gully's advice on smoking Fitz to W. H. Thompson, 15 July 1861, Terhune 2.408. 'I remember some twenty years ago . . . if he went on smoking.'
'inglorious pipe 'etc. Fitz to E.B. Cowell, 13 Jan. 1848, Terhune 1.592.
'water cure' Eliza T to FT, 7 Dec. 1847, Harvard, *Letters to FT*, p. 81.
'the life of the family' AHH to ETJ, 4 May 1833, Kolb, p. 758.

177 'AT is very little restive' A de Vere to Mrs Villiers, *Aubrey de Vere*, p. 146, Ward, L&S 1.283.
'Another night there was a dance' 'penniless marriage' A de Vere, *Memoir* 1.288.

178 'Caroline Standish married' AT to A de Vere, n.d., Yale. L&S 1.321, dates mid-Feb. 1859; I prefer Nov. –Dec. 1849.
'The Spinster's Sweet-Arts' Ricks 3.115.
'Their grandson once stated' see *Aldworth* by CT (Tennyson Society 1977), p. 5, based on oral evidence? Farnham Museum told me the local tradition is that AT stayed at the George Inn at 121 West Street. When *CTAT* was published, CT had apparently not thought AT visited Hale (see p. 240).
'this wild region' Journal, 14 Sept. 1866, TRC.
'heather-scented air' AT to Argyll, 8 Nov. 1866, L&S 2.445.
At Lincoln there survive in a collection of miscellaneous papers in ET's hand at TRC. They are not dated but are similar in appearance to ET's first Narrative for her sons, dated 1869. Even Catherine Barnes Stevenson in 'Emily Tennyson in her own right: the unpublished manuscripts' does not mention her stories; she appears to have missed them. But the paper in *Victorians Institute Journal* vol. 8 (1979) 31–44, is worth reading for her comments on ET's 'poetry'.

180 'a gigantic sick-house' *Times*, 5 July 1849, draws attention to sewage problems: 'Disease threatened social collapse' – people in the centre of London, not far from Somerset House, were living 'in muck and filth'.
'The room smokes' AT to Matilda Jesse, 14 Jan. 1849, L&S 1.296.

181 'bearing the look of one' *Palgrave*, 31 March 1849, ed. G. F. Palgrave (1899), p. 41.
'six-weeks-long influenza' AT to Mary Howitt, ?29 April 1849, L&S 1.299.
'near a volume of poems' Fitz to W. B. Donne, 29 Jan. 1845, Terhune 1.478.
'obscure remembrance' AT to CP, 28 Feb. [1849], Yale, L&S 1.297. This letter was misdated 1850 in *Memoir* (also oddly 1.297) and *CTAT*, p. 241, which was perhaps partly responsible for dating ET's important letter at 1850 (see below).
'heightened version' 'copied it out' WA *Diary*, 18 Aug. 1849, p. 55.
'butter papers' L&S 1.277 change WA's butter-shop into a butcher-shop, presumably because the poems were written in 'a thing like a butcher's account-book'.
'Angel in the House' The first sections of CP's long poem, a celebration of married love, were published in 1854.
'Is not the highest . . . ?' CP to Alfred Fryer, quoted in cat. 36, C.R. Johnson, *Rare Book Collecting* (1994).

182 only in Kate's sons' *Memories* p. 123–4. How accurate a text this is we cannot know

for the original has apparently been destroyed. Hoge *L* (p. 44) wrongly says this letter is at Harvard. It is, almost certainly, one of the letters WFR told HDR 'are too private to be exhibited' (Rawnsley papers). The version published is likely to have been not only cut but altered without acknowledgment, judging by versions in *Memories* of other letters which do exist to prove an extraordinary disregard of the originals. *CTAT* (p. 242) first dated it 1850 without any question mark. Everyone has followed this: cf. Ricks *T*, p. 206, Ricks 2.309, *RBM*, p. 331, Shaw and Shatto, *Tennyson. In Memoriam* p. 20. L&S 1.322 at least puts the date in square brackets. All now concede there is no reason it could not be 1849.

183 'I had rather not' Kingsley to John Parker, jun., see R.B. Martin,*The Dust of Combat*, p. 162.

'willing and deliberate' review in *Fraser's Magazine* Sept. 1850, see *Critical Heritage*, p. 173.

'The principal cause' James Douglas to Bishop of Lincoln, 21 May 1849, LAO.

184 'Alfred went to Charles' A.J. Symington to HT, 11 Jan. 1894, TRC. The original letter has some alterations in HT's hand, e.g. *their* part for *his* part (a sacrifice) and an addition 'because the fear (sic) that he was too sensitive to make a good husband'. Symington's evidence is not entirely reliable; he had understood Charles Turner was present at the wedding.

185 'We never keep him long' MT to Lewis Fytche, n.d., TRC.

'I am off again' AT to CP, 2 Oct. 1849, L&S 1.309.

'We used to be wits' CTT to Brookfield, *Brookfield*, p. 239.

'I have a love' AT to THR, mid-Oct. 1845, Harvard, L&S 1.246.

'I was amused' Weston Cracroft diary, 17–21 Nov. 1849, L&S 1.311.

186 'with greater pleasure' AT to S.W. Rawnsley, n.d., L&S 1.105.

'Sweet and Low' *Memoir* 1.255, dated in *CTAT* (p. 239) 24 Nov. 1849, and Ricks 2.219.

187 'Let them be married soon' ET to JMC, *From Friend to Friend*, p. 16.

the Lancashire weaver *Memoir* 1.283–6, L&S 1.307–9.

'highest honour' AT to Forster, n.d., *Memoir* 1.284, L&S 1.309.

'would have broken stones' A. Gatty to HDR, 9 Dec. 1892, recalling talk on 1 Nov. 1859, Rawnsley papers.

St George peach ET to HS etc., 18 Aug. 1851, TRC.

188 'The longer one lives' ET to AW, 21 Feb. 1892, TRC. Emily in 1892 also wrote about the case of 'Miss Pope' – presumably Horatio's daughter Cecilia's sister-in-law, who had given up her chance of marriage to stay with her mother and then her mother died. 'She must be very desolate now.'

'great responsibility' 'lost courage' Narrative, TRC.

'We went into the study' C. K. Paul in *Charles Kingsley: His Letters and Memories of His Life* 1.225.

189 'kind and clever' AT to CR, [27 Dec. 1849], Harvard, L&S 1.316.

'marry in about a month' AT to CR, [25 Dec. 1849], TRC, L&S 1.316.

'causelessly bitter' crones AT to THR, mid-Oct. 1845, Harvard, L&S 1.248.

'One cannot mourn' ET to AW, 11 Jan. 1850, TRC. James Hoge seems to have missed this letter when preparing his 1974 edition of ET's letters. If he saw it, he obviously did not realize its importance. Elizabeth Franklin died 10 Jan. 1850.

190 'shilly-shallying' see p. 184, mentioned in Symington's letter.

'7/6 out of his income' reported in Edmund Peel to C. Bradshaw, L&S 1.328.

'use a black seal' ET to HT, 5 Nov. 1872, TRC.

'I can never forget' ET to CR, 17 Feb. 1884, TRC.

191 'formative influences' Ricks *T*, p. 246.

'lived so long unmarried' AT to R. Monteith, 10 Jul. [1850], L&S 1.330.

'I have never regretted' CR to HDR, 30 March [1877?], Rawnsley papers.

'Goethe thought it a sign' *Memoir* 2.288. ET's copy of *Faust* at TRC.

'half-dozen copies' See L&S 1.322 but also CP to WA, 17 April 1850, Champneys 2.173.

title of *IM* ET to AT, 26 June 1864, TRC.

'a month before the wedding' Narrative, TRC, 'We met at Shiplake a month before the wedding' has sometimes been taken to mean that this was their first meeting for years, which it certainly was not.

inability to 'make up his mind' WFR Tennyson Centenary Lecture (1909) offprint at TRC, p. 20.

'silence about his engagement' etc. All Mary T's comments to Mrs Burton on the marriage come only from the Rawnsleys, some existing in WFR to HDR letters (Rawnsley papers) and published in WFR's lecture, as above.

192 'Married!! is it possible?' A de Vere to AT, 21 June 1850, TRC.

'afraid of the summer' AT to SRE, 21 July 1850, L&S 1.332.

'It is settled' AT to CR, n.d., L&S 1.325.

'by dint of very great exertions' ET to LTT and CTT, 17 June [1850], TRC.

193 'long before such adornments' Miss Mitford's description of Shiplake – unidentified cutting at TRC, *Memoir* 1.329.

'The thing is to come off' CTT to ET and AT, *Memoir* 1.330, TRC.

'crowning her' ET to CR, 17 Feb. 1884, TRC, see also 15 Dec. 1886, TRC.

'maiden in the day' *IM* XL, Ricks 2.357.

'sprig of syringa' Rawnsley *Memories*, p. 126; Narrative, TRC.

Rebecca Self Her ill-spelt letter survives in Rawnsley papers – THR's version *Memories*, p. 72. *RBM* (p. 334) calls her 'old' in 1850 but she was still alive more than forty years later.

194 'She with all the charm' 'Locksley Hall Sixty Years After', Ricks 3.151.

'strange thoughts and feelings' 'brace of' 'double sister' etc. LTT and CTT to ET and AT, 13 and 20 June 1850, TRC (part of letter is used in *Memoir* 1.330).

'The peace of God' *Memoir* 1.329.

'Look through mine eyes' 'The Miller's Daughter', Ricks 1.416.

195 'the nicest wedding' Narrative, *Memoir* 1.329.

'It was very pleasant' ET to LTT and CTT, 17 June [1850], TRC. This letter is transcribed with unusual inaccuracy in L&S 3.461, and with his usual inaccuracy by Hoge *L*, p. 46.

'tedious' curate 'tedious Greville' is a variant at Harvard in a note by AT '"undisturbed by tedious Greville" would be a better rhyme' for 'level' than 'evil', 'but I do not love to be personal.' See Ricks 2.460.

crimson vase Journal, 24 Feb. 1865, TRC, 'Lionel puts snowdrops into the tall crimson glass she gave us when we were married.'

leather-bound Bible TRC. In it ET wrote 'For my Lionel when I am gone.'

dresser from Horncastle Now in north London, it houses some china reputedly from Somersby.

bread-board Wallis charged £3.13.6, a large sum. It has the initials AT and a laurel wreath at the centre. See C. Sturman: 'The Tennysons' Bread-Board' in *Lincolnshire Past and Present* no. 9, Autumn 1992. It can be seen at TRC.

'a present of £50' AT to Moxon, n.d., L&S 1.333.

Mary Tennyson's comments see note to p. 191 'silence about'.

196 'this sunny spot' in one version of 'The Vicar of Shiplake', Ricks 3.601, see below.

'baby enough' ET to LTT and CTT, 17 June 1850, TRC.

'Vicar of that pleasant spot' 'The Vicar of Shiplake', Ricks 2.459.

197 'What creatures men are!' *T and his Friends*, p. 20.

'It is clothes' Rawnsley *Memories*, p. 148.

'happy and comfortable' ET and AT to CR, 14 June 1850, Harvard. This contains a puzzling reference to *IM*. Both L&S 1.328 and Hoge *L*, p. 45 read 'going' (following HT in black notebook TRC), where I read 'giving'. ET has altered 'I am' to 'We are': 'All except the *IM* we are giving directly', i.e. straight away. *IM* was reprinting. AT asks Moxon to send copies to his aunt and HS, 17 July 1850, L&S 1.331.

198 only Alfred's bit *Memoir* 1.330. There is no evidence that the Shiplake poem was ever attached to this letter and AT's remark about the third stanza is also not part of this letter. Ricks 2.460.

'Yours is the only note' ET to LTT and CTT, 17 June 1850.

hay fever not a cold Mary T, letter quoted in Rawnsley's lecture.

'pet and nurse' LTT to ET, 20 June 1850, TRC.

'have not beaten' AT to SRE, 14 June 1850, L&S 1.328.

'What passions' *T and his Friends*, p. 115, Ricks in *Tennyson* is very good on the nature of T's 'passion' for AHH, p. 215 on.

'amatory tenderness' *The Times*, 28 Nov. 1851, *Mangles*, 20 Sept. 1870, p. 59.

199 her own copy It has not only AT's inscription but a neat contents list in ET's hand (the first line of each section and the page number) and the words, obviously written much later, 'For our Hallam when we are gone. E.S.T.', TRC.

critic who quotes Rader, p. 113.

'Happy' Ricks 3.189.

biographer's suggestion *RBM*, p. 335.

'She has loved and prayed' AT to Monteith, 10 July [1850], L&S 1.330.

'a lady only four years younger' AT to Colquhoun, [10 July 1850], TRC, L&S 1.329.

200 'so beautiful and touching' Journal, 31 March 1871, TRC.

dread of pregnancy MBrad diary, 1864, BL.

'an heir to nothing' 'You do ill' AT to THR, [Nov. 1850], Harvard, L&S 1.343.

'your good man's example' 'sounds more cozy' LTT to ET, 13 and 20 June 1850, TRC.

201 'obscure and solitary church' etc. words on AHH's memorial at Clevedon.

'walking on the terrace' voices at Thackeray's table from ATR *Records*, p. 40.

'It was my wish' ET to LTT and CTT, 17 June [1850], TRC.

AHH's tomb Lady Elton, who died soon after, told me in 1995 that there had once been a notice on Clevedon railway station saying 'ALIGHT HERE FOR ARTHUR HALLAM'S TOMB'.

'tablet in a transept' AT to Forster, [22 June 1850], TRC, L&S 3.462.

chancel to dark church See *IM* LXVII. 15, Ricks 2.382, changed in 1855.

'It seemed a kind of consecration' Narrative, TRC.

CHAPTER 6 'Happiness after so many years of trial'

202 best part of a week ET to LTT and CTT, 17 June 1850, TRC, said they had taken the lodgings till the 22nd.

'elaborate excuses' 'the weeping Devonshire climate' AT to SRE, [21 July 1850], L&S 1.332.

202 all Rawnsleys dear AT to Mary Rawnsley (Sophy's sister-in-law), ?25 Nov. 1849, Mat. 1.365, L&S 3.460.
Valley of the Rocks a favourite Victorian excursion. In 1853 Gosse's mother wrote the section on it in *Seaside Pleasures*. Gosse's friend Hamo Thornycroft visited it on *his* honeymoon in 1884. (See *Edmund Gosse*, p. 240.)
'A great deal of dressing' etc. *Glaucus, or Wonders of the Seashore* (1855) *passim*.

203 'He was almost like a child' MS Mat. 6.237.
'delightful man' WA *Diary*, 3 April 1867, p. 151.
'Conversation never commonplace' Journal, 10 Oct. 1865, TRC.
'like an angel' J. Carlyle to Helen Welsh, 31 Jan. 1845, L&S 1.233.
ET leads conversation ATR in *From Friend to Friend*, p. 38.

204 'The old order changeth . . .' Ricks 2.17, l. 240.
'revolving many memories' Ricks 2.18, l. 270.
'painful little operation' *not* laceration, as Hoge *J* reads, p. 17. The problem was not, as ET thought at the time, 'some injury to a nail', but the 'abnormal fancy' of a toenail to grow into his flesh. It caused problems again in 1853 and 1857. Narrative/Journal, TRC.
not invited to wedding In fact, AT said his mother did not even 'know of it till it was done', AT to Colquhoun [10 July 1850], TRC, L&S 1.329.
'female fortitude' 'Isabel', l. 11, Ricks 1.202.
'not angry' AT to Forster, July 1850, Mat. 4.473, L&S 1.331.
'hopes to make acquaintance' AT to Moxon, 17 July [1850], L&S 1.331. ET's thank-you letter, 2 Aug. 1850, is at BL (Ashley MS), book itself at TRC.

205 'our only living great poet' Kingsley in *Fraser's Magazine*, Sept. 1850, xlii. 245–55. See *Critical Heritage*, p. 173.
G.H. Lewes *Leader*, 22 June 1850, 1.303–4.
'monotonous' Fitz to FT, 31 Dec. 1850, Terhune 1.696.
'sceptical of grief' Charlotte Brontë to Mrs Gaskell, 27 Aug. 1850.
'appeals heart to heart' EBB to Miss Mitford, *Letters*, ed. Betty Miller (1954).
comparison with Milton and Shakespeare See *Critical Heritage*, p. 8.
'Byron is dead' *Memoir* 1.4.
Fitz on JS To Fanny Kemble [March 1881], Terhune 4.400.

206 Isabel Spedding's memories from letter to HDR, 12 Feb. 1893, Rawnsley papers.
JS 'much pleased' Fitz to FT, 31 Dec. 1850, Terhune 1.696.
sock story Mirehouse Guide.
Tent Lodge derived its name, a little ominously, from a tent set up on the site by a previous inhabitant, who believed in the fresh-air 'cure' for consumption.

207 Ruskin on CP's poems, 2 June [1850?], Champneys 2.278.
'I cannot enough value' CP to EP, [19] Aug. 1850, Champneys 1.195.
'worthy of her husband' CP to EP, [15] Aug. 1850, Champneys 1.197.
'laureate of the tea-table' Gosse, *Athenaeum*, June 1886.
Tennyson on 'The Angel in the House' AT to CP, 30 Oct. 1854, L&S 2.99.
'kill the Angel in the House' Woolf in lecture 'Professions for Women' (1931).
'a very charming person' CP to EP, [13] Aug. 1850, Champneys 1.197, L&S 1.335.

208 'After dinner,' CP to EP, [15] Aug. 1850, Champneys 1.196, L&S 1.336.
'I like Mrs T.' CP to EP, [19] Aug. 1850, Champneys 1.195, L&S 1.336.
'counts on you for a friend' and conversation CP to EP, Aug. 1850, Champneys 1.137.

209 'became rather glorious' CP to EP, Aug. 1850, Champneys 2.115.
'leaving off wine' AT to Colquhoun, 10 July 1850? TRC. The letter is mutilated. This is the best reading. L&S 1.329.

209 'It counts for so much' AT to Boyd Carpenter in *Some Pages of my Life* (1911), p. 268.

210 'Your father made me nervous' Narrative/Journal, TRC, see also *Memoir* 1.334.
Carlyle on AT Herbert Warren in *T and his Friends*, pp. 131–3.
'Alfred looks improved' Carlyle to J. Carlyle, 3 Oct. 1850, *Letters to His Wife*, ed. Bliss, L&S 1.339.
'a very nice creature' Carlyle to Fitz, 17 Dec. 1850, Terhune 1.691.

211 'one of the stars of my life' FLu to HT, 10 Aug. 1896, TRC.
'a very interesting woman' A. de Vere to Isabella Fenwick, 14 Oct. 1850, L&S 1.339.
One night at Tent Lodge *Memoir* 1.334.

212 'very greatly blessed' A. de Vere to Isabella Fenwick, 24 Sept. 1854, L&S 2.96.
'quality of its doubt' T.S. Eliot, *Selected Essays*, p. 336.
'I hate unfaith' MS Mat. 56 in ET's writing. Cf. *Memoir* 1.309.
'We have but faith:' *IM* 'Prologue' ll. 21–4, Ricks 2.317.

213 'It is He that hath made us' Psalm 100, Jubilate Deo, BCP.
'I cannot understand' *IM* XCVII, l. 36, Ricks 2.417.
'Yesterday it was too wet' CP to EP, [19] Aug. 1850, Champneys 1.195, L&S 1.337.
'driven out of the Church' AT in *Mangles*, 29 March 1871, p. 68. The parson was Isaacson at Freshwater.
family prayers In 1858 when Maurice took prayers at Farringford, AT praised his reading, *Memoir* 1.429.
'double solitude' ET to Alice Woolner, 14 June 1865, TRC.
'he rowing, she steering' HT had omitted this in his use of the Journal for *Memoir*. ET added it to proof of Materials, see *Memoir* 1.334.

214 'apple-pie creation' Journal summer 1850, TRC, omitted from Hoge *J*.
'Forsaken Merman' AT's comment, Harriette Smith to HDR, 1 Nov. 1892, Rawnsley papers, used in *Memories*, p. 122.
'among the poets' CP to EP, 15 Aug. 1850, Champneys 1.197, L&S 1.336.
'he should like to live by his Mother' Mary's letter from *T and his Friends*, p. 20.
'Dowdeswell' ET writes Dodswell in Journal, obviously Dowdeswell, just a few miles from Cheltenham. Hoge *J* omits.
Leyden House sometimes written Ladon.

215 'rather a horror to me' AT to ET, n.d., TRC, L&S 2.1.
told Walter White In WW *Diary*, p. 145.
said at Shiplake acc. to Harriette Smith to HDR, 10 Nov. 1892, Rawnsley papers.
'good airy rooms' AT to SRE, [Nov. 1850], L&S 1.343.
minor poets consumed 'like stubble' Fitz to FT, [March 1846], Terhune 1.528.

216 Harry Hallam died at Siena, 25 Oct. 1850.
AHH's sister as guest Journal, 1 Oct. 1872, TRC.
'a dream that the Queen' Journal, 6 Nov. 1850, TRC.
'as a mark of' and acceptance C.B. Phipps to AT, 5 Nov. 1850, *Memoir* 1.335–6.
'sucking at time and leisure' AT to Monteith, n.d., L&S 2.65.
'eighth year' AT to FLo, 1 Feb. 1858, L&S 2.193.
'his dread of levées' ET to L. Colquhoun, 26 Dec. 1850, Brotherton.
'shoals of trash' AT to E. Russell, 28 Sept. [1852], TRC, L&S 2.45.

217 'the week's excitement' 10 July 1850, TRC, *Circle*, p. 170.
the Hall at Warninglid The house was officially called Rockingham Hall (not Buckingham as L&S have it 2.2), but known locally as The Hall – not the Hill as *RBM* calls it (p. 356). The house itself no longer exists. The house now known as

Lydhurst is on the site listed as Warninglid Hall in the 1842 tithe survey when it belonged to Edward Stanford, the Tennysons' landlord.

218 'poor Milnes' ET to AT, n.d., TRC, *Memoir* 1.174. L&S 1.177, assumes the same servant had been with AT right through, but surely the reason she was 'howling' in 1840 was that she was leaving the Ts' service and returning to Lincolnshire. ET says specifically these two Milnes sisters came from her 'Father's house'. They were not at Horncastle in 1841 Census. In L&S 2.3 (and *TRB* quoted) Milnes was mistranscribed as Millar.

'Alas! a storm' 'the bell' Cuckfield gang Narrative/Journal. In *Memoir* 1.337 HT makes the hole in the wall sound much worse than ET does.

'The state of the country' Fanny Kingsley, *Charles Kingsley: His Letters and Memories of His Life* 1.241.

Frimley murder Kingsley wrote four papers in the *Christian Socialist*.

219 'Maud' For resemblances between 'Maud' and *Alton Locke* see J.B. Steane, *Tennyson* (1966), pp. 93–4, 111–12. (Ricks 2.516.) *CTAT*, p. 281.

interest in comparative religion ET read Maurice's *The Religions of the World and their relations to Christianity*. 2nd edn. 1848 at TRC, though not given until Nov. 1855.

'I am going in two hours' AT to Forster, [21 Jan. 1851], TRC, L&S 2.2.

'the Sorcerer-Cataleptic' Journal, 21 Jan. 1851. Hoge *J* reads 'Seizure-Cataleptic'. Both words occur in the section of *The Princess* AT was revising (Ricks 2.197), so does 'sorcerer' and ET writes 'sorcerer'.

220 'how grieved am I' AT to ET, [22 Jan. 1851], Yale and TRC, L&S.

'one of the sweetest and *justest*' AT to SRE, [22 Feb. 1851], L&S 2.4.

221 'from your cradle' AT to SRE, [8 March 1851], L&S 2.9.

a letter together AT and ET to SRE, 28 Dec. [1850], L&S 1.346.

garden chair as ET writes Journal, 2 Feb. 1851, TRC; Audrey in MS Mat. copies as 'Bath' chair and this went into *Memoir* 1.338. They would surely not have had a Bath chair at this stage.

arrived 3 Feb. 1851 Some have supposed there was a December visit, closer to the 'half a year' mentioned in the 'Vicar of Shiplake' poem – but there is no evidence of it; AT does say '*more than* half a year'.

ordered by carrier ET to 'Mr Lovejoy', 10 Feb. 1851, Library of Periodical and Eclectic Literature, Falls Church, Virginia.

222 'in a white pinafore' Harriette Smith to HDR, 10 Nov. 1892, Rawnsley papers. Struwel-Peter story WFR in *Memories*, pp. 121–2.

wedding poem See my p. 196. L&S 1.345 dates the Harvard letter on the same sheet as the poem at 'early Dec. 1850'. I date it Feb. 1851. Innumerable versions of this poem exist and much comment has been made on them. See not only Ricks 2.459 but *TRB* 4.3(1984) 114–22, R.L. Collins. WFR to HDR (Rawnsley papers, n.d. – but 1890s): 'I fancy that . . . some of it was written then [but] not given to my father until 6 months after when he added the 2 stanzas about his wife. The mother told me she watched him making them as he drove with her to Reading and then said "Now I know what you have been doing you must give me a copy of that".' Harriette Smith in two letters to HDR (Rawnsley papers, 1 Nov. 1892 and 29 Jan. 1898) remembers being at the time shown the lines 'as a profound secret'. 'I remember it all *so distinctly*' – the poem being written *after* the Ts' return from honeymoon. In 1898 she said how sorry she was HT left the two verses out of *Memoir*. Her evidence sounds convincing but she thought the Ts had been *abroad* for their honeymoon.

222 `Keep it to yourself` AT to D. Rawnsley, n.d., Harvard. L&S 1.345, guessing Dec. 1850 not Feb. 1851 as I think it.
published the story HDR in *Memories*, pp. 72–4.

223 'serious inconveniences' CP to ET, 1 Feb. 1851, TRC.

224 'not hopelessly tight' AT to ET, [6 March 1851], Yale; L&S 2.8.
'my wife begs' AT to Clifton, Nat. Lib. of Scotland; L&S 2.7 misreads 'Phrenologists'.

225 'The man was inspired' Kingsley to his wife, 12 June 1849, in *CK Letters and Memories*.
'about ten miles' AT to J.R. Thompson, n.d., L&S 2.18.
'Omnibus hourly' schedule in AT's hand, Yale.
'a mitred Bishop' ET wrote (Narrative) of 'Spoils of a French church carved in wood'. CT in *TRB*, Nov. 1973, wrote of the 'figure of a bishop carved in wood (Spanish or Austrian)'. No longer in Chapel House, now called Tennyson House and owned by Pete Townshend of 'The Who' and his family.

226 poem 'To the Queen' Ricks 2.463. Dated March 1851, it was T's first publication as Laureate – printed as dedication to 7th edn. *Poems*. The 'wild March' stanza actually not published until 1853.
'the organ rolled' AT to Robert Monteith, [*c.* 24 April 1851], L&S 2.15.
Tennyson on the stillborn child April 1851: to Emily Patmore, ELL, AW, Forster, L&S 2.13–6, see also 2.86 (*Memoir* 1.375).

227 'the nine-months neighbour' from 'Little bosom not yet cold', Ricks 2.465.
'Shadow and shine is life' 'The Grandmother', Ricks 2.601.
'happy in the thought' This is E. Russell thirty years earlier on the death of a newborn nephew (*CTAT*, p. 22) – it is typical of the consolation offered.
'Gossip is my total abhorrence' AT to SRE, [8 March 1851], L&S 2.9.
'Tennyson is married' Lucie Duff-Gordon to C.J. Bayley, 18 May 1851 (information from Katherine Frank).
'Mrs T. has had a son . . .' CP to WA, 28 April 1851, Champneys 2.175.

228 gruff words, 'his bride, long sought' etc. *Memoir* 2.486–7.
dedication *Lyrical Poems* 'A selection of the best work of the world's greatest living poet.' See my p. 557.
Treasury of Sacred Song 'Morning Hymn' and 'Evening Hymn' are both taken by Ricks to be by ET, though on the page (p. 323) it looks as if the second hymn could be by AT.
AT on Palgrave improving AT to ET, 4 Aug. [1853], TRC, L&S 2.68.
Allingham's first visit WA *Diary*, 28 June 1851, pp. 60–3.

229 'graceful little bracelet' AT to WA, 1 July [1851], L&S 2.18.
June 1851 Hoge and Pinion think the Tennysons were in Cheltenham this month, but the evidence seems to the contrary. ET's letter to JS (Hoge *L*, p. 51) should be 7 June 1852.
making inventories There are several surviving at TRC relating to Chapel House. One, obviously in a servant's hand, is ill-spelt and may be 1853 as it includes '2 babys mug', as well as 'nutcracks' 'sugger tongues' and 18 'large falks', 'dirst spoons' etc.

230 Channel stormy ET to HS, 20 July 1851, TRC.
Kers' marriage was 7 July 1851. ET to HS, 19 Aug. 1851, TRC.
Ker's career AT to ET, 18 Jan. 1852, *Memoir* 1.347, L&S 2.21.
meeting Brownings in Paris HT is misleading (*Memoir* 1.341). The only meeting was in July on the way *to* Italy.
EBB and Tennyson She had worked with R.H. Horne on an essay on AT. Four of 39 pages at Univ. of Virginia in her hand.

230 de Vere told Allingham *Letters to WA* (1911), 29 Sept. 1865.

231 gossip about PL Cf. *Athenaeum*. EBB to Miss Mitford, 15 June 1850.
'like the foot of a young bird' and curls FLo in *My Confidences*, p. 157.
'wonderful spirit eyes' ET to EL, [Sept. 1855], TRC.
'plant herself in the heart' ET to RB, 20 Dec. 1865, Yale.
'being a poet's wife' ET to HS, 20 July 1851, TRC.
Brownings on Bagni EBB to Miss Mitford, [July 1849], *Letters*, ed. Lubbock, p. 252.

232 'the kindest in the world' RB to AT, 13 Dec. 1885, *Brownings to Tennysons* (Baylor) p. 45. ET makes no mention of how they travelled. EBB travelling from Italy that summer writes (to John Kenyon, 7 July 1851) of 'calèches', 'the unfinished railroad and the diligence,' 'the coupé'. *Letters*, ed. F.G. Kenyon (1897).
route mainly from ET to EP, 3 Nov. 1851, Champneys 2.306/7.
ET on Nice ET to EL, 17 Feb. 1865, TRC.
'I am afraid our countrymen' ET to HS etc., 18 Aug. 1851, TRC.

233 'kind in helping us' and 'flies, fleas' ET to Eliza T, 13 Aug. 1851, TRC.
'out of doors roaming' ET to FT, 15 Oct. 1851, *Letters to FT*, p. 104.

234 Casa Gregorio Barsantini (*sic* ET and Murray – *not* Giorgio Basantino as *Memoir* 1.341) identified by Michael Meredith as near the English Chapel 'in the busiest and least pleasant part of the town, as the Brownings discovered in 1857, the least successful of their three visits.' The visit which led them to recommend Bagni to the Ts was to 'Casa Valeri in Bagni Caldi, high up on the hills'. The plaque commemorating the Bs' visit is on Casa Tolomia where they were in 1853; this is also in the valley. ET says the disadvantage of Bagni Caldi was 'scorpions and centipedes'.
'We get on very well' 'portantini' etc. ET to HS etc., 18 Aug. 1851, TRC. See also ET to EP, 3 Nov. 1851, Champneys 2.306.

236 'Juggernaut' at Pisa Christ, flanked by the Virgin and St John by Jacopo Turrita, dating from the turn of the thirteenth and fourteenth centuries.
Villa Torrigiani ET to HS etc., 9 Sept. 1851, TRC. There is more than one Villa Torrigiani (ET spells it Torregiani) in Florence; the place where ET and AT stayed has often been wrongly identified. It is undoubtedly on the right (going from the Arno) of what is now the via de Serragli, near the Porta Romana. The villa is shown clearly on the map in Murray's *Handbook to Northern Italy* (1858) and fits exactly with ET's description. The name can still be seen on the gate post; the villa is not open to the public.
'larger than we require' FT to ET and AT, 30 Dec. 1854, back of vol. 4, Mat., TRC.
'chilled and stunted' Robert Bulwer to EBB, 7 Jan. 1854 (*Background*, p. 125).

237 'behaves like a lady' 'chattering in English' ET to HS etc., 9 Sept. 1851, TRC.
FT's "life in Italy" MB to HT, 8 May [1898?], Yale.
misunderstandings ET to FT, 15 Oct. 1851, Harvard, *Letters to FT*, p. 105.
'another little one' AT to A. de Vere, [*c.* 17 Aug. 1852], L&S 2.40.
'before the passes close' ET to HS etc., 11 Sept. [1851], TRC.
'Marriage is often a restorer' E. Peel to C. Bradshaw, 21 June 1850, L&S 1.328.

238 'It seemed rather like a dream' ET to HS etc., 11 Sept. 1857, TRC. Although they were always together, ET's long letters make very little mention of AT, which is why they have been so little used.
'very stupid of him' FLu to Brookfield, 8 Feb. 1852, *Brookfield*, p. 370.
not going to Rome In Narrative, ET gives the 'public' reason: 'Italy was in so disturbed a state.'
'Poor things' ETJ to FT, 15 Oct. 1851, Harvard, *Letters to FT*, p. 105.

239 Milan Cathedral etc. 'rather a melancholy house' ET to EP, 3 Nov. [1851], Champneys 2.307.
'The Daisy' Ricks 2.494.
241 'Italy is the land I love' ET to MGa, 26 Oct. 1864, Boston PL.

CHAPTER 7 The births of the boys

242 'not . . . the better' ET to EP, 3 Nov. 1851, Champneys 2.307.
'house-hunting business' AT to G.F. Flowers, n.d., L&S 2.72
'ill at ease' Fitz to W.B. Donne, 1 Jan. 1852, Terhune 2.46.
'Had I Alfred's voice' Fitz to FT, [Dec. 1851], Terhune 2.45.
'no curiosity' Fitz to E. Cowell, [5 Dec. 1851], Terhune 2.43.
243 two volumes of drawings EL to ET, 2 Dec. 1851, Yale. Hoge L (p. 56), not having seen this letter, but only ET's thank you (4 Dec. 1851, TRC), assumes EL's present consisted of original drawings. The volumes of *Illustrated Excursions in Italy* (1841) are at TRC.
'National panic' FLu to Brookfield, 8 Feb. 1852, *Brookfield*, p. 369.
'on writing it out' AT to CP, n.d., Berg, L&S 2.20.
244 'Canst thou not hold on?' AT to ET, [23 Jan. 1852], TRC, L&S 2.23. This letter contains, I think, a mistranscription. AT writes '*Must* thou read *The Times* every day?', rather than '*Hast* thou?' (after '*The Times* is a fool').
'hatred of letter writing' AT to Mr and Mrs THR, 27 Jan. [1852], Harvard, L&S 2.24.
letters to John Forster three from ET to Forster at Harvard, 28 Jan., 4 Feb. and 12 Feb. 1852.
patriotic poems 'Hands All Round', *Examiner*, 7 Feb. 1852, signed 'Merlin'. See Ricks 2.475.
'Taliessin's' lines 'Suggested by Reading an Article in a Newspaper', Ricks 2.475.
245 'hit a Frenchman' JS to ET, 4 Feb. 1852, TRC, L&S 2.25. On 30 Sept. 1852 ET told JS they had put his £5 cheque in the fire – 'the rifle club does not go on.' (TRC)
'hoping to move' 'agitator' ET to CP, 28 Jan. [1852], L&S 2.24.
'quicker train' ET to EBB, 9 Aug. [1852], Hoge *L*, p. 60.
'bring my two girls' W.M. Thackeray to ET, 4 Feb. 1852, not *c.* 6 July 1851 as in L&S 2.19, Yale.
246 memories of Chapel House ATR in *From Friend to Friend*, p. 1.
John Rashdall His family came from Mavis Enderby where ET's parents were married.
mesmerism recalled in ET's journal, March 1865. Some of this entry in green journal is in HT's writing.
'waking trance' AT to B.P. Blood, 7 May 1874, Harvard, L&S 3.78.
'letters on Mesmerism' ET to FT, 9 Dec. 1852, Harvard, L&S 2.54. (William Gregory, *Letters to a Candid Enquirer on Animal Magnetism*, 1851.)
247 outing to Kew ET to JMC, 25 June 1852, *From Friend to Friend*, p. 2.
'moving tales' ET to JS, 7 June [1852] (*not* 1851 as Hoge *L*, p. 51), TRC.
'made peace' J. Carlyle to ET, n.d., Yale.
'send a sovereign' AT to ET, 13 July [1852], L&S 2.32. This letter carries a mistranscription that began in Mat 11.69. Audrey had copied Redcliffe. ET altered 'cliffe' to 'car', but instead of ending up with the correct 'Redcar', HT read it as Redcliffe Scar, which does not exist. See *Memoir* 1.350. They go to Redcar together in 1853, Journal, July.

247 'Daddy' took him to Grimsby Extract from letter in *Memoir* 1.353. The original, presumably full of other personal details, does not survive. L&S 2.35.

248 'her thought, not mine' AT to EP, [12 Aug. 1852], Champneys 1.304, L&S 2.38.
'incomplete without' EBB to ET, 21 July 1852, Yale.
'move into lodgings' ET to a Mr Robertson, 7 July 1852, Rochester.
'may move to town' ET to EBB, 9 Aug. [1852], microfilm, Univ. of Virginia. L&S 2.36, not having seen ET's letter above, print 'may have to turn'.
JMC's 'great kindness' AT to JMC, 11 Aug. 1852, transcript at TRC, L&S 2.37.

249 'My wife is in labour' AT to EBB, n.d., Pierpont Morgan.
HT's birth apparently took place 'in the room at the top front' of Chapel House, the 'two left hand windows'. Scrap of letter at TRC by his second wife, May Prinsep Hichens.
letters on HT's birth L&S 2.36–42, *Memoir* 1.356–8.
AT on infant Hallam *T and his Friends*, p. 144.
'more than he ever wrote' baby's name ET to JS, 30 Sept. 1852, TRC.
'How happy I am' RB to AT, 11 Aug. 1852, Yale.

250 'nurse *our* baby' *Brookfield*, p. 307, wrongly dated 1850.
'De Profundis' Ricks 3.67.
on naming child AT to A de V, L&S 2.40, cf. AT's poem for his grandson, Ricks 3.70.

251 'names . . . united in . . . infant' H. Hallam to AT, 24 Aug. 1852, Yale, 'afraid he might be a fool'. ET tells the story (Journal and to Colquhoun, Brotherton, Dec. 1852) adding 'like many other good stories this is too good to be exactly true'. Cf. *CTAT*, p. 270.
'these little creatures' EBB to ET, 29 Sept. 1852, Yale.
'Tennysons never could' Catherine Tennyson to FT's son Alfred, 4 Feb. 1884, Lilly.
'Emily and the boy' AT's worries to E. Russell, 28 Sept. [1852]. TRC, L&S 2.45.
'nothing but babies' ET to JS, 30 Sept. 1852, TRC.

252 F.D. Maurice See *Life of FDM*, ed. F. Maurice (1884), pp. 62–3, letter to AT, 30 Aug. 1852, Yale, L&S 2.76 (AT to Kingsley). HT admired his godfather's ideals, but protested (not in *Memoir* but in a speech after his return from Australia, TRC) 'that the word socialism had come to be used by communists who want to seize all capital . . .' He named FDM as his godfather in this speech – 'one of the fathers of the old Christian Socialism'.
HT's christening L&S 2.43–8; *Memoir* 1.359–61; Robert Morier, *Memoirs and Letters* (1911); ET's notes at Yale; Domett *Diary*, p. 68.

253 Baptismal Breakfast FT to ET, 5 Nov. 1852, Mat. back of vol. 4, TRC.
'too late lingering' EBB to Mrs Newham, 9 Oct. 1852.
Gunter's of Berkeley Square. In my childhood still a famous caterer.
Thackeray on brown cob ATR *Records*, p. 40.

254 RB nursing HT EBB to Miss Mitford, 6 Oct. 1852.
'happy beside a cradle' EBB to Mrs Martin, 2 Sept. 1855.
'Don't bother yourself' AT to Tom Taylor, 21 Nov. 1852, L&S 2.51.
'choking smell' ET to L. Colquhoun, 12 Oct. [1852]. This letter, recently come to light, shows that FT was with them, apparently arriving just after the christening – 'for whose sake we are here'. 'We shall be off to the sea as soon as we can.' In my possession.
'so happy here' ET to JS, 21 Oct. [1852], TRC.

255 'far from Skeggie' 'looks pleasantly' ET to FT, 9 Dec. 1852, Harvard, L&S 2.53.
'all my life' ET to L. Colquhoun, Dec. [1852], Brotherton.
'Roman Catholic doll' ET to EL, 19 March 1873, TRC.

255 'What a life of wonder' *T and his Friends*, p. 144.
Lear's project EL to ET, 5 Oct. 1852, Pierpont Morgan.
256 HT's leg and arm, etc. ET and AT to FT, 9 Dec. 1852, Harvard, L&S 2.53.
eating books AT to H. Hallam, 11 Feb. [1853], Princeton, L&S 2.58.
257 petition ET to L. Colquhoun, Dec. [1852], Brotherton. ET refers to 'Brother
Jonathan' (a US equivalent of John Bull) in the letter. The first all-women convention
on women's rights had taken place in Seneca Falls, NY, in July 1848.
'Alfred nurses him' 'As heroines go' Fitz to E. Cowell, 29 Dec. 1852, Terhune 2.83.
'An old Housekeeper' Fitz to R.M. Milnes, 12 April 1874, Terhune 3.487.
'single in Lincolnshire' Fitz to W.F. Pollock, Dec. 1864, Terhune 2.538.
'never writes, nor indeed cares' Fitz to FT, 31 Dec. 1850, Terhune 1.696.
258 'dear old Fitz' WA *Diary*, 1883, p. 320.
'entire management' ET to Mrs Scholfield, 15 March [1853], Huntington, L&S
2.61.
'abominable Twickenham' ELL to AT, 31 March 1853, *Circle* p. 181, TRC.
'afraid of this coast' Fitz to ET, 25 Sept. 1853, Terhune 2.106.
'Your face' Fanny Kingsley to ET, [6 May 1853], TRC.
259 Maurice's essays See Florence Higham, *FDM* (1947).
'black fingers' Journal, 10 March 1861, TRC.
visiting Edward CTT and LTT visited in 1856. ET comments on the fact; LTT's letter
to which she refers has been destroyed. ET and AT would never be in York again.
'trying the congregation' ET to AW, 14 Aug. 1889, TRC.
260 'one of the guards' AT to ET, [27 July 1853], TRC, L&S 2.66. Alfred writes from
Richmond on 25 July (L&S 2.65) and is at Edinburgh on the 27th. So they must have
been at York both before and after Richmond. Why did he not catch the train at
Darlington?
'I did not get further' ET to JS, 11 Oct. 1853, TRC.
'ill and weary' 'The Daisy', l. 96, Ricks 2.497.
leaving out 'dearest' AT to ET, 4 Aug. [1853], TRC, L&S 2.67.
'not near so pretty' AT to ET, 6 Aug. [1853], TRC, L&S 2.68.
'a nice little place' AT to ET, 22 July [1852], *Memoir* 1.352, L&S 2.34.
'like a backbone' Grasby generally *Glimpses*, pp. 6–11.
261 'poisoned the cow' from a Lincolnshire story told by HDR, *Memories* p. 115, and
used by AT in 'The Church-Warden and the Curate', Ricks 3.228.
Louisa's writing Roger Evans, whose PhD thesis on CTT at TRC explored these
diaries, agrees with the likely identification of E. as Emily. In another entry: 'I do
distrust and blaspheme my sister in flesh and spirit' dated only '12th'. 12 Aug. 1853
seems to have been the only '12th' they were together at this period.
names of servants' children from the Census 1861, when they were four and one.
'writing and hearing' ELL to ET, 31 Aug. 1858, TRC.
262 report from WA WA *Diary*, 1 Nov. 1853, p. 63.
Giulio's letter to his mother, 3 Aug. 1853, Lilly. Giulio (known later as Julio or
Julian) born 30 June 1840. His parents were married after his birth though 1839 is
always given as the date. His younger brother Alfred would exploit the situation.
black blood of the Tennysons Horatio to ETJ, 22 Dec. 1853, TRC.
'talking of buying' H. Hallam to ET, 7 Nov. 1853, TRC.
263 rejected the offer George Seymour to ET, 29 Oct. 1853, TRC.
renting with an option ET to Seymour, 31 Oct. 1853, draft TRC.
'Beginning to faint' from 'Come into the garden' 'Maud' Part I. XXII, l. 858, Ricks
2.563.

264 'concluding a bargain' 'changeable mind' AT and ET to Harry Lushington, 8 Nov.
[1853], Virginia, not all in L&S 2.74.
'chalk and sand' Ruskin to AT, Yale (AT uses them in his poem 'To FDM').
'far from the haunts of men' *Memoir* 1.364–5.
utter solitude AT to Milnes, [30 June 1853?], Yale, L&S 2.64.
'nothing but sea and stars' AT to Moxon, 28 Feb. [1854], L&S 2.80.
265 'no fishing' AT to ET, [31 Dec. 1855], TRC, L&S 2.139.
'half hid in the gleaming wood' 'Maud' Part I. VIII, l. 258, Ricks 2.536.
history of Farringford built for Edward Rushworth, MP for Yarmouth 1780–97. Julia
Crozier to AT, 18 May 1875: 'I think you may depend on the year 1806 for I saw
yesterday, quite by chance, the carpenter who was apprenticed to "Stephens of
Yarmouth" who built Farringford.' TRC. The 1812 engraving (see Wheatcroft, *The
Tennyson Album* (1980), p. 72) was published by Sherwood, Neely and Jones of
Paternoster Row. Directories call it Farringford *Hill*, Ts simply Farringford.
266 'most beautiful in the spring' ATR quoted in *Thackeray's Daughter* (1951), p. 112.
'drawn down to the bay' ET to JMC, March 1856, *From Friend to Friend*, p. 8.
267 worrying about money Academics with tenure and regular salaries have often
criticized AT for his caution about money. It seems to me understandable, even his
holding on to his Civil List Pension.
'bore and bother' AT to E. Russell, [24 March 1854], L&S 2.83.
poem for FDM 'To the Rev. F.D. Maurice', Ricks 2.497.
'Mars culminating in the Lion' AT to E. Cowell, 17 March 1854, Trinity, L&S 2.81.
Other letters about LT's birth, L&S 2.81–7.
268 'only son a perilous gift' ET to Annie Fields, 26 May 1891, Huntington.
'The kiss, The woven arms' 'The Miller's Daughter', Ricks 1.417, l. 231.

CHAPTER 8 'Equally mated'

269 'winning children' ET to JMC, *From Friend to Friend*, p. 8.
happy childhood 'his desire was to make H & L's childhood as happy as possible',
Thomas Wilson, *Memoir* 1.512.
'brutality of old nurses' Mat. 4.48.
'Our boys are healthy' ET to EBB, 14 Sept. [1857], Wellesley.
270 'a happier boyhood' *A Child's Recollections*.
Hallam's eyes/monk *Memoir* 1.378 (Mat. 3.37).
'vexations enough' AT to CP, [April 1854], Yale, L&S 2.87.
'joy as a virtue' ET to JMC, *From Friend to Friend*, p. 9.
richness of one's possessions ET to TW, 15 Feb. 1859, TRC.
'beating and kissing' ET to AT, 16 June 1858, TRC.
271 T's views on handling children Notebook N6 at TRC.
painful to punish ET to Agnes, 8 Nov. 1895, TRC.
discourtesy to servant HT remembers, *Memoir* 1.370.
twins story Journal, 25 Jan. 1858, TRC.
272 'one servant less' ET to AT, 20 Sept. 1856, TRC.
'lighting fires' with books AT to R.J. Mann, n.d., L&S 2.167.
E angel, A public writer WA *Diary* quoting AT, 21 Oct. 1880, p. 303.
'treating domestics' EL to Fortescue, 21 Dec. 1884, *Later Letters of EL*.
eleven men, seven women ET to Agnes, 4 May 1895, TRC.
'*too* kindly' AT to ET, [8 May 1857], TRC, L&S 2.174.
'vines and roses' 'and myrtles instead of flagstones' ET to MGa, 1 Oct. 1863, Boston PL.

273 'secretary and business manager' Sir Charles Tennyson in foreword to Hoge L.
'equally mated' ET to MGa, 12 Jan. 1859, Boston PL.
'in thy hands' AT to ET, [20 June 1864], TRC, L&S 2.371.
'so clever' Mangles, 29 March 1871, p. 71.
274 'insulting lies' ET to TW, 1 Feb. 1856, TRC.
groaning about letters Mangles, 28 March 1871, p. 62.
'poor Turner' ET to AT, 19 Aug. [1854], TRC. AT would compare himself to Turner
in another way: they both made 'rough sketches' first in order to work them up. 21
Nov. 1882, L&S 3.239.
bottles of port H. James to W. James, 29 March 1877, Henry James, Letters, ed. Percy
Lubbock, 1920, p. 53.
'Cardboard resolves' FT to AT and ET, 24 Jan. 1861, TRC.
275 'a labour of love' ET to AT, 28 June 1864, TRC.
'many a line on the north wind' AT to S.E. Dawson, 21 Nov. 1882, L&S 3.239.
first words Journal, 5 Dec. 1863.
'Reading . . . impossible' ET to D. Rawnsley, 13 Nov. 1856, TRC.
Reading . . . 'is so much better' ET to TW, 5 Dec. 1862, TRC.
'pain-provoking pages' EL to ET, 6 May 1868, TRC.
violent letter quoted in Richard Jesse letter at Rochester, 21 May n.y.
'Pity me!' ET to TW, 6 Feb. 1859, TRC.
276 'work. . . now measurable' ET to ELL, c. Dec. 1863, TRC.
'not so hopeless' ET to MGa, 1 Oct. 1863, Boston PL.
'Very darling chaps' EL diary, 7 June 1859, Harvard.
'feet pattering' ET to AT, 17 Aug. 1854, TRC.
'Nothing in the way of . . .' ET to J.M.F. Ludlow, 14 March 1859, Pierpont
Morgan.
277 'I love you all the same' AT to Forster, 29 March 1854, Memoir 1.373, L&S 2.85.
'supply The Times' TW to JMC, 16 Aug. n.y., Rochester.
'to his unfortunate wife' FT to MBro, 6 April 1861, Lilly.
'kill a pig' AT to Manns, [Dec. 1858], draft Mat. iv. 74, L&S 2.211. but word order
as here.
'better than a poem' Traubel, Walt Whitman in Camden (1906), p. 36. The letter is
reproduced in facsimile.
'a monticule of letters' AT to ?, 18 March 1862, L&S 2.299.
written by ET, signed by AT to J. Simeon, 15 June 1865, Syracuse, not so indicated in
L&S 2.399.
278 Tennyson autographs Martin Tupper to collector, see L&S 3.214.
280 'wild with delight' John Barrington Simeon, to be 4th baronet, would continue in this
vein. At the time of his father's death, when the heir was twenty, Lionel would
describe him as 'very wild'.
Louisa Simeon's memories Louisa Ward, Memories for my Children, privately
printed, 1889.
'No one except my own' ET to LTT, Aug. 1870, TRC.
'a fine high-natured girl' etc. MBrad diary, 28 Jan. 1868, BL.
'Love Love Love' ET to EL, 5 June 1857, TRC.
'most delightful spirits' ET to E. Cowell, 3 Aug. 1854, CUL.
281 Maud ringing in his ears Fitz to ET, [Dec. 1872], Terhune 3.388.
the sharp shock See my p. 582.
'want of orthodoxy' ET to D. Rawnsley, 3 May 1854, Harvard.
'the greatest favour' ET to FLu, 2 Sept. 1855, TRC.

282 'the most perfect character' EL to ET, 9 Oct. 1856, TRC.
'more as a relative' ET to EL, [late Sept. 1855], TRC.
'you *good* people' FLu to ET, 20 June 1856, TRC.
'I grow just as silent' ET to EL, 25 Sept. 1855, TRC.

283 'Morn broadened' ET to EL, [Nov. 1855], from 'A Dream of Fair Women', 1.265.
EL to ET, 11 Nov. 1855, TRC, tells of the sale of this picture. See Ruth Pitman, *Edward Lear's Tennyson*, pp. 100–1.
settings of T's songs In Holman Hunt's painting 'The Awakening Conscience', the music on the floor (with the dedication to ET clearly visible) is 'Tears, Idle Tears'. See 'Edward Lear sings Tennyson Songs' by A.H. Ehrenpreis, Harvard Lib. Bull. vol. xxvii, 1979.
letter on prospectus 8 Oct. 1853, by which time the songs were published.
'I can only talk' ET to AT, 15 July 1870, TRC.

284 'Good gracious!' EL to ET, n.d. [Aug. 1860?], TRC.
health after childbirth The Victorians were well aware of the beneficial effects. Poor Effie Ruskin was told by two doctors that having children would benefit her health; she could only reply that Ruskin disliked children. *The Order of Release*, (1947), p. 163.
boys on her back ET to EL, 30 Aug. [1855], TRC.

285 popular medical text book *Medical Knowledge* printed for J. Smith, High Holborn, disguised (on spine) as *Aristotle's Works*, n.d.

286 'Most unwise' ET to EL, 22 Feb. 1871, TRC.
only infirmities AT's annotations to H.J. Jennings, *Lord Tennyson: a biographical sketch* (1884), pp. 105–6, TRC.

287 pining for mountains ET to Forster, 9 June [1854], TRC, L&S 2.93.
'hardly seen a human face' AT to CP, [April 1854], Yale, L&S 2.87.
'I feel sick at heart' ET to AT, 19 Aug. [1854], TRC.
preferred not to leave ET to EL, 27 Aug. 1855, TRC (not 62.5498).

288 settings of AT 'Tennyson in Song', *Musical Times*, 1 Nov. 1892, lists 573 published settings. Cf. AT to Argyll, 29 July 1859, of 'Hands All Round' 'She has set it to music far more to the purpose than most of Master Balfe's.' Balfe set a dozen T songs including 'Come into the garden, Maud'.
'Sweet and low' AT to Tom Taylor, 16 July 1852, L&S 2.33.
'song in four time' ET to A. Macmillan, 25 Jan. 1860, Berg, L&S 2.249.

289 'beaten black and blue' AT to R.J. Mann, [Sept. 1855], L&S 2.127.
'People bother him so' ET to Forster, 9 June 1854, TRC, L&S 2.92.
'a couple of thousand pounds' Moxon to AT. See June Steffensen Hagen, *T and His Publishers*, p. 100. Perhaps £100,000 in current money.
'to take little Hallam' AT. to ET, 18 May [1854], L&S 2.89.
bonfire Millais' painting 'Autumn Leaves' belongs to Manchester City Art Galleries. It is reproduced in *Voices in the Gallery*, ed. Abse (1986) opposite a poem 'The Bonfire' by Anthony Thwaite.
'A hates overrealism' is in HT's hand in epitome Journal as if it were part of the original journal which he felt should not be left out. See *Memoir* 1.380.
Millais' portrait is now in Wellington, New Zealand where I saw it in the home of ET's great-grandson, James Tennyson, son of A.B.S. Tennyson ('golden-haired Ally'). It could have been painted later than 1854–5; there is no record of Emily posing for Millais. A letter attached to the back suggests it was given to AT in 1861. Contradicting that letter, is a remark in a letter from Lionel in 1879 saying Millais had offered to give them his portrait of ET; LT would collect it the following week. This

suggests that ET and AT never possessed it and it went down Lionel's side of the family.

290 'I positively loathe' ET to TW, n.d. [early 1857], Bodleian.
'Not knowing anyone' HS to ET, 12 Oct. 1853, Harvard. This seems to be the only surviving letter from HS to his daughter Emily.

291 'Oh! that 'twere possible' puzzles See Ricks 2.20 and 2.514–16. If AT had available, not a copy of *The Tribute*, but only HS's copy of AT's own poem, parallels in 'Maud' with other poems in the collection, such as the ballad 'The Wicked Nephew', seem irrelevant.
'weave a story' Notes to 'Maud' in Eversley edn.
Kate Rawnsley's claim WFR in *Memories*, p. 122–3.
as his daughter suggested Louisa Simeon Ward's story is quoted in *Glimpses*, p. 57.
ELL's visit mid-May? Cecilia's letter – see *Circle*, p. 187. Journal is not clear about the exact date.
'strange, wild story' Mary G diary, 22 March 1879, BL.
'called out to his wife' *Mangles*, 29 March 1871, p. 69.
AT's study AT to Tuckerman, 6 Feb. 1855, Harvard, L&S 2.106. His first-floor study, which can be seen today in the Farringford Hotel, was not built until 1871.

292 'It seems that I am happy' 'Maud' Part I, XVIII,VI, l. 648, Ricks 2.555.
'I have led her home' 'Maud' Part I, XVIII, I, l. 599, Ricks 2.553.
'pet bantling abused' T to MBrad, diary 1860, *Memoir* 1.468.
'to read things to oneself' Journal, 8 Feb. 1859, TRC.
'the case with Alfred's wife' Monteith to Milnes, 12 Nov. 1855, Trinity.
'violent scenes... false' ET to HT, 13 March 1874, TRC.
'It is people's own fault' ET to Forster, 6 Aug. 1855, TRC, L&S 2.118.

293 'surrealistic lunacy' Ricks *T*, p. 253.
'I hate the dreadful hollow' 'Maud' begins: Ricks 2.519.
'nothing of Lincolnshire' HT to J.C. Walters, 5 Feb. 1890, L&S 3.410.
'deeply pessimistic view of marriage' Ricks *T* p. 251.
'the mouth of a madman' AT to A.T. Gurney, 6 Dec. 1855, L&S 2.137.
Westminster Review George Eliot, Oct. 1855, viii. 596–615 (anonymous).
'death and destruction to the enemy' ET to Forster, 6 Dec. 1854, TRC.

294 'true feeling about war' ET to LTT, 9 May 1879, TRC.
HT and chimney sweep ET to AT, 17 Aug. 1854, TRC.
'Frenchman, a hand in thine!' Ricks 3.627, *Memoir* 1.380.

295 'Only one's friends' ET to JMC, 13 Jan. 1855, TRC. *From Friend to Friend*, p. 11, wrongly dates part 1 Jan. 1885.

296 'The Charge of the Light Brigade' ET's letters to Forster at TRC. Many at the time called it 'horrid rubbish' (AT's uncle Charles), 'very unworthy of him' (CLD); others admired, including survivors of the 'blunder'. Proof at Yale corrected by both AT and ET. See E.F. Shannon and C.B. Ricks, *Studies in Bibliography* xxxviii (1985), 1–44 and Ricks 2.510.

CHAPTER 9 Friends and relations

298 'such a thing in his life before' F. Tuckerman to E. Tuckerman, 20 Jan. 1855, Yale.
'Locksley Hall' sold to Yale in 1947 for $2,000.
'very fine and strong' Leonée Ormond in her useful *Tennyson and Thomas Woolner* (Tenn. Soc. 1981), unfortunately (p. 8) follows Hoge in his misreading 'fine and shiny'. TW had made an earlier medallion of AT, finished at Coniston in 1850.

298 'I never in my life' TW to ET, 22 March 1855, TRC.
   'in the strongest words' CP, Champneys 1.84.
299 'on my lean face' ET to TW, 21 Nov. [1855], TRC.
   'take to poisoning' ET to TW, 26 June [1856], TRC.
   'give Alfred something to do' ET to TW, 16 Nov. 1859, TRC.
   'always with me' TW to ET, 24 June 1860, TRC.
300 Franklin family feud Jane Franklin diary, SPRI. In April 1860 Lady F. would record
   seeing a notice in *The Times* asking people who had a claim against Franklin's estate
   to contact HS: 'a last fragment of past years of suffering'. See *The Fate of Franklin*,
   pp. 329–30. HS was the sole executor.
   'dearest friend' JF to HS, 22 Feb. 1825, *John Franklin's Bride*.
   Spilsby shop *Illustrated London News*, 20 Oct. 1859. See p. 42.
   'simple devout nature' ET to Lady Richardson, 2 Oct. 1871, Rochester. The search
   for remains continues. In 1993 the Lady Franklin Memorial Expedition investigated
   in vain some possible burial mounds. See 'Signs of Life', Wadhams & Casarini,
   Geographica, April 1994.
301 'few I love so well' Louisa Lushington's death. See *Circle*, p. 189. Letters in
   Lushington family papers. ET 'writing and weeping' see AT to ELL, 26 July 1854,
   L&S 2.94.
   Henry Lushington's death See *Circle*, pp. 51–2 for beginning of Lushington/Tennyson
   friendships. Henry is one of the three dead friends (with AHH and J. Simeon)
   commemorated in 'The Garden at Swainston'. ELL was even closer; he outlived AT.
   'The women are my portion' C. Jebb, 17 July 1876, quoted in *Dearest Love to All*, p.
   125.
   'Thank you for staying' ET to EL, 17 Aug. 1855, TRC.
302 'I am sick at heart' ET to EL, 30 Aug. [1855], TRC.
   'Open thy mouth' Psalm 33, v. 10.
   losing umbrella etc. AT to ET, [31 Aug. 1855], TRC, L&S 2.125. Anyone who fails to
   feel sympathetic towards AT and towards ET as his wife should read this letter in its
   entirety.
   'It is a pity' ET to EL, [early Oct. 1855], TRC.
   'speaking out to me' ET to GSV, 5 Oct. 1855, Nat. Lib. of Wales, L&S 2.129.
303 'a vast pile' friendship Bradley to ET, 21 Nov. 1881, TRC.
   Bradley picnic etc. MBrad diary, BL.
304 'supercilious habit' FLu to ET, 13 April 1856, TRC.
   'the true spirit' *Memoir* 1.413.
   notebook ET's notebooks from this period include Natural History notes, e.g. 'on
   what can flourish near the sea'. *Conversations with Goethe* (1850) had been given to
   AT by Carlyle, TRC.
   'not superior' 'very pleasant' FLu to ET, 14 Sept. 1856, and 20 June 1856, TRC.
   'dust of the world' Proverbs 8:26, used with 'crust of conformity' 'love of
   Mammon' etc. at different times in MBrad diary, BL, together with description of ET
   etc.
305 'The more intimately' 'a sort of good angel' 'my darling' MBrad diary, 20 June 1861,
   20 Jan. 1861, 1 Jan. 1864, BL.
   'No friends can be nearer to us' Journal, 7 Jan. 1869, TRC.
   'Between Ally and myself . . .' ET to EL, 25 Sept. 1855, TRC. Ann Colley in
   Tennyson and Madness (1983) uses this statement out of context (p. 42) to suggest
   that Emily shared Tennyson's tendency to gloom and depression, a mental instability,
   even a feeling that black blood ran in her own veins. There is really very little evidence

of this as I hope this biography makes clear. Like everyone, she did have some dark hours. Colley attributes Emily's physical problems to 'spinal neuromimesis', hysterical in origin. See pp. 42–3 ibid.

306 'for many a long day' EL to ET, 28 Oct. 1855, TRC.
'One would be all' ET to EL, 17 Nov. 1855, TRC.

307 'your friend Miss Cotton' FLu to ET, 13 April 1856, TRC.
'Alack! for Miss Cotton!' 'sliding pleasantly out of life' EL to ET, 28 Oct. 1855. For the reference to not being what he seems, cf. Maria Edgeworth's *The Purple Jar*.
'The pasting and ironing' Christmas ET to EL, 11 Jan. 1856, TRC. The buyer at Sotheby's of Lear's alphabet is not known to TRC.

308 'rarely in bed' See e.g. John Tyndall, *Memoir* 2.472. 'Two fine little boys – probably in T's estimation his best poems – joined us at dinner.' This was April 1858 when the boys were only five and four.
'racing round the table' FP in *Nineteenth Century*, Feb. 1899, proof at TRC.
'We admire the place' ET to EL, 7 April 1855, TRC.
sending him the changes ET to Moxon, [Aug. 1855], Harvard, L&S 2.116.

309 'the gauntlet of much stupidity' AT to Weld, Oct. 1855, TRC.
'seven-inch hailstones' ET to EL, [Oct. 1855], TRC.
'strong in the conceit' ET to AT, 31 Oct. 1858, TRC.
'too much his second self' EBB quoted in *Authors and Friends*, p. 352.
'I am proud of her intellect' *Memoir* 1.331.
'utterly against' ET to JS, 27 June 1856, TRC.
'our own things' ET to TW, n.d., Bodleian.
purchase of Farringford agreements at TRC. AT to Simeon [20 March 1856], Yale. ET to GSV, 19 April 1856, Nat. Lib. of Wales.

310 'We have agreed to buy' The passage from Journal was cut out (HT's note: 'CUT OUT FOR MEMOIR'). MS Mat. has a copy in Audrey's hand, not Emily's. The version here from Printed Mat. not *Memoir* 1.412, slightly different, and giving date as 24 April 1856. The whole sequence is rather confused. L&S actually print a letter to Alan Ker about the purchase *twice*, vol. 2, p. 75 and p.148. The latter date is correct.
'I fear Tilly' 'You have done quite right' ET to AT, [30 Jan. 1856], TRC, is wrongly dated at 1854 by Hoge and AT's letter in reply at Yale is wrongly dated in L&S 2 at [? Oct. 1853] on p. 72. It should be a day or two before the one on p. 144 (both Feb. 1856), which discusses books at Chapel House as lease was expiring.

311 'I pray thee say nothing' ET to AT, 1 July 1856, TRC.
'Where your treasure is' Matthew 6:21.

312 the Red House High Down Villa, a red brick house ('a most unwelcome sight opposite our farm gate' in Sept. 1855) was later called both the Red House and Villa Doria. It belonged to John Dore and was often rented by the Tennysons.
Emily on the chaos that summer to TW, Bodleian, to AW, TRC.
Prince Albert's visit *Dear and Honoured*, p. 41, wrongly suggests the chaos was because redecoration was taking place, and that the furniture in ET's description was the Tennysons' own. That did not arrive until after the Seymours' sale.
'the new fort' ET to AW, 15 May 1856. See Jenkinson's *Practical Guide to the Isle of Wight*: 'It was completed in 1856 and is principally beneath the surface of the ground.'
'I write to make you laugh' ET to GSV, 21 May [1856], Nat. Lib. of Wales.

313 'any pawnbrokers?' 'overprizing' 'we have so much' AT unpacking all ET to TW summer 1856, TRC.

314 'played our welcome' ET to EL, 5 June 1857, TRC.

315 'as I was getting into bed' crossed out in epitome Journal.
   'But hither shall I never come' 'Guinevere', Ricks 3.544, l. 575.
   at Eastbourne with invalids Welsh sea ELL to ET, 26 Aug. 1856, TRC.
316 'these idle tales' unpublished draft by ET of a possible epilogue to the Idylls, TRC.
   worthy subject 'No story in the world is to be compared with it.' ET to AT, 17 Sept.
   1856, TRC.
   'My wife has a great fancy' The text of this undated note to W. B. Donne (Mat. 2.
   181) is put by L&S as early as Feb. 1854. The books were finally returned in April
   1857. (See L&S 2.171–2 and ET to AT, 30 April, TRC.)
   'I can always write' AT to Knowles, *Nineteenth Century* xxxiii (1893).
   Mabinogion Lady Charlotte Guest translated (1838–49) a collection of Welsh stories.
   No mention of Arthur in the *Mabinogion* proper, but he is in other stories she
   collected.
317 'Both years' ET to EBB, 14 Sept. 1857, Wellesley.
   'The climate disagreed' etc. ET to TW, 31 July and 1 Oct. 1856, TRC.
   'Wales . . . crowded' ET to EL, Sept. 1856, TRC.
318 'Our purse' ET to JS, 15 Sept. 1856, TRC.
   'how real the story' admiring both boys ET to EL, 18? Sept. 1856, TRC.
   Patmore 'improved' ET to TW, 20 Oct. 1856, TRC.
319 Patmores copying CP to AT, 4 Nov. 1856, L&S 2.164, and ET to EP, 6 Nov. [1856],
   Champneys 2.308–9.
   HT 'splendid' EP to TW, 14 Sept. [1855]. On 14 Sept. the Tennysons were still in
   Wales so the letter presumably dates from the year before, when HT was indeed three.
   Bodleian.
   'stopped strangers' CP to ET, 25 Jan. 1856, TRC.
   'exceeding anxiety' ET to AT, 30 Jan. 1856, TRC.
   'Not Shakespeare' story ET to EL, 28 Nov. 1856, TRC. I love this story because my
   own grandchildren at two were similarly familiar with Shakespeare – from a
   Staffordshire figure of him they identify every time they visit.
320 'may you ever be spared' 'Cissy absent' ELL to AT and ET, 6 and 31 Oct. 1856, TRC.
   urgent entreaties ET to D. Rawnsley, 13 Nov. 1856, TRC.
   'the sadness of the house' ET to EL, 28 Nov. 1856, TRC.
   'Nothing can be made of her' ELL to ET, 9 May 1865, TRC. (*Circle* p. 210.)
   'a good strong wife' CL to ELL, August 1855. (*Circle* p. 199.)
   try 'to keep her up to' her promises ELL to ET, 29 Oct. 1859, TRC.
   'ground hollow' 'open graves' ET to GSV, 29 Jan. 1859, Nat. Lib. of Wales, L&S
   2.213.
321 trial copies destroyed BL has a trial copy of *Enid and Nimuë: the True and the False*
   (1857).
   'that kind of woman' JS to AT, 15 July 1856, TRC, L&S 2.159.
   '"Merlin" seems to me' ET to JS, 15 Sept. 1856, TRC.
   'poems of grand moral feeling' ET to GSV, 12 June 1857, Nat. Lib. of Wales.
   'a grain of dispraise' ET to EBB, 14 Sept. 1857, Wellesley.
322 'proving the poet's home' ET to JS, 27 June [1856], TRC.
   adultery, fornication, etc. MS Mat. 4. 69 and Mat. 11.129. It is in HT's hand but by
   the 1896 proof it has been reduced to 'Criminal I may be, suicide I am not yet.' And
   it did not appear in *Memoir*. See Philip L. Elliot, *The Making of the Memoir*, Tennyson
   Society (1993), p. 13.
   'a failure' 'in a money point of view' ET to TW, 3 Oct. 1856, 13 Feb. 1857, Bodleian.
   'towards the improving of Farringford' FLu to ET, 18 Jan. 1857, TRC.

323 Ruskin *Memoir* 1.420, and P. FitzGerald, *Burne Jones*, p. 66.
unsold copies money owed Weld to AT, 27 Oct. 1858, and Weld to ET, 30 Oct., 4 Nov. 1858, TRC. The issue was complicated by the proposed illustrated edn. of *The Princess*, which AT said had gone ahead without his consent.
'I will . . . copy anything' ET to Forster, n.d., draft, TRC.
'brain aches' ET to TW, 28 Oct. 1858, TRC.
'Until eleven' 'much annoyed' ET to Weld, 3 Nov. 1858, TRC.
324 'facts respecting' ET to Forster, 31 Oct. 1858, TRC.
'Should you decide' Weld to ET, 4 Nov. 1858, TRC.
'energetic kindness' Journal, 27 Nov. 1858, TRC.
'guinea Xmas book in Routledge's advertisements' FLu to ET, 25 Dec. 1858.
'fresh troubles' ET to MGa, 18 April 1859, Boston PL.
'I wish you could persuade' TW to ET, 19 April 1859, TRC.
325 'A selection made' ET to MGa, 25 Feb. 1859, TRC.
'workman's letter' AT to Moxon, 8 Feb. 1858, Brotherton.
servants' wages ET's accounts (TRC) show servants paid quarterly. Even Andrews the cook earned only £5.5s a quarter. But ET would pay for many extras beyond their keep – outings, fares home, etc.
ordered a carriage For many years the Ts relied on a local man to provide transport. I have a note in ET's hand: 'Will Mr Lambert be good enough to send a one horse carriage with a good horse to take Mr Tennyson to Brooke this evening for a seven o'clock dinner. The carriage to be here at six with lamps as the nights are dark.'
326 AT letters to HT ?29 April 1857 and 8 May 1857, TRC.
'Why does he go?' 'I look after calves' Journal, 8 Dec. and 27 April 1857, TRC.
came from next village ET to EP, 19 March 1857, Champneys 2.308.
observed the Tennysons *Autob. of Elizabeth M. Sewell*, ed. E.L. Sewell, pp. 158–9.
327 'small pleasure' ET to TW, 1 April 1857, TRC.
needing to see a doctor ET to GSV, 12 June 1857, Nat. Lib. of Wales, L&S 2.180.
Mother and Tilly not visiting ET to AT, 20 Sept. 1856, TRC.
HT drawn by EL. Previously unpublished. TRC.
'rolling into the sea' MT to Lewis Fytche, 24 June 1857, TRC.
Tennysons at Farringford *RBM* (p. 365) says: 'Tennyson gradually drifted away from most of his family after his marriage,' but many of them were only too often guests of the house over the years.
sharing a house In April 1858 Eliza T and MT were with Horatio and his new wife at 42 Gloucester St., Belgravia, but the arrangement did not last long. By Oct. 1858 they were with the Jesses at Rose Mount, Hampstead. (See Eliza T to M. Lushington, 5 April 1858, Virginia, and AT to Mrs Hodgson, 25 Oct. 1858, TRC, L&S 2.209.)
328 'a crazy state' ET to TW, 1 April 1857, TRC.
'My dear little Grandsons' Eliza T's verse at Yale.

CHAPTER 10 'A blessed solace to him'

329 'sigh for the warm south' ET to EL, 1 June 1857, TRC.
'staying at a great house' Fitz to E. Cowell, 7 May 1857, Terhune 2.272.
330 Watts's portraits of ET *The Windsor Magazine*, June 1901, has an article on Watts, which refers to 'a sketch of Lady Tennyson signed "Signor, Little Holland House, July 28, 1858" '. None of the three surviving portraits have this inscription in the form I have seen them. Watts painted AT seven times and also made the great statue by Lincoln Cathedral.

331 'willingly have spent a week' AT to W. Fairbairn, n.d., L&S 2.187.
   'Your time of recognition' ET to EL, n.d. Aug. 1857, TRC.
   'do not defend the beard' ET to JS, 27 June 1856, TRC.
   'lazy monks' ET to EL, 5 June 1857, TRC.
   'Dirty Monk' JMC, *Annals of my Glass House*: 'he himself designates as "The Dirty Monk".' In Helmut Gernsheim, *JMC, her life and photographic work* (1975), p. 180. James Mudd's portrait appears to have been the one shown in the Exhibition. It is not clear when it was taken.
   Hawthornes' observations *The English Notebooks*, L&S 2.183–6; letters home, Sophia Hawthorne to E. Peabody, Aug. 1857, Berg, Boston PL.
   'I asked my wife' Sir Henry Craik, MS Memoir (1891), Nat. Lib. of Scotland (*RBM*, p. 416). In fact, on 31 July they had been miles apart when AT put on his shirt that morning.
332 Hawthornes' marriage See Harold Beaver in *TLS*, 14 Jan. 1994.
333 'I am as stupid' ET to WA, 8 Sept. 1857, TRC.
   'crying for joy' all ill ET to EL, 8 Aug., 18 Sept. 1857, TRC.
   'scarcely a day alone' ET to EL, 17 Nov. 1857, TRC.
334 'like a snail' ET to TW, ?16 Dec. 1857, TRC.
   'Only Mrs Tennyson' 'begging me to destroy' interested in grouping CLD diary, 18 Sept. 1857, 3 Dec. 1857. *The Diaries of Lewis Carroll* ed. R. Lancelyn Green (1953).
   'Any details' CLD to R.H. Collins, 9 Aug. 1890, *Letters of CLD.*
   'loveliest child' L. as benchmark: 'What a number of sham Lionel Tennysons you seem to meet with and what failures they all turn out when one comes to look at them.' CLD to his sister Mary, 20 Feb. 1861.
335 'going to Scotland' ET to EL, 18 Sept. 1857, TRC.
   'superhuman strength' *RBM*, p. 412.
336 'glad to get home' ET to EL, 17 Nov. 1857, TRC.
   seven guineas a week rate fixed by Lambert of the Freshwater Hotels. 'It should be more for only a month, he says.' ET to MGa, 9 July 1859, Boston PL.
   unsatisfactory lodgings damp Britannia Cottages, found for them by Jesses. Journal, 9 July 1858.
   to get Alfred to Corfu ET to EL, 13 July 1858, TRC.
   'splendid long curls' H. Lushington to R.M. Milnes, Trinity, *Circle*, p. 176.
337 regrets Grasby J. Simeon to ET, 29 Aug. 1859, Yale.
   forbidden to write ET to TW, 20 Oct. 1859, TRC.
   'I get very crazy' ET to MGa, 14 Sept. 1859, Boston PL.
   'a deep admirer' Alfred Gatty's account (9 Dec. 1892, Rawnsley papers) does not fit in exactly with ET's letters to MGa in Boston PL, but is true in essence. AT did not return from London as promptly as Gatty suggests. ET kindly wrote to MGa, 17 Nov. 1859, 'If it would be more agreeable to you to wait for him here than where you are, I hope you will come tomorrow to me.' There are over eighty letters at Boston PL from ET to the Gattys.
   boys will read them AT to MG, n.d., L&S 2.193.
   'in this one visit' ET to MGa, 26 Nov. 1858, Boston PL.
   'Your poor mad woman' ET to MGa, Feb. 1859, Boston PL.
338 'The Grandmother' AT to ET, [25 June 1859], L&S 2.231.
   'disliked sending poems to Magazines' ET to MGa, 26 May 1860, Boston PL.
   'your hand-writing' Watts to ET, 14 July 1859, NPG.
   'making Bay-windows' ET to MGa, 3 June 1859, Boston PL.
   'a will of my own' ET to TW, 29 March 1859, TRC.

339 'settling anything' ET to AT, 26 March 1859, TRC.
340 John Tyndall's story not *Henry*, as CT has it in his Foreword to Hoge *L*. See *Memoir* 2.472. Cf. 'Will', Ricks 2.492.
'unwillingly and longing for home' AT to ET, [1 April 1859], Yale, L&S 2.221.
'one of the wishes of my life' ET to AT, 22 June 1859, TRC.
341 'a constant sense' A. Gatty to HDR, 8 Dec. 1892, Rawnsley papers.
'best when not' together EL to ET, 9 Oct. 1856, TRC.
builders in the house They started 10 May and agreed not to be paid if they weren't finished by the time AT got back from London on about 18 June. 9 July 1859: ET to MGa (Boston PL) 'We have not yet got the workmen out of the house.'
'work unfit for poets' ET to TW, 9 May 1859, TRC.
342 'sensitive excitement' 'when I leave Farringford' EL diary, June 1859, Harvard.
'rare flashes of light' EL to ET, 28 Oct. 1855, TRC.
343 Fields' visit to Farringford 14–16 July 1859 J.T. Fields to Longfellow, L&S 2.234.
Annie Fields' published account in *Authors and Friends* (1897) based on her diary at the time, MS at Massachusetts Historical Society, Boston.
344 'of the Imogen sort' Fitz to W.F. Pollock, 7 Dec. 1869, Terhune 3.177.
345 'never fear, never cry' BJ to boys, Feb. 1860, TRC.
stopping them singing HT to TW (in ET's hand), 19 June 1859, TRC.
'frightening taciturnity' G. Faber, *Jowett*, p. 292.
'I often lament' BJ to AT, 29 Dec. 1855, TRC.
'a peculiar, gentle soft voice' MBrad diary, Jan. 1861, BL.
'All the great questions' ET to EL, 11 Jan. 1856, TRC.
346 'ecstacy of love' BJ to AT, 29 Dec. 1855, TRC.
'in spite of what the clergy' M. Asquith, *Autob.*, p. 136.
Isaacson AT grumbled over a period of a dozen years, recorded by both *Mangles* (p. 68 and p. 74) and A. Gatty (AG to HDR, 9 Dec. 1892, Rawnsley papers).
'awful contrast' BJ to ET, 23 April 1864, TRC.
'more than Political Economy' *Memoir* 2.467.
'wild-beaming benevolence' AT to ET, 1 Oct. 1855, TRC.
supervising garden 'played the game of life' *From Friend to Friend*, p. 20 and p. 5.
347 'a power of loving' H. Taylor, *Autob.* 2.48.
'a great honour' WA *Diary*, 24 June 1865, p. 117.
'against our rule' Journal, 1 Feb. 1860, TRC.
'What a dreadful friend' J. Wedgwood to RB, 24 Aug. 1864 and reply. *RB and Julia Wedgwood Letters*.
'When your Father is with her' JMC to HT, n.d., TRC.
'I should have been dreary' Journal, 2 Dec. 1868, TRC.
348 'playfellows for our boys' Journal, 21 Feb. 1857, TRC, rendered 'plays pelican' in *Farringford Journal* (1986) and omitted in Hoge *J*.
'mad pranks' *From Friend to Friend*, p. 20.
Mrs Cameron's piano Journal, June 1860 (Hoge oddly transcribes ET resting '*after* dinner' when it is clearly 'before'), EL diary fixes date at 18 June.
Benson's cup of tea EL to ET, 19 July 1860, TRC.
349 'never to feel happy' EL diary, 16 June 1860, Harvard.
bawdy talk EL diary, 17 June 1860, Harvard. Not only was AT 'snubby and cross' but after dinner he spoke, not only of Norway and Portugal and seasickness, but of 'I am ashamed to say it – other things'. This last is in Greek.
'Poets are birds' TW to ET, 16 March 1860, TRC.
Millais exchange from G.H. Fleming, *John Everett Millais: A Victorian Biography*

(read in MS without source notes) 'muttered': Millais to Dalziel. *RBM*'s comment (p. 425) that ET showed 'a profound ignorance' of the way poetry works does not seem justified.

349 'They do not understand' ET to MGa, 21 Dec. 1861, Boston PL.

'The trees too are luxuriant' JMC to C.H. Cameron, 15 May 1860, NPG (copy in JMC's own hand).

350 'I assume vivacity' *From Friend to Friend*, p. 28.

'ancient instrument' EL to ET, 16 Feb. 1862, TRC.

arsenic in wallpaper Stephen Bamber, my own doctor, says arsenic might aggravate a cough, but any ingestion of arsenic would normally cause death rather than coughing. On 9 May 1860 ET told Annie Fields she had had 'the whooping cough nearly ten weeks'.

351 'to hear the Idylls praised' BJ to FN, 11 May 1861, Balliol.

20,000 sold 'of the Arthur poem', TW to RB, 19 Jan. 1860, copy at Bodleian.

the boys in their blouses Journal, 1 Sept. 1858.

'villainous centre-bits' 'Maud' Part 1. XI, l. 41, Ricks 2.522, 'centre-bits': 'a boring tool with a centre point and side cutters' *OED*.

snail story Journal, June 1858, ET to AT, 16 June 1858, TRC.

happy memories nearly all from Journal, also ET to TW, 25 May 1859, TRC.

CHAPTER 11 'Before partings began'

353 'The boys are rosy' ET to EL, 14 Nov. 1859, TRC.

'Learn your lessons' AT to HT, 25 Aug. 1860, Yale, L&S 2.263.

Greek the foundation EL to ET, 15 Dec. 1861, TRC.

354 'Are you now bond or free?' Bradley to GD, 23 Jan. 1861, *Dakyns*, p. 3.

'over-dazzled' MBrad diary, Jan. 1861, BL.

'far deeper and wilder' *T and his Friends*, p. 204.

'Nothing could be kinder' *Life and Letters of Sydney Dobell* 2.178, L&S 2.270.

355 Jowett's 'heresy' ET to TW, 10 April 1861, TRC.

'This year he has written' BJ to Margaret Elliott, *Letters of BJ*, pp. 171–2, L&S 2.271.

'lift Lionel out of the baby' ET to Bradley, 4 Feb. 1861, TRC, *Dakyns*, p. 6.

'Your mother was seated' Dakyns in *T and his Friends*, p. 189.

'promises very well' ET to AG, 21 Feb. 1861, Boston PL.

356 'a great favour' ET to GD, 6 Feb. 1861, *Dakyns*, p. 7.

'I cannot but miss' Journal, Feb. 1861, TRC.

'life in life' 'The Miller's Daughter', l. 217, Ricks 1.417.

'the most peculiar manner' *Brookfield*, p. 294.

'I am his true widow' FN to Mdme Mohl, 13 Dec. 1861.

'You must come' ET to EL, March 1861, TRC.

357 'Cold and sad' EL diary, 18 March 1861, Harvard.

'finished as a poet' The Greek word EL uses is 'Khalasmenos', which presumably he meant in that sense. It can mean 'broken', 'decayed', 'out of order'.

'difficult to go' EL diary, 24 March 1861, Harvard.

one recent biographer Peter Levi, *Tennyson*, p. 271.

358 'introduced a lady' 'relief which all who have business' Sabine to Sharpey, 26 March 1861, Royal Society Library. Weld's 'resignation' was accepted on 11 April.

'The offence' ET to EL, 15 April 1861, TRC.

358 'Your affectionate dedication' ET to Weld, 29 May 1859, TRC.
359 'poor CRW was so ill' ET to EL, 22 April 1861, TRC.
   'more than you can help' ET to EL, 2 April 1861, TRC.
   'reading and thinking' ET to TW, 10 April 1861, TRC.
   'shake off London smut' AT to Weld, 21 Nov. 1855, L&S 2.135.
360 'not yet muster courage' 16 Nov. 1861, W. *White's Journal* (1898).
   ode sung at the opening of the International Exhibition Ricks 2.622.
   'Anne adds that "Charles"' Jane Franklin diary, Oct. 1865, SPRI.
   'worried out of their house' FP to AHC, 3 July 1861, Bodleian.
361 fair copy of HT's 1861 holiday journal photocopy at TRC, original presumably still
   in possession of the family (in 1967 with Mrs Evans of Gainsborough).
362 'haunted' by illness delicious air ET to EL, 10 Oct. 1861, TRC.
   'perpetual illness' ET to MGa, 1 Oct. 1861, Boston PL.
363 'Whom should I see' AHC to Blanche Clough, 21 July 1861, Bodleian.
   'I make no plans' AHC to ET, 13 Aug. 1861, Yale.
   'a kind of sacredness' Journal, 18 July 1871, TRC.
   no kinder companion, houses and carriages, etc. Journal, Aug. /Sept. 1861, TRC.
   'to amuse my sick boys' ET to MGa, 1 Oct. 1861, Boston PL.
   'continually doubtful' ET to EL, 10 Oct. 1861, TRC.
364 'ill placed in the Pyrenees' FP to AHC, 5 Aug. 1861, Bodleian.
   'People flaunt about' AHC to Blanche Clough, 22 Aug. 1861, Bodleian.
   Cauterets GD from *T and his Friends* pp. 204–5 (F. M. Stawell), Journal and AT to
   Lady Augusta Bruce, 12 May 1863, Rochester, L&S 2.327; AHC to Blanche Clough,
   Sept. 1861, Bodleian; Weld in *The Pyrenees* (1859), p. 124; HT diary, TRC.
365 'All along the valley' 'the little piece' AT to Lady Augusta, as above. ET to John
   Simeon, 8 Oct. 1861, Syracuse, Ricks 2.618.
366 'chatter like a Frenchman' LT to GD, 3 Oct. 1861, *Dakyns*, p. 14.
   Swiss Family Robinson was written in German by J.D. Wyss, published Zurich
   1812–13.
   Pau C. Jebb to her sister, 8 Feb. 1883, *Dearest Love to All*, p. 185.
   'his one wish was to get home' ET to GD, 3 Oct. 1861, *Dakyns* p. 14.
   travelling on the same train RB to G. Barrett, [30 Sept. 1861], L&S 2.280; and RB to
   AT, 9 June 1863, and 13 Oct. 1864, Baylor Browning letters.
   AHC's death 'of a relapse of malaria-fever', 13 Nov. 1861, *Memoir* 1.480.
   looking back on holiday ET to EL, 10 Oct. 1861, and ET to TW, 8 Oct. 1861, TRC
   and to MGa, 1 Oct. 1861, Boston PL.
367 'one who will fit so well' ET to GD, 1 Jan. 1862, *Dakyns*, p. 22.
   verses for Dufferin 'Helen's tower' AT to Dufferin, copy at TRC, L&S 2.280. See
   also L&S 2.313. Ricks 2.621.
   'it exposes him' ET to GD, 3 Oct. 1861, *Dakyns*, p. 14.
   AT worries (liver, building, poems) AT to Argyll, 10 Nov. 1861, TRC (copy), L&S
   2.282.
368 'Our beautiful views' ET to F. G. Tuckerman, 25 Jan. 1860, Harvard.
   buying land Two days earlier ET had told EL they had paid '£320 to prevent people
   from cutting off a great slice of sea-view'. Only one-third of an acre at the price she
   quotes, this may have been land adjoining the Terrace, a site for one house in the same
   lane as Dimbola, JMC's house.
   'More and more lodging houses' ET to TW, 10 April 1861, TRC.
   'very slovenly' ET to Lewis Fytche, 9 Dec. 1861, TRC.
   Isaac Merwood The reason for his lack of attention to the farm was, I think, that he

was the butcher at Middleton who appears in the 1861 Census, with his wife and five children, immediately after the Tennyson entry. Middleton is the part of Freshwater in which the farmhouse stands. L&S 2.72 identify him tentatively as [Jeremiah?] where the Feb. 1856 letter is wrongly dated [? Oct. 1853].

368 Charles Heard photographed by 'Lewis Carroll' on 27 July 1864 with the caption 'Hurd, Mr Tennyson's head man'.
'new source of interest' ET to EL, 10 Oct. 1861, TRC.
'get out more' ET to J. Simeon, 8 Oct. 1861, Syracuse.
'very niggard of manure' AT to R.J. Mann, 3 Feb. 1858, L&S 2.194.

369 cattle have 'only beet' obviously referring to what we call sugar beet, ET actually wrote 'beet-root', Journal, Sept. 1864, TRC.
'riding home on the farm horses' etc. Journal, 28 Oct. 1861.
AT had not met the Queen CT in *Dear and Honoured*, p. 30, guesses 'no doubt he was formally "presented"' in March 1851. CT, understandably, pays no attention to the report in *The Times*, 9 Aug. 1847, copied from the *Cork Constitution*, that the Queen and Prince had called on AT at Esher. *RBM* (pp. 309–10) does. See 'That tale about the Queen is pure moonshine,' AT to [A?] Bain, n.d., and note, L&S 3.454.
'more than one occasion' MBrad diary, 20 Jan. 1861, BL, records another occasion (after the much recorded 1856 expectation) when the Queen was at Freshwater fort and sent word she might call.
'Much soothed and pleased' *Dear and Honoured*, p. 67.

370 'her aching, bleeding heart' Princess Alice to AT, *Dear and Honoured*, p. 65.
valued by Prince Albert AT to Princess Alice, n.d., *Dear and Honoured*, p. 63, and 'he held them dear' in dedication to the Prince, Ricks 3.263.
'a woman to live and die for' Journal, May 1863, TRC.
'I would that I were dead' 'Mariana', Ricks 1.207.
'Enoch Arden' Ricks 2.625.
Eliot: 'no gift at all' and Arnold See Ricks *T*, p. 277, Eliot, *Selected Essays* p. 331.
'at the good moment' Fitz to ET, 5 July 1862, Terhune 2.443.
'the old wretch' Fitz to ET, [Feb. 1862?], Terhune 2.429.

371 'What! the great Poet' Journal, 8 Aug. 1862, TRC.
'Twenty earnest youths' Virginia Woolf, *Freshwater* ed. L.P. Ruotolo (1976), p. 8.
'gentleman squatting and peering' Journal, 20 April 1863, TRC, WA *Diary*, 4 Oct. 1863, p. 89.
HT's copy of ET's original journal in MS Mat. has details not in surviving epitome. And, typically, HT wrote 'A. finds' where ET had 'A. and I find'. HT wrote 'A. bids me come down' which ET alters to '*him*', proving how carefully she read the MS Mat. for the *Memoir*. As is usual, when two versions survive, it is impossible to tell which is closer to the destroyed original.
'in a magazine' 'anxious about the title' *The Reader*, see ET to AT, 25 and 26 June 1864, TRC.

372 'Dear, near and true' Ricks 2.683.
'loving Mrs T. singularly' and reply RB to Julia Wedgwood, 2 Sept. 1864, *RB and Julia Wedgwood Letters*, reply 9 Sept. 1864.
told W. White *Journals of Walter White* (1898), pp. 158–9, L&S 2.383.
'done what is right' ET to EL, 17 Feb. 1865, TRC. *Letters of EL* (1907).
'I found all that quiet part' EL to Fortescue, 19 Oct. 1864.

373 'good Mrs Cameron' ET to GD, 20 April 1862, *Dakyns*, p. 28.
'slender-stalked tea-rose' Ellen Terry in *The Story of my Life* (1908).
'never-ending oneness' ET to J. Simeon, 28 Aug. 1860, Syracuse.

373 'I think we can understand' ET to J. Simeon, 8 Oct. 1861, Syracuse.
'the first meeting' ET to GD, 6 Jan. 1862, *Dakyns*, p. 25.
'the lady had more money' AT to ET, [2 Nov. 1861], Yale, L&S 2.281.

374 'Poor Frank and Katie' ET to EL, 17 Feb. 1865, TRC.
'passionate tears' ET to GD, 22 Nov. 1886, *Dakyns*, p. 120.
GD's character ET to GD, 21 May 1862, *Dakyns*, p. 37.
'They are not his pupils' Journal, 25 April 1862, TRC, and to GD, 20 April 1862, *Dakyns*, p. 28.

375 'To whom has one to apply' Francis Atkinson to GD, [July 1862], *Dakyns*, p. 43.
RBM (p. 437) extrapolates from this one occasion the suggestion that it was a regular occurrence for ET to forget to pay the tutors. The tutors were also not all recent graduates; both Wilson and Lipscomb were in their late thirties. It is also not true to say that 'most of them left before their time.'
'Lionel flies to the Piano' ET to GD, [June 1862], *Dakyns*, p. 39.
'rather rough colts' Atkinson to GD, 20 May [1863], *Dakyns*, p. 67.
'share his thoughts' ET to TW, 9 Feb. 1863, TRC.
'the Noble Poet' Atkinson to GD, [July 1862], *Dakyns*, p. 44.
'turned quite rebellious' ET to BJ, 12 May 1863, Balliol.
'their really serious faults' not 'backed up' Atkinson to GD, 5 May 1863, *Dakyns*, p. 61.

376 'It was a very difficult bargain' Quotation by S.D. Collingwood of CLD's now missing diary for April 1862 in his biography of CLD.
cut himself 'a good deep cut' CLD to HT, 23 Jan. 1862, *Dakyns*, p. 23.
'great friends' ET to EL, 9 Oct. 1860, TRC.
riding the boys' pony ET to MGa, 5 Dec. 1862, Boston PL.

377 scolding ET BJ to ET, 12 May 1862, TRC.
Patmores, EP's death Champneys 1.184–6, L&S 2.312 and 3.210.

378 written to Woolner: 'It is a terrible thing for him indeed' ET to TW, 10 July 1862, Bodleian.

379 'do something for the Poles' ET to GD, 24 Feb. 1863, *Dakyns*, p. 59.
'as our great financier' AT to WEG, 30 Oct. 1862, BL, L&S 2.317.
'Political Economy can allow' BJ, *Memoir* 2.467.
ET's proposals BL (Gladstone papers).

380 annuity tables in *The Times* 4 March 1865.
'set all the bells ringing' ET to TW, 28 March 1865, TRC.

381 'shake my two boys by the hand' *Memoir* 1.490.
'I found myself on my knee' ET to Eliza T, 11 May 1863, TRC.
Hallam's account as a boy TRC.

382 Effie Ruskin on Victoria 21 June 1850.
'I never felt it so easy' ET to BJ, 12 May 1863, Balliol.
Queen Victoria's diary 9 May 1863, *Dear and Honoured*, p. 79.

383 'good for her to see people' BJ to ET, 28 May 1863, TRC.
'a luncheon the Tennysons gave' *Anne Gilchrist*, p. 169.
'Things get so repeated' ET to HS and AW, Feb. 1867, TRC.
'never-ending oneness' ET to J. Simeon, 28 Aug. 1860, Syracuse.
'a remarkable woman' ET to Eliza T, 11 May 1863, TRC.

384 'She spoke a little' Jane Franklin diary, 19 July 1863, SPRI.
talk of classic metres MBrad diary, Dec. 1863 and Jan. 1864, BL, WA *Diary*, 27–28 Dec. 1863, pp. 93–5 (also describing boys).

386 'baby-soles' 'Aylmer's Field' Ricks 2.664, l. 186.

386 Edith Bradley's memories *A Child's Recollections*.
387 'the anomaly of high souled . . .' EL diary, 17 Oct. 1864, Harvard.
     'a jolly woman' Fitz to W.F. Pollock, Dec. 1864, Terhune 2.538.
     Rejlander's visit In Journal, 1 May 1863, ET had already seen some of the
     photographs: 'Lionel's very fine'. None survives of him alone from this batch.
     'for faithful portraits' Journal, 9 Sept. 1868, TRC.
388 'like them but not their very selves' Journal, 14 Oct. 1865, TRC.
     JMC's photograph of boys together See Wheatcroft, p. 79.
     'No woman should be photographed' *Three Freshwater Friends* quoted in Brian
     Hinton, *Immortal Faces*, p. 94.
     Watts's portrait See Plate section. Journal, Nov. 1862, GFW to ET, n.d., TRC.
     comments, Argylls, Lady Grant Journal, 24 June 1863, TRC.
     'a subtle alchemist' ET to GFW, 24 June 1863, Virginia.
     'unliker than Watts' ELL to ET, 5 May 1864, TRC. One is reminded of Mary G's
     story of GFW's portrait of WEG 'because he was Watts everyone raved', until Mary
     herself said 'It's awful', Mary G, *Diaries and Letters*, p. 491.
389 Garibaldi's visit *Memoir* 2.1–4, Journal, April 1864, *Illustrated London News*, etc.
     Letters at TRC.
     'expected to see a hero' AT to Argyll, May 1864, L&S 2.364.
390 'given your stories well' ET to TW, 11 July 1864, TRC. TW's marriage to Alice
     Waugh 6 Sept. 1864.
391 sad summer ET to GD, 2 Sept. 1863, *Dakyns*, p. 70; ET to W.H. Thompson, 9 Dec.
     1863, TRC; ET to MGa, 14 Aug. 1863, Boston PL. At Harrogate 30 July–10 Sept.
     'If you wish to kill yourself' *Memoir* 1.512.
     'your evermore delight' HT to T. Wilson, [April 1866], TRC.
392 French holiday LT diary at TRC as well as Journal. Letter to FP in Mat. 2. HT to GD,
     19 April [1865], *Dakyns*, p. 85.
393 sal volatile used as smelling salts, 'a restorative against faintness'.
     'and we know' ET would have had no idea, for instance, of JAS's involvement in Dr
     Vaughan's resignation from Harrow five years before – succeeded by Montagu Butler.
     Even JAS's sister Charlotte (to whom GD was at this time trying to pay some
     attention) did not know. It was through GD that JAS first met 'Norman', the boy who
     came to obsess him. He was one of GD's pupils at Clifton. In his *Memoirs*, pp. 148–9
     JAS calls GD 'masculine to the backbone'. He was not as 'pained and terrified' by
     JAS's homosexuality as Henry Sidgwick was; they were very close friends and shared
     a great deal. HT remained devoted to GD. In 1910 he called him 'the welcomest of all
     men'. *Dakyns*, p. 275. See also Phyllis Grosskurth, *John Addington Symonds* (1964),
     p. 40 (skeletons) and p. 77.
394 'I have been today to Farringford' JAS to GD, 23 Nov. 1864, 'We found Mrs
     Tennyson' JAS to Charlotte Symonds, 24 Nov. 1864, *Letters of JAS*, ed. Schueller
     and Peters (1967), p. 510–1.
395 'they want more discipline' BJ to ET, May 1863, TRC.
     'I was ill last night' HT to GD, 17 April 1862, *Dakyns*, p. 27.
     'too old for the matriarchal' BJ to ET, 14 July 1863, TRC.
     Gladstone's concern AT to ET, [12 Feb. 1864], Mat. 2.393–4, L&S 2.352–3, and AT
     to ET, [23 Nov. 1864], TRC, L&S 2.384.
396 'We put ourselves in his hands' ET to EL, 14 July 1863, TRC.
     'sending him to a Mr Paul' Mrs Henry Taylor to ET, 2 Aug. 1864, Yale.
     'the end of this month' C. Kegan Paul to ET, 14 Oct. 1864, Yale.

396 'come in their long hair' AT to Duchess of Argyll, 26 Dec. 1864, TRC, L&S 2.388.
'Mr Paul does not wish' ET to MGa, 26 Oct. 1864, Boston PL.
'Ally says had he known' ET to TW, 20 March 1865, TRC.
Watts – without fee – Watts, who had heard of the Tennysons' wish from a letter from JMC to her sister Mrs Prinsep wrote to ET 'the price shall be the pride I shall feel in giving pleasure to so great a man'. GFW to ET, 25 Feb. 1865, Yale.

397 'crossing the water' diary of A.J. Munby, 23 May 1865, Trinity. Munby apparently saw the Tennysons on the 4.30 boat from Yarmouth to Lymington on 23 May. Both Journal and *Memoir* 2.23 say they crossed on 22 May, but a letter from ET to J.S. Blackie (2 Dec. 1865, Nat. Lib. of Scotland, L&S 2.411) says the boys began near Wimborne on 24 May. They presumably stayed night of the 23rd in Wimborne, visited the Minster next morning before going to the school. ET recorded the monument of Margaret Beaufort 'with her hand in her husband's'. The green journal has most of a page missing at this point and it is not in MS Mat. – HT presumably thinking it too intimate.

CHAPTER 12 Searching for escape

398 'talking of "Devil's Jumps"' ET to MGa, [Dec. 1864], Boston PL, L&S 2.389.
ninety acres etc. scenery splendid *Journals of Walter White*, p. 159, and AT to ET, [28 Nov. 1864], Yale, L&S 2.386 ('What an address', MS Mat.).
encouraging letter A. Gilchrist to ET, 11 Dec. 1864, TRC.

399 'the Laureate is rather tired' AG to W. Haines, 20 Nov. 1864, *Anne Gilchrist*, p. 152.
'threatened with villas' ET to EL, 17 Feb. 1865, TRC.
'a sentry at *my* gates' ET to HS and AW, 16 Feb. 1867, TRC, *Dear and Honoured*, p. 84. ET told the story to the boys too. See also WA *Diary*, 18 Feb. 1867, p. 150.
'for the sake of *IM*' AG to W. Haines, 24 July 1864, *Anne Gilchrist*, p. 150.
'His poems are worthless' AT in *Mangles*, 25 Aug. 1871, p. 96.
'How you would have loved him' BW-C, *London Mercury* v., 1921–2, *Interviews*, p. 113.
'more delicate' MBrad diary, 14 Jan. 1865, BL.

400 rejected BJ's idea BJ to FN, *Jowett*, pp. 336–7.
'all night' fishing HT's schoolboy handwriting is so terrible, I may have misread 'all right', HT to ET, 28 May [1865], TRC.
'so new a life' C.K. Paul, 29 May 1865, TRC.

402 'Feel her spirit etc.' LTT diary, Feb. 1865, TRC.
'All her sons' CR to HDR, 30 March ?1877, Rawnsley papers.
'the departure' AT to ET, [27 Feb. 1865], TRC, L&S 2.394.
'*pretty* cheerful' AT to ET, 25 Feb. 1865, *Memoir* 2.18, L&S 2.393.
'much depressed' EL reporting to Fortescue, 21 April 1865, after ET to EL, 19 April 1865, TRC.
'How soon did the sisters' CTT to Lewis Fytche, 27 March 1865, TRC.
'a delightful proof' *Glimpses*, p. 14. Agnes quoting ET.
'nonsense and ignorance' G. Eliot, Journal, 23 April 1877, particularly 'on vivisection'.
'a dear noble creature' ET to GD, 14 Oct. 1865, *Dakyns*, p. 91.

403 'She settles here' AT to Viscountess Boyne, 8 Nov. 1865, L&S 2.408.
'such heavy shocks' MT to Lewis Fytche, 12 May 1865, TRC.
'so nervous' ET to AT, 15 June 1870, TRC.
'sonorous roar' LT to ET, May 1869, TRC.

403 'Uncle Toby' LT's journal, 26 Nov. 1884, TRC, CT in *Background*, p. 169 rewrites this, leaving out 'idiocy'.

MT stories from Eustace Jesse's scrapbook, TRC. *Background*, p. 169.

'blowing up' his sister 'Relations step in' ATR to Millais, in *Thackeray's Daughter* p. 115. *Mangles* also records AT's impatience with his sisters.

'Poor Aunt Tilly' ET to HT, 2 Nov. 1869, TRC.

'always complaining' ET to LTT, 25 Jan. 1867, TRC.

origins of Norse story ET to J. M. Ludlow, 1 Nov. 1865, CUL. ET to GD, 14 Oct. 1865, *Dakyns*, p. 91.

404 'So here she goes' ETJ to AT, n.d. [1875], Yale.

'a deeper hiding' AT of Mary Bourne's death to Louis T. d'Eyncourt, n.d., L&S 2.363.

'the most morbid' *CTAT*, p. 199.

'HURRAH AUNTY NANNY' ET to AW, 13 July 1863, TRC.

Anne lately at Farringford Jane Franklin diary, 19 July 1863, SPRI.

405 'continually thinking' ET to AW, 15 Oct. 1863, TRC.

Aubrey House/Weld problems ET to MGa, 4 Feb., 7 March, 26 July 1864, Boston PL.

406 'strongly against Aubrey' ET to AT, 26 June 1864, TRC.

selling Aubrey ET to EL, 19 June 1866, TRC.

'better than the Milford set' Agnes to LT, 5 Sept. 1866, TRC.

wringing AT's hand etc. ET to HT, 8 June 1869, TRC, Journal, 23 July 1865.

407 1865 holiday ET to GD, 14 Oct. 1865, *Dakyns*, p. 91; Journal and *Memoir* 2.24–7 (and MS Mat.) and ET to TW, 16 Sept. 1865, TRC.

409 'trampling over my grounds' AT to Lewis Fytche, 17 June 1865, TRC, L&S 2.400.

'The place is cockney' AT to Argyll, 3 Oct. 1859, L&S 2.244.

'cockney raptures' AHH to ETJ, 26 May 1832, Kolb, p. 582.

Locker a Cockney FLo, *My Confidences*, p. 410.

arbutus and strawberry AT to Mary Rawnsley (of 'a great Editor'), Nov. 1849, L&S 3.460.

rooks not nightingales from Laura Troubridge, *Memories and Reflections* (1925).

410 servants dancing at night on the Downs A.J. Munby diary, 23 May 1865 (under 2 June), Trinity.

'receiving the Queen' ET to HS and AW, 18 Sept. 1865, TRC.

Queen Emma's visit Journal; *Glimpses*, p. 100; Jane Franklin diary, July 1865 on, SPRI; Jane Franklin to ET, 5 Oct. 1865, Yale; *Memoir* 2.27–8; ET to Annie Fields, 5 Oct. 1865, Huntington.

'amatory tenderness' *The Times*, 28 Nov. 1851, 'The Poetry of Sorrow'.

412 'ludicrous foreshadowings' Jane Franklin diary quoting letter from ET, 5 Oct. 1865.

'caught that morning' AT to ET, [5 Dec. 1865], TRC, L&S 2.412.

'his way is scarcely ours' ET to HS and AW, 18 Sept. 1865, TRC.

'idleness is the root of all evil' ET to HT and LT, 9 Nov. 1865, TRC. Boys' letters at TRC.

413 Lionel stammering AT to ET, [6 Dec. 1865], TRC, L&S 2.413. I can find no evidence that Lionel was bullied at Paul's, as *RBM* suggests (p. 465). The stammering (which may have been the result of Paul's methods) was certainly one reason for his withdrawal. *RBM* suggests (p. 456) that he stammered *before* he went to Paul's.

414 plans for Lionel to go to Bristol see *Dakyns*, pp. 94–8.

415 'Get me into Marlborough this Easter' Pinion (p. 109) is misled by Hoge *J*, p. 241.

Marlborough may not be a slip of ET's. The boy could have gone for an interview; he was definitely still at Paul's in the first term of 1866.

415 'deep and real' C.K. Paul to ET, 13 March 1866, TRC.
'Gladstone and Browning' In the epitome of the Journal, ET wrote at the end of Feb., 'Lionel's two wishes for London were that he might see Mr Browning and Mr Gladstone.' Hallam wrote this same wish in a letter from Paul's at the time; it seems likely it was primarily *his* wish.
'a bad influenza' ET to MGa, 1 May 1866, Boston PL.
'the waving of red flags' AT to Duchess of Argyll, 26 Dec. 1863, TRC, L&S 2.346.

416 'just what she was' RB to Isa Blagden, 19 Feb. 1866, *Life and Letters of RB*, p. 273.
Jowett on RB BJ to FN, 6 April 1866, Balliol.
'most eloquently' ET to HS and AW, 22 Feb. 1866, TRC.
Eyre case; evening at TW's house JAS's description, *Century Magazine*, May 1893, L&S 2.415. Edwin Hodder, *The Life of a Century* (1901), says 'the defence of Eyre' was 'led by such men as Carlyle, Ruskin, Tennyson and Kingsley,' a curious assessment.

417 'tipsy' talk 'tipsy' was the word AT used himself of someone who had had too much to drink. *Mangles*, Aug. 1870, p. 30.
'quarrelling about Eyre' BJ to FN, 6 April 1866, TRC.

418 'Lucretius' ET wrote to Fields, T's US publisher on 4 March 1868 saying '"Lucretius" will be sent by the next mail tho' it is not to be published until May.' Virginia. 'Lucretius' in E's hand with a few corrections by AT at Yale.
'Do bundle the Lushingtons out' HT to ET, 26 Sept. 1866, TRC.
'Remember to send for me' 'I take my book' AT to ET, 29 May 1866, TRC.
'another sort of illness' ET to MGa, 1 May 1866, Boston PL.
'a most gentle lady' 30 June–1 July 1866, Trench in Mat. 6.56.

419 AT's behaviour MBrad diary, 3 May 1866, BL; Holman Hunt, *Memoirs* 2.168.
keeping cloak on ET to HS and AW, 22 Feb. 1866, TRC.
bunch of grapes *Mangles*, 3 Sept. 1871, p. 102.

420 not smoking and drinking TW to ET, 23 Sept. 1860, *Memoir* 1.465.
'violent' EL diary, 27 Feb. 1869, Harvard.
'a look in his face' MBrad diary, 30 Dec. [1863], BL, L&S 2.349.
'ludicrous things' WA *Diary*, 22 Nov. 1866, p. 146.
pulling down hair MS Mat., *Memoir* 2.85. But is it HT's 'take'? It could be ET's.
'not chipped to the smooth pattern' ATR *Records*, p. 60.
'One evening at Farringford' J. Comyns Carr, *Some Eminent Victorians* (1908). JCC says he was seventeen, which would make the year 1866.

421 'received with particular kindness' A.M. Brookfield, *Annals of a Chequered Life* (1930). AMB was born in 1853.

422 'a novel of Mrs Braddon's' M.E. Braddon (1837–1915) was at this time notorious as the author of *Lady Audley's Secret* and other 'inventive, lurid novels', as the *Oxford Companion* puts it. She was attacked for corrupting young minds, but had many admirers.
'making endless Madonnas' ET to EL, 17 Feb. 1865, TRC.
Andrews as model ET to HT and LT, Oct. 1865, TRC.

423 'sure to do well' T's visit MB to ET, [May 1866], TRC, and MBrad diary, BL.
parting with Lionel Journal and ET to LT, 27 Aug. 1866, TRC. Other letters to and from boys all at TRC.

425 'an elixir for me' ET to MGa, 21 Dec. 1865, Boston PL.
'He looks older' *Anne Gilchrist* pp. 161–5.

426 'A grand view' Journal, Sept. 1866, TRC.
'back in delightful home' Journal, 15 Nov. 1866, TRC.
'I wish it to be kept secret' AT to FP, 23 March 1867, L&S 2.456. The address was Greyshott, Headley, Liphook, Hants. The original building no longer exists, but walks in the area are well worth taking.

427 'doing nothing' BJ to FN, Jan. 1867, Balliol.
going to Rome ET to TW, 21 and 23 Dec. 1866, TRC.
'his uncertainty' 'To read the Scriptures' WA Diary, 1–3 Feb. 1867, pp. 149–50.
Bayard Taylor's visit Sadly, Taylor's letter to E. C. Stedman, on which this passage is based, was seen by a journalist who used it. AT told Fields furiously that BT 'saw in me not a man but a paragraph'. L&S 2.454 and 514.
making George Eliot weep Journal, 31 Aug. 1871, TRC, L&S 3.12.

428 Lionel ill at Ore House ET to LT, 9 Oct. 1866, TRC.
Hallam's illness ET's letters to LT, HS, LTT, AW and Journal, all at TRC; MBrad diary, BL; ET to J. Simeon, March 1867, Syracuse.

430 'It's no good thinking' ET to HT, 14–16 Feb. 1871, TRC.

432 'much improved in speech' ET to MGa, 10 June 1867, Boston PL.
'We must not complain' ET reports HT's words to EL, 22 Feb. 1871, TRC.

433 Hallam and the washing up ET to HS and LTT, 22 May 1867, TRC.
'if he had the solitude' JMC to J. Simeon, 27 April 1868, Syracuse.
'an inspired person' BJ to ET, 23 May 1868, TRC.
'not without regret' BJ to FN, 22 June 1867, Balliol.

434 AT snubs the boys EL diary, 30 Sept. 1867, Harvard.
'impossible not to like him' R. Jebb, Life and Letters, pp. 93–4, L&S 2.481.
'He did not say' G. Grove to Bradley, 8 Jan. 1868, L&S 2.475.

435 'Lucretius' Ricks 2.708.
'She says does not think it will shock' AT to G. Grove, [17 Jan. 1868], L&S 2.480.
describing Anne Gilchrist Journal, Nov. 1866; ET to HS and AW, 15 May 1867.
'comfortable and cheerful' AG to W. Haines, Anne Gilchrist, p. 169.
'I must tell you about Greenhill' ET to HS, LTT, AW 12 June 1867, copy TRC.
position of Greenhill 'When Emily set out from Greyshott Farm in June 1867 in the "basket-carriage", she would have descended 300 feet to pick up Anne Gilchrist at Brookbank and then reascended the same amount to get to Greenhill – although the horizontal distance travelled would be no more than three miles,' Dr R.W. Trotter to me 14 Dec. 1994. On 10 July 1871 ET told AT that a surveyor 'measuring heights says that our house is 800 feet above the sea, 'the top of the down just above us more than a thousand feet.'

436 'the sea distinctly' 'a poet to live' AG to W. Haines, 7 July 1867, Anne Gilchrist, p. 171.
Surrey, Sussex Aldworth is just on the Sussex side of the county boundary, with Haslemere its post town. It was unnecessary for Philip Collins to be alarmed by L&S's 'mistake' in locating Aldworth in Surrey (his important review THES, 23 April 1982), when they had read dozens of letters headed Aldworth, Haslemere, Surrey.
'a great river looping' 'years of negotiation' Knowles, T and his Friends, p. 248.
'a paper found after his death' deposited by his biographer Priscilla Metcalf at TRC.

437 meeting at Haslemere station T and his Friends, p. 247. It may not have been entirely chance. See Metcalf, pp. 199–200.
JK's own account T and his Friends, pp. 247–51.
a more complex story ET to TW, 21 and 23 July 1867, TRC.

437 'I made a plan' Mat. at TRC has 'Mr Knowles . . . looked at our sketch and plans and took them home to put them in "working form", as he said.'

438 'This fellow makes me' *Mangles*, Aug. 1870, p. 29.
'He is the cleverest man' ET to Welds, 15 Feb. 1893, TRC.
'His active nature . . .' Journal, 11 Nov. 1871, TRC, *Memoir* 2.110.
'designed by Lady Tennyson' e.g. in *Memories and Memorials of William McCabe* 2. 349–50, L&S 3.299.

440 'tile or slate' Fitz to ET, 3 Nov. 1868, Terhune 3.108.
'two of the prettiest places' BJ to HT in HT diary, 27 Jan. 1889, L&S 3.391.
'two more delightful homes' ET to AT, Journal, Dec. 1870, TRC.
'like cannon balls' WA to C. [Jebb], 17 Dec. 1872, *Dearest Love to All*, p. 90.
Green Hill LT still calls it Greenhill in May 1870.
If Grandpapa die HT to ET, [Sept. 1867], TRC.

441 Louisa's letter to a friend LTT to Richard Wilton, 10 Nov. 1878, TRC.
Henry Sellwood's death Journal and ET to GD, 20 Jan. 1868, *Dakyns*, p. 107; ET to MGa, 22 Nov. 1867, Boston PL; ET to J. Simeon, 28 Sept. 1867, Syracuse; ET to LTT and AW, 28 Sept. 1867, TRC.
'Speak to Him thou' 'The Higher Pantheism', Ricks 2.705.

442 Swinburne's parody 'The Higher Pantheism in a Nutshell' in *The Heptalogia* (1880).
'Body and spirit are twins: God only knows which is which. The Soul squats down in the flesh, like a tinker drunk in a ditch.'
'What I said in "The Princess"' MBrad diary, 13 Jan. 1870, BL.

443 'We are all at your command' ET to Longfellow, 17 July 1868, Harvard.
'a very lovely and attractive lady' Anne Longfellow Pierce, 16 July 1868, L&S 2.495.
'angelic Mrs Tennyson' Tiny Cotton to Agnes Jones, 18 July 1868, L&S 2.497.
Mary Ryan's wedding Journal, 1 Aug. 1867; ET to HS and AW, 15 Aug. 1867, TRC; ET to J. Simmons, 1 Aug. 1867, Haslemere Museum.

445 Lionel's grandson at Eton CT in *Stars and Markets*, p. 11, reporting his eldest son in 1925.
'Well, it is no use pining for the past.' ET to AT, 22 Nov. 1868. TRC.

CHAPTER 13 'Beset by work of many kinds'

446 'doubly provoking' ET to LT, 25 Sept. 1868, TRC.
'confounded photographs' WA *Diary*, 11 Aug. 1868, p. 185.
'the most overworked person' BJ to ET, 10 Nov. 1868, p. 185.
'to have improved them' AT to Francisque Michel, L&S 2.504.

447 'perseverance' LT to ET and AT, 26 May 1870, TRC.
fires to pass through MBrad to ET, 3 Oct. 1868, TRC.
'Money runs away' LT to ET and AT, 23 Oct. 1868, TRC.
'being of a careless nature' LT to ET and AT, 16 Oct. 1868, TRC.
'Do take care' LT to ET, 3 Dec. 1868, TRC.

448 Horatio looks better ET to EL, 10 Nov. 1868, TRC.
'the smallness and egotism' EL diary, Nov./Dec. 1868, Harvard.
'little possibility of quiet' ET to AT, 22 Nov. 1868, TRC.
'Do not worry' HT to ET, Nov. 1868, TRC.
'let other people' LT to ET, 2 Dec. 1868, TRC.
'San Graal' ET to EL, 18 May 1869, TRC.
scarcely knows what she does ET to EL, 10 Nov. 1868, TRC.

449 'thanks to an embrocation' ET to Welds, 20 Dec. 1868, TRC.

449 Emily Lushington's death ELL to ET and AT, 26 Dec. 1868, TRC.
450 'Is it not a blessing' ET to EL, 6 Feb. 1869, TRC.
'the scene of so much sorrow' ET to Welds, 23 Jan. 1869, TRC.
'so many strong individualities' ET to HT, 18 May 1869, TRC.
'As to Aunty Nanny' LT to ET, 21 May 1869, TRC. Lionel's arithmetic seems a little strange but he makes his point.
451 'quick and sharp' ET to HT, 22 May 1874, TRC.
'in opposing' ET to HT, 28 Sept. 1869, TRC.
'take porter and port' ET to Agnes, 6 April 1865, TRC.
Mrs Cameron in a similar state ET to AW, 6 Feb. 1865, TRC.
send business papers ET to AW, Jan. 1868, TRC. AW saw Weld's last book *Notes on Burgundy* (left in a shorthand MS) through the press. Her preface is dated 17 July 1869. It is dedicated to CTT.
452 reporting a headache LT to ET etc. 5 Feb. 1869, TRC.
453 taxation ideas ET to WEG, 14 Feb. 1869, BL.
a prompt reply WEG to ET, 16 Feb. 1869, TRC; *Memoir* 2.63.
'half dead of fatigue' AT to FLo, May 1869, Harvard; L&S 2.522.
454 'an immense contempt' 'donkey drawing-room' CT, *Stars and Markets*, p. 33.
455 on Stenton Eardley ET to J. Simeon, 4 June 1869, Syracuse.
AT 'has not complained' FLo to ET, 2 July 1869, Yale.
'18 or 20 souls' ET to EL, 29 July 1869, TRC.
'With thy leave' ET to AT, 16 June 1869, TRC.
456 'everybody a genius' ATR to Walter Senior, [Easter 1865], *Letters of ATR*, ed. Hester Ritchie (1924)., p. 126. ATR really got to know ET in Oct. 1868 when she first stayed overnight at Farringford. 'She is much much nicer than I used to think her and younger.' ATR to Minny, n.d. [Oct. 1868], Eton.
agree in our notions ET to LT, 21 Oct. 1868, TRC.
'this little dream' ATR to G. M. Smith, n.d., *Letters of ATR*, p. 133.
'this pitiable class' Journal, 21 Oct. 1868; 'comical lines' Journal, 25 Oct. 1868. These are not known to Ricks and may have been destroyed.
'immoral wish' FLu to ET, 20 June 1856, TRC.
457 'metaphysical speculations' e.g. Journal, 16 May 1873, TRC.
Christ's example e.g. ET to HT, 21 March 1871, 19 Nov. 1872, TRC.
'entirely suits his father' ET to EL, 22 Feb. 1871, TRC.
458 helping with HT's essays e.g. 16 Feb. 1871, ET to HT, 31 March 1871, TRC.
'a perennial stream' AT to FLo, 6 Aug. 1869, L&S 2.530.
'innocent sight' ET to HT, 6 June 1870, TRC.
'rather compunctious' AT had no scruples about also digging up common land on Blackdown ('patches of heath and heather') to cover bare patches in his own grounds. *Mangles*, p. 92.
459 planted trees ET's list of what they planted with cypresses and 'other spiral trees' – 'Lambertiana, Douglas, Nobilis, Grandis, Insignis, Smithiana and Cedars.' TRC.
boys' reading n.d., TRC.
on Darwin ET to HT, 14 March 1871, TRC.
Evolution and the ant WA *Diary*, 6 Nov. 1885, p. 343.
believed in Darwin's theory *Mangles*, 28 March 1871, p. 63.
'great relief' 'terrace squints' ET to HT, 28 Sept. and 22 Oct. 1869, TRC.
460 General John Yaldwyn 1803–79; the Yaldwyn family had for centuries owned the entire Blackdown estate, over 1300 acres. See J.O. Randell, *Yaldwyn of the Golden Spurs* (1980).

460 on spiritualism and ET and AT Journal, 19 Oct. 1869, TRC; FT to MBro, 21 March
1872, 8 Jan. 1875; MBro to FT, 1 Oct. 1874, 13 Jan. 1875, 6 Feb. 1876, 22 July
1883, 19 Oct. 1892. 'All my friends . . .' MBro to FT, 1 Oct. 1874. All letters at Lilly.
Mangles, 25 Aug. 1871, pp. 91, 93; 30 Oct. 1872, p. 132.

461 'Papa does not settle' ET to HT, 1 July 1870, TRC.
'Admirably they have worked' the new piano Tilly ET to AT, 20 June 1870, TRC.
'that beast the Builder' *Mangles*, 7 June 1871, p. 81.

462 'growing weary of Blackdown' *Mangles*, 28 Oct. 1872, p. 128.
'Aldworth doesn't do' Fitz to ET, [Nov. 1873], Terhune 3.456.
'comfort, every discomfort' Milnes to his wife, 30 July ?, L&S 3.11.
'top of a mountain' AT to WEG, 12 Aug. 1869, BL.
overpowering at times FP journal, 14 Oct. 1871, *Palgrave*, p. 135.
'before we built here' ET to HT, 10 Dec. 1869.
'I must have nooks' *Mangles*, 4 Sept. 1870, p. 35.
'I like a cock and a hen' ATR *Letters*, p. 147.

463 'Underneath that soft' AG to William Rossetti, *Anne Gilchrist* pp. 211-2. The text as
published (in ET's lifetime) omits 'Poet Laureate's' and their names.
'that tormenting stream' Walt Whitman, AG's great hero, inevitably thought it was
deep male companionship AT needed. 'With a personality such as his, what a pity not
to give himself to men.' *Anne Gilchrist*, p. 23.
'return hospitalities' ET to HT, 1 Nov. 1872, TRC.

464 T's diet Journal, 1 Sept. 1868, 19 Feb. 1871, TRC; *Mangles*, 29 March 1871, p. 67.
'And once for ten long weeks' Ricks 3.106, l. 14 on.
simplicity e.g. BW-C, *London Mercury* v., 1921-2, p. 148. 'exceedingly
simple' Longfellow's sister, L&S 2.496.
'the happiest state' MBrad diary, 1 Jan. 1870, BL; Mat. 2.118 has 'mood' for 'state'.
In *Memoir* 2.93 HT renders this 'My father was extraordinarily happy now.'
'tired of guests' ET to HT, 21 Oct. 1870, TRC.

465 attacked his sister *Mangles*, Aug. 1870, p. 30.
'the most wonderful woman' James Knowles in the *Nineteenth Century* xxxiii Jan.
1893, *not* included in N. Page's reprint in *Interviews*.
velvets fade *Mangles*, 15 Sept. 1870, p. 52. Knies identifies the sister as ETJ but she
left on 30 Aug.
Leaves of Grass Mangles, 25 Aug. 1871, p. 96.
'large and lovable' AT to Whitman, 12 July 1871, L&S 3.9.
'I never read' *Letters of Emily Dickinson*, 25 April 1862.
language of sisters *Mangles*, 20 Sept. 1870, pp. 59-60.

466 Villa Emily Noakes, *Edward Lear*, p. 249.
Lear's first visit to Aldworth EL diary, Sept. 1869, Harvard; and EL to Simeon, 27
Oct. 1869, Syracuse.
buying pictures The following June AT bought from TW 'pictures for the dining
room' apparently without anguish. AT to ET, 18 June 1870, TRC; L&S 2.550.
Madame D'Arblay Fanny Burney's real name.

467 'comeatable' AT to JS, 19 Jan. 1870, TRC; L&S 2.540.
ringing and no one coming AT to ET, 21 March 1870, TRC; L&S 2.544.
supplying Albert Mansions ET to AT, 16 March, 22 March, 25 March 1870, TRC.

468 Pistol, 'the foul-mouth'dst rogue' 2 *Henry IV*, II. iv. 77-8. AT to FLo, n.d. ; L&S
2.513.
Holy Grail and *Idylls* ET to HT, 5 Nov. 1869, TRC.
£4,300 AT to Messrs Strachan, 31 Dec. 1868; L&S 2.512.

469   rap over the knuckles ET to CLD, [*c.* 5 March 1870], Yale; L&S 2.543. Ricks 2.697.
     'Make a stand' ET to AT, 20 Nov. 1868, TRC. 'The Last Tournament' appeared in
     the *Contemporary Review* in Dec. 1871.
     'talking machines' 'clatter' from one of ET's own stories, TRC.
     'in the smallest degree' 'seeing people' ET to AT, 14 June 1870, TRC.
     'refreshed by the society' ET to AT, 16 March 1870, TRC.
     people to call on List at TRC, n.d., L&S date it *c.* 15 Feb. 1873. Could be earlier.
     'rusty' in Isle of Wight *The Life and Work of Thomas Hardy*, ed. Millgate (1984) p.
     141.
     'distressingly plain' MBrad's description of Louisa Simeon, diary, Jan. 1868, BL.
470   'Let me come' 'being in bed' ET to AT, 15 and 17 July 1870, TRC. Emily's numerous
     surviving letters from this summer, referring to AT's, give a good indication that many
     of his were destroyed.
     'tinting of cornice' 'home is not home' ET to AT, 19 and 20 July 1870, TRC.
     'overdone in many ways' MBrad to ET, 24 July 1870, TRC.
     'He has seen a homeopath' LT to GD, 10 Oct. [1870], *Dakyns*, p. 110.
471   'the happiest time' ET to HT, 25 Oct. 1870, TRC.
     'closest friend' To the widow, AT said, 27 June 1870, L&S 2.551, Simeon was
     'the only man on earth . . . to whom I could, and have more than once opened my
     heart.' Others claimed similar hours of such intimacy, including Alfred Gatty.
     'Such is modern life' ET to LT, 1 June 1870, TRC.
     'much more languid' ET to EL, 22 Feb. 1871, TRC.
     'what I hear about Jack' Sir John Barrington Simeon (1850–1909) would himself be
     an MP 1895–1906.
472   AT at Dickens's funeral See also *T and his Friends*, p. 253.
     'talk to people' ET to AT, 29 March 1870, TRC.
     deeply loving natures ET to EL, 22 Feb. 1871, TRC.
     'I do love that boy' ET to HT, 17 Feb. 1871, reporting Mrs Grosvenor Hood.
     'This long break' ET to AT, 29 March 1870, TRC.
473   'blown out with glory' AT to W.H. Thompson, *c.* 15 Jan. 1868, Trinity; L&S 2.477.
     'easily satisfied' Arthur Bradley, satisfying them not long after his mother had
     confided in ET her despair not only of his algebra, but of his intellect. See A.G.
     Bradley, *When Squires and Farmers Thrived* (1927).
     'grow up stronger' ET to HT, 21 March 1871.
474   'codifying' 'originality' ET to HT, 15 Nov. 1872, TRC.
     'mass of moth's eggs' ET to HT, 13 Dec. 1870, TRC.
     'grown no bigger' AT to J.R. Thompson, 25 March 1871, L&S 3.3.
     on Dimbola ET to HT, 21 Feb. 1871, TRC.
475   Kennet's estimate This is at Virginia: £386.17.4. Contract dated 14 March, the whole
     to be completed 'to the entire satisfaction of Mr Waterhouse'.
     Kennet's progress ET to HT, 16 May 1871, TRC. The plaster was still not dry when
     they returned in Dec. ET observed AT 'drying places where the wet showed with a hot
     poker' Journal, 11 Dec. 1871, TRC.
     'political' comments ET to HT, 21 Feb., 28 Feb., 10 March, 19 May 1871; BJ to ET,
     10 March 1871, TRC.
476   write to thank ET to I. Mangles, 7 Apr. 1871 (with note from AT), Ohio.
     packed only socks how clever his wife *Mangles*, 29 March 1871, pp. 71–2.
477   'Miss Weld's illness' BJ to ET, 3 April 1871; ET to HT, 6 April 1871; ET to AT, 19
     March 1870, TRC. With hindsight in Journal: 'The last day poor Agnes comes here I
     think before her dreadful illness,' 21 Dec. 1871, TRC. Many references in March

1872; 'paralysis' 1 Oct. 1872. AT to Whitman, not naming Agnes, [8 July 1874], L&S 3.80; walking with AT 'most days', ET to LTT, 7 March 1874, TRC.

478 Agnes on AT Argyll to ET, 7 March 1893, TRC; HT to T. J. Wise, 24 April 1908, BL.

479 'Where rosemary flourishes' *Glimpses*, p. 83.
hexameters from Wales *Memoir* 2.109; L&S 3.12.
Mrs Creak *Mangles*, 2 Oct. 1871, p. 114.
'We have room for more' ET to WEG, 21 July 1871, BL.

480 'O that Gladstone . . .' ET to HT, 1 Sept. 1871, TRC.
'delightful abode' WEG diary, 24 July 1871, BL.
'What an ugly boy' ET reporting HT to AT, 7 July 1871, TRC.
'tall loutish youth' Swinburne, *Letters*, ed. C.Y. Lang, 1959–62, 2.191.
'handsome son' *Mangles*, 29 March 1871, p. 71.
'waiting for an Eton boy' Beef *Mangles*, 25 Aug. 1871, p. 97.

481 'theological discussions' ET to HT, 15 March 1872, TRC.
'The Captain's chatter' ET to HT, 19 Sept. 1871, TRC.
'clearly disliked' mouse story *Mangles*, 1 Oct. 1871, p. 107; see also *Memoir* 2.355.
'flutter and fluster' ET to HT, 8 Sept. 1871, TRC.
'found us out' GE to J. Blackwood, 24 July 1871, *G. Eliot Letters* (Haight) 5.169.
'greatest living poet' G. H. Lewes, 22 June 1850, *Leader* in *Critical Heritage*, p. 7.

482 'I called there' ET to HT, 29 Aug. 1871, TRC. In Journal, when rewritten in the 1890s, ET's own visit is not recorded. See *Mangles*, 3 Sept. 1871, p. 102. It was in Mat. but was eventually wiped out of *Memoir* 2.107 or 109.
'the making of Lewes' *Mangles*, 24 Aug. 1871, p. 92.
'Poor soul!' Jane Carlyle to Alexander Gilchrist, 31 July 1861 in *Anne Gilchrist*, p. 86.
'Almost anything' BJ to G. Eliot, 7 May 1878, Virginia.
'I am grieved' GE to FLo, 6 Feb. 1872, *G. Eliot Letters*.

483 'My want and my trial' ET to HT, 27 Feb. 1872, TRC.
chapel at Aldworth *Mangles*, 25 Oct. 1871, p. 116.
'Another Idyll' BJ to ET, 3 April 1871, TRC.
'so many poems' BJ to ET, 3 April 1871, TRC.
'a pattern youth' Journal, 7 Oct. 1869, TRC.

484 'plain Mr and Mrs' 'wear the honour' AT to WEG, 30 March and 16 April 1873, BL; L&S 3.57.
letters to Hallam 11 Feb. 1871, 28 March 1871, 5 Nov. 1872, TRC.
'house witout thee empty' ET to AT, 6 July 1871, TRC.

485 Lionel's 'HHHC stupor' ET to HT, 5 March 1872, TRC. (Henry Herschel Hay Cameron)
stolid worthy Cf. *RBM*, p. 506 (HT's 'self-effacing resignation') and Millgate, *Testamentary Acts*, p. 39: 'dutiful, dependable . . . doggedly conformist.'
namesake nephew Lionel Tennyson, third Lord Tennyson (1889–1951), England cricketer, gambler, who at twenty-two lost £12,000 on horses in a week. *From Verse to Worse*.

486 'learning stupid parts' MBrad diary, 2 Jan. 1872, BL.
acting for Mrs Cameron *A Child's Recollections*.
HT starting university See L&S 3.16, which does not make it clear that AT is writing about the possibility of sending HT to his old master's *college* – Bradley was Master of University College, Oxford. ET to HT, 27 Sept., 28 Nov. 1871, etc.
Louisa Prinsep (sister of May – who would be HT's second wife – and Annie) was

actually a niece of Thoby Prinsep, JMC's brother-in-law. Her father was Charles Robert Prinsep, who had died in 1864.

487 scandal at Eton LT to AT and ET at TRC; Probyn's history from Michael Meredith, Eton.

488 'Papa is quite ill' ET to HT, 1 April 1872 (ET's last letter to Marlborough), TRC. Eton and Marlborough at this period Lady Augusta Stanley wrote to her sister about a young master, Prothero, who 'is disgusted with the world in general, but Eton in particular . . . He says that it is all but impossible to be trained at Eton with a chance of taking a good place at a difficult examination. Marlboro' and Cheltenham he thinks far the best.' *Later Letters of Lady Augusta Stanley 1864–1876*.
asking about Lionel ET to HT, 23 May 1872, TRC.

489 'perfectly ludicrous' etc. ET to HT, 12 March 1872, TRC.
'a racketing and junketing' See *The Letters of JAS* 2.216, 8 April 1872. It has to be the Prinsep/Bowden Smith wedding to which JAS refers, though the note is misleading. JAS was definitely there. JAS to ET, 2 Nov. 1872, refers back.
'honorary hostess' JMC to HT, ?18 March 1872, TRC.
a ball at Farringford Journal and AT to Knowles, 5 April 1872, L&S 3.28.

490 eighteen this year Eleanor born 21 Aug. 1854.
'if he were a woman, and washed' Blakesley to Thompson, 16 April 1833, Kolb, p. 749. I have not found evidence for *RBM*'s unsourced statement (p. 366) that Mary Ker disliked Emily and thought her 'overly ambitious' for AT. It is not true (as has been seen in this book) that AT 'gradually drifted away from most of his family after marriage' (p. 365). It would undoubtedly have made life easier for ET if they had seen less of the Tennyson siblings.
'given to shifty ways' letter quoted in WFR's 1909 lecture, TRC. Mary's ability to do without men is illustrated by the fact that she and Alan Ker spent thirteen years of their marriage without seeing each other (*Background*, p. 161).

491 'spiritual sun' E. Jesse to FT, 9 July 1884, Lilly.
'slightly deranged' ET to HT, 18 Aug. 1872, TRC.
'two skulls side by side' Journal, Aug. 1872, TRC.
'finds out everything' ET to EL, 19 March 1873, TRC.

492 'a man of his age' *Mangles*, 21 Sept. 1872, p. 120.
two sets of rooms HT to F. Jenkinson, 18 Sept. 1872, CUL. The lodgings were at 36 Market Hill. Information on FJ from obituary in *Cambridge Review*, 26 Oct. 1923. ET to EL, 19 March 1873: 'The best and most intellectual of the fellow students are his companions at Trinity.' TRC.
'What a picture' HT to FJ, Oct. 1878, CUL.
'When Walter and I' n.d., scrap at Yale.
'a history of thy day' ET to HT, 18 Oct. 1872, TRC. Other letters to HT at Cambridge all at TRC.

493 women and degrees ET to Agnes, 7 March 1896, TRC.
'the head of the woman' 1 Corinthians 11:3. See ET to AW, 27 March 1892, TRC.
'bits of paper' HT's note to ET's 7 March 1896 letter.
'No son could well be' Journal, 7 Oct. 1872, TRC.
'like the Paltry Poet' Fitz to ET, [Dec. 1872], Terhune 3.388.
Laurence portrait Fitz to ET, sending it off, 19 Nov. [1876], Terhune 3.721. Another version, bitumenized, belonged to Moxon. Portrait in Plate section. NPG.
See *RBM*, p. 553 who bases his accusations on comparison between the existing portrait and the lithographs made after the original. See his plate viii (opp. p. 149).

494 'wholesome flattery' AT to ET, 4 Nov. [1872], TRC; L&S 3.40.

494   ET worth '20 P. L. s' AT to ET, 7 Nov. 1872, TRC; L&S 3.40.
      'when she is alone' JMC to HT, n.d., TRC (3500) 'They are so complete in their lives'.

495   JMC and Henry ET to HT, 19 Feb. and 3 March 1873, TRC.
      'given to every sort of vice' quoted in Brian Hinton, *Immortal Faces* (1992), p. 104. The original source of this is mysterious.
      ET and shop for JMC's photographs *From Friend to Friend*, p. 27.
      on JMC's photographs MBrad to FT, New Year's Eve 1873, Lilly.
      'I will not bemoan' ET to LT, 21 Nov. 1873, TRC.

496   'until after he will care to go' ET to EL, 23 June 1873, TRC.
      'You must let Aldworth' HT to ET and AT, 15 Feb. 1873, TRC.
      exam results *Cambridge University Reporter*, 4 April 1873. I can find in HT's letters from Cambridge no suggestion that he was 'homesick' (*RBM*, p. 502).
      not to worry about writing ET to HT, 1 March 1873, TRC.
      HT letters from Cambridge 15 Feb., 6 June 1873, TRC.

497   *Undergraduates' Journal* The only surviving copy at CUL is No. 1 (New Series) price 6d, broadsheet, Friday May 9, 1873.
      national insurance, taxation ET to HT, 1 Dec. 1873, TRC.
      'Excuse my presumption' ET to HT, Nov. 1873, TRC.
      'if Mamma could revise' ET declined the suggestion, 6 May 1873, 'If I did it, it would be no longer his for I must write from an entirely different point of view . . . I think if you admit speculative articles they ought all to be likewise practical in order to give them a living interest.'
      fatigued from the number of visitors ET to GD, 15 May 1873, *Dakyns*, p. 111.

498   'marred by no intruding Jesse' LT to ATR, 24 May 1873, Eton.
      calms irritable nerves, family movements ET to HT, 6 and 16 May 1873, TRC.
      the Knights' baby Sadly, she did not go on very well, though William remained devoted to this 'idiot' daughter. When she died, he refused Emily's offer of the landau for the funeral, preferring the dogcart.

499   Frank and the 'disgraceful' clothes ET to HT, 16 May 1873.
      'grown and developed a new love' Journal, 27 Jan. 1873, TRC. All ET's letters to HT and LT at Cambridge at TRC.

500   'People are very kind' ET to EL, 27 Nov. 1873, TRC.
      hopes Knowles had not spoiled ET to HT, 13 Nov. 1873, 'of whom you say you are jealous'. J. Franklin to ET, n.d., TRC.
      'two days with the Tennysons' Richard Jebb to C. Slemmer, 26 Dec. 1873, from *Dearest Love to All*, p. 87.

501   'fragile and worn' CR diary, 5 Oct. 1873, copy at LAO.
      encouraged him to go, sewage book ET to HT, 7 and 24 March 1874, TRC.

CHAPTER 14 Weddings

503   dramatic collapse *CTAT* (p. 414) puts the collapse in September 1874 and suggests Hallam then came home 'to take his mother's place'. Other biographers have understandably telescoped the chain of events, e.g. Harold Nicolson in *Tennyson*, p. 197 – 'fortunately HT had only just gone to Cambridge. He was at once recalled to fill his mother's place.' HT in *Memoir* 2.208 does suggest the long process: April 1874 to 'after Christmas 1875'. But in MS Mat. 1.8 there is a scrap suggesting that on his mother's illness, 'I was summoned home from Cambridge'. See my p. 513, in this chapter.

503 'Papa is really better' HT to AT and ET, 28 May 1874, TRC.
'the present iciness' LT to ATR, n.d., Eton.
the rent too high £500 a year or £300 to £400 for the summer – a huge amount. Aldworth was let to Earl Russell.

504 'We all went to Tours' HT to Fitz, 23 Dec. 1874, L&S 3.91, HT's travel diary, TRC.
make use of servants LT to ET, 6 Feb. 1875, TRC.
Dr Dabbs and phosphorous AT to Sophie Cracroft, 10 Nov. 1874, Syracuse; L&S 3.89.
'see Dr Dabbs oftener' LT to ET, 15 Nov. 1874, TRC. Dr Dabbs became a personal friend, e.g. LT's 1875 diary (Harvard) LT walks for 2¼ hours on 23 April to Newport to 'rehearse at Dabbs'.
mysteriously ill Michael Millgate, Testamentary Acts, p. 39.
Paget's lecture published in the Lancet, 11 Oct. 1873. I am indebted to Ann Colley, Tennyson and Madness (1983), for drawing my attention to Paget's lectures.

505 'She has overwrought herself' quoted in James Knowles, Nineteenth Century, Jan. 1893, p. 188. Not in Interviews reprint.
'letters for five hours a-day' 'lie all her length' AT to Duchess of Argyll, 3 June and 12 July [1875], L&S 3.103/7.
comments on her health I made an analysis of every reference to her health in Journal and letters surviving. She suffered from weak lungs, persistent cough, painful breathing, 'the old pain in the brain'. The references to her problems with walking are never related to her back.

506 'anything but be patient' ET to Agnes, 6 Dec. 1894, TRC.
banished from modern translations The New English Bible has 'How blest are those of a gentle spirit.'
'the root of gentleness' ET to HT, 7 March 1874, TRC.
'The only prescription' BJ to ET, 13 April 1876, TRC.
Lionel's diary for 1875 and notebook Harvard.

507 'in ragged patches' MBro to FT, 13 March 1875, Lilly.
Lucy Lushington died 1 Oct. 1874.
'not the child of her affections' FT to MBro, 8 Jan. 1875, Lilly.

508 sonnet for Brookfield Ricks 3.15; WHB died 12 July 1874.
'the circle grows smaller' ET to GSV, 12 March 1874, Nat. Lib. of Wales.
fog-excluder invention AT to Knowles, 6 Jan. 1875, Harvard; L&S 3.93.
Browning's acknowledgment See Memoir 2.181.
'After-dinner talk' AT to RB, [early July 1875], Berg; L&S 3.106.

509 RB's sister delighted Alfred Domett's version of Sarianna's version: Domett Diary pp. 153–4.
'upwards of a year' AT to SRE, 25 March 1875; L&S 3.100.
'for two years' AT to Duchess of Argyll, 3 June 1875, TRC; L&S 3.103.
just as his father Memoir 1.71. 'In February 1831 my father left Cambridge, for my grandfather was somewhat ailing and wished that he should return to help his mother.'
the new game The equipment and rules had been patented by Major W.C. Wingfield only the year before (1874). The court was originally 'shaped like an hour-glass'. Anne Thackeray playing I presume ATR though Annie Prinsep also features in the letters.
epitaph for Franklin Ricks 3.16.

510 'An indomitable woman' CR diary, 18 July 1875, copy at LAO.

510 'Peace and health' AT to FLo, 23 June 1875; L&S 3.104. Godfrey Locker-Lampson, b. 19 June 1875. His father was b. 1821.

engagement 'the greatest event' LT to H.H.H. Cameron, 30 Sept. 1875, Brotherton. HT's and Eleanor's letters at TRC. LT diary and notebook, Harvard.

511 At the time. . . with joy e.g. ET to GSV, 'share in our joy', 14 Jan. 1876, Nat. Lib. of Wales.

'written by Emily herself' This is part of the outline (in the green bound journal at TRC) ET wrote after AT's death to help HT with *Memoir*. It appears first in MS Mat. 7, Cf. *Memoir*. 2.211–12.

'affection beyond all idea' EL diary, July 1877, Harvard.

512 'as short for Pater' HT's hand in MS Mat.

'half a Bruce' AT to Argyll, 13 Feb. 1876, *Memoir* 2.212; L&S 3.122.

'only twenty-one' LT was twenty-two the following month.

'slowly recovering' AT to WEG, 22 Nov. 1875, BL; L&S 3.115.

'a perfect holiday-time' BW-C, *London Mercury* v., 1921–2. *Interviews*, p. 116. She dates this reminiscence as the early autumn of 1875. The Ts were back at Farringford on 20 Sept. ; the boys to Cambridge on 13 Oct. It does not tally with ELL's letter to FT, 11 Oct. 1875 (Lilly): 'Emily rather better but very weak. Visitors forbidden.' Perhaps the tennis players were simply kept away from her, though at Aldworth that summer she had sat out watching them.

I have been offered HT to AT and ET, 24 Nov. 1875, TRC.

513 'decidedly better' LT to ET, 14 Nov. 1875, TRC.

one business letter 'Dear Sir,' as from AT, 27 Oct. 1875, Virginia, in ET's hand; L&S 3.111.

'I shirked' HT to AT and ET, n.d. [Dec. 1875], TRC.

'My mother was seriously ill' MS Mat. 1.8. See my note to p. 503.

'Hallam did not return' dated 16 April 1878 in green journal, TRC, copied 1893–4.

'I go back late' HT to Knowles, 13 Jan. 1876, Pierpont Morgan.

'Lionel . . . has gone back' MT to Mrs Craik, 8 Feb. [1876], TRC.

514 'our absolute need' AT to W.H. Thompson, 29 March 1876, Trinity; L&S 3.126.

as has been suggested *RBM*, p. 505.

Shoreditch lectures programmes, lists, Eleanor's letter, 23 March 1876, CTT's diary, 16 March and 7 April 1876 comments; all at TRC.

515 'feared . . . a fiasco' MBro to FT, 6 Feb. 1876, Lilly.

'regenerate the British Stage' LT to H.H.H. Cameron, 9 May 1875, Brotherton.

'a domestic tragedy' LT to ET, A, HT, 27 April 1876, TRC.

Queen Mary HT reported to ET 4 May 1876 on his visit with 'Papa, Eleanor, Lionel' and others the night before, TRC.

516 ET as composer Dr Ian Copley, *Music Review* vol. 41, 1980 and *Lady Tennyson, Composer* (n.d.) TS at TRC. Oliver Davies (of the Royal College of Music) wrote to me (31 Jan. 1996) of ET's 'almost total harmonic ineptitude', but confirms the songs record the 'vanished style of authentic delivery. ET's lack of musical knowledge, and inability to polish or tidy up her inspirations, then becomes a plus.' 'Wealth dropt in by the window' is, he considers, 'the most inventive melodically'. Davies has looked at the music ET played (at TRC) and writes, 'Her repertoire was quite demanding – not unusually so for an English lady of her generation, but indicating a great deal of study and practice nonetheless.' See p. 288 and note.

517 Lionel's exam results Second General Examination for the ordinary BA degree 1875 Class I Tennyson, L. Trinity. BA(Ord) 1876 2nd in history, *University Reporter* 1872–77. His son, Charles, *Stars and Markets* (p. 101) advises us not to be superior

about these ordinary degrees, which produced 'a better educated man'. *RBM*, p. 506 calls LT's degree 'undistinguished'.

517 'My father bids me say' LT to GSV, 10 Jan. 1876, Nat. Lib. of Wales; L&S 3.119.
'You are most welcome' BJ to ET, 13 April [1876], TRC.
'Fishmongers or Letter carriers' EL to ET, 5 Jan. 1876, TRC.

518 'The needless charlock' wild mustard MS Mat. 6.50 (1866).
'Blessed is he . . .' Carlyle on work, as epigraph to *Anne Gilchrist*. Hymn to the delights of work, TRC.

519 'Eleanor is as good as can be' ET to LT, 17 March 1876, TRC.
Lionel went to France 'Thou must stay in Paris as long as Scoones will let you', ET to LT, 28 Jan. 1877. AT apparently joined LT in France in Feb. 1877 (not in Pinion).
'Papa is mildly happy and well,' LT wrote, asking for letters to the Hotel d'Angleterre at Rouen. 'Tell us what train to expect you by at Amiens' – 'you' being probably HT and Eleanor.
'What pleased me most' Eleanor to LT, 17 Jan. 1877, TRC.

520 moral actresses LT to H.H.H. Cameron, 7 Jan. 1877, Brotherton.
'obliged to come out' 'enjoying measles' LT to Mrs Field of Philadelphia, n.d., scrap at Yale.
Lionel a very good nurse AT to FLo, 12 June 1877, L&S 3.147.
'referred to by his father' Mary G diary, 1 Nov. 1876, BL.
arrangements that winter The letter to Knowles, 22 Dec. 1876, Rochester, L&S 3.139, is in Hallam's hand not ET's as L&S have it. But 'My dear Mr Knowles' suggests ET dictated it.
'performed by eating' AHH to ETJ, 21 April 1832, Kolb, p. 554.

521 India Office status of entrants system altered in 1886.
'two big fellows' ET 'younger' EL diary, July 1877, Harvard.

522 'like a sort of miracle' ATR to Andrew Hichens, *Thackeray's Daughter*, p. 154.
Thackeray/Ritchie wedding 5 Aug. 1877; Emily Ritchie to ET, *Thackeray's Daughter*, p. 151.

523 immensely tedious In Mat. there is the sentence 'he unfortunately disliked the routine work' – a telling phrase, which disappears in *Memoir* 2.322, which gives a rose-coloured view of LT's career.
'With the natives of India' FP, *Nineteenth Century*, Feb. 1899, p. 6.
Indian friends There are a number of mentions in LT's letters, including Sirdar Dilar and Syed Mahmood (Judge of the High Court of Allahabad).

524 'quarrels over public matters' MBro to FT, 7 Feb. 1879, Lilly. The 'Indian highlanders' must be Afghans. Britain had invaded Afghanistan that winter after the Emir in Kabul had established a relationship with Russia. (Cf. LT's Russian lessons.) The Treaty of Gundamik was signed in May 1879.
calming AT down See e.g. Domett *Diary*, Nov. 1883, p. 280 'Oh, he's exaggerating it.'
'Who says that wars are over?' from 'A Call to Arms' (1852), later 'Adapted to the melody of Emily Lady Tennyson', as 'The Penny-Wise', Ricks 2.467.
whether war ever just ET's notes at TRC on 'The Army' are in *CTAT*, p. 417 'only wars of defence . . . can be Christian wars'.
'War for War's sake' 'Charge of the Heavy Brigade', Ricks 3.96.
'toothache all over the body' CTT to HDR, *Memories*, p. 228.
'Don't fret yourself' LT to ET, 14 Jan. 1878, TRC.

525 Charles and Louisa Turner's last months I am indebted to Dr Roger Evans for much information (PhD thesis, TRC). Also Harriet Tennyson to FT, Feb. 1878, Lilly.

525 'under the care of Dr Dabbs' recommended by ET. The measure of George
Dabbs's reciprocal admiration for ET is suggested by his dedication to her memory of
'a phantasy', *The Dream* (1900). It is full of angels. He also wrote children's stories
and plays.
loving stream of letters quoted 24 Oct. 1878, 13 Nov. 1878. ET destroyed nearly all
LTT's self-lacerating letters to her.

526 Fitz's suggestions of wives for AT 'jolly woman' Terhune 2.538, 'old
Housekeeper' Terhune 3.487.
'ambitious flight' Fitz to Fanny Kemble, 22 Feb. [1878], Terhune 4.100.
'does not like her' Fitz to Anna Biddell, [28 Feb. 1878], Terhune 4.105.
FT's notion of ET's ambition Fitz to FT, 11 April [1878], Terhune 4.113.
great gun's wife AT jun. to his father FT, July 1879, Lilly.
'The dear Dean was ill' Journal, TRC. ET's hand in HT's 'voice' for *Memoir*.

527 'As the throng was very large' F.W. Farrar, *Men I have known* (1897), pp. 35–8
[slightly different in L&S 3.152].
'tongues wagged' Mrs T late Mary G diary, BL.
'Tennyson had chosen' Domett *Diary*, p. 212. Farrar's account suggests the choice of
witnesses was his own.

528 'a bunch of violets' Agnes to CTT, n.d., TRC (2400).
'we want to go to Shiplake' LT to All, 15 May 1878, TRC.
Sabine Greville described Henry James, *Letters* (Edel) 2.196, 17 Nov. 1878.
'your Mother's grace' Sabine Greville to HT, 28 Feb. 1878, MS Mat., TRC.
a glimpse of AT George Gissing to Algernon Gissing, 28 Feb. 1878, *Letters of GG*
(1927).
honeymoon letters, mouse 'sitting on my pillow' Eleanor to All, 10 March 1878 etc.,
TRC.

529 'She used to flirt' Caroline Jebb to Polly, Nov. 1894, *Dearest Love to All*, p. 237.
'later in returning' Journal, 2.222, TRC.
'Dearest Mama' Eleanor to ET, 20 June 1878, other letters Eleanor to ET, all at TRC.

530 'christening robe' ET to LTT, 5 Nov. 1878, TRC.
Hallam's legal studies 'a heavy burden of names' ET to EL, 15 Jan. 1879, TRC.
(Temple dinners mentioned again in May.)

531 'never was a baby before' MBro to FT, 30 March 1879, Lilly.
'as good as a lady' MT to ET, 18 Aug. 1884, TRC.
on baby Lionel LT to ET, Eleanor to ET, ET to EL, Dec. /Jan. 1878–9, all at TRC.
'Gold-head curly head' early version of 'To Alfred Tennyson, My Grandson', Ricks
3.70. The dedication to *Ballads and Other Poems* (1880) begins 'Golden-haired Ally
whose name is one with mine.' The last line uses 'wronged' rather than 'harmed'.

532 'extremely cheerful' ET to EL, 15 Jan. 1879.
'you are a grandmother' EL to ET, 24 Nov. 1878, TRC.
'the infirmities of the Grandmother' ET to EL, 15 Jan. 1879.
'never see her like again' LT to H.H.H. Cameron, 24 Feb. 1879, Brotherton.
'colder and darker' MBro to FT, 30 March 1879, Lilly.
'coming across the Park' Journal, 1 July 1862, TRC.
'so loving and strong' ET to LTT, 26 Feb. 1879, TRC.
'God bless you' CTT to LTT, n.d. [Feb. 1879?], TRC.

533 'a sister, has to minister' LTT to Richard Wilton, Nov. 1878, TRC.
'Mary did her duty' Arthur Tennyson to FT, 13 May 1879, Lilly.
'Thy beloved one' 'Thou hast been' ET to LTT, 27 and 30 April 1879, TRC.

534 'Keep your heart up' AT to LTT, May 1879, TRC, L&S 3.172.

534 'And through this midnight' from 'Prefatory Poem to My Brother's Sonnets' 'Midnight, June 30, 1879', CTT, *Collected Sonnets*, 1880, Ricks 3.45.
'I was dreaming of you' ATR to ET, 27 May 1879, *Letters* ed. H. Ritchie, p. 179.

535 'Japanese writing table' FLu to HT, 7 Aug. 1879, TRC.
The Tennyson Turner marriage Sir Charles Tennyson (*T. and his Friends*, p. 60) suggested 'the devotion of the pair was remarkable', that their love retained 'a certain youthful ardour to the end' but evidence suggests it was fundamentally an unhappy marriage, however much they both devoted themselves to their parishioners at Grasby and however much their faces 'beamed with a heavenly light', as ET put it. CTT seems to have been a saintly, forgiving and delightful man, as well as a good poet. Only once does he write (27 Dec. 1866, Memorandum Book, TRC) 'Louisa's lachrymosity me miserrimo atq. irato' – but it must often have been the case, and Louisa's vast jottings (eighteen little diaries and much else) have no word of happiness.
ended in tears '11th hour bouleversement' MBro to FT, 26 Oct. 1881, Lilly.
'much more congenial' ET to CR, 15 Dec. 1886, TRC.
'such hard work to get on' Harriet Tennyson to FT, New Year's Eve 1879, Lilly.
Harriet Tennyson was herself dead by June 1881, mourned by the poor she visited (Horatio Tennyson to FT, 21 June 1881, Lilly).

536 Turner money Eleanor to ET, 10 June 1881, TRC.
'without available legs' MBro to FT, 15 Nov. 1879, Lilly.
helped to feed and dress ET to Eleanor, 17 April 1879, TRC.
'Child-Songs' *St Nicholas* vol. VII no. 4, Feb. 1880.
ET as Humpty Dumpty LT to ET, 12 Dec. 1880, TRC.

537 soap bubbles, straw hat and sombrero story WA *Diary*, 8 Sept. 1884, p. 331, 5 Aug. 1880, p. 286. WA says little Alfred in AT's hat is aged three. He was not two until the following November. This story has often been repeated inaccurately; Peter Levi in his *Tennyson* (1993) seems to be half-remembering it on p. 259. Even *CTAT* (p. 451) has little Charles himself present when he is not in WA's description.
hairbrushing etc. I tell this story to counteract the impression Lionel's grandson, the later Hallam Tennyson, gives of him in *The Haunted Mind*. ('Not, one feels, a genial paterfamilias,' p. 11.) Eleanor's letters to ET, several hundred at TRC.
reviewing for Knowles Eleanor to ET, 10 June 1880, TRC.
anonymous reviews. There is no trace of Eleanor's work in the *Nineteenth Century*.
'Tennyson worried' HT to ET, 23 June 1880, Yale.
Jane Harrison *DNB* reveals she actually took a second but was nonetheless remarkable. In her *Reminiscences* (1925) she says AT's 'daughter-in-law' 'was among my closest friends.' She stayed at Aldworth but did not describe ET.

538 failure to secure a secretaryship LT to All, 3 May 1880: 'No secretaryship for Lord Lansdowne.' TRC.
'as good to them as you used to be' ET to EL, 7 June 1881, TRC.
arriving for lunch from Henry James, *The Middle Years* (1917) p. 92. If it was Eaton Place, as HT says, it must have been 1879. James dates it at 1877 or 1878. *RBM* suggests it must have been after 1880 when Lowell came to London as Minister, but he was in Madrid in 1879 (LT had met him there in 1878) and was frequently in London. A letter at TRC records a recall to Madrid not long after the lunch. See L&S 3.186. HJ, knowing London as he did, was more likely to get the date wrong and the place right.

539 'as if in a coffin' Thomas Hardy at 9 Upper Belgrave St., from *The Life and Work of TH*, ed. Millgate (1984), p. 140.

539 'They know we are away' HT to ET, 14? June 1880, Yale.
'make his own conditions' ET to ELL, 11 May 1880, TRC. Two letters (L&S 3.191)
are both in ET's hand, but may only be drafts or copies.

540 'London society' 'ceaseless chaff' Mary G diary, 24 Feb. 1888 and 14 May 1883, BL.
Mary's visit to Farringford Mary G diary, June 1879, BL; L&S 3.174–7 is not
accurate to the original in the BL as it comes from a faulty published text.
'Farringford did me one good turn' Mary G, 1 July 1879, letter in Clwyd Record
Office, Hawarden. Maggie Warren, Mary's close friend, daughter of Lord de Tabley.

542 'Mary the fascinating' LT to All, 21 June 1879, TRC.
Mary overworking HT to Mary G, Dec. 1882, BL. All HT's letters to Mary G are in
the Gladstone papers at the BL. Quoted 2 March 1882, 28 Aug. 1883, 27 Sept. 1883.

543 Lionel's smile Mary G diary, 5 April 1879, BL.
'black beard and no manners' Margot Asquith, Autobiography (1920), p. 194.
'a career of his own' CT (for instance, as reported in TRB Nov. 1982, p. 14) suggests
HT never had any thought of his own career. 'He regarded his duty to his father as
paramount.' Contemporary records show this was not true; he tried hard to get
work of his own and his parents encouraged him.
'a student of the Inner Temple' e.g. in biographical entries years later. One (a proof
for Chatto and Windus) has the addition in ET's hand 'is a JP for Hants', Virginia.
'willingly have set me free' Memoir 2.208.
'likely to be a vacancy' ET to WEG, 15 Dec. 1881, BL; L&S 3.215.

544 'as big a print' HT to Macmillan, 9 Jan. 1884, BL.
'desire to see more of you' WEG to ET, 28 March 1881, TRC.
disillusioned with I.O. LT to All, 30 Jan. and 15 April 1881, etc., TRC.
'He drew the curtains' A.V. Baillie (1864–1955) later Dean of Windsor, from The
Making of a Man, p. 71; L&S 3.206.
The Promise of May The Times, 13 Nov. 1882; Daily News, 16 Nov. 1882. An
unidentified cutting in the Dykes Campbell scrapbook at Harvard says The Times was
'an exaggerated report'.

545 'cadging' 'a good thing' LT to H.H.H. Cameron, 17 Dec. 1881, Brotherton.
'the only way to get anything' Eleanor to ET, 8 Dec. 1881, TRC.
'not altogether wisely' AT to Sir Louis Mallet, 26 Jan. 1883, Mat. 4.135; L&S 3.243.

546 news of Lionel LT to All, 8, 20, 28 Feb. 1883, TRC.
problems for HT as MP EL diary, 17 Aug. 1880, Harvard.
loves WEG but hates his politics To G.W. Prothero, TRC, L&S 3, 333. Also in
Rawnsley Memories, p. 103, and to Times, 28 June 1892.
WEG's fanaticism ET to Welds, 12 Feb. 1886, TRC.
parliamentary aspirations ELL wished HT luck with the 'Industrials' when he went
for his Leeds interview. Telegram to H. Gladstone is 22 May 1883 (TRC) from
Headingly to Downing Street. It seems likely they did not think the Poet Laureate's
son a suitable representative. Colin Matthew suggests the reorganization of the Leeds
constituency in 1884–5 as another possible reason why HT never stood for it.
'Your advice followed' HT to Mary G, Oct. 1883, BL.

547 Alfred Tennyson's Works HT to Macmillan, 14 Jan. 1884, BL.
many times in the past AT had refused a baronetcy at least three times. A seat in the
Lords was not just grander but would give HT the chance of doing a real job. A
peerage was in AT's mind as early as 1871. See Mangles, p. 85.
'against the thing' ET to HS and AW, 6 Feb. 1865, TRC.
Governor-General of Australia As 2nd Lord Tennyson, HT was Governor of South
Australia from 1899 (three years after his mother's death) and acting Governor-

General for his final year 1902–3. He won golden opinions at that difficult period of early Federation and declined to stay on 'wholly and solely on your account and the boys', as his wife wrote to *her* mother. 12 Jan. 1903, *Vice-Regal Days*, p. 263.

547 'the sound of a title' BJ to ET, 7 Dec. 1883, TRC.
carping *PMG*, 12 Dec. 1883, *Spectator* quoted in *PMG*, 15 Dec. 1883.

548 'a solemn thing' 'as long as the race lasts' ET to EL, 23 Jan. 1884, TRC. There is a certain irony as subsequent holders of the title have lived abroad and not sat in the House of Lords. The heir to the title now lives in New Zealand.
LT and HT advice to ET e.g. 28 Feb. 1883, 18 July 1884, TRC.
'Certainly fresh' ET to Julia Lennard, n.d. *c*. Feb. 1884, Ch. Ch. Oxford. See also L&S 3.270.

549 'a new source' ET to EL, 23 Jan. 1884, TRC.
'That Hallam should inherit' ET to WEG, 27 Sept. 1883, BL.
'As to the Peerage' FT to his son Alfred, 4 Jan. 1884, Lilly. FT's son Alfred, information from FT archive at Lilly.

550 Maria's death ET to FT, 25 Jan. 1884, Lilly.
'delighted and relieved' I can find no evidence for *RBM*'s suggestion (p. 550) that ET found it 'painful' 'to lose her favourite son'. She was *not* losing him. She never travelled 'to Farringford from Aldworth' in the summer so there was no question of her being too ill to do so. HT and his wife did not have to come home early from their honeymoon as the passage suggests. Audrey did not always stay at home with ET when HT and AT were away. In 1886 she was with them in Norfolk and in both 1887 and 1889 she went on cruises with them.
'a very happy nature' Audrey to her mother, 25 Jan. 1903, *Vice-Regal Days*, p. 264.
'a devoted daughter' HT to FT, 22 Nov. 1883, Lilly.
'royal in her sweetness' AT to Mary Boyle, [24 Sept. 1883], TRC; L&S 3.262.

551 Mary Gladstone's engagement and marriage HT to Mary G, 30 Dec. 1885, 17 Jan. 1886, 1 Feb. 1886, BL.
masses of childish letters TRC.

552 'wiped out of the record' Both Edward and Michael Tennyson appear only in the family tree in *Memoir*. Even ET's great-grandson, the present HT, in *Studies in Tennyson* says Alfred and Charles 'were the poet's only grandchildren until Hallam's eldest son was born in 1889'. He thinks Michael may have been schizophrenic. His confinement – after ET's death – was said to have been because of 'violence'. In *The Haunted Mind* (pp. 14–15) Hallam Tennyson says his father, Sir Charles, only mentioned Michael after his brother's death in 1953. But see *CTAT*, p. 488: 'three small boys.'
'he talks but very little' ET to Mrs John Field, 14 Sept. 1886, Pierpont Morgan.
'very different' ET to AW, 7 Sept. 1890, TRC.
The Times review of LT's report 11 April 1884. The same issue carried a report of the death of Mary Ker, the eldest of AT's sisters and the first to die, at seventy-three on 4 April. 'Well on the Sunday, a corpse on the Friday,' ETJ to FT, April 1884, Harvard.
'I have written to Mary' LT to All, 16 Feb. 1884, TRC.

553 AT's will copy at TRC. A codicil after LT's death refers to his children. No one seems to have commented on this will. Surely in 1884 AT must have made some other provision for LT.
'sprained his ankle' MBro to FT, n.d. [spring 1884], Lilly.
a 'quiet country wedding' ET to EL, 4 June 1884, TRC. Audrey's father, Charles Boyle, died at Hawkhurst on 20 Aug. 1884.
'strikingly handsome' unidentified cutting at Harvard.

554 'a friendly wink' WA *Diary*, 25 June 1884, p. 323.
'a raree-show' MBro to FT, 4 Aug. 1884, Lilly.
'composed by my mother' HT to John Field, 16 Aug. 1884, Yale.
'struck by the beauty' HT to ET, 26 June 1884, TRC.
'It was hard to bear' ELL to AT, June 1884, TRC; 'the two little boys', Alfred and Charles, were now five and four.
'good work in the world' 'My darling' ET to HT and Audrey, 26 June 1884.
555 'She likes being read to' HT to ET and AT, 27 June 1884, TRC.
'peace of mind' HT to John Field, 16 Aug. 1884, Yale.

CHAPTER 15 'The deepest cloud of human sorrow'

556 'the paths leading' AT to Princess of Wales, [Jan. 1885], copy at TRC; L&S 3.309.
'crave wary walking' *Julius Caesar* II.i.15.
when he was a boy ET to LT, 25 Nov. 1865, TRC.
'a touch of his father's genius' *A Child's Recollections*, p. 67.
'a true personal devotion' ET to Dufferin, 29 Sept. 1884, draft TRC.
'all appointments' ET to Dufferin, 13 Oct. 1884, TRC.
557 'anxious to be of service' 'some way to be useful' Dufferin to ET, 2 and 17 Oct. 1884, TRC.
'almost carried' WA *Diary*, 5 Dec. 1884, p. 340.
'the old bright intelligence' FP journal, 10 Jan. 1885, *Palgrave*, p. 179.
dedication Selection of *Lyrical Poems of Alfred Tennyson*.
'a reminder' ET's letter quoted in *Palgrave*, p. 270.
Lear's dedication The long dedication, in the form of a letter dated 24 Nov. 1885, is reproduced in Ruth Pitman, *Edward Lear's Tennyson*, p. 33.
558 'most frightfully anxious' HT to Mary G, 30 Jan. 1885, BL.
'a subject for Alfred' BJ to ET, 6 July 1885, TRC. The resulting poem was called 'The Ancient Sage', Ricks 3.138. HT: 'My father considered this as one of his best later poems.' The Chinese philosopher's name can be rendered in many different ways. BJ used Laotsee.
559 'Think of me' in Margot Asquith, *Autobiography* (1920), p. 194.
Lionel's diary In the same notebook marked 'PRIVATE' in which he had written out poems as an undergraduate, 18 pages Nov./Dec. 1884, Jan./March 1885, TRC.
560 'his necessity her great opportunity' Annie Fields. See my epigraph, p. xiii.
had not forgotten Lionel Dufferin to ET, 5 May 1885, TRC.
Lionel's Indian diary TRC. Other information on travels from ET to Welds, 18 Dec. 1885, TRC.
561 Lionel's death The 'official' story of Lionel's illness was as inaccurate as the suggestion that Lionel went to India as part of his work for the India Office. HT asked Macmillan to tell the papers on 4 April 1886 that Lionel had been 'seized with a dangerous malaria while staying at Government House, Calcutta'. Letters and telegrams including Dufferin to ET, 28 March and 10 May 1886. The archive includes a dark curl: 'Lionel's hair cut off when he was dead by the nurse.' All at TRC.
562 Pentedatelo Lear's spelling. Today it is Pentedattilo. *EL's Tennyson*, p. 59.
Telling Lear HT to EL, 11 March 1886, TRC.
563 time of Lionel's death and burial *Memoir* has three, not four, but four was written at the time. Burial sometimes seven, sometimes nine. Nine in HT's hand in a letter to John Field (Pierpont Morgan). This account comes mainly from a letter from Audrey reporting to Hallam what Eleanor had told her (Pierpont Morgan). In 1955,

travelling on another P&O liner, I saw a burial in the Red Sea, the most moving of all funerals.

563 'Christ is risen' Horatio Tennyson to All, 28 April 1886, TRC.
'Such sorrows' ET to ELL, June 1886, TRC.
'no words' ET to J. Mangles, 5 July 1886, Ohio.
'to bid my boy farewell' from poem 'To the Marquis of Dufferin and Ava', Ricks 3.198–201.
'poor rags of comfort' ET's phrase in a letter to FT on the death of his wife, 25 Jan. 1884, Lilly.
'I myself have always felt' AT to SRE, 26 June 1871; L&S 3.6.

564 'All sadness *should* be lost' ET to Mr and Mrs J.W. Field, 5 Feb. 1887, Pierpont Morgan.
'This world's hope' ET to CR, 15 March 1887, TRC.
published a letter This letter, which the present Hallam Tennyson thinks is at Lincoln, is not catalogued and I could not find the original. The part quoted is on p. 12 of this HT's autobiography, *The Haunted Mind*, and on p. 6 of *Studies in Tennyson*.

565 'fall in love' See Winifred Gérin, *Anne Thackeray Ritchie* (1981), pp. 214–15. 'There remains no written trace of the ordeal.' Gérin had the benefit of the co-operation of Belinda Norman-Butler, ATR's grand-daughter, to whom her book is dedicated.
'just to Eleanor' ET to HT, 30 Nov. 1889, TRC.
'such brothers!' EL to Audrey, 29 April 1886. A recent book suggests that Lionel and Hallam were the originals of Tweedledum and Tweedledee, a contentious theory.
'never could understand' 'strong, tall young man' Caroline Jebb to her sister, Nov. 1894, April 1886, *Dearest Love to All*, p. 237 and p. 221.

566 'Mr Dittmor said' ET, n.d., Ashley MSS, BL.
'the blessed hope' ET to EL, 22 Oct. 1886, TRC.
'Words weaker than' from 'To J.S.', AT's poem on the death of Edward Spedding, quoted by HT in letter of sympathy to F. Jenkinson, 8 Jan. 1888, CUL.
'instrument through which' Dufferin to ET, 10 May 1886, TRC.
'a terrible nightmare' HT to General Sir George Higginson; photocopy kindly sent to me by David Holmes, book and autograph dealer, Philadelphia.

567 'the thousand snares' ET to HT, Feb. 1873, TRC.
'calm and resigned' Eleanor to J. & E. Field, 20 Jan. 1886, Pierpont Morgan.
'It is bliss' *CTAT*, p. 489.
'The thought of Lionel' In ET's handwriting as HT (in the continuation of Journal at TRC) begins 'My Father says sometimes . . .'.
on the cover of Froude From scrap in ET miscellaneous box, TRC. 'Words written by AT on the cover of *Oceana*' etc. 'finished on that day'. Copy of the book, TRC. Published in 1886, subtitled 'England and her colonies', it no longer has its cover.
'strength to support' quoted by Edmund Gurney to HT, 5 May 1886, TRC.
'good for all of us' ET to Mangles, 5 July 1886, Ohio. (It could be to *Mrs* Mangles. ET's Mr and Mrs are often indistinguishable.)
'our highest weal' ET to EL, 14 Aug. 1883, TRC.
'source of strength' HT to A de Vere, 10 May 1886, Pierpont Morgan.
'peace and comfort' BJ to ET, 27 April 1886, TRC.
'companions to our boy' ET to J. and E. Field, Sept. 1886, Pierpont Morgan.
'Audrey a comfort' HT to Mary Fraser Tytler, 11 Nov. 1886, NPG.
'half my life' HT to F. Jenkinson, 8 Jan. 1888, CUL.

568 'one whom I loved' HT to Mary G, 26 April 1886, BL.
Lionel's notebook TRC. Shakespeare sonnet 71, 'The Sailor Boy', Ricks 2.301.

568 how can it be selfish?' ET to HT, n.d. [c. May 1873], TRC.
'excellent spirits' HT to ET, [21 July 1886], Yale. This letter is in L&S 3.338–9 but they read it differently: 'exuberant'.

569 *Jack and the Beanstalk* It was published by Macmillan. AT shared in the dedication. 'To my Father in recognition of what this booklet owes to him, And to my nephews, "Golden-hair'd" Ally, Charlie, and Michael, who have so far condescended as to honour it with their approbation.' It was probably through the Gattys that HT came into contact with Caldecott. He illustrated many books by their daughter, Mrs Ewing, and also designed the cover for MGa's magazine.
Eleanor's letters to ET all at TRC, e.g. 'Please insist', 7 Sept. 1890.
pleasure and privilege ET to Sarah [Prinsep?], 12 Nov. 1889, Rochester.
Charlie's cooking etc. ET to Welds, 10 Sept. 1889, 25 Aug. 1890, TRC.

570 'a model for all National schools' ET to Agnes, 14 Dec. 1895, TRC.
'in need of discipline' Eleanor to ET, 27 June 1886, TRC.

571 'my dearest Lady Tennyson' e.g. 4 Jan. 1889, TRC.
'entirely altered' HT to ET, [21 July 1886], Yale; L&S 3.338–9.
'deeply wronged us' ET to HT, 30 Nov. 1889, TRC.

572 'walk till you die' CT quotes this at the end of his Foreword to Hoge's unsatisfactory edition of *The Letters of Emily Lady Tennyson* (1974).
Birrell's background from CT's talk on 28 Sept. 1962 to the Rowfant Club (copy at TRC). See also *Stars and Markets*.

573 'two spirits bound on earth' ET's lines as a 'subject' for AT at the time of the fiftieth anniversary of Queen Victoria's marriage. TRC.
'You must forgive me' ET to AW, 9 June 1888, TRC.
Eleanor's second marriage Caroline Jebb to her sister, Nov. 1894, *Dearest Love to All*, p. 237.
'force an entry' *CTAT*, p. 497. Charles must have heard this from Birrell himself. In Journal, 4 Aug. 1890 'A. very nervous and upset at meeting Birrell. All goes off well.'
glad of Eleanor's happiness ET to Agnes, 15 May 1890, 27 Feb. 1896, 'All that concerns her is a matter of affectionate interest to me.' ET to Agnes, 21 Oct. 1895.

574 comforted Emily Eleanor to ET, 7 Oct. 1892, at AT's death, TRC.
'affection and helpfulness' BJ to ET, 1 May 1887, TRC.
'sweet and aged saint' BJ to FN, 22 May 1887, Balliol.
'the strong one of the family' Argyll to ET, 17 Oct. 1889, TRC.
'far sterner stuff' MBro to FT, 18 Oct. 1892, Lilly, and MBro to ATR, 10 Oct. 1892, Eton.
'bad times together' ETJ quoted in Kolb, p. 802. Emily Jesse's grave at Margate bears no reference to the Tennyson connection.

575 'impressed me more' J.H. Shorthouse to ET, 5 April 1888, Yale.
'looking into the other world' AT would be much taken with WA's words when he was dying in Nov. 1889: 'I am seeing things that you know nothing of.'
'the old beloved home' ET to EL, 25 Dec. 1887, TRC.
Hallam's diary of 1888–9 illness TRC.
scarcely move Wilfrid Ward, *New Review*, July 1896 of 1 Jan. 1889.
'as near death' Mat. 4.323.

576 'three stone' HT to Craik, 12 Dec. 1888, BL.
'words of consolation' BJ to HT, 11 Nov. 1888, TRC.
'leave his father and mother' Genesis 2:24, Matthew 19:5, Mark 10:7.
'best help and comfort' ET to ELL, 22 Oct. 1886, TRC.
revealing letter money ET to Welds, 23 March 1888, 3 Sept. 1891, TRC.

577 'the burdens on his shoulders' MBro to FT, 26 Dec. 1888, Lilly.
no need for tuck A.B.S. Tennyson to Eleanor, 27 May 1888, TRC.
boys singing ET to AW, 27 Oct. 1889, TRC.
'for his own peace of mind' AT to E. Russell, 10 March 1833, L&S 1.90.

578 'Dear little Michael' ET to AW, 11 Nov. 1890, TRC. There is a particularly
disturbing letter about Michael from Eleanor to ET (n.d. but c. March 1890) with a
desperate hope of Michael's 'growing up like other boys'.
FLo's reading from his autobiography, My Confidences.
letters about Michael ET to Agnes, 26 Jan. 1895, 21 Sept. 1894, 10 Jan. 1890, TRC.
'peculiar' brothers e.g. GT on Arthur's 'gestures and twitchings' L&S 1.62.

579 'good solid desk' 'French' ET to Craik, 1 Nov. 1889, 24 Nov. 1889, TRC.
'Locksley Hall Sixty Years After' Ricks 3.151. Cf. p. 194 and p. 587.
'too delicate and tender' Reported to ET by ATR, 25 Nov. 1892, TRC.
'a tender, spiritual face' CTAT, p. 514.
'the awful group' HT to Craik, 16 Jan. 1890, BL. Witch of Endor: 1 Sam. 28:7. There
is an unpublished poem by Mary T at TRC in which the witch is described.
'Your brother seems turning' MBro to FT, 23 Jan. 1890, Lilly.
Helen Allingham pictures The one of AT makes a fine cover for Peter Levi's Tennyson
(1993) and is also in Helen Allingham's England (1990) by Ina Taylor, a delightful
book with many local scenes near both Aldworth and Farringford. Her late painting
of ET is on p. 64. Helen Allingham illustrated The Homes of Tennyson (1905), with a
text by her brother, Arthur Paterson.

580 'calm sunshine' T and his Friends, p. 184 – quoted by Daisy Bradley (Margaret
Woods).
crying over 'Surly Tim' London Memories of Brander Matthews in Scribner's
Magazine, Nov. 1916.
'cared to make me happy' T.M. Lee, 27 June 1892, Mat. 4.353–5; L&S 3.444/6.
brusque but pretty things WFR in Memories, p. 148.
'too grotesque' JAS to Margaret Symonds, 29 Aug. 1892, Letters, p. 745.
shocking stories Miss Rundle's diary; 'Marlborough' notebook at TRC. See Memoir
1.279.

581 on servants ET to AW, 20 Oct. 1890, TRC.
'your wife and my husband' ET to RB, 22 July 1889, Yale.
T's 'second self' EBB quoted in Annie Fields, Authors and Friends, pp. 352–3.
'my truest critic' AT to HDR, quoted Memories, p. 116.
'her husband's best critic' BJ in Memoir 2.467.

582 'Fitz is Fitz' ET to HT, Nov. 1889, TRC.
'Mrs Browning's death' Fitz to W.H. Thompson, 15 July 1861 in Letters and
Literary Remains of Edward FitzGerald ed. W. Aldis Wright (1889).
RB in Athenaeum 13 July 1889.
'Edward FitzGerald's friends' ET to ATR, 16 July 1889, Eton.
most sympathetic RB to ATR, 20 July 1889, Thackeray's Daughter, p. 166.

583 nothing could excuse RB to ET, 21 July 1889, The Brownings to the Tennysons, ed.
T.J. Collins, Baylor Browning 22 (Waco, Texas,1971), p. 48.
'cruel work' ET to RB, 22 July 1889, Yale.

CHAPTER 16 'The dead are not dead but alive'

584 'shadowy' ET to Annie Fields, 26 May 1891, Huntington.
wanted by all of them ET to HT, 16 Nov. 1889, TRC. Lionel Hallam Tennyson born

7 Nov. 1889. AT said 'I am very glad', which ET thought 'a great deal' for 'the dear darling' to say.

584 'cannot be in two places' ET to ATR, 17 Dec. 1889, Eton.

'feeling the footing' ET to Welds, 14 Dec. 1889, TRC.

dealing with *Demeter* ET to Craik, 5 Nov. 1889, BL; ET to HT, 6 Nov. 1889, TRC.

article in *I.O.W. County Press* 4 Feb. 1888; for 'Happy', Ricks 3.190. 'Forlorn', Ricks 2.508.

585 'overtasked and knocked up' ET to AW, 30 Dec. 1889, TRC.

'touching in his care' ET to HT, 27 Oct. 1889, TRC.

'Darby and Joan fashion' ET to BJ, 14 Nov. 1891, Balliol. 'Darby and Joan' from the ballad 'The Happy Old Couple', *Gentleman's Magazine*, March 1735.

'a loving scolding' ET to HT, 20 Nov. 1889, TRC.

'a blessing to all' ET to Sarah Prinsep, 12 Nov. 1889, Rochester.

'long to see him' ET to HT, 11 Nov. 1889, TRC.

family accounts ET to Agnes, 12 July 1895, 'As to money matters, of which I have since my marriage had chief management till lately . . .', TRC.

586 hiring of new servants letters in May 1894 from Frances Dann of Sheffield, granddaughter of one of the staff involved.

'both names' ET to HT, 29 Nov. 1889, TRC.

'quite a different person' ET to AW, 13 April 1890, TRC.

'live a few more years' BJ to ET, 14 Dec. 1889, TRC.

20,000 copies June Steffensen Hagen, *Tennyson and His Publishers* (1979), p. 182.

'persistence of the gift' *Nineteenth Century*, March 1889.

'far more plangent' W.E. Henley, 'Tennyson', *Views and Reviews* (1890). See *Critical Heritage*, p. 445.

comments on *Demeter* ET, 12 Dec. 1889, TRC.

'The Moaning of the Bar' ET's misnomer of AT's poem and his use of 'moaning' is interesting to me as 'The Tide on the Moaning Bar' is an early story by F.H. Burnett, written at the same period as 'Surly Tim', a story AT was known to admire.

587 'The Roses on the Terrace' Ricks 3.216. Christopher Ricks is one of those who thinks there is no question that 'it is to Rosa Baring'. Jack Kolb, TRB, Nov. 1991, says the only surviving holograph version (Harvard) does not address 'Rose'. It reads: 'Here on this terrace fifty years ago . . .'. But Kolb agrees with Rader and Ricks that it is 'a public acknowledgment of his attraction to, and affair with, Rosa Baring'. To me a 'public acknowledgment' seems highly unlikely, particularly in 1889. Fifty years before this, if we are to be literal, the love of Tennyson's life was Emily Sellwood. Lionel Tennyson in *From Verse to Worse*, p. 17; Harold Nicolson in *Tennyson*, p. 160.

'the Imagination of a Poet' ET to AW, 30 Dec. 1892, TRC.

'the localising craze' headline in the *Athenaeum*, 15 Feb. 1890. J.C. Walters, *In Tennyson Land* (1890), was particularly guilty.

'Let the poems speak' ET to HT, 7 Nov. 1889, TRC.

'not one touch of autobiography' AT to Charles Esmarch, 18 April 1888; L&S 3.366.

588 'June Bracken and Heather' Ricks 3.234. This sounds like Aldworth, but there is a note in Trinity Notebook 37 that it was written in T's eighty-second year (i.e. in June 1891) when ET was indeed seventy-seven, nearly seventy-eight. Tennyson was away on a cruise in the south-west that June. Pinion (p. 175) has suggested it was Exmoor heather.

'a rich man to enter' Luke 18:25.

588 'a useful way of spending' ET to Agnes, 17 Feb. 1896, TRC.
carpets for the Bishop ET to AW, 9 Aug. 1892, TRC.

589 'Courage Faith and Love' ET to HT, 16 Nov. 1889, TRC.
Letters to Agnes about charity and money 22 Nov. 1893, 17 Feb. 1896, 4 May 1895, 14 Dec. 1895, TRC. No records of ET's charity work seem to exist. One can gather a certain amount only from her letters and her obituaries. The records of the Royal Literary Fund show that Agnes Weld, after many years of helping those worse off than she was, became almost destitute and in need of charity herself; her application was refused (perhaps because of her cousin Lord Tennyson's wealth) in Jan. 1903.
'Sullivan to write the music' ET to BJ, 14 Nov. 1891, Balliol.
'never seen a play' ET to BJ, 26 Nov. 1891, Balliol.

590 needing applause ET to EL, 12 Feb. 1887, TRC.
'a wild genius' ET to Sophie Tennyson, 10 Sept. 1892, Lilly.
'cracky' HT to Craik at Macmillan, 14 June 1894, BL.
'passionate being' Mary G diary, 28 Oct. 1889, BL. Natalie Janotha had been born in Warsaw 8 June 1856. Lionel and Eleanor heard 'the new pianist' in Feb. 1879.
some had been published Only *The Song of the Alma River* (1864), *Two Child-Songs* (1880) and *Hands All Around* (1882).
several recitals One of them was in Freshwater Assembly Rooms, 6 Aug. 1891. The story of Janotha's involvement with ET's music is complex and is fully told in I.A. Copley's 'A Tennysonian Anecdote' in the *Music Review*, vol. 41, 1980, p. 257. None of Janotha's adaptations appear to survive but there are three volumes of ET's own music at TRC. Janotha's letters also at TRC. *PMG*, 19 May 1891. In an unpublished TS at TRC, I.A. Copley says ET's 'harmonic vocabulary rarely extended beyond the three basic chords of the "vamping" pianist.' He found many blunders. See also note to p. 516 of this book.

593 'a perilous gift' ET to Annie Fields, 26 May 1891, Huntington.
'Blessing to parents' TRC.

594 'tired of London' WA *Diary*, 19 Sept. 1880, p. 299.
'sheaf fully ripe' HT to Queen Victoria, 16 Aug. 1896, copy at TRC.
'the suffering life' ET to AW, 15 Oct. 1892, TRC.
Edison's phonograph (shouting laughing) Journal, 15 May 1890 (ET's hand, HT's 'voice'), TRC. The grandson's own description: *From Verse to Worse*, p. 13.
rising quickly, dancing Andrew Hichens notes on April 1891 at Yale; *Memoir* 2.384.

595 'our tablet' The lines 'Speak living Voice' are not attributed and I have not been able to discover who wrote them. They are not on the CD-Rom poetry database at the London Library. I would like to think ET wrote them herself, but no doubt someone will tell me otherwise.

596 'shared the life' BJ to ET, 20 Oct. 1890, TRC.
'how hard the road' See also *Stars and Markets*, p. 14. 'Her expression made one feel she had suffered intensely.' 'more than a month' EL diary, Oct. 1864, Harvard.
Abbey bust C. Jenner to ET, 20 Sept. 1893; Yale; Bradley to ET, Oct. 1894, TRC.
'a comfort to my Mother' HT to Queen Victoria, *Dear and Honoured*, p. 146.
Emily's nourishment ET to Agnes 8 June 1893, 19 May 1894, TRC.
'Her silky hair' Daisy Bradley (as Margaret L. Woods), *T and his Friends*, p. 180.

597 'same spirited sweep' Annie Fields, *Authors and Friends*, p. 355.
'wonderful serenity' CT in Foreword to Hoge *L*.
'I see the face of God' BJ in *Memoir* 2.466.
'a stronger faith' BJ to ET, 5 Oct. 1892, TRC.

598 'old character of an hotel' 'closely packed' ET to Agnes, 16 Aug. 1893, 10 July 1895, TRC.

'I see no one' ET to Agnes, 29 Dec. 1892, TRC.

'Chaucer don't mind' MBro to FT, New Year's Eve 1873, Lilly.

'vomit morally' etc. Talks and Walks (Audrey's hand), TRC.

'How people do love' ATR to ET, 25 Nov. 1892, TRC.

'thankful for what is left' ET to Mary Watts, 29 May [1894], NPG.

599 'agreeing as we do' proofs Note and Mat. at TRC.

600 'Life of the Life' Ricks 1.549 (quotes J.M. Kemble), *Memoir* 1.59.

'There's no hurry' HT to BJ, 15 Sept. 1893, Balliol.

'I will not add more' ET to FP, 13 Nov. 1893, *Palgrave*, p. 247.

601 'still to keep my interest' ET to Lady Martin, 1 Sept. 1893, Rochester.

'not a very useful one' ET to Agnes, 10 July 1895, TRC.

'a joy it is to me' ET to Agnes, 7 Feb. 1894, TRC.

602 'to appear among *His* poems' ET to Craik, 24 Sept. 1893, TRC.

'who wrote the Bible' ET to Agnes, 23 Feb. 1895, TRC.

603 'guessed guinea pigs' ET to Agnes, 28 April 1896, TRC. Both the new baby, Harold, and his older brother, Aubrey, were killed in the First World War.

'the best talker' FP to Warren, May 1897, *Palgrave*, p. 254.

'The Grandmother' Ricks 2.599 ('tired a little', 'this room into the next', 'I shall go in a minute').

W.E.H. Lecky I am indebted to Ann C. Colley for her emphasis on Lecky's importance to ET (see 'ET's Death Bed', *TRB*, Nov. 1991).

'highest pleasure in sacrifice' See the first chapter: 'The Natural History of Morals'.

604 'Almost to the last' HT to Lecky, Trin. Coll. Lib., Dublin, quoted by Ann Colley.

'just begun the second volume' The volume begins with the 'growth of priestly influence in Irish politics' – a subject which had always intensely interested ET.

'golden sovereigns' *Stars and Markets*, p. 15.

ET's last words pasted in front of bound copy of Materials vols 1 and 2, TRC. HT does not mention the grandsons Charles and Alfred, who were also in the house, but only his own sons.

605 repeats in *Memoir* *Memoir* 2.432.

held back from evil HT to Rollo ?, 19 Aug. 1896, Rochester.

Knowles's surviving diatribe Deposited by his biographer Priscilla Metcalf at TRC.

'Charlie's face' Eleanor to HT, 10 Aug. 1896, TRC.

Agnes at ET's funeral Agnes to HDR, n.d. [Aug. 1896], Rawnsley papers.

606 'one of the few people in the world' HT to Craik, 12 Aug. 1896 (in my own possession).

607 'Vastness' Ricks 3.134; *Memoir* 2.343.

Index

━━━